JAPAN

PROFILE

OF

A

NATION

JAPAN
PROFILE
OF
A
NATION

Kodansha International
Tokyo · New York · London

Published by Kodansha International Ltd., 17-14 Otowa 1-chome,
Bunkyo-ku, Tokyo 112 and Kodansha America Inc.

Distributed in the United States by Kodansha America, Inc., 114
Fifth Avenue, New York, NY 10011 and in the United Kingdom
and continental Europe by Kodansha Europe Ltd.,
95, Aldwych, London WC2B 4JF

First edition, 1995

95 96 97 98 10 9 8 7 6 5 4 3 2 1
ISBN4-7700-1890-8

Printed in Japan

Library of Congress Cataloging-in-Publication Data
A catalog record for this book is available from the Library of Congress

During the closing years of the twentieth century, we have seen worldwide interest in Japan grow as the nation takes on a more prominent and active role on the international stage. Many have felt the need for an accurate and reliable reference source that is both comprehensive and accessible to the general reader. With this in mind, JAPAN: PROFILE OF A NATION was compiled from the valuable and detailed resource *Japan: An Illustrated Encyclopedia* published by our parent company Kodansha Ltd. A generous selection of entries from this treasure trove of information has been reorganized into thematic sections such as

Editor's Preface Geography and Nature, History, Government and Diplomacy, Economy, Society, Culture, and Life. Cross-references are provided within the entry to lead the reader to related material, and an index of entry titles and key words is included as part of the supplementary materials. Those readers requiring more specialized information about Japan are advised to consult *Japan: An Illustrated Encyclopedia*.

We sincerely hope that the publication of JAPAN: PROFILE OF A NATION will promote better international understanding through an authentic and fascinating portrayal of all that is Japan.

Kodansha International

June 1995

Explanatory Notes

Organization

This book is divided into seven thematic sections which, except for History, are further divided into a number of sub-sections. For example, the Society section consists of four parts: Social Environment, Education, Transportation, and Mass Communications. Each of these sub-sections in turn comprises a number of in-depth entries on specific subjects.

Entry Titles

Entry titles are, wherever possible, given in English followed by the same title in Japanese characters. In most cases the romanized equivalent of the Japanese title is included in parenthesis at the head of the entry. Where a romanized Japanese title is used for the main entry title, a parenthetical English translation is given when appropriate.

Sub-Headings

Within many of the longer entries, sub-headings are used to indicate major divisions. A Japanese translation of each sub-heading is given to the right.

Romanization and Italicization

Japanese words are spelled in this book according to the Hepburn system of romanization used in most English-language publications on Japan. Chinese words and names are given in the official *pinyin* system of romanization. Sanskrit is transliterated in the system most widely used in English-language scholarly publications.

Japanese words are italicized only where they first appear in an entry.

Cross-References

Cross-references are included within the entries themselves in the form of words set in SMALL CAPITALS to inform the reader that the book contains an entry on the subject named.

Money

Post-1945 yen values are followed by their US dollar equivalents, with the dollar figure based on the average exchange rate pertaining during the year or years in question.

Personal Names

Japanese, Chinese, and Korean personal names are given surname first, the normal order used in those languages (e.g., Kawabata Yasunari rather than Yasunari Kawabata or Kawabata, Yasunari).

Supplementary Materials

Photographs, Graphs, and Tables
In addition to the numerous photographs, graphs, and tables presented throughout the book, a collection of full-page color photographs of Japan and a map showing regions and cities are included just prior to the main text.

Constitution of Japan
The full text of the Constitution of Japan is presented in both English and Japanese.

Chronology of Japanese History
Lists major events in Japan's political, social, and cultural development. Major events in world history are listed in a separate parallel column for comparison and reference.

Index
The index includes entry titles (in both English and Japanese) and key words from the text.

Contributors

James C. ABEGGLEN
AKIYAMA Terukazu
AMANO Ikuo
Walter AMES
J. L. ANDERSON
AOKI Eiichi
Haruo AOKI
ARAI Naoyuki
James T. ARAKI
ARAMAKI Shigeo
Janet ASHBY
Hans H. BAERWALD
James C. BAXTER
Harumi BEFU
BEKKI Atsuhiko
Andrea BOLTHO
Gordon T. BOWLES
Robert H. BROWER
John Creighton CAMPBELL
Thomas W. CLEAVER
Martin C. COLLCUTT
Walter Ames COMPTON
Michael COOPER
Heinrich DUMOULIN
H. Byron EARHART
Earle ERNST
Lee W. FARNSWORTH
Scott C. FLANAGAN
FUJII Toshiko
FUKUDA Hideichi
Haruhiko FUKUI
FUKUSHIMA Yasuto
Robert GARFIAS
Van C. GESSEL
Allan G. GRAPARD
Willem A. GROOTAERS
David HALE
Ivan P. HALL
Robert B. HALL, Jr
William B. HAUSER
HAYAKAWA Zenjiro
HAYASHI Hikaru
Benjamin H. HAZARD
HIRASAWA Yutaka
Frank HOFF
Leon HOLLERMAN
Inger-Johanne HOLMBOE
HOSOYA Chihiro

IBARAGI Naoko
Hiroko IKEDA
IMAMICHI Tomonobu
IMAIZUMI Yoshinori
INOKUCHI Shoji
ISHIYAMA Akira
ITO Nobuo
IWADARE Hiroshi
Donald JENKINS
Eleanor H. JORDAN
KAMINOGO Michiko
KANEKO Yoshimasa
KARASAWA Tomitaro
KARIYA Takehiko
KATA Koji
KATO Masashi
KATO Shumpei
KATO Tsuneo
KATO Yukitsugu
KAWAMOTO Takashi
KIDA Hiroshi
KIMURA Kiyotaka
KINOUCHI Kiyoko
KONO Tomomi
KOTANI Kozo
KUDO Masanobu
KUMAKURA Isao
KURITA Ken
KURIYAMA Shigehisa
Edward J. LINCOLN
Victor D. LIPPIT
Leonard LYNN
Kathleen McCARTHY
Terry Edward MacDOUGALL
Theodore McNELLY
MAKABE Tetsuo
John M. MAKI
William P. MALM
Wimmer MANFRED
MASUI Ken'ichi
MATSUDA Osamu
MERA Koichi
MIHARA Takeshi
MIYANO Nobuyuki
Ross MOUER
Hugo MÜNSTERBERG
NAKAGAWA Koji
NAKAGAWA Toshihiko
NAKAMURA Hajime

NIIRA Satoshi
NISHIMATA Sohei
NISHINO Teruhiko
NIWATA Noriaki
Agnes M. NIYEKAWA
NOGUCHI Takenori
NOGUCHI Yukio
Edward NORBECK
NOZAKI Shigeru
ODA Takeo
OGAWA Yoshio
OGURA Michio
Frank Masao OKAMURA
OKAMURA Tadao
OKI Yasue
P. G. O'NEILL
ORITA Koji
OTSUKA Shigeru
OTSUKA Sueko
OWADA Hisashi
Allan PALMER
Hugh PATRICK
T. J. PEMPEL
David W. PLATH
William V. RAPP
C. Tait RATCLIFFE
Coleman REX
Bradley RICHARDSON
Thomas P. ROHLEN
John M. ROSENFIELD
SAITO Shizuo
Robert K. SAKAI
Mitsugu SAKIHARA
Kazuo SATO
SATO Tadashi
SAWADA Takahiro
C. Franklin SAYRE
Marc SCHULTZ
A. C. SCOTT
SEIKE Kiyosi
SHIKI Masahide
SHIMBORI Michiya
SHIMIZU Hideo
SHIMIZU Yoshiaki
SHIMOKAWA Koichi
SHINADA Yutaka
SHINJI Isoya
SHIODA Nagahide
Michael J. SMITKA

SOEDA Yoshiya

Norman SPARNON

Kurt STEINER

William E. STESLICKE

SUGIYAMA Yasushi

SUZUKI Masao

SUZUKI Yukihisa

Barbara Bowles SWANN

TAGUCHI Yoshiaki

TAKAGI Noritsune

TAKAKUWA Yasuo

Ted T. TAKAYA

TAKEUCHI Hitoshi

TANAKA Jiro

TANAKA Tsutomu

TERAI Minako

John E. THAYER III

David A. TITUS

TOMIKI Kenji

TSUCHIDA Mitsufumi

TSUJI Shizuo

TSUKUBA Hisaharu

TSUTSUI Michio

UDAGAWA Akihito

Makoto UEDA

USHIOGI Morikazu

Allie Marie UYEHARA

Suzanne H. VOGEL

WAGATSUMA Hiroshi

WATANABE Hiroshi

WATANABE Takeshi

WATANABE Toru

Herschel WEBB

Stanley WEINSTEIN

William WETHERALL

YAGI Natsuhiko

YAMADA Makiko

YAMADA Toshio

YAMAGUCHI Kazuo

YAMAGUCHI Makoto

YAMAMOTO Kazuhiro

YAMASHITA Kikuko

Kenneth YASUDA

YONEKURA Mamoru

YOSHIDA Aya

Masatoshi M.YOSHINO

Michael Y. YOSHINO

Managing Editor

WAKAYAMA Hitoshi

Book Design

Katsui Design Office

Editor

SUZUKI Setsuko

Translator

Marc SCHULTZ

Editorial Service

Guild

Photo Credits

Steve GARDNER

HIBI Sadao

Kodansha Photo Library

PANA

TAKAHASHI Nobuyuki

TATEISHI Akira

TATEUCHI Toshinobu

TOYOTAKA Ryuzo

YAMAMOTO Ikuo

Shinjuku, Tokyo

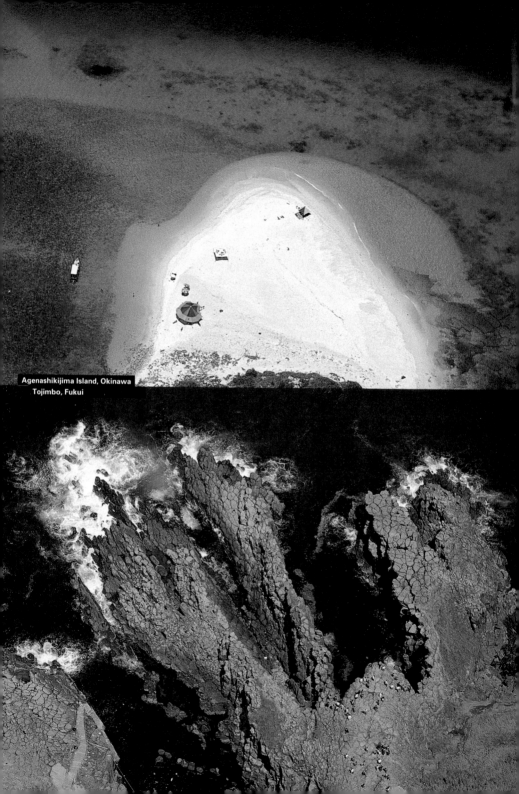

Agenashikijima Island, Okinawa
Tojimbo, Fukui

Mt. Fuji

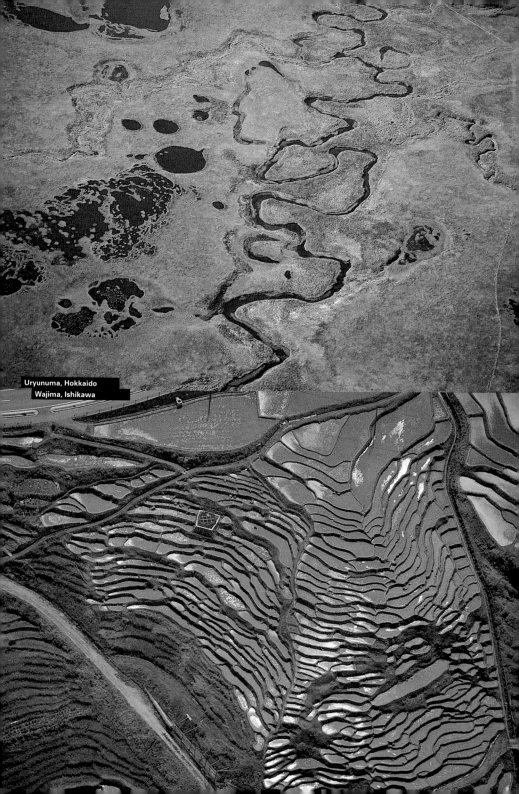

Uryunuma, Hokkaido
Wajima, Ishikawa

Yururito Island, Hokkaido
Makinohara, Shizuoka

Toshimaen, Tokyo
Shinobazunoike, Tokyo

Seibu Stadium, Saitama
Yoyogi Park, Tokyo

Regions and Cities

RUSSIA

CHINA

Yuzhno-Sakhalinsk

Etorofu

Wakkanai

Abashiri   Kunashiri

Asahikawa

Daisetuzan

Vladivostok

Sapporo   Kushiro

Hakodate

Sea of Japan

Aomori   Hokkaido

NORTH KOREA

Akita

P'yongyang

Morioka

Honshu

Sendai

Chugoku region

Seoul

Niigata

Tohoku region

SOUTH KOREA

Toyama   Mito

Kanazawa

JAPAN

Fujisan   Tokyo

Kyoto   Yokohama

Okayama   Kobe   Nagoya

Hiroshima   Osaka

Kita Kyushu   Takamatsu

Fukuoka   Kochi

Kanto region

Asosan

Kumamoto

Chubu region

Kagoshima

Kinki region

Pacific Ocean

Shikoku region

Kyushu region

Naha

Ogasawara Islands

Nansei (Ryukyu) Islands

Okinotorishima

GEOGRAPHY
AND
NATURE

Land

Areas and Cities

Plants and Animals

Coral reef in the sea near
one of the Ryukyu Islands,
Okinawa Prefecture.

Land

Japan (Nippon or Nihon)   日本●

TERRITORY AND
ADMINISTRATIVE DIVISIONS   領土と行政区分●

Japan consists of an archipelago extending approximately from northeast to southwest. It lies off the east coast of the Asian continent. The total land area as of October 1992 was 377,800 square kilometers (145,869 sq mi), only slightly larger than that of Finland or Italy and about the same size as the US state of Montana. The four major islands of Japan are Hokkaido, Honshu, Shikoku, and Kyushu. Claimed by the Japanese, the northernmost islands of Kunashiri (Kunashir), Etorofu (Iturup), the Habomai Islands, and Shikotan were occupied by the Soviet Union at the end of World War II and are still occupied by the Russian Federation. The Ogasawara Islands and Okinawa Islands, under American rule after World War II, were returned to Japan in 1968 and 1972, respectively. The areas of the main geographical divisions of Japan (including offshore islands under their administrative control) are as follows: Hokkaido 83,451 sq km (32,220 sq mi), Honshu 231,033 sq km (89,202 sq mi), Shikoku 18,782 sq km (7,252 sq mi), Kyushu 42,151 sq km (16,275 sq mi), and Okinawa Prefecture 2,265 sq km (875 sq mi). Following the recent tendency among countries to enlarge territorial waters, Japan set its territorial limit at 12 nautical miles from the coast in 1977.

Population   人口●

At the time of the Meiji Restoration (1868) Japan's population was about 33 million. In 1994 it was 124,323,000, seventh largest in the world. The density per square kilometer (0.386 sq mi) was 334 persons in 1992. Although this figure is comparable to 359 persons in the Netherlands and 325 in Belgium, the density of the Japanese population per unit area under cultivation is the highest in the world, because over two-thirds of Japan is occupied by mountainous terrain, and alluvial plains occupy only 13 percent.

The population was distributed comparatively equally all over the country about a century ago, when Japan was still predominantly agricultural. With industrialization, however, there was a strong tendency toward regional concentration. As a result, 43.1 percent of Japanese live in the three major urban areas of TOKYO, OSAKA, and Nagoya. The Tokyo Metropolitan Area in particular, although less than 2.0 percent in terms of area, has a concentration of 23.4 percent of the national population.

Population of Japan's
Ten Largest Cities
(1994)
日本の10大都市
(in thousands)

City	Population
Tokyo	11,573
Yokohama	3,265
Osaka	2,481
Nagoya	2,091
Sapporo	1,719
Kobe	1,479
Kyoto	1,391
Fukuoka	1,221
Kawasaki	1,171
Hiroshima	1,077
Kita Kyushu	1,015

Formation of the Country 　　　　　　　国家の成立●

Among the various theories on the formation of Japan as a nation-state, one school holds that, because of its proximity to the Asian continent, northern Kyushu was the site of the first political center. By the 4th century a sovereign court had emerged, which by conquest and alliance eventually unified the country. The Yamato court (ca 4th century–ca mid-7th century) repeatedly dispatched expeditionary forces to northeastern Honshu and succeeded in subduing it in the 7th century, thus establishing the prototype of a unified Japan consisting of Honshu, Shikoku, and Kyushu. Under the Taika Reform of 645, the *kokugun* system of administration was instituted, and the country was divided into 58 (later 66) provinces (*kuni* or *koku*) with subunits called *gun*. This division remained in effect nominally until the Meiji Restoration (1868). However, during the Edo period (1600–1868), the *bakuhan* (shogunate and domain) system was superimposed on the kokugun system.

Changes in Territory 　　　　　　　　　領土の変遷●

The territory of Japan has remained essentially the same from the 7th century, but its history is nonetheless one of numerous modifications. In 1609 the *daimyo* of the Satsuma domain (now Kagoshima Prefecture) established control over the Ryukyu Kingdom of the Okinawa Islands (see OKINAWA PREFECTURE). The Ogasawara Islands (also known as the Bonin Islands) were discovered by the Japanese in 1593 and were officially incorporated into Japan in 1876. Hokkaido, once called Ezo, was settled by the Japanese in the Edo period. As trade developed with the Ainu people (an indigenous people of Hokkaido) in the interior, the Japanese gradually made their way into the southern part of Sakhalin (J: Karafuto) and the Kuril Islands, where they came into conflict with the Russians. In 1875 Japan concluded the Treaty of St. Petersburg with Russia and gave up the southern part of Sakhalin in exchange for the Kuril Islands. After the Sino-Japanese War of 1894–1895 Japan acquired Taiwan, and after the Russo-Japanese War of 1905 it acquired the southern half of Sakhalin and leased the southern part of the Liaodong Peninsula. It annexed Korea in 1910 and secured a mandate over former German territories in the South Sea Islands after World War I. Thus at the time of the outbreak of World War II, the total land area was 680,729 square kilometers (262,830 sq mi). However, after its defeat Japan was stripped of all territories acquired during its period of colonialism and, until the restoration of Okinawa in 1972, was left with essentially the four main islands.

Ceremony marking the twentieth anniversary of the return of Okinawa to Japan by the United States in 1972.

Modern Prefectural System 　　　　近現代の都道府県制度●

After the Meiji Restoration the country was administratively reorganized into the prefectural system. Tokyo, Osaka, and Kyoto were made *fu* (urban prefectures) in 1871, and the rest of the country was divided into 302 *ken* (prefectures). By 1888 this system had been integrated into a system of 3 fu and 43 ken. Hokkaido was initially administered directly by the central government but later came to be treated equally with other prefectures, although it was called a *do* (circuit) rather than a ken. In 1943 Tokyo Fu was designated as a special administrative area and named Tokyo To (officially translated as Tokyo Metropolis). At present Japan is administratively divided into 1 to (Tokyo To), 1 do (Hokkaido), 2 fu (Osaka Fu and Kyoto Fu), and 43 ken.

NATURAL FEATURES OF JAPAN   日本の自然●
Topography   地勢●

The chief feature of the Japanese archipelago is its geological instability, including frequent volcanic activity and many earthquakes. Another distinctive characteristic of the topography is the fact that the Japanese archipelago is made up almost entirely of steep mountain districts with very few plains.

High, precipitous mountains of about 1,500–3,000 meters (5,000–10,000 ft) run along the Pacific Ocean side of southwestern Japan. Deep, V-shaped valleys are cut into these mountain districts. In contrast, on the SEA OF JAPAN side of southwestern Japan are groupings of plateaus and low mountain districts with a height of about 500–1,500 meters (1,600–5,000 ft), such as the Hida, Tamba, and Chugoku mountain districts; the Kibi Highland; and the Tsukushi Mountains.

The large number and variety of volcanoes found throughout the Japanese archipelago constitute another remarkable feature. There have been 188 volcanoes active at some time or another since the Quaternary geological period, and more than 40 of these remain active today. Among these are volcanoes that have had numerous violent eruptions, such as Asamayama and Bandaisan. Further, a special characteristic of Japan's volcano zone is the development of large craters or calderas such as those at Akan, Daisetsu, Hakone, Aso, and Aira. The caldera at Aso is on a scale unrivaled anywhere in the world.

A small number of large rivers, such as the Ishikarigawa, Shinanogawa, Tonegawa, Kisogawa, Yodogawa, and Chikugogawa, have fair-sized delta plains at their mouths. Diluvial uplands and river and marine terraces have developed in many coastal areas of Japan, and these are utilized along with the plains for both agriculture and habitation.

Five Highest Mountains
主な山

Fujisan	3,776 m
Kitadake	3,192 m
Hotakadake	3,190 m
Yarigatake	3,180 m
Akaishidake	3,120 m

Five Longest Rivers
主な川

Shinanogawa	367 km
Tonegawa	322 km
Ishikarigawa	268 km
Teshiogawa	256 km
Kitakamigawa	249 km

Climate 気候●

Located in the monsoon zone of the eastern coast of the Asian continent, the most notable features of the climate of the Japanese archipelago are the wide range of yearly temperatures and the large amount of rainfall. However, because of the complexity of the land configuration, there are numerous regional differences throughout the seasons.

Spring (春) When low-pressure areas pass over the Pacific coast of Japan in March, the temperature rises with each rainfall. When low-pressure areas start to develop over the Sea of Japan, the strong wind from the south called *haru ichiban* (the first tidings of spring) blows over Japan. This wind causes flooding due to suddenly melting mountain snow and the foehn phenomenon, which sometimes results in great fires on the Sea of Japan side.

Summer (夏) The onset of the rainy season (*baiu* or *tsuyu*) takes place around 7 June. It starts in the southern part of Japan and moves northward. With the end of the rain around 20 July, the Ogasawara air masses blanket Japan, and the weather takes on a summer pattern. The peak of summer is late July, and the summer heat lingers on into mid-August.

Fall (秋) September is the typhoon season. Weather resembling that of the rainy season also occurs because of the autumnal rain fronts. The weather clears in mid-October, and the winter winds start to blow.

Winter (冬) In December, when the atmospheric pressure configuration has completely changed to the winter pattern, northwest winds bring snow to the mountains and to the plains on the Sea of Japan side, and a dry wind blows on the Pacific Ocean side. The peak of winter comes around 25 January.

Spring: Cherry-blossom viewing in Ueno Park, Tokyo.

Summer: Morning glory festival.

Autumn: Grape picking.

Winter: Snow shoveling in Shinjuku, Tokyo.

Life and Nature 生活と自然●

Japan's land area is small but its configuration is complex, so that the climate and the flora and fauna vary regionally, extending from the subarctic zone in the north to the subtropical zone in the south; there is also much seasonal change. An abundance of hot springs, which are popular as health resorts, accompany the many volcanoes.

Japan's seasonal changes and geological structure bring many natural disasters. Heavy rains due to the baiu front and the autumn typhoons bring about landslides, floods, and wind damage. Heavy winter precipitation causes snow damage as well as flooding and cold damage. In addition, earthquakes on the scale of the Tokyo Earthquake of 1923, which was assigned a magnitude of 7.9, strike somewhere in Japan every several decades. Typhoons and the tidal waves accompanying earthquakes also inflict damage on heavily populated, low-lying coastal areas. Flooding and land subsidence have also occurred as the result of land reclamation and excessive pumping of groundwater.

GEOLOGICAL STRUCTURE 　　　　地質構造●
Topography 　　　　地殻●

Topographically, the Kuril Arc; the Sakhalin-Hokkaido Arc; the Honshu Arc, connecting Kyushu, Shikoku, Honshu, and the western part of Hokkaido; and the Ryukyu and Izu-Ogasawara arcs make up the Japanese islands. The Kuril, Japan, and Izu-Ogasawara trenches constitute one continuous trench. This trench is a narrow, submarine channel with a depth of about 9,000 meters (30,000 ft) in some areas. The Japan Trench, however, is not connected to the shallower Nankai Trough in the offing of Shikoku and Kyushu, nor is the Nankai Trough connected to the Ryukyu Trench. The Philippine Basin is separated from the Pacific Ocean by the Izu-Ogasawara Arc, and the Nankai Trough and the Ryukyu Trench together correspond to the northern edge of the Philippine Basin.

The Sea of Okhotsk, the Sea of Japan, and the East China Sea separate Japan topographically from the Asian continent. They are generally shallow, although some basins in the Sea of Okhotsk and the Sea of Japan are 3,000–4,000 meters (9,800–13,000 ft) deep.

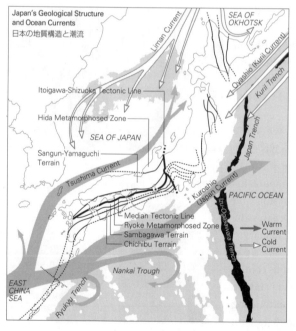

Japan's Geological Structure and Ocean Currents
日本の地質構造と潮流

The border of northeastern Japan and southwestern Japan is a great fault called the Itoigawa-Shizuoka Tectonic Line. The beltlike area east of this fault and running from the western part of Niigata Prefecture to the central part of Nagano Prefecture and from Yamanashi Prefecture to the eastern part of Shizuoka Prefecture forms a single valley crossing Honshu that is called the Fossa Magna. The mountain ranges and volcanic zones that form northeastern Japan turn south-southeast at the Fossa Magna and are connected to the Izu Islands. Southwestern Japan is divided into an inner belt (the side facing the Sea of Japan) and an outer belt (the side facing the Pacific Ocean) by the great fault called the Median Tectonic Line, which runs lengthwise along the axis of southwestern Japan from the Ina Mountains to Oita Prefecture. These belts can be traced as far as the Ryukyu Islands. In southwestern Japan there are fewer volcanoes than in northeastern Japan, and they are concentrated in the area facing the Sea of Japan and Kyushu. Volcanic activity is vigorous in northeastern Japan.

Crustal Movement   地殻運動●

The Japanese islands have severe crustal movements, which are still progressing. Crustal movements include movements of short duration, such as seismic activity, and also slow movements of long duration. Volcanic activity, gravity anomaly, and crustal heat flow are also directly caused by the crustal deformation. VOLCANOES have been particularly active in northeastern Japan since the Quaternary period. There is a narrow nonvolcanic zone along the Pacific coast, the rest of the region being volcanic.

Sea of Japan (Nihonkai)   日本海●

One of the three marginal seas (the others are the East China Sea and the Sea of Okhotsk) around Japan. It is situated between the Asian continent and the Japanese archipelago and is connected to adjacent seas by the straits of Mamiya, Soya, Tsugaru, Kammon, and Tsushima. It is the smallest of the three seas (1,008,000 sq km; 389,000 sq mi) and the deepest (maximum depth: 3,712 m; 12,178 ft; average depth: 1,350 m; 4,430 ft). The Sea of Japan provides good fishing grounds and is an important factor in the heavy winter snowfalls on parts of Honshu.

Volcanoes (kazan)   火山●

The many active volcanoes in Japan form a part of the so-called circum-Pacific volcanic zone, which surrounds the Pacific Ocean. While volcanic eruptions have significantly influenced the life of the Japanese people since earliest times, causing heavy loss of life, they have also produced beautiful natural views and features and provided fertile soil.

Distribution of Volcanoes　　　　　　　　火山の分布●

The volcanoes are located in a line that generally runs parallel to the Japanese archipelago. The eastern edge of volcano distribution in Hokkaido and northern Honshu forms a line running almost parallel to the central mountain range that forms the backbone of the archipelago; to the west of this edge line, called the volcanic front, volcanoes are distributed as far as the SEA OF JAPAN. The volcanic front turns abruptly southward in the northwest corner of the Kanto region of Honshu near Mt. Asama (Asamayama) and, by way of the Yatsugatake volcano group, Fuji-Hakone-Izu National Park, and the eastern side of the Izu Peninsula, goes through the Izu Islands to the volcanic islands of the Marianas. In southwestern Japan the distribution is not so dense, but a volcanic front runs across western Honshu, extends southward to central Kyushu, and is connected to the volcanoes of Taiwan by way of the Ryukyu Islands.

Structure and Activity of Japanese Volcanoes　　　日本の火山の構造と活動●

Many Japanese volcanoes have a conical shape similar to that of Mt. Fuji (FUJISAN), which has become a symbol of Japan. These volcanoes, called stratovolcanoes, were formed by the alternate accumulation of lava flows and of volcanic blocks and bombs emitted from the summit crater. One characteristic of this type of volcano is its profile, which consists of a beautiful exponential curve with wide, gentle skirts.

Many of the smallest volcanoes were formed by a single eruption and have never resumed activity. One such type, the pyroclastic cone, is usually formed over a period ranging from several days to several years by an effusion of pumice, scoria, and volcanic ash. Another type is the lava dome, in which highly viscous lava is gradually pushed up as a huge mass. Most pyroclastic cones and lava domes are no more than 200 meters (650 ft) in height, and they often occur in groups.

Crater wall of Mt. Bandai.

Two rarer kinds of eruption activity are known for their destructive power. One is a large steam explosion, which is a characteristic feature of the stratovolcano toward the end of its life. In the 1888 eruption of Mt. Bandai (Bandaisan), a series of violent explosions lasting several minutes each was followed by a huge landslide. The other type of destructive eruption is caused by the effusion of an enormous amount of magma onto the ground within a brief period. The magma contains large quantities of gaseous components (mostly water vapor) that, during volcanic eruptions, separate themselves from the magma in the form of foam, much like the foam of beer that rises when a bottle is opened. The foamy magma splits into pieces and is violently ejected as a mixture of rocks, pumice, volcanic ash, and gas known as a pyroclastic flow.

Disasters Due to Eruptions and Their Prevention　噴火による災害と防災●

In a vulcanian eruption, which is the most common type of eruption in Japan, it is only rarely that volcanic rocks and bombs are ejected from the crater over a horizontal distance of several kilometers. It has become possible to foretell explosive eruptions, and when warning signals occur, entry into the danger area around the crater is prohibited. At a greater distance from the volcano than the range of volcanic bombs, damage to buildings from other factors, such as the shock wave of the eruption, is a major concern. Even more dangerous, however, is the fall of pumiceous rocks that have been blown high into the sky and drift with the wind to land in areas far from the crater. Damage to crops from accumulation of volcanic ash is a serious economic hardship, and several famines are attributed to destruction of rice paddies by volcanic eruptions.

The eruption at Fugendake, May 1991.

Microearthquakes and any change in the earth's crust are observed regularly and continuously at 19 active volcanoes throughout Japan, including Asamayama, Miharayama, Asosan, and the Unzendake group. At these volcanoes instruments such as seismometers, tiltmeters, extensometers, and laser beams are used to make precise measurements of any changes. The Global Positioning System (GPS), which uses artificial satellites, is also utilized to monitor conditions. Thus, it is unlikely that a major eruption could occur without some forewarning. However, means of preventing disasters stemming from volcanic eruptions remain inadequate, as volcanic eruptions are natural phenomena involving the release of huge amounts of energy.

In November 1990 there was an eruption at Fugendake, the highest peak of Unzendake, which last erupted in 1792. During the 1991 eruption pyroclastic flows claimed 44 lives.

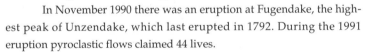

Earthquakes (*jishin*)　地震●

Earthquakes are a frequent phenomenon in Japan; nearly 10 percent of the energy released worldwide by earthquakes each year is concentrated in and around the Japanese islands. In the last century Japan has experienced 24 destructive earthquakes with magnitudes of 6 or higher on the scale used by the Meteorological Agency of Japan. This scale roughly approximates the better-known Richter scale used in the West. Both scales measure the magnitude of an earthquake by the energy released from its epicenter.

The most famous earthquake was the great Tokyo Earthquake of

Geography and Nature

1923 (Kanto Daishinsai), which was later given a magnitude of 7.9 on the Japanese scale. Centered near metropolitan Tokyo and Yokohama, the quake resulted in more than 100,000 deaths and billions of dollars in property loss. In Tokyo alone it took the lives of more than 60,000 people, of whom more than 50,000 died in quake-related fires.

Causes and Distribution of
Earthquakes in Japan　　　　　　日本における地震の原因と分布●

The Tokyo earthquake was caused by movement along a fault, that is, a fracture in the earth's crust. The upper layer of the fault zone shifted about 6 meters (20 ft) east and about 3 meters (10 ft) south with respect to the lower layer. The surface of the earth moved upward and toward the Pacific Ocean. This same type of movement is seen in virtually every earthquake that occurs along the Pacific coast of Japan.

Earthquakes tend to recur periodically, the interval between occurrences varying with the locale. Seismologist Kawasumi Hiroshi (1907–1972) estimated that the mean time between major earthquakes in the southern Kanto region is 69 years. There are also "swarms," sustained periods of numerous small quakes. The longest recorded swarm took place in the mid-1960s at Matsushiro in Nagano Prefecture.

Earthquake activity in Japan is accompanied by various forms of crustal distortion and fault displacement depending on the geographic and geologic area involved. For example, the tips of such peninsulas as the Boso, Miura, and Kii, all of which jut out into the Pacific Ocean, slowly sink into the ocean at the rate of 1 centimeter (0.4 in) a year, but a major earthquake would lift the tip to compensate instantly for the accumulated depression. On the other hand, earthquakes occurring in southwestern Japan, west of the Fossa Magna, are created by sudden movements of the earth along an existing fault zone, and unlike earthquakes on the Pacific coast, these quakes are not preceded by crustal movement.

The crustal distortion accompanying Pacific coast quakes is caused by mantle convection within the earth. In the southeastern Pacific Ocean there is a ridge, toward which mantle convection surges from the earth's core and then moves horizontally toward Japan before creeping downward again to the core. When mantle flow gets into the core, the movement causes one plate on the mantle to subduct, or dive under the other, and become absorbed in the underlying mantle. The involvement of peninsula tips in this movement causes their slow depression between earthquakes, the rate of depression being equal to the speed of mantle convection. The sudden upheaval of a peninsula's tip in an earthquake is due to "elastic rebound."

The Western Nagano Earthquake of 1984 was assigned a magnitude of 6.9.

The Southwest Hokkaido Offshore Earthquake of 1993 was assigned a magnitude of 7.8.

Pacific coastal areas are gradually compressed by mantle convection in the intervals between earthquakes, and in a large earthquake they rebound toward the Pacific. Accordingly, the greater the accumulation of pressure from the Pacific Ocean, the greater the probability that an earthquake will occur in the region.

Earthquake Prediction   地震予知●

Since 1965, funds have been allocated for research on earthquake prediction, most of it centering on characteristic crustal distortions. In 1969 the Meteorological Agency, the Geographic Survey Institute, and several national universities formed the Coordinating Committee for Earthquake Prediction to pool the results of their research. It was decided to conduct surveys over the entire area of Japan and to repeat measurements of geologic changes at short intervals by means of leveling and triangulation in comparatively small areas of the country deemed important, such as the southern Kanto area and the Tokai region (Shizuoka and Aichi prefectures). Distortion and faulting also have been monitored continuously, using sensitive instruments such as the tiltmeter and extensometer. It is known that microelastic impact waves are generated in considerable numbers before rock fractures under the accumulation of strain, which is thought to resemble foreshock activity preceding large earthquakes. The flow of heat that is transmitted from the core of the earth to the surface is closely related to crustal phenomena; further, terrestrial magnetism and earth current are said to change in relation to a large earthquake. Therefore, these phenomena are being measured to determine if there is some connection that will contribute to earthquake prediction.

Toppled train cars and burning houses in the aftermath of the Kobe Earthquake of 1995 (Hanshin Daishinsai). Assigned a magnitude of 7.2, this earthquake caused massive destruction of buildings, roads, and other facilities and resulted in more than 5,000 deaths.

Three factors: when, where, and how severe are essential to earthquake prediction. Although quakes do occur periodically and are accompanied by characteristic crustal movements, the difficulties of predicting precisely when a quake will strike are not likely to be solved soon, and the likelihood of a quake's occurrence will continue to be based on statistical probability.

Most of the enormous damage accompanying large earthquakes comes from fire following building collapse, and also from the effects of *tsunami*, a large sea wave. Earthquakes are particularly destructive in Japan because closely packed structures, usually of wood, make for inadequate firebreaks, while the popularity of small space heaters fueled by gas or kerosene increases the chance of fire.

Areas and Cities

Hokkaido　北海道●

The northernmost and second largest of Japan's four main islands. It is separated from Honshu to the south by the Tsugaru Strait and bounded by the SEA OF JAPAN on the west, the Sea of Okhotsk on the northeast, and the Pacific Ocean on the south and east. Several mountain ranges cross Hokkaido, and those belonging to the Ezo Mountains run from north to south across the center of the island, separated into two strands by a series of basin areas. To the west of these mountains lies the broad Ishikari Plain. To the southwest of the plain is a long peninsula, which is the area closest to Honshu. The climate is unlike that of the rest of Japan, being notably colder and drier.

Hokkaido

The prehistoric culture of Hokkaido seems to have shared many of the characteristics of the early culture of Honshu, except that it lacked the culture of the Yayoi period (ca 300 BC–ca AD 300). Hokkaido, or Ezo, as it was known, was inhabited by the Ainu and not included in Japan proper. In the Edo period (1600–1868) the Matsumae domain was established in the extreme southwestern corner of the island. After the Meiji Restoration of 1868, the new government placed great emphasis on Hokkaido's economic development, setting up a colonial office (Kaitakushi) and encouraging settlers to come from other parts of Japan. The name of the island was changed to Hokkaido (literally, "Northern Sea Circuit") in 1869. The present prefectural form of administration was established in 1886. (Within Japan's prefectural system, Hokkaido alone is called a do [circuit] rather than a ken [prefecture]; however, it is the equivalent of a prefecture.)

The main agricultural crop is rice; grain and vegetable farming as well as dairy farming are active. Fishing and forestry have long been an important part of Hokkaido's economy. They also form the basis for much of Hokkaido's industrial activity, including food-processing, woodworking, pulp, and paper industries.

Lake Mashu, a caldera lake in eastern Hokkaido.

Hokkaido is noted for its dramatic and unspoiled scenery, which includes active volcanoes, large lakes, and vast virgin forests. Major tourist attractions are Shikotsu-Toya, Akan, Daisetsuzan, Shiretoko, and Rishiri-Rebun-Sarobetsu national parks. Area: 83,451 sq km (32,220 sq mi) in 1992; pop: 5,665,699 in 1994; capital: Sapporo. Other major cities include Hakodate, Asahikawa, Otaru, Muroran, Tomakomai, Obihiro, and Kushiro.

Tohoku region (Tohoku *chiho*) 　　　　　東北地方●

Region encompassing the entire northeastern part of Honshu and consisting of Aomori, Iwate, Akita, Yamagata, Miyagi, and Fukushima prefectures. The region is largely mountainous, and most towns and cities are concentrated along the Pacific and SEA OF JAPAN coasts and in the centers of several basins. The climate is highly seasonal, with short summers and long winters.

The area is primarily an agricultural area and forestry and fishing are also important. There is some petroleum and natural-gas production, and the iron, steel, cement, chemical, pulp, and petroleum-refining industries have been developing. The principal city is Sendai. Area: 66,883 sq km (25,824 sq mi) in 1992; pop: 9,834,548 in 1994.

Tohoku region

Kanto region (Kanto *chiho*) 　　　　　関東地方●

Located in east central Honshu, consisting of TOKYO, Chiba, Saitama, Kanagawa, Gumma, Ibaraki, and Tochigi prefectures. This is Japan's most heavily populated region and is the political, economic, and cultural center of the nation. The regional center is the metropolitan area that includes TOKYO, Yokohama, Kawasaki, and Chiba. The region is dominated by the Kanto Plain.

The term Kanto (literally, "east of the barrier") originally referred to the area east of the barrier station (*sekisho*) at Osakayama in what is now Otsu, Shiga Prefecture; the term was used in contradistinction to the KANSAI REGION west of the station. The border was later moved twice, finally being set much farther east at the barrier station at Hakone (in what is now Kanagawa Prefecture).

Kanto region

The Tokyo-Yokohama district in the center of the region is Japan's leading commercial and industrial area. Agriculture plays a declining but still important role in the region's economy. Coastal fishing in the Pacific Ocean and Tokyo Bay has declined because of increased pollution and land reclamation in Tokyo Bay. Area: 32,413 sq km (12,515 sq mi) in 1992; pop: 38,902,262 in 1994.

Tokyo 　　　　　東京●

Capital of Japan. Located on the Kanto Plain, on the Pacific side of central Honshu. Bordered by the prefectures of Chiba on the east, Saitama on the north, Yamanashi on the west, and Kanagawa on the southwest, and by Tokyo Bay on the southeast. Under its administration are islands scattered in the western Pacific, among them the Izu Islands and the Ogasawara Islands.

Tokyo Prefecture comprises the 23 wards (*ku*) of urban Tokyo, 27 cities (*shi*), 1 county (*gun*), and 4 island administrative units (*shicho*). The county and the island units contain 14 towns and villages (*cho, son*). Area: 2,183 sq km (843 sq mi) in 1992; pop: 11,573,029 in 1994.

The residents of Tokyo live in a total of 5,003,985 dwellings, with an average floor space of 63 square meters (645 sq ft). The average household has 2.3 members.

Geography and Climate　　　　　　　　　　　　地形と気候●

Tokyo was known by the name Edo (literally, "Rivergate") before the Meiji Restoration (1868), and the principal rivers of the Kanto region—the Edogawa, Arakawa, and Sumidagawa—still flow to the sea through eastern Tokyo. Along the alluvial plains of the old river Tamagawa, volcanic ash emitted from the Fuji-Hakone Volcanic Range accumulated to form the Musashino Plateau, where the western wards (commonly known as the Yamanote district) and outlying districts are located. Some areas in the eastern wards (the *shitamachi* district) lie 2–3 meters (6.5–10 ft) below sea level.

The four seasons are sharply delineated, and the climate is generally mild, with the highest average monthly temperature in August (26.7°C; 80.1°F) and the lowest in January (4.7°C; 40.5°F). The annual precipitation is 1,460 millimeters (57.5 in).

Fauna and Flora　　　　　　　　　　　　　　　動物と植物●

Pollution and unchecked land development ravaged the animal and plant population in Tokyo Prefecture during the 1960s, but, with stricter pollution controls, 370 out of the approximately 570 bird species found throughout Japan have been sighted within Tokyo. Other wildlife found in the mountainous areas include the Japanese antelope, raccoon dog, fox, flying squirrel and rabbit.

The official tree of Tokyo is the ginkgo, which is utilized as a shade tree throughout the city. Other common trees in Tokyo include the cherry, zelkova, and Japanese oak.

History　　　　　　　　　　　　　　　　　　　歴史●

Where Tokyo now stands relics have been found dating from the Jomon (ca 10,000 BC–ca 300 BC), the Yayoi (ca 300 BC–ca AD 300), and the Kofun (ca 300–710) periods. During the 7th century Japan was divided into some 50 provinces, and Musashi Province was established in what is today Tokyo, Saitama, and eastern Kanagawa prefectures. Its administrative center was located in what is now the city of Fuchu, which served as the political center of the province for nearly 900 years. During the civil wars of the 15th century, the warrior Ota Dokan (1432–1486) constructed the predecessor of Edo castle at the present site of the Imperial Palace.

After nearly a century of warfare, Toyotomi Hideyoshi (1537–1598) partially united the country and dispatched Tokugawa Ieyasu (1543–1616) to Kanto in 1590 as lord of Edo Castle. After Hideyoshi's death Ieyasu completed the unification of Japan and established the Tokugawa shogunate in Edo in 1603. He constructed a castle town there with a *samurai* residential district on the castle's western side. To the east marshland was reclaimed, and a commercial and industrial area came into being. As the city flourished merchants and artisans flocked to Edo; the population reached one million by 1720, making Edo the largest city in the world at that time.

In 1867 the Tokugawa shogunate came to an end, and, with the Meiji Restoration the following year, Edo, renamed Tokyo ("eastern capital"), became the national capital. The imperial family took up residence at Edo Castle in 1869. In the following years Tokyo grew steadily in importance as the political, commercial, and financial center of Japan. Almost completely destroyed in the Tokyo Earthquake of 1923, the city was largely rebuilt by 1930 and administratively enlarged in 1943, merging surrounding districts and suburbs into Tokyo To (Tokyo Prefecture; officially, Tokyo Metropolis).

A portrait of Tokugawa Ieyasu, the warrior chieftain who survived Japan's late-16th-century wars to set up the Tokugawa shogunate in Edo (now Tokyo).

Much of Tokyo was destroyed during World War II by American bombing. After Japan's defeat Tokyo remained the seat of government, with the General Headquarters of the Supreme Commander for the Allied Powers (SCAP) located there until the end of the Occupation in 1952. During the period of economic recovery starting in the 1950s, large enterprises increasingly concentrated their managerial operations in Tokyo. This resulted in an increase in population from 6.3 million in 1950 to 9.7 million in 1960.

The city undertook a feverish building program in preparation for the 1964 Tokyo Olympic Games, and by 1965 the population had reached 10.9 million, resulting in serious housing problems and skyrocketing land prices. A program of building urban subcenters has since been carried out to alleviate the concentration of company head offices in the central Tokyo area, and the pollution problems that were severe in the late 1960s and early 1970s have now been alleviated to a degree; the waters of the river Sumidagawa in eastern Tokyo are relatively clean

Geography and Nature

once more. The four-lane intracity expressway system that was begun in the 1960s is still often severely congested, however, and a further period of rapidly spiraling land prices since the mid-1980s has put home ownership beyond the reach of most Tokyoites.

Local and Traditional Industry 地場産業と伝統産業●

Local industries were long centered in the three shitamachi wards of Taito, Sumida, and Arakawa, but in recent years are expanding to the surrounding wards, particularly Adachi and Katsushika. Products include clothing, knitted goods, precious metals, toys, and leather goods. Among traditional industries, fabric making has been prominent. Cities within Tokyo Prefecture such as Hachioji, Ome, and Musashi Murayama have been noted for the production of fabrics since the Edo period (1600–1868), and the island of Hachijojima is noted for its *kihachijo* dyed fabric. Many of the craftsmen making traditional products face the problems of weak consumer demand and the difficulty of financing successors.

Modern Industry and Finance 現代の産業と金融●

Tokyo developed into a center of manufacturing and heavy industry from the Meiji period (1868–1912) until the end of World War II. After 1965, however, tertiary industries—commerce, finance, transportation, communication, wholesale and retail stores, and service industries—began to surpass secondary industries. As of 1992 primary industries constituted only 0.1 percent of the total industries in Tokyo; secondary industries, 24.5 percent (compared to 50 percent in the 1960s); and tertiary industries, 72.2 percent. Tokyo boasts a total of approximately 765,600 enterprises employing nearly 8.2 million workers. Most of these enterprises are small and medium-sized concerns. The total output of Tokyo Prefecture in fiscal 1991 was ¥86.6 trillion.

As new office buildings take over the central part of the city, small shops and permanent residents have been forced out to suburban areas, creating the so-called doughnut phenomenon. The pollution of the 1970s also forced large manufacturing plants and related factories from the shitamachi lowlands to the outlying districts or to reclaimed land in Tokyo Bay and adjacent prefectures. With the soaring urban and suburban land prices in recent years, more companies have been relocating their research and development centers and some of their head office departments to buildings equipped with the latest communications technology in outlying areas of Tokyo. However, most large Japanese corporations, foreign companies, and the national press and mass media still have their head offices in Tokyo; these are particularly concentrated in Chiyoda, Chuo, and Minato wards.

Downtown Tokyo.

Tokyo Metropolitan Government Offices, Shinjuku, Tokyo. Completed in March 1991.

Another recent development has been the growth of the Shinjuku, Shibuya, and Ikebukuro districts. Now known as satellite city centers or urban subcenters, they have become flourishing business and recreation districts. The doughnut phenomenon, originally confined to the old city center, has spread to these satellite centers, and between 1985 and 1990 the population of the 23 urban wards of Tokyo Prefecture fell by 190,000.

Tokyo is also a major financial center. The Tokyo Stock Exchange is one of the largest in the world in terms of aggregate market value and total sales, and deposits in Tokyo banks constituted 24 percent of the nation's total deposits in 1993.

Transportation　　　　　　　　　　　　　　交通●

Tokyo is served by two AIRPORTS: Tokyo International Airport (commonly called Haneda Airport), the main terminal for domestic flights in the southern end of the city, and New Tokyo International Airport (commonly called Narita Airport), located 66 kilometers (41 mi) east of Tokyo.

Tokyo Station.

The nation's main railway lines are concentrated in Tokyo, with terminals at Tokyo, Ueno, and Shinjuku stations. Trains for the west (Nagoya, Osaka, Kyoto) leave from Tokyo Station (Tokaido and SHINKANSEN "bullet train" lines); trains for Tohoku, Hokkaido, and Niigata originate from Ueno Station (Tohoku, Joban, Takasaki, and Joetsu lines; the Tohoku and Joetsu Shinkansen lines originate from Tokyo Station). From Shinjuku Station trains connect the city with the mountainous regions of central Japan (Chuo trunk line).

The principal commuter railway lines in Tokyo are the Yamanote line, a loop around the heart of the city; the Keihin Tohoku line, running through Tokyo and Saitama and Kanagawa prefectures; the Chuo line, running through western Tokyo; and the Sobu line, connecting Tokyo and Chiba. A network of private railway lines radiates outward from the principal stations on the Yamanote line, and 12 private and metropolitan SUBWAY lines have replaced the old network of streetcars. Tokyo is also well served by bus lines, and expressways connect the city to various regions.

Education　　　　　　　　　　　　　　　　教育●

In recent years a number of colleges and universities have moved away from the crowded city, but Tokyo is still a major educational center, with 78 junior colleges and 107 universities as of 1993. The city is also the location of numerous academic societies, including the Japan Academy and the Japan Art Academy.

Cultural and Recreational Facilities　　文化及びリクリエーション施設●

The arts （芸術） Western culture was introduced into Japan

through the gateways of Yokohama and Tokyo after the Meiji Restoration, and Tokyo today offers a variety of modern arts as well as traditional arts such as KABUKI (drama), *nagauta* (singing), *buyo* (dance), and RAKUGO (a form of comic storytelling). There are eight large-scale theaters in Tokyo, including the Kabukiza and the National Theater. There are also numerous concert halls, museums, and art galleries.

The media （マスメディア） Tokyo is also a major information center. Eight general newspapers are published in Tokyo (including four in English), as well as three economic and industrial newspapers and seven sports newspapers; an average of more than 6,685,000 newspaper copies were printed each day in 1989. In addition, it is estimated that roughly 2,400 monthly and weekly magazines were being published in Tokyo in the early 1990s.

Parks and sports facilities （公園とスポーツ施設） Although most parks are small by Western standards, a considerable number are scattered throughout Tokyo. Major parks in central Tokyo include the Imperial Palace grounds, Hibiya Park, Ueno Park, and the Meiji Shrine Outer Garden. There are also some 10 zoological and botanical gardens in the metropolitan area. Major national parks in Tokyo Prefecture include Chichibu-Tama National Park, Ogasawara National Park, and part of Fuji-Hakone-Izu National Park.

Points of Interest 観光名所●

Situated in the center of Tokyo and surrounded by a moat and high stone walls is the Imperial Palace, still retaining vestiges of its former glory as the residence of the Tokugawa family. To the east lies the Ginza, an area known for its fine shops, department stores, and numerous restaurants, bars, and cabarets.

North of the Ginza is Nihombashi, the commercial hub of the city, from which all distances from Tokyo to places throughout Japan are measured. Nearby are the districts of Kanda, renowned for its bookshops and universities, and Akihabara, famous for its discount stores selling all kinds of electrical appliances. Further to the north lie Ueno and Ueno Park that houses the Tokyo National Museum, the National Science Museum, the National Museum of Western Art, the Ueno Zoological Gardens, and the temple Kan'eiji. To the east of Ueno is the oldest temple in Tokyo, Asakusa Kannon, in the heart of the shitamachi district, with its many shops still selling traditional handicrafts.

Sensoji temple, Asakusa, Tokyo.

Another point of interest in the capital is the Diet Building in Nagatacho. Nearby Roppongi and Azabu, situated close to Tokyo Tower, house many foreign embassies. Neighboring Akasaka is known for its luxurious nightlife. Near Shibuya Station lie Meiji Shrine, Yoyogi Park, the National Stadium, and Harajuku, a fashionable district popular with young people.

The area around Shinjuku Station—which has the highest rate of passenger turnover in the country—is rapidly being developed, with restaurants and theaters in the Kabukicho area on the eastern side of the station and numerous skyscrapers on the western side, including the new Tokyo Metropolitan Government Offices in the striking 48-story twin-tower building (243 m; 797 ft) designed by the world-famous architect Tange Kenzo (1913–). Another fast-growing commercial center is Ikebukuro, where the 60-story Sunshine City complex was completed in 1980.

A major project under way in the Tokyo Bay area is the Tokyo Frontier Project. This is a huge development on landfill sites that are planned for completion in the early 21st century. The Ariake and Daiba sites (448 hectares; 107 acres) will include blocks of high-technology "intelligent" buildings, sports and leisure facilities, and international conference centers. Complementing this colossal undertaking is the equally ambitious Tokyo Bay Bridge and Tunnel project, construction on which began in 1989 and is due for completion in 1996. Connecting the city of Kawasaki in Kanagawa Prefecture with Kisarazu in Chiba Prefecture, this project will serve as a key link in the Tokyo Bay ring road, which, it is hoped, will reduce traffic congestion in central Tokyo.

Chubu region (Chubu *chiho*) 中部地方● Chubu region

Encompassing Niigata, Toyama, Ishikawa, Fukui, Yamanashi, Nagano, Gifu, Shizuoka, and Aichi prefectures in central Honshu. Geographically divided into three districts: the Hokuriku region on the SEA OF JAPAN side, the Central Highlands (or Tosan), and the Tokai region on the Pacific seaboard. The principal city of the region is Nagoya. The region, largely mountainous, is dominated by the Japanese Alps and contains numerous volcanoes including Mt. Fuji (FUJISAN). Some of Japan's longest rivers, the Shinanogawa, Kisogawa, and Tenryugawa, flow through the region. The Niigata Plain along the Sea of Japan is one of the largest rice-producing areas in Japan, and the Nobi Plain on the Pacific coast is the most densely populated and highly industrialized area in this region. Numerous inland basins have very cold winters. The Pacific side is generally mild, and the Sea of Japan side has long snowy winters.

The Chubu region includes three industrial areas (the Chukyo Industrial Zone and the Tokai and Hokuriku industrial regions). Among

Geography and Nature

traditional products of the district are lacquer ware and ceramics. Agricultural products include rice, tea, mandarin oranges, strawberries, grapes, peaches, and apples. Fishing is important all along its coast. Area: 66,775 sq km (25,782 sq mi) in 1992; pop: 21,170,706 in 1994.

Kinki region (Kinki *chiho*)　　　　　　　　近畿地方●

Located in west central Honshu and consisting of Osaka, Hyogo, Kyoto, Shiga, Mie, Wakayama, and Nara prefectures. It is the nation's second most important industrial region. The terrain is mountainous with many small basins in between and numerous coastal plains on the Inland Sea, Osaka Bay, and the Kii Channel. The Kii Peninsula is warm even in winter. The northern part of the region faces the SEA OF JAPAN and is noted for its heavy snowfall.

Kinki region

The Kyoto-Nara area was the cultural and political center of Japan in ancient days, but it lost its political significance after the capital was moved to Tokyo in 1868. The Osaka-Kobe district is the center of commerce and industry for western Japan. This area is called the Hanshin Industrial Zone. Rice and citrus fruit production, lumbering, and fishing are important activities. Principal cities include OSAKA, KYOTO, and Kobe, one of the country's most important ports. Area: 33,090 sq km (12,776 sq mi) in 1992; pop: 22,142,576 in 1994.

Kansai region (Kansai *chiho*)　　　　　　　関西地方●

A term loosely applied to the area centering on the cities of Osaka, Kyoto, and Kobe. It is sometimes defined as equivalent to the KINKI REGION, but the latter is an official geographical designation with clearly defined boundaries. The term Kansai is rather a cultural and historical one, the definition of which has changed over the years. Kansai (literally, "west of the barrier") was first used sometime before the 10th century in contradistinction to the word Kanto. Kanto ("east of the barrier") referred to the area east of the barrier station (*sekisho*) at Osaka (in what is now Shiga Prefecture), and Kansai referred to the area west of the station. It was later fixed farther east at the barrier station at Hakone (in what is now Kanagawa Prefecture). The term is also used to describe local speech patterns (as in Kansai *ben* or Kansai *namari*) and manners and customs. See also KANTO REGION.

Kyoto 京都●

City in southern Kyoto Prefecture, in the Kyoto fault basin. The ancient capital of Japan from 794 to 1868, Kyoto, rich in historical sites, is today the seat of the prefectural government and one of Japan's largest cities. Kyoto is renowned for its fine textiles and traditional products and is also a thriving center for industry.

Natural Features 地形●

The low Tamba Mountains surround the city to the north, east, and west. Two peaks, Hieizan and Atagoyama, dominate the northeast and northwest of the city. The rivers Kamogawa and Katsuragawa flow through the central and western districts of the city. Kyoto's landlocked location accounts for its cold winters and hot summers. The annual average temperature is 15.2 °C (59.4 °F) and annual precipitation is 1,600 mm (63 in).

History 歴史●

The Kyoto fault basin was first settled in the 7th century by the Hata family, immigrants from Korea. In 603 Koryuji, the family temple of the Hata, was constructed at Uzumasa in the western part of the basin. In 794 Kyoto, then called Heiankyo, became the capital of Japan. The plan of the new city was patterned after China's Tang dynasty (618–907) capital of Chang'an (modern Xi'an). Its rectangular shape measured 4.5 kilometers (2.8 mi) east to west and 5.2 kilometers (3.2 mi) north to south.

Nijojo, a residential castle located in the city of Kyoto, erected by Tokugawa Ieyasu.

Kyoto was temporarily eclipsed as the center of national power by Kamakura during the Kamakura period (1185–1333), but during the Muromachi period (1333–1568) a shogunate was established in Kyoto, and the city regained its status as the nation's political center. During the Onin War (1467–1477), which signaled the end of the Muromachi shogunate, a large part of the city was destroyed.

During the Edo period (1600–1868) the Tokugawa shogunate was firmly established in Edo (now Tokyo) and the political focus of the country again shifted away from Kyoto. However, the city still prospered as an artistic, economic, and religious center. Particularly notable were fabrics such as *nishijin-ori* (brocade) and *yuzen-zome* (printed-silk), pottery, lacquer ware, doll making, and fan making. The city received a great blow when the capital was transferred to Tokyo after the Meiji Restoration (1868), but responded with a rapid program of modernization.

Kyoto Today 今日の京都●

Lacking a harbor and surrounding open land, Kyoto was slow in developing modern industries, but today, as part of the Hanshin

Industrial Zone, Kyoto has numerous electrical, machinery, and chemical plants. The city is also an educational and cultural center. There are some 37 universities and private institutes of higher learning, including Kyoto and Doshisha universities. Kyoto has 24 museums, including the Kyoto National Museum, and it possesses a total of 202 National Treasures (20 percent of the country's total) and 1,684 Important Cultural Properties (15 percent). In addition the city itself is a veritable historical storehouse. The Kyoto Imperial Palace and the Nijo Castle are both remarkable examples of Japanese architecture. The Katsura Detached Palace with its lovely pond and teahouses, and the Shugakuin Detached Palace, famed for its fine garden, draw visitors from afar. Located close to Kyoto Station are two temples of the Jodo Shin sect, Nishi Honganji and Higashi Honganji, both imposing examples of Buddhist architecture, as well as Toji, noted for its five-tiered pagoda.

East of the Kamogawa are the temple Kiyomizudera, with its wooden platform built out over a deep gorge; the Yasaka Shrine, where the annual Gion Festival is held in July; and the Heian Shrine, where the annual Jidai Festival is held in October. Other noted temples include Chion'in; Ginkakuji, built in 1482 and famed for its garden; and Nanzen-ji, situated in a pine grove east of the Heian Shrine. In the northern part of the city are the Kamo Shrines, where the Aoi Festival is held in May each year. To the northwest are the Zen temple Daitokuji, with its priceless art objects; Kinkakuji, with its three-story golden pavilion; Ninnaji, renowned for its cherry blossoms; and Koryuji. The natural beauty of the Hozukyo gorge, the Sagano district, and the hills of Takao also attracts visitors. Kyoto is the national center for the tea ceremony and flower arrangement and is the birthplace of NO, kyogen, KABUKI, and other traditional performing arts. Area: 610.2 sq km (235.6 sq mi) in 1992; pop: 1,390,607 in 1994.

Maiko san (*geisha* apprentices).

Osaka 大阪●

Capital of Osaka Prefecture. The third largest city in Japan after TOKYO and Yokohama, it is the financial center of western Japan. In the 7th and 8th centuries Osaka was a port for trade with China and the site of several imperial residences. The national unifier Toyotomi Hideyoshi (1537–1598) built Osaka Castle as his headquarters in 1583. In the Edo period (1600–1868) Osaka served as the entrepôt for goods, especially tax rice, for the entire nation and was called Japan's "kitchen."

Osaka is the center of the Hanshin Industrial Zone. Its principal industries are textiles, chemicals, steel, machinery, and metal. Besides Osaka Castle, attractions include the Osaka Municipal Museum of Fine Arts, the remains of the ancient capital of Naniwakyo, the temple Shitennoji, and the Sumiyoshi Shrine. Cultural attractions include the BUNRAKU puppet theater as well as kabuki. Area: 220.5 sq km (85 sq mi) in 1992; pop: 2,481,464 in 1994.

Chugoku region (Chugoku *chiho*)   中国地方● Chugoku region

Encompasses the entire western tip of Honshu, comprising Hiroshima, Okayama, Shimane, Tottori, and Yamaguchi prefectures. With the Chugoku Mountains as the dividing line, the Inland Sea side is called the San'yo region and the SEA OF JAPAN side, the San'in region. It is a mountainous region with many small basins and coastal plains. The most heavily populated areas are along the Inland Sea coast, around the cities of Hiroshima, Kurashiki, and Okayama. The Inland Sea coast is a major area of industry and commerce. The Okayama Plain and the coastal plains along the Sea of Japan are important rice-producing areas. The warm, dry climate of the Inland Sea coast is also ideal for citrus fruit and grapes. The waters off the coast were once among Japan's richest fishing grounds, but catches have declined because of industrial pollution. Area: 31,907 sq km (12,319 sq mi) in 1992; pop: 7,755,125 in 1994.

Shikoku region (Shikoku *chiho*)   四国地方● Shikoku region

Region consisting of Shikoku, the smallest of Japan's four main islands, and numerous surrounding islands. Shikoku lies across the Inland Sea from western Honshu and across the Bungo Channel from northeastern Kyushu. It consists of Kagawa, Tokushima, Ehime, and Kochi prefectures. Shikoku's high mountains and steep slopes severely limit agriculture, habitation, and communication. The climate is subtropical and on the Pacific Ocean side of the island there is heavy rainfall in summer.

Much of the island is a thinly populated agricultural region, with little large-scale industry. Two recently completed chains of bridges linking Shikoku with Honshu are expected to bring in many new industries. Extensive land reclamation in Kagawa and Tokushima prefectures should provide more room for this industrial expansion. Takamatsu and Matsuyama are the largest cities. Area: 18,796 sq km (7,257 sq mi) in 1992; pop: 4,220,019 in 1994.

Kyushu region (Kyushu *chiho*) 九州地方●

Region consisting of Kyushu, the third largest and southernmost of the four major islands of Japan, and surrounding islands. Kyushu comprises Fukuoka, Nagasaki, Oita, Kumamoto, Miyazaki, Saga, and Kagoshima prefectures. OKINAWA PREFECTURE is sometimes included in the term Kyushu. Geographically divided into north, central, and south Kyushu, the region has a mountainous interior with numerous coastal plains, volcanoes, and hot springs. The climate is subtropical with heavy precipitation.

Kyushu region

Rice, tea, tobacco, sweet potatoes, and citrus fruit are the major crops, and stock farming, hog raising, and fishery also flourish. Heavy and chemical industries are concentrated in northern Kyushu. The major cities are Kita Kyushu and Fukuoka. Area (including Okinawa Prefecture): 44,416 sq km (17,149 sq mi) in 1992; pop: 14,631,866 in 1994.

Okinawa Prefecture (Okinawa Ken) 沖縄県●

Composed of a chain of some 60 islands generally referred to as the Ryukyu Islands; located south of Kyushu and surrounded by the East China Sea and the Pacific Ocean. The islands are generally subdivided into the Okinawa, Miyako, Yaeyama, and Senkaku groups. Okinawa, the main island of the Okinawa group, is by far the largest in terms of both size and population and is the prefecture's economic, administrative, and cultural center. With the exception of the northern portion of the main island, most of the terrain is fairly level. The climate is subtropical, with abundant rainfall; typhoons are frequent.

While the people of Okinawa are of the same ethnic strain as those of mainland Japan, they have developed outside the framework of the Japanese state for much of their history. In the 15th century the Ryukyus developed into a unified kingdom, whose ruler paid tribute to the Chinese emperor. In 1609 the kingdom was conquered by the Shimazu Family of the Satsuma domain (now Kagoshima Prefecture).

Ryukyu Islands

However, tribute missions continued to be sent to China. After the Meiji Restoration (1868) the Japanese government claimed formal sovereignty over the Ryukyus and incorporated them as Okinawa Prefecture. This was not recognized by the Chinese until the conclusion of the Sino-Japanese War in 1895. The invasion of Okinawa by American troops in 1945 resulted in some of the bloodiest fighting in World War II, with great loss of life among the civilian population. The islands were administered by the American military from 1945 until 1972, at which time they were returned to Japan.

Economic development has been made difficult by the fact that much of Okinawa, including prime agricultural land, has been occupied by American military bases. Remoteness from mainland Japan and lack of fresh water have also hindered progress. Tourism is the primary source of revenue. Okinawa's warm climate, subtropical vegetation, and beaches, as well as its unique arts and handicrafts, attract visitors. The International Ocean Exposition was held here in 1975. Area: 2,265 sq km (875 sq mi) in 1992; pop: 1,266,898 in 1994; capital: Naha. Other major cities include Okinawa, Ginowan, and Urasoe.

Fujisan (Mt. Fuji)   富士山●

The highest mountain (3,776 m; 12,388 ft) in Japan and the most loved by the Japanese. Located on the border of Shizuoka and Yamanashi prefectures in central Honshu, Fujisan boasts a superb conical form that has become famous throughout the world as a symbol of Japan and has inspired generations of Japanese artists and poets. Although dormant since 1707, it is classified by geologists as an active volcano.

At the summit of Fujisan is a crater with a diameter of about 800 m (2,600 ft) and a depth of about 200 m (660 ft). The diameter at the base of the mountain, including the broad lava fields of the piedmont zone, is roughly 40–50 km (25–30 mi). Lava from Fujisan has been discovered in the seabed near Tagonoura, indicating that there is a vertical range in the lava distribution of nearly 4,000 m (13,100 ft).

In broad perspective Fujisan is part of the Fuji Volcanic Zone. The timberline is found in the altitude range of 2,400–2,800 m (7,900–9,200 ft); between this line and the peak are naked slopes of lava and lapilli. Fujisan has few alpine plants compared with other mountains exceeding 2,500 meters (8,200 ft) in central Japan.

Climbing of Fujisan started as a religious practice. Adherents of Fujiko, a syncretic sect with both Buddhist and Shinto elements, regard the mountain as sacred. The Shinto shrine Fujisan Hongu Sengen Jinja, whose main shrine is in the city of Fujinomiya, south of the mountain, also treats Fujisan as sacred. Nowadays many people climb Fujisan for

Mt. Fuji in winter.

pleasure. It is crowded with tens of thousands of climbers daily during the climbing season, which runs from 1 July to 31 August.

Plants and Animals

Plants (*shokubutsu*) 植物●

Extending north to south for some 3,500 kilometers (2,175 mi), the Japanese archipelago has a great diversity of climate and vegetation. Botanists estimate that there are 5,000 to 6,000 native species of plants. This article deals chiefly with certain seed plants (spermatophytes) that are of particular importance to the Japanese people.

Types of Plants in Japan 日本における植物の種類●

In terms of plant distribution, Japan is included in the East Asian temperate zone and may be roughly subdivided into the following five zones:

1. The subtropical zone, which includes the Ryukyu and Ogasawara island groups. Characteristic plants are the *gajumaru* (*Ficus microcarpa*) of the Ryukyus and the *himetsubaki* (*Schima wallichii*) of the Ogasawaras.

This Japanese cedar on the island of Yakushima is known as Jomon Sugi. It is estimated to be 3,000 to 7,000 years old.

2. The warm-temperate zone of broad-leaved evergreen forests, which covers the greater part of southern Honshu, Shikoku, and Kyushu. The *yabutsubaki* (*Camellia japonica*), the *shiinoki* (*Castanopsis sieboldii*), and the *kusu* (*Cinnamomum camphora*) are among its characteristic plants.

3. The cool-temperate zone of broad-leaved deciduous forests, which covers central and northern Honshu and the southwestern part of Hokkaido. Characteristic plants include the *konara* (*Quercus serrata*) and the *buna* (*Fagus crenata*).

4. The subalpine zone, which includes central and northern Hokkaido. Characteristic plants include the *kokemomo* (*Vaccinium vitisidaea*) and the *tohi* (*Picea jezoensis*).

5. The alpine zone, which covers the highlands of central Honshu and the central part of Hokkaido, with the *haimatsu* (*Pinus pumila*) and *komakusa* (*Dicentra peregrina*) among the characteristic plants.

Although some plants came to Japan very early in the nation's history, most of the naturalized plants were introduced in rapid succession after the beginning of the Meiji period (1868–1912). The number of naturalized plants is said to be between 200 and 500. Although most came from Europe, the United States has in recent years become a major source.

Uses of Plants in Japan 日本における植物の利用●

Throughout their recorded history, the Japanese have utilized plants for food and for countless other purposes, including clothing, medicines, dyes, oils, tools, roofing, sculpture, paper, matting, hats, ropes, baskets, and fuel. Most plants now being put to such uses are indigenous to Japan, but the majority of edible plants are thought to have been introduced from the Asian continent.

Plants in Literature 文学と植物●

The beauty of nature, embodied in the term *kacho fugetsu* ("flowers, birds, wind, and moon"), has been a principal theme in Japanese literature, especially WAKA (31-syllable poetry) and HAIKU. The fact that flowers have been given first place in this phrase does not seem to be coincidental. *The Tale of Genji*, written about the year 1000 and noted for its superb descriptions of nature, makes reference to 101 kinds of plants. Frequent use of trees and plants in similes is often considered one of the characteristics of Japanese literature.

For the Japanese, nature has not only been an object of aesthetic appreciation but also an agent evoking intense poetic sentiments. They have loved flowers not so much for their fragrance and color as for their form and emotional import. The special significance Japanese have attached to the seasons in their poetry is an expression of their close observation of and affection for plants as signs of the ever-vanishing, ever-perpetuating pattern of nature. An understanding of this attitude is essential to the appreciation of traditional Japanese literature.

Plants in the Visual Arts 芸術と植物●

Pictorial and other arts in Japan have also traditionally relied heavily on the artist's sensitivity to nature and have generally tended toward the simple, compact, and sparely graceful. Traditional Japanese renditions of landscapes do not display the wide range of color seen in Western-style oil paintings. In sculpture, too, works are in general delicately carved and small in scale. Plants, flowers, and birds or their patterns are frequently reproduced in lifelike colors on fabric, lacquer ware, and ceramic ware. A love of natural form and an eagerness to express it ideally have been primary motives in the development of traditional Japanese arts, such as FLOWER ARRANGEMENT, the TEA CEREMONY, tray landscapes (*bonkei*), BONSAI, and landscape gardening.

Plants and Folklore 植物と民俗学●

In the hope of avoiding natural disasters, early people formulated sacred rites of exorcism, ablution, and divination. These mystico-religious activities and an awe of nature in general led people to see symbols of the divine in trees and flowers. An excellent example is the once widely practiced worship of primeval evergreen trees—pines (*matsu*), cedars (*sugi*), cypresses (*hinoki*), and camphor trees (*kusunoki*)—which the early Japanese believed offered habitation (*yorishiro*) to deities who descended from heaven. The practice of decorating the gates of houses with pine branches (*kadomatsu*) on New Year's Day (see NEW YEAR) derives from the belief that this was a means of welcoming deities.

Another folk custom involving flowers, the flower-viewing party (HANAMI), also dates back to antiquity. Originally an event closely related to agricultural rites, it later became a purely recreational activity. The most popular flower for viewing has been the *sakura* (flowering cherry). An annual cherry-viewing party sponsored by the imperial court became an established custom in the Heian period (794–1185). During the Edo period (1600–1868) the practice of holding annual flower-viewing parties spread among the common people. Besides the sakura, the *ume* (Japanese plum), *fuji* (wisteria), *kiku* (chrysanthemum), and *hasu* (lotus) are common objects of viewing.

Plants and Religion   植物と宗教●

Plum blossoms.

The early Japanese worshiped nature as divine. They believed that natural features such as mountains, rivers, stones, and plants all had spirits and offered prayers to and sought salvation from them. For religious festivals, evergreen trees such as pines and *sakaki* (*Cleyera japonica*) were used because they were thought to be dwellings of gods, and marine products (seaweed, fish, and shellfish) and fresh farm vegetables were offered to the deities instead of animal flesh. These traditions survive in present-day Shinto. Buddhism, which was introduced to Japan in about the 6th century, banned the destruction of living creatures, so flowers and plants were used for its rituals, a practice that is still followed.

Plants in Modern Japan   近現代の日本における植物●

During the Meiji period, the Japanese became preoccupied with modern and Western values and much less concerned with nature. At one time this change was generally regarded as a sign of progress, but a major consequence of Japan's rapid industrialization (especially since World War II) has been the indiscriminate exploitation of nature, including reckless deforestation. This in turn has led to widespread pollution that has affected every element of Japanese society. People have recently come to realize that the "progress" they once believed to be entirely beneficial is not necessarily so and that conservation and rehabilitation of the natural environment should be a major priority. Many Japanese now feel strongly that their country's great wealth of plant life should be protected and reconsidered in light of old values.

Animals (*dobutsu*) 動物●

The Japanese islands are inhabited by Southeast Asiatic tropical animals, Korean and Chinese temperate-zone animals, and Siberian subarctic animals. Japan's fauna includes many species and relicts not found in neighboring areas. Some of these relicts are found on Honshu, but a larger number inhabit the Ogasawara Islands and the islands south of Kyushu.

Overall Characteristics 全体的な特徴●

In zoogeographic terms, the sea south of central Honshu belongs to the Indo-Western Pacific region, which is part of the tropical kingdom; it abounds in bright coral fish, sea snakes, and turtles and is inhabited by the dugong and the black finless porpoise. The sea north of central Honshu belongs to the Northern Pacific region, part of the northern kingdom, which extends along the southern coast of the Aleutian Islands and the west coast of the United States down to California and is inhabited by the fur seal, Steller's sea lion, and Baird's beaked whale. Finally, Hokkaido, which largely faces the Sea of Okhotsk in the Arctic region, is visited occasionally by animals indigenous to the Arctic region, such as the walrus.

In the zoogeographical division of the Japanese islands by land animals, the Ryukyu Islands south of Amami Oshima are sometimes regarded as part of the Oriental region extending from the Malayan Peninsula to India and sometimes as a transition zone from this region to the Palaearctic region; the area north of Yakushima off southern Kyushu is considered part of the Palaearctic region. The Ryukyu Islands are inhabited mostly by tropical animals, such as the flying fox, crested serpent eagle, variable lizard, and butterflies of the family Danaidae. In mainland Japan (Honshu, Shikoku, and Kyushu) and Hokkaido, which belong to the Palaearctic region, two groups of animals are predominant: those of deciduous forests of Korea and central and northern China, such as the raccoon dog, sika deer, Japanese crested ibis, mandarin duck, and hairstreak; and those of coniferous forests of Siberia, such as the brown bear, pika, hazel grouse, common lizard, and nine-spined stickleback.

The *kamoshika*, a herbivorous animal found only in Japan.

Of these animals, those of the Korean and Chinese group are confined mostly to the Japanese mainland and those of the Siberian group to Hokkaido. Consequently, it is common to include the mainland in the Manchurian subregion of the Palaearctic region and Hokkaido in the Siberian subregion. However, the geological history of the Japanese islands, marked by repeated separation from and reunion with the Asian continent, is exceedingly complex, giving rise to a corresponding complexity of animal migration and, as a result, noncontinuous distribution. The fauna of Japan differs slightly from those found in corresponding areas of the continent and not a few species are endemic to Japan.

For the protection of endangered species, countermeasures such as the conservation of habitats, artificial breeding, and feeding have been reviewed by the Environment Agency, and some proposals already have been implemented. In order to protect animals and insects, in 1979 the agency started a quinquennial survey of the status of animal populations.

Animals in Japanese Culture   日本文化と動物●

Many of the beliefs and views held in Japan about various animals stem from native traditions, Buddhist sources, and the classic works of Chinese literature. Such traditional animal symbols as cranes and turtles (for felicity and long life) and swallows (for faithful return) were adopted from the Chinese by the Japanese ruling class in the protohistoric and ancient periods. It was not until the late medieval period (mid-12th–16th centuries) that a set of animal symbols that were truly Japanese evolved.

Until the late 19th century, the vast majority of Japanese refrained from slaughtering four-legged animals and relied chiefly on fish for animal protein. This practice derived mainly from Buddhist teachings. The Japanese view of animals includes the role played by *jikkan junishi*, or the sexagenary cycle of the ancient Chinese calendrical system. The cycle is broken down into subcycles of 12 years, each of which is represented by an animal. Even today, it is common practice to associate a person's character and fortune—based on his or her birth date—with those of the corresponding animal in the sexagenary cycle (e.g., "the year of the dragon"). In addition, animals and flowers are often used in artistic and poetic descriptions to elicit a sense of time and season.

The *noguchigera* of
Okinawa.

Birds (*chorui*)   鳥類●

There is no endemic genus among the 490 bird species found in Hokkaido and Honshu. The only genera endemic to Japan are those represented by the *meguro* (Bonin honeyeater; *Apalopteron familiare*) and the extinct Ogasawara *mashiko* (Bonin grosbeak; *Chaunoproctus ferreorostris*) of the Ogasawara Islands and the *noguchigera* (Pryer's woodpecker) of Okinawa, all of which are native to islands far from the Asian continent.

Mainland Species   固有種●

The four truly endemic mainland species are the *yamadori* (copper pheasant), the black *karasubato* (Japanese wood pigeon; *Columba janthina*), the red-cheeked *aogera* (Japanese green woodpecker), and the black-backed *seguro sekirei* (Japanese wagtail). The *komadori* ("horse bird"; Japanese robin) and the *nojiko* (Japanese yellow bunting; *Emberiza sulphurata*) breed only in Japan and can be classified endemic, but they migrate to warmer climes in winter.

Seabirds   海鳥●

Among seabirds seldom seen outside Japan are the very rare *ahodori* (short-tailed albatross; *Diomedea albatrus*) found in Torishima and the Senkaku Islands; the *umineko* (black-tailed gull), which breeds in Hokkaido and Honshu; and the *kammuri umisuzume* (Japanese auk; *Synthliboramphus wumisuzume*), which breeds in the mainland and the Izu Islands.

Nonendemic Species   固有種でないもの●

Japan's common, nonendemic birds include the *tancho* (Japanese crane), which breeds in Hokkaido; the *oshidori* (mandarin duck); the *karugamo* (spotbill duck), found year round throughout Japan; the *sashiba* (gray-faced buzzard eagle), which breeds in the mainland; the mountain-dwelling *kumataka* (Hodgson's hawk eagle), a mainland inhabitant used for hawking; the giant *shimafukuro* (fish owl; *Ketupa blakistoni*) in Hokkaido; the *kijibato* (eastern turtledove; *Streptopelia orientalis*) and the *hiyodori* (brown-eared bulbul; *Hypsipetes amaurotis*), found all over Japan; the sweet-voiced *uguisu* (bush warbler); the lemon-breasted *kibitaki* (narcissus flycatcher; *Ficedula narcissina*); the long-tailed *sankocho* (black paradise flycatcher; *Terpsiphone atrocaudata*); the trainable *yamagara* (varied tit; *Parus varius*); and the nectar-sucking *mejiro* (Japanese white-eye; *Zosterops japonica*).

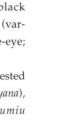

Japanese cranes at Kushiro Marsh in Hokkaido.

Other birds worthy of mention are the rare *toki* (Japanese crested ibis; *Nipponia nippon*), the *onaga* (azure-winged magpie; *Cyanopica cyana*), the giant *owashi* (Steller's sea eagle; *Haliaeetus pelagicus*), the *umiu* (Temminck's cormorant; *Phalacrocorax filamentosus*), several species of *hototogisu*, the *akashobin* (ruddy kingfisher; *Halcyon coromanda*), the *raicho* (ptarmigan), the high-mountain-dwelling *iwahibari* (alpine accentor; *Prunella collaris*), and the *kiji* (common pheasant).

Fishes *(gyorui)*   魚類●

There are about 3,000 species of freshwater and seawater fishes in and around the Japanese islands. Important freshwater fish include the river-dwelling *ayu* (sweetfish); the *iwana* (charr; *Salvelinus pluvius*), of

Geography and Nature

mountain streams; the *moroko* (*Gnathopogon elongatus*), of rivers on plains; the *wakasagi* (*Hypomesus olidus*), of lakes and swamps; the *koi* (carp), distributed intermittently in Europe and East Asia; the *funa* (crucian carp), found throughout the world; the *medaka* (Japanese killifish; *Oryzias latipes*); and the *dojo* (loach; *Misgurnus anguillicaudatus*). More than 10 species of the beautiful *tanago* (bitterling; *Acheilognathus moriokae*) inhabit rivers and swamps in northern Japan and lay eggs in the gills of such shellfish as the *karasugai* (*Cristaria plicata*); many of these are endangered endemic species, such as the *miyako tanago* (*Tanakia tanago*) in rivers on the Kanto Plain. The *mahaze* (goby) is found along the coast from Hokkaido down to Kyushu, and the *tobihaze* (mudskipper; *Periophthalmus cantonensis*) is found in the western part of Tokyo Bay and along the coasts of South Asia, Australia, and Africa.

Natural monuments and protected species
(*tennen kinembutsu*) 天然記念物●

The Japanese term tennen kinembutsu, usually translated as "natural monument," has a wider range of meaning than any one English equivalent. In the strict sense it refers to natural objects and phenomena (including species of animals and plants) characteristic of or peculiar to Japan that have been designated for preservation under the Cultural Properties Law of 1950 or similar local laws. These include certain geologic or mineral formations and areas (other than national parks) of special historic, scenic, or scientific interest, as well as certain species of animals and plants found only in specific areas of Japan. Natural monuments and protected species are classified into two categories: those designated for preservation by the national government under the Cultural Properties Law (953 in 1992, including 75 classified as "special natural monuments") and those set aside for protection by the laws of local public bodies such as prefectures, cities, towns, and villages.

Protected Areas 保護区域●

Areas of specific interest that have been set aside as tennen kinembutsu are classified under a number of official designations such as Nature Protection District, Primeval Forest, and Shrine Forest. Nature Protection Districts include Lake Towada; the river Oirasegawa; the Kurobe gorge; the Oze, Torishima, and Kushiro bogs; and the island of Minami Iojima. Primeval Forests include the Daisetsuzan area, the Sarugawa Headwaters Primeval Forest, and the Maruyama Primeval Forest (all in Hokkaido), and the Kasugayama Primeval Forest in Nara

Lake Towada in the Towada-Hachimantai National Park.

and the Aso Kitamukidani Primeval Forest. One Shrine Forest is the Miyazaki Kashima Forest in Toyama Prefecture.

Plants   植物●

Certain rock-zone flora found in specific locations and the boundary zones of distribution of certain plants found only in limited areas are also classified as tennen kinembutsu. A great number of very old or very large individual trees have also been designated as natural monuments.

Geologic formations that have been designated as natural monuments include the group of cirques (deep, steep-walled basins) at Yakushidake, the limestone cave known as Akiyoshido in Yamaguchi Prefecture, and the upthrust coasts of Kisakata in Akita Prefecture. A number of unique mineral formations and fossil sites have also been designated.

Animals   動物●

Indigenous species of Japanese wildlife designated as tennen kinembutsu include the Amami *no kurousagi*, the *meguro* (Bonin honeyeater), and the giant salamander (*o sanshouo*). Other tennen kinembutsu include cranes and their migration grounds in Kagoshima Prefecture, the natural habitat of sea bream in the waters of Tainoura in Chiba Prefecture, and the breeding grounds of the horseshoe crab in the waters near Kasaoka, Okayama Prefecture. Naturalized species include the magpie, the turtledove and domestic birds and animals (such as certain varieties of fowl), the *misaki* horse (*misaki uma*), Mishima cattle (Mishima *ushi*), and the long-tailed cock (*onagadori*).

The *o sanshouo* salamander is the world's largest amphibian.

Ise Shrine in Mie Prefecture. One of two treasure repositories of the Outer Shrine. The shrine is razed and rebuilt every 20 years in a rite called *shikinen sengu*.

History of Japan (*nihonshi*) 日本史●

Observers in Europe and the United States are naturally tempted to view Japanese history in terms of its encounters with the West. From this perspective, the "Christian Century" from ca 1540 to ca 1640, and the century and a half from the arrival of Commodore Matthew Perry's fleet and the "Opening of Japan" in the mid-19th century to the present, tend to be viewed as the major phases of Japanese history. The Japanese themselves, of course, see these periods of contact with the West, especially in modern times, as vital phases of their historical development, but they also look to their relations with the Asian continent. They prize the formative contacts with China and Korea in the premodern era and recall with regret Japan's imperialist aggression in Korea, China, and Manchuria in the period leading to World War II, a tragic episode that has shaped their modern history in numerous ways and with which they are still coming to terms.

Despite the importance of these contacts with other societies, however, it is the unfolding history of the Japanese people within the islands of the Japanese archipelago itself that must take center stage in any discussion of the Japanese past. That past can be divided into seven major phases: prehistoric (*senshi*), protohistoric (*genshi*), ancient (*kodai*), medieval (*chusei*), early modern (*kinsei*), modern (*kindai*), and contemporary (*gendai*).

Major Period of Japanese History
時代区分

Western calendar	Periods (*jidai*)
10,000 BC	Paleolithic (pre-10,000 BC)
300 BC	Jomon (ca 10,000 BC–ca 300 BC)
AD 300	Yayoi (ca 300 BC–ca AD 300)
400	Kofun (Yamato; ca 300–700)
500	
600	Asuka (593–710)
700	Nara (710–794)
800	Heian (794–1185)
900	
1200	Kamakura (1185–1333)
1300	Northern and Southern Courts (1337–1392)
1400	Muromachi (1333–1568)
1500	Sengoku (1467–1568)
1600	Azuchi-Momoyama (1568–1600)
1700	Edo (Tokugawa; 1600–1868)
1800	
1900	Meiji (1868–1912)
	Taisho (1912–1926)
	Showa (1926–1989)
	Heisei (1989–)

The Prehistoric Period 先史時代●

Archaeologists who specialize in the earliest phase of Japanese social development usually divide the prehistoric phase into four major periods: a long paleolithic preceramic period prior to ca 10,000 BC; the Jomon period (ca 10,000 BC–ca 300 BC), which saw the introduction of ceramics; the Yayoi period (ca 300 BC–ca AD 300), when metals and sedentary agriculture became widespread; and the Kofun period (ca 300–710), age of the great burial mounds and the beginnings of political centralization. However, this latter period, which was one of transition to the era of written records, is also known as the protohistoric period.

The first inhabitants of the Japanese islands were paleolithic hunter-gatherers from the continent who used sophisticated stone blades

but had no ceramics or settled agriculture. This paleolithic culture persisted until the close of the Pleistocene epoch, about 13,000 years ago, when
the Japanese climate ameliorated and sea levels began to rise. In these
changing climatic circumstances a new culture began to overlay the older
paleolithic culture. This new culture is known as Jomon (literally, "cord
marked") from the magnificent pottery that characterized it. Although it
has been commonly thought that the Jomon people were hunter-gatherers
who did not practice cultivation, recent research suggests that by about
1000 BC in Kyushu they were cultivating a green-leaf condiment known as
shiso and had begun to cultivate rice, which was not native to Japan.

From about 300 BC Jomon culture was overlaid by a distinctly different culture, the Yayoi, characterized by less flamboyant ceramics, a
knowledge of bronze and iron technologies, including fine weaponry, and
the systematic development of wet-field rice agriculture. These developments laid the basis for the strong martial current found in Japan's early
history and for the agricultural way of life that profoundly shaped
Japanese society into the modern era. They also contributed to greater
social stratification and the emergence of a hierarchy of local clans (*uji*),
ruling service groups (*be*), and slaves. Yayoi culture had spread through
Kyushu, Shikoku, and Honshu by the mid-3rd century AD.

Jomon pottery from
Fukushima Prefecture.

The Protohistoric Period   原始時代●

Before the close of the Yayoi period, from about the mid-3rd century, clans in the Yamato region and other areas of central and western
Japan were building impressive mounded stone tombs, called *kofun*, for
the burial of their chieftains. The largest of these kofun, built in the
Yamato region, are said to be the mausoleums of the first powerful political dynasty in Japan, the Yamato, which eventually asserted political
control over the entire country.

Tumuli continued to be built in Japan until the end of the 7th century. By then, however, the old clan society was being restructured and
Japan was already well on the way to the articulation of a Chinese-inspired
centralized imperial administration. The Asuka period (593–710) marks
the final phase of this transition between protohistory and history proper.
The Asuka period dates from the establishment of the court of Empress
Suiko (r 593–628) in the Asuka region of Yamato, south of the present-day
city of Nara. That same year (593) Prince Shotoku (574–622) began to serve
as her regent. For more than a century the area was the site for the palaces
of the rulers of the Yamato lineage and the powerful uji supporting it.
Buddhism had been introduced to this region in the mid-6th century and
it was here that Prince Shotoku labored to elevate the power and prestige

One of the many
representations of Prince
Shotoku, the great Asuka-
period statesman.

of the imperial line and set the country on the course of centralized reform heralded in his Seventeen-Article Constitution. The Japanese court sponsored Buddhism; built temples, palaces, and capitals after Korean and later Chinese models; began to write histories using Chinese characters; and laid out a blueprint for a Chinese-style imperial state structure later known as the *ritsuryo* (legal codes) system.

The Ancient Period   古代●

In 710 a magnificent new capital, called Heijokyo and modeled on the Chinese Tang dynasty (618–907) capital at Chang'an, was established at Nara. During the course of the Nara period (710–794) Japan received even more direct cultural and technological influences from China. Japan's first chronicles, the *Kojiki* (712, Records of Ancient Matters) and *Nihon shoki* (720, Chronicle of Japan), were compiled at this time. Buddhism and Confucianism were harnessed to support political authority, and temples were constructed in the capital and in each of the provinces. Centralized systems for the administration of taxation, census, and landholding were instituted. By the closing years of the 8th century, however, the centralized imperial administration and public land system were showing signs of strain. Politics in Nara were upset by rivalries among nobles and clerics. In 784 Emperor Kammu (r 781–806) decided to make a new start and tried to revive the ritsuryo system by moving the capital to a new site. In 794 a new capital, called Heiankyo (literally, "Capital of Peace and Tranquillity"), was established where the modern city of Kyoto now stands. This was to serve as the home of the imperial court and the capital of Japan until the 19th century, when the capital was moved to Edo, which was renamed Tokyo.

Kojiki (Record of Ancient Matters).

The period from 794 to 1185, which was the heyday of the imperial government's rule of Japan from Heiankyo, is known as the Heian period. It saw the full assimilation of Chinese culture and the flowering of an elegant courtly culture. Politically, however, the imperial court and the imperial office itself came to be dominated by nobles of the Fujiwara family, and the court had difficulty in maintaining its control over the administration of the provinces. In the absence of an effective centralized military system, warrior bands began to assume more power, first in the provinces and then over the court itself when the Taira family seized power in the capital in the mid-12th century.

The Medieval Period   中世●

The Taira were overthrown in 1185 by warriors led by Minamoto no Yoritomo (1147–1199), who was granted in 1192 the title of shogun and established a military government, called the Kamakura shogunate, in the small town of Kamakura in eastern Japan. The first four centuries of warrior domination, covering the Kamakura period (1185–1333) and the Muromachi period (1333–1568), are usually described as Japan's feudal era. The court was not displaced by the creation of a military government in Kamakura but its influence steadily weakened. The shogunate assumed control of the administration of justice, the imperial succession, and the defense of the country against the attempted Mongol invasions of Japan in the late 13th century. Headed first by Yoritomo, the Kamakura shogunate was overthrown in 1333 by a coalition led by Emperor Go-Daigo (r 1318–1339), who was seeking to restore direct imperial rule .

Go-Daigo himself was ousted in 1336 by Ashikaga Takauji (1305–1358), who had helped bring him to power. Takauji, using a rival emperor as a puppet sovereign, established a new shogunate in the Muromachi district of Kyoto. After several decades of civil war between the rival Northern and Southern courts the shogunate was put on a firm footing by Ashikaga Yoshimitsu (1358–1408), the third Ashikaga shogun. Later Ashikaga shoguns were less successful in controlling the feudal coalition. Beginning with the Onin War (1467–1477), the country slipped into the century of sporadic civil war known as the Warring States period (Sengoku period; 1467–1568), in which local feudal lords (*daimyo*) ignored the shogunate and the imperial court and struggled with each other for local hegemony.

Ashikaga Takauji.

The Early Modern Period
近世●

From the mid-16th century, a movement toward national reunification gradually emerged out of the violence of the warring feudal domains and was carried through by three powerful hegemons, Oda Nobunaga (1534–1582), Toyotomi Hideyoshi (1537–1598), and Tokugawa Ieyasu (1543–1616). The short but spectacular epoch during which Nobunaga and Hideyoshi established their military control over the country and began to reshape its feudal institutions is known as the Azuchi-Momoyama period (1568–1600). This was an age of gold, grandeur, and openness to the outside world. Hideyoshi had visions of conquering Korea and establishing an enduring dynasty, though he lived to see his Korean invasions end in brutal failure. His death in 1598 left his heir vulnerable to rival daimyo. One of these, Tokugawa Ieyasu, after a striking victory over pro-Toyotomi warriors at the Battle of Sekigahara in 1600, assumed the title of shogun and established a powerful and enduring shogunate in the city of Edo (now Tokyo), ushering in the Edo period (1600–1868) in Japanese history.

Toyotomi Hideyoshi, warlord of humble origins, who in 1590 completed the work of national reunification begun by Oda Nobunaga.

Ieyasu's victory gave him preponderant power and allowed him to rearrange the political map of Japan. He established a carefully balanced political structure known as the *bakuhan* (shogunate and domain) system in which the Tokugawa shogunate directly controlled Edo and the heartland of the country while the daimyo (classified on the basis of their loyalty to the Tokugawa) governed the 250 or so domains (*han*). Ieyasu and his shogunal successors were able to maintain a strong centralized feudal structure by balancing the daimyo domains; enforcing status distinctions between samurai, merchants, artisans, and peasants; instituting a hostage system of alternate-year attendance by daimyo in Edo (*sankin kotai*); eradicating Christianity; controlling contacts with the outside world, especially the West; and enforcing regulations for samurai, nobles, and temples. This structure was dominated by samurai and relied heavily on the tax yield of the peasants, but it also gave scope to the merchants of Edo, Osaka, Kyoto, and the castle towns to develop commerce and a lively urban culture.

The Modern Period 近代●

An Edo-period illustration of Nihombashi, starting point of the Tokaido and the symbolic center of Japan during the Edo period.

The Tokugawa system, oppressive as it was in many respects, gave the country more than two centuries of peace and relative seclusion from the outside world. This was threatened in the 19th century as Russian, British, and American vessels began to probe Asian waters and press for trade with China and Japan. The shogunate's failure to "expel the barbarians," the concession of unequal treaties, and the opening of ports after Perry's visit in 1853 set in motion a chain of events that led the powerful domains of Satsuma, Choshu, and Tosa to use the imperial court to challenge the shogunate, which was overthrown in the Meiji Restoration of 1868. The young samurai who carried through the restoration wanted to preserve, revitalize, and strengthen the country. This process moved ahead rapidly during the course of the Meiji period (1868–1912). The slogan of the new leadership of Japan was *fukoku kyohei* (Enrich the Country, Strengthen the Military). This meant reforming most social, political, and economic institutions along Western lines. Japan adopted a constitution in 1889, opening the way to parliamentary government. It achieved industrial progress and built up sufficient military power to defeat China in 1895 and Russia in 1905, and to annex Korea in 1910, emerging as the major imperialist power in East Asia.

The Taisho period (1912–1926) was marked by Japan's acceptance as a major power and a period of party government sometimes known as Taisho Democracy. The Showa period (1926–1989) began on a note of optimism but quickly descended into military aggression in Manchuria and China and Japan's departure from the League of Nations. Ultranationalism and political oppression at home eventually led to war with the United States and the Allied powers in Asia and the Pacific.

The Contemporary Era　現代●

The defeat of Japan in 1945 under atomic clouds brought the Allied Occupation, demilitarization, dismantling of the old industrial combines (*zaibatsu*), renunciation of divinity by the emperor, a new constitution, democratization, and a new educational system. After a painful period of postwar rehabilitation, the Japanese economy began to surge ahead in the 1960s and 1970s. The Tokyo Olympics in 1964 brought Japan renewed international recognition. The nation's continued prosperity has been based on a security treaty with the United States, a consistent stress on economic growth and business-oriented policy making, an emphasis on education, and the frugality, energy, and sustained efforts of the Japanese people. In recent years the Japanese, under international pressure to liberalize trade, have been moving from an export-oriented economy to one that is more accessible to foreign imports. This is part of a larger effort by the Japanese to overcome a strong historical tendency to view themselves as somehow unique and aloof from other nations. They are now attempting to truly internationalize their society and bring it into fuller cooperation with an increasingly interdependent world.

Origin of the Japanese people (*nihonjin no kigen*)　日本人の起源●

Thousands of artifacts and caches of broken animal bones have been recovered from rock shelters, limestone fissures, and glacial loam sites, some dating from as early as the end of the second glacial period a half a million years or more ago. The oldest identified human (*Homo sapiens*) remains, although incomplete, date from about 30,000 BC. The oldest remains satisfactory for comparative analysis are from the early part of the Jomon period (ca 10,000 BC–ca 300 BC), but Jomon skeletal assemblages satisfactory for statistical analysis date from about 5000 BC.

The Jomon population was generally short-statured with heavy skeletal structure; skulls were longheaded, and faces were short and broad with markedly concave nasal profiles. Multivariate discriminant analyses place Jomon skulls between those of the native Ainu and modern Japanese but closer to the Ainu and more variable.

The historical Japanese known as the Yamato (Yamatobito) are probably mainly descendants of the cultivators of the Yayoi period (ca 300 BC–ca AD 300) with regionally varying admixtures of the earlier Jomon population and a continually increasing immigrant population from the insular south and, more especially, Korea and China.

GOVERNMENT AND DIPLOMACY

Members meet in the main chamber of the House of Representatives. The speaker of the house sits on the raised dais behind the central podium.

Constitution

Constitution of Japan (Nihonkoku Kempo)　　　日本国憲法●

The Constitution of Japan, successor to the Constitution of the Empire of Japan (1889; also known as the Meiji Constitution), became effective on 3 May 1947. It is notable for its declaration that sovereignty resides with the people, its assertion of fundamental human rights, and its renunciation of war and arms. A thoroughly democratic document, it revolutionized the political system, which under the Meiji Constitution had been based on the principle that sovereignty resided with the emperor.

Enactment　　　　　　　　　　　　　　　　　　　　　　　　　制定●

The Japanese surrender in World War II took the form of acceptance of the terms of the Potsdam Declaration, which called for the removal of obstacles to democratic tendencies and the establishment of a peace-loving government in accordance with the freely expressed will of the Japanese people. In October 1945 Prime Minister Shidehara Kijuro appointed Matsumoto Joji (legal scholar and minister of state) to head a committee to investigate the question of constitutional revision. The following February the staff of US General Douglas MacArthur, the supreme commander for the Allied powers (SCAP), became convinced that the Matsumoto committee was incapable of adequately democratizing the constitution and that the Far Eastern Commission (representing the Allied powers) might soon intervene in the matter. MacArthur directed his Government Section to formulate a model constitution for Japan. The Government Section's hastily drafted constitution was based in part on a policy paper of the American State-War-Navy Coordinating Committee (SWNCC). On 13 February 1946 Government Section officials delivered their draft to the Japanese cabinet.

Shidehara Kijuro advocated international cooperation during his two terms as foreign minister in the 1920s. He was Japan's second postwar prime minister (1945–1946).

After difficult negotiations the SCAP and Japanese officials agreed on a draft constitution based on the SCAP model. On 6 March 1946 the Shidehara cabinet published the text as its own handiwork.

To ensure legal continuity with the imperial constitution, the proposed new constitution was passed in the form of a constitutional amendment almost unanimously by both houses of the Imperial Diet, and on 3 November 1946 it was promulgated by the emperor, to become effective 3 May 1947.

Provisions　　　　　　　　　　　　　　　　　　　　　　　　　条項●

The new Constitution of Japan declares that the emperor shall be "the symbol of the State and of the unity of the people, deriving his position from the will of the people with whom resides sovereign power."

All acts of the emperor in matters of state now require the advice and approval of the cabinet, and the emperor has no "powers related to government." The emperor appoints as prime minister the person selected by the Diet and appoints as chief judge of the Supreme Court the appointee of the cabinet.

The new constitution enumerates the rights and duties of the people, such as freedom of speech. Discrimination "in political, economic or social relations because of race, creed, sex, social status or family origin" is forbidden. The people have the right to maintain "minimum standards of wholesome and cultured living," and the state is expected to promote social welfare and public health. The right to own property is declared inviolable. The most famous provision of the constitution is article 9, which states that the Japanese people "forever renounce war" and that "land, sea, and air forces ... will never be maintained." See RENUNCIATION OF WAR.

If the lower house passes a resolution of no confidence in the cabinet, the cabinet must resign or the lower house must be dissolved within 10 days. Thus the new constitution established the parliamentary-cabinet system of democracy, similar to that of Great Britain. The two houses of the Diet designate the prime minister, but if the two houses are unable to agree, the choice of the House of Representatives (lower house) prevails. The defeat of a bill by the House of Councillors (upper house) may be overridden by a two-thirds majority vote of the lower house, except that a lower-house simple majority may prevail where the budget, a treaty, or the designation of the prime minister is involved.

The Japanese Supreme Court has explicit authority to determine the constitutionality of legislation and government acts.

The New Constitution in Practice　　　　　　　　新憲法の運用●

Shortly before and after the new constitution became effective, the Diet passed 45 laws to implement its provisions. This legislation included the new Imperial Household Law, the Cabinet Law, the Diet Law, the Local Autonomy Law, electoral laws, and amendments to the Civil Code and the Code of Civil Procedure.

Since the Occupation ended in 1952, the government has interpreted the constitution to mean that it may dissolve the House of Representatives without having to wait for a vote of no confidence. The government, which until recently has been dominated by the conservatives, has dissolved the lower house at times advantageous to the conservatives. Since the governing conservatives usually held majorities in both houses, they were able to dominate the system.

Ceremony on Constitution Memorial Day (3 May) in 1950.

Over the years, the constitutionality of the Self Defense Forces has been frequently challenged in the courts, but the Supreme Court has avoided ruling definitively on this issue. Although conservatives have advocated amendments that would clarify the right to maintain military forces, the Japanese people have thus far not altered a word of their democratic constitution.

Democracy (*minshu shugi*) 　　　　　　　　民主主義●

Japan has a functioning democratic system, that is, a system in which sovereignty resides in the people, who exercise it through elected representatives and who are guaranteed the civil liberties essential to its exercise.

History 　　　　　　　　　　　　　　　　　歴史●

Itagaki Taisuke, leader of the Freedom and People's Rights Movement during the Meiji period.

Japan's democratic tradition stretches back to the early Meiji period (1868–1912). In the 1870s dissatisfied former *samurai* and landowners who were not represented in the new government launched a movement for representative institutions, or "popular rights". Led by such people as Itagaki Taisuke (1837–1919), they formed several political parties. Ideologically, Itagaki and his followers were influenced by the ideals of French radicalism, while Okuma Shigenobu (1839–1922), based his platform on the ideas of English liberalism and parliamentary goverment.

In 1889 the Japanese government adopted a constitution that permitted a weak House of Representatives and a limited franchise. Political parties gradually became accepted in government after the first party cabinet was formed in 1898, reaching a peak of power during the Taisho period (1912–26).

The end of World War I, with the apparent victory of democracy in the West and of Marxism in Russia, coupled with a postwar recession in Japan, stimulated a movement for social, economic, and political reform in Japan among many students, writers, intellectuals, journalists, politicians, and labor leaders. They called for reforms ranging from the introduction of socialism and Marxism and the formation of labor unions to the development of true liberal democracy. The Sodomei (Japan Federation of Labor) was formed in 1919 and a communist and several socialist parties were formed in the 1920s.

Okuma Shigenobu, an important politician of the Meiji and Taisho periods and founder of Waseda University.

The Japanese government responded to demands for reform with a series of both conciliatory and repressive acts. Some progressive factory and labor laws were adopted and the Universal Manhood Suffrage Law was passed in May 1925, but these acts were coupled with the repressive

Peace Preservation Law of 1925 and a series of police raids that destroyed many left-wing groups or drove them underground by the early 1930s.

From 1930 on army and navy officers involved themselves in a series of incidents that indicated their ability to intervene in civilian affairs. Key events included the Manchurian Incident in 1931 and the assassination of Prime Minister Inukai Tsuyoshi (1855–1932) in 1932, and a full-fledged military insurrection in 1936. Political parties lost their power and prestige and the military held sway over Japan politically, economically, and socially until the end of World War II.

Postwar Development   第二次世界大戦後の発達●

Japan's present democratic system centers on the primary author-ity of a bicameral Diet (parliament) of representatives elected by the people. Executive power is exercised by a prime minister (chosen by the Diet) and by a cabinet he appoints. Judicial power resides in the Supreme Court and lower courts. Popular control over local government is exer-cised through a system of local and prefectural assemblies and executives elected by the people. A system of checks and balances distributes power among the executive, legislative, and judicial branches and assures the people of a voice in government.

However, public confidence in democracy has been severely tested in postwar Japan. A series of scandals from 1970s to 1990s, includ-ing the Lockheed Scandal and the Recruit Scandal, and other corrupt practices have occasioned a certain amount of disillusionment and dis-content with the actual workings of Japan's political system.

Former prime minister Tanaka Kakuei on his way to court on charges connected to the Lockeed Scandal.

The infrequency with which elected legislative bodies initiate leg-islation has also been a problem. Representation rarely means the intro-duction of bills, since at all levels of government most bills are introduced by the executive branch after limited consultation with parties and inter-est groups. The subsequent process of negotiating a consensus occurs behind closed doors, and even the legislative committee "hearings" are not really open either to the public or to interest groups. A predictable conse-quence of this situation has been a general loss of public confidence in gov-ernment and increasing feelings of apathy and detachment from the polit-ical process. Politicians sensed this trend and responded to public demands for more thorough democratic practices. Evidence of this can be found in the 1994 election districting system reform; the first significant change since 1945 (see POLITICAL REFORMS OF 1994).

Renunciation of war (*senso no hoki*)   戦争の放棄●

Doctrine arising out of article 9, the most famous and most controversial article, of the Constitution of Japan (1947). Article 9 reads as follows:

"Aspiring sincerely to an international peace based on justice and order, the Japanese people forever renounce war as a sovereign right of the nation and the threat or use of force as a means of settling international disputes."

"In order to accomplish the aim of the preceding paragraph, land, sea, and air forces, as well as other war potential, will never be maintained. The right of belligerency of the state will not be recognized."

The San Francisco Peace Treaty of 1951 specifically stated that the Allied powers "recognize that Japan as a sovereign nation possesses the inherent right of individual or collective self-defense." With that provision as the basis, the Diet in 1954 passed a law creating the Self Defense Forces (SDF). The twin questions of the development of the SDF and the possible violation of article 9 have been highly controversial issues in Japanese politics.

Prime Minister Yoshida Shigeru signs the San Francisco Peace Treaty formally ending the state of war between Japan and the Allied powers.

The Supreme Court of Japan has not dealt directly with the constitutionality of the SDF, only on the constitutionality of the United States-Japan security treaties that permit US bases in Japan. However, the court has refused to declare such bases unconstitutional, arguing that matters relating to national security are by their nature political and must therefore be decided by the sovereign people, who can express political judgments on security matters by exercising their suffrage in free elections.

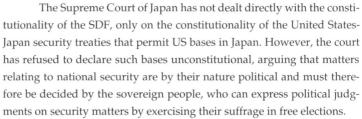

Emperor

Emperor (tenno)   天皇●

The title *tenno* was first assumed by Japanese rulers in the 6th or 7th century and has been used by all subsequent Japanese sovereigns.

Japan's imperial institution, the oldest hereditary monarchy in the world, was already in existence when Japan emerged into recorded history and has since been perpetuated in a predominantly male line of descent. Although the emperor has almost always been regarded as the titular head of the national government, the most striking feature of the office through most of Japanese history has been the tendency to emphasize instead the emperor's role as chief priest in the indigenous Japanese religion, Shinto, and to delegate most of the effective powers of government to others.

titular

From Early Historical Times
to the Mid-12th Century   古代から12世紀中頃まで●

The emperor figures centrally in a mythology preserved in the historical chronicles *Kojiki* (712, Record of Ancient Matters) and *Nihon shoki* (720, Chronicle of Japan). According to these, the sun goddess Amaterasu Omikami, chief divinity of the Shinto pantheon, bequeathed to her grandson Ninigi no Mikoto a mirror, jewels, and a sword, which he in turn passed on to his descendants, the emperors of Japan, the first of whom was the emperor Jimmu.

According to the ancient chronicles of the *Kojiki* and *Nihon shoki*, the emperor Jimmu was the legendary first sovereign (*tenno*) of Japan.

The emperor was thought to possess magical powers to propitiate or intercede with divinities. But because of the awe surrounding his person, it was also considered inappropriate for the emperor to concern himself with the secular business of government. That business, including both the making and execution of policies, belonged to ministers serving the emperor, and there was a tendency from very early historical times for those ministers to form political dynasties of their own.

The only extended period of Japanese history in which the emperor combined the roles of both high priest and functioning head of government was from the reign of Tenji (r 661–672), in the latter half of the 7th century, through the reign of Kammu (r 781–806) at the end of the 8th century and the beginning of the 9th. It was Tenji who, in the Taika Reform of 645, made the first major attempt to bring the powerful provincial clans (*uji*) under the control of a strong central regime.

This period of direct imperial rule was characterized by the effort to establish a centralized bureaucratic state in Japan patterned on the example offered by Tang dynasty China. The key instrument in this process was the adoption of law codes, known collectively as the *ritsuryo* (legal codes) system, that established an elaborate hierarchy of offices headed by the emperor and prescribed the procedures of governmental administration at both national and provincial levels.

However, in the 9th century several efforts to personalize imperial rule by freeing it from the entrenched bureaucracy backfired, beginning a process in which the emperor was increasingly isolated from the machinery of government.This tendency was exacerbated by the creation or revival of two other extrabureaucratic posts to which the emperor delegated the authority he had formerly wielded personally: *sessho* (regent for an emperor still in his minority) and *kampaku* (regent for an adult emperor). From the late 9th century onward, both posts were dominated by members of the powerful Fujiwara family, who, while making no claim to the emperor's title or ritual role, ruled in his name.

The last century of the Heian period (794–1185) saw a waning of the power of the Fujiwara regents and a brief return of power to the imperial house. The leading figures through most of this period, however, were not reigning emperors but retired sovereigns who retained headship of the imperial house after abdication.

Medieval Period (mid-12th–16th centuries) 中世●

Three more families, again nonimperial, held sway over the national government and the imperial institution from the closing years of the Heian period to the end of the Kamakura period (1185–1333), ushering in the age of warrior rule that was to last until the Meiji Restoration of 1868.

The first of these, the Taira family, ruled from Kyoto and legitimated themselves by occupying high offices within the imperial court. The second, the Minamoto family, destroyed the Taira in 1185 in a bloody war they waged from their base at Kamakura in eastern Japan. Remaining there after their victory, they established a wholly new pattern of national government, the Kamakura shogunate. The emperor remained in Kyoto and continued to preside over the imperial government, but these institutions were now reduced to almost complete impotence, real power devolving on the shogunate. Imperial legitimization for this situation took the form of a commission from the emperor naming the head of the Minamoto family to the office of *seii tai shogun*, or "barbarian-subduing generalissimo", and thus by implication granting him absolute authority over territories and population beyond the reach of the much reduced imperial power.

The third family to dominate the national government in this period was the Hojo family, whose members ruled from 1203 as shogu-

Minamoto no Yoritomo, who founded the Kamakura shogunate, beginning a 700-year period of warrior rule during which the emperor wielded little direct power.

nal regents (*shikken*). This initiated a complex and many-tiered delegation of power that has few parallels in world history. The emperor in Kyoto reigned, but the imperial government was controlled by a Fujiwara regent. The effective national government was in Kamakura, nominally headed by a shogun, but also in fact controlled by the Hojo regent. To complicate matters further, from the mid-13th century the shogunate began to interfere actively in the imperial succession, creating schisms within the imperial house that further decreased its power.

A clean sweep of this meaningless institutional complexity was undertaken by Emperor Go-Daigo (r 1318–1339) in 1333, who made war on the Hojo, destroying the Kamakura shogunate, and became head of a reinvigorated imperial government. This revival of imperial authority was, however, pathetically brief. In 1336 Ashikaga Takauji (1305–1358), Go-Daigo's chief military commander, turned against the emperor, deposed him, and set up in his place a puppet from a different branch of the imperial house, the Northern Court. The latter then appointed Takauji shogun, initiating the 240-year Muromachi shogunate.

Go-Daigo established a rival court, the Southern Court, that maintained a precarious existence until 1392, when the rivalry between the two Courts was finally resolved by the third Muromachi shogun, Ashikaga Yoshimitsu (1358–1408). The material circumstances of the imperial house reached their nadir in the course of the Muromachi period (1336–1573). The Imperial Palace was destroyed in the disastrous Onin War (1467–77).

Early Modern Period (mid-16th–mid-19th centuries)   近世●

The restoration of the court's fortunes awaited the reunification of Japan, accomplished between 1568 and 1603 by three men, Oda Nobunaga (1534–1582), Toyotomi Hideyoshi (1537–1598), and Tokugawa Ieyasu (1543–1616)—each of whom derived sanction for his rule from the imperial institution. After the collapse of rule by the senior two men, Ieyasu followed long precedent in having himself named shogun in 1603, commencing more than 250 years of rule by the Tokugawa shogunate.

The shogunate devoted great attention to the maintenance and control of the imperial institution. The Imperial Palace was restored to its former grandeur, and residences were provided for the entire court nobility (*kuge*). Income from designated lands was earmarked for the imperial treasury. Yet at the same time rigorous restraints were imposed on the freedom of the imperial family and court nobility.

The imperial court in Kyoto had little if any influence on practical state affairs, but the emperor continued to perform certain functions

Oda Nobunaga, the leading figure in Japan's 16th-century reunification, acquired several imperial court titles to legitimate his power.

important to the shogunate. The public acts of the court consisted wholly of the performance of rituals associated variously with Shinto, with Buddhism, or with Confucianism.

Quite apart from this, however, the imperial institution came to play a new symbolic role in Japanese political thought, constructed in the course of the Edo period (1600–1868) by writers and thinkers known as *kinnoka*, or "imperial loyalists," who drew their ideas chiefly from various modifications of Confucian theory or from the indigenous intellectual tradition of Kokugaku (National Learning). Their stress on the centrality of the imperial house within the Japanese polity proved to be an explosive concept in the mid-19th century, when it combined with the crisis touched off by Western pressure to "open" Japan to foreign trade and diplomacy. The result was a political movement aimed at fending off the foreign threat, abolishing the shogunate, and replacing it with a new national government under direct imperial rule. Within 15 years of Commodore Matthew C. Perry's arrival in Japan in 1853, this upsurge of imperial loyalism proved a key factor in the toppling of the Tokugawa regime and the initiation of the Meiji Restoration of 1868.

Modern Period (1868–1945)   近現代●

The leaders of Meiji Japan engaged in 20 years of pragmatic political experimentation to redefine the imperial institution. With the proclamation of the Constitution of the Empire of Japan on 11 February 1889, the emperor became a constitutional monarch in a centralized and unitary state that was to exercise greater political power than any previous form of government in Japan's history.

Succeeding to the throne in 1867, Emperor Meiji became the symbolic focus of the movement to overthrow the Tokugawa shogunate.

According to the constitution, the emperor was "sacred and inviolable," and sovereignty rested with him as the head of the Japanese empire. He commanded the armed forces, declared war, made peace, and concluded treaties; he had emergency powers to maintain public order and declare a state of siege. All laws required the emperor's sanction and enforcement.

Paradoxically, however, the supreme authority accorded the emperor in the constitution, and the other efforts made to bolster his centrality to the Japanese polity, were not accompanied by real political power. In fact, the system was designed instead to preserve the emperor's political immunity while he served as the sacrosanct basis for rule by others, namely, the ministers of state and the chiefs of the armed forces. The emperor's primary political role from 1889 to 1947 was to ratify the policies and personnel decisions reached by his government leaders and to put the seal of the imperial will on political decisions they had forged, not to actually make decisions or dictate policy himself.

Contemporary Monarchy (1945–)　　　現在の天皇制（1945年以降）●

Japan's defeat in World War II and the subsequent Allied Occupation wrought momentous changes in the imperial institution and its place in Japanese politics and society. In the early years after the surrender the issue of imperial responsibility for the war was a subject of heated debate, leading to calls for outright abolition of the "emperor system." A more moderate approach prevailed, however, and the 1947 CONSTITUTION OF JAPAN retained the emperor, though in a drastically altered relation to the state and made the emperor "the symbol of the State and of the unity of the people, deriving his position from the will of the people with whom resides sovereign power." He was to have no political powers. All acts by the emperor in matters of state were reduced to merely formal and ceremonial functions, requiring the advice and approval of the cabinet. The autonomous Imperial Household Ministry was demoted to the status of an agency of the Prime Minister's Office, the peerage was eliminated, and Emperor Showa (Hirohito, r 1926–1989) himself declared on New Year's Day 1946 that he was "not divine". Thus the prewar Japanese state with its theory of imperial prerogative was thoroughly dismantled.

Emperor Showa and General Douglas MacArthur in September 1945.

Along with these fundamental changes in the legal and institutional relationship of the emperor to the political system, efforts were made to "popularize" the imperial family as the nation's first family, united with the people in warmth and affection. No longer was the emperor to be surrounded by an aura of sanctity, elevated in transcendence above his people who were now no longer subjects, but citizens. As a symbol the "new" emperor was to mirror a modern, democratic, and middle-class Japan.

Doubts about the imperial institution have remained. A small but vocal minority of Japanese believe that the emperor, by his very nature as a hereditary monarch, contradicts democracy, while others believe that a resurgence of Japanese fascism or absolutism is possible so long as the imperial institution is permitted to exist. But the vast majority of Japanese citizens favor the status quo. This was confirmed when, in January 1989, Emperor Akihito (r 1989–) became the first emperor to succeed to the throne under the present constitution. Despite dissenting voices, it seems clear that the consensus in Japan continues to support the retention of the imperial house, within a carefully defined legal framework.

Emperor Akihito (1933– ; Akihito Tenno) 明仁天皇●

The present emperor and the 125th sovereign (*tenno*) in the traditional count (which includes several legendary emperors). Eldest son of Emperor Showa (1901–1989) and Empress Nagako (1903–), the present empress dowager. From 1946 to 1950 he was privately tutored in the English language and Western culture by Elizabeth Gray Vining, an American teacher known for her authorship of children's books. In 1952 he entered the Department of Politics at Gakushuin University, and in November of that year his coming-of-age ceremony and his investiture as crown prince were conducted. While still a college student, he left Japan in the spring of 1953 for a state visit to the United Kingdom to act as his father's representative at the coronation of Queen Elizabeth II. On his tour, he visited 13 countries in Europe and North America before returning to Japan in October. He completed his course of studies at Gakushuin University in March 1956.

Emperor Akihito and
Empress Michiko waving
to the crowd during a
parade in 1991.

In April 1959 Crown Prince Akihito married Shoda Michiko, eldest daughter of Shoda Hidesaburo, then president of the Nisshin Flour Milling Co, Ltd, breaking with the long-established tradition that the wife of the crown prince should be chosen from among the ranks of the imperial family or the former peerage. In their family life they have achieved a relative freedom from the restrictive precedents of court tradition.

While still crown prince, Akihito represented Emperor Showa on a number of state visits overseas, visiting 37 countries in the course of 22 separate trips. He also served as the honorary president of Universiade 1967 in Tokyo and of Expo '70 in Osaka. During Emperor Showa's tour of Europe in September 1971 and his tour of the United States in 1975, Crown Prince Akihito conducted affairs of state in his absence. In 1975 he was the first member of the imperial family to officially visit Okinawa after its reversion to Japan in 1972.

On 7 January 1989 he became Emperor Akihito, succeding to the throne after his father's death. The following day he adopted the formal reign title Heisei ("Establishing Peace").

Like his father, Emperor Akihito is known as a scholar of marine biology and ichthyology and for his research into the fishes of the family Gobiidae. He also enjoys sports and is a lover of music, playing cello in impromptu performances with other members of the royal family. He and Empress Michiko have three children: Crown Prince Naruhito, Prince Akishino, and Princess Sayako.

Empress Michiko (1934– ; Michiko Kogo)　　　　美智子皇后●

Wife of EMPEROR AKIHITO. Eldest daughter of Shoda Hidesaburo, founder of the Nisshin Flour Milling Co, Ltd, and his wife Fumiko. She is a graduate of the University of the Sacred Heart in Tokyo. In April 1959 she married then crown prince Akihito. As the first imperial bride to be selected from outside the circle of the imperial family and the former peerage, her marriage to Crown Prince Akihito was broadly welcomed by the Japanese people as a symbol of the democratization of the imperial house. On 7 January 1989 she became empress upon her husband's ascension to the throne as Emperor Akihito. Empress Michiko maintains a lively interest in literature, arts , and music and serves as honorary president of the Japan Red Cross Society.

Crown Prince Naruhito (1960– ; Naruhito Kotaishi)　　徳仁皇太子●

Princely title Hiro no Miya. Eldest son of EMPEROR AKIHITO and EMPRESS MICHIKO. The crown prince graduated from Gakushuin University in 1982 and completed his initial coursework for the doctorate in history there in 1988. From 1983 to 1985 he studied at Merton College, Oxford University, where he conducted research into the sea trade routes and port cities of medieval Europe. On 7 January 1989 he became crown prince when his father ascended to the throne as Emperor Akihito. In June 1993 Crown Prince Naruhito married Owada Masako (b 1963).

Crown Prince Naruhito.
Princely title Hiro no Miya.

Imperial Palace (Kokyo)　　　　　　　　　　皇居●

Official residence of the emperor. Situated in Chiyoda Ward, Tokyo, occupying 1.15 square kilometers (0.44 sq mi). Japanese emperors and their families have resided here since after the Meiji Restoration of 1868, when Edo Castle was designated the official imperial residence (before the Meiji Restoration, emperors resided in Kyoto). A new palace was completed in 1888, but this was destroyed in air raids in 1945. The present palace complex, the Kyuden, was completed in 1968. Its individual buildings include the Omote Gozasho, the emperor's office for affairs of state; the Seiden, for official ceremonies; the Homeiden, for banquets entertaining guests of state; and the Chowaden, for evening receptions. These buildings are connected by corridors surrounding a large central courtyard. To the northwest is the Fukiage Gosho, formerly the private residence of Emperor Showa, now occupied by his widow. A new palace residence for EMPEROR AKIHITO was completed in May 1993. Part of the palace grounds is open to the public.

National anthem (kokka) 国歌●

The de facto Japanese national anthem is "Kimigayo" (His Majesty's Reign). Basil H. Chamberlain (1850–1935), author of *Things Japanese* (1890), translated the anthem as follows: *Kimi ga yo wa Chiyo ni yachiyo ni Sazare ishi no Iwao to nari te Koke no musu made* :

> Thousands of years of happy reign be thine
> Rule on, my lord, till what are pebbles now
> By age united to mighty rocks shall grow
> Whose venerable sides the moss doth line

The words of the song are from the 10th-century anthology *Kokinshu*. The author is unknown. The tune was composed by Hayashi Hiromori (1831–96) in 1880. In 1893 the Ministry of Education made it the ceremonial song to be sung in elementary schools on national holidays. Soon it was sung at state ceremonies and sports events. Although popularly identified as the national anthem for many years, "Kimigayo" has never been officially adopted as such.

National flag (kokki) 国旗●

The national flag of Japan has a crimson disc, symbolizing the sun, in the center of a white field. It is popularly known as the Hinomaru (literally, "sun disc"). The Tokugawa shogunate (1603–1867) adopted the flag for its ships in the early 1600s. In the mid-19th century the shogunate decreed that all Japanese ships fly flags with the sun on a white field. In 1870 the Meiji government officially designated it for use on Japanese merchant and naval ships. It has never been officially designated as the national flag; however, it has become so by customary use.

Hinomaru
日の丸

The design and proportions of Japan's national flag were fixed in 1870 by the Meiji government. The vertical to horizontal ratio was set at 2:3, the disk was to be placed at the exact center, and the diameter of the disk was to equal three-fifths of the vertical measurement of the flag.

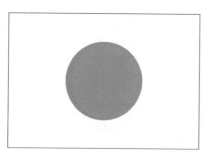

Major Components of the Government

Diet (Kokkai)   国会●

The legislative branch of the Japanese government. According to the CONSTITUTION OF JAPAN, the Diet is "the highest organ of state power" and the "sole law-making organ of the State." The Diet consists of two chambers: the HOUSE OF REPRESENTATIVES (Shugiin), or lower house, and the HOUSE OF COUNCILLORS (Sangiin), or upper house. All Diet members are selected in popular elections. The Imperial Diet (Teikoku Gikai), the direct predecessor of the present Diet, was established in 1890 through provisions in the Constitution of the Empire of Japan (1889) and consisted of a House of Peers (Kizokuin) and a House of Representatives. Constitutionally, the Imperial Diet was weak, primarily because the power of legislation was vested in the emperor and because the cabinet was responsible to the emperor rather than to the Diet. Initially, the House of Representatives reflected the opinions of a highly restricted segment of the public, representing only the 1.5 percent of the population who paid an annual tax of ¥15 or more. Not until the passage of the Universal Manhood Suffrage Law in 1925 did all male citizens over the age of 25 obtain the right to vote and thus the possibility of influencing their legislative representatives.

The Diet Building, completed in 1936.

During the Taisho period (1912–1926), substantial changes occurred in Japan's body politic, including its national assembly: Sovereignty might be constitutionally vested in the emperor, but legislative power was exercised by him and his advisers with the consent of the Diet. Diet Members formally organized themselves into parliamentary parties and articulated alternative policies that were covered by the newspapers and thus helped shape public attitudes.

Possibly the best indication of the Diet's growing powers in the 1920s was the energy that its opponents devoted to circumscribing them. Members were accused of being the corrupt tools of vested corporate interests, incapable of protecting the "national polity" (*kokutai*). Terrorist groups plotted assassinations, some of which were successful. By the end of the 1930s, parliamentarianism was a flame that flickered uncertainly. Parliamentary parties were forced to serve the interests of the nation's predominantly military rulers. The Diet became a rubber stamp, but those in power did not take the final step of abolishing it altogether.

The transformation of the Imperial Diet into the present Diet was set forth initially in the postwar constitution (effective in May 1947). Unlike the previous constitution, the new constitution gave supreme legislative power to the Diet and made it the most important organ of the government.

Government and Diplomacy

Organization

組織●

Bicameralism was retained at the insistence of Japanese authorities, but the hereditary and appointive House of Peers was replaced by the elected House of Councillors, which consists of 252 members who serve six-year terms. The prime minister and a majority of his cabinet ministers were required to be members of the Diet and, "in the exercise of executive power, shall be collectively responsible to the Diet"; this is in direct contrast to the relationship that had prevailed under the Meiji Constitution. A revolution in constitutional doctrine had taken place: the entire membership of the Diet would be publicly elected, and the cabinet, in which executive authority was vested, would be responsible to the Diet. The doctrine of parliamentary supremacy had supplanted that of imperial prerogative.

At the same time, the new constitution altered the relationship between the two chambers. The House of Representatives and the House of Councillors share legislative power: "A bill becomes a law on passage by both Houses..." However, the 500 representatives of the lower house, whose term of office is four years unless the house is dissolved, have authority in three important areas. First, in the designation of the prime minister, if there is disagreement between the two chambers, "the decision of the House of Representatives shall be the decision of the Diet." Second, the national budget must first be submitted to the House of Representatives. Furthermore, if the two houses fail to reach agreement on the budget, and if joint committees fail to resolve the matter or no decision is made by the House of Councillors within 30 days, the will of the lower house prevails. Third, while international treaties may first be introduced for approval in either chamber, the decision of the lower house prevails over a contrary judgment by the upper house if joint committees fail to resolve the matter or no decision is made by the House of Councillors within 30 days. Also, in all fields of legislation, the House of Representatives can override the House of Councillors by a two-thirds vote. Thus the Diet is bicameral, but the House of Representatives is predominant in certain crucial spheres.

Members meet in the main chamber of the House of Councillors.

The Workings of the Diet

国会の権能●

A Diet session convening after an election for the House of Representatives or House of Councillors entails the following sequence of five events. First, the presiding officers are elected. Normally, each party nominates its own candidates, with those of the majority party being elected. On occasion, the speaker (or president) will share power with a deputy who is a member of the leading opposition party.

Second, the prime minister is elected. When a single party is unable to obtain an absolute majority in both chambers, two or more parties agree to a coalition to support the election of a prime minister whose cabinet ministers reflect the political groups that voted for him. See PRIME MINISTER AND CABINET.

Third, the emperor appears at an opening ceremony to read an imperial edict formally convening the Diet.

Fourth, the prime minister and selected members of his cabinet—normally including at least the minister of finance and minister of foreign affairs—read their statements of basic policy to each of the chambers. Reviews of past achievements and a catalog of new legislative goals are the usual content of the prime minister's message.

Fifth, each of the parliamentary parties states its own legislative program. These statements tend to be a series of alternatives to or criticisms of the proposals by the prime minister and his ministerial associates. This pattern of challenge and response continues throughout the session, but rarely in plenary meetings of either house. Much more frequently, it occurs at meetings of the Budget Committee or of a subject-matter committee that is conducting hearings on a particular legislative bill or government policy.

These formalities establish the overall tone. Once they have been completed, the respective houses move into a routine, periodically punctuated by impasses and confrontations. Legally, the presiding officers in each chamber have the responsibility and power to "maintain order in the house, adjust its proceedings, supervise its business, and represent it." They are assisted by a secretary-general who has the dual responsibility of supervising the secretariat of each chamber and acting as its chief parliamentarian.

If an item of legislation is not controversial, the system usually works smoothly. Legislation is drafted by government bureaucrats in various ministries and follows a process leading to final approval that is carefully programmed by the majority party (or coalition of parties).

House of Councillors (Sangiin)   参議院●

One of the two elective bodies that make up the Diet. Under Japan's post-World War II constitution, the House of Councillors replaced the hereditary, appointive House of Peers, which had been established under the Meiji Constitution. Although the House of Councillors and the House of Representatives share power, the latter predominates in decisions on legislation, designation of the prime minister, budgetary matters, and international treaties. Every three years, half of the 252 representatives in the House of Councillors are elected by popular vote to a six-year term of office that is not terminated in the event of dissolution of the House of Representatives. One hundred of the seats are filled on a proportional representation system; the remaining 152 seats are filled on a system of prefectural districts.

House of Representatives (Shugiin)　　　　衆議院●

The lower house of the Diet. According to the provisions of the Constitution of Japan, the House of Representatives and its collective decisions take precedence over the upper house (the House of Councillors) in the areas of legislation, the budget, treaty ratification, and the selection of the prime minister. The representatives, who have numbered 500 since December 1994, are elected by popular vote. Their term of office is four years, unless the House has been dissolved before their term has elapsed.

Prime minister and cabinet (shusho to naikaku)　　　首相と内閣●

The chief executive officer of the Japanese government and his cabinet. The cabinet system was adopted in Japan in 1885 and has continued without interruption until the present. There have, however, been a number of fundamental changes in the powers, functions, and composition of the cabinet, particularly when the prewar cabinet system under the Meiji Constitution is compared with the postwar cabinet system under the 1947 constitution. In the postwar system the constitution vests supreme executive authority in the cabinet, which is responsible to the legislature. In the prewar system the cabinet was not responsible to the legislature and the legislature had no power either to select a prime minister or dissolve a cabinet.

The Prewar Cabinet System　　　　第二次世界大戦前の内閣制度●

Following the Meiji Restoration (1868), a Grand Council of State (Dajokan) was established in 1868 as the supreme political authority which evolved into a central deliberative body consisting of three state ministers who had direct access to the emperor and seven councillors, or *sangi*. Heads of the various government ministries often served as sangi as well, so that by the end of 1881 real power was in the hands of a virtual oligarchy.

Organization of the Executive Branch of the Government

行政府

- Cabinet
  - Cabinet Secretariat *2
  - Cabinet Legislation Bureau
  - Security Council of Japan
  - National Personnel Authority *1

- Board of Audit

- **Prime Minister's Office**
  - Fair Trade Commission
  - National Public Safety Commission *2
  - Environmental Disputes Coordination Commission
  - Imperial Household Agency
  - Management and Coordination Agency *2
  - Hokkaido Development Agency *2
  - Defense Agency *2
    - Defense Facilities Administration Agency
  - Economic Planning Agency *2
  - Science and Technology Agency *2
  - Environment Agency *2
  - Okinawa Development Agency *2
  - National Land Agency *2

- **Ministry of Justice**
  - National Bar Examination Administration Commission
    - Public Security Examination Commission
  - Public Security Investigation Agency

- **Ministry of Foreign Affairs**

- **Ministry of Finance**
  - National Tax Administration *3

- **Ministry of Education**
  - Agency for Cultural Affairs

- **Ministry of Health & Welfare**
  - Social Insurance Agency

- **Ministry of Agriculture, Forestry, & Fisheries**
  - Food Agency
  - Forestry Agency
  - Fisheries Agency

- **Ministry of International Trade & Industry**
  - Agency for Natural Resources and Energy
  - Patent Office *3
  - Small and Medium Enterprise Agency

- **Ministry of Transport**
  - Central Labor Relations Commission for Seafarers
  - Maritime Safety Agency
  - High Marine Accidents Inquiry Agency
  - Meteorological Agency

- **Ministry of Posts & Telecommunications**

- **Ministry of Labor**
  - Central Labor Relations Commission

- **Ministry of Construction**

- **Ministry of Home Affairs**
  - Fire Defense Agency

*1 auxiliary organ
*2 headed by cabinet ministers
*3 considered an agency

The change to the cabinet system in 1885 appears to have been motivated by the effort to strengthen the executive branch in the face of the projected establishment of an independent legislative branch. The prime minister and the various cabinet ministers were made responsible only to the emperor, not to the Diet. Moreover, upon the promulgation of the constitution in 1889, the oligarchs announced their intention to remain aloof from party politics by adhering to the principle of nonparty or "Transcendental" cabinets (*chozen naikaku*).

For the seven cabinets between 1885 and 1898 the prime minister-ship was rotated among the oligarchs. As the oligarchs retired from the day-to-day administration of cabinet affairs they assumed the role of elder statesmen (*genro*).

The prewar prime minister enjoyed extensive appointment powers, including the appointment of cabinet ministers and vice-ministers, judges, prosecutors, and prefectural governors. Nevertheless, the prime minister was not a strong chief executive but rather had to share the right to advise the throne with the genro, the officers of the imperial household, the privy councillors, and the military chiefs of staff.

Until the Taisho Political Crisis of 1912–1913, the oligarchs coordinated the decision-making process behind the scenes through the vehicle of the informal, extraconstitutional genro council and through their position on the Privy Council. Following World War I, this single dominant coordinating oligarchy was gradually replaced by a much larger and more diverse set of institutional elites, composed of the parties, the military, the bureaucracy, the peerage, and the court. Much of the political history of the 1918–1945 period can be viewed as a competition among these institutional elites for control of the government. From the mid-1930s the military dominated the cabinet until Japan's defeat in World War II.

Postwar Changes in the Cabinet System　　　　戦後の内閣制度の変遷●

The postwar constitution introduced two major kinds of change in the cabinet system. First, executive power was vested solely in the prime minister and his cabinet. All real executive authority was removed from the emperor, and the throne became a purely symbolic and ceremonial institution. The prime minister is now empowered to appoint and remove all cabinet members at his own discretion. Moreover, to ensure civilian control of the military, the Defense Agency has formally been made a subordinate part of the Prime Minister's Office.

The second major change was the clear establishment of cabinet responsibility to the elected representatives of the people. The prime minister is elected by the DIET, and either house of the Diet may adopt a resolution of impeachment against any individual cabinet member. Moreover, if the lower house passes a nonconfidence resolution or rejects a confidence resolution, the cabinet must resign en masse within 10 days or dissolve the lower house, call an election, and resign following the opening of the new Diet. Finally, the constitution requires that the prime minister and the majority of all cabinet members be elected members of the Diet.

The Making of the Prime Minister and His Cabinet   首相の誕生と組閣●

The prime minister is selected by a majority vote in each House of the Diet and is formally appointed by the emperor. If the two Houses disagree on their selection or the upper house fails to act within 10 days after the lower house has voted, the choice of the lower house stands as the decision of the Diet. Since the Liberal Democratic Party (LDP) maintained majority control of both houses of the Diet from its inception in 1955, the president of the LDP was routinely installed as prime minister until the downfall of the 1955 status quo in 1993 (see POLITICAL PARTIES). New official cabinets come into being following the selection of a new prime minister and after each election of the House of Representatives. In practice, cabinet posts are reshuffled much more frequently, with virtually annual major reconstructions of the cabinet in which over half its personnel are changed. The reasons for this frequent turnover are based on factional politics. Continuity is maintained by the Conference of Administrative Vice-Ministers, composed of the highest civil-service career officers in each ministry. Most policy matters are in effect decided at this level and forwarded to the cabinet for fairly routine approval.

Cabinet Powers and Organizations   内閣の権限と組織●

The prime minister and his cabinet have important judicial and legislative powers as well as executive responsibilities. In the judicial area they are empowered to select the chief justice and the other judges of the Supreme Court and to appoint lower-court judges from a list nominated by the Supreme Court. In the legislative area the cabinet determines the convocation of extraordinary sessions of the Diet, enacts cabinet orders to execute the provisions of the constitution and Diet laws, and, most important, prepares and submits bills to the Diet. The various cabinet staff offices and government ministries and agencies assist the cabinet in the exercise of this extensive concentration of powers.

As of 1994 the cabinet was composed of the prime minister and the heads of the 12 ministries: Justice; Foreign Affairs; Finance; Education; Health and Welfare; Agriculture, Forestry, and Fisheries; International Trade and Industry; Transport; Posts and Telecommunications; Labor;

Construction; and Home Affairs (Jichisho). Another 8 ministers of state without portfolios head other important executive offices and agencies such as the Cabinet Secretariat, the Defense Agency, and the Economic Planning Agency.

Elections (*senkyo seido*)   選挙制度●

Japan has had a national election system since the promulgation of the Constitution of the Empire of Japan on 11 February 1889. The extension of the franchise, limited at first to a small proportion of the adult male population, took place gradually, culminating in the adoption of universal suffrage shortly after the end of World War II.

The Prewar System   第二次世界大戦前の制度●

Rally to celebrate passage of the Universal Manhood Suffrage Law of 1925.

The first national election for the House of Representatives took place in 1890, but the right to vote was restricted to males who paid annual taxes of ¥15 or more. Over the next three and a half decades the number of enfranchised voters grew from fewer than 500,000 to about 3 million. The Universal Manhood Suffrage Law of 1925 expanded the electorate to about 12 million by granting the vote to all male citizens 25 years of age or older, though women were not enfranchised until December 1945.

Before 1945 there were fewer opportunities for popular participation in Japanese government. Members of the House of Representatives were elected, but seats in the House of Peers were either appointive or hereditary. Local government was directly subordinate to the central government. Local assemblies were popularly elected, but prefectural governors were appointed by the national government. City mayors were appointed by prefectural governors from a list of names submitted by city assemblies. Headmen and mayors of villages and towns were elected by their respective local assemblies.

Current Practices   現在の制度●

As a result of the Public Office Election Law of April 1950, all Japanese citizens are eligible to vote if they have reached the age of 20 and have met a three-month residency requirement (for voting in local elections). Candidates for political office must meet the stated age requirement for each office. Members of the House of Representatives and of prefectural and local assemblies must be at least 25 years old. Members of the House of Councillors and prefectural governors must be at least 30.

Japan has had a comprehensive election system incorporating all levels of government since the end of World War II. Under current election laws, members of all legislative bodies, including both houses of the Diet and prefectural, city, town, and village assemblies, are selected by popular vote. Political executives, including prefectural governors and mayors or other chief officials of local governments, are also chosen in popular elections. The prime minister, who is elected by the Diet, is the only political executive not chosen by direct popular vote.Today elections for half of the 252 members of the House of Councillors are held every three years in a combination of nationwide and prefectural districts. In the House of Representatives, 500 members are elected for four-year terms, typically in elections held irregularly after the dissolution of the House. Of these 500, 300 are elected from single-seat constituencies, and 200 are elected under a proportional representation system. Elections are held every four years for most prefectural and local executive offices and assemblies.

Administration   選挙管理●

Japan's electoral system is overseen by election administration committees within each administrative division of the country, i.e., prefectures, cities, towns, and villages. Administrators in local-government election sections assist the election committees in carrying out the day-to-day tasks of managing the system. The Ministry of Home Affairs regulates the system as a whole.

Laws specifying acceptable campaign practices are extremely detailed and strict in Japan. The period within which campaigns can be conducted, campaign funding and expenditures, and such matters as the number of posters permitted are precisely spelled out. Such practices as sponsorship of parties for constituents, door-to-door visits to solicit voter support, and gift-giving by candidates and their supporters are prohibited.

Political Reforms of 1994 (Seiji Kaikaku)   政治改革（1994年）●

Public anger over political corruption in the Liberal Democratic Party (LDP) has continued since the Lockheed Scandal (1976) and reached a new peak with the Recruit Scandal (1988). At the beginning of the 1990s reform-minded members of the LDP were putting most of the blame for the ongoing corruption on the medium-sized constituency system (*chu senkyoku sei*) in which each district sends between three and five representatives to the lower house. Claiming this system makes it difficult for power to change hands, they began serious deliberations over

Government and Diplomacy

reform measures that would introduce proportional representation and smaller election districts into elections for the HOUSE OF REPRESENTATIVES.

The LDP failed twice in its efforts to carry out political reforms—under Prime Ministers Kaifu Toshiki (1931–) and Miyazawa Kiichi (1919–). This resulted in the LDP's ouster in 1993 after four decades as the governing party. In 1993, a coalition of opposition parties formed a government under Prime Minister Hosokawa Morihiro (1938–), and the LDP became an opposition party. In early 1994, the Hosokawa cabinet finally succeeded in passing a political reform package through the Diet, but only after negotiating a major compromise with the LDP. The legislation calls for a fundamental change in the electoral system of the House of Representatives, an inevitable result of which will be a radical realignment of Japan's political map. The major parts of the political reform bills are as follows:

Hosokawa Morihiro, prime minister (1993–1994).

The Electoral System (選挙制度) The number of seats in the House of Representatives will be reduced from the present 511 seats to 500. These will consist of:

(1) Single-Seat Constituencies: The nation will be divided into 300 electoral districts, each of which will elect and be represented in the House of Representatives by a single seat.

(2) Proportional Representation: Separately, the entire nation will be divided into 11 regional blocs, and the remaining 200 members of the House will be elected from these multi-seat blocs on a proportional representation basis. A party must win at least 2 percent of the proportional representation votes to win a seat.

Fund Raising (政治資金) After a 5-year period all fund raising by individual candidates will be prohibited. During this transitional period each candidate will be permitted to set up one fund-raising body. This body can then accept annual contributions of up to ¥500,000 from any single company or organization.

State Subsidies for Political Parties (政党への国家補助) The government will subsidize recognized political parties to the limit of two-thirds of the party's total income from political contributions during the preceding year. The purpose of this subsidy is to offset the tighter limits imposed on campaign contributions from the private sector.

Political parties (*seito*)   政党●

Political parties emerged in Japan after the Meiji Restoration (1868), gained increasing influence with the opening of the Imperial Diet

(1890), and attained temporary political ascendancy following World War I. Outmaneuvered by the military, they declined in the 1930s and were dissolved and absorbed by the Imperial Rule Assistance Association in 1940. Political parties were revived under the Allied Occupation in the wake of World War II, and since 1952, when Japan regained its independence, they have been the primary force in national and local politics.

Parties in the Making   政党の発達●

"Political associations" (*seisha*), which arose in the 1870s and were usually groups of disgruntled former *samurai*, rural landowners, and urban intellectuals, were the precursors of political parties. Their demands for a popularly elected national assembly brought them into confrontation with the Meiji oligarchs or *genro*, who reacted by promulgating repressive laws to control publications, political libel, and public assemblies.

The two major party builders of the early Meiji period (1868–1912) were Itagaki Taisuke (1837–1919) and Okuma Shigenobu (1838–1922). Itagaki had joined the government in 1871 but resigned in 1873 and in the following year founded the first protoparty, the Aikoku Koto (Public Party of Patriots), which memorialized the government on the need to institute an elected assembly. Itagaki and his compatriots also established a regional group in Osaka called the Aikokusha (Society of Patriots), which was the basis for the founding in 1881 of Japan's first national party, the Jiyuto (Liberal Party). Many emulators among disaffected former samurai set up similar parties and between 1882 and 1886 mounted armed revolts against the government, whose reaction was the enactment of the Peace Preservation Law of 1887, which tightened restrictions on political activity.

Okuma resigned from the government in 1881 and in 1882 formed the Rikken Kaishinto (Constitutional Reform Party), which drew its membership mainly from the fledgling urban intelligentsia. It remained active until 1896. More conservative parties, such as the Rikken Teiseito (Constitutional Imperial Rule Party; 1882), represented themselves as defenders of the oligarchic government.

Parties in the Diet   国会と政党●

Parliamentary politics in the Diet, which opened in November 1890, was marked by an intense rivalry between the oligarchic government, which reserved the right to appoint cabinets, and the Liberal and Constitutional Reform parties. The Constitutional Reform Party, which was initially overshadowed by the Liberal Party and even by some of the pro-oligarchy groups, such as the Kokumin Kyokai (Nationalist

Association; 1892), was reconstituted as the Shimpoto (Progressive Party) in 1896 and consolidated its position as the second party. In common parlance the Liberal and Progressive parties were termed *minto* (popular parties), while groups of supporters of the oligarchic bureaucracy were referred to as *rito* (bureaucrats' parties). Neither of the popular parties had representation in the hereditary and appointive House of Peers, nor did they control local politics, for key local officials were appointed by the central government. Yet despite the popular parties' intransigent opposition to the antiparty policies of the oligarchs, the minto platforms reflected the interests of the rural elite and were no less conservative and nationalistic than the pronouncements of the oligarchs.

The Politics of Compromise   妥協の政治●

Rapprochement between parties and oligarchs was spurred in 1898 when Prime Minister Ito Hirobumi (1841–1909), who was a genro, dissolved the Diet due to opposition by the popular parties to his proposal for extra land taxes. The Liberal and Progressive parties merged to form the Kenseito (Constitutional Party), which won a majority in the Diet in the succeeding election. Ito resigned and invited Okuma and Itagaki to form a cabinet, Japan's first party cabinet, which was led by Okuma as prime minister and Itagaki as home minister. The alliance collapsed within months and the Progressive Party faction reorganized as the Kensei Honto (True Constitutional Party; 1898) and later as the Rikken Kokuminto (Constitutional Nationalist Party; 1910). However, in 1900 Ito formed the Rikken Seiyukai (Friends of Constitutional Government Party; commonly called Seiyukai), a coalition of former Jiyuto members and bureaucrats that won a majority in the Diet, marking the forthright entrance of oligarchs and bureaucrats into party politics on a basis of compromise with conservative factions of the popular parties. In 1913 General Katsura Taro (1847–1913), protege of the authoritarian oligarch Yamagata Aritomo (1838–1922), formed the Rikken Doshikai (Constitutional Association of Friends), absorbing the wealthier half of the Rikken Kokuminto; in 1916 it was reconstituted as the Kenseikai (Constitutional Association). From 1922 onward, rivalry between the Kenseikai and the Seiyukai, rather than between parties and oligarchs, became the dominant pattern.

With the increasing incidence of cabinets formed by parties during the first quarter of the 20th century, control of local assemblies by parties was achieved even more swiftly than in the Diet, and by 1910 some 90 percent of prefectural assemblymen were affiliated with one of the two major parties.

Ito Hirobumi, preeminent statesman of the Meiji period.

In the late 19th and early 20th centuries a number of proletarian parties appeared, but they evoked hostile reactions from the leaders of the major parties as well as the oligarchs, and many were banned soon after their formation by the invocation of such repressive laws as the Public Order and Police Law of 1900. Following the Bolshevik Revolution of 1917 and the emergence of labor unions, the Nihon Shakai Shugi Domei (Japan Socialist League) was established in 1920 and the Japan Communist Party (JCP; Nihon Kyosanto) in 1922. The chief threat to the major parties was not the proletarian parties, popular support of which was limited, but the military. The political power of the military was made clear in 1912 when the army minister Uehara Yusaku (1856–1933) resigned to protest the government's decision not to provide funds for two new army divisions. The army's refusal to name a successor to Uehara brought down the cabinet.

Ascendancy of Parties and the Military Takeover　政党の優位と軍の支配●

The cabinet formed in 1918 by Hara Takashi (1856–1921), largely made up of members of the Seiyukai, was the first viable party cabinet, and from then until 1932, the premiership was almost always held by the leaders of major parties. Nevertheless, the selection of prime ministers and cabinets was not a democratic process; candidates for the premiership were nominated by the genro and their protégés and appointed by the emperor, while ministers, except for those of the army and navy, were chosen by prime ministers in consultation with imperial advisers and confirmed by the emperor.

The two major parties, the Kenseikai (reorganized in 1927 as the Rikken Minseito) and the Seiyukai, alternated in power until the assassination in 1932 of Inukai Tsuyoshi (1855–1932), Seiyukai president and prime minister. Although prime ministers throughout the period were nominally designated by Saionji Kimmochi (1849–1940), protégé of Ito Hirobumi, it was the influence of parties upon the formation of cabinets that distinguished this brief era of Taisho Democracy in the early-20th century.

By the early 1930s there had emerged two legal noncommunist proletarian parties, which united in 1932 to form the Shakai Taishuto (Socialist Masses Party), a party that soon began to compromise step by step with the emergent forces of militarist authoritarianism. The JCP, which had been dissolved under government pressure in 1924, was reestablished underground in 1926 and remained active until about 1935, by which time arrests had decimated its membership.

Inukai Tsuyoshi, prime minister assassinated in 1932 during a failed military coup.

The number of voters quadrupled with passage of the Universal

Government and Diplomacy

Manhood Suffrage Law in 1925 and political campaigns became vastly more expensive. The industrial and financial combines Mitsui and Mitsubishi, the two largest *zaibatsu*, funded the Seiyukai and the Rikken Minseito, respectively, but both parties tapped additional sources, legal and illegal, and well-publicized malfeasance and corruption among politicians made it easier for the military to denounce party politicians. It was Inukai's death in 1932 at the hands of young naval officers that signaled the end of party cabinets. From that point until the end of World War II, there was a succession of "national unity" cabinets led by military men or their collaborators. In 1940 all political parties were absorbed by the Imperial Rule Assistance Association.

The Postwar Period
戦後期●

With the conclusion of hostilities in August 1945 efforts were made to resuscitate the major prewar parties, and by November all had reappeared, most under new names. The abolition of the military and the replacement of the House of Peers with an elected HOUSE OF COUNCILLORS left the civil bureaucracy as the only major institutional rival of the parties, while the new CONSTITUTION OF JAPAN made the National DIET the "highest organ of government" and provided for control of the cabinet by the Diet.

The Occupation Purge, which began in 1946, had a debilitating effect on the postwar conservative parties and also removed many local leaders from positions of influence, requiring all of the parties to rebuild their bases of local power. Revision of the election laws lowered the voting age, granted suffrage to women, and increased the number of members elected from constituencies. This encouraged the participation of independents and minor parties and provoked fierce competition among the major parties, leading to unstable cabinets and frequent stalemates until February 1949, when Yoshida Shigeru (1878–1967) of the Minshu Jiyuto (reorganized in 1950 as the Liberal Party) formed a stable cabinet that endured until October 1952. The land reforms of 1946 eliminated large landed estates and vested title in former tenants, removing an important stimulus to radicalism in rural areas and creating an electorate that became a dependable source of support for the conservatives. However, political corruption, particularly "money politics," was as common as before the war. Moreover, all parties remained ridden with the factionalism that had afflicted their forebears.

Prime Minister Yoshida Shigeru speaking at a Liberal Party campaign rally in 1950.

The most striking change in party membership was a dramatic increase from 1949, especially in the Minshu Jiyuto, of conservative members who were retired government bureaucrats. The entry of former senior bureaucrats into party politics became a permanent pattern, and while it testified to the new influence and prestige of the Diet, it also brought about an increasingly cozy relationship between the conservative parties and the upper levels of the administrative bureaucracy.

The 1955 Status Quo　　　　　　　　　　55年体制●

Following the restoration of Japan's independence in 1952, division among the conservatives made it impossible for either the Liberal Party or the Nihon Minshuto (Japan Democratic Party; successor of the prewar Rikken Minseito) to form a stable majority in the Diet, while the Japan Socialist Party (JSP) had split in 1951 into parties of the Left and the Right. In 1955, however, the JSP reunited and a month later the conservatives merged to form the Liberal Democratic Party (LDP), thus giving birth to the "1955 status quo" (*gojugonen taisei*), with the LDP controlling both Houses, the JSP holding roughly half the number of LDP seats in each, and the LDP mounting a series of one-party cabinets. From then on, antagonism between the two parties became a dominant pattern in the Diet over almost all major political programs.

During the late 1950s the LDP took controversial stands in favor of the revision of the new constitution, the augmentation of police powers and the revision of the United States-Japan Security Treaty. When the last of these was settled in 1960 after considerable turmoil, the government turned to the problems of economic growth and foreign trade, and in these areas its policies were in general popular.

By the late 1960s, however, the 1955 status quo was showing strain. LDP popularity waned due to a series of political scandals and the party's failure to deal satisfactorily with social and economic issues, such as a housing shortage, environmental pollution, and rising land prices. With the JSP racked by factionalism, the power vacuum was filled by splinter groups, such as the Democratic Socialist Party (DSP; Minshu Shakaito), founded in 1960 by right-wing members of the JSP, and newcomers such as the Komeito (Clean Government Party), which, with the support of members of the religious organization Soka Gakkai, gained an increasing number of seats in the Diet in the 1960s. In 1967 the LDP failed for the first time since 1955 to receive a majority of the popular vote, and its share continued to decline, as did that of the JSP, until the late 1970s.

Headquarters of the Liberal Democratic Party.

From the late 1960s the Komeito, the DSP, and the JCP gained increasing support among residents of cities, and they consistently controlled a third of all votes cast. The formation of a multiparty system was further spurred by the establishment of splinter parties: in 1976 critics of the LDP's "money politics" broke away to found the Shin Jiyu Kurabu

(New Liberal Club), while in 1977 a group of right-wing members of the JSP founded the United Social Democratic Party. Continuing corruption and factionalism contributed to diminishing popular support of the LDP, and in the periods 1976-80 and 1983-86 the party failed to win a majority of seats in the House of Representatives, while the JSP found its share reduced to 20 percent in the 1970s and 1980s.

However, in the 1986 elections for the House of Representatives the LDP won 300 of the 511 seats, and in the wake of the election the dissident Shin Jiyu Kurabu returned to the fold. The LDP lost its majority in the House of Councillors in 1989, but in the 1990 elections it did well, retaining a solid majority in the House of Representatives. The JSP also gained a sizable number of new seats in this election; the losers were the other opposition parties such as the Komeito, JCP, and DSP.

The Downfall of the 1955 Status Quo　　　　55年体制の崩壊●

Miyazawa Kiichi, prime minister (1991–1993).

The LDP's repeated failure to carry out political reforms led to the breakaway of dissidents who formed the Shinseito (The New Life Party) and the Shinto Sakigake (The Harbinger Party) in 1993. This, in turn, paved the way for breaking the LDP's grip on the government. The LDP Cabinet under Prime Minister Miyazawa Kiichi (1919–) made an outright promise to institute reforms. Its failure to do so opened the way for an overwhelming defeat on a non-confidence vote in the Diet and dissolution, followed by a call for national elections in July 1993. The election resulted in an unprecedented defeat for the LDP and an equally unexpected setback for the JSP which found its seats reduced almost by half. The electoral defeats suffered by these two political parties marked the end of the 1955 status quo. After political maneuvering among the opposition parties, a coalition government was formed in August 1993 under Prime Minister Hosokawa Morihiro (1938–), the head of the Nihon Shinto (Japan New Party, established in 1992), with the Shinseito holding the key posts and the remaining posts going to the other seven coalition parties, including the JSP.

Murayama Tomiichi, prime minister (1994–).

Despite its relatively high popularity, the Hosokawa government lasted only eight months with Hosokawa resigning in April 1994 after being attacked by the LDP concerning questionable loans he had received. Selected by the same group of coalition parties, Shinseito member Hata Tsutomu (1935–) replaced Hosokawa as prime minister. Almost immediately, however, the JSP and the Shinto Sakigake left the coalition, turning it into a minority government and forcing a general resignation in June 1994. The LDP immediately joined with the JSP and the Shinto Sakigake to form a coalition government with JSP member Murayama Tomiichi

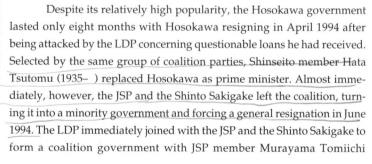

(1924–) as prime minister. The alliance between the LDP and the JSP, two parties which had fought bitterly up until one year before, surprised not only the public but the politicians involved as well.

In December 1994 six opposition parties, including the Shinseito, the Komeito, the Nihon Shinto, and the DSP, joined together to form the Shinshinto (New Frontier Party). This action left two large conservative parties, the LDP and the Shinshinto, with 200 and 178 House of Representative seats, respectively, followed by the JSP with 72 seats. In this situation, the JSP should be able to wield considerable influence; however, it has been forced to compromise on many of its traditional policies, such as its opposition to the SELF DEFENSE FORCES and nuclear power.

Bureaucracy (kanryosei)　　　　　　官僚制●

Japanese public bureaucracy comprises a national government bureaucracy, various local government bureaucracies, and the bureaucracies of public and semipublic corporations.

During the Meiji period (1868–1912) creation of a cabinet system and promulgation of Imperial Ordinance No. 37 (1887) and the Constitution of the Empire of Japan (1889) established the outlines of a national bureaucracy modeled on that of Prussia. Architects of the Meiji regime viewed a powerful parliament, local autonomy, and party government as threats to national cohesion and the development of urban-based industrialization. To protect public administration from the perceived dangers of localism and politics civil servants were selected through competitive examinations. Civil service became a lifetime career, with service being to emperor and nation rather than to domain or class. Virtually essential to a high-level bureaucratic career was graduation from an elite state university, such as Tokyo or Kyoto University, with these two schools providing the vast majority of senior civil servants.

Under the Meiji regime, each minister was appointed by—and was directly responsible to—the emperor. Collective cabinet responsibility was further diminished by the emperor's right of supreme command (tosuiken), which meant that the emperor, rather than the prime minister or any other civilian authority, had control over the military. This resulted in two national bureaucracies, one civil, the other military, with the latter manipulating its privileged access to control cabinet composition and government policy making.

Although every law required the consent of the Imperial Diet, few originated there. Most were drafted within agencies of the bureaucracy and then presented for ratification. An imperial ordinance, while technically issued by the emperor, provided extralegislative means for direct bureaucratic control over much public policy making.

During the Allied Occupation of Japan (1945–52), proscription of the military and significant change to the constitutional powers of the emperor, DIET, and local governments bore upon both national and local bureaucracies. Under the new CONSTITUTION OF JAPAN (1947), bureaucrats were responsible to the PRIME MINISTER AND CABINET rather than to the emperor. Most public employees were also prohibited from striking or even engaging in collective bargaining.

The National Government Organization Law of 1948, still the basic outline for the country's civil service, provides for four types of administrative organs: ministries, offices on the ministerial level, agencies, and commissions. The first two are the primary administrative organs of national government. The latter two oversee areas of administration different from the main work of a ministry or involving overlap, or potential conflict, with other ministries. Unable to submit proposed legislation or cabinet orders directly to the Diet, or to issue ministerial orders, these hold less formal power than the ministries.

As of 1995, there were 12 main ministries in the Japanese government, each headed by a minister who is almost invariably a member of parliament. Each minister is assisted by one or two parliamentary vice-ministers, usually members of parliament who serve as liaison between their ministry and the Diet. Career civil servants constitute the remainder of the ministry and are headed by an administrative vice-minister who oversees all administrative matters within the ministry. Each ministry is typically divided into 6 to 12 functional bureaus, headed by bureau chiefs, plus a secretariat responsible for ministerial records, statistics, personnel, public relations, and financial accounts. Bureaus may be subdivided into several departments, or directly into sections, the basic working units of the ministry. Most ministries also include auxiliary organs, and many oversee detached agencies or commissions. Each ministry has advisory committees composed of representatives of private interest groups and individual experts to provide advice on matters under ministry jurisdiction.

The Prime Minister's Office is responsible for the overall coordination of government policies. Under the Prime Minister's Office is the Management and Coordination Agency, which provides overall coordination of government departments, overseeing such operations as administrative inspection, personnel, and government pensions.

LOCAL GOVERNMENT is a two-tiered system comprising 47 larger units, known as prefectures, and their approximately 3,250 cities and smaller units, known collectively as municipalities. Almost all of the more than 3 million local public officials are local civil service personnel, appointed and paid by local public bodies.

In principle, local government entities are autonomously governed and administratively independent of the national government. In fact, a good deal of national governmental work is often delegated to local government agencies, and their actions are often directly overseen by the central government. Relying heavily on central financing, local government accounts for about two-thirds of total government disbursements, yet collects only about one-third of the nation's tax receipts.

There are approximately 100 public corporations in Japan, each legally independent but supervised by a national government agency and subject to Diet budgetary control. Performing wide-ranging functions in such diverse fields as transportation, public broadcasting, cultural exchange, energy development, etc, these public corporations employ some 620,000 individuals. About half of their top officials are retired senior civil servants.

Taken together, national government, local government, and public corporations have about 5 million full-time employees. Although this number constitutes a nearly 10-fold increase over the size of Japan's wartime bureaucracy, it is still significantly lower than those for most other industrialized countries.

National civil service is overseen by the Management and Coordination Agency, which handles organizational issues, and the National Personnel Authority (NPA), responsible for enforcement of the National Civil Service Law. Entrance and promotion are based primarily on written and oral examinations administered by the NPA. Although theoretically any Japanese citizen is eligible, graduates of Tokyo and Kyoto universities predominate.

Once appointed to a post, an individual typically remains with the same agency throughout his career. Advancement is primarily a function of seniority: members of an entering class move upward as a cluster through a variety of positions within an agency. The most senior positions are held for only two or three years before early retirement at age 51 to 55. In a practice called *amakudari* ("descent from heaven"), many retired bureaucrats find second careers, in private industry or public corporations overseen by the agencies for which they worked. A small proportion go on to politics. Their influence, locally and nationally, is considerable: approximately 20 percent of Japan's postwar cabinet ministers have been former bureaucrats, and the prime ministership has been held by more ex-civil servants than professional politicians.

Because service in a single ministry is the rule and lateral entry rare, loyalty to one's agency or section runs deep, often exaggerating bureaucratic tendencies toward tunnel vision and compartmentalization. Even sections within the same agency frequently resist cooperation, each seeking to maximize its sphere of influence. Some coordination is achieved through an informal weekly conference of administrative vice-ministers. Interministry teams are also established ad hoc to analyze and make policy recommendations on short-term problems.

The technical expertise of Japan's bureaucrats allows them to exercise substantial power in public policy formulation: approximately 90 percent of all legislation passed by the Diet since 1955 was drafted within the bureaucracy. Individual agencies have the power to issue ministerial ordinances, and the cabinet can issue a cabinet order, both of which supplement but can also bypass the legislative process. Although advisory commissions theoretically provide agencies with outside expertise, the ministerial staff defines the problem being investigated, oversees the investigation, and generally writes up the final report. "Retired" agency personnel who go on to second careers outside the bureaucracy perpetuate its influence: rarely are links to the former home agency severed; instead, they are used to facilitate coordination with private sector groups.

In contrast to the intimacy between the top levels of the bureaucracy and the Japanese political and economic establishment, the lower levels have been highly unionized since the Occupation. Although largely denied the right to strike, public employees once played a key role in the spring wage offensive. However, the public sector unions were weakened by the privatization of leading public corporations.

Efforts to improve efficiency by reducing the size and complexity of the national bureaucracy have enabled Japan, alone among the major industrialized countries, to stabilize the size of its national civil service. On the other hand, local bureaucracies have grown rapidly, and the trend in recent years has been to reassign centralized functions of national government to local levels of administration.

Local autonomy (chiho jichi)   地方自治●

The concept of local autonomy in government involves the right of local entities, such as prefectures, cities, towns, and villages, to decide and administer a range of public policies on their own initiative, with relative freedom from supervision ("corporate autonomy"), and the right of local citizens to participate in the formation of such policies ("civic autonomy"). Although the term chiho jichi had been widely used ever since the Meiji period (1868–1912), little local autonomy in either sense existed before 1945. The 1947 constitution contains a chapter on "local autonomy," implemented by the Local Autonomy Law (Chiho Jichi Ho) of the same year. In 1949 a successor to the Home Ministry, which had supported the prewar centralization, the Local Autonomy Agency (Chiho Jichi Cho), was created and became the Ministry of Home Affairs (Jichisho) in 1960. Education and police, decentralized under the Occupation, were recentralized to some extent thereafter. Many functions that could be considered local are governed by national laws. The administration of these laws is often delegated to governors and mayors as agents of the national government.

The types and standard rates of local taxes are determined by the Local Tax Law (Chihozei Ho). Local taxes account for about one third of total revenues, the rest being transfers of funds from the national government. The transfers often fall short of local requirements, and financial dependence and financial stringency limit local autonomy.

Local government (chiho seiji) 地方政治●

The general trend in local government since the Meiji Restoration (1868) has been for the expansion of local decision-making authority in areas of local concern and the fuller participation of citizens in the local process except for an interlude during the World War II years.

Establishment of the Prefectural System 廃藩置県●

Following the Meiji Restoration, the government began replacing the approximately 260 domains (han) and local administrative organs of the bakuhan (shogunate and domain) system with a centralized administrative structure consisting primarily of prefectures (ken) and urban prefectures (fu). In 1871 the government instituted a nationwide administrative system consisting of 72 prefectures with prefectural governors appointed by the central government. Local administration within prefectures was provided by large and small census districts. The Home Ministry, created in 1873, had the authority to sanction or disapprove of the actions of prefectural governors and became the central administrative element in state control of local government.

In 1878, legislation known as the Three New Laws was promulgated to unify local administrative organization and governance. The first law called for the institution of districts (*gun*) in rural areas and wards (*ku*) in populous urban areas as units of local administration. Prefectural governors appointed and supervised the chief officers of gun and ku, while citizens selected ruling chiefs on a more local level, such as town or village. The second law established representative assemblies in all prefectures, but reserved for the governors the power to originate bills. Less than 5 percent of the population was enfranchised to vote in these elections. Nevertheless, prefectural assemblies marked the establishment of elective representative institutions in Japanese government. The third law established rules for the collection of taxes at the prefectural and subprefectural levels. Amalgamations reduced the number of prefectures to 47 (3 fu, 43 ken, and 1 administrative province or *do*) by 1888, further promoting uniformity in subnational governance.

In 1888 the Local Autonomy System superseded the first of the Three New Laws and established a Municipal Code and Town and Village Code declaring that these units of local government should administer their own affairs "subject to the supreme control of the central government." The codes provided for the establishment of a mayorship and elected assemblies and specified that male citizens who met certain criteria of age, family, and taxpaying status could vote or hold elective office. In 1890 the Prefectural Code and District Code made further revisions to the structure of local government. Prefectural councils were created to handle business delegated to them by the prefectural assemblies. The District Code made the district (gun) a unit of local government with a chief, an elected district assembly, and a district council.

Districts were abolished as local government entities in 1923 and as state administrative units in 1926. Universal male suffrage, adopted in 1925, expanded citizen participation in local government. In 1929 local self-government powers were strengthened when the home minister lost the authority to make peremptory cuts in prefectural budgets and local and prefectural assemblies were given more legislative authority.

Wartime Centralization of Government Authority　戦中の中央集権●

Following the outbreak of conflict with China in 1937, the government required localities to take on more delegated tasks in an attempt to strengthen the state through centralization. In 1940 the Home Ministry ordered that community councils (*chonaikai*) be organized in city block areas and villages, with mayors and town and village chiefs as heads. Neighborhood associations (*tonarigumi*) were made responsible for the policing and welfare of their areas. Laws enacted in 1943 reduced the powers of prefectural assemblies and enlarged the power of the governorship. The last modification in the local government system before the end of World War II came in July 1943 when the government created nine Regional Administrative Councils to coordinate the action of local bodies and further strengthen central authority.

Postwar Local Government System　戦後の地方政治制度●

Decentralization of governmental authority and the strengthening of local government emerged early in the Allied Occupation. The new system of local government was intended to break up concentrated bureaucratic power revolving around Home Ministry-appointed governors, increase citizen participation and control, assure fairness in the conduct of local affairs, and expand the scope of autonomous local jurisdiction. The Home Ministry was eliminated and in December 1947 educational and police affairs were placed largely in local hands. The new CONSTITUTION OF JAPAN (1947) in essence guaranteed the decentralization of political authority by confirming the "principle of local autonomy" and by establishing such basic features of the new system as the separation of local from national administration and the direct popular election of prefectural governors and of mayors, as well as local assemblies. The latter provision gave voters the potential for controlling the executive authority, thereby providing incentives for governors and mayors to address the concerns of the local electorate. Further steps were sought to deconcentrate authority at the local level by creating prefectural and municipal commissions in charge of public safety, election management, and inspection of local administration. However, there was a strong bureaucratic resistance to administrative and financial decentralization and skepticism on the part of conservative governments concerning the administrative capacity of local authorities.

Post-Occupation Evolution　占領終了後の発展●

The legacy of local governmental reforms under the Allied Occupation was a mixed system combining aspects of prewar centralized administration with postwar local autonomy, an institutional separation between levels of government, and an intensified need for local governmental responsiveness to popular constituencies. During the first postwar decade, controversy centered on the relative merits of the Occupation reforms and on the efforts of central government bureaucracies and conservative parties to recentralize administrative authority. Recentralization of the police and educational systems, completed by 1956, stirred strong opposition from socialists, unionists, and intellectuals fearful of a reversion to prewar authoritarianism. On the other hand, central government elites encouraged amalgamations of municipalities, upgraded the overall quality of public administration, and facilitated the implementation of economic plans and national functions delegated to local authorities.

Beginning in the mid-1950s, local governments became participants in the national drive for economic growth. National authorities created a variety of national and regional development banks to promote public financing and investment in new industrial sites, water resources, and industrial infrastructure. Local authorities joined this effort by trying to attract industry with ordinances that provided for corporate tax breaks and other incentives for industrial development. Furthermore, new national laws for regional development were established in the early 1960s. In response, local authorities competed with each other to receive national government designation as target areas for development, thereby furthering the nationwide spread of the petrochemical, steel, machinery, and other heavy and chemical industries.

By the late 1960s and early 1970s, many local governments began reordering their priorities. Economic growth encouraged a rapid urbanization of the population and urban land prices spiraled, making the provision of an adequate social infrastructure difficult. At the same time, new urban problems such as pollution-related diseases, traffic congestion, and uncontrolled urban sprawl proliferated.

The intensity of such problems resulted in substantial grass-roots protests and efforts by citizens to seek ameliorative policies from local government. Opposition representation in assemblies increased and coalitions of opposition parties formed around new urban issues succeeded in electing reformist local heads in major areas. Under these circumstances, local authorities began to pioneer new forms of communication with residents, pollution-control measures, and social welfare programs. As a result, local priorities diverged significantly from national ones and contributed to the eventual shift in national priorities from unrestricted economic growth to establishing a higher quality of life.

Moreover, government reform efforts of the late 1970s and early 1980s led to an increased reliance on local authorities for the implementation of national social and environmental programs. There emerged, in effect, a broad recognition that local governments had matured in their administrative competence, had a unique role in setting local priorities and coordinating public programs, and were necessary partners of the national government in creating livable communities.

Judicial system (*shiho seido*) 司法制度●

The unified national structure of courts for the administration of justice. The 1947 constitution (art. 76) provides that "the whole judicial power is vested in a Supreme Court and in such inferior courts as are established by law." All courts on all levels are parts of a single system under the sole and complete administration of the Supreme Court. A jury system does not exist.

The structure of the judicial system is as follows: the Supreme Court (Saiko Saibansho); 8 high courts (*koto saibansho*) in the eight principal geographical subdivisions of the country; 50 district courts (*chiho saibansho*) in the principal administrative units; 50 family courts (*katei saibansho*); and 452 summary courts (*kan'i saibansho*) located throughout the country. The DIET as the sole law-making organ can change the organization of the courts by passing the necessary legislation, but the administration of the court system remains constitutionally vested in the Supreme Court.

The Supreme Court is headed by the chief justice, who is appointed by the emperor after designation by the cabinet. The other 14 justices are appointed by the cabinet. The court is organized into a grand bench consisting of all 15 justices and three petty benches of 5 justices each. All cases before the Supreme Court are appeals; it possesses original jurisdiction over no cases. The constitution (art. 81) also provides that the Supreme Court is the court of last resort "with power to determine the constitutionality of any law, order, regulation or official act."

The Supreme Court Building, Chiyoda Ward, Tokyo.

The high courts are essentially appellate courts. They are courts of first instance for the crimes of insurrection, preparation for or plotting of insurrection, and of assistance in the acts enumerated.

District courts have original jurisdiction over most cases with the exception of offenses carrying minor punishment and a few others reserved for other courts. In addition, they are courts of appeal for actions taken by the summary courts. Family courts came into existence in 1949. They have jurisdiction over such matters as juvenile crime (the age of majority being 20), problems of minors, divorce, and disputes over family property. Summary courts have jurisdiction over minor cases involving less than ¥900,000 in claims or fines or offenses carrying lighter punishments.

Police system (*keisatsu seido*) 警察制度●

Japan's approximately 260,000 (1994) police officers are organized into prefectural forces coordinated and partially controlled by the National Police Agency in Tokyo. They enjoy wide community support and respect.

Historical Development 歴史●

Until 1600, social control was performed essentially by the military and by groups of citizens organized for mutual defense. During the Edo period (1600–1868), the Tokugawa shogunate developed an elaborate police system based on town magistrates, who held *samurai* status and served as chiefs of police, prosecutors, and criminal judges. The system was augmented by citizens' groups such as the *goningumi* (five-family associations), composed of neighbors collectively liable to the government for the activities of their membership.

Tokyo Metropolitan Police Department headquarters.

After the Meiji Restoration (1868), the Home Ministry was established in 1873. With jurisdiction over the Police Bureau, it effectively controlled the police. This new, centralized police system had wide-ranging responsibilities far beyond the essential police duties, including the authority to issue ordinances and handle quasi-judicial functions. It also regulated public health, factories, construction, and businesses and issued permits, licenses, and orders. To help control proscribed political activities, the Special Higher Police (Tokubetsu Koto Keisatsu or Tokko) were established in 1911 in Tokyo and in 1928 in all prefectures. With the outbreak of the Sino-Japanese War of 1937–1945, the police were given the added responsibilities of regulating business activities for the war effort, mobilizing labor, and controlling transportation. Even fire fighting came under police direction, as did the regulation of publications, motion pictures, political meetings, and election campaigns.

After World War II, leaders of the Allied Occupation required the Diet to enact a new Police Law. This 1947 law abolished the Home Ministry. It also decentralized the system by establishing about 1,600 independent municipal police forces in all cities and towns with populations of over 5,000. Smaller communities would be served by the National Rural Police. Popular control of the police was to be ensured by the establishment of politically neutral, civilian public safety commissions.

This attempt at decentralization was unsuccessful. In June 1951, the Police Law was amended to allow smaller communities to merge their police forces with the National Rural Police. Eighty percent of the communities with autonomous forces did so. The system was further centralized with passage of a new Police Law in 1954.

Present Structure　　　　　　　　現在の組織●

Today the Japanese police system is based on prefectural units that are autonomous in daily operations yet are linked nationwide under the National Police Agency.

Prefectural police headquarters, including the Tokyo Metropolitan Police Department, control everyday police operations in each prefecture. In effect, the prefectures pay for the patrolman on the beat, traffic control, criminal investigation, and other routine functions but have little control over domestic security units, which are funded by the national government, as are the salaries of senior national and prefectural police officials.

Prefectures are divided into districts, each with its own police station under direct control of prefectural police headquarters rather than linked administratively to the government of the town or city in which it is located. There are about 1,250 of these police stations nationwide. Districts are further subdivided into jurisdictions of urban *koban* (police boxes) and rural *chuzaisho* (residential police boxes).

The mainstay of the Japanese police system is the uniformed patrol officer (*omawari san*). The patrol officers man the police boxes and patrol cars and comprise 40 percent of all officers. They are the generalists who usually respond first to all incidents and crimes and then funnel them to the specialized units for further investigation.

Police box.

The scope of police responsibilities remains broad, though considerably narrowed from the prewar period. Besides solving ordinary crimes, criminal investigators establish the causes of fires and industrial accidents. Crime prevention police bear added responsibility for juveniles, businesses such as bars and Mah-Jongg parlors, and the enforcement of "special laws" regulating gun and sword ownership, drugs, smuggling, prostitution, pornography, and industrial pollution. Public safety commissions usually defer to police decisions.

Contact with the community is augmented by the requirement that koban-based police visit every home in their jurisdiction twice a year to gather information, pass on suggestions regarding crime prevention, and hear complaints. Neighborhood crime prevention and traffic safety associations provide another link between police and community, further promoting extensive public involvement in law and order.

Taxes (*sozei seido*) 租税制度●

The most significant tax by far is the national income tax, producing some 67.5 percent of the ¥64 trillion in total national tax revenue received for fiscal year 1993. This tax can be classified into two categories. The first is the individual income tax defined in the Income Tax Law (Shotokuzei Ho) and its supporting enforcement orders and regulations. This tax produced 42.1 percent of fiscal 1993 national tax revenue. The second category of national income tax is the corporate income tax imposed on all legal entities (known as *hojin* or juristic persons). This tax is defined in the Corporation Tax Law (Hojinzei Ho) and its supporting enforcement orders and regulations; it provided some 25.4 percent of fiscal 1993 national income tax revenue.

Although historically the major emphasis of the Japanese tax system had been on direct rather than indirect taxation, six tax reform bills were enacted in December 1988 that, among other things, introduced a new major indirect tax, the national consumption tax. The consumption tax provided 8.5 percent of national tax revenue in 1993.

Income taxation in Japan is based on self-assessment, and therefore, all corporate taxpayers must file a final corporate tax return with the tax office within two months of the end of their business year. However, most individual taxpayers need not file a tax return provided that they have received only remuneration income and all or almost all of that income is from one employer. Their employer calculates their tax amount, which is withheld at source, and makes a year-end adjustment, either collecting additional tax or refunding tax to the taxpayer. Individual taxpayers who have significant renumeration income from two or more sources or who have other types of income are required to file a final income tax return by 15 March of the year following the calendar year for which they are being taxed.

The national Japanese domestic tax system is administered by the National Tax Administration, a semi-independent agency of the Ministry of Finance. This body oversees 12 regional taxation bureaus and 517 local tax offices. Tax policy and international tax negotiations are handled by an internal bureau of the Ministry of Finance called the Tax Bureau. Customs matters come under the Customs and Tariff Bureau of the Ministry of Finance.

National Tax Administration headquarters.

Revenue Estimates, 1993
国税(1993年度、当初予算)

Direct taxes	Amount (in billions of yen)	percent
Income tax	27,046	42.1
Corporate tax	16,313	25.4
Inheritance tax	2,699	4.2
Land price tax	623	1.0
Subtotal	46,681	72.6

Indirect taxes	Amount (in billions of yen)	percent
Consumption tax	5,458	8.5
Stamp revenue	1,756	2.7
Gasoline and fuel taxes	2,197	3.4
Liquor tax	2,051	3.2
Stock exchange and securities taxes	390	0.6
Tobacco tax	1,019	1.6
Customs duty	923	1.4
Motor vehicle and other tonnage taxes	692	1.1
Other *1	3,123	4.9
Subtotal	17,609	27.4
Total	64,290	100

*1 Taxes appropriated for special accounts.
Source: Ministry of Finance.

For local tax matters, a general framework is established by the Local Tax Law, which is overseen by the Local Tax Bureau of the Ministry of Home Affairs. The type of local taxes that can be imposed and their rates are regulated by the national government.

A formal procedure exists for settling tax disputes with the government. Protests must first be filed with the chief of the tax office or the director of the regional taxation bureau. If this proves unsatisfactory, the taxpayer may claim review by the tax court called the National Tax Tribunal. A ruling by the tax court may then be appealed to the regular judicial courts.

International Relations

History of international relations (*kokusai kankei shi*)　国際関係史●
　　Japan's relations with foreign nations, following abandonment of the shogunal policy of National Seclusion in 1854, can be divided into the period before and the period after the close of World War II. The earlier period includes the entrance of Japan into the community of nations, its participation as an equal in international affairs, and the creation and collapse of the Greater East Asia Coprosperity Sphere. The later period embraces the Allied Occupation (1945–1952), the San Francisco Peace Treaty (1951), admission to the United Nations (1956), and the gradual reestablishment of an independent diplomatic policy.

The Opening of Japan
and the "Unequal Treaties"　　　　　日本の開国と不平等条約●

The "black ships" of Commodore Matthew Perry.

　　The arrival in Japan of Commodore Matthew Perry and his "black ships" (*kurofune*) in 1853 led to the signing by representatives of the United States and the Tokugawa shogunate of the Kanagawa Treaty of 1854, which effected the opening of Japan. Formal diplomatic relations were soon established with the United Kingdom, Russia, the Netherlands, and other Western countries. The various friendship and commercial treaties that Japan concluded with these countries provided for broad grants of extraterritoriality and restrictions on Japan's right to levy customs duties and were the means by which Japan was forcibly incorporated into a system of international relations developed by the Western powers. Following the formation of the Meiji government in 1868, Japan embarked on a program of forthright Westernization, with the goal of establishing Japan as a great power. Revision of the Unequal Treaties became a crucial concern, and the issue was raised by a succession of foreign ministers, but the nations of the West were disinclined to relinquish their vested privileges. It was not until the signing of the Anglo-Japanese Commercial Treaty of 1894 that the extraterritorial rights of a foreign power were first abolished. Japan did not fully recover autonomous customs rights or attain equal status with Western nations until 1911.

Expansion on the Asian Mainland　　　アジア大陸への進出●

　　In 1876 Japan compelled Korea to sign the Treaty of Kanagawa, gaining for itself access to three Korean ports, extraterritorial rights, and full exemption from customs duties. Japan thus succeeded in concluding an unequal treaty with Korea ahead of the Western powers. China, however, held considerable influence over Korean diplomatic and domestic affairs, and rivalry with Japan was inevitable. After a series of political coups inside Korea in 1884, Japan and China agreed to withdraw their troops from Korea; however, in the spring of 1894 the Tonghak Rebellion broke out, and the Korean government called on the Chinese for military assistance. Japan too sent an expeditionary force, which clashed with the Chinese in July 1894, leading to the Sino-Japanese War of 1894–1895. The Treaty of Shimonoseki (1895), which ended hostilities, provided for the cession by China of Taiwan and the Pescadores. Reparation money received from China played a significant role in the industrialization of Japan, while the opening of numerous Chinese ports and cities to Japanese commerce and industry enabled entrance into the Chinese domestic market. The Tripartite Intervention by Russia, Germany, and France, however, forced Japan to relinquish the Liaodong Peninsula, which it had also obtained from China.

Following the severance of China's interest in Korea, a new rivalry developed between Russia and Japan. After 1900, Russia now stationed troops in Manchuria, which Japan considered a grave threat to its position on the Korean peninsula. It was under these circumstances that Japan signed with Britain the Anglo-Japanese Alliance (1902), the first military treaty concluded by Japan with a foreign country. Renewed in 1905 and 1911, for 20 years it remained the pillar of Japanese foreign policy.

On 6 February 1904 Japan broke off diplomatic relations with Russia over the issues of China and Korea and on 10 February declared war (Russo-Japanese War of 1904–1905). The terms of the Treaty of Portsmouth (1905), which ended hostilities, gave to Japan the southern half of Sakhalin and the Russian lease concessions in China, including the Liaodong Peninsula; the latter provided a foothold for eventual Japanese political domination of southern Manchuria. Russia also agreed not to intervene in Korean affairs, and in 1910 Korea became a Japanese colony.

In a series of agreements with Russia in 1907, 1910, and 1912, Japan established a sphere of influence in southern Manchuria and the eastern part of Inner Mongolia. By means of the South Manchuria Railway, Japan strengthened its position in the area. This activity, however, was in conflict with the Open Door Policy of the United States, which was based on the principle of equal access to Chinese markets, and led to a dispute between Japan and the United States over the issues of railway rights and interests in Manchuria. Friction was exacerbated by restrictions placed by the United States on immigration from Japan, as well as by rivalry between the US and Japanese navies in the Pacific Ocean.

US president Theodore Roosevelt (center left) and Japanese diplomats Komura Jutaro (center right) and Takahira Kogoro (far right) at the conference where the Treaty of Portsmouth was signed in 1905.

Government and Diplomacy

World War I and Its Aftermath 第一次世界大戦とその結果●

With the attention of the Western powers turned to Europe, Japan moved to strengthen its position in Asia. In the Twenty-one Demands presented to China in 1915, Japan sought formal recognition of its occupation of German holdings on the Shandong Peninsula, extension of tenure for its leaseholds in China, and appointment by the Chinese government of Japanese as political, financial, and military advisers.

Following World War I, Japan was one of the five victorious nations at the Paris Peace Conference in 1919; it received confirmation of its occupation of the Shandong Peninsula and the mandate for the Pacific Islands formerly held by Germany. However, because of Japan's strong pressure on China, confrontation between Japan and China increased. Following the Bolshevik Revolution in Russia in November 1917, Japan joined the Allied Siberian Intervention (1918–1922). By November 1918 more than 70,000 Japanese troops were entrenched in northern Manchuria and the Maritime Province. The forces of the United States, the United Kingdom, and France completed their withdrawal by April of 1920, but Japan, which had hoped to establish a sphere of influence in eastern Siberia, did not follow suit until October 1922.

Japanese troops departing Tokyo on their way to take part in the Siberian Intervention.

At the Washington Conference of 1921–1922 a plan for international cooperation in East Asia, the so-called Washington System, was formulated. Japan agreed to remove its military forces from the Shandong Peninsula, and during the 1920s, while also working to develop its established interests, Japan made an effort not to disturb the political equilibrium in Asia. However, when the Chinese Nationalist Party (Guomindang) extended its sphere of activity to Manchuria and Inner Mongolia, Japan replied with extreme measures such as the assassination of Zhang Zuolin.

Growing Japanese Military Activity
in China 中国における軍事活動の拡大●

The Manchurian Incident of September 1931 and the establishment of the Japanese-controlled puppet state Manchukuo in 1932 brought the Japan-United States confrontation in Asia close to the flash point. Japan ignored the Nine-Power Treaty, which it had signed at the Washington Conference in 1922. The United States, which opposed all of Japan's activities in Manchuria, responded with the Stimson Doctrine.

The Japanese challenge to the Washington System was denounced by a large majority of the member countries of the League of Nations. Japan responded by leaving the League of Nations in March 1933. Japan's economy suffered due to its estrangement from Britain and the United States, and to compensate for its losses Japan extended its influence from Manchuria into northern China. The military dominance of Japan over the entire area of Manchuria created tension with the Soviet Union and led to the signing of the Anti-Comintern Pact in 1936 by Germany and Japan. Triggered by the Marco Polo Bridge Incident of July 1937, Japan's expansion into northern China escalated into general armed conflict. As the scope of military activity in China increased, the United States reacted by declaring an embargo against Japan.

World War II   第二次世界大戦●

The 1938 declaration of the Toa Shinchitsujo (New Order in East Asia), which encompassed China, Manchukuo, and Japan, and the announcement in August 1940 of the Greater East Asia Coprosperity Sphere, which included Southeast Asia as well, gave notice of Japan's intention to create a new non-Western political order throughout Asia. It was in the context of the "New Order" that the Japanese-backed Reorganized National Government of the Republic of China was established in 1940.

Commemorative photograph taken at the time of the announcement of the Greater East Asia Coprosperity Sphere.

The sweeping victories of Germany, following the outbreak of World War II in September 1939, convinced Japan of the value of an alliance, and in September 1940 it negotiated the Tripartite Pact with Germany and Italy. In the same month, Japan invaded the northern part of French Indochina.

The collapse of Japan-United States relations appeared imminent; negotiations in Washington proved fruitless. The Soviet-Japanese Neutrality Pact, concluded in April 1941, provided assurance against an attack from the north, and Japan advanced into the southern part of French Indochina. In retaliation the United States froze Japanese assets and banned oil exports to Japan. On 26 November the US secretary of state, Cordell Hull, replied with the Hull Note, which called for radical changes in Japan's Asia policy. This was construed by Japan as an unacceptable ultimatum that left it with no alternative but war.

Overwhelming victories in the Pacific theater in the initial stages of World War II opened the way for Japanese occupation and military administration of French Indochina, the Philippines, the Dutch East Indies, Malaya, and Burma. However, defeat in the Battle of Guadalcanal (August 1942–February 1943) put Japan on the defensive, and imperial Japan was on the verge of collapse.

**Allied Occupation and Dependence
on US Military Strength**   連合国占領と米国軍事力への依存●

Japan conceded defeat on 15 August 1945 and formally surrendered to the Allied powers on 2 September. The right of Japanese to rule their nation was made subject to the authority of the supreme commander for the Allied powers (SCAP). As supreme commander, Douglas MacArthur presided over General Headquarters (GHQ) and set about implementing plans for the demilitarization and democratization of Japan.

Following the victory of the communists in China in 1949 and the establishment of the People's Republic of China (PRC), and the outbreak of the Korean War in 1950, the United States moved to restore Japan's independence. In September 1951 Japan and the Allied powers (excluding the Soviet Union, China, India, and Burma) signed the San Francisco Peace Treaty, which became effective in April 1952, enabling Japan to reenter the community of independent nations. Prohibited by the new CONSTITUTION OF JAPAN from possessing land, sea, or air military forces, Japan was faced with the problem of national security. The issue was partially resolved when, at the signing of the peace treaty, it concluded the first of the United States-Japan security treaties, bringing Japan under the protective umbrella of the US military. Bases used by the army of occupation remained in the hands of US forces, and during the Korean War the Japanese economy was stimulated by massive US military procurements. With US backing, Japan was accepted in 1955 as a member of the General Agreement on Tariff and Trade (GATT) and in 1956 as a member of the United Nations. At the end of the 1950s, Japan announced its intention to adhere to "three principles" in the determination of its foreign policy: membership in the Asian community, diplomacy centered on the United Nations, and maintenance of Japan's position in the free world. Throughout the 1960s, however, Japan's foreign policy was strongly influenced by that of the United States. Opponents of this relationship were particularly vocal in 1960, when the United States-Japan Security Treaty was revised, and again following the outbreak of the Vietnam War.

Emergence of Japan as an Economic Power　　　　経済大国日本の出現●

In the postwar era Japan's expanding foreign trade has played an increasingly influential role in the formation of its diplomacy. In the latter part of the 1960s Japan's economy reached a level competitive with those of the United States and the European Community (EC). Friction over trade issues caused Japan-United States relations to enter a new phase. In the midst of a textile dispute between the two countries in 1969–1971, President Richard Nixon announced in July 1971, without prior consultation with Japan, that he would visit Beijing to negotiate the establishment of diplomatic relations with China. Out of deference to US anticommunist policy and despite domestic agitation for the normalization of relations with the People's Republic of China, Japan had maintained close ties with the Republic of China on Taiwan, and this radical shift in policy was construed as a shock. On the heels of this "shock" came the announcement by President Nixon, again without consultation, of his New Economic Policy, which resulted in a major appreciation of the yen and the unsettling of Japan's foreign trade.

In the late 1970s friction with the United States, which continued to be Japan's chief trade partner, again grew heated due to several factors: the trade balance was overwhelmingly in favor of Japan; increasing imports of Japanese steel and electronic products had grave consequences for corresponding US industries; and the United States criticized Japan for not opening domestic markets to US goods. Economic friction with the United States persisted through the 1980s, and the criticism was voiced in the US Congress that Japanese trade practices were "unfair".

A similar trade dispute developed between Japan and the nations of Western Europe. Trade imbalances arising from the enormous export volumes of Japanese steel, electronic products, ships, and automobiles caused friction, which intensified in the 1980s and was stimulating the formation of a new protectionism and of new economic blocs in the early 1990s.

Relations with the Soviet Union and China ソ連・中国との関係●

The conclusion of the first United States-Japan Security Treaty in 1952 inevitably brought Japan into confrontation with the Soviet Union and China. In 1955, during the post-Stalin-era thaw in the cold war, the Soviet Union initiated negotiations on the restoration of normal relations with Japan. However, the talks were suspended in mid-1956 due to a dispute over a number of islands off the coast of Hokkaido that had come under Soviet dominion at the close of World War II and that Japan demanded be returned. Afterward it was decided that an interim agreement terminating the state of war between the two nations would be put into effect, while negotiations continued on a peace treaty. The Soviet-Japanese Joint Declaration to this effect was signed in October 1956, and diplomatic relations were resumed.

In the 1980s, following the emergence in the Soviet Union of Mikhail Gorbachev, international tensions were reduced, bringing an end to the cold war that had dominated world politics for more than 40 years. The state visit to Japan by President Gorbachev in April of 1991— the first ever by a Soviet leader—contributed to the amelioration of Soviet-Japanese relations. However, after many twists and turns such as the dissolution of the Soviet Union and Boris Yeltsin's succession to the

President Gorbachev visits Japan (1991).

Government and Diplomacy

Presidency, the issue of the Northern Territories has still to be resolved and there is no prospect for the early conclusion of a peace treaty with Russia.

When the San Francisco Peace Treaty was implemented in April 1952, Japan established diplomatic relations with the Nationalist government on Taiwan, which it recognized as the official government of China. Until 1972 contact with the People's Republic of China was maintained on a largely nongovernmental basis, and only limited and intermittent trade was conducted.

In the 1970s dissension within the communist bloc began to grow and the eruption of armed conflict between China and the Soviet Union in 1969 was a factor in the decision of the United States to negotiate with China for the establishment of diplomatic relations. The China-United States rapprochement paved the way for the issuance of a joint communiqué in September 1972 establishing formal diplomatic relations between Japan and the People's Republic of China (of which Japan recognized Taiwan to be a territory) and the signing in 1978 of the China-Japan Peace and Friendship Treaty.

Relations with Korea  朝鮮・韓国との関係●

China and Japan agree to establish formal diplomatic relations (1972).

In 1948 the Korean peninsula was divided at the 38th parallel between the Democratic People's Republic of Korea (North Korea) and the Republic of Korea (South Korea), with which Japan established diplomatic relations. This effort, however, was fraught with difficulties due to the deep resentment felt by Koreans toward the nation that had colonized it. The sentiment culminated in the anti-Japanese policies of the first President Syngman Rhee. Following the assumption of power by the government of Pak Chong-hui, negotiations were resumed and resulted in the signing of the Korea-Japan Treaty of 1965, in which Japan recognized South Korea as the only lawful government on the Korean peninsula. Contacts with North Korea have been largely unofficial, but in 1990 negotiations were initiated to normalize relations.

Relations with Southeast Asia and the Pacific Basin

東南アジア・太平洋地域との関係●

Japan's postwar relations with Southeast Asia began with negotiations concerning war reparations. The first country with which Japan reached an agreement was Burma, followed by the Philippines, Indonesia, and the Republic of Vietnam, all between 1954 and 1959. In the 1960s Japan established close economic relations with many countries in the region, and since then, attaching importance to a special relationship with these nations, Japan has placed particular emphasis on foreign aid. In 1967 Thailand, Malaysia, Singapore, Indonesia, and the Philippines organized the Association of Southeast Asian Nations (ASEAN) to increase economic cooperation. ASEAN industrial development has been accelerated by Japanese capital funding and technology.

With the ASEAN countries, Japan, and a number of other nations in the East Asia-western Pacific area, the NIEs (newly industrializing economies) have become the most dynamic regional influence upon the world's economy. As providers of raw materials, Australia, Canada, New Zealand, and Mexico have become increasingly important to Japan and the other industrialized nations of the region, and growing economic interdependence has lent itself to the idea of a "Pacific Basin Economic Sphere". In November 1989 government representatives of Canada, the United States, New Zealand, Australia, South Korea, Japan, and the six ASEAN nations (Brunei joined in 1984) met for their first conference, at which they established principles for economic cooperation. Japan considers the advancement of regional economic stability and expansion of the international system of free trade to be essential to its well-being.

Japan and the Middle East   日本と中東●

Japan is almost totally dependent on the import of oil to meet its needs. In the years since the oil crisis of 1973, Japan has established strong economic relations with the countries of the Middle East, not only in regard to the import of oil but also the export of refining plants and other industrial goods. During this period Japan chose to support the Arab nations vis-a-vis Israel, but in the wake of the Persian Gulf War of 1990–1991 it is likely that Japan's foreign policy will assume a broader view.

Economic Assistance to Developing Nations   開発途上国への経済援助●

Total direct government economic assistance to developing nations provided by Japan has steadily increased, reaching US $11.2 billion in 1992 and exceeding that of all other economically advanced nations. Nevertheless, because in 1990/1991 less than 40 percent of Japanese aid— as opposed to 98.9 percent of British foreign aid and 73.9 percent of US aid—was in the form of outright grants, critics have argued that its effectiveness was severely circumscribed. In step with government aid, private investment by Japanese in developing countries is also increasing, and the scope of Japanese technological cooperation with the developing nations is also expanding (see OFFICIAL DEVELOPMENT ASSISTANCE).

United Nations and Japan

(Kokusai Rengo *to* Nihon)　　　　　　　　　国際連合と日本●

Japan was admitted to the United Nations on 18 December 1956, and its foreign policy has since then included "the centrality of the United Nations" as one of its basic guidelines. Japan has established a UN bureau at the Ministry of Foreign Affairs and a permanent mission to the UN headquarters, as well as a permanent delegation to the United Nations' European subheadquarters in Geneva, Switzerland. Since 1958 Japan has been elected to the UN Security Council as a nonpermanent (two-year-term) member six times and since 1960 has been a regular member of the Economic and Social Council. Tokyo has been the base of the network of research facilities known as the UN University since its founding in 1974, and in 1994 there were 12 other UN organizations operating in Japan, including the United Nations Information Center, the United Nations Children's Fund (UNICEF) Office in Japan, the Japan branch office of the United Nations High Commissioner for Refugees (UNHCR), and the United Nations Development Program (UNDP) Tokyo Liaison Office. The nongovernmental organizations registered with the United Nations in Japan include the Japan Red Cross Society, the United Nations Association of Japan, and the National Federation of UNESCO Associations in Japan. In 1994 Japan was the second largest payer of UN operating expenses, contributing over 12 percent of total expenses.

Ogata Sadako, the United Nations High Commissioner for Refugees, visits a refugee camp in Cambodia in 1993.

Despite the increasing importance of Japan's role as a member of the United Nations, until 1992 it had not sent troops to participate in UN peacekeeping activities because of its renunciation of arms as embodied in article 9 of the Japanese Constitution. That Japan's contribution was limited to an economic one met with criticism from countries overseas during the Persian Gulf War of 1990–1991. In 1990 and again in 1991 the ruling Liberal Democratic Party proposed legislation in the Diet that would enable SELF DEFENSE FORCES troops to participate in UN peacekeeping activities. In June 1992 the Diet passed the Law on Cooperation in United Nations Peacekeeping Operations, and, after a formal request from the United Nations, Japanese troops were sent to Cambodia in October of that year. Since then, Self Defense Forces personnel have also participated in UN peacekeeping operations in Mozambique, and, at the request of the UNHCR, have taken part in the refugee relief effort in Rwanda.

As its role in overall UN operations expands, there have been increasing calls within Japan for a permanent

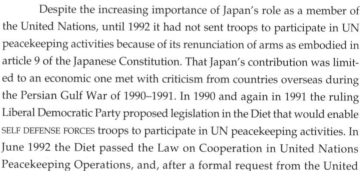

Japan's Contribution to the UN Budget
国連の通常予算と日本の分担　　(in millions of US dollars)

Years	Japan's contribution	UN budget
1970–71	13.79	363.59
1980–81	103.78	1,339.15
1990–91	194.85	2,134.07
1992–93	254.11	2,389.24

Source: Ministry of Foreign Affairs.

seat on the UN Security Council. As of the end of 1994 the outcome for Japan of UN deliberations on Security Council membership was uncertain.

International cultural exchange

(*kokusai bunka koryu*) 国際文化交流●

Between the opening of Japan to foreign contact in the late 19th century and World War I, Japan stressed the importation of Western culture rather than the introduction abroad of its own culture. Behind this effort was the intention of creating a modern state based on the Western model. Following World War I, the importance of promoting international understanding of Japan through cultural exchange was recognized, and in 1934 the Kokusai Bunka Shinkokai (KBS; the Society for International Cultural Relations) was established.

Following World War II, rapid economic growth and increased visibility of Japan in the international community prompted greater interest in Japanese culture and society among countries overseas. With the aim of conducting Japan's international cultural relations on a more systematic basis, the Japanese government created a new cultural exchange organization, the Kokusai Koryu Kikin (JAPAN FOUNDATION), in 1972.

Japan's international cultural exchange activities are handled mainly by the Cultural Affairs Department of the Ministry of Foreign Affairs, the Science and International Affairs Bureau of the Ministry of Education, and two public corporations attached to these ministries: the Japan Foundation and the Japan Society for the Promotion of Science. Among the programs administered by these governmental and semi-governmental agencies are (1) educational exchange, including the exchange of students, teachers, and trainees; (2) academic exchange, including the exchange of scholars and researchers, support of Japanese studies, and promotion of Japanese language teaching abroad; (3) artistic exchange, including the exchange of artists and artworks and the sponsorship of visual- and performing-arts programs; (4) cultural materials exchange, including the exchange of books, films, and radio and television programs; and (5) multilateral cultural exchange, including cooperation with UNESCO, the Southeast Asian Ministers of Education Organization, and other international cultural exchange organizations.

There are also some 500 private organizations and foundations in Japan today that are engaged in the promotion of international cultural exchange. They include such organizations as the International House of Japan, the Japan Association of International Education, the Japan Center for International Exchange, the Commemorative Association for the Japan World Exposition, the Hoso Bunka Foundation, the Toyota Foundation, and the Yoshida International Education Foundation.

The Japan Foundation (Kokusai Koryu Kikin)　国際交流基金●

In 1972, the Japan Foundation was established as a special corporation under the jurisdiction of the Ministry of Foreign Affairs, and since that time it has served as the pivot point for Japan's international cultural exchange. Throughout its history, it has continued to work toward truly global international cultural exchange through everything from the development of all types of bilateral exchange between Japan and other nations to the promotion of exchange between third nations. Headquarters are in Tokyo.

Japanese-Language Teaching　日本語教育●

Cooperation in overseas Japanese-language education has been one of the major pillars of the activities of the Japan Foundation since its founding. A broad-ranging response has been made to the requests from local overseas educational institutions including the dispatch of specialists to Japanese-language education institutions in numerous foreign countries; the granting of aid for the salaries for local overseas instructors; and the conducting of proficiency tests for people whose native language is not Japanese. Also, in areas such as Bangkok, Jakarta, and Sydney, where demand is high, overseas Japanese-language centers have been established to promote the creation of a comprehensive overseas Japanese-language education network and to provide daily-life support to on-site instructors.

The Japanese-Language Proficiency Test is given both in Japan and abroad.

The Japan Foundation
Japanese Language Institute　国際交流基金日本語国際センター●

The Japan Foundation Japanese Language Institute was opened at Urawa in Saitama Prefecture in 1989 as a subsidiary organ of the Japan Foundation responsible for providing comprehensive support and cooperation for overseas Japanese-language training. At this institute, training programs are given for overseas Japanese-language instructors and diplomats from Asia and the Pacific area. The institute also donates Japanese-language teaching materials appropriate to the conditions of the country of their destination; develops language teaching materials and teaching methods; carries out surveys on the present conditions in overseas Japanese-language education; and promotes information exchange.

Introducing Japanese Culture and Arts   日本文化の紹介●

One of the most important activities is the broad-scale introduction overseas of all fields of art, from classical and traditional to contemporary. This includes such Japanese formative arts as painting, sculpture, and video art; stage arts such as dance, music, and drama; such visual arts as feature films; and life-culture arts including flower arranging, tea ceremony, *origami*, kites, and fireworks. Also, in recent years, there has been an increase in the number of large-scale events held in order to provide comprehensive introductions to Japanese culture.

The Japan Foundation
Center for Global Partnership   国際交流基金日米センター●

The Center for Global Partnership (CGP) was established in April 1991 in order to administer a ¥50 billion fund for the purpose of deepening and broadening dialogue between the Japanese and American people in various fields.

The major work of the CGP will be to promote intellectual exchange for global partnership through joint research projects and dialogues on such issues as the environment, north-south problems, and other problems held in common, and to develop better understanding through regional and grass-roots level activities.

Official development assistance

(ODA; *seifu kaihatsu enjo*)   政府開発援助●

In Japan ODA is synonymous with foreign aid and includes grants-in-aid, technical assistance, loan aid, and financial support contributed to international organizations engaged in development and relief work.

Japanese foreign aid following World War II began in the1950s in the form of reparations payments to Burma, the Philippines, Indonesia, and Vietnam and grants resembling reparations to several other Asian nations, including South Korea. This was followed by a period in the 1960s when strong export expansion was a principal interest in foreign aid programs. In the late 1960s and early 1970s the provision of aid and investment aimed at securing agricultural and raw material supplies, called "development import" (*kaihatsu yunyu*) assistance, became a dominant emphasis.

The marked contrast between the stances taken by Japan at the First United Nations Conference on Trade and Development (UNCTAD I), held in Geneva in 1964, and the fifth conference (UNCTAD V), held in

reparations

Government and Diplomacy

Manila in 1979, illustrates clearly the significant change in the Japanese approach to economic cooperation with developing countries as a focus in foreign economic policy. The former meeting saw Japan, preoccupied with its own program of heavy industrialization and economic relations with advanced powers, adopting a very negative attitude toward development assistance and the developing countries' case for preferred access to export markets in developed countries. By the time of the 1979 meeting, however, development issues were at the forefront of Japan's foreign policy interests; Japan had become the fourth or fifth largest aid donor, with ODA spending of about US $2.6 billion.

With an ODA outlay of US $11.3 billion in 1993, Japan became the world's largest aid donor, as measured by the disbursement of official development assistance by the industrial countries represented in the Development Assistance Committee (DAC) of the Organization for Economic Cooperation and Development (OECD). However, measured as a percentage of gross national product (GNP), at 0.26 percent Japanese aid ranked 18th among DAC nations and was slightly less than the DAC average of 0.29 percent. Japanese aid in 1993 was 20.5 percent of the total disbursed by all DAC nations.

The government has emphasized that a priority will be increasing the grant aid component of ODA in accordance with the international view that grants ought to be the principal form of aid, and also in response to requests from poorer countries that are in urgent need of this form of aid. In response to Japan's increasing worldwide economic impact, the government has gradually moved beyond narrow economic objectives in an effort to shoulder greater responsibility in the international economy.

Aid Administration   援助機関●

The administration of official Japanese aid programs and policies rests with a number of government ministries and agencies, in particular the Ministry of Foreign Affairs, the Ministry of Finance, the Ministry of International Trade and Industry (MITI), and the Economic Planning Agency. They are backed up by three government-funded institutions, the OVERSEAS ECONOMIC COOPERATION FUND (OECF), the Export-Import Bank of Japan, and the JAPAN INTERNATIONAL COOPERATION AGENCY (JICA), which respectively oversee the disbursement of soft loans, export

Regional Distribution of ODA
二国間ODAの地域配分
（支出純額ベース）　　　　　(net disbursements in millions of US dollars)

Region	1980	1990	1991	1992	
Asia	1,383	4,117	4,521	5,524	(65.1%)
Middle East	204	705	1,807	364	(4.3%)
Oceania	12	114	111	166	(2.0%)
Africa	223	792	910	859	(10.1%)
Latin America	118	561	846	772	(9.1%)
Europe	-15	158	14	103	(1.2%)
Unclassified	23	494	663	696	(8.2%)
Total	1,962	6,940	8,870	8,484	(100%)

Source: Ministry of Foreign Affairs.

credits, and technical assistance and grant aid. There is no central aid agency as in some other donor countries. See also JAPAN OVERSEAS COOPERATION VOLUNTEERS.

Overseas Economic Cooperation Fund

(OECF; Kaigai Keizai Kyoryoku Kikin) 海外経済協力基金●

Special public corporation that provides financial assistance to developing countries. The OECF is the principal agency administering Japanese official development assistance (ODA), managing about 40 percent of the net disbursements of ODA funds. It was established in 1961 under the provisions of the Overseas Economic Cooperation Fund Law.

The OECF's main functions fall into two categories. First, it provides loans to governments and government agencies in developing countries. Approximately 80 percent of all loans in this category have gone to countries in Asia, mostly for the development of infrastructure facilities (transportation, electric power, gas, etc) and for the purchase of commodities. Second, the OECF extends loans to, or makes equity investments in, Japanese corporations involved in overseas development projects.

The Economic Planning Agency directs the activities of the OECF, acting in conjunction with the Ministry of Foreign Affairs, the Ministry of Finance, and the Ministry of International Trade and Industry (MITI). The OECF has its head office in Tokyo and maintained 17 overseas offices as of 1994.

Japan International Cooperation Agency

(JICA; Kokusai Kyoryoku Jigyodan) 国際協力事業団●

Special public corporation established to promote international cooperation through the provision of overseas development assistance. It was founded in 1974 in accordance with the International Cooperation Agency Law.

JICA's main activities include (1) the strengthening of technical assistance programs to developing countries provided by the Japanese government by bringing technical trainees to Japan and by dispatching specialists and providing needed equipment and materials for projects overseas, (2) the facilitation and promotion of grant assistance programs, (3) the extension of loans and equity investment related to development projects, (4) the training and dispatching of Japan Overseas Cooperation Volunteers (JOVC).

JICA's activities are administered by the Ministry of Foreign Affairs; the Ministry of Agriculture, Forestry, and Fisheries; and the Ministry of International Trade and Industry (MITI). Its head office is in Tokyo, with subsidiary agencies, such as the International Training Center, spread throughout the country. JICA maintains 52 offices overseas. In 1994, its staff numbered 1,213, of whom about 303 worked abroad.

Japan Overseas Cooperation Volunteers

(JOCV; Seinen Kaigai Kyoryoku Tai)　　　　　　青年海外協力隊●

Often called the Japanese Peace Corps. Program founded by the Japanese government in 1965 to provide technical services and instruction to developing countries. Financed exclusively by the Japanese government, the JOCV sent out 10,255 volunteers between 1965 and 1990.

The volunteers, all young people, serve a term of two years and receive a monthly living allowance; their housing is provided by the host country, and they work as members of that country's government. The JOCV places strong emphasis on technical qualifications and experience, and nearly half of its volunteers have been in agriculture, fishing, and other areas of primary industry.

Territorial waters (ryokai)　　　　　　　　　　領海●

Japan's first official declaration concerning territorial waters came in 1870, when the Franco-Prussian War broke out in Europe and the Japanese government issued a proclamation of neutrality stipulating that "the contending parties are not permitted to engage in hostilities in Japanese harbors or inland waters, or within a distance of 3 nautical miles (1 nautical mile = 1.85 km or 1.15 mi) from land at any place, such being the distance to which a cannonball can be fired." After that, Japan continued to adhere to the 3-mile limit not only for its own territorial waters but also as a rule of international law that should be applied throughout the world.

The Law on Territorial Waters (Ryokai Ho) enacted in 1977 provides for a limit of 12 nautical miles, except for the Soya Strait, the Tsugaru Strait, the eastern channel of the Tsushima Strait, the western channel of the Tsushima Strait, and the Osumi Strait, for which the 3-mile limit remains in effect pending the outcome of the Third United Nations Conference on the Law of the Sea.

Territory of Japan (*ryodo*) 領土●

The territory of a state in international law comprises the land, the territorial waters, and the territorial airspace to which the sovereignty of the state extends.

In the land area of Japan bordering Russia there have been territorial disputes concerning the Kuril Islands and Sakhalin. These have been the subject of several treaties, most notably the Sakhalin-Kuril Islands Exchange Treaty of 1875, the 1905 Treaty of Portsmouth, and the San Francisco Peace Treaty of 1951, by which Japan renounced claim to the Kuril Islands and Sakhalin. By the San Francisco Peace Treaty Japan also renounced claim to Korea, which it had attached in 1910, and to Formosa (Taiwan) and the Pescadores, acquired from China in 1895.

Japan acquired the Ryukyu Islands when the lord of the Satsuma domain forced the ruler of the Ryukyus to swear allegiance in 1609. The Ryukyus became Okinawa Prefecture in 1879. The Ogasawara Islands (Bonin Islands) were put formally under the administration of Japan in 1875. Other islands were annexed to the territory of Japan in the late 19th and early 20th centuries, including Minami Torishima (Marcus Island), the Volcano Islands (Kazan Retto), the Senkaku Islands, the Daito Islands, and Takeshima.

There is ongoing dispute over the Northern Territories, which comprise the islands of Kunashiri, Etorofu, Shikotan, and the Habomai Islands, occupied by the Soviet Union at the end of World War II and, as of 1995, still occupied by the Russian Federation; Takeshima, occupied by the Republic of Korea; and the Senkaku Islands, claimed by the People's Republic of China and Taiwan.

Northern Territories issue (Hoppo Ryodo *mondai*) 北方領土問題●

Dispute concerning Japan's Northern Territories, which consist of Kunashiri, Etorofu, Shikotan, and the Habomai Islands, occupied by the Soviet Union since 1945 and still occupied by the Russian Federation in 1995. The Japanese government maintains that the Russian occupation is illegal and demands the return of these islands.

The Habomai Islands.

After Japan's defeat in World War II, it signed the San Francisco Peace Treaty with 48 Allied nations (but not the Soviet Union) in September 1951. In the treaty Japan renounced all rights and title to the Kuril Islands, but the text did not stipulate which islands made up the Kuril chain nor which government was to exercise sovereignty over them.

Asserting that Kunashiri, Etorofu, Shikotan, and the Habomai Islands are not included in the term "Kuril Islands" as used in the San Francisco treaty and that they have historically constituted an integral part of the territory of Japan, the Japanese government sought their return. The Soviet Union refused, contending that the territorial issue had already been resolved. Then during Soviet president Mikhail Gorbachev's visit to Tokyo in 1991, both sides confirmed in a joint communique that final resolution of the issue would be carried out as a part of a future peace treaty between the two countries. However, the Soviet Union was dissolved at the end of that year.

In October 1993, President Boris Yeltsin, the successor to Mikhail Gorbachev, visited Tokyo for two days and met Prime Minister Hosokawa Morihiro, but no progress was seen on the Northern Territories issue.

National defense (*kokubo*) 国防●

The Japanese term kokubo encompasses the maintenance of military forces as well as such nonmilitary aspects of a nation's security as economic strength, political stability, and the international environment.

The international environment has changed profoundly since the end of World War II, bringing Japan to realize that the increasing complexity and diversity of threats to world and regional peace call for keener attention to questions of national defense. Instead of relying solely on its own forces to maintain peace, Japan has emphasized the United States-Japan security treaties, peaceful diplomacy, economic relations of mutual interdependence, and cultural exchange with other nations.

Evolving Attitudes 国防に対する考え方の変遷●

It is said that General Douglas MacArthur, the supreme commander of the Allied forces occupying Japan after World War II, intended to dismantle completely the old military forces and military industries and to transform Japan into "the Switzerland of the Far East". But in 1950, after the outbreak of war in Korea and hardening of the cold war, a National Police Reserve of 75,000 men was formed. In the early days of the cold war, as the United States requested a considerable degree of Japanese rearmament, Prime Minister Yoshida Shigeru resisted on grounds that such action would "suppress the economy and make for domestic instability." In 1952, with Japan's independence restored, the National Police Reserve, adding maritime and air branches, became the National Safety Forces, later reorganized as the SELF DEFENSE FORCES (SDF).

This combination of the relatively small Self Defense Forces with a bilateral security treaty with the United States remains the core of Japan's national defense. Japan has pursued Yoshida's policy of "inexpensive defense" and achieved economic development by favoring peaceful coexistence and promoting an international environment favorable to free trade.

National Defense Policy 国防政策●

The Japanese government's basic policy for national defense, enunciated by its National Defense Council (now Security Council) in 1957, sets forth the objectives of preserving Japan's peace and independence, deterring direct or indirect aggression, and repelling any assaults. International cooperation, stabilization of public welfare, a gradual increase in defense capabilities, and reliance on the security treaties were among the original means to achieving those objectives. Since then, a few new principles have been added. These include the Hikaku Sangensoku (the three nonnuclear principles of not manufacturing, possessing, or introducing into Japanese territory nuclear weapons, as approved by the Diet in 1971), a prohibition on the dispatch of troops overseas, a prohibition against conscription, the three principles regarding the export of arms, and the maintenance of a "strictly defensive posture" (*senshu boei*), signifying a passive defense strategy. The strategy centered on the concept of keeping military capabilities to a minimum level necessary for self-defense. The National Defense Program Outline adopted in 1976 called for a limited attack into Japanese territory to be repelled by Japan's own defensive forces, with assistance from the United States should these prove to be inadequate. When this outline was adopted, the Miki Takeo cabinet also enunciated a policy of limiting defense spending to 1 percent or less of Japan's gross national product, a precedent followed by almost all succeeding governments.

In November 1978 the United States and Japan concluded an agreement called The Guidelines for Japan-US Defense Cooperation. Based on the United States-Japan security treaties, the guidelines further defined the conditions and plans for defense cooperation between the two countries. As tension between the United States and the Soviet Union grew in the early 1980s, Japan increased its defense expenditures and promoted additional military cooperation with the United States under the above-mentioned guidelines. Since the end of the cold war in the early 1990s, however, concern with military matters in Japan has shifted from defense against invasion to the country's new role in cooperating with United Nations peacekeeping operations to resolve regional conflicts.

Self Defense Forces (SDF; Jieitai) 自衛隊●

Armed forces responsible for the ground, sea, and air defense of Japan. The term "Self Defense" is used in the official title because the 1947 Constitution of Japan prohibits the nation from possessing military forces (see RENUNCIATION OF WAR), but, according to the government, does not prohibit the nation from maintaining the ability to defend itself.

Historical Development 成立●

After World War II, Japan's army, navy, and air force were dismantled, but, with the outbreak of the Korean War in 1950, General Douglas MacArthur, commander of the Allied Occupation of Japan, ordered the establishment of a National Police Reserve of 75,000 men to fill the gap created by the dispatch of Occupation forces to Korea. From its inception, this force was recognized as possessing greater firepower and mobility than the regular police force. In 1952 its name was changed to National Safety Forces and, together with the Maritime Guard, it was administered by the newly established National Safety Agency.

With the passage of the Self Defense Forces Law in 1954, the Safety Agency became the Defense Agency, and the existing forces were reorganized as the Self Defense Forces, with three services: the Ground Self Defense Force (GSDF; J: Rikujo Jieitai), the Maritime Self Defense Force (MSDF; J: Kaijo Jieitai), and the Air Self Defense Force (ASDF; J: Koku Jieitai).

Organization and Command 組織●

Supreme command rests with the prime minister, who represents the cabinet. The director-general of the Defense Agency, a member of the cabinet, receives his orders from the prime minister and is assisted by civilian and military personnel and by the Joint Staff Council. The chiefs of staff of the three forces carry out within their commands the orders of the director-general and supervise the activities of their respective branches.

Personnel 人員●

Self Defense Forces personnel enlist between the ages of 18 and 25 for voluntary two- or three-year terms. In 1970 the SDF formed a reserve corps of volunteers on inactive status, and in 1974 it began recruiting women. Officers are selected from among graduates of the National Defense Academy, graduates of regular universities who have passed a qualifying examination, and noncommissioned officers who score high on the qualifying examination. Each service has its own officer candidate school, but there is also a National Institute for Defense Studies for higher study by selected officers.

Female members of the Self Defense Forces.

Defense Budget 防衛予算●

Defense appropriations totaled approximately ¥4.7 trillion (US $44.7 billion) in 1994, or 0.948 percent of the estimated gross national product. Since its inception the SDF's share of the GNP has decreased, though real appropriations have continued to climb. In 1994 the breakdown of expenditures by organization was GSDF, 36.4 percent; MSDF, 23.7 percent; ASDF, 24.2 percent; Defense Facilities Administration Agency, 11.6 percent; and others, 4.1 percent. Of the overall defense budget, 42.6 percent went for personnel expenses and 57.4 percent for non-personnel-related expenses (equipment, training, bases, research and development, etc).

Units and Their Deployment   部隊と配置●

The GSDF is divided into 12 infantry divisions and 1 armored division, which are grouped into 5 regional armies. The greatest emphasis has been placed on the defense of Hokkaido. In 1994 GSDF personnel numbered about 146,000. The force is equipped with 1,200 medium tanks and helicopters.

The MSDF comprises the Self Defense Fleet and five district units. It regards antisubmarine warfare as its most important mission. In 1994 personnel numbered about 43,000 and the MSDF deployed 60 destroyers and destroyer escorts, 15 nonnuclear submarines, and about 200 antisubmarine anticraft and helicopters.

The men and equipment of the ASDF are divided into four air zones. Operational emphasis is placed on the swift identification of aircraft encroaching on Japanese airspace and on quick response to a possible consolidated air attack. In 1994 personnel numbered some 45,000, and the ASDF possessed some 360 fighter planes as well as Patriot surface-to-air missiles.

The Constitution and the SDF   憲法と自衛隊●

Since its inception the SDF has faced the charge that its existence is a violation of article 9 of the constitution. To this, the government has responded that although the constitution forbids war as a means of resolving international disputes, it does not negate the right of self-defense. Although criticism continues, the SDF has won general acceptance from the Japanese public, and the voices calling for abolition are fewer.

Self Defense Forces personnel on patrol as part of UN peacekeeping operations in Cambodia.

With the end of the cold war, there have been increasing calls in Japan for a reduction in the size, and a rethinking of the role, of the SDF. The deployment of forces overseas had been prohibited since its founding, but with the June 1992 enactment of the Law on Cooperation in United Nations Peacekeeping Operations, the SDF is now able to participate in UN peacekeeping activities and humanitarian relief efforts abroad. As of the end of 1994, the SDF has taken part in peacekeeping operations in Cambodia (September 1992–September 1993) and Mozambique (May 1993–January 1995) and refugee relief operations in Rwanda (September–December 1994). See also NATIONAL DEFENSE.

ECONOMY

The Tokyo Stock Exchange in the Kabutocho district of central Tokyo.

Contemporary economy (*gendai* Nihon *keizai*) 現代日本経済●

The Japanese economy is the world's second largest market economy, with a gross domestic product (GDP) of ¥421 trillion (US $3.8 trillion) in 1993. The same year Japan's per capita national income, at ¥2.9 million (US $26,079), was third in the world behind Switzerland and Luxembourg. With the economy in a recession, however, growth has stagnated and the 1993 GDP increased only 0.1 percent over the previous year. While export levels in the 1990s have remained high (US $351.3 billion in 1993), import volume has fallen because of the slow domestic economy, and as a result the trade surplus grew from US $63.5 billion in 1990 to US $141.5 billion in 1993.

The High-Growth Era 高度成長期●

At the end of the Allied occupation in 1952, Japan ranked as a less-developed country, with per capita consumption a mere one-fifth that of the United States. During the period 1953-73, the economy grew with unprecedented rapidity (average growth was 8.0% per annum overall and 10.6% during the 1960s) and Japan became the first less-developed country in the postwar era to graduate to developed status. Real output per person in 1970 was 2.5 times higher than in 1960, and by 1968 Japan had surpassed West Germany to become the world's second largest economy. This rapid growth resulted in significant changes to Japan's INDUSTRIAL STRUCTURE. First, production shifted from a heavy reliance on AGRICULTURE and light manufacturing to a focus on heavy industry and, increasingly, services. In 1954, when recovery from World War II was largely complete, the primary sector (agriculture, fisheries, and mining) still accounted for 24.5 percent of output and 37.9 percent of the labor force; in contrast, manufacturing (the secondary sector) accounted for only 23.8 percent of output and 19.5 percent of employment. By 1970, agriculture and mining had fallen to 8.3 percent of output and 17.8 percent of the labor force, while manufacturing had risen to 30.2 percent of output and 27.0 percent of employment. In 1985, 9 percent of the labor force was in primary sector occupations, 33 percent in secondary, and 58 percent in tertiary. Urbanization also progressed rapidly, with the proportion of people living in cities escalating from 38 to 72 percent of the population between 1950 and 1970.

Until 1952 economic policy was dictated by the Occupation. Reforms in 1949 under the Shoup mission and Dodge line put in place the postwar tax system, balanced the government budget, normalized the financial system, and brought Japan into the world trade system at a fixed exchange rate of ¥360 per US dollar. These reforms cured the post-war hyperinflation but at the cost of a sharp recession. While profits generated by the large number of special orders (*tokuju*) for goods and services in Japan to support United Nations forces during the Korean War helped end the recession, the economy continued to alternate between periods of prosperity and recession.

The first major expansion—the Iwato Boom (1959–61, average growth 12.2%), spurred by Prime Minister Ikeda Hayato's 1960 Income-Doubling Plan—touched off an investment spree. Growth reached 14.5 percent in 1961, but as in the 1950s this led to increased imports, and the government was forced to slow growth during 1962 because of the result-ing balance-of-payments crisis. Further expansions occurred in 1963–64 (average growth 11.8%), 1967–70 (the Izanagi Boom, average growth 11.2%), and 1972–73 (the Tanaka expansion, average growth 8.9%).

Many factors contributed to rapid growth, including the shift in employment from low-productivity primary sector pursuits to manufac-turing and the entry of an increasingly skilled and better-educated postwar-baby-boom generation into the labor force. In addition, macro-economic policies were conducive to growth, the international environment was blessed with stable commodity prices and expanding trade, and investment was high. Together with the introduction of better technology, productivity increased rapidly.

The contribution of government industrial policy to economic growth is less clear, and on net was probably not large. The government was heavily interventionist during the early years of the Occupation, but direct controls were eased after 1949 and largely eliminated by 1955. Industrial policy was implemented via indirect controls, requiring licenses for imports and technology transfer. Japan became a member of the International Monetary Fund (IMF) in 1952 and the General Agreement on Tariffs and Trade (GATT) in 1955. Around 1960, Japan committed itself to TRADE LIBERALIZATION by seeking IMF article 8 status and deciding to join the OECD, both of which were realized in 1964. Tariffs and quantitative controls on most goods were removed by 1970, and, with the exception of agriculture and some high-technology prod-ucts, most nontariff barriers were eliminated by the 1980s. Nevertheless, the overall bias was for a greater degree of protection of domestic pro-ducers than in the United States.

Indirect government assistance also came in the form of tax breaks, treasury investment and loans, and the Ministry of International Trade and Industry's policy of administrative guidance. An important example is the Machinery Industries Promotion Law of 1956, which supported the machine tool industry as well as automotive parts and other metalworking sectors. Ultimately, most industries obtained some government favors, and it is unclear that any industry was effectively promoted relative to its rivals. However, domestic policies did result in a minimal presence by foreign firms in most sectors, and permitted some industries to survive that would otherwise have succumbed to foreign competition.

Financial assets were wiped out by the 1945–49 hyperinflation, but from the 1950s the banking system was gradually rebuilt, largely along pre-World War II lines. In 1949 the stock exchange was reopened, but it did not develop into a major source of new funds until the 1980s, and a bond market was not allowed to develop. Banks sought customers in emerging industries, encouraging the entry of new firms into the market and hence the presence of vigorous interfirm competition. Corporate finance depended on bank financing as the major source of outside funds, giving rise to a capital structure dominated by debt. To prevent takeovers, enterprise groups, or *keiretsu*, actively sought cross-shareholdings with a variety of firms, including major financial institutions (banks in Japan are permitted to purchase up to 5% of the shares of a client firm). Small and medium enterprises remained relatively important during this period, employing nearly three-quarters of the labor force. However, unlike the larger enterprise groups, small and medium-sized firms were tied to local banks, employed less-skilled or older workers (or temporary and female workers), and paid lower wages. In manufacturing, they often functioned as subcontractors (*shitauke*) to larger firms.

During the 1950s the major exporters—and thus the leading firms—were in textiles and other light industries, whose products were marketed by general trading companies; government promotion, however, focused on heavy manufacturing located in major coastal industrial complexes. During the 1960s the IRON AND STEEL INDUSTRY and the shipbuilding industry came to the fore, followed by the chemical industry and in the early 1970s the electronics industry; the AUTOMOTIVE INDUSTRY rose to prominence in the late 1970s. Exports were important, especially for textiles and shipbuilding, which were aided by a rapid increase in world trade throughout the 1960s.

But growth was fueled above all by investment based on increased consumer spending. As incomes grew, consumption shifted from basic products such as radios, fans, and scooters to more expensive and luxurious items such as color televisions, air conditioners, and cars. In the case of manufacturing, a mature industrial base made it feasible to purchase new machinery and to concentrate on improving managerial performance. New machinery meant new technology, which meant lower costs and higher profits. Furthermore, in the case of many industries, no firm could afford to lag behind its rivals in installing new equipment. Growth fueled investment, which in turn fueled further growth.

To facilitate the adoption of new technology, after 1955 large firms adopted the modern employment system and trained their "lifetime" employees in new skills. Labor unions based on an enterprise rather than an industry or a craft cooperated in this, since new skills led to higher incomes and assured future jobs. Labor disputes were of minor importance after 1960, and annual contract negotiations occurring during the spring wage offensive (*shunto*) helped to keep workers aware of the link between wages and productivity. As a consequence, inflationary hikes within the wage system were generally avoided.

Rapid growth was not without its problems. Until the late 1960s, Japan faced chronic balance-of-payments difficulties, due variously to surging imports when the economy grew too fast, or poor exports when foreign markets were in recession. The government therefore used monetary policy to slow the economy in 1953–54, 1957, 1961, 1963, and again in 1967. Inflation and price stability also proved to be problematic, at least comparatively: during the 1960s, consumer prices rose at an average annual rate of 5.8 percent in Japan, versus 2.7 percent in the United States. The spread of pollution and pollution-related diseases went unchecked until the late 1960s, when abysmal air quality in Tokyo and multiple fatalities from mercury and cadmium poisoning prompted more stringent pollution control laws. Government provision for SOCIAL WELFARE also lagged; only from about 1970 did social security coverage become universal, so until then workers had to rely entirely upon private savings. Only in the late 1980s did corporate and national PENSIONS reach a level sufficient to help the average retiree. On the other hand, income distribution remained remarkably even; no underclass emerged.

Labor union protest against high prices and inflation during the 1974 spring wage offensive.

Toward a Mature Economy:

1973–1990　　　　　　　経済の成熟に向けて：1973年～1990年●

By 1973, many of the factors that supported rapid growth lost their strength. First, Japanese industry had caught up with the best practices abroad; improving productivity required more resources than in the past. This in turn lowered the profitability of new investment, which fell to a permanently lower level after 1974. By 1973, the growth of the now urban and better-educated labor force had peaked. Finally, the international environment became less favorable, due mainly to the revaluation of the yen and trade friction with the United States. The Japan-United States textile talks of 1969, the Nixon Shocks of 1971, a worldwide commodity price boom that culminated in the quadrupling of oil prices during the oil crisis of 1973, and the movement of the yen to a floating rate in 1973 all worked to slow growth.

Domestic macroeconomic policy was also less conductive to growth. The government made a major policy blunder in 1971–72, when it permitted exporters to convert their dollars to yen, which rapidly increased the money supply. This was magnified by Prime Minister Tanaka Kakuei's plan to rebuild the Japanese archipelago (Nihon Retto Kaizo Ron), which interacted with easy money and rising international commodity prices to touch off a speculative binge in real estate and domestic commodity markets. Japan was thus already suffering from double-digit inflation by October 1973, when the first oil crisis touched off sharp price increases and hoarding.

Even before the October 1973 oil crisis, the government had started to slow the economy in response to rising inflation; combined with the impact of a quadrupling of oil prices, gross national product (GNP) fell 1.4 percent in 1974, the first actual decline since the 1950s. More significant, the oil shock and recession lowered expectations of future growth: private investment fell from 31 percent of GNP in 1973–74 to under 25 percent of GNP from 1977 on. Growth slowed from the 10 percent level to an average of 3.6 percent during 1974–79 and 4.4 percent during 1980–90. Consumer prices stabilized after 1975, and Japan experienced comparatively low inflation following the second oil crisis in 1978. Furthermore, unemployment never surpassed 3 percent.

The decline in investment by 6 percent of GNP after 1973 threatened the economy with recession, particularly since consumption failed to increase and savings remained high. Tax cuts in 1974, 1975, and 1977, however, served to stimulate the economy, while increases in central government expenditures continued at a steady pace. The central government budget deficit ballooned to 6.1 percent of GNP in 1979, which kept the economy out of recession. The overall government deficit, however, peaked in 1978 at 5.5 percent of GNP, as local and provincial surpluses partially offset the central government deficit.

Gross National Product
実質国内総生産

(trillions of yen)

1955 1960 1965 1970 1975 1980 1985 1990 1993
Source: Economic Planning Agency; Bank of Japan

The deficit was held in check from 1979; in addition, monetary policy turned restrictive, with the Bank of Japan raising the discount rate in stages from 4.25 percent to 9 percent. Indeed, continued concerns about large deficits led to a succession of tight budgets throughout the 1980s, though tax increases were held in abeyance until 1987 and 1988. The primary exceptions granted in the tight budgets in the 1980s were for social security, NATIONAL DEFENSE, and foreign aid. By 1985 the consolidated government deficit shrank to 0.8 percent of GNP, and turned into a surplus from 1987. Again, a decline in fiscal stimulus by 6 percent of GNP might be expected to drag the economy into a recession. This time shifts in international trade offset the decline in domestic demand. The trade balance remained relatively stable during the 1970s, and in 1980 actually showed a slight deficit. But by 1985, the current account surplus in Japan's BALANCE OF PAYMENTS reached 3.7 percent of GNP. While the economy was weak in 1981–83, exports increased sharply during 1983–85, due in part to the strengthening of the US dollar.

After the 1985 Plaza Accord, the yen rose sharply in value, reaching ¥120 to the US dollar in 1988, twice its average 1984 value and three times its 1971 value. As a result, after 1986 the trade surplus gradually shrank. But this time around, domestic demand increased to pick up the slack. Monetary policy was eased four times during 1986, as the Bank of Japan lowered the discount rate from 5.0 percent to 2.5 percent, the lowest level since World War II. Consumption began increasing in 1986, and investment took over during 1987–90; in fact, corporate investment rose to 19.6 percent of GNP in 1988 and 21.7 percent in 1989, far above the 15.3–17.5 percent that had prevailed during 1980–87, and exceeding total investment in plant and equipment in 1989 for the entire United States in both percentage and value.

With higher stock prices, new equity issues skyrocketed to ¥16.8 trillion (US $116 billion) in 1987 and ¥24.8 trillion (US $177 billion) in 1989, becoming a significant source of finance for corporations for the first time since the crash of the Tokyo market in 1961. Banks found a new outlet for funds in real estate development. In turn, corporations attempted to maximize the productivity of their assets using real estate holdings as collateral for stock market speculation in a method referred to as *zaitech* ("financial technology"). In the ensuing speculative binge (1986–89), land prices doubled and the Tokyo Nikkei stock market index rose 2.7 times.

Japan tightened monetary policy beginning in May 1989, and higher interest rates touched off a collapse of stock prices. By the end of 1990, the Tokyo stock market had fallen 38 percent from its peak, wiping out ¥300 trillion (US $2.3 trillion) in value in the space of a few months. Financial deregulation measures—such as allowing banks and securities firms to establish subsidiaries in each other's fields—were implemented in the early 1990s, but as of the end of 1994 the Tokyo stock market showed little sign of recovery.

By 1993 land prices in Tokyo had fallen 49.3 percent from the 1990 speculative peak, leaving major Japanese banks saddled with a large volume of bad debt as borrowers are unable to pay back loans on real estate purchased at inflated prices.

Japan's International Role　　　　　　　　　　　日本の国際的役割●

Investment abroad, together with trade flows, is shifting Japan's international economic role. First, Japan is now either the number one or number two trading partner for the other countries of the Pacific Rim, including the United States. At the same time, manufactured products constituted over 50 percent of Japanese imports in 1990. Japan is thus a significant market for manufacturers in East and Southeast Asia, including textiles and low-end consumer electronics.

Alongside direct trade flows, Japanese national saving has continued to outstrip domestic borrowing needs, leading to the conspicuous presence of Japan as a major source of portfolio investment in the United States and elsewhere. In the first six months of 1989, for example, Japanese investors purchased US $39.1 billion of US Treasury and other foreign bonds; more visible were purchases of real estate and companies, notably Rockefeller Center, CBS Records, and Columbia Pictures Entertainment. Equally important has been overseas direct investment in manufacturing, tied to protectionist threats or (given the volatility of exchange rates) the

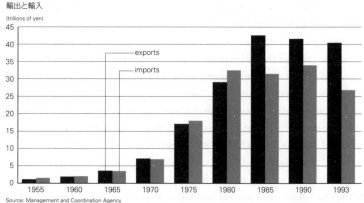

Exports and Imports
輸出と輸入
(trillions of yen)

exports
imports

1955　1960　1965　1970　1975　1980　1985　1990　1993

Source: Management and Coordination Agency.

need to produce in major markets rather than export to them. Japanese firms now operate 11 automotive assembly plants in North America. After the end of the 1986 to 1991 boom period known as the "bubble economy," new overseas direct investment fell sharply and by 1992 it had dropped to slightly over half the 1989 level. In 1993, however, there was a slight upturn as the rising value of the yen forced Japanese companies to move some of their manufacturing operations overseas.

One result of Japan's heightened presence has been trade friction, accentuated by the concentration of much of Japan's exports within a narrow range of goods, such as automobiles. In addition, Japan is strong in certain high-technology products that are perceived in the United States and Europe as critical for strategic reasons. The United States, for example, has been instrumental in the implementation of protectionist measures such as voluntary export restrictions and orderly marketing arrangements within the Japanese steel, machine tool, automobile, and semiconductor industries. At the same time, the United States has also pushed for more open Japanese markets in high-technology products (satellites and supercomputers), lumber, agriculture, and financial services. These efforts were systematized during the mid-1980s in the bilateral MOSS talks, followed in 1989–90 by the Structural Impediments Initiative talks, and in 1993 by The Japan-United States Framework Talks for a New Economic Partnership.

Future Growth and a Stronger Yen 将来の成長と円高●

Japanese firms are perceived as the world leaders in a range of industries, such as automobiles, laptop computers, and semiconductor memory chips. Furthermore, Japanese industry is now playing a greater role in developing and applying state-of-the-art technologies in areas ranging from precision machinery to robotics and new materials. Research and development expenditures have grown faster than the overall economy and in 1992 reached ¥12.8 trillion (US $101 billion), of which 75 percent was funded by industry. That same year Japan accounted for 22.5 percent of all patents registered in the United States.

There are major challenges ahead, however. Changes in the traditional distribution system and increasing competition from imports are forcing prices and profit margins down and leading to questions about the long-term feasibility of carrying non-essential employees under the lifetime employment system.

Another set of issues lies in the problems raised by Japan's rapidly aging population. Projections show no growth in the labor force after 1996, while 14 percent of the population will be over age 65 (nearly dou-

Economy

ble the US proportion, though similar to that in Germany and Scandinavia). This shift in labor supply will be exacerbated by the reduction in hours worked by the average employee as Japan moves toward a five-day workweek. By 2020 there will be only three workers for each retiree, and supporting such a large nonproductive population will entail a massive transfer of resources.

The Yen Continues to Climb （円の高騰） After falling back to an average value of ¥145 to the US dollar in 1990, the yen again began to climb. It averaged ¥135 per US dollar in 1991, ¥127 in 1992, and ¥111 in 1993. In June 1994 it passed the ¥100 per US dollar mark, and in March 1995 exceeded ¥90. Although the cause of this dramatic rise is unclear, the large Japanese trade surplus, the US budget and trade deficits, and a general lack of confidence internationally in the US dollar appear to be contributing factors.

The rise of the yen is a strong blow to the Japanese economy, which in 1994 had only just begun to recover from the recession that began in 1991. Manufacturers have been forced to raise the prices of their products abroad, thereby hurting sales, and some Japanese companies are shifting production operations to Asia and elsewhere in order to remain price competitive in domestic and world markets. This has raised fears of the hollowing out of Japanese industry.

The Yen-Dollar
Exchange Rate
円－ドル換算相場

1970	360.00
1975	296.79
1980	226.74
1985	238.54
1990	144.79
1993	111.20
1994	102.18

From 1949 to 1970, the fixed rate of exchange was ¥360 per US Dollar.
Source: Bank of Japan.

Economic history (Nihon *keizaishi*) 日本経済史●

PREMODERN ECONOMY (to 1868) 前近代の経済（1868年まで）●
Economic History before 1600 1600年までの経済史●

Jomon culture, which flourished from around 10,000 BC to around 300 BC, provides the first evidence of economic activity. Early Jomon people formed a hunting and gathering society that left behind shell mounds containing pottery, tools, and other artifacts. Agriculture entered Japan in the 3rd century BC, and a new culture emerged, Yayoi culture, marking a transition to a settled agricultural society.

Around AD 250 a powerful elite group, known for its great tomb mounds (*kofun*) and an advanced material culture, appeared within Yayoi society. Social differentiation was first visible during the Kofun period (ca 300–710). The ruling clans (*uji*) controlled support groups (*be* or *tomo*) composed of craftsmen, warriors, ceremonial personnel, or cultivators. By the mid-5th century the Yamato uji, forerunner of the imperial house, which claimed descent from the sun goddess, was dominant in western Japan. The emergent Yamato Court, centered in the Yamato Basin, showed evidence of barter and foreign trade.

The 6th and 7th centuries saw new tensions in Yamato society as the Soga family attempted to usurp political leadership. The coup in 645 against the Soga family, which resulted in the Taika Reform, however, reasserted the authority of the sovereign. A new *ritsuryo* (legal codes) system of government, modeled after that of Tang China (618–907), was eventually developed. The state took title to all agricultural land. An elaborate system of land management (the *handen shuju* system) rationalized field boundaries and assigned rights to income and cultivation.

In 723 the government offered tenure for three generations to those who reclaimed lands. Later this was extended to perpetual tenure rights as an incentive for reclamation. These policies undermined state control over agricultural land and contributed to the eventual breakdown of the handen shuju system. Economic expansion in the 8th century is indicated by the issuance of coins by the central government in 708. Japan was not yet a monetary society, and coins circulated largely in the Kinai or capital region. Official missions to and from China encouraged the growth of foreign trade.

Private control of land spread in response to government efforts to develop new farmland. Many elite houses and major shrines and temples exceeded their allotments and reclaimed vast tracts of land for private use. While these lands were subject to taxes, permanent tenure was the first step toward the creation of private landed estates (*shoen*), in which the proprietor assumed the duties of governance. By the 12th century 5,000 shoen existed, comprising most of the agricultural land in Japan.

Depiction from the 12th century of a *shoen* estate in Kii Province (now Wakayama Prefecture).

Foreign trade increased in the Heian period (794–1185), and, until it was restricted after 1254 at the request of the Chinese authorities, Song dynasty (960–1279) copper coins (*sosen*) circulated widely in Japan and brought great profits to their importers. The use of coins for transactions became more common during the 13th century. Shoen tax goods were increasingly sold at local markets for cash. Members of the *samurai* (warrior) class were increasingly dependent on cash in the Kamakura period (1185–1333), obtaining cash loans from moneylenders. Market towns appeared in the period. Retail shops emerged, and wholesalers (*toimaru*), who began as merchant-officials charged with marketing and storing shoen tax goods, appeared to supply them with goods.

The 14th century saw the diffusion of intensive cultivation methods in agriculture, resulting in more monetary transactions in the economically advanced Kinai region. As commerce and the monetary economy grew, the *sake* brewers and pawnbrokers (*doso*) became tax collectors for the shogunate and provincial warlords (*shugo daimyo*). They loaned funds to both daimyo and the urban nobility and amassed great economic power. By the time of the Onin War (1467–1477), wealthy urban residents (*machishu*) administered much of Kyoto, and their authority increased as the power of the Muromachi shogunate declined.

The Onin War destroyed the shoen system and the authority of the Muromachi shogunate. Shugo daimyo were replaced by local military leaders (Sengoku daimyo). Sengoku daimyo domains were autonomous and independent of central authority. They instituted a new tax system that replaced shoen revenues. All taxing authority was in their hands, and local and absentee power holders were eliminated.

The 16th century was a period of major urbanization. Trade and handicraft production were concentrated in the castle towns (*joka machi*) of the daimyo. Samurai were assembled in the castle towns, leaving village administration in the hands of the farmers. The castle towns became political, economic, and transportation centers of the domains. Daimyo eliminated trade barriers and broke up the monopolistic powers of the guilds , which encouraged trade expansion and accelerated commercial activity. In the 1540s European traders entered Japanese waters bringing new commodities such as European luxury goods and firearms.

By the late 16th century, Oda Nobunaga (1534–1582) and his successor, Toyotomi Hideyoshi (1537–1598) surveyed all land under their control and replaced the *kandaka* system of taxes computed in cash with the *kokudaka* system, in which productivity was measured in rice as the tax base. After Nobunaga's death in 1582 and unification of the country by Hideyoshi in 1590, the kokudaka system was extended to the entire country. A four-class system (*shi-no-ko-sho*; warrior-farmer-artisan-merchant) was implemented, with warriors, farmers, artisans, and merchants as the major divisions of society.

Edo-Period (1600–1868) Economy   江戸時代（1600年–1868年）の経済●

Following the death of Hideyoshi in 1598, Tokugawa Ieyasu (1543–1616) emerged as the most powerful warlord in the country. In 1603 his shogunate was headquartered in Edo (now Tokyo), which soon developed into the largest city in Japan. In order to secure allegiance of the other daimyo, the Tokugawa instituted the *sankin kotai* system, whereby daimyo were required to spend alternate years in Edo to attend on the shogun. This political measure was to have profound economic effects. Edo became the center of a new economic network as all kinds of commodities were shipped to the city for consumption by the daimyo, their samurai retainers, and other service personnel. By the mid-18th century, Edo had a population of over 1 million. Osaka, with its easy access to waterborne transport, became the primary commodity market in the central Kinai region. Daimyo from western Japan shipped tax rice to Osaka for sale to obtain the cash necessary to support their Edo residences and their travels to and from the capital. In time Osaka merchants hired by the daimyo as warehouse managers (*kuramoto*) or account agents (*kakeya*) also provided the daimyo with long-term credit as well.

Urbanization progressed during the Edo period, and population growth continued from the early 17th through the mid-18th century. Demands for food, textiles, utensils, housing, and other essentials led to a rapid expansion in commercial activity. This in turn required increases in the volume of currency and banking facilities. The Osaka money changers (*ryogaesho*) organized an official association, and, by 1670, 10 moneylenders supervised financial activity in the city. Bills of exchange and certificates of deposit circulated like paper money within and between cities, and daimyo domains issued paper currency (*hansatsu*) for circulation within domain boundaries.

Paper currency (*hansatsu*) issued by the Awa domain.

Foreign trade during the Edo period was subject to new controls imposed by the shogunate. The shogunate in the early 17th century prohibited foreign voyages by Japanese, and concentrated foreign trade in Nagasaki. There was trade with Korea through the daimyo of Tsushima, and the Satsuma domain also traded with the Ryukyu, but all other trade was monopolized by the shogunate at Nagasaki where limited trade with Holland was carried on through Dutch traders.

Enterprise size ranged from large merchant houses such as the Mitsui and the Sumitomo, with hundreds of employees and family members, to small retail or craft shops. A wide range of artisans and entertainers made urban life possible and attractive, and many village residents derived their incomes exclusively from wage labor or nonagricultural employment. Trade and craft production were clearly separated from farming. This separation of economic roles, which was the foundation of the Edo-period class system, increasingly became a legal fiction.

Until the late 16th century, there had been few large towns outside the Kyoto-Osaka region, but by the mid-18th century the urbanized population had increased to over 10 percent. Urban life, however, proved difficult for the daimyo and samurai as revenues and incomes failed to keep pace with the costs of city existence. Daimyo were forced to borrow from their retainers, further reducing samurai disposable income. The incomes of both the daimyo and the samurai were based on land taxes paid in kind, while their expenditures were in cash. As tax receipts proved inadequate, the best sources of credit were the merchants who managed their rice warehouses. Merchants thus became major creditors to daimyo and samurai.

By the mid-19th century Japan, which had entered the Edo period as an agrarian society, had become a highly monetized and commercialized economy. The economic policies of the shogunate, however, were out of step with economic realities. Land taxes no longer supported the needs of the shogunate or the domain governments. Currency debasement, forced loans, debt abrogations, and temporary levies helped defray immediate crises, but no long-term solutions existed. The stage was set for dramatic changes; the demand of foreigners for trade would totally transform the social and economic order of Tokugawa Japan, forcibly thrusting it into a growing world economy.

EARLY MODERN ECONOMY
(1868–1945)　　　　　　　　　近代の経済（1868年－1945年）●

At the time of the Meiji Restoration (1868), a number of conditions that had coalesced over time during the Edo period provided a favorable base for industrialization. Among these were the growth of a large educated population; a surplus of labor in the agricultural sector; a highly monetized economy controlled by a wealthy and capable merchant class; and the large samurai class, capable of filling leadership and administrative positions.

The opening of Japanese ports to foreign trade in 1859 exposed the still-underdeveloped economy to the threat of colonial domination by the West. In an effort to avoid the fate of other Asian nations colonialized by Western powers, the Meiji-period (1868–1912) government imposed a number of controls on the economic activities of foreigners in Japan, including travel restrictions and bans on land ownership.

Industrialization and Economic Modernization　　工業化と経済の近代化●

In preparation for the rapid development of Japanese industry, much of the socioeconomic system of the Edo period, including the complex shi-no-ko-sho class system was dismantled. The *sekisho* (barrier stations) were abolished, and other restrictions on transportation and communication were lifted. Land ownership rights for farmers were established; and restrictions on the planting of crops other than rice were abolished. These reforms led to the modernization of agricultural management. The government also implemented land tax reform, under which land taxes, which had been paid chiefly in rice since the early Edo period, were made payable in currency. In 1876 the stipends of former samurai (*shizoku*) were converted into government bonds and hereditary pensions were paid off on a sliding scale.

In addition, the Meiji government first abolished the old, complex currency system and established a new, unified national currency system with decimal denominations and standardized units. It also introduced new systems of banking and company organization. The banking system was modeled on the US system of national banks, and in 1882 a central bank, the Bank of Japan, was founded.

Private Sector Development Efforts 民間部門発展の努力●

The private sector leadership played a key role in the modernization of the economy. Among these entrepreneurs were a number of members of such wealthy merchant families from the Edo period as the Mitsui and the Sumitomo. Most of them, however, came from the ranks of the former samurai, peasant, or merchant classes and became modern businessmen amid the turmoil of the early Meiji period.

The Development of the Factors of Production 生産要因の充実●

Large amounts of capital accumulated in the hands of merchants and landowners in the late Edo and early Meiji periods. This capital was invested in new companies and business ventures, primarily in factories, machinery, and other fixed assets. A large surplus of workers developed during the depression that accompanied the unification of the currency system from 1881 to 1885. These people, chiefly former farmers, provided a portion of the industrial labor force; low-ranking former samurai and small businessmen also experienced a high rate of bankruptcy, and many then became workers.

Tokyo office building built by Mitsubishi in 1894.

Growth Industries 成長産業●

The centerpiece of Japan's expanding industrial development was the textile industry. The Meiji government strongly promoted the modernization of this industry in order to reduce dependence on imports, employing foreign technicians to supply technical know-how and assistance. In 1897 cotton yarn exports exceeded imports for the first time. By 1918 six giant spinning firms had been formed.

The first major production facility in the IRON AND STEEL INDUSTRY began operation around 1890 at Kamaishi, Iwate Prefecture. The government-run Yawata Iron and Steel Works began operation in 1901 and became Japan's leading ironworks after the Russo-Japanese War of 1904–1905. The shipbuilding industry grew rapidly at the turn of the century, fostered by supportive government policies and the efforts of such firms as Mitsubishi Shipbuilding (now Mitsubishi Heavy Industries,

Ltd), Kawasaki Shipyard Co (now Kawasaki Heavy Industries, Ltd), and Osaka Iron.

A number of special banks were established after 1897, including the Nippon Kangyo Bank (now Dai-Ichi Kangyo Bank, Ltd); the Industrial Bank of Japan, Ltd; the Bank of Taiwan; and the Bank of Korea. Bank deposits increased, and, with the cancellation of excess loans, five giant banking concerns had come to dominate by 1917: the Dai-Ichi Bank; the Mitsui Bank (now Sakura Bank, Ltd); the Mitsubishi Bank, Ltd; the Sumitomo Bank, Ltd; and the Yasuda Bank (now Fuji Bank, Ltd).

The Problems of Growth 成長の問題点●

Behind the rapid growth in the industrial sector was the sluggish development of agriculture, which continued to be characterized by a pre-modern tenancy system with small farms averaging less than 1 hectare (2.47 acres). In commerce and industry, alongside the emerging large modern enterprises, numerous small enterprises and cottage industries continued to exist. (This dual structure has continued to be a central feature of the Japanese economy.) Despite the modernization of important industries, the income level of the common people remained low.

In the West, as industrialization spread, so too did the socialist and labor movements. In Japan this was not the case, as the government took active steps to suppress them at home. The Public Order and Police Law of 1900 (Chian Keisatsu Ho) was largely effective in suppressing organized union activity by government surveillance before World War I. Its replacement, the Peace Preservation Law of 1925 (Chian Iji Ho), which was directed against communists and anarchists, suppressed the more radical elements within the labor movement.

Economic growth came to a halt in 1920, when the Japanese economy fell into a severe depression following its rapid expansion during World War I. A tolerable recovery had been achieved when, on 1 September 1923, a massive earthquake struck the greater Tokyo region. In 1927 an unprecedented financial crisis occurred when a number of important banks failed. Then in 1930–1931 the Japanese economy was engulfed by the worldwide depression that followed the 1929 crash of the US stock market.

Throughout this period of crisis, bankruptcies of small and medium-sized enterprises were common in almost all economic activities. There was also a push for the concentration of capital, resulting in a striking growth in the power of the industrial and financial combines known as *zaibatsu*. The Mitsui, Mitsubishi, Sumitomo, and Yasuda zaibatsu developed into conglomerates between 1909 and 1920, and in the following decade they expanded their affiliated enterprises and established positions of firm dominance over the Japanese economy.

The farm economy also suffered. The depression gave independent farmers, as well as tenant farmers a severe level of debt. Tenant farmer disputes increased in number, and there was an overall growth in social unrest. Against this background the Manchurian Incident occurred in September 1931, and the government soon embarked on a program of increasing military expenditures. Military demand contributed to the recovery of strategic industries, employment, and the farm economy.

On the other hand, the Manchurian Incident was the first in a series of Sino-Japanese conflicts leading to the outbreak of the Sino-Japanese War of 1937–1945 and then Japan's entry into World War II in 1941. Throughout the war the government strengthened its control over the economy and promoted the development of strategic industries, but production in important manufacturing industries dropped, especially after 1943, until it collapsed under aerial bombardment in 1944 and 1945. The wartime economy itself collapsed with Japan's surrender on 15 August 1945. Overall production at the end of 1945 was only one-sixth of prewar (1935–1937 average) levels. At the war's end more than 25 percent of Japan's physical capital stock and 45 percent of the prewar empire had been lost.

OCCUPATION AND RECOVERY
(1945–1960s) 占領と復興（1945年—1960年代）●

The Allied Occupation of Japan lasted 80 months, from 15 August 1945, when Japan accepted the Potsdam Declaration, to 29 April 1952. It is often divided into four periods: reform (August 1945–February 1947), reverse course (February 1947–December 1948), Dodge Line (December 1948–June 1950), and Korean War (June 1950–April 1952). It was a time of economic and political reform, as well as recovery from the physical destruction and economic exhaustion of World War II.

The Reform Period 改革の時代●

While economic recovery was left largely in Japanese hands, the activities of SCAP (the Occupation authorities) during 1945–1947 were concentrated upon a series of reforms. The most important of these reforms concerned agriculture (the land reforms of 1946, encouragement of agricultural cooperative associations, and rice price controls), labor (legalization of trade unions and collective bargaining, and enforcement of labor standards), and industry (passage of an Antimonopoly Law, zaibatsu dissolution, and deconcentration of economic power).

As a simple matter of avoiding famine, massive aid was essential to Japan, with the United States the almost exclusive source. The aid program included a wide range of industrial raw materials and paid for more than half of Japan's total imports through 1949.

Although the occupation purge was directed primarily at political and military leaders of the Japanese war effort, an "economic purge" was extended to cover industrial, commercial, and financial leaders judged to have cooperated actively with the Japanese military. The effect of the purge on economic recovery was questionable, and over 200,000 of those purged were later officially depurged by appeals boards and administrative action.

Because Japan financed its political and economic reforms largely by printing new money, the country experienced accelerating inflation in 1945–1949. An initial Occupation effort to check this inflation in February 1946 took the form of an abortive "new yen" currency reform. All pre-1946 currency was invalidated, with new notes issued yen-for-yen but only for limited amounts. Both demand and savings deposits were also frozen. However, budgetary deficits of the Japanese government and credit creation by the Bank of Japan continued to be financed by an excessive printing of currency and expansion of bank credit.

Two important agencies of economic recovery and expansion were set up by the Japanese in late 1946, after the failure of the "new yen" experiment. These were the Keizai Antei Hombu, or Economic Stabilization Board (ESB; the present Economic Planning Agency), and the Fukko Kin'yu Kinko, or Reconstruction Finance Bank (RFB). The ESB planned and supervised a revived system of price controls and rationing and also subsidized increased production. The RFB made longer-term loans to public and private institutions to increase their productive capacities. A characteristic of Japanese planning was to select particular industries as keys to the next stage of economic expansion, and to concentrate assistance on such industries with little regard for short-term market forces. Priorities shifted from coal and food in 1946 to iron, steel, and fertilizer production in 1948.

The Reverse Course Period　　　　　　　　逆行の時代●

The reverse course may be dated from 1 February 1947, the scheduled date for a general strike by a united front of government workers' unions. SCAP decided to forbid the strike, and a pattern of hostility between SCAP and the Japanese Left crystallized and continued for the remainder of the Occupation. Whereas SCAP had been antimilitarist, antinationalist, and antifascist before February 1947, anticommunism and antiunionism came to overshadow these earlier ideologies after that date.

With partial revival of Japanese production by 1948, international trade became increasingly important, but under SCAP's supervision all commercial imports as well as exports required licensed approval by the Japanese authorities. Only in 1948 did SCAP begin to permit the entry, and then the permanent residence, of foreign private traders.

The Dodge Line Period ドッジ・ラインの時代●

In the fall of 1948 a Detroit banker Joseph M. Dodge was appointed a special adviser to SCAP on economic matters. The measures undertaken during this period were known collectively as the Dodge line. Under the Dodge program, the price control system, production subsidies, and the RFB loans were terminated. Dodge advocated free-market economics, balanced budgets, lower taxes, stabilization of the exchange value of the yen (at ¥360 to the US dollar), and strict regulation of the money supply. His drastic anti-inflationary measures, combined with a recession in world markets for Japanese exports, brought on a severe decline in aggregate demand; the results were business failures and unemployment. By the spring of 1950 the short-term outlook for the Japanese economy was bleak.

The Korean War Period 朝鮮戦争時代●

The outbreak of the Korean War caught both SCAP and the Japanese authorities by surprise. After the war began on 25 June 1950 the semimilitary economy that Japan almost immediately became was dominated by *tokuju* (special procurement demand) for the United Nations forces in Korea; the Japanese economy thus returned to full capacity, boom conditions, and high growth. The money supply was freed from its Dodge line fetters. As for the Dodge line as a whole, three main pillars remained in place: an annually balanced budget, a stable yen-dollar exchange rate, and the dissolution of the price-control and rationing machinery.

Recovery and Growth 回復と成長●

War procurements during the Korean conflict and a general expansion of world trade enabled Japan to earn the foreign exchange to pay for the imports so essential for growth. The Japanese rate of growth in the 1950s and 1960s was without historical precedent and came to be called an "economic miracle." Japan was the second largest borrower from the World Bank in the late 1950s, and it was classified as a less-developed nation in the early 1960s. Yet by 1964 it was recognized as one of the advanced industrial nations, and by 1968 it had surpassed West Germany to become the world's second largest market economy. Business optimism began to emerge as the economy moved beyond postwar recovery. Actual performance exceeded expectations, and the rates of growth and labor productivity accelerated. The average annual growth of the gross national product (GNP) rose, despite occasional slowdowns, from 7.1 percent between 1952 and 1957 to 9.8 percent between 1957 and 1962. Prime Minister Ikeda Hayato proposed a 10-year Income-Doubling Plan in 1960, only to see income double in 7 years. The size of the emerging Japanese economy in the 1960s and its concentration on exports and GNP growth provoked international complaints and retaliation (even from the United States), which played a major part in shaping Japan's economic policies and performance in the 1970s and 1980s. See also CONTEMPORARY ECONOMY.

Economic agencies (keizai kancho)　　　　経済官庁●

Ministry of Finance headquarters.

Government ministries and agencies concerned with economic policies, in particular, the Ministry of Finance, the Ministry of International Trade and Industry (MITI), and the Economic Planning Agency (EPA). The Ministry of Finance helps prepare the national budget and revisions to the tax system and also provides supervision and guidance to banks and securities companies. MITI supervises individual industries and is responsible for the formulation and enforcement of international trade policies. It influences the industrial world through its administrative guidance powers. The EPA coordinates economic policies and prepares long-term economic plans, annual economic forecasts, and the White Paper on the Economy.

Since the Japanese government often manipulates public works expenditures as a way to control business fluctuations, the Ministry of Construction and the Ministry of Transport also have important economic roles. The Ministry of Foreign Affairs, MITI, the EPA, and the Ministry of Finance divide the responsibility for overseas economic aid.

National budget (kokka yosan)　　　　国家予算●

The general account budget of the national government's revenues and expenditures is usually regarded as the most important of all government budgets. In addition to this budget, there are also individual budgets for a group of special accounts created to implement government policies. Thirty-eight special accounts were operative in 1994.

Social Security　　　　社会保障関係費●

Various outlays for public assistance programs, social welfare programs, social insurance programs, public health services, and unemployment measures are included in this category, which represented 18.4 percent of the 1994 general account budget. Public assistance provides support to individuals who are unable to meet the cost of living. The national government provides 75 percent of this assistance and local governments 25 percent. Social welfare programs are intended to support those people for whom care is necessary, such as children, the aged, and the physically and mentally disabled.

Social insurance can be classified into health insurance, pensions, and unemployment insurance. The health insurance system consists of employee insurance and national health insurance. The pension system, similarly, has two classes. National pension insurance provides basic, mandatory coverage for all citizens, while other programs provide additional benefits for private- and public-sector employees. While these programs depend mainly on contributions made by employers and employees, subsidies from the general account are also substantial. Measures to combat tuberculosis, poliomyelitis, and other communicable diseases; cancer; and mental illness are carried out by the public health service. To cope with unemployment, there are unemployment insurance, unemployment relief works, and special measures to promote employment. See also SOCIAL WELFARE.

Public Works　　　　　　　　　　　　公共事業関係費●

One of the features of Japanese public expenditure is a relatively high level of government investment (10.6 percent of the 1994 general account budget). The main emphasis since the late 1960s has been on public works aimed at increasing social overhead capital. Social capital includes erosion and flood-control projects; road construction; port, harbor, and airport facilities; housing; public service facilities; improvement of conditions for agricultural production; forest roads; and water supply for industrial use. Of these, the heaviest investment is in road construction, which is managed primarily through the Road Improvement Special Account. The expenditures in this special account consist of expenses for projects under the direct control of the national government, subsidies to local governments, and investments in public expressway corporations. The main sources of revenue for these expenditures are transfers from the general account.

Education and Science　　　　　　　　文教・科学振興費●

Expenditures in this category were 8.2 percent of the 1994 general account budget. Schools for compulsory education (elementary schools and middle schools) are operated by local authorities; the national government is required by law to provide one-half of the teachers' salaries in these schools. Other government outlays are expenses for public school facilities, school education assistance, transfers to the National Schools Special Account, loans to students, and the promotion of science and technology. The revenue and expenditures of national universities and hospitals attached to national schools are managed through the National Schools Special Account.

Transfers to the Foodstuff Control Special Account　　食料管理費●

The Foodstuff Control Special Account was originally created to stabilize the prices of agricultural products by controlling the purchase and sale of rice, wheat, barley, and other commodities. However, sale prices of domestic rice and some other crops are not high enough to cover the government's purchase price and overhead expenses. As a result, a large deficit has developed in this special account, and funds are transferred from the general account each year to cover the deficit.

Economic Cooperation　　経済協力費●

In fiscal 1994 the government expenditure for economic cooperation was estimated at ¥999 billion (1.4 percent of the general account budget). Government economic assistance to developing countries has increased rapidly. See also OFFICIAL DEVELOPMENT ASSISTANCE.

Local Allocation Tax　　地方交付税交付金●

This expenditure—which equals 30 percent of income, corporation, liquor, and consumption taxes and which represented 7.5 percent of the 1994 general account budget—is distributed by the national government to assist local governments through a special account for allotment of the local allocation tax and transferred tax. Local governments can use these grants at their discretion. The national government allocates these grants according to the financial needs of each local government.

National income (kokumin shotoku)　　国民所得●

The national income measures used in international comparisons are gross national product (GNP) and gross domestic product (GDP). Japan's GDP in 1993 was ¥421 trillion (US $3.8 trillion), making it the second largest market economy in the world. In the same year per capita income was ¥2.9 million (US $26,079), comparable with that of Western nations after adjusting for Japan's high cost of housing and other goods. This high economic scale was achieved largely due to high economic growth from 1955 to the late 1960s, during which period the nation's average annual growth rate was around 10 percent, about double that of Western nations. Although this rate declined, it still remained higher than that of most other industrialized nations in the 1970s and 1980s. After the end of the 1986 to 1991 boom period known as the "bubble economy," growth slowed drastically, with the GDP growth rate falling to 0.4 percent in 1993 and 0 percent in 1994. New corporate investment stagnated as a result of both the economic slowdown and a sharp rise in the value of the Japanese yen. As of the end of 1994, prospects for recovery were uncertain.

Structure of National Income   国民所得の構造●

The Japanese economy can be understood by examining three aspects of the national income: production, distribution, and disposition. Regarding production, primary industry (agriculture, forestry, and fishing), which accounted for 26.0 percent of the GDP in 1950, fell to 2.1 percent in 1992, while the share of secondary industry (manufacturing) rose from 31.8 percent to 36.7 percent, and tertiary industry (services) rose from 42.3 percent to 61.2 percent in the same years. In recent years, the share of secondary industry appears to have reached a ceiling, and that of tertiary industry has continued to develop, creating a service-oriented economy (see INDUSTRIAL STRUCTURE).

As for distribution, the proportion of employee compensation has increased, whereas that of income from private corporations and private unincorporated entrepreneurial income has decreased. In 1950, employee compensation stood at 41.8 percent, while private unincorporated entrepreneurial income was 45.6 percent. In 1992, these figures were 69.0 percent and 9.3 percent, respectively.

When expenditures, or disposition of national income, are broken down into consumption and savings, the share of savings in national disposable income steadily increased from about 20 percent in the 1950s, peaking at 30.3 percent in 1970. It then fell to an average of 22.8

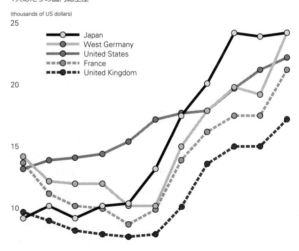

Per Capita GDP of Selected Countries
1人あたりの国内総生産

(thousands of US dollars)

Japan
West Germany
United States
France
United Kingdom

1980 1981 1982 1983 1984 1985 1986 1987 1988 1989 1990

Source: Economic Planning Agency.

percent in the 1990–92 period. Even now, however, this figure is higher than that of other advanced nations.

Income distribution (*shotoku bumpu*)   所得分布●

Household income differentials in Japan narrowed sharply after World War II, especially in the high-growth period of the 1960s and 1970s. However, income differentials have started to widen in recent years. There are a number of factors accounting for this trend. First, wage levels of workers in large corporations often differ markedly from those of their counterparts in smaller firms. In the 1950s this situation was referred to as the dual structure of the economy, which was more or less eliminated in the high-growth period. In the 1980s, however, wage differentials based on corporate size began to expand again. The considerably higher levels of nonmonetary compensation provided by large corporations, including expense accounts and housing and other benefits, further exacerbate the effects of the dual structure.

A second feature of wage differentials in Japan is that they are far greater among different age groups than in other developed countries. This is primarily due to the seniority system followed by most Japanese corporations.

The third factor concerns the fact that an increasing number of Japanese women in households with lower incomes sought employment in order to supplement their husbands' limited incomes. This development originally served to equalize Japanese family incomes. Recently, however, supplementary incomes earned by working women have tended to widen income differences between families, as many women in high-income-bracket households are now also gainfully employed.

The wage gap between the sexes remains conspicuous in Japan. In 1993 the average monthly salary of a female worker amounted to only 62 percent of the salary of her male counterpart. This is primarily because the average working woman's career is only about 60 percent as long as the average man's, a definite disadvantage in a wage system based on seniority; women are more often employed in comparatively low-paying industries and smaller firms; and many women are part-time workers.

Although income distribution in Japan is still relatively equal in terms of employment income, the gap between rich and poor is seen as much wider when considered in terms of asset ownership. The gaps in asset ownership widened markedly in the second half of the 1980s because of skyrocketing land prices. While falling land prices in the early

1990s have narrowed the disparity somewhat, there continues to be a big prosperity gap between property haves and have-nots.

Modern employment system

(*gendai no koyo seido*)   現代の雇用制度●

The employment system in the post-World War II period has been based on three essential institutions: lifetime employment (*shushin koyo*), the SENIORITY SYSTEM (*nenko joretsu*), and enterprise unionism.

Lifetime Employment   終身雇用●

In the characteristic Japanese employment system, companies recruit workers immediately upon graduation from a school or university, and these workers continue in the same company until retirement. This is considered to be the ideal employment relationship, but it is mostly limited to larger firms.

Regular employees can expect to be employed until retirement unless they violate any of the rules of employment. When business is depressed, regular employees are dismissed only as a last resort. In return for this job security, employees are expected to accept transfers to other departments or to subsidiaries when business is bad and to respond positively by working overtime when the company is doing well. As long as employees maintain such a commitment, it is commonly understood to be the employer's responsibility to maintain stability of employment.

Seniority System   年功序列●

This system bases an employee's rank, salary, and qualifications within an enterprise on the length of service in that company. Wage increases and promotions are highly dependent on the employee's school background, sex, and type of work. This system can be traced to a period of serious labor shortages during World War I when the Yokosuka Naval Shipyard adopted it as a means of securing enough technical and skilled workers.

Enterprise Unionism   企業組合主義●

The third basic feature of the Japanese employment system is the prevalence of enterprise unions. This form of unionism was established after World War II because of the following factors: (1) strong paternalism among postwar employers of all sizes and types; (2) a wide variety of working conditions, which prevented the development of a unitary wage structure based on technical qualifications and competence; and (3) the interest of union members in secure jobs and income, owing to the inadequacy of government social security. These factors led Japanese union members to prefer to bargain with management at the level of the individual enterprise. Paternalistic management and enterprise unionism have both supported lifetime employment and promoted labor-management harmony.

Temporary Employees 臨時雇用者●

The Japanese employment system is dependent on a variety of temporary employees. Because the number of regular workers is limited, companies take on temporary workers for a fixed period in response to business upturns. If the situation deteriorates, the companies simply release the temporary workers. In addition to temporary employees who work the same hours as regular employees, there are part-time workers, students, and those on loan from employment agencies, who work a limited number of hours only. When regular employees reach retirement age, some are retained with the special status of "nonregular staff" (*shokutaku*), but they are regarded as temporary employees. There is a strict demarcation between regular and temporary employees in terms of working conditions, job status, wages, and benefits.

Smaller firms operate welfare systems similar to those in large companies, but in many small companies working conditions do not improve with increasing length of service. As a result, labor mobility among small firms is high and many workers are hired in mid-career. Lifetime employment, therefore, is a system operating mainly in large private companies and the public sector.

Corporations (*kigyo*)   企業●

Japan has more than 1.5 million corporations. There is, however, considerable concentration of economic power in a small number of corporations. Of the 1,561,300 corporations existing at the time of the 1991 census, only 1,162 had more than 2,000 employees. There were 1,681 corporations listed on the Tokyo Stock Exchange as of November 1994.

Financial Characteristics   資本調達の特徴●

The huge capital requirements of many corporations during the period of rapid economic growth, which began in the 1950s, led to a dependence on debt financing. Since Japan's capital markets were still undeveloped at that time, companies were forced to rely on the banks for financing. Banks were then able to exert considerable influence over management decisions, while holders of common shares exerted little control. Because banks, in turn, had to rely on the Bank of Japan, the country's central bank, for additional funds, the government was able to exercise a major influence on important corporate decisions using direct credit expansion controls known as *madoguchi shido* ("window guidance").

In the 1980s, however, development of the capital markets and substantial liquidity in the total economy led to a reduction in dependence on debt financing. With deregulation, companies became better able to raise funds on their own utilizing financial instruments such as convertible bonds.

Enterprise Groups and Subsidiaries   企業グループと子会社●

Following World War II, the *zaibatsu* (financial and industrial combines) were dissolved by Occupation fiat. Many groups later recombined, however, because of traditional ties and an urgent need for the capital that could be obtained from the banks of the group. Although mutual shareholding reinforces the connections, there is no central ownership, and group coordination is much looser than in prewar zaibatsu.

Of more importance to the operations of the corporation than its connections with other large companies is the pattern of subsidiaries and subcontracting firms that has developed. These smaller firms not only pay lower wages, but also provide a smaller package of benefits. Hence, there is a considerable economic advantage to using smaller firms as suppliers of those components or subassemblies that require less-skilled labor. The subsidiary or subcontractor relationship also gives the parent company flexibility in scheduling and allows cyclic downturns in demand to be displaced onto the smaller firms.

Employment Practices   雇用形態●

The pattern of Japanese employment has as its basis a mutual commitment by the corporation and the employee. The corporation undertakes to retain each person that it selects until retirement, despite later temptations to terminate employment. Employees undertake to remain in the employ of the corporation once they make their choice, however attractive alternative positions might appear. Large corporations recruit employees directly from school, and hiring is not for a particular skill or job. Each assumes that over time the individual will fill a range of positions. Compensation is based on seniority, with rank, performance, and other special conditions as additional considerations.

The effect of this pattern is to establish an unusual identity between the interests of the individual employee and the interests of the corporation itself. The employee's security and assurance of continued improvement in income depend directly on the success of the firm. Midcareer moves from one firm to another for more money are relatively rare. The enterprise union system also tends to reinforce rather than dilute employee identification with the company.

It should be noted that this employment pattern applies primarily to the regular employees of large corporations, never to temporary workers and seldom to employees in small firms (see MODERN EMPLOYMENT SYSTEM). Changes in the pattern are occurring, but only slowly. Some companies have tried to shift the emphasis from seniority to performance when determining promotions and raises. The recession in the early 1990s has put additional pressure for change on the traditional pattern, and under the label "restructuring" some corporations are trying to reduce their population of high-paid older employees.

Corporate history (kigyo no rekishi)   企業の歴史●

An analysis of the development of Japanese business from the Meiji period (1868–1912) to the eve of World War II.

The Legacy of the Edo-Period Merchants   江戸時代の町人の遺産●

The activities of the merchants of the Edo period (1600–1868) facilitated the use of money throughout Japan and resulted in an increasingly unified market. Osaka became the commercial and financial center of the country, and developed highly advanced trading and financial techniques. Central to the commercial activities of the period was the concept of the household (ie), composed of the owner-family and all those employed by it, who, in exchange for absolute loyalty, were guar-

anteed permanent employment. Within the household each member had
his place in a strictly ordered hierarchical system.

The Leaders of the Meiji Government
as Modernizers   近代化を進めた明治時代の指導者達●

The leaders of the Meiji Restoration of 1868 superimposed
selected Western-style institutions on traditional Japanese society. Class
privileges and class restrictions were abolished, and former *samurai* were
helped toward gainful employment; merchant guilds were prohibited;
freedoms of enterprise and migration were proclaimed. In 1871 a unified
currency, based on the yen, was established. The Ministry of Public
Works (Kobusho), established in 1870, planned the importation of technology and the promotion of industry; it employed more than 500
foreign experts as technicians and instructors.

After 1884, most government enterprises were sold to private
concerns—such as Mitsui, Sumitomo, and Mitsubishi—which would
later develop into *zaibatsu* (financial cliques). Western-style businesses,
notably factories and banks, were hailed as part of the new era of
"Civilization and Enlightenment". The government, however, saw modern business primarily in terms of strengthening the state rather than in
terms of satisfying consumer demands.

The Growth of Modern Business (1868–1937)   現代的ビジネスの成長●

The overall growth of modern business passed through four
major stages in Japan. There was a pioneering period from 1868 to 1884,
when sound financial conditions were restored after the government initiated deflationary policies in 1881. Many firms collapsed during the
period of deflation. The second period, from 1884 to 1919, was one of
accelerated growth that was stimulated by Japan's policy of imperial
expansion, notably after the Sino-Japanese War of 1894–1895 and the
Russo-Japanese War of 1904–1905. The latter gave a particular impetus to
the shipbuilding industry and to heavy industry in general. Industrial
paid-up capital tripled during World War I, when the Asian market was
left totally open to Japanese trade. Worldwide economic dislocation following World War I led to the prolonged depression that was the major
feature of the third period, which ended in 1931. There were waves of
bankruptcies, mass unemployment, and a growing concentration of capital in the hands of the zaibatsu. After 1931, the fourth period saw a
reflation under the influence of war preparations. Exports were strongly
promoted, and the economy reflated toward full employment.

Modern banks were launched in 1876 in the form of national
banks. The Bank of Japan, established in 1882, acted as the central bank,

and a few government-run banks granted long-term loans for foreign trade, industry, and agriculture. The main weakness of Japan's banking system was the large number of small banks that were tied to individual firms by continued extension of large loans. In periods of crisis, many such banks failed, and this in turn led to a heavy concentration of banking capital. Between 1926 and 1929 the number of banks decreased from 1,417 to 897, and, by 1935, 40 percent of all deposits were held by the "Big Five" (Dai-Ichi [now Dai-Ichi Kangyo Bank, Ltd], Mitsui [now Sakura Bank, Ltd], Mitsubishi, Yasuda [now Fuji Bank, Ltd], and Sumitomo).

During the 1920s and 1930s general trading companies, notably those of the zaibatsu, played the key role in expanding Japan's international trade. The Mitsubishi, Kawasaki, Ishikawajima, and Hitachi shipyards grew and integrated vertically into large industrial enterprises that produced heavy machinery, railway engines and coaches, electric cables, and other heavy iron and steel products. Shipping received some subsidy but was left to private initiative. Nippon Yusen Kaisha (controlled by Mitsubishi), Osaka Shosen, and Toyo Kisen emerged as the three major shipping companies.

By 1886 a total of 32 railway companies had come into existence, and by 1905, 67 percent of some 7,800 kilometers (4,846 mi) of railway lines were operated by private companies. Nationalization of all but 9 percent of the lines was carried out in 1906–1907.

Main Tokyo branch of Sumitomo Bank.

Forms of Business   ビジネスの形態●

The joint-stock company (*kabushiki kaisha*) received strong backing from the Meiji government. The Commercial Code of 1899 distinguished three types of company: limited liability company (*yugen kaisha*), limited partnership company (*goshi kaisha*), and unlimited partnership company (*gomei kaisha*). The zaibatsu holding companies controlled the expanding network of financial and industrial companies through a system of direct and interlocking stockholdings and through the appointment of loyal top managers.

There were four main reasons for the growth of Japan's zaibatsu. First, they had large initial capital resources. Second, the holding-company system itself gave them ready access to financial resources (banks), raw materials (mines), and direct lines of foreign trade. Third, they were led by able individuals who were entrepreneurs and who actively secured new managerial talent. Fourth, they were family-based organizations that applied the concept of the household (*ie*) to the new business environment. They delegated decision making but demanded the unswerving loyalty of their managers and employees.

Corporate culture (*kigyo bunka*)   企業文化●

The unique style and policies of a company. Japanese corporate cultures tend to share certain basic understandings and managerial ideologies that differ from those of Western corporations, including conceptions of such crucial matters as profits, dividends, contractual obligations, and company personnel practices. These features reflect the values and characteristics of Japan's social and economic systems.

Background   背景●

In the early Meiji period (1868–1912) there was considerable foreign influence on the Japanese business community, but it was only a part of larger and more complex developments, in which the legacies of premodern Japan and particular processes and markets played significant roles in shaping the character of emerging companies. Two sources of indigenous organizational influence were the official *han* (domain) and Tokugawa shogunate bureaucracies and the successful merchant houses (*shoka*). The supreme ideal of serving political authority and thus society was espoused by merchants as well as bureaucrats.

Confucian thought—with its conception of the social order as one of many parts working together for the common good, its acceptance of hierarchy, and its emphasis on social identity—was easily adapted as an ideology for modern organizations. The close-knit agricultural hamlet (*buraku*) and the work-oriented forms of the patron-client (*oyabun-kobun*) relationship are two elemental social institutions influencing Japanese corporate consciousness.

Typical Corporate Ideology   典型的な企業イデオロギー●

The contemporary Japanese company generally possesses an official company ideology expressed in the company song, in essays by company elders, in catechismlike lists of primary goals and values, and in annual celebrations and public events. Each company's leader seeks to create an ideology which portrays the company as a big family, or in terms that underline common interest, comradeship, and long-term relationships. Harmony, cooperation, and hard work will bring prosperity and growth despite a fiercely competitive and changing environment. The company is clearly the highest priority, and the morality of membership is judged in terms of loyal service to the company.

It is also common for company ideologies to contain lofty pronouncements stressing that business success must be honestly won with the best interests of society in mind. The company's work is seen as contributing to the glory and prosperity of Japan. The money, the people, the company's history, and the results of business are all seen as merged into one organic social entity.

Socialization and Reinforcement 社会化と強化●

Japanese have little trouble accepting that companies will try to mold their members to fit a particular ethos and style. The worker's character, attitudes, and values are properly subjects of company concern. Therefore, new employees usually undergo intensive corporate education and training programs.

Training represents a conscious effort on the part of management to reinforce corporate culture. Most employees are willing to participate in informal company-sponsored activities. Relations within small work groups are expected to be personal, warm, and actively developed outside working hours. The ideal boss is one who will aid subordinates in personal problems, give advice, and enter into a close association.

Corporate culture is reinforced by routine behavior. A prime example is the simple matter of morning greetings among workers. Typically company policy calls for a brief ceremony to begin the day in each office or workshop and, however seemingly mundane it may become, its absence can create difficulties.

One of the most characteristic qualities of Japanese corporate culture, in fact, is the degree to which it is managed. Japanese of all ages and stations in life tend to defer to the group, particularly its leaders. Due to the general absence of strong personal religious beliefs and concomitant ideological committment, the governance of daily social conduct has typically become a matter of rather particularistic group and institutional norms. Japanese companies fulfill this role through the sponsorship of their own lively subculture.

Management (*keiei kanri*) 経営管理●

In Japan, the origins of the professional manager go back to the pre-World War II period. As the *zaibatsu* (the large prewar financial combines) expanded and diversified, the families owning them began to turn over the operation of these vast enterprises to professional managers, and by the 1930s professional managers had come to assume the major management responsibilities. This trend became firmly established in the postwar era, as the zaibatsu were dissolved and stock ownership became widely disbursed. With few exceptions, large Japanese enterprises are now managed by professional managers.

Organizational Structure and Decision Making 組織の構造と意思決定●

In Japan the individual, at least historically, existed only as a member of a group and not as a strong, clearly identifiable, and distinct entity. The basic unit of Japanese organizations remains the group. A task is assigned to and performed by a group rather than by individuals. The task is defined on the basis of the group, the assignment is carried out by the group, and the responsibility is shared by all. Under such an organizational arrangement, a leader must first create and then maintain a climate in which every member of the organization can work together harmoniously.

The decision-making process commonly followed in large bureaucratic organizations is known as the *ringi* system, which has often been described as an approval-seeking process. In it a proposal, known as a *ringisho*, is prepared by a lower functionary. The ringisho works its way up through the organizational hierarchy in a highly circuitous manner, often at a snail's pace, and at each step is examined by the proper officials, whose approval is indicated by affixing a seal (see NEMAWASHI). Out of this process a decision emerges. The dynamic but informal interaction that characterizes every stage of decision making is the essence of the ringi system. From the very stage during which a decision is first being shaped, various ideas and alternatives are explored, albeit very informally. Different interests are accommodated, and compromises are sought. At the same time, a process of education, persuasion, and coordination among various groups takes place.

An elusive element in the ringi system is the role of the formal leader. In this system the formal leader is not a decision maker in the classical sense. In the Japanese organization, while the status of a leader is meticulously defined, his role in the decision-making process is little differentiated from that of other members of the organization. In other words, the leader participates with his subordinates in the decision-making process. Thus, the degree to which the leader's view is incorporated into a decision depends largely on how well he is accepted and respected by his subordinates and on the kind of relationships he enjoys with them.

Another basic condition for making the ringi system effective is the need for a high degree of shared understanding and values among the participants. In large Japanese companies, the development of such shared understanding and organizational commitment begins with the recruiting system and is reinforced through subsequent personnel practices. Young men are carefully selected from among the graduates of the best universities and have thus already survived a series of rigorous

Economy

screening processes and are highly homogeneous in ability, training, background, and values. Once they have been recruited by a company, they go through an intensive socialization process during which they are indoctrinated with the values of a particular firm and through which, after a number of years, they develop a high degree of shared understanding and commitment. Japanese practices are undergoing gradual change, but the patterns outlined here are found today in almost every large Japanese corporation.

Corporate decision making (*kigyo no ishi kettei*) 企業の意思決定●

The *ringi* system, a process of decision making through the use of circular letters, is known as a system unique to Japanese enterprises. More formal decisions, however, often are made in a meeting of company executives, as is the case in other countries. Top management decides fundamental managerial policy; proposals for and research on actual measures to be followed are assigned to each responsible division. Middle management takes a leading part in planning a measure, and after informal negotiations with other related departments the plan is formally presented in the form of a *ringisho*, a letter bearing the proposal that is circulated among the various departments of the organization. Since information is reported to the top level, the upper management, including the CEO, is well acquainted with the plan when it is finally submitted at a board of directors' meeting. Consequently the support of the plan in such a meeting is, in principle, unanimous.

As a company increases in size and the business diversifies, decision-making authority is passed down to each responsible division. However, at the very least fundamental plans for the corporate group and decisions on important matters are made at meetings of the parent company's top-level management. In addition, the CEO of the parent company controls the whole group by retaining control over important personnel appointments and budget allocations to each division or subsidiary. In Japan it is the company's main bank, its principal customer, and its employees' union, rather than its stockholders, that exercise outside influence on the decision-making process.

Corporate recruitment (*saiyo*) 採用●

Large Japanese corporations have adopted a general pattern of long-term employment for both workers and management. This has allowed firms to plan for their projected employment needs and hire on a highly systematic basis. Large companies recruit new employees (the company's future managers) almost exclusively from the finest universities. The graduates are hired on the assumption that they will be with the same company until they retire, are given on-the-job-training, and are promoted within the company. Most companies begin holding company information seminars for undergraduates about eight months to one year before college graduation in March; official hiring begins after graduation and employment begins in April. However, some companies "decide" on students unofficially well before their actual graduation from college. This practice has been officially discouraged by universities and the Ministry of Labor, but many companies continue to recruit undergraduates secretly.

Small and medium-sized companies are generally more flexible in hiring executive staff and may hire people who have had prior work experience. The main reason for this is that almost all of the most promising new graduates are recruited by the large companies. In the first half of the 1990s, however, the recession has caused most large firms to cut back on their hiring of new graduates, and some small and medium-sized companies have taken advantage of this to aggressively recruit talented people.

Seniority system (*nenko joretsu*) 年功序列●

System of employment in Japan in which an employee's rank, salary, and qualifications within a firm are based on the length of service in the company. Workers, upon hire, are expected to stay with the company until their retirement. Starting wages are determined by educational background, age, sex, and type of job, while wage increases are primarily governed by age and length of service; retirement pay is based on length of employment, position, and wage level at the time of retirement. Seniority is also an important factor in promotions.

The seniority system enables employees to benefit from stability of employment: the longer they work at a single company, even at comparatively low wages, the greater their overall remuneration. Employers can benefit from strong worker loyalty and stability and the resultant ease with which they can formulate personnel plans. They suffer, however, from the necessity of carrying along surplus workers and growing inflexibility within their organizations.

With the steady increase in numbers of employees in higher age brackets, the pyramidal personnel structure has started to crumble as

Japanese corporations begin to suffer from skyrocketing labor costs. The problem will only get worse as the average age of Japan's population continues to grow, putting increasing pressure on companies to place more emphasis on employee ability and less on seniority. See also MODERN EMPLOYMENT SYSTEM.

S*ettai*

(entertaining; particularly entertaining of business clients)　　　接待●

In Japan one of the most common ways of showing gratitude to a company's best customers is to provide entertainment. This typically consists of an invitation to a substantial meal at a Japanese or Western restaurant, followed by one or more visits to Japanese-style hostess bars. Because of the high cost of these evenings, the change to less favorable tax treatment of such expenses, and the trend among younger persons to spend more time with their families, there has been a tendency toward less conspicuous consumption.

Settai is mainly carried out at expensive Japanese-style restaurants (*ryotei*). The typical ryotei is patterned after the traditional Japanese house, with, of course, waitresses dressed in *kimono*. An evening at a ryotei with a valued client usually begins with a meal of 10 or more courses (all rather small in volume) lasting between two and three hours. If the guest is to be particularly honored, the host may call a group of *geisha* to play the *shamisen* (lute) and dance for the party.

The most common alternative to an evening of eating and drinking is an invitation to a round of golf. Since memberships in golf courses can run from nearly ten million yen for a new but distant course to several hundred million yen for courses convenient to Tokyo, golf is regarded as an appropriately prestigious activity with which to reward customers.

Foreign trade (boeki)　　　　　　　　貿易●

Narrowly defined, foreign trade refers to the export and import of goods and services from and to Japan. However, in the sense of international commerce, it can be considered to include financial or capital flows as well.

The Opening of Japan　　　　　　　日本の開国●

Japan's modern foreign trade officially began in 1859. The Tokugawa shogunate (1603–1867) until then had maintained a policy of National Seclusion. However, with the signing of the Harris Treaty (United States-Japan Treaty of Amity and Commerce) in July 1858, Japan opened its doors to Western commerce. At the outset the most important Japanese export was raw silk, which was welcomed in the European market. Other exports were primarily raw material goods, semimanufactures, and foodstuffs; these included tea, copper ware, marine products, medicine, oil, and lacquer ware. Key imports were cotton thread, cotton and wool textiles, ironware, sugar, medicinal herbs, military ships, and guns. Approximately 80 percent of Japan's trade was with the United Kingdom, the next largest trading partners being the United States and the Netherlands.

Initially Japan maintained a continual surplus balance of trade. However, after lowering import tariffs by the signing of the Tariff Convention of 1866, imports of manufactured goods increased, and Japan entered a period of deficit trade balances. Trade treaties concluded during this period did not recognize Japan's right to set its own customs duties, and Japan did not obtain tariff autonomy until 1911.

From the Meiji Restoration (1868)
to World War I　　　　　明治維新から第一次世界大戦まで●

After the Meiji Restoration, Japanese foreign trade increased dramatically every year. As part of its efforts to increase production and modernize Japanese industry, the government actively worked to further foreign trade and promoted overseas such products as raw silk, tea, hemp, tobacco, camphor, and soy. Considering individual products, raw silk's percentage of total exports gradually declined from the level of more than 70 percent in 1863. Manufactured goods such as matches, silk products, and cotton textiles began to be exported around 1890. After 1900, raw cotton imports replaced cotton thread, iron became the primary metal import, and ship imports were supplanted by various types of machinery.

In the early Meiji period (1868–1912) almost all commercial trading rights were held by foreign merchants, primarily English traders. According to an 1877 study, 94 percent of all exports were handled by foreign firms.

Japan's trade volume, which in 1870 had been less than ¥30 million (US $84,000), exceeded ¥500 million (US $1.4 million) by World War I. During the 47 years from 1868 to 1915, there were only 12 years in which Japan had a surplus balance of trade.

From World War I Prosperity to a Wartime Trading System

第一次世界大戦による繁栄と第二次世界大戦中の貿易システム●

World War I provided the opportunity for a major increase in export business. The war caused a sharp decrease in exports of European and US products and an increase in demand for Japanese products. There was also an increase in exports of military supplies to the countries at war. As a result, the structure of Japanese exports changed, with a decrease in the percentage of raw materials and semimanufactures and an increase in the percentage of finished goods. Compared to prewar statistics, Japan's exports doubled by 1916, and in 1918, the last year of the war, exports were three times prewar levels. The cumulative trade surplus during the four years of the war was ¥1.4 billion (US $3.9 million).

After the war, however, because of an increase in Japan's domestic demand, the foreign trade balance changed from a surplus to a deficit. The worldwide Great Depression, which began with the New York stock market crash of 1929, dealt a serious blow to Japan's foreign trade. The adverse effect was heightened by a steep increase in the value of Japanese currency resulting from Japan's ill-timed return to the gold standard in January 1930. Japan's 1930 exports declined 31.6 percent compared to the previous year, and 1931 exports declined another 46.6 percent compared to 1930. Import levels also dropped severely. Imports in 1930 declined 30.2 percent compared to the previous year, and 1931 imports declined 40.3 percent compared to 1930.

Following the Manchurian Incident (1931) Japan adopted foreign trade and exchange controls in the course of organizing its war economy. With the development of trading blocs within the world trading system, the 1930s were marked by a great expansion of Japan's trade with its colonies. After the outbreak of the Sino-Japanese War of 1937–1945, Japan's foreign trade began increasingly to take on a wartime character. Imports became a means of obtaining military materials, and exports were promoted in order to acquire the foreign currency needed for imports.

Japanese trade controls were imposed progressively from 1937 on, and in 1941, with the issuance of the Trade Control Order, Japan began a program of general mobilization. Consequently, Japan became heavily dependent on trade within the "yen bloc," which included its colonies, and trade with countries outside this bloc was cut drastically. Japan had a trade surplus with respect to yen bloc countries and a large trade deficit with other countries.

Foreign Trade after World War II　　　　第二次世界大戦後の貿易●

Immediately following World War II, the devastation of Japan caused a continuing foreign trade deficit as well as a chronic lack of foreign currency. It was not until the high-growth period of the late 1950s and early 1960s that export power increased significantly because of dramatic advances in manufacturing capacity and technology. Japan's trade balance began to show a surplus starting in the second half of the 1960s, although oil crises in 1973 and 1979 caused a temporary balance-of-trade deficit. After 1983 Japan's trade surplus grew rapidly, reaching US $120.2 billion in 1993. Factors behind this success include both the competitive strength of the Japanese company and the nature of the Japanese economy, which tends to encourage exports and discourage imports.

Postwar Exports　　　　第二次世界大戦後の輸出●

In the 1960s, Japan's average dollar-base export increase of 18.4 percent per year was 2.3 times the overall rate of increase in world trade. The makeup of Japan's exports continued to shift to the heavy-industry fields of steel, machinery, and chemical products and away from textiles and light-industry products. In the 1970s, exports of machinery and electronics jumped as increasing emphasis was placed on high-value-added products. As a result, the focus of TRADE FRICTION shifted from textiles and steel to products such as color televisions and automobiles.

In the 1980s, exports of advanced-technology-intensive products including computers, semiconductors, videocassette recorders, machine

Japan's Exports to and Imports from Major Trading Partners, 1970–1990
主要貿易相手国別輸出及び輸入 (in millions of US dollars)

Country	1970		1975		1980		1985		1990	
	Exports	Imports	Exports	Imports	Exports	Imports	Exports	Imports	Exports	Imports
United States	5,939.8	5,559.6	11,148.6	11,608.1	31,367.3	24,408.0	65,277.6	25,793.0	90,322.4	52,368.6
West Germany	550.2	617.0	1,660.7	1,139.0	5,756.4	2,500.8	6,937.8	2,928.0	17,782.0	11,487.1
South Korea	818.2	229.0	2,247.7	1,308.0	5,368.3	2,996.3	7,097.2	4,091.9	17,457.2	11,706.7
United Kingdom	479.9	395.2	1,473.2	810.5	3,781.9	1,954.4	4,722.8	1,816.8	10,786.1	5,238.7
Australia	589.0	1,597.7	1,738.9	4,156.1	3,388.9	6,981.6	5,379.0	7,452.2	6,900.3	12,368.8
Canada	563.3	928.6	1,150.8	2,498.8	2,436.6	4,724.2	4,520.2	4,722.9	6,726.5	8,392.2
China	568.9	253.8	2,258.6	1,531.1	5,078.3	4,323.4	12,477.4	6,482.7	6,129.5	12,053.5
France	127.3	186.4	699.2	500.8	2,021.2	1,295.6	2,083.1	1,323.7	6,127.8	7,589.6
Italy	192.1	134.4	333.6	365.2	955.3	938.5	1,116.7	1,049.8	3,408.6	5,008.2

Note: Exports are calculated on a free on board (FOB) basis, and imports are calculated on a cost, insurance, and freight (CIF) basis.
Source: Japan Tariff Association.

tools, and facsimile machines continued to increase sharply, and trade friction over these products began to occur. Many Japanese companies, the most conspicuous being the automobile manufacturers, established local production facilities in the United States and Europe, partly in response to growing protectionist sentiments there. This caused a partial shift in the makeup of Japanese exports from finished goods to parts and subassemblies. In an effort to maintain price competitiveness after the sharp rise in the value of the yen which began in 1985, many Japanese companies also moved the manufacturing of labor-intensive and technically less-complex parts and products to China and other Asian countries in order to take advantage of the low labor costs there. In 1993, 29 percent of Japanese exports went to the United States, and 36 percent to Southeast Asia.

Postwar Imports   第二次世界大戦後の輸入●

In the period immediately following World War II, raw fuels and textile raw materials made up the bulk of the imports. The relative importance of textile raw material imports decreased and that of mineral fuel and metal raw materials increased along with the development of Japanese heavy industry. As a result of the 1973 and 1979 oil crises, crude oil prices soared, and in 1980 mineral fuels were approximately 50 percent of total imports. By 1990 mineral fuels had fallen to 24.2 percent of imports due to lower oil prices and the successful energy-conservation efforts of Japanese industry.

At the beginning of the 1980s, manufactured goods represented only 25 percent of Japanese imports. This share increased rapidly during the second half of the decade, exceeding 50 percent in 1990. Part of the increase was due to large-volume imports from the production facilities that Japanese companies established in Asia in response to the rising value of the yen. In 1993 color television imports exceeded exports for the first time. In the 1990s, there have also been cases of Japanese automobile companies "re-importing" into Japan vehicles manufactured in the United States and elsewhere.

Government policy on foreign trade (*boeki seisaku*)   貿易政策●

Japan's modern trade policy began in the Meiji period (1868–1912), and its first major objective was the achievement of parity with the West. Until the end of the Unequal Treaties, tariffs and trade were in the hands of the Western powers, so the Japanese government was limited in the measures it could take to improve the nation's trade position. The government promoted industrialization and economic development through subsidies, loans, and technical assistance. This necessitated the import of equipment, ships, steel, and other commodities that Japan itself did not make and that had to be paid for by exports. Thus evolved what has remained a fundamental part of Japan's trade policy: Japan exports in order to import.

After 1899 tariff protection of specific industries was undertaken. At the same time, tariffs on raw materials were kept low, increasing the effective protection and further stimulating manufacturing. Protection of the home market was later extended to colonies and occupied territories. The need to secure raw material and markets in a hostile international trading environment led to efforts to form the so-called Greater East Asia Coprosperity Sphere in the years immediately preceding World War II.

Following the war there was an immediate need to resuscitate the economy, especially trade. Priorities for imports were set by the government in conjunction with business. There were protective tariffs on manufactured goods, while raw materials were allowed in essentially duty-free. Specific assistance was given or removed as industries developed or gained strength. Thus steel was given priority first, then automobiles in the 1950s, and computers in the 1960s and 1970s. Industries with either export potential or strategic economic importance were favored, and the government encouraged exports via special tax and credit incentives.

Fundamental economic policies have had as much of an impact on trade as trade-specific policies. The government's push to industrialize placed a premium on investment and growth. Financial resources were channeled through the city banks, the government development banks, the tax structure, and the government's expenditure patterns to such areas as steel, chemicals, shipping, and shipbuilding. The primary architect of the plan was the Heavy Industry Bureau of the Ministry of International Trade and Industry (MITI), along with the Ministry of Finance. The focus on growth and industrialization in turn led to rapid increases in manufacturing investment and productivity, which enhanced Japanese competitiveness.

Import liberalization continued slowly through the 1960s and 1970s as Japan's industrial strength and export surplus developed further. After 1968, Japan's export surplus developed rapidly due to the Vietnam War, rising US inflation, and Japan's improving productivity. In turn, external pressures, especially from the United States, for real and substantive liberalization increased markedly. But the government still did not embrace full liberalization quickly.

Since the 1980s the major trade issue has been the growing trade surplus, and Japan's current trade policies are thus increasingly oriented toward encouraging imports while keeping the volume of exports down. This has created the need for major institutional reversals, which have been difficult to achieve. Some obvious policy steps have been taken to encourage imports, including unilateral tariff cuts, removal of import restrictions, reform of the system for standards certification, and import promotion campaigns. In addition, there have been periodic voluntary export restrictions on items such as automobiles to specific markets. Liberalization of agricultural imports, particularly rice, continued to be a politically sensitive issue, since almost all political parties' owe a considerable part of their support to agriculture. However, the coalition government of Prime Minister Hosokawa Morihiro (1938–) finally decided at the end of 1993 that it would partially open the rice market to imports. The decision was part of the last-minute agreement reached at the Uruguay Round as well as an emergency measure to make up for a poor rice crop that year.

Much remains to be done to change ingrained procedures. Many of the gains in import liberalization have come only as a result of direct foreign pressure. See also FOREIGN TRADE.

Trade friction (boeki masatsu)　　　　　　　貿易摩擦●

Trade friction has been a recurring issue in Japan's relationships with other nations since the mid-1950s. Until the early 1980s, friction primarily involved efforts to control rising Japanese exports and to prevent alleged dumping of Japanese products. In contrast, during most of the 1980s Japan's trade disputes with the United States typically involved attempts to gain greater access to the Japanese market. The Structural Impediments Initiative talks, which began in 1989, marked a new phase by addressing so-called nontariff obstacles to trade between the United States and Japan.

The history of Japan's trade friction is both lengthy and broad in scope. For example, Japan has placed voluntary limits on exports to the United States of cotton goods (1957), steel (1969), wood and synthetic fibers (1972), color televisions (1977), and automobiles (1981). Japan also agreed to restrain its steel exports to Europe in 1972. To counter dumping, the United States instituted a formula to trigger penalties on steel and machine tools imported at unfairly low prices (1978).

Through the late 1970s and the 1980s, as a result of the US objective of improving access to the Japanese market, the following accommodations were reached: increases in Japanese import quotas in beef and oranges, revision of Japanese import standards and certification procedures, the Japanese government's Action Program to Improve Market Access, the Japan-United States Semiconductor Agreement, and the Market-Oriented Sector Selective agreement covering Japanese markets for telecommunications equipment, electronics, pharmaceuticals, medical equipment, forest products, and transportation equipment. Similarly, the "Super 301" clause of the US Omnibus Trade and Competitiveness Act (1988) was applied to improve access to Japan's supercomputer, satellite, and wood product markets (1988). In contrast with the market-opening approach adopted by the United States, Japan has had a number of disputes with the EU countries and Australia concerning Japanese exports of videocassette recorders and semiconductors.

As Japan's huge trade surplus with the United States continues to grow in the 1990s, the emphasis in talks between the two countries has expanded from specific products to include comprehensive negotiations on macroeconomic policies. Under the Structural Impediments Initiative agreement of 1990, Japan and the United States established a wide-ranging basis on which each country will address structural issues affecting bilateral trade. A new series of negotiations, called The Japan-United States Framework Talks for a New Economic Partnership, began in July 1993. These talks are to cover three areas: macroeconomic policies such as Japanese tax rates and public investment and the US budget deficit, specific industries such as computers and automobiles, and cooperation on global problems such as the environment and AIDS. Progress has been slowed by the issue of numerical targets—the United States seeks a concrete way to measure the success of Japan's market opening measures, but Japan takes the position that numerical targets are unacceptable because they lead to managed trade.

Disagreement among the nations of the European Union, the United States, and Japan over agricultural trade has stalled General Agreement on Tariffs and Trade (GATT) talks since the start of the so-called Uruguay Round of 1986. In particular, since the mid-1980s the United States has been strongly urging Japan to liberalize its rice market. Despite continued opposition from farmers, the Japanese government partially opened the rice market as part of a last-minute agreement reached at Uruguay Round talks held in 1993.

Japanese farmers in front of GATT headquarters in Geneva, Switzerland, protest liberalization of agricultural imports (1993).

The series of negotiated settlements covering Japan's trade friction has in turn spawned a number of significant economic developments. For example, Japan has responded to restrictions on exports by moving pro-

Economy

duction of some products such as color televisions and automobiles to the United States. Japanese companies also increased the number of automobiles manufactured in Europe, notably the United Kingdom.

Trade liberalization (*boeki jiyuka*) 貿易自由化●

Immediately after World War II, Japan was allowed to maintain import restrictions. As a condition for joining international organizations such as the General Agreement on Tariffs and Trade (GATT) and the International Monetary Fund (IMF), however, Japan was required to liberalize substantially its trade policies. In 1955 the percentage of liberalized products was only 15 percent, but this figure rose to 90 percent by 1963. International trade was liberalized further in the 1960s as the result of multilateral tariff negotiations by GATT. In 1967 Japan instituted the across-the-board tariff reductions agreed to during the talks known as the Kennedy Round and removed tariffs from 2,147 items. Discussions in the mid-1970s known as the Tokyo Round removed more tariffs.

In the 1980s Japan adopted other measures to open its domestic market to imports. In the Action Program to Improve Market Access in 1985, tariffs were reduced on or removed from 1,853 items. Japan's tariff rates are the lowest among the advanced industrialized countries. As of 1993, Japan still protected 12 agricultural products through import quotas. However, in the Uruguay Round talks held in December 1993, Japan agreed to gradually remove these remaining restrictions on agricultural imports. See also GOVERNMENT POLICY ON FOREIGN TRADE.

Balance of payments (*kokusai shushi*) 国際収支●

A statistical record of all economic transactions between residents of the reporting country and residents of all other countries.

Merchandise Trade Balance 貿易収支●

Defined as the difference between exports and imports, this is one of the most frequently used measures of a country's balance-of-payments performance. Japan ran a deficit in merchandise trade in the early postwar years through the mid-1950s, a time when the national economy underwent gradual recovery. By the mid-1960s Japan had increased its international competitiveness to the point where it began consistently to run a surplus in its merchandise trade balance. The surplus expanded rapidly in the 1980s although it dropped somewhat near the end of the decade before starting to increase again in 1991. In 1993 Japan's total trade surplus was

US $141.5 billion, including a surplus of US $56.3 billion with the United States, US $28.9 billion with the European Union, and US $61.9 billion with the developing economies of East and Southeast Asia.

Trade Balance in Invisibles 貿易外収支●

Invisible items include expenditures and receipts for transportation, insurance, business travel and tourism, investment income, and interest on loans. Data on Japanese transactions in invisibles since 1961 show a consistent trend toward larger and larger deficits. A number of factors account for the deficits. First, it took a long time for Japan to build up foreign assets to the point where earnings on those assets had a perceptible impact on the net invisibles account. Second, because of Japan's imports of raw materials, transportation payments tend to be high. Third, for years Japan has paid a considerable amount in licensing arrangements for technology to foreign firms. In the second half of the 1980s, Japan's deficit in invisible trade increased rapidly because of the rise in the yen's value and increases in overseas tourism. Japan's deficit in unilateral transfers, a part of invisible trade, also grew quickly during this period because of increases in official development assistance (ODA).

Current Account Balance 経常収支●

This balance combines net merchandise trade, transfer payments, and net invisibles. Japan's current account fluctuated between deficit and surplus in the mid-1950s and mid-1960s, reflecting the business cycle. It has since maintained a consistent current account surplus except for a few years of deficit caused by the two oil crises in the 1970s. In the first half of the 1980s the current account surplus grew due to a drop in oil prices and to increases in exports. However, after peaking as a percentage of the gross domestic product (GDP) at 4.4 percent in 1986 and peaking in absolute terms at US $87 billion in 1987, it fell substantially. The fall can be attributed to several factors, including a sharp appreciation of the yen and an increase in public investment that was designed to spur domestic demand. In the 1990s the surplus has begun to expand again as a result of the increasing trade surplus and the income earned on the overseas investments made by Japanese companies in the second half of the 1980s. In 1993 the current account surplus reached US $131.4 billion and was 3.0 percent of the GDP.

Japan's International Balance of Payments
国際収支

(in millions of US dollars)

	1980	1985	1990	1993
Current account balance (total)	-10,746	49,169	35,761	131,448
Merchandise trade balance	2,125	55,986	63,528	141,514
Trade balance in invisibles	-11,343	-5,165	-22,292	-3,949
Unilateral transfer balance	-1,528	-1,652	-5,475	-6,117
Capital account balance (total)	5,465	-65,478	-22,118	-92,762
Balance of long-term capital	2,324	-64,542	-43,586	-78,336
Balance of short-term capital	3,141	-936	21,468	-14,426
Errors and omissions (total)	-3,115	3,991	-20,877	-260
Overall balance (total)	-8,396	-12,318	-7,234	38,426

Source: Ministry of Finance.

Industrial history (*sangyoshi*) 産業史●

Japan's modern industrial history can be roughly divided into two periods: first, the early modern era from the Meiji Restoration (1868) to the end of World War II, during which capitalism was established, and second, the contemporary period which has seen reconstruction and rapid economic growth.

Early Modern Industry (1868–1945) 近代の産業（1868年−1945年）●

Japan's industrial revolution began in the late 1880s. Light industry, notably the textile industry, grew rapidly between 1887 and 1896, while a second wave of industrialization between 1897 and 1906 led to the establishment of many heavy industries. The Meiji government took the lead in developing such basic industries as railroads and mining, as well as a number of manufacturing industries such as shipbuilding, iron and steel, and machine tools. Most of these enterprises were later turned over to the private sector.

During World War I Japanese industry experienced significant growth, as it benefited greatly from the inability of European suppliers, preoccupied with the war, to trade in Asian markets. Japan provided the Allies with military supplies, and there was great demand for Japanese shipping. An industrial boom took place during the period of the war as the values of Japanese exports rose threefold, and there was a rapid accumulation of capital. Industrial production overtook agricultural production during the war; capitalism in Japan had become fully entrenched.

Despite economic hardships caused by a depression in 1920, the Tokyo Earthquake of 1923, and the Showa Depression of the 1930s, the productivity of Japanese industry continued to increase as a result of technological progress, greater efficiency in production techniques, and the development of managerial techniques designed to secure employee loyalty. Japan's heavy industries, such as iron and steel and shipbuilding, grew rapidly in the 1930s. The output of the chemical, machine tool, electric machinery, and ceramics industries all increased greatly during this period. Exports rose sharply, led by shipments of textile products and sundry goods. In the precision machinery industry, which became the foundation for Japan's munitions industry, domestic products were almost meeting domestic demand.

Throughout this period there was no antimonopoly policy in Japan. Since the Meiji Restoration the overriding concern of the nation's leaders had been Japan's national survival in the face of the political and economic threat of Western domination. Therefore, in the period before Japan's defeat in World War II it is not clear that the government placed a premium on economic competition in itself. Administrations considered rather that the national interest would best be served by supporting the interests of large, powerful, and well-established companies such as Mitsui, Mitsubishi, and Sumitomo—the *zaibatsu* (financial cliques)— that had the resources to lead the nation's industrial progress. The zaibatsu dominated industry in this period, exercising an oligopolistic control over a wide range of industries such as manufacturing, mining, and transportation, as well as finance and overseas trade.

Meanwhile, a dual structure had developed within the manufacturing industry itself, between, on the one hand, the relatively small number of firms with capital-intensive production methods, and, on the other hand, vast numbers of low-capital, labor-intensive small firms and family concerns, many of which were more or less wholly dependent on the business of a single larger firm. In 1930, 60 percent of the nation's manufacturing labor force was employed by firms with fewer than 10 workers. Although this figure had fallen to just 9 percent by 1986, the "dual structure"—the high proportion of smaller-scale businesses in dependency relationships with larger firms—has continued to be a key characteristic of the Japanese economy in the post-World War II period.

A great many new industries emerged in the years between the world wars. For instance, the development of the electric power industry gave a great boost to the domestic aluminum-smelting industry. The development of the radio led to the beginning of vacuum tube production. Many new businesses entered this area, including the companies now known as Toshiba Corporation and Victor Co of Japan, Ltd. Many other major Japanese manufacturing companies of the present day were founded at this time, such as Toyota Motor Corporation, Nissan Motor Co, Ltd, and Mitsubishi Heavy Industries, Ltd.

Subsidies supported the production of military vehicles and the substitution of domestic production for the import of cargo ships. The birth of Nippon Seitetsu (Nippon Steel Co), an iron and steel trust, was the result of government guidance. Industrial growth was also fostered by laws enacted for individual industries, with emphasis placed on automobiles, petrochemicals, iron and steel, machine tools, and aircraft. For example, the infant automotive industry was promoted by the Automobile Manufacturing Industry Law of 1935.

Contemporary Industrial History (from 1945)　　現代産業史（1945年以降）●

During the reconstruction period following World War II, the recovery of key industries was aided by an industrial policy known as the Priority Production Program. Underdeveloped capacity in certain areas was seen as a bottleneck limiting overall growth, so the electric power, iron and steel, marine transportation, and coal industries were targeted for rapid reconstruction.

The Korean War (1950–1953) enabled Japanese industry to climb out of the stagnation in which it was mired at the end of the 1940s. By supplying the United Nations forces serving in Korea with vast quantities of matériel, Japan was able to earn the foreign exchange necessary to pay for vital imports; the war thus provided the stimulus for the economic recovery of the 1950s.

During the rapid-growth period from the late 1950s to the early 1970s, industries such as iron and steel, construction, and pharmaceuticals grew quickly, and the household electrical products industry and the petrochemical industry developed. The international economic environment at this time was favorable for Japanese exports; in the 1960s, Japan's average export increase of 18.4 percent per year was 2.5 times the overall increase in world trade. This period saw the establishment of an industrial structure based on imported raw materials that were domestically processed for export.

In the wake of the export successes of the iron and steel and shipbuilding industries, other industries such as precision machinery and electronic and optical equipment also turned to export-led growth. Huge investments were made in production facilities for heavy industry, located in the Tokaido megalopolis that stretches along the Pacific coast from Tokyo to Osaka and Kobe. Total plant and equipment investments exceeded profits, and the ratio of borrowed capital increased.

Kobe shipyard of Kawasaki Heavy Industries, Ltd.

Aggressive management created an increasing demand for funds, which banks satisfied using their large volumes of household savings deposits. Relationships between corporations and their main banks became closer, and industrial groups of affiliated companies formed around major banks. This aggressive corporate capitalism and strong reliance on indirect financing were characteristic of the Japanese industrial structure and were the basic mechanisms responsible for the strong economic growth. Japan's national income more than doubled in the 1960s, and in 1968 its gross national product became the second largest among the world's market economies. The spring labor offensive (*shunto*) became in the 1960s the established mechanism by which labor bargained for more equitable income distribution.

Efforts to reduce costs and increase efficiency in response to the oil crisis of 1973 strengthened the competitiveness of major export industries. Successful conservation efforts were made by both management and labor; as a result, energy demand fell by 37 percent in the chemical industry and by more than 20 percent in the iron and steel industry. In the automobile industry energy-saving efforts led to lighter automobiles and increased fuel economy, which further increased export competitiveness.

The oil crisis of 1979 also caused distinctive changes in the country's industrial structure. The heavy industries, which had supported rapid economic growth, stagnated, and the emphasis shifted to industries that utilize high technology and sophisticated machinery. Productivity increased through innovations such as the mounting of small computers on machine tools to develop numerically controlled equipment. It was also during the late 1970s that the computer industry and the semiconductor industry began to grow rapidly.

In response to growing trade friction with the United States and Europe, in the 1980s many Japanese companies in key export industries, such as electronics and automobiles, set up local manufacturing facilities overseas. The rapid rise in the value of the yen after 1985 has also forced some companies to move part of their manufacturing operations to China and Southeast Asia in order to maintain price competitiveness. Although export levels remain high in the early 1990s, the shift of manufacturing jobs overseas has provoked fear of the hollowing out of Japanese industry.

Many outside observers tend to emphasize the role of the intimate relationship between business and government in increasing the industrial competitiveness of Japan. Since the Meiji Restoration, Japanese administrations have indeed worked closely with industry to develop Japan's economy. It is argued that, particularly since World War II, the government has identified key industrial sectors for development and then actively encouraged major corporations to undertake the necessary research, investment, and development. Recent examples were the official encouragements in the early 1980s to Japanese manufacturers to overtake the US computer giant IBM. However, other observers have insisted that much of the credit for Japan's rapid economic growth must be given to the private sector rather than the government. They claim that the introduction of new technologies and the development of new products owe more to the mechanisms of market competition than they do to the leadership of government, and that in many key areas, such as robotics, the government was slow to respond to the challenge of the new technology.

Industrial structure (*sangyo kozo*)　　　産業構造●

National economies are conventionally divided into three sectors: primary industries (agriculture, forestry, and fisheries), secondary industries (mining, manufacturing, and construction), and tertiary industries (transportation, communications, retail and wholesale trade, banking, finance and real estate, business services, personal services, and public administration). In general, national economies in the early stages of development are dominated by primary production related to land. As the economy develops and income rises, the primary sector shares of output, capital, and labor tend to fall, and those of the secondary sector tend to rise. In late stages of development, the primary sector accounts for only a small fraction of total economic activities, the secondary sector begins to decline in relative terms, and the tertiary sector comes to the fore.

Historical Experience of Japan　　　日本の歴史的経験●

Japan's economic development since the Meiji Restoration (1868) is an excellent illustration of these patterns. In the distribution of the labor force between agriculture and nonagriculture, changes were slow until the early 1900s, considerably accelerated from then up to World War II, and very rapid during the decades following the war. After 1960 the agricultural labor force began to contract in absolute terms, and even those who remained on farms worked only part-time as farmers.

In the secondary sector, statistics show a continued relative expansion in employment and production until the mid-1970s. The tertiary sector maintained a relatively stable share in net domestic product before World War II, although its share of the national labor force expanded. After World War II, its share of employment continued to increase, while its share of gross domestic product (GDP) remained stable until the early 1960s when it, too, started to rise.

Changes in Manufacturing　　　製造業の変遷●

A broad comparison of light and heavy manufacturing reveals that light manufacturing accounted for as much as 85 percent of total production until 1900. From then on, the share steadily declined, and after 100 years the relative positions of light and heavy manufacturing were reversed. The textile industry was the dynamic catalyst in Japan's industrialization. Textile output was less than 10 percent of the total in the 1870s but jumped above 25 percent in the 1890s and stayed close to 30 percent until World War II. Its continued expansion through the prewar period provided significant employment opportunities, especially for surplus female labor in agriculture. This temporary migration was a salient feature of prewar labor mobility. After World War II, the textile industry began to decline, and by 1990 it accounted for only 3.1 percent of the national labor force.

In heavy manufacturing, the iron and steel industry began to expand in the decade beginning in 1910, but government protection was necessary to shield it from international competition. After World War II, basic metals maintained a stable share of manufacturing output. On the other hand, the machine tool industry, after making relatively slow progress in the pre-World War II period, experienced a spectacular expansion in the three decades after 1945; its share of manufacturing output exceeded 40 percent by 1972. Japan is now one of the world's leading exporters of machinery. The chemical industry maintained a comparatively stable 10 percent share before World War II and rose to 20 percent after the war.

The most recent stage in the development of national economies has been called postindustrialism, which is marked by a decrease in the employment share of the secondary sector and a shift from production of goods to services. This "service revolution" brings the continuing growth of tertiary industries; it seems to have begun in Japan in the mid-1970s, when manufacturing employment started to decline. In 1990 the tertiary sector accounted for 60.8 percent of total output and employed 59.0 percent of the national labor force.

Relationship to the Foreign Trade Structure　　　外国貿易との関連●

The composition of a nation's exports and imports closely reflects its stage of industrialization. Japan's main exports were tea and raw silk when the country opened its doors to foreign powers in the 1860s, and raw silk remained the most important export item until 1929. In the 1930s, cotton replaced raw silk as the most important category of Japanese exports. In the early postwar period, more than half of exports were in light manufacturing, but with the expansion of heavy industries Japanese exports continued to shift to heavy manufactured goods, which came to account for more than 87 percent of the total value of exports by 1990.

Japan's imports consisted almost entirely of manufactured products in the early Meiji period. Industrialization in the subsequent decades enabled Japan to increase imports of crude materials. Thus, in the 1930s, Japan's imports consisted of light manufactures (12 percent), heavy manufactures (30 percent), foodstuffs (18 percent), raw materials (33 percent), and fuels (7 percent). Comparable figures in 1988–1990 were 16, 31, 14, 14, and 22 percent (others 3 percent), respectively.

The Tomioka Silk-Reeling Mill was opened by the Meiji government in 1872.

Agriculture (*nogyo*)   農業●

Prior to the Meiji Restoration of 1868, as much as 80 percent of the population of Japan was engaged in farming. Rice has been overwhelmingly dominant as the main crop. The emphasis has always been on improving productivity per unit of land area in rice and other plant crops. Highly labor-intensive farming methods were developed as a result of the limited acreage allotted to each farm household. These agricultural characteristics gave rise to farming practices and folk customs that in turn profoundly affected the nature of Japanese culture as a whole. Since the Meiji Restoration, industrialization and urbanization have had a significant impact on Japanese agriculture. The proportion of farmers to the total population, the proportion of cultivated acreage to the total area of the country, and the relative importance of agriculture in the total economy have all declined, while the importation of foodstuffs has increased. With these tendencies, many of the events and customs of Japanese rural life have begun to lose their importance.

History of Agriculture   農業の歴史●

Japanese agriculture began about 2,000 years ago with the cultivation of rice. Other crops cultivated in Japan since ancient times include wheat, barley, *awa* (Italian millet), *hie* (barnyard millet), soybeans, *azuki* beans, *daikon* (radish), and cucurbits.

The oldest farm tools were made of wood or stone. When technology from the continent brought the manufacture of iron tools, rapid progress in agriculture was made and much wasteland was brought under cultivation.

From the end of the Heian period (794–1185) influential families emerged in the provinces and accumulated wealth through agricultural production. Taking control of the government in the Kamakura period (1185–1333), they showed greater concern about agriculture than did former rulers and encouraged improvements. With the emergence of a large number of cities and towns in the Edo period (1600–1868), the percentage of the population not engaged in agriculture increased, and farmers were required to produce more and more. However, more than half of the rice produced was collected as land tax, and farmers were frequently left with insufficient amounts for their own needs. They made do with wheat, barley, or millet. Agricultural output was increased with endeavors in three major areas: reclaimed lands, fertilizers, and plant breeding.

During Japan's drive toward modernization after the Meiji Restoration, Western practices in agriculture were studied closely.

However, since the natural condition of the land in Japan is quite different from the West, mere transplantation of foreign technology often did not work well. Emphasis was shifted, therefore, back to rice as the main crop and to the development of intensive farming methods. Agriculture experimental stations were built by the state to conduct most of the plant breeding of important crops.

Agricultural Modernization   農業の近代化●

Of all the reform programs that followed World War II, the Land Reforms of 1946 were perhaps the most successful in bringing about basic and far-reaching changes in Japan. A sweeping redistribution of land largely eliminated tenancy by 1949 and resulted in about 90 percent of cultivated land being farmed by owners. Postwar food shortages, high prices, a black market in rice, and general inflation all worked to the advantage of Japan's farmers. In most cases they were able to pay off the debts on their new land with relative ease and to begin investing the capital that was needed for the rationalization of agriculture. The government aided farmers by establishing price support programs, especially for rice. It also gave strong support to agricultural technical schools, experimental stations, and extension programs. Agricultural Cooperative Associations enhanced these government initiatives by extending low-interest loans and developing group marketing at the village level. The end result was a relatively affluent farming population with the education, incentive, and access to capital needed to purchase the new crop strains and fertilizers to increase yields, as well as the machinery to ease labor demand.

Mechanized rice planting.

Japan began to experience labor shortages by the late 1950s after the beginning of rapid economic growth. The demand for labor in the urban-industrial centers resulted in a growing exodus of people from rural areas. A large part of the present agricultural labor force is over 45 years of age. Part-time farmers are numerous, and well over half the labor force is female.

It seems unlikely that Japanese agriculture could have succeeded without the spread of machines, chemicals, and other labor-saving devices. Virtually all land is now cultivated by machine. Traditional methods of farming are rapidly giving way to power cultivators, tractors, and other machines. Due to all of these factors Japan's total rice crop increased from about 9.5 million metric tons (10.5 million short tons) in 1950 to over 13 million metric tons (14.3 million short tons) in 1975. Per capita rice consumption, however, has declined, and the government is now concerned with problems of overproduction and surplus storage.

Farmers protest the liberalization of Japan's rice market (1993).

Economy

Farmers have been encouraged, and in some cases subsidized, to convert their rice fields to other crops. This governmental policy of production adjustment exacerbated the shortage caused by the extremely poor rice crop in 1993. Changes in Japanese eating habits have resulted in increased production of meat, dairy products, fruits, and vegetables.

Japan's traditional labor-intensive agriculture has been transformed into a highly mechanized and capital-intensive system in less than a generation and much of its new technology serves as a model for other developing Asian nations. Yet some problems and questions remain for the future. Production costs, especially for rice, are very high, and Japanese agriculture requires heavy subsidies. Most farms are too small in scale for maximum utilization of land and capital. When and how Japanese farms will reach a more efficient size remains a question for the future.

Fishing industry (gyogyo)   漁業●

The modern Japanese fishing industry operates boats worldwide, though the principal Japanese fisheries are in the North Pacific, including the Bering Sea and the Sea of Okhotsk. Industry production for 1992—9.3 million metric tons (10.2 million short tons) of fish and other seafood—was the second largest in the world after China's.

Traditional Japanese Fishing   伝統的漁法●

Although modern commercial fishing methods are responsible for the bulk of Japan's fish production, traditional techniques are still in use. Long "fish corrals," up to 1,000 meters (3,281 ft) in length and made of bamboo or net hurdles, are used in lakes, and weirs are built into streams to catch river fish. The Japanese catch octopuses in ceramic or concrete pots suspended from lines. Japanese divers collect abalone, oysters, and sea plants, as well as pearls. Cormorant fishing, an ancient technique for catching river fish, has survived to the present day as a tourist attraction.

The State of the Industry   漁業の現状●

In 1990 there were 185,000 fishing concerns in Japan, of which 67 percent were family-run operations using boats of less than 10 tons, and 24 percent were family-run aquiculture firms, including seaweed cultivation and fish and shellfish farming businesses. Large and medium-sized fishing companies made up the remaining 9 percent. All large Japanese fishing companies (except for setnet fisheries) are licensed by the national or prefectural governments.

Modern Commercial Fishing 現代の商業漁業●

The Japanese fishing industry has adopted a host of new fishing devices and techniques to reduce operating hours and compensate for the shrinking labor force. Highly automated fishing vessels are now common, and various types of ultrasonic devices that monitor the movement of fish around boats, warn of fish entering a net, and provide information on the condition of the net are widely used. Remote-control meters show the height of a net in relation to fish movements, allowing a boat to adjust its speed accordingly, and seine net depth meters are widely used to help boats place nets in the path of oncoming fish.

In 1992 the total catch from coastal fisheries was slightly under 2.0 million metric tons (2.2 million short tons). Although the coastal fishing catch has been dropping since the early 1980s, the shortfall has been made up by aquiculture harvests, which amounted to nearly 1.5 million metric tons (1.6 million short tons) of products in 1992. See also FISH AND SHELLFISH FARMING.

Offshore fishing within about 20 kilometers (12 mi) of shore is carried out by boats of more than 10 tons using purse seines, trawls, drift nets, and hook and line. Most fish caught offshore are migrating species, so catches vary widely from year to year. In 1992 the offshore catch totaled approximately 4.6 million metric tons (5.1 million short tons), of which sardines and mackerel accounted for over 70 percent.

Open-sea (pelagic) fishing, conducted with large factory ships equipped with freezing and processing equipment, also uses such methods as purse seining, trawling, and drift netting, along with longline angling. Annual catches were large throughout the late 1960s and early 1970s.

Around the mid-1970s, however, the industry initiated self-imposed restrictions on the size of open-sea catches in anticipation of changes in international fishing zones. In 1976 the United States adopted a 200-mile fishery zone, as did Canada, the Soviet Union, and various

Japan's Seafood Production
漁業部門別生産高 (in thousands of metric tons)

Type of production	1960	1965	1970	1975	1980	1985	1990	1992
Open-sea fishing	1,410	1,733	3,429	3,168	2,167	2,111	1,496	1,209
Offshore fishing	2,515	2,788	3,279	4,469	5,705	6,498	6,081	4,619
Coastal fishing	1,893	1,861	1,889	1,935	2,037	2,268	1,992	1,983
Marine aquiculture	285	380	549	773	992	1,088	1,273	1,291
Inland fishing and aquiculture	90	146	168	199	221	206	209	188
Total	6,193	6,908	9,315	10,545	11,122	12,171	11,052	9,290

Source: Ministry of Agriculture, Forestry, and Fisheries.

Economy

European countries. This put many fishing grounds off limits to Japanese boats. The government launched a long-term program to increase the amount of fish and sea life in Japan's own 200-mile fishing zone, but in the meantime increasing demand for fish, combined with shrinking catches, boosted Japan's imports of marine products. By 1992 Japan's open-sea catch had fallen to 1.2 million metric tons (1.3 million short tons), and imports of marine products had soared to 3 million metric tons (3.3 million short tons), making Japan the world's leading importer of marine products.

Fish and shellfish farming (*yoshoku*; *saibai gyogyo*)　養殖と栽培漁業●

The artificial cultivation of marine products (also called aquiculture) plays an important role in the Japanese fishing industry. Japan has long been engaged in the farming of freshwater fish, *nori* (a type of seaweed), and oysters. In recent years the farming of such choice fish as yellowtail, red sea bream, and prawns has proliferated. In addition, a large number of fish and shellfish farming centers have been established along Japan's shores, where selected species of fish and shellfish are artificially bred and raised to a certain size, then released to the sea to grow to sizes fit for harvesting.

Freshwater Fish Culture　　　　　　　　　　　　　　淡水養殖●

The climate in Japan ranges from near subarctic to semitropical, and intensive farming of a variety of species of both cold and warm water fish has developed through the use of sophisticated fish culture techniques.

Species that have been successfully farmed in Japan include tilapia. Experimental farming of a total of eight strains of tilapia was attempted, and the results showed that *T. nirotica* was best suited to the Japanese climate.

Saltwater Fish Culture　　　　　　　　　　　　　　海水養殖●

Nori and oyster farming are said to have started in Japan about 300 years ago. However, it was only in 1957 that saltwater fish (yellowtail) farming was started in earnest. Saltwater farming is also applied to shrimp, lobsters, prawns, octopuses, oysters, scallops, and seaweed (nori, *wakame*, and kelp).

Methods of Culture　　　　　　　　　　　　　　　養殖の方法●

Methods of culture are divided into lake, river, pond, paddyfield, reservoir, canal, and shallow saltwater cultures. Methods are also classified by type of facility as follows: fish preserve, net-enclosure, embankment, pond, reservoir, and raft cultures.

Typically, seeds are bred artificially and raised in a controlled environment to commercial sizes, then shipped to the farms. The method in which artificially bred seeds are raised to egg-bearing sizes and then harvested after bearing the eggs is called full-cycle culture.

In the case of freshwater fish, composite feed is used, while fish meat is used for feeding saltwater fish (except sea bream). Ingredients for composite feed are adjusted to the nutrition requirements of different species. Such abundant and inexpensive fish as sardines, mackerel, and saury pike are used as feed, either fresh or frozen. Oxygen is supplied by exchanging the water in the fish farm, so it is necessary to maintain the fish population at a level compatible with the water-exchanging capacity of the farm.

Fish Farming   栽培漁業●

Fish farming is carried out through public projects of the central and prefectural governments. The term "fish farming" refers to an operation in which fish seeds are produced in large quantity, released in a protected sea environment for growth, and harvested when grown to a commercial size. Fish and shellfish now being raised, including those in the experimental stage, cover about 100 species, including yellowtail, harvest fish, flounder, horse mackerel, hardtail, Spanish mackerel, grouper, rockfish, rock trout, black porgy, flatfish, king crab, northern sea shrimp, and cuttlefish.

Forestry (*ringyo*)   林業●

About 70 percent of Japan's total area is wooded. Forests play a particularly important role in land conservation in Japan, as steep mountain ranges run along the midline of the islands from north to south and the rivers are short and torrential. Japan is a great consumer of wood as well as the world's greatest importer of logs and wood chips (accounting for about 20 percent of the world's wood trade). It is also notable for its exceptionally high proportion of planted forests, which occupy about 40 percent of the nation's total forest area.

Forest Conditions in Japan   日本の森林●

A great variety of trees grow in Japan because of the marked temperature differences from north to south and a high level of humidity brought about by warm ocean currents. Trees can be classified as evergreen broad-leaved types such as camellias and *kusunoki* (camphor tree), deciduous broad-leaved types such as *buna* (beech) and *tochinoki*

(Japanese horse chestnut), and conifers such as *sugi* (cedar) and *hinoki* (cypress). Of the total forest area of about 24.7 million hectares (61.0 million acres), about 9.9 million hectares (24.5 million acres) support planted forests consisting mainly of cedar, cypress, and pines.

Forestry Operations 森林の運営●

In the 18th century, exploitive forestry aiming at simply gathering wood from natural forests was replaced by sustained-yield forestry with artificial planting and cultivation of trees. After the Meiji Restoration of 1868 forestland was divided into privately owned and government-owned areas. National forests account for about 7.3 million hectares (18.0 million acres) of the total wooded area of Japan, private forests for 14.0 million hectares (34.6 million acres), and forests owned by local governments for the remainder. Private forests occupy 56 percent of Japan's entire forest area. The continued migration of young farm workers to urban areas and factories has greatly reduced the number of forestry workers.

History of Wood Utilization 木材利用の歴史●

Wood has been used for construction and fuel in Japan since early times, but the use of lumber for construction increased rapidly starting in the 8th century as wooden palaces and temples such as Todaiji and Toji were built. The city of Kyoto became Japan's center of wood consumption.

The flourishing of urban culture in the Edo period (1600–1868) accelerated an increasing demand for wood products for furniture, building, and fuel. Starting in the late 18th century, regional lumber markets developed along the lower reaches of the large rivers; these markets continued to grow in the 19th century. With the modernization of the Japanese economy following the Meiji Restoration, the demand for wood grew rapidly. Following the Tokyo Earthquake of 1923, imports, particularly from the United States, became an important factor in Japan's wood supply.

After World War II, the need for building materials escalated, as did the demand for such wood products as paper pulp and plywood. However, domestic production was on the decline. In recent years emphasis has been increasingly placed on forests as places of recreation and as natural environments in need of conservation. Thus Japan has had to rely more and more on outside sources of wood. In 1992 Japan's total wood consumption was 108 million cubic meters (3.8 billion cu ft), of which only 25 percent was domestically produced. Lumber made up 47 percent of the total, pulp and wood chips 39 percent, and plywood 13 percent.

Iron and steel industry (*tekkogyo*)

鉄鋼業●

Modern iron-making techniques and steel production began in Japan in 1901 with the opening of the state-owned Yawata Iron and Steel Works, an integrated steel plant. Later, private steel makers such as Kobe Steel, Ltd, and a branch factory of Kawasaki Shipyard Co began production, but they used separate pig-iron and steel production operations rather than integrated techniques. The worldwide economic crisis in 1929 spurred debate in Japan over amalgamation of public and private steel companies as a means of increasing the international competitiveness of the industry. In 1933 the Nippon Steel Co Law was passed, and in 1934 state-owned Yawata was combined with six private companies to form Nippon Steel. The goal was to expand the use of integrated production techniques, but most of the private steel makers did not participate. Japan's maximum yearly production of crude steel prior to the end of World War II was 7.7 million tons in 1943; this was 9.5 percent of US production for the same year.

Postwar Growth

第二次世界大戦後の成長●

Following the war, Nippon Steel was broken up into Yawata Steel and Fuji Steel, and intense competition developed within the industry. Supported by rapid economic growth, production facilities were expanded, and Japan became the world's largest steel-exporting nation.

A new Nippon Steel was created in 1970 through the merger of Yawata Steel and Fuji Steel, and today the five major Japanese steel producers are Nippon Steel Corporation, Kawasaki Steel Corporation, NKK Corporation, Sumitomo Metal Industries, Ltd, and Kobe Steel. Although Nippon Steel is a descendant of the government-owned Yawata Iron and Steel Works, the other four companies have been private steel makers since their inceptions. The product breakdown for 1993 production was pig iron, 73 million tons; crude steel, 97.1 million tons; carbon steel products, 91.4 million tons; alloy steel products, 18.1 million tons; and ferro-alloy, 0.8 million tons.

The Japanese steel industry is totally dependent on imports of iron ore and coal, but it has maintained its interna-

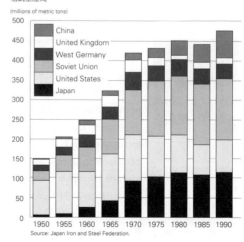

Crude Steel Production
粗鋼生産高
(millions of metric tons)

China
United Kingdom
West Germany
Soviet Union
United States
Japan

Source: Japan Iron and Steel Federation.

tional competitiveness through a high-quality labor force and the implementation of new production facilities and technology. In 1993 Nippon Steel was the largest producer of crude steel in the world.

Problems and Prospects 問題点と展望●

Although Japan remains a key steel-exporting country, voluntary export restrictions to the United States (begun in 1969), the rise in value of the yen, the increase in domestic demand, and the increase in steel production by China and South Korea have led to decreases in the quantity and monetary value of Japan's steel exports. In response to this trend many of the steel companies are restructuring through diversification into such new businesses as electronics, biotechnology, and new-materials development.

Automotive industry (*jidosha sangyo*) 自動車産業●

The Japanese automotive industry got its start in 1902 with the production of a small, low-power (12-hp) trial vehicle by two independent makers. Trial models by many other makers followed, but domestic makes, produced in small quantity, could not compete with the imported cars (mostly from the United States) that flooded Japan just after the Tokyo Earthquake of 1923. Ford and General Motors, with their superior production techniques, marketing, and service systems, established subsidiary companies in Japan in 1925–26 and started assembling trucks and passenger cars from imported parts. Soon after, foreign automobiles completely took over the Japanese market.

Before and during World War II, the Japanese automotive industry, under government direction, concentrated on producing trucks for the military. Such early manufacturers as Nissan Motor Co, Ltd; Toyota Motor Corporation; and later the forerunner of Isuzu Motors, Ltd, were licensed under the Automotive Manufacturing Industries Law (Jidosha Seizo Jigyo Ho) of 1935. This act was aimed at protecting and promoting domestic automobile production by providing tax breaks for domestic manufacturers and by imposing restrictions on (and in 1940 eliminating altogether) the activities of foreign automobile makers. Mitsubishi Heavy Industries, Ltd, and Hino Motors, Ltd, were also involved in wartime production. After the war, Occupation authorities allowed Japanese manufacturers to continue some production, mostly of trucks, but total production in 1946 was only 20,000 vehicles. Passenger car production began again in 1952, with most of the demand for passenger cars coming from the taxi business. From around this time, the government, led by

Nissan North America, Inc; facilities located in Smyrna, Tennessee.

the Ministry of International Trade and Industry (MITI), began its support and protection of the domestic auto industry.

After 1960 the domestic production of passenger cars increased at an unprecedented rate. Companies that began manufacturing passenger cars around this time included the Toyo Kogyo Co, Ltd (now Mazda Motor Corporation); Fuji Heavy Industries, Ltd; Daihatsu Motor Co, Ltd; and Honda Motor Co, Ltd. Many large new factories were built, the parts industry was integrated and concentrated (facilitating the development of an organized subcontracting system), and nationwide sales networks were strengthened.

Around 1968 Toyota and Nissan increased their exports of automobiles and light trucks. By 1975 they were joined by Honda and other Japanese manufacturers. In the wake of the oil crisis of the 1970s, demand in the American automobile market shifted from the large, high-powered, gas-guzzling models to the smaller, more fuel-efficient makes for which Japanese manufacturers were known, bringing their share of the North American automobile market to 23 percent by the late 1970s. Pressure from American domestic manufacturers led to voluntary export restrictions on Japanese auto manufacturers (1981–1994). After 1985, increasing US-Japan trade friction and a drop in export profits led more and more Japanese auto manufacturers to set up production plants in Canada and the United States. As of March 1993, eight Japanese auto companies had established 11 plants (3 of which are joint ventures) in North America, with total annual output approaching 1.83 million vehicles; in Europe, Japan's second largest automotive export market, Japanese automobile assembly plants had also started production (in the United Kingdom); and in Southeast Asia, Japanese manufacturers were either cooperating with domestic automobile producers or setting up multinational diversified assembly operations. Japanese parts suppliers followed the major auto manufacturers abroad, expanding their overseas production capacity and building up technology transfer and cooperation networks. In 1993 the Japanese automobile industry produced 11.2 million vehicles, of which 5 million were exported.

Precision machinery industry (*seimitsu kikai sangyo*)　精密機械産業●

Japan's precision machinery industry is best known for its watches and cameras, but it also produces precision instruments, measuring equipment, medical equipment, sewing machines, and optical equipment. Japan's experience in producing *wadokei* (classic Japanese-style clocks), which dates back to the 17th century, provided a springboard for the development of the modern chronometer industry. Japan started to produce Western-style watches and clocks in the early Meiji period (1868–1912), and by the 1920s exports had exceeded imports.

Japanese cameras were of very poor quality until after World War II. By the 1950s, however, manufacturers had raised the quality of their products to world standards, dramatically expanded production, and carved out a considerable share of the international market. Japan now ranks first in the world in production of cameras and is second only to Hong Kong in timepieces. As the two industries depend heavily on exports, they have been hurt by the recent appreciation of the yen. They are also facing growing competition from the newly industrializing economies (NIEs). However, in many cases Japan exports crucial high-technology parts to producers in the NIEs for final assembly with locally produced parts. As Japan's camera production is not likely to increase in the future, camera manufacturers are diversifying into the production of office automation equipment such as copying machines and facsimile machines, as well as medical equipment.

Discount camera shop in Tokyo.

Computer industry (kompyuta sangyo)   コンピュータ産業●

Japan has the second largest data-processing industry in the world after that of the United States, with large-scale subsectors producing mainframe computers, minicomputers, personal computers, peripheral equipment, and software. Total domestic production in 1991 reached ¥6.0 trillion (US $44.5 billion) , and exports amounted to ¥2 .7 trillion (US $20.0 billion) . In 1992 the top five computer makers in Japan were Fujitsu, NEC, IBM Japan, Hitachi, and Toshiba.

Japan's computer market is the second largest in the world after the United States. Overall, the hardware market consists of 50 percent mainframes, 25 percent minicomputers (including workstations), and 25 percent personal computers. Partly as a result of the downsizing trend among corporate users, mainframe demand has fallen steadily since the mid 1980s. In contrast, during the same period workstation and personal computer demand has grown at an average of over 20 percent a year. In 1991 over 2.3 million personal computers were produced, and the market—dominated by NEC's 50 percent share—was valued at ¥1.4 trillion (US $10.4 billion).

History   歴史●

Although Osaka University launched Japan's first computer development program in 1947, the first electronic digital computer was not constructed until 1956, 10 years after ENIAC, the first electronic computer, was developed in the United States. Following the first exports of US computers to Japan in 1954, the Ministry of International Trade and Industry (MITI) organized the Research Committee on the Computer to coordinate computer industry development, but computers did not attain urgent priority in Japanese industrial policy until the mid-1960s.

In 1960 IBM was granted permission to manufacture in Japan in return for licensing basic patents to all interested Japanese manufacturers; 13 Japanese companies immediately entered cross-licensing agreements with IBM. By 1964 RCA, TRW, Honeywell, General Electric, and Sperry Rand had all entered technical assistance agreements with Japanese makers.

The Japanese government's vigorous promotion of the computer industry dates from 1964. In that year IBM's introduction of its System 360 and its success at the Tokyo Olympic Games graphically demonstrated to Japanese political and business circles the strategic potential of computers. Interest was also stimulated by the purchase of the largest French computer manufacturer by the US firm General Electric. Computers came to be seen in Japan as a strategic industry whose fate held profound implications for Japan's future.

To achieve rapid advancement in domestic computer technologies, MITI launched several national priority projects. The FONTAC project (1962–1964), undertaken by Fujitsu, Oki, and NEC, was the first prototype manufacturing project of a general-purpose large-scale computer system in Japan. Another project, aimed at prototype manufacture of a super-high-performance computer system, was undertaken from 1966 to 1972. This was the result of the Electronics Industry Deliberation Council Report of 1966, prepared under the aegis of MITI. As a result of the commercial agreements with US firms and the success of these vigorously coordinated domestic projects, the Japanese computer industry made rapid strides in the late 1960s. Epitomizing the new priority given to computers, government research and development (R&D) subsidies by 1967 were four times 1960 levels.

In the early 1970s, prior to liberalizing the Japanese computer market, MITI organized the six mainframe makers into three specialized R&D groups with the aim of developing a computer to match IBM's 370 series; the groups were provided with government R&D subsidies amounting to 50 percent (US $195.9 million) of the expenses incurred. When IBM brought out its fourth-generation computer utilizing VLSI (very large scale integration) technology, MITI responded by organizing another "national project": two new cooperative research groups consisting of Fujitsu, Hitachi, and Mitsubishi Electric in one group, and NEC and Toshiba in the other. The project was so successful that by the late 1970s Fujitsu and Hitachi were selling computers to their US and European rivals. By the early 1980s the Japanese computer industry had in many respects closed the 10-year gap in hardware sophistication that had existed in relation to IBM in the 1950s, although its software remained inferior in most applications. IBM was in Japan by the early 1990s no more than one among several major manufacturers; in 1990 it had to yield its leading position in the mainframe market to Fujitsu.

Structure of the Industry   産業の構造●

In contrast to US and European patterns, there are virtually no specialized major computer makers in Japan. Except for Fujitsu, there is not a single major Japanese computer maker for which computers provide over 35 percent of total sales. Three of the six major producers, Fujitsu, NEC, and Oki, are telecommunications firms that diversified into computers. The other three, Hitachi, Mitsubishi Electric, and Toshiba, are general electronics firms that diversified into computers in the early 1960s.

For structural reasons, it has been the bureaucracy, especially MITI, that has been the constant initiator of policy on computers, rather than individual firms. MITI has frequently taken the initiative at key stages in the development of the computer industry by providing strategic direction and by organizing and subsidizing industry research groups.

The character of Japanese government R&D assistance to computers has been somewhat different from that of the United States. US manufacturers receive aid in connection with projects designed primarily for governmental end-use, especially in the defense and aerospace sectors. Japanese makers receive aid, often in the form of direct subsidies, for commercial R&D, although the amounts are relatively modest by international standards.

A further crucial factor greatly contributed to the development and competitiveness of the Japanese computer industry. During the so-called calculator war that began in the mid-1960s, a furiously competitive process of cost cutting and progressive miniaturization brought down the price of calculators from ¥400,000 (US $1,100) in the mid-1960s to a mere ¥1,000 (US $4) in the 1980s, 1/400th of their original price. In the same 20-year period calculators were reduced from the size of television sets to that of credit cards. It was this ferocious competition among the leading manufacturers that enabled them to develop the kind of high-quality, low-cost mass-production manufacturing techniques that served them so well when they moved into the computer market.

Construction industry (*kensetsugyo*)   建設業●

Japan has the world's largest construction market, with 1993 domestic construction investment estimated at ¥90 trillion (US $809 billion), or 19 percent of the gross national product. This construction investment was 40 percent civil engineering works and 60 percent (building) construction works. Nationally there are some 530,000 construction companies, and the approximately 6.4 million construction industry workers represented 9.6 percent of all workers in 1993.

In 1992 overseas construction orders were ¥853 billion (US $6.7 billion). In the past most overseas orders came from the industrialized countries, primarily the United States, but by the beginning of the 1990s more than half were from Asia. Two factors behind the strong growth in Asian orders are the growing demand from Japanese companies building factories in Asia and the increase, beginning in the 1980s, in Japanese overseas development assistance to the region. Foreign construction companies have difficulty in breaking into the Japanese domestic market, but extended negotiations have produced some results: by September 1993, 75 foreign companies had received construction licenses.

Energy Sources

Natural resources (*tennen shigen*) 天然資源●

Japan's industrial complex is built on one of the world's weakest resource bases. Although in variety Japan's resources are surprisingly rich, their amount, availability, and quality limit domestic production to a fraction of the country's needs.

The degree of Japan's dependence on imported raw materials is illustrated by the following import figures from 1989: petroleum, 99.7 percent; coal, 91.4 percent; bauxite, 100 percent; nickel, 100 percent; iron ore, 99.8 percent; copper, 98.4 percent; and lead, 90.0 percent. Japan also relies on outside sources for 100 percent of its raw cotton, wool, and rubber, as well as large and growing amounts of forest products, agricultural commodities, and seafood. Japan's exceptionally high rate of economic and industrial growth since the 1960s has resulted in ever greater reliance on foreign sources.

Coal 石炭●

Japan's coal reserves were estimated at about 7 billion metric tons (7.7 billion short tons) in 1990, but the largest fields are located at opposite ends of the country in Hokkaido and Kyushu, adding transportation fees to relatively high production costs.

Japanese coal is generally low-grade bituminous of inferior heating value. High-grade coking coal supplies are negligible, so virtually all of the nation's needs must be imported. Coal seams are generally deep below the surface, steeply inclined, and plagued by inflammable gases, all of which make mechanization difficult. High production costs, bitter labor-management strife, dangerous operations, and competition from other energy sources have led to a sharp drop in output and in the number of mines and miners. Production in the 1950s and 1960s averaged 50 to 55 million metric tons (55 to 60.5 million short tons) annually; by 1990 it had dropped to 8.3 million metric tons (9.1 million short tons). Coal-mining labor has similarly declined from a force of roughly 244,000 in 1960 to about 5,000 in 1990, and the number of operating mines has dropped from 682 to 26. Despite greatly improved productivity, the domestic coal industry has a doubtful future, notwithstanding government subsidies.

Miners hold a ceremony following the closing of the Mitsui Mining Co, Ltd, coal mine at Ashibetsu in Hokkaido (1992).

Petroleum and Natural Gas 石油と天然ガス●

Japan's petroleum-refining industry is the third largest in the world, but virtually all crude oil must be imported from China, Indonesia, and the Middle East. A trickle of domestic oil comes from the Niigata fields along with smaller fields scattered through northern

Honshu and Hokkaido.

Small natural gas fields and wells are also scattered, with the largest concentrations in Hokkaido, northern Honshu, and Chiba Prefecture. But as with coal, most of Japan's increased demand for petroleum and liquefied gas will have to be met by foreign sources, often through joint development projects with countries having surplus energy resources.

Hydroelectric Power   水力発電●

Rugged terrain, abundant precipitation, and fast-flowing streams have made it possible for Japan to develop one of the world's largest hydroelectric industries. Numerous small hydroelectric plants once produced the largest share of Japan's electricity, but in 1991 they accounted for only a little over 20 percent.

Nuclear Power
and Alternative Energy Sources   原子力発電と代替エネルギー●

Japan is among the world leaders in the development of nuclear power plants. Despite growing concern and an increasingly vigorous anti-nuclear-energy movement, the government has pressed ahead with its nuclear power program. By 1993, 48 atomic reactors had been built, supplying 31.2 percent of its total electrical power output through nuclear generation. Japanese electrical power producers have signed agreements with suppliers in Canada, the United Kingdom, Australia, and Niger to secure reserves of unprocessed uranium amounting to a total of 200,000 metric tons (220,000 short tons).

Alternative sources account for only a small fraction of the nation's energy supply, but research and development proceed in such areas as solar and geothermal power, gasification and liquefaction of coal, and the separation of hydrogen from seawater.

Metal and Minerals   金属と鉱物●

Japan's metal resources have become almost totally inadequate for such a large industrial complex. In 1991 Japan ranked third in steel production, and it also had the world's third largest aluminum industry. The small size of Japan's deposits of metal ores, coupled with the scale of production for both export and domestic consumption, makes it impossible to reduce the nation's dependence on overseas supplies.

In the steel industry, for example, Japan imported 99.8 percent of its iron ore requirements in 1989, mainly from Australia and Brazil; it also imports 99.5 percent of the coking coal essential to steel production.

Similarly, though more than 3 million metric tons (3.3 million short tons) of aluminum is produced annually in Japan, production is totally dependent on imported bauxite, mainly from Australia. Japan in 1989 imported 98.4 percent of the materials used in making copper and 82.2 percent of those used by the zinc industry. Domestic supplies of lead meet only 10.0 percent of the demand. In other minerals, Japan is virtually wholly dependent on foreign sources.

Wood and Pulp　　　　　　　　　　　　　　　木材とパルプ●

Even though Japan's forests cover about 60 percent of the land, lumber supplies have grown tight, forcing Japan to look to outside sources for over half of its lumber supply. Nor are domestic supplies adequate for one of the world's largest producers of pulp, paper, and other wood products; pulp imports now constitute roughly 20 percent of consumption.

With the growth of tourism, Japan's forest lands have become valuable as parks. But heavy demand has led to overcutting. Any further expansion of domestic wood and pulp production would result in heavy environmental damage to Japan.

Future Outlook　　　　　　　　　　　　　　　将来の展望●

Without continued access to foreign resources, Japan has no chance for economic survival. Virtually all its natural resources are of such small quantities as to make it impossible to expand production without quickly exhausting them. In addition, Japan also faces the challenges of increasing international competition for resources and rising global concern over ecological issues, factors that are likely to have a significant impact on Japan's resource policies in the years to come.

Energy sources (*enerugi shigen*)　　　　　　エネルギー資源●

Japan's energy options are seriously limited by its lack of domestic energy sources coupled with the huge energy demands of its industries. Japan's dependence on imports for its energy supply rose from 43.4 percent in 1960 to 84.4 percent in 1970 and then stabilized at about 91 percent in the 1980s.

Oil　　　　　　　　　　　　　　　　　　　　石油●

From 1965 to 1974 the rapid growth of the Japanese economy led to a 10.2 percent average annual increase in energy demand, more than twice the world average of 4.8 percent. During the same period there was a shift from coal to oil as an energy source because of the depletion of domestic coal mines and the relative efficiency of oil; as a result the increased energy demand had to be met almost entirely by imported oil.

The fourfold increase in oil prices brought on by the oil crisis of

1973 led to profound changes in Japanese energy policy. In 1973 Japan was importing 99 percent of its crude oil, and the imported oil represented 77 percent of the total energy supply. Eighty-five percent of the imported oil originated in the Middle East and northern Africa. Because of its overdependence on imported oil, the impact of the "oil shock," as it was commonly called, was felt even more strongly in Japan than in many other countries. It affected all sectors of the economy, causing aggravated inflation, prolonged recession, rising unemployment, and business failures. Facing the threat of disruption in the oil supply, the government announced an oil emergency policy in November 1973 aimed at reducing dependence on oil, increasing geographical diversification of oil sources, and conserving energy. At the same time a new policy more sympathetic toward Arab countries was also announced, with a view to improving Japan's relationship with key oil-producing nations.

Although Japan remains heavily dependent on imported oil, as a result of conservation efforts and development of alternative energy sources oil's share of the country's total energy supply dropped to 58.3 percent by 1990.

This poster from the time of the 1973 oil crisis urges people to conserve oil.

Coal 石炭●

Coal provided 16.6 percent of Japan's energy in 1990. Coal mining is a declining industry in Japan, and, even with maximum effort and government support, domestic production can at best be maintained at the 1990 level of some 8 million metric tons (8.8 million short tons) per year, owing to depletion of resources, higher costs, and the scarcity of skilled mine workers. Thus, any increase in demand must be met by imports, which stood at some 105 million metric tons (115.5 million short tons) in 1990.

Natural Gas 天然ガス●

The share of natural gas in Japan's total energy supply was 10.1 percent in 1990. The domestic production of natural gas, like that of oil, is very limited, and if natural gas is to play a significant role in the future as an alternative energy source it will have to be in the form of imports of liquefied natural gas (LNG). In 1990 Japan imported 36 million metric tons (40 million short tons) of LNG, more than double LNG imports for 1980. Liquefied gas has various advantages as an energy source, including cleanness and convenience. Its areas of production are more evenly distributed around the world than is the case with oil.

Nuclear Energy 原子力エネルギー●

In Japan, because of its lack of domestic energy resources, nuclear energy has received the highest priority in the search for alternatives to oil.

Economy

Japan's first nuclear power plant was built in 1963. As in other countries, the antinuclear movement, with its concerns over the location, safety, and waste products of nuclear power plants, has many supporters in Japan.

Other Energy Sources and Conservation   その他のエネルギー源と資源保護●

Hydroelectric power accounted for 4.2 percent of the total energy supply in 1990. New energy sources such as geothermal energy, solar power, and wind hold promise for the future, but, while they may be technically feasible and research is proceeding, they are not yet economically practical. These new energy sources provided only 1.4 percent of the total power supply in 1990.

Energy conservation constitutes one of the pillars of Japan's energy policy and many efforts are being made to increase efficiency in energy use. However, great conservation efforts have already been made in industry, which is the major energy-consuming sector in Japan, and most industries will find it extremely difficult to raise efficiency further. Per capita energy consumption in Japan in 1991 was at the relatively low level of about 3.5 metric tons (3.9 short tons) oil equivalent, as against 7.7 metric tons (8.5 short tons) oil equivalent in the United States, which alone indicates that there is limited potential for major benefits from conservation in the future.

Electric power (*denryoku*)   電力●

Electric power was introduced to Japan in the form of thermal power in 1887; hydroelectric power followed in 1890. From 1887 to 1911, thermal power predominated. Most hydroelectric power plants were located far from cities, and electricity could be transmitted only over short distances, making hydroelectric power unsuitable for city use. Hydroelectric power became more important than thermal power after 1912 and continued to predominate during an almost 50-year period that spanned the two world wars. In the 1920s, electric utilities began selling surplus electricity inexpensively, encouraging the expansion of electrochemical and other industries.

The Kurobe Dam in Toyama Prefecture is the highest in Japan and the fifth largest in the world.

During the reconstruction period that followed World War II, development of new power generating sites, both thermal and hydroelectric, rapidly increased. Large dam power plants began to be used in the development of hydroelectric power. In spite of these innovations, thermal power generating facilities took on more importance because construction of hydroelectric generating facilities required a good deal of time and capital.

After 1960, a period of high economic growth in Japan, iron and steel, chemical, machinery, and other heavy industries expanded rapidly. With the resulting rise in individual incomes, electric appliances became common household items and demand for electricity rose accordingly. Japan's first nuclear power plant for commercial use began operating in July 1966, and after the 1973 oil shock there was an upsurge in the development of nuclear power (see NUCLEAR POWER PLANTS).

In 1993 total power generated for commercial use amounted to 795.7 billion kilowatt hours, of which thermal power plants (oil, LNG, and coal) supplied 56.3 percent; nuclear power plants, 31.2 percent; hydroelectric power plants, 12.3 percent; and alternative energy sources such as geothermal power, 0.2 percent.

In Japan maximum transmission voltage has been 500 kilovolts since 1974 because of the increase in the number of nuclear and other generating facilities built far from cities. Increasingly, safer underground transmission lines have replaced overhead power lines close to urban areas.

Nuclear power plants (*genshiryoku hatsudensho*)　原子力発電所●

As of December 1993 there were 17 commercial nuclear power plants operating in Japan, with a total of 25 boiling water reactors, 22 pressurized water reactors, and 1 advanced thermal reactor; total electrical capacity was 38.5 million kilowatts. In 1993 Japan was the world's fourth largest producer of nuclear power with 248.2 billion kilowatt-hours produced (31.2 percent of the nation's total output).

Although Japan has depended on Britain, the United States, and France for all of the enriched uranium used as fuel, in 1991 Japan Nuclear Fuel Industries, Inc, completed construction of Japan's first nuclear fuel plant in the village of Rokkasho, Aomori Prefecture. The plant began operations in 1992, meeting a portion of Japan's demand for enriched uranium.

Mihama nuclear power plant in Fukui Prefecture.

Following the catastrophe at the Chernobyl nuclear power plant in the Soviet Union, many Japanese expressed concern over the safety of such facilities. Although the Japanese government revised its safety inspection standards, it made no policy changes concerning the nuclear generation of electricity. It is estimated that by the year 2030 the demand for electricity will require the expansion of nuclear power output to 137 million kilowatts.

Omote Sando at Harajuku, Tokyo. Lined with cafes and boutiques, this avenue forms the main approach to Meiji Shrine.

Social Environment

Social welfare (*shakai fukushi*)　　　　　　社会福祉●

Social welfare in Japan is designed to guarantee a minimum standard of living and to protect citizens from certain types of social and economic risk. Japan's social welfare system consists of four major components: public assistance, social insurance, social welfare services, and public health maintenance. In 1994 social welfare–related expenses accounted for 18.4 percent of the national budget.

Development of Social Welfare　　　　　　社会福祉の発達●

Modern social welfare in Japan began in the early Meiji period (1868–1912), when a system of disability and retirement allowances for military personnel and public officials was instituted. Aid for the general work force did not come until some years later. The Poor Relief Regulation of 1874, a government reaction to popular unrest, provided limited support to workers, but it was not until the passage of the Health Insurance Law of 1922 (implemented in 1927) that Japan had its first true social welfare legislation for workers. In 1938 the National Health Insurance system was established to cover those excluded by the 1922 law. Though these steps were important in the development of social welfare in Japan, they were largely conciliatory gestures by the government to appease labor during a period of social unrest caused by rapid industrialization and modernization.

Post-World War II Reforms　　　　　　第二次世界大戦後の改革●

After World War II, the Allied Occupation established new legal and philosophical bases for social welfare in Japan and extensively reformed the administration of the existing welfare system. The philosophy of this time is set forth in the Constitution of Japan, which states that "All people shall have the right to maintain the minimum standards of wholesome and cultured living", and is further codified in the Livelihood Protection Law of 1946. Although the initial social welfare programs established were small-scale, the postwar legal reforms clearly established the responsibility of the government to promote and improve social welfare. Through subsequent legislation, mainly in the 1950s and 1960s, and through a series of reforms in the 1980s, Japan has established a comprehensive welfare system that is comparable in most respects to systems in other advanced countries.

Categories of Social Welfare　　　　　　社会福祉の種類●

Programs designed to assure a minimum level of security to those who are unable to generate subsistence-level income are classed as public assistance. In recent years the number of people receiving public assistance has decreased steadily, with only 0.8 percent of the population receiving such assistance in 1990.

Social insurance, the second component of Japan's system of social welfare, covers four main areas: health and medical insurance, public pensions, unemployment insurance, and workers' compensation. All citizens are entitled to coverage under one of Japan's basic health insurance programs, depending on employment status or place of residence. The main program, based on the Health Insurance Law of 1922, automatically covers all employees in firms with more than five workers. The National Health Insurance program covers many of the remaining noninsured, including the self-employed, the elderly, and foreign residents. Seamen, public officials, and schoolteachers are covered by separate insurance programs. Health insurance is financed by contributions from employers and employees, as well as by subsidies from the national treasury. See also MEDICAL AND HEALTH INSURANCE.

Since 1961 all Japanese of working age have been legally required to be covered by one of the public pension programs, all of which provide old-age, disability, and survivor benefits. In 1986 public pensions were organized into a two-tiered system. At one level, the national pension provides mandatory basic pensions for all citizens. Aside from this basic pension, a second level of support that includes the employees' pension insurance program and mutual aid association pensions provides additional coverage and benefits for private- and public-sector employees. See also PENSIONS.

Legislation protecting workers against unemployment began when the government passed the Employment Security Law of 1947, which set up a network of government-operated employment offices. In the same year the Unemployment Insurance Law was passed, providing for benefits for those unemployed persons actively seeking employment. Programs are funded jointly by employees and employers.

Current workers' compensation programs, based on the Factory Law of 1911 and two postwar laws, the Labor Standards Law and the Workers' Compensation Law, assign liability to employers to provide compensation for workers in the event of injury or death resulting from work-related accidents.

Social welfare services, the third main component of the Japanese welfare system, are of three major types: services for the handicapped, services for the aged, and services for children, which include aid to fatherless families. Government programs for the handicapped include pensions, institutional care, rehabilitation programs, special education, and cash subsidies. Emphasis is given to services for the handicapped outside of institutional settings, including medical counseling and "home helper" programs. Programs for vocational guidance and employment opportunities are offered by the Ministry of Labor.

Japan's rapidly aging population has made welfare services for the elderly a pressing social problem. The Old-Age Welfare Law of 1963 introduced nursing homes, free annual health examinations, a system of home helpers, and local welfare centers for the aged. In 1973 the government introduced free medical care for all persons 70 years or older. However, the 1983 Law Concerning Health and Medical Services for the Aged reintroduced the requirement that certain health-care fees be paid by the individual.

Welfare services are also offered to needy families with children. The Child Welfare Law of 1947 established the government's responsibility to protect children in need. The 1964 Law for the Welfare of Mothers, Children, and Widows provides financial assistance and such services as vocational counseling and homes for fatherless families.

Public health maintenance, the fourth component of the social welfare system, includes public sanitation and the prevention and treatment of infectious diseases, including pollution-related diseases. Rapid economic growth has brought about considerable progress in all aspects of public health in Japan. See also ENVIRONMENTAL QUALITY.

Housing for the elderly.

Administration 運営管理●

Most social welfare–related activities are administered by the Ministry of Health and Welfare, although the ministries of labor and education also fulfill important social welfare functions. The Social Insurance Agency administers the key public pension programs. However, implementation of most programs is left to local governments: independent bureaus for health and welfare services operate at prefectural, city, town, and village government levels. In addition, welfare offices at the city and district level administer public assistance and engage in other welfare activities. At the private level, social welfare councils coordinate local welfare activities under contract with local governments. Volunteer welfare commissioners designated by the welfare minister carry out much of the casework investigation, counseling, and referral services.

Pensions (*nenkin*)   年金●

The Japanese pension system centers on public pensions administered by the national government, providing old-age, disability, and survivor benefits. Public pensions are supplemented by individual pension plans provided by private enterprises. By law, all Japanese citizens of working age must subscribe to a public pension plan.

Japanese pensions started in 1875 with the *onkyu* system for retired army and navy servicemen. This system was later expanded to cover government officials, schoolteachers, and policemen. In 1939 the first pension program for private-sector employees, the Seamen's Insurance Law, was enacted. From 1942 Laborers' Pension Insurance provided coverage for general workers; this was the precursor to the current Employees' Pension Insurance. In 1959 the National Pension Law was passed; it covers farmers, the self-employed, housewives, and other categories of people who had been excluded from employees' pensions.

In 1986 the pension system was greatly simplified and was reorganized into a two-tiered system. The NATIONAL PENSION was extended to provide basic, mandatory pension coverage to all Japanese citizens. Spouses of employees' pension subscribers are now required to enroll in the National Pension program. As of 1993, 68.9 million citizens were enrolled in this program. Two supplemental programs provide additional coverage and benefits. The Employees' Pension Insurance program provides coverage for 32.5 million private-sector employees. Mutual Aid Association Pensions enroll an additional 5.8 million public employees and teachers. A declining number (now under 3.0 million) still receive

Japan's Pension System (March 1993)
日本の年金システム

Type of pension	Insured person	Insurer	Number of insured persons (in millions)	Average monthly pension benefits (in yen)
National Pension (basic)	Self-employed workers	Nation	18.51	37,000
	Spouses of salaried workers	Nation	12.11	37,000
	All salaried workers	Nation	38.32	— *1
	Total		68.94	—

Supplemental pensions received by salaried workers				
Employees' Pension Insurance	Private-sector salaried workers	Nation	32.49	156,000
Mutual aid association pensions (MAAs)	Public employees and employees of groups that have MAAs	MAA	5.83	158,000 to 217,000 *2
	Total		38.32	—

*1 Salaried workers' National Pension benefits are included in the figures given below for Employees' Pension Insurance and mutual aid association pensions.
*2 This is a range of averages for seven different associations.   Source: Ministry of Health and Welfare.

onkyu pensions. Additional coverage for employees of certain companies is provided by privately funded corporate pensions.

The National Pension and Employees' Pension Insurance are administered by the Ministry of Health and Welfare. The smaller mutual-aid-association programs are under the jurisdiction of various ministries. One-third of the costs of contributory National Pension benefits are provided by the national treasury, with the rest supplied by contributions from the insured and from other pension plans. The costs of employee insurance are usually covered by equal contributions of employer and employee proportionate to the employee's wage rate.

National Pension (Kokumin Nenkin)   国民年金●

Introduced in 1959, the National Pension was originally designed for those not covered by other existing pension programs, especially farmers and the self-employed. Since reform of the pension system in 1986, joining the National Pension program is mandatory for all Japanese citizens between the ages of 20 and 60. Employed persons also receive additional benefits from Employees' Pension Insurance or Mutual Aid Association Pensions. In 1993, 68.9 million people were covered under the National Pension system.

The National Pension consists of three components: a basic old-age pension, a disability pension, and a basic survivor's pension. Contributions from insured persons and employers cover two-thirds of the cost of National Pension benefits, with the remainder paid by the national treasury. In 1993 the monthly payment required of all individual contributors to the National Pension system was ¥11,100 (US $99.8). The basic old-age pension of ¥37,000 (US $333) per month (as of 1993) is paid to people aged 65 and over who have fulfilled the minimum contributory requirement of 25 years.

Medical and health insurance (*iryo hoken*)   医療保険●

Central component of Japan's medical care security system, designed to provide nationwide health care coverage. The cornerstone of the present system of public health insurance is the 1922 Health Insurance Law, providing coverage primarily for factory workers and miners. Since 1961 all Japanese citizens and aliens resident in Japan have been entitled to coverage under one of six alternative health insurance plans. Chief among them are employees' health insurance, which covers most private-sector employees, and NATIONAL HEALTH INSURANCE, for people ineligible for employee health insurance. Other plans provide coverage for seamen, national public-service employees, local public-service employees, and private-school teachers and employees. The 1982 Law concerning Health and Medical Services for the Aged provides for medical care for citizens aged 70 and over. By 1980, 99.3 percent of the total population was covered under one of the six plans; the remaining 0.7 percent was covered by the medical assistance program. Under most Japanese medical insurance plans, members are required to pay 10 to 30 percent of their medical expenses, depending on the type of treatment provided; the insurance carrier then remunerates the doctor, hospital, clinic, or other medical care provider directly for the remainder on a fee-for-service basis determined by the Ministry of Health and Welfare.

The nationwide cost of health care has been rising faster than national income, with medical costs accounting for 3.1 percent of national income in 1960 and 6.3 percent in 1985. Increased costs incurred by the aged, hospital inpatients, and hospital outpatients accounted for the majority of this growth. The rapid expansion of Japan's aged population since the 1970s and its effects on medical care and costs is one of the major issues that the medical and health insurance system must face in coming decades.

Medical examination.

National Health Insurance
(Kokumin Kenko Hoken)   国民健康保険●

National Health Insurance covers the self-employed and their dependents, retired persons, and various other categories of individuals ineligible for employees' health insurance or any of the other medical and health insurance plans. In 1958 a new law gave the responsibility of overseeing the insurance to local governments. Under the present system premiums are paid solely by the insured; they consist of a fixed portion and a means-proportional portion. The amount of the premium varies from one municipality to another. The system also receives financial assistance from the national treasury. The insurance covers 70 percent of medical costs incurred by the principal insured or the principal's dependents (the rate is 80 percent for an insured retiree). As of 1992 there were 42.6 million people enrolled in National Health Insurance plans.

Society

Aging population (*koreika shakai*)   高齢化社会●

The aging of Japan's population is expected to become an increasingly acute problem as the number of elderly grows at the rate of approximately 650,000 per year. Longevity for both sexes first exceeded 50 years in 1947, 60 years in 1952, and 70 years in 1971. Figures for 1993 show a life expectancy of 82.5 years for women and 76.3 years for men. These figures are expected to increase to 84 years for women and 78 years for men by 2025. Due to the growing number of elderly within the working population, most large corporations have raised their mandatory retirement age to 60 years or above since the mid-1980s. In 1986 a more unified pension system, based on revisions of the National Pension Law, the Employees' Pension Insurance Law, and laws affecting other types of public pensions, was put into effect to respond to problems created by the aging population. Revisions were designed to assure the long-term stability of the nation's pension system and establish 65 as the uniform starting age for public pensions (see NATIONAL PENSION).

It is estimated that by 2020 only three workers will be supporting each retiree. Due to the disproportionately large burden that health care for the elderly was beginning to place on the medical care system as a whole, existing provisions for a national system of free health care for the elderly were replaced in 1983 by the Law concerning Health and Medical Services for the Aged. The law stipulated that health care expenses for the elderly were to be covered partly by fixed rate contributions from local governments, the NATIONAL HEALTH INSURANCE program, employee insurance plans, and the individual. A 1986 amendment further increased costs borne by the elderly for health care. In 1986 and 1988, however, expenses began to rise again, and in 1991, more than 29 percent of national medical care expenditure was devoted to caring for the elderly.

Other issues that are expected to accompany Japan's growing elderly population include the development of facilities and resources to care adequately for the senile and bedridden and the projected drop in economic vitality and tax revenues. Finding acceptable solutions to these problems will be one of Japan's greatest challenges as it approaches the 21st century.

Ratio of People 65 and Older to the Total Population
65才以上人口の総人口に占める割合

Country	1970	1980	1990	2000
Japan	7.1 (%)	9.1	12.0	17.0
United States	9.8	11.3	12.6	12.8
France	12.9	14.0	13.8	15.4
Sweden	13.7	16.3	18.1	17.1

Note: Figures for 2000 are projections.
Sources: Ministry of Health and Welfare; United Nations.

5/3

Life cycle (*raifu saikuru*)   ライフサイクル ●

Society's schedule of stages for an individual's life. The cycle is generally thought to extend from birth to death, although an individual is considered a social entity before birth, and many religions posit continuing life for the soul after death. Stages of the cycle mark a person's readiness to participate in social roles and institutions. The schedule has evolved over time and has been altered radically by the institutions of 20th-century mass society and by the greater longevity of modern populations.

entity

Age Reckoning   年齢認識 ●

For social purposes age is reckoned in both relative and absolute terms. Relative age is set by order of birth: one is senior, peer, or junior to someone else. Japanese often claim that theirs is a uniquely "vertical" society, pervaded by rules of seniority. Seniority rules, however, are common to modern institutions such as schools, corporations, and bureaucracies in all societies.

Certain ages traditionally have been considered favorable, others dangerous. The most favorable years—60, 70, 77, and 88—mark successful aging. The danger years (*yakudoshi*) occur earlier: 19 and 33 for women, 25 and 42 for men. Although most Japanese scorn the danger years as superstition, many continue to observe them. To ward off danger, people obtain protective amulets and purifications at Shinto shrines and avoid new ventures during the year.

The following outline depicts life stages as a typical individual might pass through them.

Infancy   幼児期 ●

In Japan it is common for an expectant mother to don an abdominal sash in the fifth month of pregnancy: this is society's first overt recognition of a new individual. One month after birth the infant is taken to a local Shinto shrine to be introduced to the guardian gods and symbolically to all of society. Annual celebrations for children occur on 3 March for girls (Doll Festival), 5 May for boys (Children's Day), and on 15 November for girls aged seven and three and boys aged five (Shichigosan).

Childhood (about 7-13 years)   幼年期（7～13才）●

In the past, when children reached the age of seven they were expected to help their parents with household tasks and to assume community duties as members of the children's group (*kodomo-gumi*). Today, however, a child's first duty is to study. Under the modern school system in Japan the most important rites of passage are matriculation and gradu-

matriculation

ation. During this stage of life one's "age" is reckoned more by years-in-school than by years-since-birth.

Youth (about 13-25 years) 青年期 (13〜25才) ●

Although only nine years of schooling are required, more than 90 percent of Japanese young people complete high school, and 40 percent enter college. In middle school and high school many students also attend special tutoring academies (*juku*) to prepare for entrance examinations for the next level of schooling. The demands of this "examination hell" have had a great impact on the daily lives not only of students but of their families and friends as well.

Today one attains legal maturity at age 20, and municipal governments celebrate Coming-of-Age Day (Seijin no Hi) for 20-year-olds on 15 January.

Maturity (about 26-60 years) 成熟期 (26〜60才) ●

A man's pace of life and focus of ambition are caught up in promotions, raises, and occupational skills, and less in the family dynamics. Most women find paid work after leaving school, but few are able to sustain long-term occupational careers because social expectation dictates that they attend to housekeeping and child-rearing duties. In contrast to a century ago, however, today the typical woman gives birth to only two or three children, spaced closely together, so that she has completed the period of intensive child care within about a decade after marriage. Many women later take up paid employment, though they are at a disadvantage in the labor market.

Old Age (about 61 and over) 老齢期 (61才以上) ●

The 60th birthday, when the zodiac signs complete a full cycle, was the traditional beginning of old age; today many Japanese celebrate this birthday with family and friends. In some organizations, retirement (*teinen*) occurs before age 60, and long-term employees receive pension benefits. Most men and many women, however, take other jobs and remain in the labor force for another 10 years. Often this is because retirement incomes are thought to be inadequate.

After Death 死後●

In Buddhist tradition, at death an individual is given a posthumous name by the priest of the family temple. This is inscribed on the tombstone and on a personal memorial tablet (*ihai*) kept in the home. In the early weeks and months after death, frequent rites are held to comfort the soul. Thereafter, deathday anniversaries are honored for up to 50 years. After that, one's individuality dissolves into the collective body of the household ancestors, and, except for the famous or notorious, social recognition ceases.

Change 変遷●

Under the impact of modernization different parts of the life-cycle schedule have changed in ways that may often be contradictory. Legal maturity is granted at age 20, but popular opinion regards anyone as immature until married or embarked on a working career. Family versus work is a serious issue for many men and women. Retirement before 60 seems unduly early when life expectancy is now 80 years.

Family (kazoku) 家族●

The most common Japanese terms for family are *ie*, kazoku, and *setai*; although these words are often used interchangeably today, in the past they had different meanings. Ie (often translated as "household") has come to be used by scholars for Japan's traditional type of family, especially as it existed during the Edo period (1600–1868); it means a united or corporate group of people who share residence and economic and social life and who regard themselves as a continuing unit of kin. The term kazoku appears to be more recent than ie. When used distinctively, it means a corporate domestic group consisting only of genetic and affinal kin or in-laws. Setai denotes a residential group or household, regardless of the relationships of its members, although these are most commonly kin. Neither kazoku nor setai carries the connotation of continuity of the term ie. See also MARRIAGE.

The Traditional Family 伝統的家族●

The family was organized as a hierarchy with the male household head at the apex, theoretically in a position of absolute authority over others. Until after World War II, this authority was supported by law. The authority of the wife of the family head related to domestic matters. Seniority in age conferred prestige, but sex and specific position of authority strongly affected status. A retired household head was respected but had little or no authority. Generally, when the head retired, his eldest son succeeded him, remaining with his parents after marriage and maintaining the continuity of the family line. The future household head held a status much superior to that of his younger siblings. A bride, who traditionally held the lowest status in the family, might be divorced if she failed to please her in-laws or produce a child.

Most Japanese families today have only one or two children.

Authority meant responsibility as well as privilege. The family head was responsible for the economic welfare and also the deportment of other members. He exercised control over family property and the conduct of farming or other occupations, and he was also responsible for the welfare of deceased ancestors, seeing that proper ceremonies were conducted in their honor.

The welfare of the family ideally took precedence over the needs of any individual member. Confucian views on relations between husband and wife and between parent and child were explicitly taught. Religion, whether Shinto or Buddhism, with its emphasis on reverence for ancestors, also gave support to the traditional family organization. The functions of the family related to almost every aspect of life. Close emotional bonds have continued to characterize the Japanese family and Japanese society in general.

The Contemporary Family 現代の家族●

The typical Japanese family today is a nuclear family, with a mother, father, and two children, in a two- or three-bedroom apartment or house in an urban area. Most typically, the father commutes by train to his job in the city, while the wife cares for the children and the house, creating a nurturing environment for the whole family.

Western culture and values have had a large influence, inspiring postwar legal reforms and general social change. The ancient distinctions between eldest and younger sons, and between sons and daughters, have decreased, although they have not disappeared. Eldest sons are no longer universally expected to live with and take care of their parents, and daughters-in-law have been freed from the absolute authority of their mothers-in-law. Women, less restricted to the home, are freer to pursue education, jobs, and hobbies, and to initiate divorce.

Despite such rapid change, however, the Japanese family is characterized by stability and continuity. Growing individualism still gives way to the needs of the group, and roles within the family remain clearly differentiated. The divorce rate remains low compared to that of the United States. Children still feel an indebtedness (*on*) to their parents and care for them in their old age.

As a result of Japan's postwar prosperity, almost all families consider themselves middle class and, in fact, the urban middle-class family is the dominant type and model for all Japan. Middle-class ideals and standards of living have penetrated rural areas as well.

The company is the center of the husband's life.

Husband-wife relationships (夫と妻の関係) In contrast to the past, today a woman's relationship with her husband is much more important than her relationship with any of his relatives. Most young people, influenced by the West, want to have a more companionable and romantic marriage than their parents had. Nevertheless, after a year or two of marriage, most couples settle into a pattern of separate social worlds and a clear-cut division of labor. The husband's life is absorbed in his company; he works long hours and socializes with his work group. The wife becomes absorbed in her mothering role as soon as she becomes pregnant. Her social life revolves around her children but may include female relatives and friends.

The husband nominally heads the family and bears clear responsibility for financial support. However, far from being a strong authority figure, he is more likely to let his wife take effective charge of everything concerning the house and children. The husband often turns his salary over to his wife, and she controls the finances, including the allocation of her husband's spending money.

Though some couples are quite close and companionable, emotional intimacy is less important than in the West. Fulfillment of one's duties as a parent takes precedence over affective needs. The continuity of the family is thought to be more important than marital gratification. Accordingly the divorce rate in Japan has remained rather low (around 1.3 per 1,000 persons in 1990), although the number fluctuates slightly.

The wife often spends her time shuffling the children to and from private tutoring schools.

Child rearing and education （育児と教育） Not only is the rearing and education of children the responsibility of the mother, but it is a task that does not allow for substitutes. Motherhood and the careful nurturing of children are valued as supremely important in Japan. Mother and child are usually inseparable when the child is young, and even in later years the mother-child relationship continues to be the strongest and closest within the family.

In order to assure a child's success in the Japan of today, whether the child is a boy or a girl, the mother must spend much time and thought on education. Though Japanese complain about the examination system and often make fun of the so-called education mother (*kyoiku mama*) who single-mindedly drives her children toward educational achievement, most middle-class mothers feel they have no choice but to be one. See ENTRANCE EXAMINATIONS.

The largest percentage of female employees work in clerical jobs.

Working women （働く女性達） Economic growth has produced an increase in the number of women in the work force. In 1990, 50.1 percent of women of working age were in the labor force, and 64.9 percent of all women working were married. Women want to work for a variety of reasons such as to increase the family's ability to pay for better housing, children's education, or personal luxuries. Some better-educated women want to work in order to pursue careers of their own. See WOMEN IN THE LABOR FORCE.

Grandparents（祖父母） Filial piety is no longer the cornerstone of Japanese morality. Still, most Japanese consider it "natural" to take care of their parents in their old age. There are a few nursing homes, but most middle-class adults would consider it shameful to allow their parents to live in one. Elderly parents ideally live with or near one grown child, and while there remains some tendency to choose an elder son, many parents now prefer to live with a daughter, since mother-in-law problems are avoided.

Nuclear family *(kaku kazoku)* 核家族●

The nuclear family has become far more common in Japan with the changes in industrial structure and increased urbanization of the country after World War II. The traditional pattern in Japan was that of the extended family, in which the head of the household *(kacho)* lived not only with his wife and children but with his parents, grandparents, and occasionally other relations as well. After the end of the war the concept and the legal system supporting it gradually lost their power, and the nuclear family has come to predominate. The shift away from primary industries, which involved the labor of all family members, toward secondary and tertiary industries in which the husband became the sole breadwinner has also accelerated this trend. In 1955 nuclear families constituted 45.3 percent of all households, a figure that rose to 59.6 percent by 1991.

Marriage *(kon'in)* 婚姻●

Marriage in Japan has been characterized as centering on arranged marriage *(miai kekkon)*, in which a man, a woman, and their families are formally introduced to each other by a go-between, or *nakodo*. Allied to this is the traditional Japanese concept of marriage as the creation of links between two households rather than the joining of two individuals. Put simply, marriage has traditionally been more of a family affair in Japan than it has in most Western cultures.

In recent years, however, the Japanese attitudes to marriage have changed in response to a host of new social situations, some of which are the result of influence from the West. While traditional ideas concerning the mechanics of making a match in Japan have not been completely abandoned, marriage in contemporary Japan is much more of a private decision between two people than it was before World War II. Households, in particular the parents of a couple contemplating mar-

A formal meeting of prospective marriage partners and their families (*miai*).

riage, do not have as final a say in the matter as they did 50 years ago; and the function of the nakodo, while still important, has in many cases shrunk to a largely ceremonial role.

Marriage in the Premodern Period   前近代の婚姻●

During the Nara and Heian periods (710–1185), among the court aristocracy marriage was essentially matrilocal, with a man moving into his wife's house after they were married. Men of rank and importance could divide their time between two or three different houses, and marriage practices among the ruling elite are thought to have been largely polygynous.

An aristocratic woman usually conducted herself with discretion, since her pregnancies needed recognition by a man for her children to have any importance in society. Children might be confirmed to the rank of their father, or they could be adopted into other households to achieve rank.

It was much more difficult for lower classes to follow the marriage practices of the elite. Farmers, artisans, and low-ranking warriors had a better chance of maintaining their status through permanent marriage with one wife.

By the late 12th century the *samurai* class had become the ruling elite in both central and provincial affairs throughout Japan. The political imbalances, warring factions, and military reprisals that had brought the samurai to power frequently involved households related through marriage. It was during this politically unsettled time that marriage, that is, *seiryaku kekkon* (marriage of convenience) began to assume importance as a means of ceremonially establishing military alliances between families, reaching the height of its importance in the period of intense interfamily political struggle known as the Sengoku period (1467–1568).

Among samurai families the practice of maintaining multiple wives became less common. Samurai marriage customs also stressed the immediate transfer of the wife from her parents' home to her husband's residence. Family concerns became important in the selection of a spouse, intensifying the need for professional nakodo to ensure an appropriate match.

The marriage practices of rural commoners were less affected by the rise of the military elite. Practices that lent a more casual air to marriage customs, such as night visiting (*yobai*) and multiple liaisons, continued in the provinces.

Gifts exchanged between families at the time of the *yuino* engagement ceremony. Both the gifts and the wrapping are symbolic of an auspicious union.

With the establishment of the Tokugawa shogunate in 1603 and the return of political stability, the samurai emphasis on arranged marriage continued throughout the Edo period (1600–1868) and urban commoners increasingly emulated samurai custom. The miai, a formal meeting of prospective marriage partners and their families, became popular. The *yuino*, a ceremonial exchange of engagement gifts between families, also became an important part of marriage practice among urban commoners.

Legally, marriage in the Edo period was subject to a number of rules and regulations designed to preserve the status quo of the ruling military elite. Central among the many laws created was the mandatory reporting of proposed marriages before any ceremonies took place. Marriages had to be cleared through officials and the appropriateness of the match confirmed.

Marriage and Industrialization   婚姻と工業化●

After the Meiji Restoration of 1868, Japan began an all-out effort to industrialize and catch up with the West. Cities, the centers of industry, also became centers of migration from all parts of Japan, further increasing the need for a nakodo to ensure the appropriateness of a marriage.

The increased mobility of the population during the Meiji period (1868–1912) was a key factor in changing attitudes toward marriage in many rural areas. As in urban centers, the miai, yuino, the use of nakodo, and other practices that had originated with the samurai became more common in rural areas. Parental arrangement of and authority over marriages increased.

In the Meiji period, under the Civil Code of 1898 marriage was legally conducted under the so-called ie (household) system, which necessitated the agreement of the heads of the two households involved in a marriage, rather than the man and woman to be married. Under Meiji civil law husband and wife were far from equal: through marriage, the wife lost her legal capacity to engage in property transactions; management of her own property came under her husband's control; and only the wife had the duty of chastity. The Meiji Civil Code remained the law of the land until after World War II, when the new Civil Code of 1947 abolished the ie system and eliminated the legal inequality of husband and wife.

Number of Marriages
婚姻件数と初婚平均年齢

	Number of marriages (thousands)	(per 1,000)	Average age for the first marriages Male	Female
1965	955	9.7	27.2	24.5
1975	942	8.5	27.0	24.7
1985	736	6.1	28.2	25.5
1993	793	6.4	28.4	26.1

Source: Ministry of Health and Welfare.

Post-World War II Japan   第二次世界大戦後●

Though the legal requirements of marriage in Japan changed radically after the war, marriage practices were slower to respond to outside influence. The traditional marriage pattern continued relatively unchanged, especially in high-status families. Very few Japanese of the mid-20th century expected to find a spouse through casual meeting or dating.

Even in contemporary Japan, where Western marriage practices seem to have affected a sizable number of Japanese, the traditional system has not completely disappeared. Rather, Western influence has worked its way into a traditional system that has modified itself to meet contemporary preferences. Many people still seek the advice of a nakodo on a potential spouse; dating then confirms or disallows previous judgments concerning the individual's suitability. The nakodo is especially useful when a person is near or past what is considered the "appropriate" age for marriage (statistically, the average age for the first marriage has been on the rise since 1970; in 1993 it was 26.1 for females and 28.4 for males).

More Japanese now say they prefer a *ren'ai kekkon*, or "love marriage," over the traditional arranged marriage. Individual choice has in many cases become the deciding factor in settling on a marriage partner, and the level of familial involvement in the marriage process has come to resemble that found in Western countries; that is, not completely absent, but not nearly as deep as it was in prewar Japanese society.

Women in the labor force (*fujin rodo*)   婦人労働●

Women were traditionally an important part of Japan's agrarian labor force, but the industrialization that followed the Meiji Restoration of 1868 initiated the flow of female workers into the textile industry. Most received very low wages; some even were indentured by their families in return for a lump-sum payment. Buttressed by growing nationalism, their working conditions deteriorated while their numbers increased.

The textile industry's poor working environment and overcrowded dormitories first received widespread attention with the 1903 publication of *Shokko jijo* (Conditions of Factory Workers), a report by

Men and Women in the Japanese Labor Force
性別労働力人口と就業率

Year	Population aged 15 and older (millions)		Labor force (millions)		Labor force participation rate		Percentage of the labor force occupied by women
	Male	Female	Male	Female	Male	Female	
1965	35.29	37.58	28.84	19.03	81.7	50.6	39.8
1970	38.25	40.60	31.29	20.24	81.8	49.9	39.3
1975	40.99	43.44	33.36	19.87	81.4	45.7	37.3
1980	43.41	45.91	34.65	21.85	79.8	47.6	38.7
1985	46.02	48.63	35.96	23.67	78.1	48.7	39.7
1990	49.11	51.78	37.91	25.93	77.2	50.1	40.6

Note: The labor force perticipation rate is the ratio of males or females in the labor force to the total population of males or females aged 15 or over. Source: Ministry of Labor.

Society

the Ministry of Agriculture and Commerce, and *Nihon no kaso shakai* (1899, Japan's Lower Classes) by Yokoyama Gennosuke. A movement for legislation to protect women and minors, begun in the 1890s but stalled during the Russo-Japanese War (1904–1905), revived as part of a budding labor movement. The Factory Law of 1911, implemented in 1916, limited workdays for women to 12 hours, forbade night work between 10 pm and 4 am, and required a minimum of 2 days off per month.

Although concentrated in the textile industry, women outnumbered men in the total labor force until about 1930. Women also moved into other manufacturing jobs and skilled occupations as growing numbers of men joined the military.

After World War II, with many women left single and impoverished by the war, women's participation in the labor force remained necessarily high. Before World War II, most working Japanese women were young and single, but with rapid economic growth many companies began to offer part-time employment, and the number of married women employees rose considerably. Since 1955 the percentage of married women in the female labor force has almost tripled, rising to 64.9 percent in 1990.

Until about 1950, over 60 percent of working women were "family workers," mainly in agriculture. By 1990, family workers had declined to 16.7 percent. Conversely, women's entry into "prestige professions" such as law and medicine has been slow, and fewer than 1 percent of female civil servants occupy managerial posts.

In 1990 clerical and related jobs accounted for the largest percentage of female employees (34.4 percent, excluding self-employed and family workers), followed by craft and production workers (20.6 percent), professional and technical workers (13.8 percent), sales workers (12.5 percent), service workers (10.7 percent), and other occupations (8.0 percent). The order of distribution has not changed for some time, although the number of women in each occupation has varied, increasing in professional and technical fields while decreasing in manual labor.

The treatment of women in Japan's labor force resembles their treatment in other industrialized countries. In both Japan and the West, female workers make up more than one-third of the total labor force and earn lower wages than men. Residual prejudice against women, however, has resulted in somewhat more discrimination against them in Japan than in the West. Tradition holds that women should devote themselves to the home after marriage, a view that causes the length of

University students discuss career prospects with a corporate recruiter.

uninterrupted employment at the same firm to be rather short. Japanese court decisions have ruled against forcing women to retire upon marriage or upon having passed the "appropriate" age for marriage (commonly set at 30).

Japan's Labor Standards Law of 1947 stipulates equal pay for equal work, but this is rare in practice because of continuing tendencies to channel women into dead-end jobs and favor men at promotion time. According to one survey, the average monthly wage paid to female employees in 1990 was somewhat over 60 percent of that paid to male employees. The difference in Japan between men's and women's wages is still the greatest in the industrialized world, although it has narrowed slightly.

This disparity is due largely to the seniority system that presupposes "lifetime" employment of men, whereas the length of uninterrupted employment, average age, and educational level of women have tended to be lower than those of men. Very few women attain positions of high responsibility in business. Businesses still generally employ women only in low-level or temporary jobs because of the view that they should work only until marriage or childbirth.

The Equal Employment Opportunity Law for Men and Women of 1985 removed all restrictions for management and specialist positions except certain regulations applying to women workers in the period prior to and following childbirth. It is anticipated that the new law will encourage the employment and advancement of women on merit.

Sarariman サラリーマン●

Loanword derived from the English "salaried man." The term was coined in the Taisho period (1912–1926) to distinguish the emerging class of white-collar workers, who received a regular salary, from blue-collar workers, usually paid an hourly wage. Today, sarariman is often used in reference to middle-class, white-collar workers employed by private companies or government agencies. The sarariman usually works for the same company or organization until he reaches retirement age, although midcareer company changes have become increasingly common. Status is strongly influenced by the employee's academic background, and advancement is a gradual upward movement within the company. The model sarariman is expected to be intensely loyal to his employer, putting company considerations before those of family and personal life, working many hours of overtime, and taking only the minimum number of holidays each year.

Society

Foreigners in Japan (*zainichi gaikokujin*)   在日外国人●

The number of foreign nationals resident in Japan steadily increased throughout the 1980s and was 1,320,748 in 1993. This figure includes only foreigners registered in accordance with the Alien Registration Law; tourists in Japan for less than 90 days, children under the age of two months, and members of foreign diplomatic services are not included. The largest national group, accounting for 51.7 percent of the total, is composed of North and South Koreans (682,276), followed by citizens of China and Taiwan (210,138), Brazil (154,650), the Philippines (73,057), and the United States (42,639).

Since the revision of the Immigration Control Law in 1990, regulations governing employment of foreigners have been more strictly enforced; however, the revised law also makes foreign nationals of Japanese descent eligible for permanent resident status, and their numbers have suddenly increased. For example, the number of Brazilians of Japanese descent residing in Japan increased almost 29 times between 1985 and 1990.

Fifty-two percent of all foreigners in Japan live in the four prefectures of Tokyo, Osaka, Hyogo, and Aichi, with the highest concentration in Tokyo. Of registered aliens in Japan, 60.0 percent were permanent residents in 1989; the rest were temporary residents, drawn to Japan by increasing foreign direct investment, by employment opportunities offered by the growing demand of Japanese firms for foreign workers, and by the chance to study in Japan. The influx of workers from South America, South and Southeast Asia, and the Middle East, a significant number of whom are employed illegally, has become a much-discussed trend.

The number of international marriages increased 4.6 times between 1970 and 1990. From 1975 onward, the number of marriages involving Japanese men and foreign women, many from China, Korea, or the Philippines, surpassed the number of Japanese women marrying foreign men.

A number of Japanese local governments have begun to implement new services to respond to the needs of foreign residents, such as the publication of information pamphlets in English, Chinese, and Portuguese and the assignment of English-speaking personnel to provide assistance. Since many foreign nationals of Japanese descent bring their families with them to Japan, special courses are being set up in elementary schools in areas where their numbers are especially concentrated. See also FOREIGN STUDENTS IN JAPAN; FOREIGN WORKERS.

Foreign Nationals in Japan (1993)
国籍別外国人登録者数

Nationality	Number
North and South Korea	682,276
China and Taiwan	210,138
Brazil	154,650
Philippines	73,057
United States	42,639
Peru	33,169
United Kingdom	12,244
Thailand	11,765
Vietnam	7,609
Iran	6,754
Others	86,447
Total	1,320,748

Source: Ministry of Justice.

Alien registration (*gaikokujin toroku*)   外国人登録●

The Alien Registration Law (Gaikokujin Toroku Ho, 1952) requires all foreigners residing in Japan for more than one year to apply for registration to the mayor or headman of the village, town, or city where they live and to present a passport and copies of a photograph within 90 days from the date of entry into Japan. The information required on the application form includes the applicant's name, date and place of birth, sex, nationality, occupation, port of entry, passport number, and address while in Japan.

Upon registration by the local government official, registrants are issued a Certificate of Alien Registration that must be renewed every five years or whenever visa status changes. Each registrant, excluding children under the age of 16, is required to carry this certificate at all times and to present it upon demand to police officers, maritime safety officials, railway police officers, or other public officials.

A growing number of noncitizens in Japan have objected strongly to the requirement that fingerprints be taken as part of the registration procedure, arguing that fingerprinting is the treatment given to criminals. By December 1991, 156 people had refused to be fingerprinted, and several prosecutions had resulted in guilty verdicts and fines. In response to growing protests the Ministry of Justice abolished the fingerprinting requirement for persons with permanent resident status, effective January 1993.

Emigration and immigration control
(*shutsunyukoku kanri*)   出入国管理●

Immigration into and emigration from Japan are both regulated by the Immigration Control Order (Shutsunyukoku Kanri Rei) of 1951 (originally a government order, but a law after 1952). In regard to foreigners' entry into Japan, it states that no alien shall enter Japan without a valid passport or crewman's pocket ledger (art. 3). The Ministry of Justice grants visas, often renewable, of no more than three years' duration; only those in special categories such as diplomats and government officials may receive longer visas. Permanent residence is rarely granted. Entry is denied to aliens judged unsuitable by the authorities, and certain undesirable aliens may be deported. All Japanese nationals may emigrate from Japan to any other country except North Korea. Japanese nationals with a known police record have difficulty obtaining a passport.

Society

Foreign students in Japan (*gaikokujin ryugakusei*) 外国人留学生●

In 1949 the Japanese government began granting scholarships to students from Asian countries. In 1954 Japanese government scholarships for foreign students (the so-called Mombusho scholarships) were established. At present Japan accepts foreign students in two categories: those receiving Japanese government scholarships and those receiving government or private support from their own countries. Students receiving Japanese government scholarships are themselves divided into two categories: research students, who pursue graduate-level studies, and undergraduate students, who enroll in university departments, technical colleges, or special training schools. Japanese government scholarship students in 1992 numbered 5,699, of whom more than 90 percent were Asians. Students not on Japanese government scholarships numbered 42,862 in 1992.

Since 1980 the total number of foreign students in Japan has grown each year, increasing from 6,572 in 1980 to 48,561 in 1992. However, these figures are still small when compared with the 449,700 foreign students in the United States in 1993. Hoping to admit 100,000 foreign students into Japan by the year 2000, the Ministry of Education is increasing the number of Japanese government scholarship recipients.

Nationality of Foreign Students (1992)
国籍別外国人留学生

Nationality	Students	(%)
China	20,437	42.1
Korea	11,596	23.9
Taiwan	6,138	12.6
Malaysia	1,934	4.0
U.S.A.	1,245	2.6
Indonesia	1,154	2.4
Others	6,057	12.5
Total	48,561	100

Source: Ministry of Education

Foreign workers (*gaikokujin rodosha*) 外国人労働者●

Paid employment of workers who are citizens of foreign countries is strictly regulated by the Immigration Control Law, the revisions of which were implemented in 1990. Except for spouses of Japanese nationals and people of Japanese descent, permission to work is granted to foreigners only in 28 skilled employment categories such as education, communications, medicine, finance, and computer software design. In principle, manual workers are not allowed entry, and students from overseas who work part-time are also subject to restrictions.

The majority of illegal foreign workers in the early 1980s were women who had entered the country with tourist visas and worked in bars and entertainment districts. However, severe shortages of labor triggered by the economic boom of the late 1980s have attracted a large influx of male foreign workers, mostly from Asian countries such as the Philippines, Bangladesh, and Iran. In recent years Japanese have been avoiding the so-called "3K" jobs (those that are *kitsui, kitanai, kiken*; "difficult, dirty, dangerous"), and there has been a significant increase in the number of construction and small engineering firms that are prepared to employ foreign manual laborers illegally.

The revision of the Immigration Control Law extended the right of long-term residence to descendants of Japanese emigrants and removed restrictions on their ability to work in Japan. Due to high inflation in Brazil, many Brazilians of Japanese descent have sought to take advantage of this change in the law; twice as many were working in Japan in 1990 as in the previous year. However, the recession in the Japanese economy in the early 1990s has resulted in fewer jobs for foreign workers.

Environmental quality (*kankyo mondai*)   環境問題●

Environmental pollution in Japan has accompanied industrialization since the Meiji period (1868–1912). One of the earliest and well known cases was the copper poisoning caused by drainage from the Ashio Copper Mine in Tochigi Prefecture, beginning as early as 1878. The subsequent development of the textile and paper and pulp industries led to water pollution, and the use of coal as the major fuel for industry in general contributed to widespread but still localized air pollution. In the period of rapid growth following World War II, however, the isolated cases coalesced into a national crisis, with Japan becoming one of the most polluted countries in the world.

At first there was widespread ignorance on the part of the public and apathy on the part of the government concerning environmental protection. Although the pollution-related Minamata disease was first reported in May 1956, the existence of the disease had been concealed and patients secretly hospitalized in municipal isolation wards. A Kumamoto University research team identified mercury from the Chisso Corporation plant as the cause of the disease in 1959, but the government did not officially recognize this as the cause until 1968. By the late 1960s, however, the degradation of the environment had deeply struck the national consciousness, and a series of strict environmental protection measures were taken.

These were quite successful in some areas, most notably in the removal of toxic substances from the water and the reduction of sulfur oxides in the air, measures that helped to dull the public's sense of urgency. At the same time other concerns came increasingly to the fore, especially such economic issues as the sharp increase in oil prices following the oil crisis of 1973, the prolonged slump in industries such as steel and shipbuilding, and the ending of the period of rapid growth. Under

Victims of Minamata disease hold a news conference.

these conditions, public pressures for a clean environment became sub-dued and the government weakened its standards. Thus, whereas in May 1973 the Environment Agency set a maximum permissible level for nitrogen oxides (a major contributor to photochemical smog) of 0.02 ppm (parts per million), the world's strictest standard, it agreed in June 1978 to a request by the Ministry of International Trade and Industry (MITI) and business circles to relax the standard to 0.06 ppm in cities and 0.04 ppm elsewhere. Still, much of the struggle against pollution had already been institutionalized, and further moderate improvement seemed in store, although the long-range outlook remained uncertain.

In four major lawsuits regarding pollution-related diseases, the right of the victims to compensation was established. The decisions in cases involving *itai-itai* disease (1971), Niigata Minamata disease (1971), Yokkaichi asthma (1972), and Kumamoto Minamata disease (1973) eased the burden of proof on the victims. These decisions clarified the responsi-bility of the companies to ensure that their activities were nonpolluting and to prevent pollution from actually taking place.

Four major factors have especially contributed to the emergence in Japan of water-pollution problems: rapid industrialization, rapid urbanization, the lag in constructing such social overhead capital facili-ties as sewage systems, and the fact that water pollution in Japan emerged from a public policy that heavily favored economic growth over public health and a clean environment.

As a consequence of the increased concern with pollution prob-lems, there has been an overall improvement in water quality, but the progress has been uneven. Strict emission controls on waste industrial waters have reduced cases of toxic-substance pollution to a very small number. On the other hand, rivers and coastal waters within metropoli-tan districts continue to suffer considerable pollution from organic substances. The problem is even more severe in bays, inland seas, lakes, and other water areas, including Tokyo, Ise, and Osaka bays and Lakes Biwa, Kasumigaura, and Suwa. In these areas there is relatively little "transfusion" of water, so the enormous amounts of nutritive salts of nitrogen and phosphorus poured into them lead to a multiplication of plankton or algae and eutrophication.

Investigators check the river Watarasegawa for pol-lution from the Ashio Copper Mine.

Another water-pollution problem is that of thermal pollution. As an increasing number of power plants are being built on an ever-larger scale, their heating of surrounding waters poses a threat to marine life and the fishing industry. Although heavy-metal pollution is no longer a serious problem, Japan's coastal waters remain highly polluted; in addition to household and industrial wastes discharged, oil dumped by ships, often deliberately, is a significant source of maritime pollution.

A number of measures have been taken to improve the quality of the water in Japan. These include the setting of national standards for toxic substances and of variable standards for the living environment (depending on the use and type of water area) and the establishing of strict effluent controls and of a comprehensive surveillance and monitoring system. Also, many laws fixing responsibility for pollution damages have been passed, court decisions favorable to victims have reinforced these, and projects to improve sewers have extended sewer service to a greater proportion of the population.

Japan's efforts to control air pollution have also met with mixed results. The greatest success has been attained in limiting pollution by sulfur oxides and carbon monoxide. The relatively successful control of sulfur oxides reflects a long-term commitment on the part of the government to reduce their concentrations. In the case of nitrogen oxides, the overall relaxation of standards in 1978 suggested that the delay in significantly reducing nitrogen oxide concentrations in the air could be prolonged indefinitely. Photochemical smog, to which nitrogen oxides are a principal contributor, first appeared in Tokyo in July 1970; since then it has appeared regularly in different parts of Japan.

In addition, the government has taken measures to cope with a variety of other forms of pollution or environmental disruption, including noise, vibration, waste disposal, ground subsidence, offensive odors, soil pollution, and pollution by agricultural chemicals. The number of complaints about noise is greater than for any other type of pollution. The greatest number of complaints concerns noise from factories, but construction, traffic, airport, and railroad (especially the high-speed Shinkansen line) noise have all generated a considerable number of complaints.

In response to the sharp deterioration in the natural environment caused by the postwar period of rapid economic growth, the Nature Conservation Law was passed in 1972 to serve as the basis for all legal measures to protect the natural environment. To protect nature and promote recreation, an extensive system of national parks, quasi-national parks, and prefectural natural parks was established. In urban areas, the government has sought to expand city park areas.

Environmental deterioration has led to sharp decreases in the number of such birds as hawks and owls, while various species, including the Japanese crested ibis, the stork, and the red-crested crane, have become threatened with extinction. Since 1972, however, the observed number of migratory birds—ducks, swans, and geese—has generally been increasing, suggesting that environmental protection measures are bringing favorable results.

The Pollution Countermeasures Basic Law in 1967 sought to create common principles and policies for pollution control in all government agencies and to promote an integrated effort to clean up the environment. The Basic Law indicates the responsibilities of the central government, local governments, and business firms with regard to controlling pollution. In addition, the Basic Law laid the framework for establishing environmental quality standards, drafting pollution-control programs, and aiding victims of diseases caused by pollution.

Although antipollution policies are mainly national, much of the enforcement is done at a prefectural or municipal level. Moreover, the designation and classification of pollution or environmental protection zones are often done by local governments, which are also empowered to adopt standards stricter than national ones if necessary. In the 1970s Japan adopted the Polluter Pays Principle, according to which polluting enterprises had to accept financial responsibility for damages they inflicted on the community. Even so, the tolerable limits remained high for many substances, and when environmental goals conflicted with "stable" growth, the latter would prevail.

In the late 1980s a growing body of scientific evidence suggested that the ozone layer of the atmosphere is being destroyed by chlorofluorocarbons and that an increase in carbon dioxide in the atmosphere is causing a general rise in world temperatures. Concern over these findings in Japan, which produces 10 percent of the annual world supply of chlorofluorocarbons, led to the passing of the Ozonosphere Protection Law of 1988.

In the 1990s damage to Japan's forests, presumably caused by acid rain, was recognized as a problem, and the Environment Agency has held international conferences with neighboring countries, including China and South Korea, to address the issue. The increasing concentrations in the air of the nitrogen oxides emitted by motor vehicles continue to be a serious problem, and in 1992 a law was passed that attempts to reduce pollution levels by restricting the types of vehicles registered in the Tokyo and Osaka areas.

Housing problems (*jutaku mondai*) 住宅問題●

Urban housing problems in Japan arose as the country entered the stage of industrialization and urbanization around 1900. Before the end of World War II, no public measures were taken, but in the 1950s three major pieces of legislation established a general framework for Japanese housing policy. The Government Housing Loan Corporation (Jutaku Kin'yu Koko) founded in 1950 was a means of channeling public funds for low-interest, long-term loans for owner-occupied housing. Under the Public Housing Law (Koei Jutaku Ho) of 1951 local authorities were empowered to build public housing for rental to low-income households with subsidies from the central government. Finally, the Japan Housing Corporation (Nihon Jutaku Kodan) was founded in 1955 as a public nonprofit developer to supply housing units for urban dwellers.

In 1966 the Housing Construction Planning Law (Jutaku Kensetsu Keikaku Ho) was enacted to coordinate public policy measures for housing. The act mandated that the central government formulate five-year comprehensive housing construction plans at five-year intervals starting in 1966. The first Five-Year Housing Construction Plan aimed at constructing a total of 6.7 million housing units.

The second Housing Construction Plan, initiated in 1971, aimed at achieving "one room for each member of the household." Although the plan was to construct 9.6 million housing units in five years, only 8.26 million units were actually built.

The third Housing Construction Plan, approved in 1976, stated explicitly that the main priority of housing policy should be shifted from an emphasis on quantity to the improvement of quality. The purpose of the fourth Housing Construction Plan, begun in 1981, was to continue to improve housing quality, especially in urban areas.

High prices for land have forced many people to buy housing at a considerable distance from their workplaces, particularly in the Tokyo metropolitan region. In all of Japan's intensely crowded urban areas it is becoming increasingly difficult for the average "*sarariman*" (middle-class workers) to purchase a single-family dwelling. Multistory buildings with individual units for sale, similar to condominiums in

Housing Units in Selected Prefectures, 1993
住宅の総数と広さ

Prefecture	Number of housing units	Ownership ratio (%)	Average size of housing unit	
			Number of rooms	Total area (m²)
Tokyo	4,669,600	39.6	3.53	63.06
Osaka	3,062,100	47.9	4.22	71.99
Toyama	317,800	79.8*	6.91*	155.52*
Nationwide	40,834,700	59.8	4.86	92.55

* Largest in Japan. Source: Ministry of Construction.

the United States, have become the standard form of urban housing.

The fifth Housing Construction Plan (1986–1990) set forth a number of guidelines, including new standards for residential housing floor space and facilities. The sixth Housing Construction Plan (1991–1995) was again concerned with housing quality and also gave special attention to the promotion of a housing environment in which the elderly can continue living in areas they are familiar with. Many issues remain, in addition to the challenge of housing the growing number of elderly, there are also the problems of the nearly 10 percent of all Japanese families who live in substandard private rental housing, as well as the obstacles faced by the handicapped and other socially disadvantaged members of Japanese society in securing adequate housing.

AIDS (acquired immune deficiency syndrome)   エイズ●

The first confirmed case of AIDS in Japan was reported in May 1985. As of December 1993 the Ministry of Health and Welfare had confirmed the existence of 685 AIDS patients and 2,914 carriers of the virus. Among patients, 418 were hemophiliacs who had contracted AIDS through infected blood preparations that had been imported, largely from the United States. Blood preparations are now sterilized by heating and are no longer a source of infection. Medical costs of hemophiliac patients of AIDS are borne by the firms that sold the infected blood preparations. The Law concerning the Prevention of AIDS, effective in 1989, was created as a part of efforts to arrest the spread of the disease.

Law concerning the Prevention of AIDS
(Eizu Yobo Ho)   エイズ予防法●

AIDS prevention campaign poster.

Law enacted in 1988 to prevent the spread of the AIDS virus in Japan. It became effective in 1989. The law requires doctors to explain to anyone who tests positive for the AIDS virus, and who, in the judgment of the doctor, is considered likely to spread the disease, the methods necessary to prevent its transmission. Doctors are further required to report the patient's name, age, and address, and information about the manner in which the virus was contracted, to the prefectural governor within seven days. If a patient fails to follow the doctor's instructions, the governor will urge or order the patient to undergo a second medical examination, during which methods to prevent transmission will again be explained. A report to the prefectural governor is not required in the case of a patient who has contracted the AIDS virus from imported blood preparations. Critics have, however, pointed out that the law represents a danger to the human rights and to the right to privacy of AIDS patients.

History of education (*kyoikushi*) 教育史●

Education in the sense of reading and writing began in Japan after the introduction of the Chinese writing system in the 6th century or before. The aristocracy was educated in Confucian thought and Buddhism in the Nara (710–794) and Heian (794–1185) periods. Buddhist priests were the first teachers in ancient Japan, and temples became centers of learning. Education spread to the military class during the Kamakura period (1185–1333); at the same time, through the growth of popular forms of Buddhism, the peasantry was also increasingly exposed to education. During the Edo period (1600–1868) both the shogunal and domainal governments established schools; the official systems were supplemented by private schools at shrines and temples. Education was widely diffused by the time of the Meiji Restoration of 1868.

Nationalism and the drive toward modernization were strong influences on education during the late 19th century. The nationalist influence was predominant after Japan militarized in the 1930s, while the post-World War II period brought decentralization and new democratic influences to education. The postwar system provides nine years of compulsory schooling, and high school education is also nearly universal. Some 40 percent of Japanese students continue their education in universities. The schools are administered by local autonomous bodies under the broad supervision of the Ministry of Education. Education plays a critical role in preparing students for employment, and career opportunities are determined largely according to school performance.

EDUCATION BEFORE 1600 1600年までの教育●

Prior to the introduction of written language to Japan, education was carried out primarily through an oral tradition of stories concerning history and customs. The introduction of writing to Japan necessitated a more conscious and systematic form of education.

Ancient Japan 古代●

Education in ancient Japan was fostered by the imperial family. Prince Shotoku (574–622) constructed Horyuji, a temple in Nara, as a place of learning. The emperor Shomu (701–756; r 724–749) constructed temples in each province; monks were sent to these temples by the government as instructors. Of particular importance in the period was the education of clergy, who were among the leaders of society.

The role of priests in spreading education among the masses during the Nara and Heian periods was considerable. Gyogi (668–749) built places of training (*dojo*) in the various regions he visited. Other priests, including Kuya (903–972) and Ryonin (1073–1132), continued this tradition of teaching.

With the establishment of the Chinese-inspired *ritsuryo* (legal codes) system of centralized government in the late 7th century, two types of schools for the nobility were established: the Daigakuryo, to educate the children of the nobility in the capital, and the *kokugaku*, to educate the children of the provincial nobility.

Medieval Education   中世●

During the Kamakura period (1185–1333) when political power shifted to the provincial military class, *samurai* drew up *kakun* (house laws) to educate their children and ensure family solidarity.

The Christian missionaries who came to Japan in the 16th century founded schools where both general and vocational education were conducted. By this time the Daigakuryo and the provincial kokugaku had declined. The most representative educational institution of this period was the Ashikaga Gakko, where monks made up a large part of the students body and the curriculum concentrated on Confucian learning. The school flourished during the late 1500s, when enrollment reached 3,000.

EDO-PERIOD EDUCATION   江戸時代の教育●

The civilizing effect of two and a half centuries of peace and modest economic growth during the Edo period (1600–1868) was nowhere more apparent than in the field of formal education. At the beginning of the period the literacy rate was very low. Tutors, mostly priests, could be found for the children of noble families, but there were virtually no schools.

The contrast at the end of the period was great. Large schools organized by the domainal authorities (*hanko*) gave a graded instruction in the Chinese classics to almost every samurai child, and local *terakoya*, the schools for commoners, taught reading and writing to villagers as well as townsmen. Other private schools and academies called *shijuku* provided more advanced instruction in a variety of disciplines and schools of thought to both samurai and commoners. Books abounded. Japan had almost certainly reached the 40 percent literacy threshold that some consider a prerequisite for modern growth.

For the Japanese of the Edo period the Chinese classics were the repository of wisdom and knowledge. Learning painfully to "construe" these classics was the central business of the domain schools. The Buddhist temples yielded authority in the moral sphere to the new Confucian schools. The school during the Edo period thus came to combine the functions shared in Western society between school and church, with continuing consequences for the educational system of modern Japan.

Confucian Scholarship and School Formation　　　儒学と学校の形成●

The establishment of Confucian scholarship as a separate branch of learning, and of the role of the Confucian scholar-governmental adviser-teacher as a distinct profession, was the work of a number of distinguished men of the 17th century: Fujiwara Seika (1561–1619), Hayashi Razan (1583–1657), and Ito Jinsai (1627–1705). Fujiwara was the first to cut himself off from his temple roots and to declare himself an adherent of the philosophy and ethic of Confucianism as something incompatible with Buddhism.

By the end of the 17th century the idea was generally established that every self-respecting *daimyo*'s band of retainers should include a *jusha* (Confucian adviser) to advise on tricky questions of historical precedent or political morality, and to tutor the daimyo's heir. Some daimyo gave financial assistance to help transform the band of disciples who gathered at the feet of any scholar into the framework of a formal school. Some 20 domains had founded schools by 1703. The number was over 200 by 1865.

Heterodoxy and New Orthodoxy　　　異端と新正統●

An emphasis on moral virtue developed, becoming the dominant but by no means the only strand of Confucian thought or of educational philosophy in the Edo period. The leader of a reaction against this trend away from mastery of ancient Chinese texts and commentaries was Ogyu Sorai (1666–1728). He rejected the entire Neo-Confucian notion that the purpose of study was the moral cultivation of the individual. He took the Legalist view that one kept men in order not by winning over their individual hearts and minds to virtue but by establishing institutions that channel their self-interest in socially beneficial directions. Scholarship was the rigorous, intellectual study of such institutions, but in addition to that practical purpose it was also an end-in-itself pursuit of intellectual and literary excellence.

For over half a century the followers of Sorai coexisted with the Neo-Confucianists until Matsudaira Sadanobu's (1758–1829) famous Ban on Heterodox Learning (Kansei Igaku no Kin) of 1790. This edict was specifically an instruction to the shogunate's school, but it had much wider effect. Henceforth, it ruled that the teachings of Zhu Xi's Neo-Confucian school should be adhered to. The ban was part of Matsudaira's plan to revitalize the Hayashi school, which he expected to play an important role in his attempts to reform the shogunate. As other domains followed suit, the "Sorai school" practically disappeared, but the new orthodoxy was in fact a relatively tolerant and eclectic one that had room for political economy as well as for moral improvement.

Other Edo-Period Schools   江戸時代のその他の学校●

　　　There were two other forms of education. The first was Japanese studies. About 15 domains, those most influenced by the National Learning (Kokugaku), had established schools of national studies around the end of the period. The other much more consequential innovation was the establishment of schools that specialized in Dutch, later Western, studies. From the first spurt of interest in Dutch science—particularly medical science—in the 1770s until the mid-1850s, these exotic studies were largely carried on by individual doctors and low-ranking samurai. A number of special schools for Western studies were begun in the 1850s, notably the shogunate's Bansho Shirabesho, which rapidly developed into a flourishing school that admitted pupils from all over Japan.

　　　Parallel to these developments was the laying of foundations for mass literacy by the simple private reading-and-writing schools (terakoya) that helped prepare the way for Japan's transition to an industrial society.

An Edo-period *terakoya* school where commoners could learn to read and write.

　　　Convinced that knowledge would enhance the strength of the nation, the Meiji government decreed an entirely new educational system based upon imported models. Almost none of Japan's great schools and colleges can trace direct links of institutional continuity back to the schools of the Edo period.

MODERN EDUCATION   近現代の教育●

　　　The history of education in Japan since the Meiji Restoration (1868) can be divided into the following five periods: the period of establishment (1868–1885), when the initial framework for a modern educational system was created; the period of consolidation (1886–1916), when various school orders were issued and a systematic educational structure was established; the period of expansion (1917–1936), based upon the recommendations of the Extraordinary Council on Education (Rinji Kyoiku Kaigi; 1917–1919); the wartime period (1937–1945) of militaristic education; and the present period (from 1945), which was ushered in by educational reforms during the Allied Occupation.

The Period of Establishment (1868–1885)   確立期（1868年－1885年）●

　　　The Education Order of 1872 (Gakusei) established the foundation for a modern public education system. Many Edo-period schools were incorporated into the new educational system. Terakoya and shijuku, schools for the common people, became primary schools; the shogunate-controlled, elite school called Kaiseijo developed into a university that later became Tokyo University, while many domain schools became public middle schools, which eventually developed into universities. Most of the schools of Western Learning developed into private *semmon gakko* (professional schools).

The educational reform effort based on the Gakusei was overambitious and was thus revised two times, in 1879 and 1880. A significant development was the 1879 issuance of the Kyogaku Taishi (Outline of Learning), which emphasized Confucian values of humanity, justice, loyalty, and filial piety. Education in *shushin* ("moral" training) took on new importance. The utmost priority came to be placed on nationalistic moral education. This formed the basis for national educational policy until the end of World War II.

The Period of Consolidation (1886–1916)　整理統合期（1886年−1916年）●

In 1885 the cabinet system was created, and Mori Arinori (1847–1889) became the first minister of education. In 1886 he issued in quick succession the Elementary School Order, the Middle School Order, the Imperial University Order, and the Normal School Order. The imperial universities were intended to be the institutions that would create capable leaders who would absorb advanced Western Learning necessary for the modernization of the nation. Middle schools (especially the higher middle schools that became higher schools in 1894) were designed to prepare students for the Imperial University.

In these ways a comprehensive school system was established for the purpose of modernization on one hand and the spiritual unification of the people on the other. In 1890 the Imperial Rescript on Education (Kyoiku Chokugo) was issued in the name of Emperor Meiji. The rescript served as a powerful instrument of political indoctrination and remained in effect until the end of World War II. The text states that the fundamental principles of education are based upon the historical bonds uniting its benevolent rulers and their royal subjects. The Rescript was given ceremonial readings at all important school events. Later, with the development of industry after the Sino-Japanese War (1894–1895) and the demand for industrial education, Inoue Kowashi (1844–1895), who became minister of education after Mori, established systems of vocational and girls' schools. In this period a variety of private semmon gakko (later to become universities) was also established. In 1898 the

Mori Arinori, Japan's first minister of education.

attendance rate for compulsory education reached 69 percent. Compulsory education was extended to six years in 1907.

The Period of Expansion (1917–1936)   発展期（1917年－1936年）●

Stimulated by the Russo-Japanese War (1904–1905) and World War I, capitalism developed rapidly in Japan. During this period the governmental Rinji Kyoiku Kaigi (Extraordinary Council on Education) issued several reports that formed the basis for the expansion of the education system over the next decade or so. Until 1918 universities had been limited to the imperial universities, but the reforms contained in the University Order of 1918 extended recognition to colleges and private universities. In accordance with this order many national, public, and private semmon gakko were raised to the status of university.

With the inflow into Japan of new currents of thought, including socialism, communism, anarchism, and liberalism, the teachers' union and student movements rose up in opposition to nationalistic education. These trends intensified in the late 1920s with the deepening of economic crisis and political confrontation. The government attempted to counteract the influence of leftist ideology by promoting the so-called Japanese spirit.

The Wartime Period (1937–1945)   第二次世界大戦中（1937年－1945年）●

After the Manchurian Incident of 1931, educational policy soon became ultranationalistic; after the beginning of the Sino-Japanese War of 1937–1945, it became militaristic. Elementary schools were changed to *kokumin gakko* (national people's schools), which were to train subjects for the empire, and *seinen gakko* (youth schools, for vocational education) became obligatory for graduates of elementary schools. Normal schools were raised in status to semmon gakko. After Japan entered World War II, militaristic education became even stronger. In order to enhance nationalistic indoctrination, control over learning, education, and thought was strengthened.

Tokyo Imperial University (renamed Tokyo University in 1947).

Educational Reforms
after World War II (1945–)   戦後の教育改革（1945年－　）●

After defeat in 1945 Japan was placed under the Occupation of the Allied forces until the San Francisco Peace Treaty of 1952. Reports of the United States education missions to Japan, which came to Japan in 1946 and 1950, became the blueprints for educational reform. The core of the reform was the Fundamental Law of Education (1947), which took the place of the Imperial Rescript on Education as the basic philosophy of education. Based on this law, the School Education Law of 1947 was promulgated in the same year, and a new school system was established.

Society

The essential elements of the new system were the replacement of the existing dual-track (popular and elite) system with a single-track 6-3-3-4 system (six years of elementary school, three years of middle school, three years of high school, and four years of university), compulsory education in elementary and middle schools, the establishment of the principle of coeducation, and the creation of the board of education system. There have been calls for further educational reforms in response to the social and economic changes that have occurred in Japan since the late 1940s, and in 1984 the Nakasone cabinet established its own advisory council, the Provisional Council on Educational Reform (Rinji Kyoiku Shingikai; also called Rinkyoshin), which presented a final report in 1987. It stressed the principle of respect for and encouragement of individuality as a fundamental goal.

School system (*kyoiku seido*) 教育制度●

The first modern school system in Japan was established by the Education Order of 1872 (Gakusei). Curricula for pre-World War II schools were established by the government, and textbooks for elementary and middle schools were either compiled or authorized by the government. Employees of public schools were considered government officials, and even private schools were required to conduct their educational activities according to government guidelines. The Japanese school system has undergone substantial change since World War II. The Educational Reforms of 1947, carried out under the direction of the American Occupation, decentralized control of education, authorized

The Japanese Education System
学校教育制度

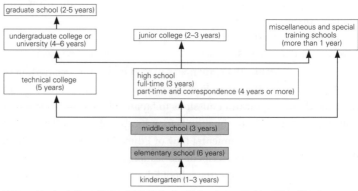

compulsory education from age 6 to the end of the school year in which the student turns 15. Source: Ministry of Education.

autonomous private schools, and encouraged the development of community education. Textbooks for elementary, middle, and high schools are now compiled under the sponsorship of private publishing houses; however, authorization by the Ministry of Education is still required (see also SCHOOL TEXTBOOKS).

The nucleus of the school system is the system of six-year elementary schools, three-year middle schools, three-year high schools, and four-year universities. In addition there are kindergartens, five-year technical colleges for graduates of middle school, and schools for the handicapped. Universities include undergraduate colleges, junior colleges, and graduate schools. Aside from these regular schools there are miscellaneous schools, most of which are vocational or technical training schools. Education is compulsory through middle school, and over 95 percent of elementary and middle schools are public; private schools play a larger role at the secondary and university level (24 percent of Japan's high schools and 73 percent of its universities are private institutions).

School curriculum (kyoiku katei)   教育課程●

The modern Japanese educational system was established in the early Meiji period (1868–1912) with the assistance of such American advisers as David Murray and Marion Scott. In 1886 the government set up the first regular curriculum. Under Japan's system of compulsory education (initially four years of elementary school), the required subjects were *shushin* (courses instilling patriotism), arithmetic, reading and writing, composition, penmanship, and physical education. Drawing and singing were sometimes included.

In 1890 the government issued the Imperial Rescript on Education. This document, based on traditional Confucian tenets, articulated the guiding principles of education in Japan; it remained in effect until the end of World War II. After the Sino-Japanese War of 1894–95, the government consolidated the school system and introduced more up-to-date subject matter into the curriculum. After 1907 compulsory education was increased to six years and the courses taught were shushin, Japanese, arithmetic, physical education, Japanese history, geog-

Standard Curriculum for Elementary Schools
小学校教育課程

| Subjects | Year | | | | | |
	1	2	3	4	5	6
	(school hours per year)					
Japanese language	306	315	280	280	210	210
Social studies	–	–	105	105	105	105
Arithmetic	136	175	175	175	175	175
Science	–	–	105	105	105	105
Life envirnomental studies	102	105	–	–	–	–
Music	68	70	70	70	70	70
Arts and crafts	68	70	70	70	70	70
Physical education	102	105	105	105	105	105
Homemaking	–	–	–	–	70	70
Moral education	34	35	35	35	35	35
Extracurricular activities	34	35	35	70	70	70
Total	850	910	980	1,015	1,015	1,015

Source: Ministry of Education.

raphy, science, drawing, singing, and, for girls, sewing. This curriculum continued basically unchanged until 1941, when elementary schools were reorganized as *kokumin gakko* (national people's schools), and the curriculum was drastically revised to meet the objective of "training loyal subjects of the emperor." Such courses as shushin and history were infused with a strong militaristic and nationalistic tone, and almost every aspect of schooling stressed absolute loyalty to the emperor.

After Japan's defeat in 1945, Occupation authorities suspended the teaching of shushin, Japanese history, and geography and forbade the formal reading of the Imperial Rescript on Education. In 1946 a team of American education specialists visited Japan and made a number of recommendations for the reorganization of the school system. Following this visit a new curriculum was developed, and the school system was decentralized and revised to accord with regional differences and individual needs. The educational reforms of 1947 established social studies as a part of the curriculum and emphasized educating students to be responsible members of society. The School Education Law of 1947 provided for the basic framework and organization of the postwar Japanese school system, while school course guidelines, first issued in 1947, stated the aim of each subject taught and the contents of teaching in each grade.

Under the contemporary system, compulsory education consists of six years of elementary school and three years of middle school; three years of high school are optional. The elementary school curriculum is uniform: all students in the same year study the same topics; no special classes or groups based on different attainment levels are formed; and students are not allowed to skip grades. The middle school curriculum includes basic vocational and technical classes geared to the students' needs and aptitudes, some on an elective basis. High schools stress matching electives to each student's abilities, aptitudes, and future course of study. Both primary and middle school curricula include one hour of moral education per week, and additional guidance is provided in all educational activities. Religious education is not included in the public school curriculum. Extracurricular activities receive strong emphasis. Curriculum standards are reviewed by the Curriculum Council (Kyoiku Katei Shingikai) of the Ministry of Education and are usually revised every 10 years, most recently in 1989.

The Structure of Education   教育科目●

Elementary schools teach Japanese language, social studies, arithmetic, science, music, arts and crafts, physical education, and homemaking. The 1989 course guidelines mandate life environmental studies, rather than social studies and science, to teach first- and second-graders about society and nature through activities and experiences geared to their immediate environment. In middle school, Japanese language, social studies, mathematics, science, and industrial arts and homemaking (one course for boys and girls) are required subjects; music, art, and health and physical education are partly required and partly elective. Foreign language is an elective, but nearly all middle school students study English; a few schools offer other languages (generally French or German). In high school, Japanese language, geography and history, civics, mathematics, science, health and physical education, the arts, and home economics (for boys and girls) are common required courses. Foreign language, usually English, is an elective taken by the majority of students; far fewer students take French or German, although more high schools than middle schools offer these languages. Specialized vocational courses are available, and extracurricular activities are required in all grades. The contents of the principal courses are as follows:

Japanese language（国語） Reading and writing is stressed. By the time students complete their elementary and middle school education, they are expected to have learned the 1,945 characters known as the *joyo kanji*. In middle and high schools the reading and appreciation of classical Japanese (*kobun*) and *kambun* (classical Chinese) are included. Composition using the *kana* syllabary and Chinese characters is taught from first grade; calligraphy, using a brush, begins in third grade.

Social studies（社会） Social studies was included in the postwar curriculum to teach democracy and pacifism, but the subject is now divided into geography, history, and civics. In elementary school, third- to sixth-graders learn about their community, their nation, and Japanese history in a combined course. In middle school children study geography and history concurrently in the first and second years; in the third year they study civics (politics, economics, and society). Social studies in high school was divided into two subjects in 1989: geography and history (taught as one course) and

Standard Curriculum for Middle Schools
中学校教育課程

	Year 1	2	3
Required subjects	(school hours per year)		
Japanese language	175	140	140
Social studies	140	140	70–105
Mathematics	105	140	140
Science	105	105	105–140
Music	70	35–70	35
Fine arts	70	35–70	35
Health and physical education	105	105	105–140
Industrial arts or homemaking	70	70	70–105
Elective subjects			
Foreign language[1] or other special subject	105–140	105–210	140–280
Other subject[2]	–	–	35
Moral education	35	35	35
Extracurricular activities	35–70	35–70	35–70
Total	1,050	1,050	1,050

1 Nearly all middle school students study English. 2 Students are required to take one of the following subjects; music, fine arts, health and physical education, industrial arts, or homemaking.
Source: Ministry of Education.

Society

civics. The initial focus of geography education is on one's own community (as in the life environmental studies course for first- and second-graders) and then gradually expands to cover a larger sphere. In middle and high school students begin with a view of the world as a whole and then study Japan and their own city in the geography and history and civics courses.

Mathematics（算数・数学）Elementary school programs cover four areas: numbers and calculation, quantity and measurement, geometry, and quantity relationships. In middle school numbers and formulas, functions, geometry, and qualitative relationships including probability and statistics are taught. High schools offer general math, algebra, geometry, basic analysis, differentiation and integration, and probability and statistics.

Science（科学）To learn about the world around them, third- to sixth-graders study living things and their environment, matter and energy, the earth and the universe. In middle school, science comprises physics, chemistry, biology, and earth science. High school students must take two of the following: comprehensive science, basic science, physics, chemistry, biology, or earth science.

Music and art（音楽・美術）Singing, instrumental music, composition, and appreciation of both Western and traditional Japanese music are taught. Elementary school students learn to play the harmonica in the lower grades and later the recorder. Elementary and middle school students are taught to appreciate and express themselves through drawing, sculpture, design, and handicrafts. High-schoolers choose two from among music, art (painting, drawing, sculpture, graphic design), calligraphy, and crafts.

Health and physical education（保健体育）In physical education students may take gymnastics, track and field, swimming, various kinds of ball games, *kendo, sumo, judo,* and dancing. There are swimming pools in 78.1 percent of the public elementary schools and 67.6 percent of the public middle schools, and swimming is required from the fourth grade on. In health classes, students study the functions and development of the body and mind, the prevention of accidents and illness, and, at the middle school level, the effects of smoking, alcohol, and recreational drug use on health.

Elementary school athletic meet.

Home economics（家庭科）Students acquire basic knowledge and skills relating to food, clothing, shelter, child care, and welfare for the aged. Both boys and girls must take home economics from the fifth grade through high school; the middle and high school courses are coeducational. Classes in industrial arts and homemaking teach middle school students the rudiments of cooking and sewing, the child-parent relationship, consumer life, and computer use. From the preparation of simple egg dishes in elementary school, or practical skills such as sewing on buttons, students progress during the high school years to more complex tasks such as making their own skirts and shirts, or cooking full meals.

Foreign language（外国語） English is taught in middle and high school, and German and French are offered in some middle and high schools. See ENGLISH LANGUAGE TRAINING.

Extracurricular activities（課外活動） Additional student activities include class assemblies, club activities, ceremonies, athletic meets (*undokai*), school plays and concerts (*gakugeikai*), excursions (*shugaku ryoko*) and field trips (*ensoku*), and educational guidance relating to student life, such as traffic safety guidance and training in the use of the school library. See also HISTORY OF EDUCATION.

School textbooks (*kyokasho*)   教科書●

In Japan all elementary, middle, and high schools are obliged to use government-approved textbooks. Textbooks are compiled by private publishers, who are given a certain amount of freedom in the style of presentation, but are also required to conform to government-issued school course guidelines. Authorization is given only after evaluation of the texts by Ministry of Education specialists and appointed examiners and a final review by the Textbook Authorization and Research Council, an advisory organ of the ministry.

A system of free distribution of textbooks for compulsory education was established in 1963. The textbooks used in each school district are chosen by the local board of education from among those authorized by the central government; in the case of private schools the responsibility lies with the school principal.

Ienaga Saburo addresses supporters after a partial victory in his third suit challenging the Ministry of Education's textbook review system.

The purpose of the official authorization of textbooks, a system that has been in effect in Japan since 1886, is the standardization of education and the maintenance of objectivity and neutrality on political and religious issues. The textbook approval process has engendered considerable controversy and has led to one famous court case, a suit brought against the government by historian Ienaga Saburo (1913–) in 1965, charging that the authorization process was both illegal and unconstitutional.

English language training (*eigo kyoiku*)   英語教育●

English is the most widely studied foreign language in Japan. During the Meiji period (1868–1912), the study of English was considered essential for importing the Western technology necessary for modernization. Language training was chiefly based on reading ability and not on conversation.

Because the written entrance examinations for universities and high schools test for English ability, grammar and reading comprehension are stressed in the English classes offered by most high schools and middle schools. However, there is a growing awareness that neglecting speaking and listening during the first six years of English language training leads to problems. The school course guidelines introduced in 1992 stress spoken communication, and the Ministry of Education has brought in native English speakers as assistant teachers of middle and high school English classes. In 1990 there were 2,146 such assistant teachers invited to Japan.

English conversation schools, courses on television and on radio, and company-run classes for employees offer further training in English. In 1992, some 2.8 million people took the Test in Practical English Proficiency (approved by the Ministry of Education since 1963).

School lunch program (*gakko kyushoku*)   学校給食●

During the post-World War II food shortage the Allied Occupation started a nationwide school lunch program. With the School Lunch Law of 1954 the practice was established on a permanent basis. The school lunch menu was based on bread until 1976, when a rice-based menu was introduced. In 1993, 99.4 percent of elementary schools and 82.4 percent of middle schools had lunch programs.

School lunch.

Entrance examinations (*nyugaku shiken*)   入学試験●

Entrance examinations are given great weight in Japan's educational system. Although nursery, primary, and middle schools also conduct such tests, Japanese society attaches the most importance to entrance exams for high schools and universities.

High school is attended by 97 percent of middle school graduates, so the function of high school entrance tests is not to weed out unqualified applicants, but to determine which school a student may attend. Private high schools design their own tests and conduct applicant interviews to select students, while public high school entrance standards are determined by the local school system. Generally, achievement test results in five categories (English, mathematics, Japanese, social studies, and science) are evaluated, along with the student's junior high school records.

Objective achievement-test performance is the key factor in university applicant selection, but certain universities may include essay-writing tests, or performance tests for applicants in music or physical education, in their evaluation process. All national and other public universities (and a few private ones) require prospective applicants to take the University Entrance Examination Center Tests—a series of standardized multiple-choice examinations measuring competence in the Japanese language, social studies, mathematics, science, and foreign languages. Based on the results, students may then make a more informed choice as to which schools to apply to. Ultimately, admission is based on the combined results of the general test plus the independent examination offered by the university in question. Entrance examinations for both high schools and universities are administered each year during the period from January through March. Students may apply to more than one high school or university.

Entrance examination for Tokyo University.

The Japanese entrance examination system does not establish in advance a target score that, if achieved, assures admission; those applying at the same time compete for a limited number of openings. In Japanese society it is generally accepted that the school one attends will decisively influence the course of one's life and career (GAKUREKI SHAKAI). Entrance tests are therefore regarded as major events in determining one's fate, and the battle to qualify for the best schools is waged with fierce intensity. The competition is seen as having assumed excessive proportions in the 1980s. This has not only led to enormous prosperity for the operators of JUKU (private tutoring schools) and CRAM SCHOOLS, but is also thought to have helped precipitate many education-related problems. These include increasing juvenile delinquency, apathy on the part of students not targeted as high achievers, and school allergy, a phenomenon whereby some students are unable to attend school for emotional reasons.

Rate of Advancement to Higher Education
高等教育進学率 (%)

		1960	1970	1980	1990	1993
University	Men	13.7	27.3	39.3	33.4	36.6
	Women	2.5	6.5	12.3	15.2	19.0
Junior College	Men	1.2	2.0	2.0	1.7	1.9
	Women	3.0	11.2	21.0	22.2	24.4
Total	Men	14.9	29.3	41.3	35.1	38.5
	Women	5.5	17.7	33.3	37.4	43.4

Source: Ministry of Education.

Gakureki shakai ("credential society") 学歴社会●

Term used in Japan to refer to the great emphasis the Japanese place on a person's educational background. In Japan an individual's social and occupational status is generally considered to be determined not only by the level of education completed, but also by the rank and prestige of the particular universities attended. Factors such as class, race, religion, and personal wealth, which are important determinants of social status in other societies, are not quite as significant in Japan because of the country's high level of homogeneity and lack of extreme inequalities in the distribution of wealth. A person's educational career, on the other hand, provides a convenient determinant of status. With a high percentage of students attending universities, the status distinctions among schools have become increasingly pronounced. As a result of this, the competition to gain entrance to the most prestigious schools has intensified markedly.

Hensachi (deviation) 偏差値●

Statistical term frequently used in Japanese education to express a student's performance on a standardized examination relative to a mean average score. Since the early 1960s hensachi figures have been used in Japan to calculate an individual's percentile ranking for practice ENTRANCE EXAMINATIONS. Guidance counselors often base their assessment of how likely a student is to gain admission to certain schools by comparing the student's hensachi with the average hensachi of other students applying to the same schools. The industry of private tutoring schools (JUKU) and CRAM SCHOOLS also calculates hensachi figures for students, based on the results of large-scale practice examinations, to advise them on test-taking strategies.

Cram schools (yobiko) 予備校●

Schools whose primary purpose is preparing students to pass the highly competitive entrance examinations of Japanese universities. Most cram school enrollees are recent high school graduates who are seeking admission to colleges and universities and failed in their first sitting for the entrance examination.

Recently competition among those hoping to pass college entrance examinations has become intense, and large numbers of students commute to cram school while still in high school. The information regarding university entrance examinations provided by the major yobiko is indispensable not only to their enrolled students but to all prospective test takers.

Juku (private tutoring schools)   塾●

In the Edo period (1600–1868) the term juku referred to small schools for the teaching of martial arts or the doctrines of a particular school of philosophy. Modern juku may offer lessons in nonacademic subjects such as arts and sports or in the academic subjects that are important in school entrance examinations. Juku for high school students must compete for enrollments with *yobiko* (cram schools), which are solely geared to helping students pass university entrance examinations. According to a 1989 survey, 38.2 percent of elementary school students, 74.9 percent of middle school students, and 37.6 percent of high school students in Tokyo were attending juku. Recently there has been a trend toward expanding the major juku into chain or franchise operations. At the same time, a number of smaller, innovative juku have sprung up to help students who are unable to keep up with classwork or who have had problems.

Elementary school students studying at a private tutoring school.

Transportation (*kotsu*)   交通●

Japan has a highly developed domestic and international transportation network. The system as it now exists was developed in the century following the Meiji Restoration of 1868, but even earlier the transportation system was relatively sophisticated for a preindustrial society.

Premodern Transportation   前近代の交通●

During the early periods of Japanese history, and especially during the 7th to 9th centuries, goods and people traveled extensively by ship between Japan and the Asian mainland. Within Japan, the establishment of a rice tax system and legal system in the late 7th century was accompanied by the construction of the first major roads. The Inland Sea was a major transportation route between settlements in Japan from early times.

After the establishment of the Tokugawa shogunate (1603–1867), international transportation activity was halted by the National Seclusion policy, which was in force from 1639 to 1854. Domestic transportation, on the other hand, grew and improved greatly during the Edo period (1600–1868). Coastal shipping routes were extended to support the expanding commodity trade, and the road network was also improved.

Meiji Period (1868–1912) to World War II   明治時代から第二次世界大戦まで●

Following the Meiji Restoration of 1868, Japan absorbed Western technology at a rapid pace. The first steam-powered train ran on a narrow-gauge track between Tokyo and Yokohama in 1872, the first automobile was imported in 1899. Western vessels quickly replaced most Japanese sailing ships, as the government subsidized the shipbuilding industry. From the 1880s onward the rail network expanded rapidly and in 1906 major portions of it were nationalized. In 1927 the first subway in Tokyo began operation. Bus service and trucking companies began in the 1910s, with rapid expansion after the Tokyo Earthquake of 1923. During the 1930s taxis developed into an important means of urban transportation.

By the 1940s the mainstay of the passenger transportation system was the railroads, while freight transportation was conducted primarily through coastal shipping and the railroads.

Postwar Transportation Network   第二次世界大戦後の交通ネットワーク●

The postwar era was characterized by an explosive growth in moter vehicles and airlines. By 1990 the rail share of total domestic passenger transportation had fallen to 30 percent, with automobiles increasing from less than 1 percent in 1950 to 66 percent in 1990. Buses also compete with the railroads to some extent, but they mainly provide feeder service to train stations or operate in rural areas where there is no rail service. SUBWAYS are an important means of urban transportation. In addition to the vast network in Tokyo, there are also subway systems in Fukuoka, Kobe, Kyoto, Nagoya, Osaka, Sapporo, Sendai, and Yokohama.

Scheduled domestic airlines have grown rapidly but still occupy a small share of total passenger transportation. International air travel has also grown at a tremendous pace: the number of passengers carried by scheduled Japanese airlines was only 112,000 in 1955 but reached 11 million in 1992.

For freight transportation, the rail share of total ton-kilometers fell to 5 percent by 1990, while trucks expanded from 8 percent in 1950 to 50 percent in 1990, and coastal shipping went from 39 percent to 45 percent.

Coordination of the transportation system has been a problem because different modes of transportation are governed by separate laws and represented by different bureaus within the Ministry of Transport. In addition, certain transportation-related activities are under the jurisdiction of other ministries.

New signs being readied when the Japanese National Railways was privatized in 1987, creating the Japan Railways (JR) group.

Railroads（鉄道） The network of RAILWAYS consists of the JR (Japan Railways) group and a number of private railways. The JR group is made up of six passenger railway companies, a freight railway company, and several other affiliated companies, all of which were created when long-term financial difficulties led to the privatization of the Japanese National Railways (JNR) in 1987. In 1990 the rail system comprised 26,895 operation-kilometers (16,710 mi), of which JR companies operated 20,175 or 75 percent of the total. JR passenger service includes intercity trunk lines, urban feeder service, and a large number of rural lines. It also operates Japan's fastest passenger trains on the SHINKANSEN "bullet train" lines of standard gauge. In 1950 the JNR alone generated 59 percent of all passenger-kilometers, but this figure had fallen to 18 percent for the JR in 1990. The JR group's Japan Freight Railway Co. provides almost all of the rail freight service in Japan, but railroads can no longer effectively compete with trucks for most freight business.

In addition to the JR group companies, there are 16 large railway companies and 58 smaller railways. Unlike the JR, the other large railway companies have evolved into conglomerates of related activities, operating sports stadiums, baseball teams, department stores, amusement parks, and

Cumulative Passenger Transportation Utilization
交通機関別利用者数   (in millions)

	Railways	Motor vehicles	Vessels	Aircrafts	Total
1960	12,290	7,901	99	1	20,291
1970	16,384	24,032	174	15	40,605
1980	18,005	33,515	160	40	51,720
1990	21,939	42,628	163	65	64,795

Source: Ministry of Transport.

real estate. More of their profits often come from these related businesses than from railway businesses.

Motor vehicles （自動車） Private automobiles have been one of the fastest growing segments of passenger transportation because of three factors that became conspicuous in the 1960s: the rapid growth of income to a point where families could afford automobiles; the development of a domestic automotive industry geared to the specific needs of the domestic market (small-sized vehicles); and the improvement of roads. The number of registered motor vehicles increased from only about 1.5 million in 1960 to over 43 million in 1990. Paving on national highways was extended from 29 percent in 1960 to 98 percent in 1991. Japan also had developed a total of 4,869 kilometers (3,025 mi) of EXPRESSWAYS by 1991. Even as late as 1960, 20 percent of all automobiles were business vehicles, but by 1990 private automobiles were 97 percent of total registrations. Despite the popularity of automobile ownership, problems such as urban traffic congestion, lack of parking, and the high cost of fuel continue to restrict the actual day-to-day use of private vehicles in Japan.

As roads have improved, trucks have increased in size. Whereas most commercial trucks did not exceed a 5-ton capacity in the mid-1950s, 18-ton trucks are now common and the number of trailer trucks is also increasing.

Highway safety continues to be a major problem. Although major safety campaigns led to a steady decline in traffic deaths between 1970 and 1980, since then the trend has reversed, and in 1988 highway fatalities exceeded 10,000.

Marine transportation （海上輸送） Seaborne freight is the primary means of transporting Japan's huge volume of raw-materials imports and finished-goods exports. Total tonnage handled by Japanese ports grew at an annual rate of 15 percent from 1980 to 1990. The most important of Japan's 121 international ports are the Tokyo Bay area (Tokyo, Yokohama, Kawasaki, and Chiba), Nagoya, the Osaka Bay area (Osaka and Kobe), Kita Kyushu, and Wakayama Shimotsu (a major oil port).

View of Tokyo bay from Tokyo Tower.

Since the oil crisis of 1973 an oversupply of ships worldwide has hurt the shipping industry as a whole. Japanese shipping companies have lost international competitiveness because of rising wages and the continuing high value of the yen since 1985. Japanese-owned vessels under flags of convenience have been increasing to gain the advantage of lower-cost labor. By 1990 the total gross tons of vessels flying the Japanese flag had fallen about 42 percent from its peak of 35 million tons in 1982. The industry has responded to the difficult business environment by trying to increase efficiency through mergers and large-scale reductions in capacity.

Along with the increases in maritime freight through the mid-1970s, Japan's shipbuilding industry expanded to a point where Japan became the world's largest shipbuilder. Japan pioneered the construction of supertankers, which were instrumental in supplying Japan's energy needs at substantially reduced transportation costs. However, the oil crisis and ensuing severe recession brought depression to the shipbuilding industry. Since then the government has taken measures to reduce capacity and employment in the industry.

Air transportation (航空輸送) After World War II, passenger airlines were prohibited by SCAP (the supreme commander for the Allied powers) until 1951, when the Ministry of Transport was given control over licensing airline routes and fares. Japan Airlines Co, Ltd (JAL), was established in 1953 as an international airline (including domestic trunk lines) with 50 percent government capital participation. At the same time approval was also given to two private regional firms, which later merged to become All Nippon Airways Co, Ltd (ANA). JAL became a private company in 1987.

Japan Airlines Co, Ltd, celebrates its passage of the 10 million passenger mark on its international routes.

As of January 1991 there were 5 scheduled international airlines in Japan, including JAL and ANA, as well as 6 scheduled domestic airlines and 49 unscheduled air service companies. To handle the increased air traffic, AIRPORTS have also expanded. In the spring of 1978, the New Tokyo International Airport (Narita) replaced Tokyo International Airport (Haneda) as the main international airport for Tokyo. Kansai International Airport opened in 1994 in Osaka.

Railways (*tetsudo*)   鉄道●

Railways in Japan date from 1872, only four years into the country's modern period, but almost four decades from the time that railways first appeared in Europe and the United States. Progress was rapid after the late start, however, and in the 20th century Japan's railways have compared favorably with those of any other nation in the world. In the post-World War II period, and especially since the development of the SHINKANSEN "bullet train," Japan has been at the forefront of railway technology.

Early Development   草創期●

The first line, begun in 1870 and completed in 1872, was of modest proportions, running 28 kilometers (17.4 mi) from Shimbashi in Tokyo to Yokohama on narrow gauge track. Financing for the first state lines was obtained partly by floating bonds on the London money market, and British technicians and technology figured prominently in the early construction of both public and private railways. Domestication of technical expertise and equipment was relatively rapid and thorough, and one of the few lasting reminders of British influence is that Japanese trains run on the left, a practice that has carried over to highway traffic control.

In the KINKI REGION, a state-constructed line between Kobe and Osaka was opened in 1874. Following initial government plans calling for a trunk line between Tokyo and Kyoto, running through a coastal route, the Tokaido was first spanned by rails in 1893. Two years later the nation's first electric railway began operating in Kyoto. By 1901 tracks had been laid the entire length of the main island of Honshu, and each of the other three main islands also had some trackage by this time. By and by, gaps in the system were filled in gradually, so that, in effect, a nationwide network was in place by the eve of nationalization in 1906–1907.

Nationalization 国有化●

Although the earliest lines had been constructed by the government, after about 1885 the apparent profitability of railways was sufficient to attract a flood of private entrepreneurs into the field. During the period prior to nationalization, however, the wars with China (1894–1895) and Russia (1904–1905) raised the question of the desirability of private control of such a key national resource. The importance of foreign loans in financing railway development was thought to raise the specter of foreign control of the private lines, and this possibility was a key element in arguments in favor of nationalization, which went into effect in 1906–1907. The resulting system was known as the Japanese National Railways from 1949 until denationalization took place in 1987.

Postwar Developments 第二次世界大戦後の発達●

Ceremony at the start of operation of the first Shinkansen route in 1964.

The extension of urban commuter systems, including subways, has been a major accomplishment of the postwar period, but the most spectacular development has been the routes of the world-famed Shinkansen "bullet trains" and the infrastructure that has been created to extend these routes throughout Japan. The original section of the Shinkansen was opened in 1964 as a route between Tokyo and Osaka. Since then, extensions have been opened to Okayama (Okayama Prefecture) in 1972 and Hakata (Fukuoka Prefecture) in 1975. Two more new lines, connecting Tokyo with northern Japan, were put into operation in 1982: the Joetsu Shinkansen, from Tokyo to Niigata (Niigata Prefecture), and the Tohoku Shinkansen, from Tokyo to Morioka (Iwate Prefecture). Also the "Mini" Shinkansen, using the conventional narrow-

gauge track partially broadened into standard gauge by addition of a
third rail, started operation between Fukushima (Fukushima Prefecture)
and Yamagata (Yamagata Prefecture) in 1992. New Shinkansen routes
are under construction.

Overnight trains with sleeping car service are available on non-
Shinkansen routes. Approximately 2,300 limited express and ordinary
express trains operate on principal lines every day, along with about
23,300 local trains.

Unlike those in many countries, the Japanese rail system can be
characterized as passenger oriented. Residents of the suburbs are so
dependent on the presence of commuter railways that land values for
lots within walking distance of stations are considerably higher.

Denationalization   民営化●

The basic form of the railway system remained the same from
nationalization in 1906–1907 until 1987, when the Japanese National
Railways was privatized and broken up into six regional private passenger services and one rail freight company, known collectively as the JR
(Japan Railways) group. The JNR had been suffering an increasing burden of debt and operating deficits since the 1960s. Most of the new JR
companies returned to profitability within two to three years of privatization by cutting staff, by reducing services on loss-making lines or
abolishing them altogether, and by buying into service industries such as
restaurants and hotels.

Workers remove the
Japanese National
Railways sign from a
station after privatization in
1987.

In addition to the main JR network—20,175 kilometers (12,535
mi) of track—and the private local lines, subway systems serve the main
cities of Japan. In densely populated urban centers, the subways provide
important feeder services to the aboveground rail lines. As crowding
increases even further, subways should become an even more important
component of the urban transportation system.

Shinkansen (New Trunk Line)   新幹線●

The Shinkansen, a high-speed passenger railroad system operated by companies of the JR group, provides first-class, or "Green Car,"
service as well as reserved and unreserved ordinary-car service. There
are no sleeping facilities and few dining facilities on Shinkansen trains,
since most runs can be made in a few hours.

The first line to be completed was called the Tokaido Shinkansen,
because it was a new trunk line on the route of the Tokaido between
Tokyo and Osaka. The San'yo line has since been constructed from

Society

Osaka west to Hakata in Kyushu. The combined route, with a total length of 1,069 kilometers (664 mi), is known as the Tokaido-San'yo Shinkansen. The train has a maximum speed of 270 kilometers per hour (168 mph), and the minimum trip time between Tokyo and Hakata is 5 hours 4 minutes. A Shinkansen train departs Tokyo for Osaka or some point further west about every seven minutes throughout most daytime schedules, lasting from approximately 6 AM to 12 PM. In 1991, 278 trains were scheduled on the route per day, each with a uniform 16 cars. Between the inauguration of service on the line in 1964 and early 1991, the Tokaido San'yo Shinkansen had carried 3 billion passengers.

The Tohoku Shinkansen and Joetsu Shinkansen commenced service in 1982. The former connects Tokyo and Morioka in northern Japan, with a route length of 535.3 kilometers (332.6 mi) and a minimum trip time of 2 hours 36 minutes. On average 115 trains are scheduled daily and passengers number over 30 million per year. The latter connects Tokyo and Niigata on the coast of the Sea of Japan, with a route length of 333.9 kilometers (207.5 mi) and a minimum trip time of 1 hour 40 minutes. On average 85 trains are scheduled daily and passengers number 20 million per year. From the inauguration of service to 1991, the two lines carried over 400 million passengers.

Development of the System   システムの発達●

The railroad that serves the 500-kilometer (311-mi) corridor between Tokyo and Osaka has always been considered the main artery of Japan. Located on the Pacific coast of central Honshu, this zone is the industrial and socioeconomic nucleus of the country; almost half the population and two-thirds of the nation's industry are concentrated there.

In the 1950s innovations on the conventional Tokaido rail line, which served this district, were given priority over other lines in an effort to meet steadily increasing demand. Because of the significance of the line, it became imperative to increase the capacity. The eventual solution was to construct a high-speed railroad on a separate double track of standard gauge—the Shinkansen. Ground was broken for the project in April 1959, and construction was completed in July 1964. Service was begun on 1 October 1964, 10 days before the opening of the Tokyo Olympic Games, with initial daily service of 60 trains with 12 cars each. The total construction cost was ¥380.0 billion (US $1.1 billion), double the original estimate.

A train on the Tokaido-San'yo Shinkansen line running between Tokyo and Hakata in Kyushu.

The Shinkansen reduced the minimum trip time between Tokyo and Osaka from 6 hours and 30 minutes to 2 hours and 30 minutes. A business trip between the two cities was no longer an overnight journey, a fact that considerably altered business activities. The Shinkansen was enthusiastically welcomed by the public because of its high speed, short trip time, good ride comfort, and superb on-time operation. In the 1960s and 1970s the image of the Shinkansen speeding past a snowcapped Mt. Fuji was seen as a symbol of modern Japan.

The line's popularity and the rapid growth in traffic volume brought about a need for the westward extension of the Shinkansen system. The San'yo Shinkansen opened for service with a 160.9 kilometer (100-mi) stretch between Osaka and Okayama in March 1972. The project had taken five years to complete at a cost of ¥224.0 billion (US $739.0 million). The line was extended to Hakata in Kyushu through the Kammon undersea tunnel in March 1975. The construction for this stretch of 392.8 kilometers (244 mi) also took five years, and the cost was ¥729.0 billion (US $2.4 billion).

In 1971 the construction of two new lines was begun from Omiya in Saitama Prefecture north to Niigata and northeast to Morioka. These lines were completed in 1982 and extended from Omiya to Tokyo in 1991. Additional routes, including the Hokuriku Shinkansen (Takasaki–Kanazawa–Osaka), are under construction, and others are being planned.

Technical Aspects   技術●

Ceremony at the 1975 opening of the Kammon tunnel extending the Shinkansen line to Kyushu.

The Shinkansen track is a conventional ballasted track between Tokyo and Osaka. This track structure, however, requires a great deal of time and labor to maintain the track geometry. Consequently, concrete slab track, which is maintenance free, was adopted for further line extensions. The Shinkansen has a DC series traction motor installed on each single-wheel axle, allowing dynamic brakes to be applied to all axles at once, and uses electric multiple-unit trains fed by AC 25 kilowatts. This system was selected for a number of reasons: the even distribution of axle load results in less strain on track structure; the turnaround operation is simple; and a failure of one or two units does not interrupt the operation of the entire train. The car body is streamlined and the cars are air-conditioned and airtight. Windows cannot be opened, but the train is well ventilated throughout. Automatic Train Control (ATC) is used to prevent collisions by maintaining a safety distance between trains and to prevent excess speeds by applying brakes automatically. All trains are continuously monitored and controlled from computer-aided traffic control systems in two central control rooms in Tokyo. Electric power supply to the trains is also monitored and controlled from the same rooms by electric power dispatchers. In case of accidents or other problems, the dispatchers act promptly to secure alternative power to restore the failure.

Since it was inaugurated in 1964, the Shinkansen has had a remarkable record of high-speed operation, safety, volume of transport, and punctuality. The success of the Shinkansen revolutionized thinking about high-speed trains. It has been described as the "savior of the declining railroad industry" since its example has stimulated many other countries to take on the new construction or the modernization of railroads as national projects, among which are the French TGV, the English HST, and the Northeast Corridor Rail Improvement Project in the United States.

Subways (chikatetsu) 地下鉄●

Japan's first underground rail service started operating in December 1927 over a 2.2-kilometer (1.4-mi) route between Ueno and Asakusa stations in Tokyo under the management of the Tokyo Underground Railway Co. The line later became part of the present Ginza Line, operated by the Teito Rapid Transit Authority. The rapid concentrations of population in large cities since World War II and the resulting transport congestion have led to successive subway-network-building programs in Tokyo, Osaka, Nagoya, Kobe, Sapporo, Yokohama, Kyoto, Fukuoka, and Sendai. In 1994 there were some 34 lines totaling 560.3 kilometers (348.1 mi) operating in nine cities. More than 8 million passengers a day travel on the 12 Tokyo lines (230.3 km; 143.1 mi) and 3 million on the 7 Osaka subway lines (99.1 km; 61.5 mi). Many of the subway lines currently under construction are designed to connect directly with existing suburban surface rail networks, the intention being to ease congestion at terminus stations and to improve convenience for passengers.

Airports (kuko) 空港●

Commercial airports in Japan are classified by the government into three categories based on size and use. As of 1994, class 1 consisted of Japan's 4 major international airports: Tokyo International Airport (Haneda), New Tokyo International Airport (Narita), Osaka International Airport, and Kansai International Airport. Class 2 comprised 25 major domestic airports (some with international service), and class 3 was composed of 48 smaller domestic airports. Besides these, there were 12 unclassified airports used jointly by commercial and military aircraft or for other purposes. Of these 89 commercial and semicommercial airports, 53 had facilities for jet passenger aircraft.

Airport operations are regulated by the Airport Improvement Law of 1956, and facilities are maintained by the government's Special

Account for Airport Improvement. Landing fees and a tax on aircraft fuel are the chief sources of revenue for airports.

Tokyo International Airport 東京国際空港●

Commonly referred to as Haneda Airport. Located on the shore of Tokyo Bay in Ota Ward, Tokyo, Haneda Airport services 40 million passengers per year and is the hub of Japan's domestic air-traffic network. It is linked to 42 airports nationwide by approximately 520 incoming and outgoing flights per day. The airport began operations in 1931 as Japan's first commercial airport. The US military requisitioned the facility following World War II; however, from 1952, when it was restored to Japanese control, until 1978, when the New Tokyo International Airport was opened, it was the chief gateway to Japan.

In order to expand capacity and reduce complaints about noise, Haneda Airport has undertaken a three-stage project of land reclamation and construction in Tokyo Bay. With the completion of the second stage in 1993, a new passenger terminal opened and the airport grew from two runways to three and from 408 hectares (1,008 acres) to 894 hectares (2,209 acres) . The third stage of expansion is scheduled for completion in 1996 and will further increase the airport's size to 1,100 hectares (2,718 acres). The Tokyo Monorail runs between Haneda Airport and Hamamatsucho Station on the JR line.

New Tokyo International Airport 新東京国際空港●

Also known as Narita Airport. International airport located some 66 kilometers (41 mi) east of Tokyo in the city of Narita, Chiba Prefecture. It opened in May 1978 and replaced Tokyo International Airport as Japan's chief international airport. Construction work on the airport at Natita began in 1969, but its completion was delayed from 1971 to 1975 and its opening until 1978 because of fierce opposition from a coalition of local inhabitants and radical students.

The New Tokyo International Airport is served by two railways, the JR line and the Keisei line. Check-in procedures for most flights can be performed at Tokyo City Air Terminal, located in Hakozaki, Chuo Ward.

The New Tokyo International Airport's main runway measures 4,000 meters (13,120 ft) in length. Under a second-stage construction program, begun in 1987, a 2,500-meter (8,200-ft) parallel runway and a 3,200-meter (10,496-ft) crosswind runway are being built. Upon completion, which has been delayed by continuing opposition, the area of the airport will double in size to 1,065 hectares (2,631 acres). As of October 1993, 51 airlines of 38 countries utilized the airport, with approximately 333 flights landing and departing daily. The airport annually handles some 22.1 million passengers and 1.4 million metric tons (1.5 million short tons) of air freight.

Kansai International Airport   関西国際空港●

Located on an artificial island built 5 kilometers (3.1 mi) from shore in Osaka Bay, this airport opened in September 1994. Because of the limited size of Osaka International Airport and the continuing noise complaints from surrounding residents which resulted in restrictions on operating hours, construction of a new international airport to serve the KANSAI REGION began in 1987. The Kansai International Airport has one 3,500-meter (11,483-ft) runway and is 510 hectares (1,260 acres) in size. In addition to expressway access, the airport has rail connections to Osaka (Nankai and JR lines) and Kyoto (JR line) and high-speed passenger boat service to Kobe.

Kansai International Airport opened in 1994.

Expressways (kosoku doro)   高速道路●

Construction of expressways in Japan began in the 1960s. Intercity expressways are designed for a maximum speed of 120 kilometers (75 mi) per hour, although legal speed limits are usually lower. These four-lane, limited-access, divided highways have a 3.6-meter (11.8-ft) lane width.

Since the opening in 1965 of the Meishin Expressway between Nagoya and Kobe, the first part of the expressway system, 5,652 kilometers (3,512 mi) had been completed by March 1995, and construction of the projected 11,520-kilometer (7,157-mi) network is expected to be finished early in the 21st century. Because of the nature of the terrain and the high concentration of housing, cultivated land, and factories along the routes, the cost of highway construction has been high in Japan relative to that in other countries, and expressway tolls are also proportionately high. However, expressways are used extensively; in fiscal 1993 average daily traffic between Tokyo and Komaki in Aichi Prefecture was 384,046 automobiles. Of the total traffic in that year, 75 percent consisted of passenger cars and 25 percent of other vehicles. Measures are being taken to protect residents along routes against highway noise and exhaust fumes. Expressways are administered by the Japan Highway Public Corporation.

Osaka expressways.

Drivers' licenses (unten menkyo)   運転免許●

There are two kinds of licenses, Class I for drivers of private vehicles and Class II for drivers of commercial passenger-carrying vehicles (taxis and buses), and they must be renewed every three years. Anyone 18 years of age (20 for trucks over 5 tons and noncommercial buses, 16 for motorcycles) may obtain a Class I driver's license by passing an examination given by the Public Safety Commission in the prefecture where he or she lives. Applicants for a Class II license and for a Class I license permitting operation of trucks over 11 tons must be 21 years old. The examination is in three parts: a test for vision, color blindness, and hearing; a road test of driving skills; and a written test on traffic regulations. Anyone certified by an accredited driving school is exempt from the road test. The possessor of a foreign driver's license is exempt from the road test and the written test. A foreign national who holds an international driver's license may drive in Japan for one year after arrival without applying for a Japanese license.

Mass communications (*masukomi*)　　マスコミ●

The Edo period (1600–1868) left Japan with a superb social base for modern mass communications in its geographically compact, culturally homogeneous, politically centralized, education-oriented, and increasingly urbanized population. The spread of democratic institutions, university education, and urban lifestyle in the 20th century created enormous markets for newspapers, magazines, and books and for the electronic media.

Structures and Functions　　構造と機能●

In organization, scale, and allocation of functions, the Japanese mass media have developed uniquely out of the indigenous economic and social structure and philosophical bent. Both newspapers and book publishing display the same intensive oligopolistic competition among gigantic, tightly knit enterprise groups that is characteristic of modern Japanese business as a whole.

Competitive pressures in a basically unitary national newspaper market have led to a striking uniformity of format, content, editorial viewpoint, and reportorial style for each prefectural paper and three regional "bloc" papers as well as the five national dailies (the *Yomiuri shimbun, Asahi shimbun, Mainichi shimbun, Sankei shimbun,* and *Nihon keizai shimbun*). With a total daily publication of 52 million, Japan ranked first in the world in per capita circulation of newspapers in 1993.

Tokyo headquarters of the publisher of the daily newspaper *Asahi shimbun.*

In 1926 the Japan Broadcasting Corporation (NHK) was granted a radio broadcasting monopoly under the firm control of the Ministry of Communications. In 1950 the new Broadcasting Law made provision for a commercial sector and reorganized NHK as a strictly public service organization. Since television broadcasting started in 1953, there has been much competition between the public and private sectors of Japan's dual system. NHK is the most popular news source and provides lavish cultural and informational programming on both its general and educational channels. The five commercial chains are Nippon Television Network Corporation (NTV); Tokyo Broadcasting System, Inc (TBS); Television Tokyo Channel 12, Ltd; Fuji Telecasting Co, Ltd; and Asahi National Broadcasting Co, Ltd. These five have been strengthened by tie-ups with the five national newspapers.

The functions of wire services, weekly magazines, and monthly journals in Japan have all been affected by the character of the newspapers. With the national dailies relying mainly on their own domestic and foreign news bureaus, Japan's two news agencies, Kyodo News Service and Jiji Press, play a supplementary role except for the local press.

Journalists ジャーナリスト●

The journalists in Japan's major media firms enjoy high professional status, and they are joined by a broad public forum (*rondan*) of intellectual critics (*hyoronka*) who fuel debate through daily columns and television symposia. Japan's highly literate public, deferential toward intellectual authority and eager for information and guidance in the pursuit of personal and corporate uplift, sustains an extensive high-grade sector of "mass quality" newspapers and television programs. The surprising homogeneity, especially in news coverage, derives from the unique organization of news gathering in Japan. The typical reporter writes not so much independent stories as raw material for reprocessing at the departmental desk, and the correspondents themselves are organized into exclusive press clubs (*kisha kurabu*) attached to all major government institutions and public figures.

Censorship and Freedom of the Press 検閲と報道の自由●

The Japanese press was under constant regulation and periodic suppression from the time of the Press Ordinance of 1875 through the militaristic regime of the 1930s, the war years, and then the censorship of the Allied Occupation authorities. Democratization during the Occupation nevertheless left the press in 1952 in a far more liberated state than it had ever before experienced. Today, Japanese journalism continues to enjoy great freedom from statutory restraint, but the press has often failed to attack government and business promptly and head-on over major evils such as graft or pollution. The collaborative ties between the press and its sources in the press clubs, among club members, and between media management and big business have all joined with general group psychology to produce a more comfortable relation between journalism and established power than would be deduced from their formal adversarial relationship.

Education, Culture, and Society 教育・文化・社会●

Mass communications has contributed to political and social stability in postwar Japan. Television has virtually eliminated the urban-rural cultural gap, a divisive factor in the prewar period. The mass media and educational system together have greatly reduced the potential for class cleavage by spreading a uniform, middle-class culture throughout Japan. Recent social concerns have included information glut and "data pollution," technological threats to privacy and individual freedom, and the gradual loss of psychological space in a postindustrial society dominated by computers, telecommunications, and hyperproductive mass media. The Japanese have done a great deal to develop the concept of the "information society" (*johoka shakai*) both as a popular notion and as a new academic discipline.

In a continuing effort to reduce the depiction of sex and violence, standards of ethics, decency, and taste are monitored by the Newspaper Content Evaluation Center, the Japan Advertising Review Organization, several broadcasting program consultative committees for television, the Motion Picture Code Committee, and the National Mass Communications Ethics Council. See also BROADCASTING; NEWSPAPERS; PUBLISHING.

Freedom of the press (*shuppan, hodo no jiyu*) 出版・報道の自由●

Under the 1889 Meiji Constitution and other laws, the Japanese media were severely restricted before World War II. After the war, Japanese media came under the protection of article 21 of the 1947 constitution, which guarantees "[freedom of] assembly and association as well as speech, press and all other forms of expression" and prohibits censorship. However, the act of soliciting the disclosure of secrets from public officials is prohibited by the Public Employee Law. Regulations also exist to control violations of reputation and privacy, and others prohibit the use of obscene expressions. In addition to these general restrictions, the Broadcasting Law of 1950 regulates broadcasting on such matters as the principle of political impartiality.

Publishing (*shuppan*) 出版●

Development of Modern Publishing 近現代の出版の発達●

Books for sale.

Newspapers, magazines, and books underwent a process of Westernization after the Meiji Restoration. Following the practice in Europe and the United States at that time, the Japanese press and newspapers formed their own unique sphere from the beginning. The rest of the printed media, such as books and magazines, formed a separate world of publishing. This division has exercised a great influence on the formation of the character of Japanese journalism.

Before World War II, freedom of the press was greatly restricted by the Publications Law, the Newspaper Law, the Peace Preservation Law, and other repressive laws and regulations. A large number of publishers, editors, scholars, and writers were punished and imprisoned under these laws. After World War II, however, article 21 of the 1947 constitution guarantees freedom of speech and the press, prohibits censorship, and abolishes all the laws and regulations that had controlled the press. In 1993 Japan published 45,799 new book titles. As of 1989 Japan ranked second in the world behind the United States in the consumption of printing and writing paper.

Until 1955 weeklies had been put out by newspaper companies, but beginning with *Shukan shincho* (1956), publishing companies began to issue their own weeklies. With government, scholarly, and corporate publications included, the total number of magazine titles in Japan is estimated to be over 10,000. Magazine sales for 1990 totaled ¥1.26 trillion (US $8.73 billion).

The Publishing Industry   出版業●

As in the publishing industry throughout the world, the majority of Japanese publishers operate on a small scale. According to the 1990 edition of *The Almanac of Publishing*, the total number of publishers in Japan was 4,282, of which publishers with capital of less than ¥5 million (US $38,910)—or whose capital was not known—numbered 2,763 (64.5%) and those with 10 employees or fewer (or with unknown numbers) totaled 2,929 (68.4%). According to the same source, more than half of the new titles in Japan were published by 120 publishers. In other words, less than 3 percent of all publishers accounted for more than half of all publishing activities. This oligopolistic situation was even more clearly reflected in the respective share of sales.

The basic route of distribution for publications in Japan is from publisher to agent to bookstore. The basis of the sales system is fixed-price sales and consignment sales, by which the majority of publications are traded.

As of 1990 about 12,556 bookstores belonged to the Association of Booksellers; when nonmember stores are added, the total number exceeds 20,000. A distribution agent connects a bookstore with a publisher and handles the distribution and return of books. Books and magazines traded by this route are considered to account for 50 percent of the total; about 70 percent are handled by the two major agencies, Tohan and Nippon Shuppan Hambai (abbreviated Nippan).

Yaesu Book Center near Tokyo Station.

The buying and selling of published material by the so-called regular route has been characterized since the 1920s by strict observance of fixed retail prices and consignment sales. An antitrust law prohibits producers from compelling agents or retailers to sell at fixed prices. From its inception, however, this law exempted so-called cultural items and daily necessities and in 1953 extended exemptions to include published material as well. As a result, published materials in Japan have been sold according to price maintenance agreements. The Japanese Fair Trade Commission has begun reviewing the price maintenance system because of growing consumer pressure.

Postwar Reforms 第二次世界大戦後の変革●

In prewar Japanese publishing circles, a clear line was drawn between publications for intellectuals and those for the masses. Since the end of the war, however, the movement toward a mass society has been symbolized by television, as well as the numerous weekly magazines created by publishing companies, and the so-called masses are no longer distinguished from the intellectual elite in the prewar sense. After 1950 best-seller fiction was neither infraliterature nor subliterature but books of quality intended for the masses. Equality of the sexes, improvement of labor conditions, and an increase and leveling in income also stimulated the creation of a new class of readers.

What played the decisive role for the postwar publishing boom, however, was the spread of secondary-school and university education. Only 3 percent of all youths attended universities in 1940, while in 1975, 30 percent attended a university or junior college.

When the conditions for the development of the publishing business in Japan are reviewed, it may be concluded that favorable growth as a whole may be expected for some time to come. But it cannot be denied that the conditions that hitherto supported the publishing business may turn into brakes: the growth of the economy has slowed since the 1970s, the proportion of students wishing to go on to universities has peaked, and individual households have been hard pressed economically. Furthermore, the full-scale arrival of the television age and the revival of motion pictures are contributing to a departure from the written media. Yet there are also signs that these visual media are forcing written media forms to undergo a kind of transformation, including the popularization of "cassette books" since 1987 and the fact that one-third of all types of magazines in Japan are comics.

The 1990s has seen increasing activity in electronic publishing utilizing computer media such as CD-ROMs, IC cards, and diskettes. As of 1994 electronic publishing has concentrated mostly on encyclopedias and dictionaries as they are especially suited to the large volume storage and extensive search capabilities provided by computers. The use of electronic typesetting has facilitated the increasing number of cases of a CD-ROM version being issued simultaneous with the publication of a printed book.

Newspapers (*shimbun*) 新聞●

In the vanguard of Japan's newspaper industry are several colossal national newspaper organizations that publish either morning or evening editions of their newspapers or both morning and evening editions. In addition to these major national media companies, there is a host of local and special-interest newspapers that also help cater to the diverse interests of the world's most literate readership.

History 歴史●

The first modern newspaper was the *Nagasaki Shipping List and Advertiser*, an English paper, published twice a week beginning in 1861 by the Englishman A. W. Hansard in Nagasaki. In 1862 the Tokugawa shogunate (1603–1867) began publishing the *Kampan Batabiya shimbun*, a translated and re-edited edition of *Javasche Courant*, the organ of the Dutch government in Indonesia. These two papers contained only foreign news. Newspapers covering domestic news were first started by the Japanese in Edo (now Tokyo), Osaka, Kyoto, and Nagasaki in 1868. Yanagawa Shunsan's *Chugai shimbun*, a model for later papers, carried domestic news as well as abridged translations from foreign papers. The first Japanese daily paper, the *Yokohama mainichi shimbun*, was launched in 1871. The *Tokyo nichinichi shimbun* (predecessor of the *Mainichi shimbun*), the *Yubin hochi shimbun* (predecessor of the *Hochi shimbun*), and the oldest existing local newspaper, the *Kochu shimbun* (predecessor of the *Yamanashi nichinichi shimbun*), were all begun in 1872.

Most papers published at this time were referred to as "political forums" because they demanded the establishment of a national Diet and printed political opinions at the time of the Freedom and People's Rights Movement (Jiyu Minken Undo). However, after the establishment of the Diet, the newspapers virtually became organs of the newly formed political parties. These newspapers were called *oshimbun* (large newspapers). *Koshimbun* (small newspapers) were popular newspapers containing local news, human interest stories, and light fiction. The *Yomiuri shimbun*, which began publishing in 1874, is a typical example. Partially because strong government pressure caused the *oshimbun* to fail, new newspapers printing impartial news started springing up around 1880. The *Asahi shimbun* was launched in 1879 in Osaka, and the *Jiji shimpo* in 1882 in Tokyo. The sudden increase in circulation made possible in the 1890s by the widespread use of rotary presses and the growth of advertising turned Japanese newspapers into large business enterprises.

When the Tokyo Earthquake of 1923 destroyed much of Tokyo,

the Osaka-based *Asahi* and *Mainichi* became the two largest national newspapers overnight, virtually dominating the Japanese newspaper industry. The opinion-shaping activity of Japanese newspapers gradually declined as the papers became interested in profits and had to respond to a broader readership. The heavy pressures from the government and the military authorities also weakened the papers' capacity for strong editorial policy.

The press was placed under complete government control from the outbreak of the Sino-Japanese War in 1937 until the end of World War II in 1945. Newsprint was rationed, and many newspapers were forced to merge. The number of newspapers dropped from 848 in 1939 to 54 in 1942.

Free competition among newspapers revived after the abolition of wartime regulations and the lifting of controls on newsprint in 1951. The system of morning and evening editions of the same paper, which had been suspended, also revived, and major papers started printing local editions. When weekly magazines, comic magazines, and television became popular, most general newspapers began to concentrate on news and advertising. As in other countries, progress in broadcast media such as radio and television deprived the newspapers of their edge in prompt reporting, which forced the press to turn to in-depth articles and news commentary. In the late 1970s and 1980s Japanese newspapers greatly increased the efficiency of their operations by full computerization of all aspects of their work—reporting, editing, typesetting, and printing—and by utilizing satellite communications.

Circulation   発行部数●

According to statistics of the Japan Newspaper Publishers and Editors Association, the total circulation of daily papers as of 1991 was 52,026,372, or an average of 1.24 newspapers per household. General papers accounted for 88.5 percent and sports papers for 11.5 percent.

The five major daily general papers in order of their circulation are: *Yomiuri shimbun*, *Asahi shimbun*, *Mainichi shimbun*, *Nihon keizai shimbun*, and *Sankei shimbun*. Maintaining their own nationwide home-delivery networks, they account for 52.6 percent of the entire circulation of daily general papers. The two leading newspapers, the *Yomiuri* and the *Asahi*, had circulations of 9,764,551 and 8,255,902, respectively, in 1991 (morning editions). Their readers are concentrated in the Tokyo and Osaka metropolitan areas, where publishing offices are located. Many prefectural papers enjoy more than 50 percent of the newspaper circulation in their areas.

Circulation of
Daily Newspapers
新聞発行部数

Year	Circulation in millions	Copies per household
1960	24.44	1.18
1970	36.30	1.24
1980	46.39	1.29
1990	51.91	1.28

Source: Japan Newspaper
Publishers and Editors Association.

Home Delivery System 宅配制度●

At first, newspapers were sold on consignment to bookstores, but the *Tokyo nichinichi shimbun* initiated a home delivery system that was soon followed by other papers. The *Hochi shimbun* started exclusive dealerships in 1903 to distribute only its own papers nationwide. The dealers not only were responsible for delivery but also acted as subscription salesmen. News of the increase in circulation for the *Hochi* prompted other papers to set up their own news dealerships, and the system of monopoly newspaper dealerships peculiar to Japan was created in 1930.

Journalists ジャーナリスト●

Would-be journalists in Japan are selected from among new university graduates through examinations conducted by the individual newspaper companies. The examinations are notoriously difficult, and hundreds of applicants may compete for a single job. Once accepted, however, they can look forward to lifetime employment. Japanese companies more often than not shift the journalists to administrative positions by the time they become senior reporters. Press clubs are a significant characteristic of Japanese journalism. They function both as social clubs for journalists and as locations for important press interviews and political announcements. It is widely recognized that there exists the danger of such clubs' becoming too closely associated with the government and other public bodies to which nonmembers have difficulty gaining access.

Broadcasting (*hoso*) 放送●

Broadcasting is defined in Japan's Broadcasting Law (Hoso Ho, 1950) and Radio Law (Dempa Ho, 1950) as "wireless communication intended for direct reception by the general public."

History of Broadcasting 放送の歴史●

On 20 August 1926 the Communications Ministry (Teishinsho; now the Ministry of Posts and Telecommunications) established the Nippon Hoso Kyokai (NHK; Japan Broadcasting Corporation). NHK monopolized the country's broadcasting industry until after World War II, but it was placed under the strict supervision of the Communications Ministry.

NHK Broadcasting Center in Shibuya Ward, Tokyo.

After World War II all legislation suppressing freedom of speech and the press was abolished in an effort to further Japan's democratization. When the Broadcasting Law came into effect in June 1950, NHK was reorganized, and a new corporation was formed. This law also paved the way for private commercial broadcast stations. In April 1950 preliminary licenses were issued to a total of 16 private broadcast stations in 14 districts of the country. Despite early pessimism about their commercial viability, these ventures soon showed large profits. The way was opened for television broadcasting with the granting of a preliminary license to Nippon Television Network Corporation (NTV) on 31 July 1952. The first actual telecast in Japan was made by NHK's Tokyo station on 1 February 1953.

Present-Day Broadcasting　　　　　　　　　　現在の放送●

Japan's broadcasting system consists of two types of broadcast enterprise: NHK, which is a government-sponsored venture, and the various commercial companies (see COMMERCIAL BROADCASTING). As a special corporation, NHK is neither a state-operated enterprise nor a public corporation. However, unlike the private companies, NHK's activities are subject to restrictions by the government and the Diet. The Management Commission makes major decisions regarding NHK, including the content of programs, and is a governing organ with the authority to appoint the president and other high officials of NHK. The members of the Management Commission are appointed by the prime minister after obtaining the approval of the Diet.

Programming （番組）　The Broadcasting Law stipulates the types of programs to be broadcast domestically. NHK is required to (1) broadcast high-quality programs that will both satisfy the demands of the public and elevate the country's cultural level, (2) broadcast local as well as national programs, and (3) contribute to the preservation of traditional culture and foster and publicize modern cultural events. Programs shown by both NHK and private commercial broadcasting firms are required by the Broadcasting Law to (1) guard against disturbing public peace and order and damaging morals, (2) maintain political impartiality, (3) include truthful news broadcasts, and (4) present all sides of complex issues and maintain a balance among educational, cultural, news, and entertainment programs.

Networks （ネットワーク）　NHK operates a nationwide broadcasting network. Private broadcasting stations licensed in their respective local regions also have their own networks. As of 1992, commercial television broadcasting consisted of five networks centered on the following key stations: Tokyo Broadcasting System, Inc (TBS) (28 stations), Nippon Television Network Corporation (30 stations), Fuji Telecasting Co, Ltd (27 stations), Asahi National Broadcasting Co, Ltd (22 stations), and Television Tokyo Channel 12, Ltd (5 stations). At the center of each of these networks is a news network. General programming other than news is also distributed through these networks. In 1992 there were 115 commercial television stations, 47 commercial AM radio stations, 39 FM stations, and 1 shortwave station.

There are two major commercial radio broadcasting networks: the Japan Radio Network and the Nippon Radio Network, both established in 1965. Commercial FM broadcasting is dominated by the Japan FM Broadcasting Association, which operates a nationwide network with FM Tokyo as its key station.

Financing （財政） The ordinary operating revenues of NHK are obtained from viewer fees, government subsidies, and miscellaneous revenues from other sources, with some 98 percent of the entire revenue represented by viewer fees. The distribution of television sets, however, has almost reached the saturation point, so that it is difficult to foresee any large increase in revenue from future fees. (Radio fees were abolished in 1968.)

Private television broadcasting companies are showing large profits with the tremendous increase in revenue from television advertising. Advertisement expenditures paid to television firms exceeded those paid to newspapers in 1975, and television has been the top advertising medium ever since.

In 1993, 34.3 million households were paying reception fees to NHK. Television sets are owned by practically all Japanese families, and according to a recent survey television ownership now averages two sets per household.

New media （ニューメディア） New broadcast technology made possible the introduction of multiplex sound broadcasting in 1978 for stereo and bilingual programming and also text multiplex broadcasting for captioned news and other programs. High-definition television (HDTV) and extended definition television (EDTV) technologies have been developed to improve picture quality. Videocassette recorder ownership expanded rapidly beginning in the mid-1980s, reaching a total of 66.8 percent of the population by 1990. In 1984 NHK began direct satellite broadcasting, and in 1989 the launch of a communications satellite made possible the establishment of a commercial network combining satellite and cable transmission. Cable television has also begun to make significant inroads into urban areas. Japanese television programs are also broadcast directly to the United States and other countries via satellite.

Commercial broadcasting (*minkan hoso*) 民間放送●

Japanese commercial broadcasting, as distinguished from public broadcasting, dates from 1 September 1951, when the first privately owned radio stations went on the air in Nagoya and Osaka; commercial television followed on 28 August 1953. Beginning about 1960 radio fell on difficult times because of the rise in popularity of television. To win back their audience, radio stations changed their format, incorporating live programs that ran for several hours, celebrity shows, late-night broadcasts, and traffic reports, and began making a comeback in the late 1960s. Commercial FM broadcasts began in 1969.

It was not until around 1957 that commercial television broadcasting spread throughout Japan. Coverage of spectacular events such as the Crown Prince's wedding in 1959 and the Tokyo Olympic Games in 1964 served to increase the number of television owners. Technological developments such as color programming and satellite-relay broadcasts paved the way for further growth of the television industry.

In 1990 there were 83 radio stations (47 AM, 35 FM, 1 shortwave) and 109 television stations (48 VHF and 61 UHF) licensed for commercial broadcasting. Advertising revenue for 1992 amounted to ¥235.0 billion (US $1.8 billion) for radio and ¥1.65 trillion (US $13.0 billion) for television. There were some 28,000 people employed in commercial broadcasting. NHK, by comparison, had 15,000 employees.

Commercial radio and television networks operate as cooperatives under the leadership of certain key stations. Among AM radio networks are the Japan Radio Network (JRN), led by Tokyo Broadcasting System, Inc (TBS), and the National Radio Network (NRN), with Nippon Cultural Broadcasting, Inc, and Nippon Broadcasting System, Inc, as key stations. Television networks include the Japan News Network (JNN), again led by TBS; the Nippon News Network (NNN), led by Nippon Television; the All Nippon News Network, led by Asahi National Broadcasting Co, Ltd; and the Fuji News Network (FNN), led by Fuji Telecasting Co, Ltd.

The prime viewing hours between 7:00 and 10:00 PM, when advertising is most effective, are referred to as the "golden hours," and during these hours there is fierce competition among stations for viewers. In 1978 Japan led the world in developing multiplex television sound broadcasts, which made possible stereo and bilingual broadcasts.

Television (*terebi hoso*) テレビ放送●

Including public, commercial, and satellite stations, 111 television stations were broadcasting throughout Japan in 1990. More than 99 percent of Japanese households have one television set, and many have two or more sets. The average length of time Japanese spend watching television is three hours a day.

Television broadcasting was begun in Japan in 1953 by Nippon Hoso Kyokai (NHK), the national public broadcasting system. Black-and-white televisions spread rapidly at the time of the 1959 wedding of the present emperor and empress. Color televisions sold similarly well at the time of the Tokyo Olympics in 1964 and replaced black-and-white sets by the mid-1970s.

In the early days of television in Japan, the television set was a focal point of family gatherings. However, with the diversification of lifestyles and the number of sets per household increasing to two or more, television viewing has increasingly become an individual activity. In response, programs have increasingly been tailored to the interests and tastes of specific viewer age groups.

Especially in the 1980s, the number of after-midnight viewers sharply increased. In 1987 NHK commenced 24-hour satellite broadcasting, which was soon followed by all-night programming on commercial television stations. After midnight, information-oriented programs for young people, movies, and all-night debate shows are broadcast. Around 1985 prime-time programming, which had until then been devoted to entertainment programs, began to feature long news programs and documentaries, with considerable success. Television has also become a major advertising medium, accounting for ¥1.65 trillion (US $13.0 billion), or about 30 percent of total advertising expenses in 1992.

Recording room at Nippon Broadcasting System, Inc.

NHK broadcasts throughout Japan and private stations broadcast on a local basis. Private stations in different parts of the country, however, generally belong to one of the nationwide networks centered on key stations headquartered in Tokyo, so programs seen in Tokyo can be seen elsewhere. The number of original programs produced by local stations is very small, but creating locally centered programming has become increasingly important for local stations.

In the second half of the 1980s, television reached an important turning point: videocassette recorders came into wide use in homes, direct satellite broadcasting began, and cable television broadcasting services using communication satellites have created a multichannel television age. The development of high-definition television (HDTV) is expected to greatly increase the pleasures and potentials of television broadcasting.

Religion

Aesthetics

Social Concepts

Annual Events

Ceremonies

Literature

Fine Art

Architecture

Theater

Language

Floats are the highlight of
the Gion Festival which is
sponsored every July by
the Yasaka Shrine in
Kyoto.

Religion

Religion (*shukyo*)   宗教●

Religious life in Japan is rich and varied, with a long history of interaction among a number of religious traditions. Most of the individual features of Japanese religion are not unique; the distinctiveness of Japanese religion lies in the total pattern of interacting traditions.

Many traditional Japanese beliefs and practices hark back to prehistoric customs, and most of these form the core of SHINTO, the only major religion indigenous to Japan. Indian BUDDHISM, the Chinese contributions of Confucianism and Taoism (transmitted first through the cultural bridge of Korea), and, much later, Christianity were introduced to Japan from outside. All these foreign traditions have undergone significant transformations in a process of mutual influence with the native tradition.

The Historical Formation of Japanese Religion   日本の宗教の沿革●

In Judaism and Christianity religion entails faith in one supreme deity; revelation of the will of this deity in a sacred book; concern with sin as disobedience to the deity; relation of man to divinity through a conscious decision or act of faith; specific ecclesiastical organizations, involving regular attendance and worship; and ethical behavior linked directly to this religious commitment.

Japanese religion differs significantly on each of the aforementioned points: there are not one but many deities; there is no one sacred book, but many religious scriptures; rather than emphasis on sin as disobedience to the deity there is a concern with ritual impurity and purification; one person usually participates in more than one religious tradition; there is no regular worship day comparable to the Sabbath but many seasonal FESTIVALS; and ethical codes are more closely related to family life and philosophy than to organized religion, while ethical shortcomings are not linked directly to divine will but are considered in terms of human imperfection.

In early Japan religious life was closely related to rice agriculture. Religious rites focused on seasonal celebrations anticipating and giving thanks for agricultural fertility and on venerating ancestral spirits who were considered directly responsible for fertility. From about 500 BC to AD 500, southwest Japan was developing into a centralized kingdom headed by an imperial family. From about AD 500, the high culture of China— including written language—entered Japan and immediately became a major influence upon the elite class and eventually upon the common people. The tendency in Japanese history has not been "either-

or" exclusivity, but rather "both-and" inclusivity, in adopting foreign cultural elements. Therefore, instead of rejecting Buddhism, the Japanese eventually incorporated it into the life of the family, making Buddhist memorial rites central to the veneration of family ancestors and directly linking Buddhist divinities to Shinto gods. Confucian notions were adopted to encourage loyalty to the emperor.

By the 8th century, local myths and traditions were largely unified around one account of creation and the descent of the emperor from the gods as seen in the *Kojiki* (712, Record of Ancient Matters) and *Nihon shoki* (720, Chronicles of Japan), the two earliest Japanese historical chronicles. Partly in reaction to the highly organized Buddhist religion, Japanese rituals and practice came to be organized as Shinto, "the Way of the gods." From this time on, Buddhism and Shinto were the major organized religions and gradually penetrated more into the lives of ordinary people. Many Shinto shrines that originated as family institutions developed into territorial shrines and eventually expanded to include branch shrines in other locales. Buddhist temples for the common people also gradually arose to fulfill the need for funerary and memorial services. From about 800 to 1400, various Buddhist sects and Shinto schools developed. In the Edo period (1600–1868) Buddhist temples became closely allied with the power of the state, and families were required to belong to a specific temple; at about the same time, Confucian thought became important for providing the rationale for the state. With the Meiji Restoration of 1868, however, Shinto became prominent in justifying and maintaining the new nation-state under its emperor and was influential even in education.

The Major Features of Traditional Japanese Religion 日本の宗教の特徴●
The seven major features that characterized Japanese religion until about 1900 overlapped and interlocked to form the general pattern of what is now considered traditional Japanese religion. These features can be identified briefly as follows:

Mutual interaction among several religious traditions （様々な宗教的伝統の相互作用） Typical of religious history in Japan is both a plurality of religious traditions and simultaneous or alternate participation by one person (or family). In recent times a person might be married in a Shinto shrine, live his life according to Confucian social teachings, hold some Taoistic beliefs about "lucky" and "unlucky" phenomena, participate in folk festivals, and have his funeral conducted by a Buddhist temple.

Intimate relationship between man and the gods and the sacredness of nature （人間・神・自然の密接な関係） In Japan the relationship between man and the sacred (*kami*) is very close. In addition to the specific deities represented in mythology, natural phenomena and emperors and other special human beings were also considered to be sacred or kami. The spirits of the dead of each family, as revered ancestors, were termed either *hotoke* (Buddhas) or kami. In Japanese religion kami and Buddhas are not conceived as being in another world so much as they are thought to exist within the world of nature and in the lives of human beings.

The religious significance of the family and ancestors (氏神と先祖崇拝) The ancient Japanese emphasis on lineage or family carried with it devotion to clan kami (*ujigami*), and Confucianism, with its insistence on filial piety and social harmony, provided a philosophical rationale for strong family ties. The home was always a center of religious practice, and this became more formalized during the Edo period, when it became customary for most homes to possess both Shinto family altars (*kamidana*) and Buddhist altars (*butsudan*) for venerating ancestors. Traditional Japanese religious life was conducted by family participation rather than by individual choice.

Shinto family altar.

Purification as a basic principle of religious life (宗教生活における清め) Notions of purity and impurity (*kegare*) and procedures of ritual purification (*harae*; *misogi*) in Japan have assumed an extraordinary importance and have pervaded the culture as a whole. The Japanese people have not conceptualized sin (*tsumi*) as a violation of divine commandments, but they have had a clear sense of the impurity or defilement that separates one from one's fellowmen and especially from the kami. The traditional observance at a Shinto shrine is to rinse the hands and mouth ceremonially as a symbolic act of purification before coming into contact with the kami. In Japan no one tradition dominates ethical concerns; rather each tradition contributes its concepts of ideal behavior: for Shinto, ritual purity and sincerity; for Buddhism, compassion and liberation from desire; for Confucianism, loyalty to superiors and benevolence toward inferiors.

Festivals as the major means of religious celebration (宗教的祝典としての祭) The pattern of religious activities was determined by each religious institution observing its own special festival days, in addition to annual festivals celebrated by families and the nation as a whole. Festivals at shrines and temples often celebrate the particular kami or Buddhist divinities enshrined there, but more often festivals are part of a seasonal drama reenacted every year. Shrines usually have both a spring festival and fall festival roughly coinciding with the transplanting and harvesting of rice. The time surrounding the NEW YEAR is a long festival period marked by large crowds visiting both Shinto shrines and Buddhist temples. The summer Bon Festival in honor of the returning spirits of the dead is observed in most Japanese homes.

Religion in daily life (日常生活における宗教) In traditional Japan, religion was not an organization apart from everyday life but closely related to every aspect of economic and social life. Rituals followed a person throughout life, from birth to marriage and death. Aesthetic pursuits such as the TEA CEREMONY and FLOWER ARRANGEMENT also embodied religious notions concerning veneration of the forces of nature.

Close relationship between religion and state (宗教と国家の密接な 関係) In Japan the general rule has been for religious authority to be subservient to political power. From the beginnings of Japanese history, myth has sanctioned the unity of ritual and government (*saisei itchi*) through the notion that the kami created the Japanese islands as a sacred land to be ruled by a sacred emperor who was a descendant of the supreme kami, the sun goddess Amaterasu Omikami. Cultural influence from China, especially Confucianism and Buddhism, strengthened and modified this basic pattern.

Religion in Modern Japan   現代日本の宗教●

Religion has undergone gradual and significant change throughout Japanese history. After the remarkable changes in national life of the late 19th and early 20th centuries, religion changed even more drastically.

During the Edo period, both Shinto and especially Buddhism became more highly formalized, and the still vital folk traditions tended to attract more of the attention and enthusiastic participation of the people. In the 19th century, popular movements formed around pilgrimage associations (*ko*) and charismatic leaders. Such groups often expanded to form the so-called new religions (*shinko shukyo*). Until 1945 the government controlled religion closely, but new religious movements continued to arise and expand, and after 1945 they became the most conspicuous development of the religious scene. With urbanization and centralization, folk customs generally and folk religion in particular declined. Social mobility, especially immigration to cities, tended to weaken both local ties and family relationships, in turn impinging upon organized religion.

Buddhism (J: Bukkyo)   仏教●

According to tradition, the founder of Buddhism, Gautama Siddhartha, was born about 446 BC as the first son of King Suddhodana of the Sakya clan at the castle Kapilavastu, located in the center of the clan's domain in what is now Nepal. Some scholars, however, place the birthdate as much as a century earlier. Although raised in luxury, at age 29 he left home to seek an answer, through renunciation, to the problem of human existence. After completing six years of asceticism, he experienced enlightenment at Buddhagaya beneath the bo tree, becoming the Buddha ("one who has awakened to the truth"). Thereafter, until his death at Kusinagara at the age of 80, he traveled throughout central India sharing his wisdom. He became known by the honorary name Sakyamuni (the sage or holy one from the Sakya [J: Shaka] clan).

Early Buddhism
初期の仏教●

In the central Ganges River Basin and eastern India at the time Gautama lived, affluence had led to a decay in the traditional caste system, less reliance on the priestly Brahmin class and the authority of the Vedas, and a decline in public morality. Philosophers became involved in endless metaphysical discussions of problems that had no solutions, but Gautama asserted that such metaphysical questions were meaningless. Buddhism attempted to point to and teach dharma, the "true eternal law" or "perennial norm" that would be valid for humanity for all ages. Buddhist doctrine is not specific, established dogma, but a practical wisdom or ethic that promises us the ideal state of humanity.

A five-storied pagoda at Horyuji temple in Nara Prefecture.

In Gautama's view, life is suffering (Skt: *duhkha*), in the face of which man is helpless. We experience suffering because everything is the result of ever-changing, interrelated conditions and causes; human existence is always in flux and in transience (Skt: *anitya*; J: *mujo*). Therefore, it is impossible to claim anything as belonging to oneself, or to assert that there is a self (Skt: *atman*). By denying the existence of atman, Buddhists also rejected the dichotomy between the subjective and objective worlds. Our perplexing and painful existence stems from various causes, and if those causes are extinguished, the confusion and suffering will also dissolve. In Japanese this chain of causality is called *engi* (dependent origination; Skt: *pratityasamutpada*).

Those who wish to be free from suffering must come to a clear understanding (enlightenment) concerning suffering, impermanence, nonself (Skt: *anatman*), and reality. To attain true knowledge (Skt: *prajna*), all lust and attachment—the root of illusion—must be extinguished. In order to achieve this, one must undergo spiritual discipline, abide by the precepts, and practice meditation. Only then will one be able to free oneself from myriad restrictions and attain that freedom called *nirvana* (J: *nehan*). The two extremes of hedonism and self-mortification are rejected; the Middle Way of no suffering and no pleasure is to be taken. Buddhism also emphasized compassion, teaching that it should be extended to all sentient beings.

Upon attaining enlightenment, the Buddha gathered around him a group of disciples; this community adopted the organizational principles of the *samgha*, which generally referred to a confederate form of government or a guild. The religious samgha was composed of both mendicant monks and lay believers, male and female. The mendicants were expected to be celibate and to refrain from secular occupations and economic transactions.

Later, rules for the religious life were stipulated: 250 precepts for males (*bhiksu*; J: *biku*) and 500 for females (*bhiksuni*; J: *bikuni*). Lay believers were instructed to maintain a good household, engage in proper work, strive to help others, and secure honor and fortune through diligent effort so that, upon death, they would be reborn in heaven. Five precepts were particularly emphasized: (1) do not kill; (2) do not steal; (3) do not act immorally; (4) do not lie; (5) do not drink liquor. Sorcery, magic, and divination were strictly forbidden, and believers were told to reject the authority of the Vedas and to eschew ceremonies involving sacrifice. While monks and nuns sought the ultimate goal of nirvana, the laity aimed at a better rebirth.

Spread of Buddhism   仏教の普及●

In the 3rd century BC, under King Asoka, India was united as one country. Asoka supported the Buddhists, and Buddhism spread throughout the country. Around that time Buddhists split into two groups: the conservative elders (Theravadin), whose purpose was to maintain traditional rules; and others, who called for various changes within the religious order. By the 1st century BC there were as many as 20 factions. These groups tended to be self-righteous and aloof from the needs of the common people and in time came to be called the "lesser vehicle" (Hinayana; J: Shojo) by their opponents.

Mahayana ("greater vehicle"; J: Daijo) Buddhism developed among the common people. Mahayanists believed in a series of Buddhas (apart from the historical Buddha)—Buddhas from the cosmic past and also Buddhas-to-be, or bodhisattvas (J: *bosatsu*)—who had deferred their own salvation until the salvation of all mankind. Mahayana stressed that the path of the bodhisattva was open to both monks and laity.

Several Mahayana texts were compiled. First to appear were the *Prajnaparamita* sutras (J: *Hannyakyo*), which taught that all things are empty (Skt: *sunya*; J: *ku*). These were followed by the *Vimalakirti-nirdesa-sutra* (J: *Yuimakyo*) and the *Srimaladevi-simhanada-sutra* (J: *Shomankyo*), which propagated lay Buddhism; the *Avatamsaka-sutra* (J: *Kegonkyo*), which taught the altruistic way of the bodhisattva and idealism; the Pure Land sutras, which advocated belief in the Buddha Amitabha (J: Amida); and the Lotus Sutra (*Saddharma-pundarika-sutra*; J: *Hokkekyo* or *Hokekyo*). The latter taught that various Buddhist practices would lead practitioners to perfection and that ultimately there is one eternal Buddha.

Two major philosophical schools also arose in the Mahayana branch during this period. The Madhyamika school (J: Chuganha), founded by Nagarjuna (J: Ryuju; ca 150–ca 250), emphasized *sunyata* (emptiness). The second school, Yogacara (J: Yugagyoha), brought to doctrinal completion by Vasubandhu (J: Seshin; 4th century), taught that the basis of our existence is a spiritual principle, *alayavijnana*, from which all things become manifest.

In 320 the Gupta dynasty was established. Buddhists developed the esoteric teachings of tantrism, known as Vajrayana or Mantrayana (J: Mikkyo), which incorporated elements of Brahmanism and folk religion. Esoteric Buddhism, however, tended to be absorbed by Hinduism. At the beginning of the 12th century, when India was conquered by Muslims, many Buddhist monasteries were destroyed, and Buddhism all but disappeared from India.

The Diffusion of Buddhism in Asia　　　　アジアにおける仏教の伝播●

King Asoka had sent out numerous Buddhist missionaries. A branch of Theravadin Buddhism was transferred to Ceylon (now Sri Lanka) and then to Burma (now Myanmar), Thailand, Cambodia, and other Southeast Asian lands. The Buddhist tradition in these areas is generally called "Southern Buddhism."

In the Kashmir and Gandhara regions in northwest India, the Theravadin lineage, especially the Sarvastivadin teachings (J: Setsu Issai Ubu), was popular. Later, Mahayana Buddhism became prevalent and from here spread throughout the western region. In Nepal as well, Mahayana Buddhism, especially the esoteric branch, was disseminated.

From the 8th century, Mahayana Buddhism, predominantly esoteric Buddhism, was transmitted to Tibet and, upon fusion with indigenous folk beliefs, developed into what is popularly known as Lamaism. In Lamaism, or Tibetan Buddhism, some lamas ("superior ones") were worshiped as incarnations (*tulkus*) of their predecessors. Lamaism eventually spread even throughout Mongolia and the Rehe (Jehol) region of northeastern China.

Buddhism was introduced to China in the 1st and 2nd centuries. Buddhist literature was subsequently translated into Chinese from Sanskrit (or its vernacular) originals. The Buddhism that came to flourish in China was chiefly Mahayana and reflected the influence of Taoism and Confucianism. Among the more important Chinese schools are the Pure Land (Ch: Jingtu; J: Jodo), Chan (J: Zen), Tiantai (J: Tendai), and Zhenyan (J: Shingon), all of which were transmitted to Japan.

Buddhism in Japan   日本における仏教●

According to one of Japan's earliest chronicles, the *Nihon shoki* (720, Chronicle of Japan), Buddhism was officially introduced into Japan from Korea in 552, when the king of Paekche sent a mission to the emperor of Japan bearing presents including "an image of Sakyamuni in gold and copper" and "a number of sutras." However, current scholarship favors another traditional date for this event, 538.

The Soga family argued that Japan should accept Buddhism. Others, particularly the Mononobe family and the Nakatomi family, claimed that the native gods would be offended by the respect shown to a foreign deity. Buddhism was publicly accepted after the Soga family's political and military defeat of the Mononobe and became prominent in the 7th-century reign of the empress Suiko (r 593–628). Her regent, the devout Prince Shotoku, is considered the real founder and first great patron of Buddhism in Japan. He established a number of important monasteries, among them Horyuji and Shitennoji.

The main hall of the late-7th-century temple Horyuji is the oldest wooden structure in the world.

Studies of Buddhist teachings began in earnest as six prominent schools were introduced from China during the 7th and the early 8th centuries. These were the Ritsu Sect, the Kusha School, the Jojitsu School, the Sanron School, the Hosso Sect, and the Kegon Sect. In the Nara period (710–794), especially under the aegis of Emperor Shomu (r 724–749), Buddhism was promoted as the state religion. Official provincial monasteries (*kokubunji*) were established in each province. At Todaiji, the head monastery, an enormous image of the Buddha was erected.

Early in the Heian period (794–1185), the Tendai sect and Shingon sect were introduced to Japan. They received support principally from the ruling aristocratic class. At the beginning of the Kamakura period (1185–1333), ZEN Buddhism was introduced from China and was especially favored by the dominant military class. The popular sects of Nichiren and Pure Land Buddhism emerged around the same time.

Under the Tokugawa shogunate (1603–1867), Buddhism and its network of temples were used to eradicate Christianity, but Buddhism also came under the strict regulatory power of the shogunate. While sectarian divisions that had been established in previous times continued, there were also modernizing tendencies, such as Suzuki Shosan's (1579–1655) occupational ethics and the popularization of Zen by Shido

Bunan (1603–1676), Bankei Yotaku (1622–1693), and Hakuin (1685–1769). Another sign was the movement to return to the true meaning of Buddhism as revealed in the original Sanskrit texts, led by Fujaku (1707–1781), Kaijo (1750–1805), and Jiun Onko (1718–1804). After the Meiji Restoration (1868), the government sought to establish Shinto as the national religion, and many Buddhist temples were disestablished. Since then, Buddhist organizations have survived by adjusting to the developments of the modern age.

After World War II, many religious groups among the so-called *shinko shukyo* (new religions) were organized as lay Buddhist movements. Several of the largest of these groups (Soka Gakkai, Rissho Koseikai, Reiyukai, Myochikai, etc) draw upon Nichiren's teachings and the Lotus Sutra.

Several characteristic tendencies can be seen in the history of Japanese Buddhism: (1) an emphasis on the importance of human institutions; (2) a nonrational, symbolic orientation; (3) an acceptance of the phenomenal world; (4) an openness to accommodation with ancient shamanistic practices and Shinto; and (5) the development of lay leadership.

Statistically, Japan is a country of Buddhists. More than 85 percent of the population professes the Buddhist faith. Buddhism in Japan maintains some 75,000 temples with nearly 200,000 priests.

Zen 禅●

School of East Asian Buddhism that emphasizes the practice of meditation. The Zen school was known as the Chan school in China. It arose in China out of the encounter between Buddhism and indigenous Taoist thought and was held in high regard for several centuries after having survived the persecution of Buddhism there in 845. Zen blossomed again after being brought to Japan, where it underwent further development during the Kamakura period (1185–1333). The two major sects of Japanese Zen are the Soto sect (Ch: Caodong) and the Rinzai sect (Ch: Linji). Though they vary in teaching and methods, both schools assign a central role to meditation as the foundation of their spiritual practice. Today Zen has an estimated following of 9.7 million and more than 21,000 temples in Japan.

History 歴史●

According to legend, the meditative practices that characterize Zen Buddhism were introduced to China by an Indian monk named Bodhidharma (d ca 532). Huineng (638–713), a patriarch of the Chan movement of the Tang dynasty (618–907), is considered to be the actual establisher of Zen in China. The Platform Sutra, ascribed to Huineng, clarified the essential traits of the Chan school of Buddhism. The so-called five houses of the Chan tradition were established toward the end of the Tang dynasty and during the period of the Five Dynasties (907–960). Two of these schools, the Linji and Caodong, endured and were transplanted to Japan.

The introduction of the Chan school to Japan was one of the most important events in Japanese religious history. Together with the proclamation of faith in the Buddha Amida and the rise of the Nichiren sect, it marked a renewal of Buddhism during the Kamakura period. Although Chinese Zen masters came to Japan and attempted to propagate the Chan tradition, it did not develop into a major branch of Japanese Buddhism until the time of Eisai (1141–1215) and Dogen (1200–1253). Eisai and Dogen studied the way of Zen in China and then propagated its tenets in Japan. During this period, many Japanese Buddhist monks began to journey to China with the express intention of studying Zen. However, the Zen school did not become well established in Japan until it was forced to resist attacks of the powerful Tendai and Shingon sects of Buddhism.

Dogen, the founder of the Soto sect of Zen Buddhism in Japan.

The Zen movement was introduced to Japan through the two main channels of Rinzai and Soto. The achievements of the Rinzai school were conspicuous in the nation's imperial capital, Kyoto, and the shogunal capital, Kamakura. These cities saw the rise of the Five Great Temples (Gozan), which were active cultural centers as well as sites of religious practice. The Gozan system originally included three monasteries in Kyoto and two in Kamakura but soon expanded to comprise five monasteries in each city. Abbots of these monasteries were often granted the title "national teacher" (*kokushi*) by the imperial court. Eisai, after founding Japan's first Rinzai temple, Shofukuji, in Hakata (now in Fukuoka Prefecture) in 1191, became the first abbot of Jufukuji in Kamakura and then of Kenninji (founded in 1202) in Kyoto, both of which were to become part of the Gozan system. He exhorted people to practice Zen in a treatise entitled *Kozen gokoku ron* (1198, On Promoting Zen and Protecting the Nation), the earliest Japanese work on Zen.

The most outstanding Japanese figure in Rinzai Zen during this early period was Enni Bennen (1202–80), who returned from a stay in China with the seal of enlightenment from the Yangqi lineage of the Linji (Rinzai) school. He served as head of the Kyoto temple Tofukuji and at the same time undertook reform measures at Kenninji. The abbot Nampo Jomyo (1235–1308) received his initial training in Kamakura, studied in

China, and returned to Japan, where he eventually became abbot of two of the most important Zen temples of the period, Manjuji in Kyoto and Kenchoji in Kamakura. A characteristic of this phase of Rinzai Zen in Japan was the activity of both Chinese and Japanese monks. In the shogunal capital of Kamakura, the Chinese masters Rankei Doryu and Mugaku Sogen (1226–86) founded Kenchoji and Engakuji, respectively and in Kyoto, temples such as Daitokuji, Nanzenji, and Tenryuji became influential centers of Japanese culture.

Dogen is considered the founder of the Soto school in Japan. It was in China that he attained enlightenment and the seal of approval to succeed his master Rujing (1163–1228) in the Soto lineage. After his sojourn in China, Dogen was first active in small temples near Kyoto. He built the first completely independent Zen temple and meditation hall, Kosho Horinji, in 1233. Later, distraught by the hostility and political intrigues of the capital, he established Eiheiji in the mountains of Echizen Province (now Fukui Prefecture), which became the center of the Soto school. Another important temple of the Soto school was Sojiji, founded by Eizan Jokin in 1321 in Noto Province (now Ishikawa Prefecture).

The Zen temple Eiheiji in Fukui Prefecture.

During the Muromachi period (1333–1568) Chinese cultural influence on Japan reached its highest level. Important trade relations with the Asian mainland, carried on chiefly by Buddhist monks, began to develop. At that time Zen displayed extraordinary vitality and spread broadly. The temple Myoshinji, established in 1337 in Kyoto, became a model for the strict discipline espoused by its first abbot, Kanzan Egen (1277–1360). The most famous monk of the time was Muso Soseki (1275–1351). He was spiritual mentor to emperors and military rulers. Soseki was instrumental in the establishment of the Gozan system and, aided by his political associations, contributed to the spread of Rinzai-sect Zen throughout Japan. As Zen became established under shogunal patronage, however, criticism arose from within. Ikkyu Sojun (1394–1481) was perhaps the most notable monk in this regard. His iconoclastic directness in criticizing smug Buddhists, along with his eccentric behavior, made him a popular figure long remembered in Japanese Zen.

During the Muromachi period Zen exerted a formative influence on the arts of ink painting, NO drama, the TEA CEREMONY, FLOWER ARRANGEMENT, and landscaping. Gozan literature, cultivated by monks of the Gozan temples, had a profound influence on the culture of the ruling class and included scholarship in such areas as the study of the Chinese classics of the Song period (960–1278) and the Neo-Confucian philosophy of Zhu Xi (1130–1200) as well as religious and secular writings in both poetry and prose.

The Edo period (1600–1868) afforded peace and an environment beneficial to the popularization of Zen. During this period, ideas based on Zen found their way into the education of the common people. As part of the religious policy of the Tokugawa shogunate, temples and members of all Buddhist sects were officially registered for the first time. The Rinzai school, divided into numerous sects, claimed fewer members than did the Soto school. A third branch of Zen, the Obaku sect, was introduced to Japan during the Edo period by the Chinese master Yinyuan (J: Ingen; 1592–1673). Its practice, developed during the Ming dynasty (1368–1644), is a combination of Zen and *nembutsu*, the invocation of the name of the Buddha Amida. The Chinese architecture and ornamentation of the Obaku sect's central temple, Mampukuji, in Uji, southeast of Kyoto, attracted much interest.

Outstanding among Rinzai monks at the beginning of the Edo period were Takuan Soho (1573–1645) and Bankei Yotaku (1622–93). Takuan taught the affinity between Zen and swordsmanship; Bankei was responsible for making Zen accessible to the simplest of the unlettered. Hakuin (1686–1769), one of the greatest Japanese Rinzai monks, was also renowned as an artist of exceptional achievement. His life represents a pinnacle in the history of Zen mysticism, and no other Zen master is thought to have articulated such a wealth of inner experience.

The Zen temple Mampukuji in Uji, Kyoto Prefecture, is noted for the stylistic influence of Ming-dynasty (1368-1644) China in its temple buildings.

After the Meiji Restoration of 1868, the Meiji government favored the Shinto religion and ordered that all syncretic associations with Buddhism be dissolved. Though adversely affected by this decree, Buddhism was already deeply rooted in Japan and soon regained a position of importance. The most prominent Rinzai figure of this period was Imakita Kosen (1816–92), who became the abbot of Engakuji in Kamakura in 1875 and went on to head the Meiji government's Bureau for Religion and Education. His successor, Shaku Soen (1859–1919), is known as the teacher of D. T. Suzuki (1870–1966), Zen's principal exponent in the West.

Practice and Enlightenment   修行と悟り ●

Zen practice primarily consists of meditation in the lotus posture, known in Japanese as *zazen*, and the study of *koan*. Practice within the Soto school emphasizes the sitting meditation of zazen. The Rinzai school also acknowledges the value of zazen; however, it encourages its practitioners to exhaust their thinking in the contemplation of riddlelike koan to progress in meditation. The Rinzai school points out several dangers in the Soto emphasis on zazen, such as becoming attached to the practice of sitting or promoting a quietistic asceticism that goes only halfway—refining the mind but not attaining a dynamic breakthrough—and teaches that a perfect and spontaneous realization that does not rely on practice is also possible.

The practices of zazen and koan study are directed toward the inner experience of enlightenment (satori); however, they are not necessarily linked with it in a causal relationship. The enlightenment experience can occur without a specific practice of Zen. On the other hand, practice is not to be regarded as futile, even if years of effort do not culminate in the enlightenment experience. Practice is considered worthwhile in itself.

Meditation in the lotus posture (結跏趺座の瞑想) Zazen is not entirely of Zen origin. Its basic form is taken from the Indian tradition of yoga, which covers a wide range of meditation practices. Among the numerous postures (*asana*) of yoga, the lotus position, regarded as the most perfect posture in yoga, was adopted by the Zen school. The practitioner sits with legs crossed and drawn in, and back perfectly upright. Zen recommends breathing in a natural, rhythmical way with a prolonged exhalation. By shutting out all sense impressions and conscious thinking, the Zen practitioner seeks to attain the highest possible state of mental concentration.

Zen monks practicing *zazen* (seated meditation).

Zazen can also be said to represent the enlightened state of mind itself. This conception is found particularly in the teachings of Dogen and his school. The lotus posture is the external sign of enlightenment, just as the Buddha Sakyamuni and all Buddhas sitting in this posture reveal the enlightened Buddha-nature.

Koan study (公案) The study of questions for meditation, koan, began in China. The grotesque events, bizarre scenes, exchanges (*mondo*) between master and disciple, paradoxical expressions, and words of wisdom that make up the content of the koan stem from the early period of Chinese Zen.

A koan cannot be solved rationally. The practitioner is obliged to "hold" the koan constantly in mind, day and night. Concentration increases until the tension causes rational thinking to give way under the pressure and a breakthrough occurs. This is the "turn back to the roots of consciousness" that opens the mind to a new way of seeing. Concentration, confrontation with an inescapable situation, and a breakthrough compose the psychological progression in this practice. Because this practice can be traumatic and requires careful monitoring to advance, koan practice cannot be undertaken without the personal guidance of the master in private interviews (*dokusan*).

It was the Japanese master Hakuin who perfected the koan system. His famous koan "What is the sound of one hand clapping?" uniquely displays the paradoxical character of the enlightenment experience: "When you clap your hands together a sound arises. Listen to the sound of one hand."

Enlightenment（悟り）Satori is a mystical experience that does not lend itself to definition. The inner experience can only be described and interpreted. Certain characteristics are clearly evident in descriptions of satori, and the suddenness of the experience has been set down as one mark of Zen enlightenment. Many accounts of satori describe it as a merging or becoming one with the whole universe. Feelings of ecstasy accompany the experience of total unity or oneness. A surging joy—what Buddhists call "dharma rapture"—overcomes the enlightened person who, completely forgetting the self, feels at one with everything. The subjective certainty of such experiences is indubitable; however, when the master acknowledges that the experience is genuine, an immediate awareness of reality has most likely taken place. One who experiences enlightenment is thought to go beyond the trivial self of usual consciousness.

The Zen Movement in the West   西洋における禅●

The numerous writings and lectures in North America and Europe of D. T. Suzuki introduced Zen Buddhism to the Western public and awakened much interest and appreciation for it. Today, scholars in a variety of disciplines carry on the research he began on Zen Buddhism, but perhaps his influence is most strongly felt in the meditation movement of our day.

There are various schools and lineages within Zen Buddhism, and consequently a wide variation in practices. Different forms of Zen meditation have found their way to the West, and Zen centers have been established in North America and European countries, especially in Britain, France, and Germany.

Nourished within the great Asian cultures of India and China and reaching maturity in Japan, Zen has found a deep resonance in the West.

Shinto   神道●

Japan's indigenous religion. The word Shinto is written with two Chinese characters; the first, *shin*, is also used to write the native Japanese word *kami* ("divinity" or "numinous entity"), and the second, *to*, is used to write the native word *michi* ("way"). The term first appears in the historical chronicle *Nihon shoki* (720, Chronicle of Japan), where it refers to religious observance, the divinities, and shrines, but not until the late 12th century was it used to denote a body of religious doctrines. The worship of kami slowly emerged at the dawn of Japanese history, crystallized as an imperial religious system during the Nara (710–794) and Heian (794–1185) periods, and subsequently was in constant interaction with Buddhism and Confucianism, which were introduced from the Asian continent. This interaction gave birth to various syncretic cults that combined the worship of kami with the imported religions. In the Muromachi (1333–1568) and Edo (1600–1868) periods, however, there was a revival of Shinto as the "Ancient Way," and an attempt was made to pare away all foreign influences. This expurgated system became the state religion of Japan during the Meiji period (1868–1912), but in 1945 Shinto was disestablished and again became one among other forms of worship.

Shinto can be regarded as a two-sided phenomenon. On the one hand it is a loosely structured set of practices, creeds, and attitudes rooted in local communities, and on the other it is a strictly defined and organized religion at the level of the imperial line and the state. These two basic aspects, which are not entirely separate, reflect fundamental features of the Japanese national character as it is expressed in sociopolitical structures and psychological attitudes.

Origins and Formative Period   起源と形成期●

Archaeological evidence of the Jomon period (ca 10,000 BC–ca 300 BC) has yielded scant information concerning religious practices. However, artifacts of the Yayoi period (ca 300 BC–ca AD 300), during which important population movements occurred and contacts with the continent intensified, show that religious life was becoming complex. Wetland agriculture necessitated stable communities, and agricultural rites that later played an important role in Shinto were developed. Metal implements, such as weapons and mirrors, were deposited in burial sites as emblems of political legitimacy. Cups and jars for food offerings have been found, a significant matter in the light of later practice in which the primary form of worship consists in offering food. Oracular bones show the increasing importance of divination.

The Kofun period (ca 300–710) was marked by influences from the continent and by the emergence of Japan as a nation. The 100 or so Japanese "kingdoms" mentioned in the late-3rd-century Chinese chronicle *Wei zhi* were gradually unified as relationships of clientage and allegiance were formed around the leaders of the powerful Yamato clan, from which developed the imperial line. Not only the Yamato kings, but also the chiefs of major clans (*uji*)—each worshiping its own tutelary divinity (*ujigami*)—were buried in stone chambers covered by earthen mounds (*kofun*) and accompanied by swords, curved gemstones (*maga-*

tama), and mirrors, suggestive of the myth of the three imperial regalia (three sacred objects that are the symbols of the legitimacy and authority of the emperor). It was during this period that the Ise Shrine and Izumo Shrine, the most important shrines of the imperial tradition of Shinto, were established. The introduction of Confucianism contributed to the formalization of the Shinto moral precepts *tsumi* (hindrance of the life force) and *kegare* (ritual impurity).

On the one hand religious activity was grounded in each community and was concerned with agriculture and seasonal acts of worship, while on the other hand it was central to the ritual and political life of the leading clans. Imperial legitimacy, based on mythical, ritual, and religious coherence, was established through the compilation of the histories *Kojiki* (712, Record of Ancient Matters) and *Nihon shoki*. In the chapters of these works that recount mythology, the structure of the pantheon is connected to the structure of early society: the relationship of major clans to the imperial family is stated to be the result of relationships established between their respective ancestors. The centrality of religious practices to the *ritsuryo* (legal codes) system of government, created after the Taika Reform (645) and under which all the lands and people of Japan belonged to the emperor, is reflected in the fact that the Office of Shinto Worship (Jingikan) was in form, if not in practice, preeminent over the Grand Council of State (Dajokan). The Jingikan, presided over by the Nakatomi, Imbe, and Urabe clans, administered a system of shrines (some 3,000 in the early 10th century) at which prayers were offered for the benefit of the state. The Shinto rituals surrounding the imperial family and its satellite clans were codified at the end of the 9th century in the Jogan Gishiki and in the early 10th century in the Engi Shiki. Imperial Shinto thus achieved the status of a coherent religion, with a system of myths, rituals, sacerdotal lineages, and shrines.

Bronze mirror excavated from the Samida Takarazuka tomb in Nara Prefecture.

The official recognition of Buddhism by Empress Suiko (r 593–628) in 594 and its acceptance by the upper strata of society not only contributed to the systematization of the traditions that later came to be known as Shinto, but also initiated a process of syncretism that was formalized in the medieval period (mid-12th–16th centuries). At the beginning of the 8th century, Buddhist temples were already being built on or next to the grounds of Shinto shrines and were called *jinguji* (literally, "shrine-temples"). Buddhist monks considered the Shinto divinities (kami) to be in need of salvation and read and lectured on the Buddhist sutras in front of Shinto shrines. In 741, members of the emperor's court offered up a set of Lotus Sutra scrolls to the Usa Hachiman Shrine, and in

745 the shrine sent funds for the completion of the state-sponsored temple Todaiji. This service, among others, resulted in the granting of the Buddhist title "bodhisattva" to the kami Hachiman in 783.

Crucial developments in the interaction between Shinto and Buddhism occurred during the Heian period, following the introduction from China of the Tiantai (J: Tendai) sect by Saicho (767–822) and esoteric Shingon teachings by Kukai (774–835), founder of the Shingon sect. The Tendai sect was permeated by Shingon doctrines after Saicho died, and the two sects established a close relationship with Shinto, resulting in the development of syncretic ritual and philosophical systems in the medieval period. The facility with which esoteric Buddhism adapted itself to Shinto worship can be explained in part by the fact that it incorporated numerous syncretic practices that had developed in India and that its fundamental teaching was that all things in the phenomenal world are emanations of the Buddha Mahavairocana (J: Dainichi).

The Medieval Period   中世●

Of several pivotal theories of amalgamation introduced by Buddhism, the *honji suijaku* ("original prototype and local manifestation") theory played a key role in the evolution of Shinto-Buddhist relationships. At its core lies the notion that Shinto divinities are manifestations of Buddhas and bodhisattvas. Hence worship of a kami was worship of a Buddha in its kami form. Associations between Shinto divinities and Buddhas, such as that which obtained between Amaterasu Omikami, chief divinity of the Ise Shrine, and Dainichi, were established at the level of particular shrines and temples, and each devised its own system of rituals and practices surrounding its syncretic pantheon. Legends explaining the origin of these associations and descriptions of ritual systems were recorded in *engi-mono*, a type of picture scroll (*emaki-mono*). While these were for proselytization among the masses, there also developed between the 13th and 19th centuries a vast body of mythico-historical and philosophical treatises composed by scholarly monks and priests. Its major categories are treatises based on schools of Buddhism, especially the Tendai and Shingon sects; treatises based on shrine traditions; and treatises written by Shinto priests. Examples of the first category are works dealing with Sanno Shinto and Sanno Ichijitsu Shinto, which arose from the Tendai sect, and Ryobu Shinto, which arose from the Shingon sect. The second category includes works of cults that originated at major shrines, such as the Kumano Sanzan Shrines, Iwashimizu Hachiman Shrine, and Kasuga Shrine. The third category is represented by works of the imperial tradition of Shinto, such as Watarai Shinto at

Kasuga Shrine in Nara Prefecture.

the Ise Shrine and Yuiitsu Shinto at the Yoshida Shrine, that evince a reaction to Buddhist influence.

The Edo Period 江戸時代●

There developed in the Edo period a shift of Shinto away from Buddhism and a rapprochement with Neo-Confucianism. At the same time scholars of the Kokugaku (National Learning) movement attempted, through rigorous philological study of old texts, to gain new insights into the culture and religious beliefs of ancient Japan as they had existed before the introduction of Confucianism and Buddhism.

The Meiji Period and After 明治時代から現代まで●

The 19th century was a crucial turning point in Shinto history: on the one hand a number of religious movements emerged to form Sect Shinto, and on the other the expurgated imperial tradition of Shinto became the state religion, giving to the Meiji Restoration of 1868 the superficial appearance of a return to the Age of the Gods. The system of national shrines was reinstated, as well as the classical Office of Shinto Worship. Shrines were supported by the government, and Shinto, whose doctrines were taught in schools, took on an increasingly nationalistic coloration. Buddhism came under attack after the government decreed the separation of Shinto and Buddhism, but quickly reacted with its own brand of scholarship. After Japan's defeat in World War II, State Shinto was disestablished and replaced by shrine Shinto, which represents the bulk of Shinto shrines at the regional and local levels.

The religious picture of Japan today is complex. Statistics fail to suggest the numerous layers of interaction that have emerged, disappeared, and reemerged through history; syncretic tendencies and a general nonchalance concerning religious phenomena make it impossible for the uninitiated to come up with a clear image. There is no doubt that the identification of imperial Shinto with nationalism has hurt the tradition considerably, even though in many ways the essence of Shinto has been preserved only at the local shrines, which have had little to do with the imperial tradition. Industrialization and fundamental social changes are now confronting Shinto with what may be its greatest challenge.

Shinto Worship and Ritual 神道と儀式●

Shinto practice is circumscribed within the context of sacred space and sacred time. The oldest known form of sacred space is a rectangular area covered with pebbles, surrounded by stones, and marked off by a rope linking four corner pillars; in the middle of this area is a stone (*iwasaka* or *iwakura*), a pillar, or a tree (*himorogi*). This ritually purified place where divinities were invoked (*kanjo*) was located in the midst of a sacred grove. The typical shrine (*jinja*) is located near the source of a river at the foot of a mountain. Surrounded by a fence (*tamagaki*), its entrance is marked by a wooden gate (*torii*) of simple style, on which a rope (*shimenawa*) has been fixed.

The etymology of the term *kami*, which is often rendered as "deity" or "god" but is translated here as "divinity," is unclear. The Shinto pantheon, which is structured only at the level of the imperial tradition, consists of the *yaoyorozu no* kami (literally, "800 myriads of divinities"). Therefore, the presence of the kami is overwhelming and pervades all aspects of life. Natural phenomena—wind, sun, moon, water, mountains, trees—are kami. Specialized kami overlook and patronize human activities and even dwell in man-made objects. Certain kami are divinized ancestors or great figures of the past, and until 1945 the emperor was regarded as divine.

Each kami is endowed with an efficient force called *tama*, which is the object of religious activity and may be seen as violent (*aramitama*) or peaceful (*nigimitama*). Tama, the force that supports all life, dwells in human beings as *tamashii* and departs at the time of death. The tama of a kami is called upon at the outset of a ceremony to listen to the praise of the community and to its wishes. It is then offered food, praised again, and sent back. During ceremonies the tama of a divinity is thought to invest itself in the sacred tree or stone described above, or, more commonly, in a stone, root, branch, sword, mirror, or other object that is kept out of sight in a shrine. As the tama is inexhaustible, it may be invoked at many different locations.

Sacred time is that of the myths of the origin of the gods and of the land, as well as the time during which these origins are commemorated. Rituals and ceremonies are performed at each shrine by priests or by a rotating group of community members, on a cyclical and yearly basis. Each word uttered, each gesture and movement, and each ceremony is prescribed in ritual codes that are today set for all shrines in the *Saishi kitei*, published by the National Organization of Shrines (Jinja Honcho).

The other central aspect of Shinto ritual is purification. Grounded in mythology, it takes two forms: *misogi*, purification from contact with sullying elements (kegare) such as disease or death, and *harae*, the restoration of proper relationships after wrongdoing, through the offering of compensation. Misogi is held to have originated in the myth of the deity Izanagi no Mikoto, who, having followed his consort Izanami no Mikoto to the Land of Darkness (Yomi no Kuni; the netherworld) and seen her in a state of decomposition, returns to the world and cleanses

The gate to the Tsurugaoka Hachiman Shrine in Kamakura.

himself in a stream. As he does so, the purification of his left eye results in the birth of the solar divinity Amaterasu Omikami, the purification of his right eye results in the appearance of the lunar divinity Tsukuyomi no Mikoto, and the purification of his nose causes the appearance of the storm divinity Susanoo no Mikoto.

The second form of purification, harae, is held to derive from the myth of Susanoo no Mikoto, who, after rampaging through the palace of his sister Amaterasu, is compelled to make recompense by offering up a great quantity of goods and having his beard cut and nails pulled off. Ritual implements, such as the folded paper strips (*shide*) that are affixed to ropes, gates, and sacred trees, and offerings of hemp, ramie, salt, and rice derive from the tradition of harae and serve the function of misogi; hence the origin of the general term misogi harae for purificatory practices. The emphasis on purity in Shinto worship is also manifested in the custom of undergoing a period of interdiction (*imi* or *kessai*) of as long as 30 days, which requires avoidance of contact with death, disease, menstruating women, and disfigured persons and abstention from sexual activity and the eating of meat, as well as adherence to conventions in food preparation, clothing, and bathing.

Shinto and the Arts   神道と美術●

Important objects of Shinto art are the artifacts found in archaeological sites, such as polished gemstones (tama, magatama), mirrors, swords, earthenware statuettes (*dogu*), and other ritual implements. It has been suggested that wooden sculptures representing anthropomorphic divinities owed their appearance to the introduction of Buddhism, or, perhaps, to Chinese influence in general. In any case, a number of statues that have been preserved are of extreme beauty, characterized by august simplicity (those in the Matsunoo Shrine and Kumano Hayatama Shrine), or by stern but refined elegance (Tamayori Hime of the Yoshino Mikumari Shrine). A type of painting used in syncretic ritual is the shrine mandala. Depicting shrine-temple complexes, such mandalas served as maps for mental pilgrimages and as objects of meditation. Famous examples are the Fuji mandala of the Fuji Hongu Sengen Shrine, the Kasuga Jodo mandala of the Noman'in, and the Kumano Nachi mandala of the Tokei Shrine. Because anthropomorphic images are generally alien to Shinto practice, shrines did not support schools of painting as the ritsuryo government and later schools of Buddhism did, and, outside of syncretic iconography, one cannot find what could be called Shinto painting.

Shrines (*jinja*)   神社●

A Shinto shrine is an enclosed area containing a wooden sanctuary and several auxiliary buildings where Shinto rites are performed and prayers offered. The shrine is the focal point of organized Shinto religious practice, including annual festivals and *kagura* (sacred dance and music). In urban areas it provides a sense of community to those living within its parish. In rural areas it tends to create a feeling of kinship among villagers by stressing the common tie that all have to the shrine deity.

A typical medium-size shrine might be laid out as follows: Toward the rear of the shrine precinct, which is often rectangular and surrounded by a fence marking it off as a sanctified area, stands the *honden* (main sanctuary), which houses the *shintai*, a sacred object in which the spirit of the deity (*kami*) is believed to reside. Usually more than one deity is enshrined. Directly in front of the honden is the *haiden* (hall of worship or oratory), where the priests conduct their rituals and individuals make their offerings. Worshipers announce their presence to the deity or deities enshrined in the honden by clapping their hands and tugging on a heavy bell rope hanging from the eaves of the haiden. A wooden box stands in front of the haiden to receive money offerings. The interior of the haiden may be entered by laymen only on special ritual occasions, and the honden only by priests on rare occasions. At the entrance to the shrine stands a *torii*, the characteristic shrine gateway. A pair of highly stylized stone lions called *komainu* stand guard in front of the gate or haiden.

Christianity (Kirisutokyo)   キリスト教●

Christianity was introduced into Japan in the middle of the 16th century. The religion was generally tolerated until the beginning of the 17th century, but the Tokugawa shogunate (1603–1867) eventually proscribed it and persecuted its adherents. When relations with the West were restored in the middle of the 19th century, Christianity was reintroduced and has continued to exist in Japan with varying fortunes.

Introduction to Japan   日本への伝来●

Portuguese traders first reached Japan in 1543, to be followed by the Jesuit missionary Francis Xavier, who arrived in 1549 with two companions. Xavier's preaching met with some success, although his efforts were hampered by the language barrier. Reinforcements arrived to continue his work and were in general well received by local rulers, who often associated them with the lucrative Portuguese trade. Activity was concentrated in Kyushu, especially Nagasaki. In 1563 Omura Sumitada became the first *daimyo* to receive baptism, and by 1579 no fewer than six daimyo had been converted. In 1579 the Jesuit Alessandro Valignano arrived to conduct the first of three inspection tours of the mission. When he left in 1582, he was accompanied by four boys who formed an embassy to Rome on behalf of the Christian daimyo of Kyushu.

By this time Christianity had attracted the attention of national figures. The national unifier Oda Nobunaga favored the missionaries and granted them generous concessions. His successor, Toyotomi Hideyoshi, continued this policy until 1587, when, on realizing the extent of Christian influence in Kyushu, he abruptly ordered missionaries to leave the country. The Jesuits were eventually joined by Spanish friars; while the new influx added impetus to evangelization, national rivalries gave rise to unseemly quarrels among the religious orders.

Martyrdoms 殉教●

In 1596 the Spanish ship *San Felipe* foundered off Shikoku and the Japanese confiscated its rich cargo. A controversy among Japanese, Jesuits, and friars resulted; Toyotomi Hideyoshi once more turned anti-Christian and condemned to death the Franciscans and their parishioners in Kyoto. Twenty-six Christians—both foreigners and Japanese—were crucified at Nagasaki in 1597. No further hostile action was taken, and missionary work continued unobtrusively. By this time the Church had reached its greatest expansion, with the number of Christians being estimated at about 300,000. Tokugawa Ieyasu, who became the de facto ruler in 1600, was at first willing to tolerate the missionaries' presence for the sake of the profitable Portuguese trade, but the arrival of Protestant Dutch and English merchants allowed him to act more freely against the Catholic missionaries. As the final showdown between Ieyasu and Toyotomi Hideyori, son of the late Hideyoshi, approached, Ieyasu turned against the Church, knowing that his rival commanded considerable support in western Japan, where Christian influence was strongest. Ieyasu was victorious, and in 1614 the Tokugawa shogunate ordered missionaries to leave the country; most of them departed, but some 40, including a few Japanese priests, remained to continue their work under cover.

Persecution and Suppression 迫害と禁教●

Within a few years organized persecution commenced. In 1622, 51 Christians were executed at Nagasaki, and two years later 50 were burned alive in Edo (now Tokyo). A total of 3,000 believers are estimated to have been martyred; this figure does not include the many who died as a result of sufferings in prison or in exile. In 1633 some 30 missionaries

This memorial in Nagasaki marks the site where 26 Japanese and foreign Christians were crucified in 1597 by order of Toyotomi Hideyoshi.

were executed, and by 1637 only 5 were left at liberty. The Shimabara Uprising of 1637–38, which was seen as a Christian-inspired rebellion, prompted the government to sever contacts with the West, except for some merchants of the Dutch East India Company, confined to Dejima, an artificial island constructed in Nagasaki Harbor. Subsequent missionary attempts to enter and work in the country were unsuccessful.

The Japanese are noted for their religious tolerance, and the persecution was occasioned by social and political rather than purely religious factors. Christian exclusivism, with its unwillingness to tolerate other religions, aroused resentment in some circles. Missionaries were regarded as a potential fifth column preparing the way for Iberian colonialism. More significantly, the shogunate was on the alert for any coalition of disaffected elements that might threaten its hegemony, and Christianity was viewed as a possible catalyst.

Reintroduction 再伝来●

Japan's period of isolation ended in the mid-19th century, when Westerners were again allowed to enter the country. In 1859 a Catholic priest took up an appointment as interpreter for the French consulate in Edo, and in the same year representatives of three Protestant churches reached Japan. Ostensibly these ministers came to serve foreign residents, but their true aim was to begin direct work among the Japanese.

Social Activity 社会的活動●

At the beginning of the 20th century Christians made a notable contribution to the foundation of the socialist and trade union movements in an effort to solve the grave social problems caused by rapid industrialization. Many of the founding members of the Social Democratic Party (Shakai Minshuto; 1901) were active Christians. A Christian, Suzuki Bunji, founded the Yuaikai or Friendship Association, in 1912; this later developed into the Nihon Rodo Sodomei, or Japan Federation of Labor. The Nihon Nomin Kumiai (Japan Farmers' Union) was founded in 1922 by two Christian socialists. Despite this contribution at the time of their foundation, many of these movements were later split by disputes and much of the initial Christian influence was weakened or lost.

War and Recovery 第二次世界大戦と復興●

The growing spirit of nationalism in the 1930s raised problems of conscience for Christians, especially when the authorities urged attendance at Shinto shrines as "a civil manifestation of loyalty." Foreign missionaries of all churches were interned or repatriated at the outbreak of World War II or at best allowed limited freedom. In 1941 government pressure led to the formation of the Nihon Kirisuto Kyodan, or United

Church of Christ in Japan, a union of some 30 Protestant churches. After the war some churches withdrew from the union, but it is still regarded as the most influential Protestant body today.

Christianity Today 今日のキリスト教●

At present Christianity in Japan is characterized by unobtrusive activity, with emphasis still placed on education as a means of spreading the gospel message. In 1990, Christians numbered some 1,075,000, or less than 1 percent of the population. There were 436,000 Catholics with some 800 parishes in 16 dioceses, while Protestants numbered 639,000 with nearly 7,000 churches.

Conclusion 結論●

In popular estimation Christianity is still regarded as a "foreign" creed, preaching admirable ideals but unsuitable for ordinary Japanese. Because of its "foreign" nature, the religion has been persecuted when demands for national identity were strong; it has been widely accepted during periods of social instability (the 16th century, the early Meiji period, and the immediate postwar period), but once social equilibrium was restored interest rapidly waned. Apart from the Nagasaki region, Christianity has yet to make any appreciable impact on rural communities; it draws its strength from the urban, professional classes.

Culture

Aesthetics

F*uryu*   風流●

This term refers to the refined taste of a cultivated, sophisticated person and to works of art and other things associated with such persons. The word was derived from the Chinese term *fengliu*, which literally meant "good deportment and manner." After reaching Japan around the 8th century, it was employed in a more aesthetic sense, referring to the refined manners of an urbane person and later to all things regarded as elegant, tasteful, or artistic. The term *fuga* is sometimes employed in the same sense as furyu, but, in general, furyu is a more inclusive term, referring not just to poetry but to all the arts.

In the 12th century furyu began to follow two separate lines of semantic evolution. In one, furyu was applied to the more earthy, showy beauty manifest in popular arts. In the other, men attempted to discover furyu in the beauty of landscape GARDENS, FLOWER ARRANGEMENT, ARCHITECTURE, and Chinese nature poetry. This latter trend gave birth to the TEA CEREMONY in the Muromachi period (1333–1568).

In the modern era Koda Rohan endeavored to achieve a union of love, art, and religion in the name of furyu in the short story "*Furyubutsu*" (1889). In *Kusamakura* (1906; tr *The Three-Cornered World*, 1965) the novelist Natsume Soseki attempted to revitalize the concept by injecting it with compassion and humanism.

Novelist, essayist, and poet
Koda Rohan.

W*abi*   侘●

An aesthetic and moral principle advocating the enjoyment of a quiet, leisurely life free from worldly concerns. Originating in the medieval eremitic tradition, it emphasizes a simple, austere type of beauty and a serene, transcendental frame of mind. It is a central concept in the aesthetics of the tea ceremony and is also manifest in some works of WAKA, *renga*, and HAIKU. Its implications partly coincide with those of SABI and FURYU.

The word wabi was derived from the verb *wabu* (to languish) and the adjective *wabishi* (lonely, comfortless), which initially denoted the pain of a person who fell into adverse circumstances. But ascetic literati of the Kamakura (1185–1333) and Muromachi (1333–1568) periods developed it into a more positive concept by making poverty and loneliness synonymous with liberation from material and emotional worries and by turning the absence of apparent beauty into a new and higher beauty.

These new connotations of wabi were cultivated especially by masters of the TEA CEREMONY, such as Sen no Rikyu (1522–91), who sought to elevate their art by associating it with the spirit of ZEN and stressed the importance of seeking richness in poverty and beauty in simplicity.

S_{abi} 寂●

Poetic ideal fostered by Basho (1644–1694) and his followers in *haikai* (HAIKU), though the germ of the concept and the term existed long before them. Sabi points toward a medieval aesthetic combining elements of old age, loneliness, resignation, and tranquillity, yet the colorful and plebeian qualities of Edo-period (1600–1868) culture are also present. At times sabi is used synonymously or in conjunction with WABI, an aesthetic ideal of the TEA CEREMONY.

Fujiwara no Toshinari (1114–1204), the first major poet to employ a sabi-related word (the verb *sabu*) in literary criticism, stressed its connotations of loneliness and desolation, pointing to such images as frost-withered reeds on the seashore. With later medieval artists such as Zeami (1363–1443), Zenchiku (1405–68), and Shinkei (1406–75), the implications of sabi focused so heavily on desolation that the emerging beauty seemed almost cold. Underlying this aesthetic was the cosmic view typical of medieval Buddhists, who recognized the existential loneliness of all men and tried to resign themselves to, or even find beauty in, that loneliness.

Fujiwara no Toshinari was a famous poet, critic, and arbiter of classical poetry.

I_{ki} and *sui* (iki to sui) 粋と粋●

Aesthetic and moral ideals of urban commoners in the Edo period (1600–1868). The concept of sui was cultivated initially in the Osaka area during the late 17th century, while iki prevailed mostly in Edo (now Tokyo) during the early 19th century. Aesthetically both pointed toward an urbane, chic, bourgeois type of beauty with undertones of sensuality. Morally they envisioned the tasteful life of a person who was wealthy but not attached to money, who enjoyed sensual pleasure but was never carried away by carnal desires, and who knew all the intricacies of earthly life but was capable of disengaging himself from them. In their insistence on sympathetic understanding of human feelings, sui and iki resembled the Heian courtiers' ideal of *aware* (see MONO NO AWARE), yet they differed from it in their inclusion of the more plebeian aspects of life.

In modern Japanese sui is usually written with a Chinese character meaning "pure essence" but other characters like "sour", "to infer", "water", and "leader" were also used for transcribing the word. Sui comprised all these meanings: it described the language and deportment of a person who fully knew the sour taste of this life and was able to infer other people's suffering, adapt himself to various human situations with the shapelessness of water, and become a leader in taste and fashion for his contemporaries.

Iki originally denoted "spirit" or "heart." Later it came to mean "high spirit" or "high heart" and referred also to the way in which a high-spirited person talked, behaved, or dressed. As it became expressive of the Edo commoners' ideal, its connotations were affected by the Osaka concept of sui and moved closer to the latter. Indeed, iki was sometimes used as an equivalent of *sui*. Yet usually it carried a slightly different shade of meaning. As an aesthetic concept iki leaned toward a beauty somewhat less colorful than sui. Also, iki seems to have had a slightly more sensual connotation than sui. It was often applied to the description of a woman, especially a professional entertainer who knew exactly how much display of eroticism was desirable by the highest standard of taste.

M*ono no aware*   もののあわれ●

A literary and aesthetic ideal cultivated during the Heian period (794–1185). At its core is a deep, empathetic appreciation of the ephemeral beauty manifest in nature and human life, and it is therefore usually tinged with a hint of sadness; under certain circumstances it can be accompanied by admiration, awe, or even joy. The word was revived as part of the vocabulary of Japanese literary criticism through the writings of Motoori Norinaga (1730–1801).

Classical scholar Motoori Norinaga identified *mono no aware* as an important aesthetic ideal pervading all Heian literature.

In Norinaga's view, mono no aware is a purified and exalted feeling, close to the innermost heart of man and nature. Theoretically the meaning of mono no aware is as comprehensive as the whole range of human emotions and can be viewed as a humanistic value, but in its actual usage it tends to focus on the beauty of impermanence and on the sensitive heart capable of appreciating that beauty.

M*ujo* (impermanence, transience, mutability)   無常●

Originally a Buddhist term expressing the doctrine that everything that is born must die and that nothing remains unchanged. The phrase *shogyo mujo* (all the various realms of being are transient) is the first of the Three Laws of Buddhism. Japanese have traditionally been keenly aware of the impermanence of things, and the sense of mujo has been a major theme in literature.

Concept of nature (*shizenkan*) 自然観●

The basic, etymological meaning of the Japanese word *shizen*, which is used to translate the English word "nature," is the power of spontaneous self-development and what results from that power. The Chinese characters for the Japanese term shizen literally mean "from itself thus it is," expressing a mode of being rather than the existence of a natural order.

The term *shizen* as a general expression for nature is not found in ancient Japanese. The ancient Japanese people recognized every phenomenon as a manifestation of the *kami* (god or gods). Such terms as *ametsuchi* (heaven and earth) and *ikitoshi ikerumono* (living things) were the closest to a comprehensive word for nature in their literature.

In the mythology of the *Nihon shoki* (720) the first offspring of the primordial couple Izanagi and Izanami were neither kami nor human but islands and landmasses. Thus human beings were not considered to be superior or opposed to nature, as in Western thought, but related as if in one family.

5/14

Social Concepts

Giri and *ninjo* (*giri to ninjo*)   義理と人情●

Social obligation (giri) and human feelings (ninjo). Giri refers to the obligation to act according to the dictates of society in relation to other persons. It applies, however, only to particular persons with whom one has certain social relations and is therefore a particular rather than a universal norm. Ninjo broadly refers to universal human feelings of love, affection, pity, sympathy, sorrow, and the like, which one "naturally" feels toward others, as in relations between parent and child or between lovers.

Giri is a norm that obliges the observance of reciprocal relations—to help those who have helped one, to do favors for those from whom one has received favors, and so forth. The concept implies a moral force that compels members of society to engage in socially expected reciprocal activities even when their natural inclination (ninjo) may be to do otherwise. To feudal warriors, giri referred foremost to their obligation to serve their lord, even at the cost of their lives, and to repay *on* (favor) received from the lord. In Japan, to be observant of giri is an indication of high moral worth. To neglect the obligation to reciprocate is to lose the trust of others expecting reciprocation and eventually to lose their support.

Generally human feelings do not conflict with social norms, and observance of giri does not contradict ninjo. However, occasions sometimes arise where one is caught between social obligation and natural inclination. Though giri and ninjo as terms have outmoded connotations in modern Japan, the concepts are still important in guiding the conduct of the Japanese.

Sempai-kohai (senior-junior)   先輩・後輩●

An informal relationship ubiquitous in Japanese organizations, schools, and associations, in which older, experienced members offer friendship, assistance, and advice to inexperienced members, who reciprocate with gratitude, respect, and, often, personal loyalty.

The sempai-kohai tie is determined by the date of entrance into a particular organization. The sempai, perhaps a graduate of the same school or a senior in the work group, acts as a friend and patron, disciplining and teaching the neophyte appropriate conduct. Sempai-kohai ties permeate Japanese society.

Nemawashi (prior consultation) 根回し●

A technique used in Japan to avoid conflicts and obtain a consensus in decision making. The literal meaning of nemawashi is to dig around the roots of a tree prior to transplanting, thus making the uprooting and movement much easier. But the term is used much more widely in a figurative sense to describe maneuvering behind the scenes to reach a consensus and obtain certain objectives, especially in politics and business. When various interests are potentially in conflict, reaching a consensus and attaining political objectives are very difficult through direct, public confrontation. Instead, in Japanese politics and business the practice is to discuss decisions in advance with various interested parties and to incorporate their views, wherever possible, into any final proposals. Much of the groundwork for decisions is therefore laid well in advance of meetings where final decisions are made, and, if the nemawashi is successful, conflicts can be avoided in public discussion.

Etiquette (reigi saho) 礼儀作法●

"Etiquette" refers to conventional rules of behavior concerning interpersonal relationships. It differs from morality or ethics in that it concerns specific rules as applied to concrete situations rather than generalities and states requirements of outward conduct rather than inner beliefs or convictions. This distinction is important, because although at one level of consciousness Japanese recognize that etiquette and morality should go hand in hand, they also recognize that in reality the two may be discrepant.

Formalized Ideal and Real Behavior 形式的規範と実際の行動●

Since Japanese society is based on the notion that one's existence is dependent upon those around one, it is essential to maintain smoothly operating human relations. Society thus demands the suppression of any antagonistic feelings one may have toward another and requires an outward behavior that reflects social harmony. This dichotomy is expressed in the Japanese concept of *tatemae*, or pro forma aspects of social relationships, versus *honne*, or one's inner feelings and intentions. The two are not expected to coincide in all cases, but socially proper conduct always takes precedence. Accordingly, Japanese strive to be aware of a possible discrepancy between outward conduct and true feeling and must be able to guess the latter, while interacting as if there were no discrepancy. This is often easier said than done—a reason why intermediaries are so often used in sensitive negotiations.

Although the discrepancy between expected conduct and inner feelings exists in all societies, in Japan it is openly condoned as natural. As a corollary to this, the rules of etiquette are more fully elaborated, and the social expectation to learn and conform to rules of etiquette is very strong.

Social Organization   社会秩序●

By specifying rules of behavior appropriate for each status, etiquette helps to define social organization. Japanese etiquette specifies, for example, that the younger show deference to the older, and the female toward the male. The level of formality in speech is one of the more obvious ways in which status difference is manifested. The Japanese language is equipped with an elaborate set of expressions indicating different degrees of respect. Characteristically, Japanese wear clothes, such as uniforms, that readily manifest their social status, allowing others to interact with them in a socially appropriate manner. Seating arrangement is another way of defining status: those of higher social status are seated at a more honored place, closest to the *tokonoma* (decorative alcove) in a Japanese-style living room.

Morality (*dotoku*)   道徳●

In the West the concept of morality is based on custom and tradition, as can be seen in the derivation of the word morality from the Latin *mores*. This is not the case in China and Japan, where the corresponding word, pronounced dotoku in Japanese, is written with two Chinese characters, the first of which means "the Way." Confucius expounded the Way thus: "In the morning hear the Way; in the evening die without regrets" (Analects 4:8).

Morality in the East is not merely a system of ethics, that is, an act of human society, a model for living. It consists of the attitude of man toward absolute being (religion), other human beings (ethics), and other creatures and things (technology).

Japanese morality at present is going through a process of transition similar to what is taking place elsewhere as it seeks to come to terms with problems occasioned by the impact of technology on human life, e.g., problems of the environment, sexuality, and euthanasia.

Festivals (*matsuri*)   祭●

Japanese festivals, holidays, and other ceremonial occasions fall into two main categories: matsuri (festivals) and *nenchu gyoji* (annual events; also pronounced *nenju gyoji*). Matsuri are essentially native Japanese festivals of Shinto origin, held annually on established dates. Nenchu gyoji is a larger category of annual and seasonal observances, many of which are of Chinese or Buddhist origin. Nenchu gyoji are arranged seasonally to form an annual calendar of events. Matsuri are often included in this calendar, and there is some overlapping between the two categories.

Matsuri are chiefly of sacred origin, related (at least originally) to the cultivation of rice and the spiritual well-being of local communities. They derive ultimately from ancient Shinto rites for the propitiation of the gods and the spirits of the dead, and for the fulfillment of the agricultural round. Some of these Shinto rites were incorporated, along with Buddhist and Confucian rites and ceremonies imported from China, into the imperial calendar of annual observances (nenchu gyoji).

A parade of floats is the focus of the Gion Festival sponsored every July by the Yasaka Shrine in Kyoto.

The word matsuri includes the rites and festivals practiced in both Folk Shinto and institutionalized Shinto. A matsuri is basically a symbolic act whereby participants enter a state of active communication with the gods (*kami*); it is accompanied by communion among participants in the form of feast and festival. In a broad sense, matsuri may also include festivals in which the playful element and commercial interests have all but obliterated the original sacramental context.

Hare and *Ke*   はれとけ●

The Japanese have a concept of two dimensions of life, hare and ke. Hare correlates with the out of the ordinary, ke with the routine, and this duality extends over time, space, and things. Shinto shrines have special festival days set aside for matsuri; these, as well as such occasions as New Year's Day, the Bon Festival, birthdays, and weddings, are termed hare. Hare and ke thus resemble the idea of the sacred contrasting with the profane, but it is perhaps more accurate to define them in terms of special and everyday.

The Sanja Festival of the Asakusa Shrine is one of the largest held in Tokyo.

The Matsuri and the Seasons   祭と季節●

Matsuri are in origin and tradition closely related to rice-centered agriculture, especially the growing cycle of rice. Among annual rites, spring and autumn matsuri are the most important. The spring festivals invoke a rich harvest or celebrate an anticipated good harvest; the autumn festivals are held in thanksgiving for a plentiful harvest.

Besides spring and autumn fetes, there are summer festivals (*natsu* matsuri) and winter festivals (*fuyu* matsuri). In farming areas the summer matsuri have the role of driving away natural disasters that might threaten the crops. In the cities, especially since the medieval period (mid-12th−16th centuries), the role of such festivals has been to ward off plague and pestilence. The winter matsuri, held between the harvest and spring seeding, have elements of both the autumn and spring matsuri. Thus, Japanese matsuri are synchronized with seasonal changes and are classified according to the four seasons.

Essentials of the Matsuri   祭の本質●

Monoimi, or purificatory asceticism（物忌：清めの行為） In the center of the Shimane Peninsula on the coast of the Sea of Japan is the Sada Shrine. Each year at the end of September the shrine celebrates the Gozakae Matsuri (literally, "seat-changing rite"). In a midnight ceremony Shinto priests change the seat on which the god is to sit. Priests participating in these rites must confine themselves to the shrine for a week of purificatory asceticism prior to the rite. Monoimi serves as the symbolic gate by which the participants in a festival leave the everyday world (ke) to enter into the special realm (hare) of the matsuri. The purification rites have been greatly simplified in recent years. In premodern Japan, however, people were not allowed to participate in the matsuri unless they had undergone this purification process.

Offerings（供物） Another essential element of the matsuri is the offerings made to the gods. Typical items include regular and glutinous (*mochi*) rice, *sake* (rice wine), seaweed, vegetables, and fruits. In Japan there are no sacrifices of living creatures during matsuri.

A Calendar of Japanese Festivals
日本の祭り

	DATE	EVENT	LOCATION
January	7	Dazaifu Usokae	Dazaifu Shrine, Fukuoka Prefecture
February	early February	Sapporo Snow Festival	Sapporo, Hokkaido
March	12-13	Omizutori	Todaiji, Nara Prefecture
April	14-15	Takayama Festival	Hie Shrine ,Gifu Prefecture
May	3-4	Hakata Dontaku	Fukuoka, Fukuoka Prefecture
	15	Aoi Festival	Kamo Shrines, Kyoto
	third weekend	Sanja Festival	Asakusa Shrine, Tokyo
July	17	Gion Festival	Yasaka Shrine, Kyoto
August	1-7	Nebuta Festival	Aomori and Hirosaki, Aomori Prefecture
	4-7	Kanto	Akita, Akita Prefecture
	12-15	Awa Dance	Tokushima, Tokushima Prefecture
October	7-9	Nagasaki Suwa Festival (Okunchi)	Suwa Shrine, Nagasaki Prefecture
	22	Kurama Torch Festival	Yuki Shrine, Kyoto
December	31	Okera Festival	Yasaka Shrine, Kyoto

Communion（直会） The *naorai*, in which participants in the matsuri partake of the food offerings at the place of celebration together with the gods, is another essential element of the matsuri. In recent years the word naorai has also come to include the eating of offerings at a place separate from the matsuri site after the festival has ended, but this is essentially a banquet and not a true naorai.

The Matsuri and the Group   祭と氏子●

The matsuri presupposes the existence of a definite group of people to act it out. Generally speaking, in both the cities and villages of Japan every local community has a shrine that is its religious symbol. The members of a community, and thus of a certain shrine, are known as *ujiko*, and they in turn refer to their shrine as the *ujigami*.

Most matsuri are conducted by a ceremonial organization consisting of Shinto priests and a small group of laymen selected from the ujiko community.

Village and City Festivals   村の祭と都市の祭●

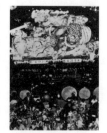

Although village festivals and city festivals resemble each other in several ways because they developed from the same origin, there are differences: village festivals tend to center on agricultural rites in the spring and autumn, and city festivals occur mostly in the summer; village festivals emphasize a man-god communion, and the city festivals stress human camaraderie. The most famous of all summer festivals is Kyoto's Gion Festival.

One of the spectacular floats at a Nebuta Festival held in Aomori Prefecture.

The Matsuri and Modern Society   祭と現代社会●

After World War II, Japan underwent rapid changes in population distribution and the structure of traditional communities. These changes had direct and indirect effects on the matsuri. Although many of the traditional patterns are still evident on closer scrutiny, human interaction has become the framework of new events, showing a move from the closed and vertical order of communion between man and god to the more open and horizontal order of interpersonal relationship.

New Year (Shogatsu)   正月●

New Year observances are the most important and most elaborate of Japan's annual events. Although local customs differ, at this time homes are decorated and the holidays are celebrated by family gatherings, visits to shrines or temples, and formal calls on relatives and friends. In recent years the New Year festivities have been officially observed from 1 January through 3 January, during which time all government offices and most companies are closed.

Preparations for seeing in the New Year were originally undertaken to greet the *toshigami*, or deity of the incoming year. These began on 13 December, when the house was given a thorough cleaning; the date is usually nearer the end of the month now. The house is then decorated in the traditional fashion: A sacred rope of straw (*shimenawa*) with dangling white paper strips (*shide*) is hung over the front door to demarcate the temporary abode of the toshigami and to prevent malevolent spirits from entering. It is also customary to place *kadomatsu*, an arrangement of tree sprigs, beside the entrance way to serve as a dwelling place for the god who brings good luck. A special altar, known as a *toshidana* (literally, "year shelf"), is piled high with *kagamimochi* (flat, round rice cakes), *sake* (rice wine), persimmons, and other foods in honor of the toshigami. The night before New Year's is called Omisoka. Many people visit Buddhist temples to hear the temple bells rung 108 times at midnight (*joya no kane*) to dispel the evils of the past year. It is also customary to eat *toshikoshi soba* (literally, "year-crossing noodles") in the hope that one's family fortunes will extend like the long noodles.

Traditional sacred straw rope making.

New Year's Days 元日●

The first day of the year (*ganjitsu*) is usually spent with members of the family. People also throng to Buddhist temples and Shinto shrines (see HATSUMODE). In the Imperial Palace at dawn or early on the morning of 1 January, the emperor performs the rite of *shihohai* (worship of the four quarters), in which he does reverence in the directions of various shrines and imperial tombs and offers prayers for the well-being of the nation. On 2 January the public is allowed to enter the inner palace grounds; the only other day this is possible is the emperor's birthday. On the second and third days of the New Year holidays, friends and business acquaintances visit one another to extend greetings (*nenshi*) and sip *toso*, a spiced rice wine.

Oshogatsu and Koshogatsu 大正月と小正月●

New Year display of *kagamimochi*.

Shogatsu refers to the first month of the year as well as to the period of the New Year's holidays. The events described above concern what is commonly referred to as Oshogatsu (literally, "Big New Year"). There is, however, another traditional New Year called Koshogatsu (literally, "Small New Year"). The former follows the date calculated by the Gregorian calendar, and the latter is set according to the lunar calendar. Koshogatsu thus starts with the first full moon of the year or more commonly on about 15 January and is largely observed in the rural areas of Japan, where the toshigami have been traditionally considered as agricultural deities.

Hatsumode ("first shrine or temple visit")   初詣●

Word used to refer to a person's first visit to a Shinto shrine or Buddhist temple during the New Year. Because it was customary to visit the shrine or temple located in the direction from one's home considered to be the most auspicious that year (*eho*), this practice was also called *ehomairi* ("visiting the shrine or temple in the eho"). Today, however, it has become more common to visit well-known shrines and temples, regardless of their location. These visits, which begin at midnight on New Year's Eve, are made annually by large numbers of Japanese. Tokyo's Meiji Shrine, Kamakura's Tsurugaoka Hachiman Shrine, and Kyoto's Yasaka Shrine each receive several million visitors over the first three days of January.

Hatsumode at Meiji Shrine, Tokyo.

Bon Festival (Urabon'e)   盂蘭盆会●

Buddhist observance honoring the spirits of ancestors; traditionally observed from 13 to 15 July (August in some areas). Also called Urabon or Obon.

Typically at Bon, a "spirit altar" (*shoryodana*) is set up in front of the *butsudan* (Buddhist family altar) to welcome the ancestors' souls; then a priest is requested to come and read a sutra. Among the traditional preparations for the ancestors' return are the cleaning of grave sites and preparing a path from them to the house and the provision of straw horses or oxen for the ancestors' transportation. The welcoming fire (*mukaebi*), built on the 13th, and the send-off fire (*okuribi*), built on the 16th, are intended to illuminate the path.

Bon and the NEW YEAR are the two high points of the Japanese festival calendar. On both occasions, custom strongly urges all members of a family, no matter how scattered, to gather together to honor their ancestors.

Buddhist family altar.

National Holidays (*kokumin no shukujitsu*)   国民の祝日●

As of 1994, there were 13 national holidays authorized under the Law concerning National Holidays (Kokumin no Shukujitsu ni kansuru Horitsu). In addition, in 1992 May 4 was designated as a principal holiday; along with 3 national holidays, it is part of the period from April 29 to May 5 that is popularly known as Golden Week. The 13 national holidays are as follows:

Ganjitsu（元日）(*New Year's Day*). 1 January.

Seijin no Hi（成人の日）(*Coming-of-Age Day*). 15 January. This holiday honors people who attain the age of 20 years anytime between 2 April of the previous year and 1 April of the current year. This is specified in the Japanese Civil Code as the age at which adulthood is reached.

Kenkoku Kinen no Hi（建国記念の日）(*National Foundation Day*). 11 February. Nationalistic commemoration of the legendary enthronement of Japan's first emperor, Jimmu.

Shumbun no Hi（春分の日）(*Vernal Equinox Day*). 21 March. Visits to family graves and family reunions occur on this day, the central day of a seven-day Buddhist memorial service (*higan*). A similar holiday is celebrated at the time of the autumnal equinox.

Midori no Hi（緑の日）(*Greenery Day*). 29 April. In 1989 this was designated as a day for nature appreciation. Prior to that the birthday of Emperor Showa was celebrated on this day.

Kempo Kinembi（憲法記念日）(*Constitution Memorial Day*). 3 May. Commemoration of the day the Constitution of Japan became effective in 1947.

Kodomo no Hi（子供の日）(*Children's Day*). 5 May. Day set aside for praying for the health and happiness of Japan's children.

Keiro no Hi（敬老の日）(*Respect-for-the-Aged Day*). 15 September. Day honoring Japan's elderly and celebrating their longevity. Established to commemorate the enactment of the Law concerning Welfare for the Aged (Rojin Fukushi Ho) in 1966.

Shubun no Hi（秋分の日）(*Autumnal Equinox Day*). 23 September. Visits to family graves and family reunions occur on this day, the central day of a seven-day Buddhist memorial service (higan). A similar holiday is celebrated at the time of the vernal equinox.

Many families with boys put up a warrior doll display on Children's Day, which is traditionally celebrated as a festival for boys and known as Tango no Sekku.

Taiiku no Hi（体育の日）(*Sports Day*). 10 October. Day on which good physical and mental health are fostered through physical activity. Established to commemorate the Tokyo Olympic Games, which were held 10–24 October 1964.

Bunka no Hi（文化の日）(*Culture Day*). 3 November. Day on which the ideals articulated in Japan's postwar constitution—the love of peace and freedom—are fostered through cultural activities.

Kinro Kansha no Hi（勤労感謝の日）(*Labor Thanksgiving Day*). 23 November. Day on which people express gratitude to each other for their labors throughout the year and for the fruits of those labors.

Tenno Tanjobi（天皇誕生日）(*Emperor's Birthday*). 23 December. Celebration of the birthday of Japan's present emperor, Akihito.

Setsubun   節分●

Traditional ceremony to dispel demons, now observed on 3 or 4 February. The practice of scattering beans (*mamemaki*) to drive away demons is one of a number of magical rites performed to ward off evil.

On Setsubun, beans (usually soybeans) are scattered inside and outside the house or building to the common chant of *oni wa soto, fuku wa uchi* ("Out with demons! In with good luck!"). It is customary for family members to eat the same number of beans as their age.

Doll Festival (Hina Matsuri)   雛祭●

Festival for girls held on 3 March. Tiered platforms for *hina ningyo* (hina dolls, a set of dolls representing emperor, empress, attendants, and musicians in ancient court dress) are set up in the home, and the family celebrates with a meal, eating *hishimochi* (diamond-shaped rice cakes) and drinking *shirozake* (made with rice malt and *sake*). Also called Joshi no Sekku, Momo no Sekku (Peach Festival), and Sangatsu Sekku (Third Month Festival).

Display of traditional *hina ningyo*.

Hanami

(literally, "flower viewing"; generally, cherry-blossom viewing)   花見●

Excursions and picnics for enjoying flowers, particularly cherry blossoms; one of the most popular events of the spring. In some places flower-viewing parties are held on traditionally fixed dates according to the old lunar calendar. The subject of flower viewing has long held an important place in literature, dance, and the fine arts.

Today radio and television stations regularly broadcast reports on the blossoming of local cherry trees. Popular viewing spots include Yoshinoyama in Nara Prefecture and Ueno in Tokyo.

Crowds flock to see the cherry blossoms at night in Ueno Park, Tokyo.

Seibo   歳暮●

Custom of giving year-end gifts and the gifts themselves; presented as an expression of appreciation for favors received in the past year. The Chinese characters for seibo mean "year end." The custom is said to have arisen from the practice of sharing with others offerings initially made to ancestors. Those in a socially superior position, such as a marriage mediator (*nakodo*), are typical recipients of seibo, as well as of midyear *chugen* gifts. Gifts are presented by those in inferior positions and are usually considered to be from family to family or from business to business. There is some discontent with the custom of seibo, probably because it is obligatory, but of all calendrically determined gift-giving occasions, seibo is by far the most important. Traditionally, seibo were personally delivered, but today people often will have stores deliver or send the gifts through the mail.

Weddings *(kekkonshiki)* 結婚式●

Weddings, perhaps the most important of the Japanese rites of passage, are one of the four major ceremonial occasions referred to as *kankon sosai* (coming-of-age, marriage, funerals, ancestor worship). For a MARRIAGE to be official, a new family register (*koseki*) must be compiled for the couple at the local administrative office. However, social and public recognition of a marriage in Japan is still often sought through the holding of extravagant weddings with elaborate formal costumes and large receptions.

Traditional Weddings 伝統的な結婚式●

Shinto wedding ceremony.

The "traditional" wedding of today was established as a pattern during the Meiji period (1868–1912). Although the marriage procedure varied a great deal with locality, most weddings included the customs described here. The day of the wedding was chosen carefully to avoid inauspicious days as determined by Chinese and Japanese astrological traditions. Traditional wedding rituals began the day before the wedding, when the bride prayed at the family shrine or temple or had a parting banquet with neighbors and parents. The wedding-day rituals primarily took place at the household of the groom, or at the household of the bride if the groom was adopted into her family in the kind of marriage called *mukoirikon*. In cases where the bride entered the groom's household, she dressed in white as she took formal leave of her parents. The white was symbolic of the death of her natal ties to them. At the household of the groom she appeared wearing a colorful *furisode*-style *kimono* and a cotton or silk head covering called *tsunokakushi* (literally, "horn-hiding"), which was supposed to suppress and hide the feminine "horns of jealousy." The groom wore a kimono with family crests and the loose trousers called *hakama*.

Modern Weddings 現代の結婚式●

Traditional weddings were basically secular rites decided upon by local customs and personal preference. Weddings today are still determined by these considerations but are more likely to include a religious ceremony, even when the couple has no particular belief or religious affiliation. Shinto weddings, which became popular after the Shinto marriage ceremony held for the crown prince in 1900, are more common than Buddhist or Christian weddings, although Christian ceremonies have become increasingly fashionable. The trend has shifted from weddings at home to weddings in shrines, temples, and (since

Culture

World War II) hotels, restaurants, churches, or special wedding halls, which are often furnished with special wedding chambers of Shinto or Christian design. Although the custom of *satogaeri* (the wife returned to her family home, bringing gifts for relatives and friends) might still be observed by some, most Japanese try to take a honeymoon of at least a week. The couple may make their ritual trip after settling into their new home. Although large-scale, expensive weddings directed and financed by the parents are still common, there are also an increasing number of weddings that more closely reflect the personal wishes of the couple.

Funerals (*sogi*) 葬儀●

About 90 percent of the funerals in Japan are conducted according to Buddhist rites. Upon death the body is washed with hot water (*yukan*), then dressed by family members in white garments (*kyokatabira*) or in his favorite clothes. More recently it has become the practice for physicians and nurses to cleanse the body and for morticians to dress it. In many cases the entire process of funeral rites is entrusted to a mortuary.

The body is laid out with the head toward the north without a pillow and is covered with a sheet of white cloth. A priest from the Buddhist parish temple recites sutras at the bedside and gives a posthumous Buddhist name (*kaimyo*) to the deceased. The body is then placed in an unpainted wooden coffin.

A notice of mourning, written on a piece of white paper with a black frame, is posted on the front door or gate of the house throughout the mourning period (*kichu*). An all-night wake (*tsuya*) or a briefer "half wake" (*hantsuya*) is held. Refreshments are served and mourners present gifts of "incense money" (*koden*). The day after the wake the funeral service is held at home, the parish temple, or a funeral hall. There are both Buddhist and Shinto forms of service.

After cremation pieces of the bones of the deceased are gathered, placed in a small jar (*kotsutsubo*), and brought home for later burial. Every 7th day until the 49th day, rites are held around the altar where the kotsutsubo is kept. The family members of the deceased express their gratitude to mourners by sending acknowledgment notes and return gifts (*kodengaeshi*) valued at about half of the koden. The kotsutsubo is buried at the grave site during this period.

Gifts of "incense money" presented by mourners at a funeral.

Literature (Nihon *bungaku*)　　　　　日本文学●

The written literature of Japan is one of the more venerable of the literary traditions of the Orient. Moreover, the oldest works in the standard canon, the histories *Kojiki* (712, Record of Ancient Matters) and *Nihon shoki* (720, Chronicles of Japan), provide in their myths, legends, and songs ample evidence of an ancient tradition of oral literature that, for the lack of a native system of writing, was not recorded until the introduction of Chinese characters.

Contact with the Asian mainland, the source of much of the material culture of the Yayoi period (ca 300 BC–ca AD 300) of Japanese history, became increasingly close during the 4th and 5th centuries. By the late 6th or early 7th century a small number of Japanese had gained an incipient mastery of Chinese writing and had developed the rudiments of a system whereby the Japanese language could be transcribed, using Chinese characters semantically to denote corresponding Japanese words or phonetically by the assignment of a Japanese sound value to individual characters. The pervasive influence of Chinese literature and its system of writing persisted until the mid-19th century, and most educated men considered it the literary language of Japan. Consequently over the course of more than a millennium a vast number of literary works were written in classical Chinese; these, as well as writings in high-classical Japanese and in hybrid forms of Sino-Japanese, of which modern Japanese is one, are all considered by the Japanese people to be elements of their literary heritage.

Early and Heian Literature　　　　　古代と平安時代の文学●

Official embassies to Sui (589–618) and Tang (618–907) dynasty China, initiated in 600, were the chief means by which Chinese culture, technology, and methods of government were introduced on a comprehensive basis in Japan. The *Kojiki* and the *Nihon shoki*, the former written in hybrid Sino-Japanese and the latter in classical Chinese, were compiled under the sponsorship of the government for the purpose of authenticating the legitimacy of its polity. However, among these collections of myths, genealogies, legends of folk heroes, and historical records there appear a number of songs—largely irregular in meter and written with Chinese characters representing Japanese words or syllables—that offer insight into the nature of preliterate Japanese verse.

The first major collection of native poetry, again written with Chinese characters, was the *Man'yoshu* (late 8th century), which contains verses, chiefly the 31-syllable WAKA, that were composed in large part between the mid-7th and mid-8th centuries. The earlier poems in the collection are characterized by the direct expression of strong emotion but those of later provenance show the emergence of the rhetorical conventions and expressive subtlety that dominated the subsequent tradition of court poetry. Although the *Man'yoshu* is today considered the great monument of early Japanese verse, contemporary literati, invariably men, chose to write their public verse in Chinese, and between the mid-8th century and the early years of the Heian period (794–1185) four imperial anthologies of Chinese poetry written by Japanese were compiled.

A revolutionary achievement of the mid-9th century was the development of a native orthography (*kana*) for the phonetic representation of Japanese. Employing radically abbreviated Chinese characters to denote Japanese sounds, the system contributed to a deepening consciousness of a native literary tradition distinct from that of China. The waka, now written with kana, was an indispensable element of social relations, and the practice arose of holding poem contests (*uta-awase*) at which pairs of verses were set against one another. Poets compiled collections (*shikashu*) of their verses, and, drawing in part on these, the *Kokinshu* (905), the first of 21 imperial anthologies of native poetry, was assembled in the early 10th century.

The introduction of kana also led to the development of a prose literature in the vernacular, early examples of which are the *Utsubo monogatari* (late 10th century), a work of fiction; the *Ise monogatari* (mid-10th century), a collection of vignettes centered on poems; and the diary *Tosa nikki* (935). From the late 10th century the ascendancy of the Fujiwara regents, whose power over emperors depended on the reception of their daughters as imperial consorts, resulted in the formation of literary coteries of women in the courts of empresses, and it was these women who produced the great prose classics of the 11th century. Written in high-classical Japanese with only the rare intrusion of Chinese characters, such works as *The Tale of Genji* (early 11th century), a fictional narrative by Murasaki Shikibu, and the *Makura no soshi* (996–1012), a collection of essays by Sei Shonagon, are considered by Japanese to be a watershed in the development of the native literary tradition. A distinctive feature of these and of many of the best of later Japanese prose works is their tendency to disregard formal structure in favor of a series of discrete scenes or discourses that present in the aggregate a comprehensive and richly detailed vision of a time and place.

Medieval Literature 中世の文学●

The chief development in poetry during the medieval period (mid-12th–16th centuries) was linked verse (*renga*). Arising from the court tradition of waka, renga was cultivated by the warrior class as well as by courtiers, and some among the best renga poets, such as Sogi, were commoners. A major development in prose literature of the medieval era was the war tale (*gunki monogatari*). The *Heike monogatari* (tr *The Tale of the Heike*) relates the events of the war between the Taira and Minamoto families that brought an end to imperial rule; it was disseminated among all levels of society by itinerant priests who chanted the story to the accompaniment of a lutelike instrument, the *biwa*. An increase in travelers along the highway connecting Kamakura, the seat of the military government, with the old capital of Kyoto gave rise to a number of travel diaries, such as the *Izayoi nikki* (ca 1280; tr *The Izayoi Nikki*) by Abutsu Ni, and the social upheaval of the early years of the era led to the appearance of works deeply influenced by the Buddhist notion of the inconstancy of worldly affairs (MUJO). Not only does the theme of mujo provide the ground note of the *Heike monogatari* and the essay collections *Hojoki* (1212; tr *The Ten Foot Square Hut*) by Kamo no Chomei and *Tsurezuregusa* (ca 1330; tr *Essays in Idleness*) by Yoshida Kenko, it is also an element of the theoretical framework of the historical work *Gukansho* (ca 1220) by the Buddhist priest Jien. The writing of literary works in Chinese continued in the hands of aristocrats and ZEN Buddhist priests of the Gozan temples.

Edo Literature 江戸時代の文学●

The formation of a stable central government in Edo (now Tokyo), after some 100 years of turmoil, and the growth of a market economy based on the widespread use of a standardized currency led to the development in the Edo period (1600–1868) of a class of wealthy townsmen. General prosperity contributed to an increase in literacy, and literary works became marketable commodities, giving rise to a publishing industry. Humorous fictional studies of contemporary society such as *Koshoku ichidai otoko* (1682; tr *The Life of an Amorous Man*) by Ihara Saikaku were huge commercial successes, and prose works, often elaborately illustrated, that were directed toward a mass audience became a staple of Edo-period literature. Commercial playhouses, patronized by commoner and *samurai* alike, were established for the performance of puppet plays (*joruri*) and *kabuki*, whose plots often centered on conflicts arising from the rigidly hierarchical social order that was instituted by the Tokugawa shogunate and underpinned by Neo-Confucian moral precepts.

Portrait of Ihara Saikaku.

The 17-syllable form of light verse known as *haikai* (later known as HAIKU), whose subject matter was drawn from nature and the lives of ordinary people, was raised to the level of great poetry by Matsuo Basho, who applied to its composition the standards of classical aesthetics. Some of the most evocative of native poetry in Chinese appeared during the Edo period; moreover, government adherence to the principles of Neo-Confucianism led to the writing in Chinese of a great number of prose works that dealt with the Neo-Confucian philosophical system. The waka, long stultified by functionless compositional conventions, was given new life when it was taken up by townsmen. A number of philologists, among them Keichu, Kamo no Mabuchi, and Motoori Norinaga, wrote scholarly studies on early literary texts, such as the *Kojiki*, the *Man'yoshu*, and *The Tale of Genji*, in which they attempted to elucidate the native Japanese world view as it existed before the introduction of Buddhism and Confucianism.

Modern Literature   近現代の文学●

The imperial restoration of 1868 was followed by the wholesale introduction of Western technology and culture, which largely displaced Chinese culture. As a result the novel, which during the Edo period had been considered a base form of literature appropriate only for the titillation or, in some instances, the moral edification of the masses, became established as a serious and respected genre of the literature of Japan. A related development was the gradual abandonment of the literary language in favor of the usages of colloquial speech, fully achieved for the first time in *Ukigumo* (1887–1889) by Futabatei Shimei. Although the *tanka* and the haiku remained viable poetic forms, notably in the hands of Ishikawa Takuboku, Yosano Akiko, Masaoka Shiki, and Takahama Kyoshi, there developed under the influence of Western poetry a genre of free verse, the first great achievement of which was the collection *Wakanashu* (1897) by Shimazaki Toson. Early stylistic influences on Japanese literature were romanticism, introduced in the 1890s by Mori Ogai; symbolism, introduced in Ueda Bin's *Kaichoon* (1905), a collection of translations of French poems; and naturalism, which reigned supreme from 1905 to 1910 and out of which developed the enduring genre of the confessional novel (I-novel or *watakushi shosetsu*).

Kawabata Yasunari, winner of the 1968 Nobel Prize for literature.

Until the 1950s a distinctive feature of the Japanese literary community was the publication of coterie magazines by writers of like mind. The humanist Shirakaba school of writers, including Mushanokoji Saneatsu and Shiga Naoya, published the journal *Shirakaba* from 1910; the early writings of Kawabata Yasunari appeared in *Bungei jidai* (1924–1927),

the organ of the modernist Shinkankaku school; and works of the proletarian writers Kobayashi Takiji and Sata Ineko were published in *Senki*
(1928–1931), a Marxist-oriented periodical. The serial publication of novels in newspapers has also been a common practice, and some of the best
Japanese novelists, from Natsume Soseki to Nagai Kafu, Tanizaki
Jun'ichiro, and Kawabata Yasunari, have written for the newspapers.
Translations of Japanese literary works have appeared in rapidly increas-
ing numbers since the 1970s, and the best creations of Soseki, Ogai, Kafu,
Akutagawa Ryunosuke, Shiga, Tanizaki, Kawabata, Ibuse Masuji, Dazai
Osamu, Enchi Fumiko, and Mishima Yukio are available in English ver-
sions. Among the foremost writers of fiction in the early 1990s were Oe
Kenzaburo, Abe Kobo, Endo Shusaku, Tsushima Yuko, Murakami Ryu,
Nakagami Kenji, and Murakami Haruki. See also MODERN FICTION.

Waka ("Japanese poetry")   和歌●

A genre of verse of various prosodic types that began to take form
in the hands of the court aristocracy in the mid-6th century. By the late 8th
century the term was used synonymously with *tanka* ("short poem"), a
type of verse that consists of five lines in 31 syllables in the pattern 5-7-5-
7-7 and that is still composed today. Early Japanese song, from which
waka arose, and the derivative genres *renga* ("linked verse") and *haikai*
(later known as *haiku*) are distinguished from waka, as is modern free
verse. The sinicized term waka, in use by the Heian period (794–1185),
replaced the previous term Yamato *no uta* (poetry of the land of Yamato),
but both imply the distinction of native verse from *kanshi*, or verse composed in Chinese by Chinese or Japanese poets.

Prosody and Rhetorical Devices   韻律と修辞的技巧●

The primary sources of our knowledge of early Japanese poetry are
the annals *Kojiki* (712, Record of Ancient Matters) and *Nihon shoki* (720,
Chronicles of Japan) and the late-8th-century anthology of poetry
Man'yoshu (Collection of Ten Thousand Leaves or Collection for Ten
Thousand Generations), most of the more than 4,000 poems in which were
culled from earlier anthologies that are no longer extant. The oldest poems
display little prosodic regularity, although there was a tendency to alternate longer and shorter lines. In the 7th century, however, possibly arising
from the influence of the five-character and seven-character lines of
Chinese verse, the number of syllables per line became standardized at
five and seven. From the mid-7th century the tanka form appears to have
been paramount, but until the middle of the 8th century it was rivaled by

the *choka* ("long poem"), consisting of an indefinite number of pairs of five- and seven-syllable lines with an extra seven-syllable line at the end. The longest choka, by Kakinomoto no Hitomaro, is one in 149 lines. Other forms were the *katauta* ("half poem"), of 3 lines of five, seven, and five syllables, to which another poet replied to form a set; the *sedoka* ("head-repeated poem"), of 6 lines in the syllable pattern 5-7-7-5-7-7; and the *bussokuseki no uta*, also of 6 lines but in the syllable pattern 5-7-5-7-7-7, the chief examples of which are inscribed on an ancient stela erected beside a stone (bussokuseki) on which the Buddha's footprints are incised.

Alliteration, consonance, and assonance are found in the earliest Japanese verses and were used by poets of all periods to provide sonority and rhetorical complexity. Until the mid-8th century the dominant cadence of waka was 5-7, but thereafter the 7-5 cadence gained the ascendancy. It also became common for the cadence to be broken, usually at the end of the third line, by a caesura. In the following 12th-century poem by the priest Jakuren, the third line terminates with a conclusive verb inflection and is followed by a noun phrase:

Sabishisa wa	To be alone—
Sono iro to shi mo	It is of a color that
Nakarikeri	Cannot be named:
Maki tatsu yama no	This mountain where cedars rise
Aki no yugure	Into the autumn dusk.

Imagery and Subject Matter　　　　　　　比喩と題材●

Classical waka employed a high proportion of images drawn from nature, personification of which led increasingly to allegory. However, unlike Western allegory, with its personified conceptual abstractions, allegory in waka tended to be concrete and personal (e.g., a poem about an orange tree that awaits the arrival of the cuckoo in early summer might also represent a lady awaiting her dilatory lover). The conventions of waka militated against the innovative use of natural images—the stock of which, in the case of insects, included the cicada and the cricket, but not the butterfly, the bee, or the firefly—and a consequence of this narrowing of content was that a new poem inevitably alluded to earlier poems in the tradition.

Waka poets concentrated on a handful of subjects, primarily human affairs (celebration, separation, grief, and especially love) and nature (natural beauty and the changing aspects of the seasons), avoiding war, physical suffering, death, and all that was ugly or low. The themes of beauty and sadness, infused by an awareness of the overarching effects of time, increasingly dominated waka. With the growing influence of a Buddhist world view holding all life to be ephemeral and all human attachment to be an impediment to enlightenment, nature poetry came typically to express a lyric melancholy, while poetry of love expressed a poignant consciousness of the impermanence of personal ties.

Historical Development 歴史●

Following the *Man'yoshu*, the next major collection of waka was the *Kokinshu* (905, Collection from Ancient and Modern Times), the first of 21 imperial anthologies. These anthologies varied considerably in size and quality, but each was considered the most important literary enterprise of its day. Among the chief sources from which poems were drawn for inclusion in the imperial anthologies were the *shikashu*, collections of poetry written and compiled by individual poets. Other important repositories of classical waka—and of critical judgments—are the records of poetry matches (*uta-awase*).

Waka of the *Kokinshu* was much influenced by the mannered elegance and precious conceits of Chinese poetry of the late Six Dynasties period (222–589), in particular the monumental *Wen xuan* (J: *Monzen*). Nevertheless, the *Kokinshu* also displays in its verse, as well as in the vernacular preface written by one of its compilers, Ki no Tsurayuki, a strong consciousness of a native poetics. Tsurayuki distinguishes between the essence or "heart" (*kokoro*) of a poem and the construct of language (*kotoba*) by means of which it is embodied. The ideal toward which the poet strives, Tsurayuki declares, is a harmony of kokoro and kotoba, of individual feeling and sincerity with rhetorical elegance and purity of diction.

The eighth imperial anthology, *Shin kokinshu* (1205, New Collection from Ancient and Modern Times), one of whose editors was Fujiwara no Teika, brought to fulfillment the organizational concepts, already apparent in the *Kokinshu*, of association and progression. Adjacent poems were linked by such devices as similarity of image or common allusion to an older poem, while all of the poems of the major divisions of the anthology, such as those devoted to individual seasons or to love, were ordered on the basis of the appearance of seasonal phenomena or the progress of a love affair. The principles of association and progression were among the influences that contributed to the development of the genre of linked verse (renga).

The last imperial anthology, *Shin shoku kokinshu* (New Collection from Ancient and Modern Times, Continued) was completed in 1439.

Following the *Shin kokinshu*, imperial anthologies displayed an increasingly sterile style, marked by a slavish veneration of the conventions of the Heian period, and by the Edo period (1600–1868) the center of waka composition had passed from the court to society at large.

Early in the Meiji period (1868–1912), the influential poet-critics Yosano Tekkan and Masaoka Shiki called for a break with the past and, following their practice, the custom arose of referring to the art of 31-syllable poetry as tanka, rather than waka. In 1899, with other young tanka poets, Tekkan founded the Shinshisha (New Poetry Society), which in 1900 initiated the publication of the literary magazine *Myojo* (Bright Star). One of the leading contributors was Yosano Akiko, whose passionate lyricism brought a new vigor to the genre.

Tanka continues in the post-World War II period to be a widely practiced form of verse; nevertheless, though today hundreds of societies and millions of practitioners carry on the tradition, the best Japanese poets have increasingly chosen to work in the genre of free verse. Moreover, the importance of convention in waka has led to the preservation of classical grammar in tanka composition, thus vitiating the immediacy of its effect on the majority of Japanese. A notable exception, however, is the vastly popular tanka of Tawara Machi (1962–), who has preserved the subtlety of feeling and expressive grace of classical waka while employing colloquial diction.

H*aiku* 俳句●

A 17-syllable verse form consisting of three metrical units of 5, 7, and 5 syllables, respectively. One of the most important forms of traditional Japanese poetry, haiku remains popular in modern Japan, and in recent years its popularity has spread to other countries.

Haiku, *Hokku*, and *Haikai* 俳句・発句・俳諧●

Loose usage by students, translators, and even poets themselves has led to much confusion about the distinction between the three related terms haiku, hokku, and haikai. The term hokku literally means "starting verse." A hokku was the first or "starting" link of a much longer chain of verses known as a haikai *no renga*, or simply haikai, in which alternating sets of 5-7-5 syllables and 7-7 syllables were joined. Hokku gradually took on an independent character. Largely through the efforts of Masaoka Shiki (1867–1902), this independence was formally established in the 1890s through the creation of the term "haiku." Haiku was a new type of verse, in form quite similar to the traditional hokku but different in that it was to be written, read, and understood as an independent poem, complete in itself, rather than as part of a longer chain.

Strictly speaking, then, the history of haiku begins only in the last years of the 19th century. The famous verses of Edo-period (1600–1868) masters such as Matsuo Basho (1644–1694), Yosa Buson (1716–1784), and Kobayashi Issa (1763–1827) are properly referred to as hokku even though they are now generally read as independent haiku.

Development of Haikai   俳諧の発展●

Renga, or linked verse, which began to be written in the Heian period (794–1185), was originally considered a diversion by which poets could relax from the serious business of composing WAKA poetry. By the time of the renga master Sogi (1421–1502), however, it had become a serious art with complex rules and high aesthetic standards. Haikai no renga, or simply haikai, was conceived as a lighthearted amusement in which poets could indulge after the solemn refinements of serious renga.

When haikai began to emerge as a serious poetic genre in the early 16th century, two characteristics distinguished it from serious renga: its humorous intent and its free use of *haigon* (colloquialisms, compounds borrowed from Chinese, and other expressions that had previously been banned from the poetic vocabulary). However, the erudite Matsunaga Teitoku (1571–1653) succeeded in establishing a more conservative and formalistic approach to haikai. For Teitoku, humor implied a sort of intellectual wit, and the distinction between haikai and renga lay ultimately only in the use or nonuse of haigon. He established strict rules concerning the composition of haikai and sought to endow the form with the elegance and aesthetic elevation of waka and serious renga.

Portrait of Matsuo Basho.

After Teitoku's death his formalistic approach was challenged by the more freewheeling Danrin School of haikai led by Nishiyama Soin (1605–1682). Soin emphasized the comic aspects of haikai. Characteristic of the Danrin style of poetry was the practice of *yakazu* haikai, in which a single poet would reel off verse after verse as quickly as possible in a sort of exercise in free association. The most renowned example of this is the legendary performance by Ihara Saikaku (1642–1693) in 1684 at the Sumiyoshi Shrine in Osaka, where he composed 23,500 verses in a single day and night.

Basho was not only the greatest of haikai poets, he was also primarily responsible for establishing haikai as a true art form. Having received instruction in both the Teitoku and Danrin styles of haikai, he gradually developed in the late 17th century a new style that, through its artistic sincerity, transcended the conflict between serious renga and

Culture

comic haikai and could express humor, humanity, and profound religious insight all within the space of a single hokku. His representative works include *Oku no hosomichi* (1694; tr *The Narrow Road to the Deep North*). Basho also had a great number of disciples. Of these, the so-called Ten Philosophers are particularly well known.

After Basho's death many of his disciples set up their own schools of haikai. In general these poets sought special effects—with some writing enigmatic, puzzlelike verse and others satisfying themselves with witty wordplay. In the late 18th century, there arose a movement of poets who sought to restore high aesthetic standards. The principal figure in this haikai reform was the talented painter-poet Buson, and the main cry of the movement was "Return to Basho!" Buson possessed great imagination and culture and a painter's eye for vivid pictorial scenes.

The number of composers of haikai grew rapidly in the early 19th century. This popularization, however, was accompanied by a general decline in quality. The most notable exception was Kobayashi Issa. Issa's poems about his poverty and about his love for small animals and insects are particularly memorable. His best known work is *Oraga haru* (1820; tr *The Year of My Life*). Today he ranks with Basho and Buson as one of the most beloved haikai poets.

Portrait of Kobayashi Issa.

Modern Haiku

現代の俳句●

The history of modern haiku dates from Masaoka Shiki's reform, begun in 1892, which established haiku as a new independent poetic form. Basic to the modernization of haiku was Shiki's most important concept, *shasei*, or sketching from life—a term borrowed from the critical vocabulary of Western painting. The magazine that Shiki began in 1897, *Hototogisu*, became the haiku world's most important publication.

Shiki's reform did not change two traditional elements of haiku: the division of 17 syllables into three groups of 5, 7, and 5 syllables and the inclusion of a seasonal theme. Kawahigashi Hekigoto who succeeded his mentor Shiki, carried Shiki's reform further with a proposal that haiku would be truer to reality if there were no center of interest in it. The logical extension of this idea was free-verse haiku, since the traditional patterning was seen as another artificial manipulation of reality. Hekigoto also urged the importance of the poet's first impression, just as it was, of subjects taken from daily life and of local color to create freshness. His style was named Shinkeiko Haiku (New Trend Haiku).

Protesting against the prosaic flatness characteristic of much of the works of Hekigoto's school, Ogiwara Seisensui maintained in 1912 that free-verse haiku must also discard the seasonal theme. He held that haiku must capture in its rhythms not the object perceived but the poet's perception. The work of many able poets appeared in his magazine *Soun* (1911–). Notably successful among them was Taneda Santoka who led a wandering life of poverty, like the beggar-priests of the past.

In 1912 Takahama Kyoshi began in the pages of *Hototogisu* (which he had edited since 1898) his lifelong defense of the traditional 17-syllable form, the seasonal theme, and the descriptive realism of Shiki. He outlined his views in a collection of essays published under the title *Susumubeki haiku no michi* (1915–1917, The Path Haiku Ought to Take). The first flowering of the traditional school was in the Taisho period (1912–1926) and featured such gifted poets as Iida Dakotsu and Murakami Kijo.

By 1920 a second generation of poets clustered about *Hototogisu*, including Mizuhara Shuoshi, Awano Seiho, Yamaguchi Seishi, and Takano Suju. The first Showa-period (1926–1989) poet to break away into subjects previously avoided was Hino Sojo, who wrote verses on romantic and sensuous love. *Hototogisu* continues to represent the central position in haiku to the present day.

Mizuhara Shuoshi broke away from *Hototogisu* in 1931, two years after having assumed the editorship of the magazine *Ashibi* (1928–). Shuoshi's talent for making imaginative use of the historical past shines in his collection *Katsushika* (1930). *Ashibi* was an important outlet for such poets as Yamaguchi Seishi, Ishida Hakyo, and Hashimoto Takako, the foremost woman haiku poet.

In the early Showa period the term *shinko haiku* (new haiku) loosely identified all groups that deviated from the traditional *Hototogisu* school. In addition to the *Ashibi* poets and the modernistic school of Hino Sojo's magazine *Kikan* (1935–41), the term also included the proletarian school.

Joining *Hototogisu* in 1933, Nakamura Kusatao deplored the shinko haiku movement for its emphasis on technique and methodology. By 1939 he was identified along with Ishida Hakyo and Kato Shuson as a member of the Ningen Tankyu Ha ("Humanness" school).

During the military-dominated prewar and World War II period, haiku was controlled by government censorship.

After the war, the effort to unite all poets was stimulated by a widely discussed 1946 article entitled "Daini geijutsuron" (On a Second-Class Art), in which the critic Kuwabara Takeo maintained that modern haiku was not a serious literary genre but only a pleasant pastime. A number of efforts to "modernize haiku"—to make it relevant to contemporary experience—were stimulated by the publicity given Kuwabara's article.

One such effort was *Tenro* (1948–94), a magazine begun in 1948 under Yamaguchi Seishi's editorship and supported by the prewar liberal Kyoto University haiku association together with some former *Ashibi* poets. *Tenro* and the prewar *Ashibi* were the two most important vehicles of the nontraditional haiku. The extreme haiku fringe of symbolism and surrealism is found in the magazine *Bara* (1952–1957) started by Tomizawa Kakio and Takayanagi Shigenobu.

Haiku Abroad   海外における俳句●

The West's first introduction to haiku came in B. H. Chamberlain's pioneer work, *Japanese Poetry* (1910), in a chapter entitled "Basho and the Japanese Epigram." William Porter's early anthology of translations was entitled *A Year of Japanese Epigrams* (1911). Haiku was first introduced to France by Paul-Louis Couchoud at the time of the Russo-Japanese War. The title of his introduction to haiku was *Les Epigrammes Lyriques du Japon*. The use of the term "epigram" in these titles is indicative of how haiku was first intepreted abroad.

Ezra Pound quickly noticed and appropriated the haiku technique of cutting up the poem into two independent yet associated images. In France Paul Eluard wrote poems in the haiku style. Haiku has rapidly become naturalized both in Europe and in the United States, and magazines of original haiku are published. Haiku magazines in the United States include *Modern Haiku*, *byways*, *Tweed*, and *New World Haiku*.

Modern fiction (*kingendai no shosetsu*)   近現代の小説●

Modern fiction in Japan has its origins in the Meiji period (1868–1912), when a flood of translations of Western literature collided with a vigorous native tradition of imaginative writing. The *gesaku* fiction of the Edo period (1600–1868) continued to have a powerful influence upon the style and content of the early Meiji fiction, and it was in reaction to this influence that Tsubouchi Shoyo produced the first critical treatise in Japanese regarding the theory and aims of the modern novel, *Shosetsu shinzui* (1885–86, The Essence of the Novel).

Fiction had been traditionally regarded as a form of vulgar entertainment, and Tsubouchi, after examining recently imported Western models of writing, sensed the need for a new kind of imaginative writing capable of depicting the realities of modern life and establishing the novel as a serious form of artistic expression. He argued the merits of realistic fiction as a medium for expressing the perceptions and aspirations of contemporary society, and discussed the need for novelists to create a written language with the vigor and comprehensibility of the spoken language, as well as the versatility and precision essential to a serious literature.

Relying upon Tsubouchi's theories and personal guidance, Futabatei Shimei produced what has been called Japan's first modern novel, *Ukigumo* (1887–89, Drifting Clouds; tr *Ukigumo*, 1967). The plot concerns an unremarkable government clerk whose tenacious adherence to old-fashioned virtues renders him a pathetic figure in the eyes of both his more opportunistic colleagues and his female cousin, who is also his presumed fiancee. What is strikingly fresh about the novel is the colloquial style of the language, Futabatei's conception of his hero's plight within the context of a quickly changing society, and his subtle psychological examination of his protagonist.

For over a decade after *Ukigumo*, few writers shared Futabatei's interest in or understanding of the modern psychological novel. But in the 1890s this quest was continued by several young writers who are usually associated with the romantic movement centering on the famous literary journal *Bungakukai* (1893–98, The Literary World). The most impressive work of fiction published in *Bungakukai* was the story "Takekurabe" (1895–96; tr "Growing Up," 1956) by Higuchi Ichiyo. Ichiyo's language is still heavily classical in diction and imagery, but the content of the story is extraordinarily modern. In this tale of children living in the shadow of the Yoshiwara pleasure quarter, Ichiyo describes the loneliness of adolescence, the confusion that attends a growing awareness of sex, and the callousness of the adult world, which must soon be theirs. The subtlety and seriousness of her handling of youthful psychology betokens something very new in her vision.

Cover of the novel
Ukigumo by Futabatei
Shimei.

But Ichiyo died too young, and it was another of her colleagues from *Bungakukai*, Shimazaki Toson, who set the pattern for one stream of modern writers by moving gradually from romantic poetry to the writing of realistic fiction to assert the authenticity of the individual personality. His first novel, *Hakai* (1906; tr *The Broken Commandment*, 1974), relates the story of a *burakumin* schoolteacher who hides his origins in the outcaste community until he realizes his only salvation as a human being lies in divulging his secret. In this powerful work, themes of bigotry, guilt, and isolation are treated with a psychological sophistication and social awareness that were new in Japanese literature.

After *Hakai*, however, Toson followed the direction set by

Culture

Tayama Katai's confessional novel *Futon* (1907; tr *The Quilt*, 1981) and retreated into his own private world to write in the genre of autobiographical or semiautobiographical novel known as the I-novel. Toson's abandonment of social realism helped to establish the genre of personal fiction, with its narrow world of limited alternatives, which for years nearly dominated the literary scene.

Thus it was not through Toson but through Natsume Soseki that the modern Japanese realistic novel was brought to full maturity. Soseki wrote a series of novels that are still among the most probing fictional accounts of the vicissitudes of modern middle-class life in Japan. His heroes are usually university-educated men made vulnerable by the new "egoism" and a too-keen perception of their separation from the rest of the world. In *Kokoro* (1914, The Heart; tr *Kokoro*, 1957), the most popular of his later novels, the hero, lonely and unable to overcome his guilt for having driven a friend to suicide because of their love of the same woman, finally kills himself. Guilt, betrayal, and isolation are for Soseki the inevitable consequences of the liberation of the self and all the uncertainties that have come with the advent of Western culture. These motifs are also explored in his novels *Mon* (1910, The Gate; tr *Mon*, 1972) and *Kojin* (1912–13; tr *The Wayfarer*, 1967).

Novelist Natsume Soseki.

Doctor, head of the army medical corps, German scholar, translator, master stylist, critic, historian, and novelist, Mori Ogai was the versatile intellectual par excellence of his time. Ironically, it is his own ambivalence toward fiction—reflecting a persistent suspicion in Japan of the artifice and unreality inherent in the genre—that seems to play a large part in the veneration with which Ogai is regarded.

Ogai first won acclaim with three romantic short stories set in Germany, each with a central Japanese character. The most popular, "Maihime" (1890; tr "The Dancing Girl," 1975), deals with the doomed love affair of a young Japanese student in Berlin with a German dancer of humble circumstances. Ogai's major novels with contemporary settings are not as dramatic as Soseki's, nor are they as rich in explicit social commentary. Yet in such works as *Gan* (1911–13; tr *The Wild Geese*, 1959), about a usurer's mistress who falls in love with a student, we find a new complexity in the psychological delineation of the characters. His most representative late works are essentially fictionalized studies in history and biography, such as the short story "Sakai jiken" (1914; tr "The Incident at Sakai," 1977) and the meticulously researched life of an Edo-period doctor presented in Shibue Chusai (1916).

Akutagawa Ryunosuke, a younger contemporary of Ogai's and

one of Japan's most famous short-story writers, also sought an outlet for his sly and supple imagination by setting many stories in the past. For Akutagawa, the past offered through its very remoteness a freedom that the present could not. Such stories as "Rashomon" (1915; tr "Rashomon," 1930), and "Yabu no naka" (1922; tr "In a Grove," 1952) are brilliantly told, combining psychological subtlety and modern cynicism with a fanciful delight in the grotesque.

Nagai Kafu was another of the major figures in modern Japanese fiction who reflected the tension between modernity and a yearning for an older Japan. His life as a writer began with travels to America and France. He is best known, however, for his elegiac works—notably *Bokuto kidan* (1937; tr *A Strange Tale from East of the River*, 1958)—depicting the fading demimonde of Tokyo with a richness of attention to place and mood that has won him a lasting place in literary history.

Shiga Naoya, who established his reputation with a body of brilliantly crafted short stories, went on to cap his accomplishments with a single full-length psychological novel, *An'ya koro* (1921–37; tr *A Dark Night's Passing*, 1976). The search for identity in the modern world is the theme of this masterwork, as the hero, born of an incestuous liaison between his mother and her father-in-law, learns this ugly fact and suddenly finds his sense of self challenged at its very foundations.

Novelist Nagai Kafu.

It was Tanizaki Jun'ichiro who took modern Japanese writing a step further into a realm of pure and playful fictionality. In early novels such as *Chijin no ai* (1924–25; tr *Naomi*, 1985) and *Manji* (1928–30), Tanizaki went far beyond the conventions of earlier realistic fiction. Both works are tales of sexual infidelity, abandon, obsession, and fantasy in which the deceptions engaged in by the characters are metaphors for the deceptiveness of fiction itself. He possessed a rare capacity to articulate through allegory the cultural confusions of modern Japan. In novels such as *Tade kuu mushi* (1928–29; tr *Some Prefer Nettles*, 1955), Tanizaki sought a sense of continuity amid contemporary uneasiness by turning to the past.

In the work of writers like Tanizaki and Kafu from the late 1920s and 1930s, a lingering aura of tradition still infuses their settings and locales, and a sense of cultural continuity, however tenuous, is still available to them. Japan's plunge into World War II and the shattering defeat that ensued, however, were sufficiently powerful to obliterate such communion with the past. The writer who most clearly reflected the sense of loss and confusion following the war, both in his writing and his tragic life, was Dazai Osamu. Dazai's early work focused upon his own dissipation and debauchery, but the chaos is intensified to the breaking point in *Shayo* (1947; tr *The Setting Sun*, 1956) and the novel published just before his suicide, *Ningen shikkaku* (1948; tr *No Longer Human*, 1958).

Not every writer after the war accepted Dazai's utterly negative response to the defeat. Ibuse Masuji was one who clung to a sense of geographical place as a mooring, but his focus was on the struggle to maintain that identification in the face of forces that threaten to obliterate it. This is clear in his finest work, *Kuroi ame* (1965–66; tr *Black Rain*, 1969), about the atomic bombing of Hiroshima. The greatness of the novel, which is narrated through the diaries of ordinary people, lies in its ability to depict all of the horrifying details of the event and yet conclude with an affirmation of humanity.

Not long after the defeat, Tanizaki Jun'ichiro also published his masterpiece, the massive novel *Sasameyuki* (1943–48; tr *The Makioka Sisters*, 1957), serial publication of which had been suppressed during the war. A chronicle of the lives of the daughters of a patrician merchant family in its last stages of decline before the outbreak of the war, it is a beautiful elegy to the final passing of all that remained of an older and more elegant world.

Writers such as Enchi Fumiko also sought to reestablish the severed links with the cultural past by calling upon such classical texts as the *Tale of Genji* and transporting them into a very different modern setting. Her novels *Onnazaka* (1949–57; tr *The Waiting Years*, 1971) and *Onnamen* (1958; tr *Masks*, 1983) describe the continuing struggle of women confined within traditional social roles.

The link between people and place has grown painfully fragile in the fiction of Nobel laureate, Kawabata Yasunari. In novels such as *Yukiguni* (1935–48; tr *Snow Country*, 1956), Kawabata creates enormous distances between his characters, suggesting a dread of intimacy that threatens even the most promising of human relationships. After the war, Kawabata took to writing what he called "elegies to the lost Japan" in such works as *Yama no oto* (1949–54; tr *The Sound of the Mountain*, 1970), in which the aging protagonist, Shingo, unable to endure the frustrating losses that surround him, opens a gulf between himself and his family by retreating into his memories of the irretrievable past.

Yet Japanese writing in the early postwar years could not be characterized solely in terms of the shock and dislocation of defeat. There was, in fact, a vigorous renascence of literary activity after 1945, and a new group of writers who debuted at this time came to be known as the "first generation" of postwar authors. They had been attracted to Marxist philosophy before the war, and returned from the war to assert the need for a type of fiction that would examine all the political, philosophical, and moral aspects of their experience. Members of this group include Noma Hiroshi, whose novel *Shinku chitai* (1952; tr *Zone of Emptiness*, 1956) depicts the military in wartime as an extension of the oppressive prewar Japanese social order, and Ooka Shohei, who in *Nobi* (1951; tr *Fires on the Plain*, 1957), a novel set in the last days of the fighting in the Philippines, depicts a solitary Japanese soldier who is reduced to the lowest level of humanity by his wartime experiences.

The "second generation" of postwar writers includes Abe Kobo and Mishima Yukio, both of whom debuted in the late 1940s. Abe would eventually create a distinctive type of Kafkaesque existential allegory in novels such as *Suna no onna* (1962; tr *The Woman in the Dunes*, 1964), while Mishima attracted an international readership with his opulent aestheticism, his vision of a postwar Japan clinging to external forms but hollow within, and his complex psychological examination of character and motivation in such works as *Kinkakuji* (1956; tr *The Temple of the Golden Pavilion*, 1959).

Critics have posited a turning point in the 1950s, after which Japanese fiction can no longer be easily characterized in terms of the early postwar consciousness. Beginning about this time, a revival and restructuring of the I-novel form was achieved by a "third generation" of postwar writers—Kojima Nobuo, who examined the collapse of the family system in *Hoyo kazoku* (1965, Embracing Family); Yasuoka Shotaro, who brought a new sense of ironic perspective to the personal narrative in *Umibe no kokei* (1959; tr *A View by the Sea*, 1984); and Shimao Toshio, whose fiction, culminating in *Shi no toge* (1960; tr *The Sting of Death*, 1985), transposes the agony and anxiety of his war experience onto his postwar marital relationship. Also included in this group is Endo Shusaku, a Catholic convert who examines the issues of betrayal, cowardice, and martyrdom in novels such as *Chimmoku* (1966; tr *Silence*, 1969), set during the Christian persecutions of early-17th-century Japan.

Novelist Endo Shusaku.

From the 1960s onward, writers have sought to synthesize various approaches to fiction or to experiment with new modes of representation. Oe Kenzaburo, who received the Nobel Prize for literature in 1994, has been a prodigiously inventive force in contemporary fiction, continuously experimenting with form and mode of presentation in dealing with both political and personal issues in such novels as *Kojinteki na taiken* (1964; tr *A Personal Matter*, 1968) and *Man'en gannen no futtoboru* (1967; tr *The Silent Cry*, 1974). Kono Taeko has examined the repressed psychology of women in *Fui no koe* (1968, Sudden Voice) and other works, while Tsushima Yuko, the daughter of Dazai Osamu, has explored the lives of women who are single parents in *Choji* (1978; tr *Child of Fortune*, 1983). And finally, the generation raised on the rebellious, rock-and-roll international culture of the last decades has found its voice in writers such as Murakami Ryu, author of *Kagirinaku tomei ni chikai buru* (1976; tr *Almost Transparent Blue*, 1977), and Murakami Haruki, whose *Noruue no mori* (1987; tr *Norwegian Wood*, 1989) sold more than 3 million copies. In Japan, as in the West, critics have periodically proclaimed the death of fiction and bemoaned the decline in the audience for serious literature, but this news has apparently not reached the Japanese public, which is buying and reading a greater number and variety of books than ever before.

Folktales (*minwa*)   民話●

Narrative literature of the people, handed down orally from generation to generation. Some tales can be traced back even before writing was introduced to Japan.

Outside of the oral tradition, there is rich documentation of folk material throughout the ages. The 8th century saw the first written records of the imperial history with the *Kojiki* (712, Record of Ancient Matters) and *Nihon shoki* (720, Chronicles of Japan), which contain many tale motifs. The *Nihon ryoiki*, *Konjaku monogatari*, and *Uji shui monogatari* of the following centuries are collections of traditional narratives, Buddhist and secular, totaling well over 1,000 in number. Also, the classic dramas of the 15th century, the NO and *kyogen*, as well as KABUKI, which originated in the early 17th century, are examples of how dramatists based their plots and themes on folk material, resulting in the preservation of tale motifs today.

Collecting Folktales   民話の採集●

Systematic collecting of folktales was started in the 1930s, following the precepts of a list of 100 major story types devised by Yanagita Kunio, who wrote *Mukashi-banashi saishu techo* (1936, Manual for Collecting Folktales).

The first attempt to tabulate the collected material in classified order was *Nippon mukashi-banashi meii* (1948, A List of Japanese Folktales). Listing the outlines of various tale types in one volume, it is useful as a handbook for tale collecting. In 1958 the original classification system of Yanagita was expanded sevenfold by Seki Keigo in a classified anthology of 8,600 folktale synopses entitled *Nippon mukashi-banashi shusei*, pub-

Yanagita Kunio, the founder of Japanese folklore studies.

lished in six volumes.

Diffusion Routes to Japan   日本への伝来ルート●

In prehistoric times Japan seems to have had closer contact with the Eurasian continent than is commonly thought. It was an era of dynamic migration from east to west along many routes. One that intimately concerns Japan was the circumpolar route that eventually populated the Americas. Situated adjacent to this route, Japan shares many cultural features with the races along this grand migration route.

The warm tides washing the shores of Japan suggest another far-reaching route of diffusion. Because many Japanese myths and legends correspond to those of ancient Greece, there is a strong possibility of an overseas route that connected the two areas by way of ports of call dotting the southern fringe of the Eurasian continent.

Again there are Japanese tales and legends that are shared by cultures on the perimeter of the Pacific Ocean. This circumpacific diffusion route follows the Japan Current, which circulates clockwise about the Pacific, north from Taiwan along the east coast of Japan, then across to the western shores of North and South America, and returns west through the Southern Pacific Ocean.

With the advent of the Yayoi period (ca 300 BC–ca AD 300), an entirely new sort of culture complex came into Japan from the southern part of Korea. A considerable number of migrants arrived with the technology of rice cultivation, weaving, the use of iron tools, bronze weapons, dolmens, pot coffins, and the making of Yayoi pottery. Yayoi culture flourished in northern Kyushu for some time and then spread eastward. From about the 3rd to the 5th centuries, the present emperor's ancestors consolidated their power in central Honshu. The *Kojiki* and *Nihon shoki* trace the imperial family history back to the mythical era and incorporate many preexistent tale motifs.

With the introduction of writing and Buddhism to Japan, first from Korea and then directly from China, Japanese folk literature gained yet another overland route to sources in Central Asia and down to India through Tibet. Tales recorded in the *Nihon ryoiki* and *Konjaku monogatari* belong to this group.

Well-known folktales of Japan include "Peach Boy"(Momotaro), "The Wen Removed" (Kobutori jijii), "The Tongue-Cut Sparrow" (Shitakiri suzume), and "Kachikachi Mountain" (Kachikachi yama).

Momotaro (Peach Boy)   桃太郎●

Popular folktale recounting the adventures of the boy Momotaro. Born from a peach found by an elderly woman washing clothes on a riverbank, Momotaro is adopted by the woman and her husband. Maturing quickly, he goes off with a dog, a pheasant, and a monkey to conquer Ogre Island and returns home with treasures for his foster parents. The tale exists in many versions; its present form has been widely popular since the late Edo period (1600–1868).

Shitakiri suzume (The Tongue-Cut Sparrow)   舌切り雀●

A sparrow owned by an honest old man eats some rice paste prepared by a greedy old woman (in some versions the man's wife). Enraged, the woman cuts out the tongue of the sparrow and drives it away. The grieving old man goes in search of his sparrow and is well treated by the sparrow's family. On leaving them, he is offered a choice of two boxes; he takes the lighter one, which turns out to be full of treasure. The greedy woman then pays a visit to the sparrows and demands the heavier box, from which emerge goblins and serpents; the woman dies of shock. The archetype of this story is found in the 13th-century collection of tales *Uji shui monogatari.*

Art (Nihon *bijutsu*) 日本美術●

Over the centuries, a wide variety of social, economic, political, cultural, and environmental factors have had an influence on the development of Japanese art. The temperate climate and four distinct seasons provided an abundance of seasonal symbols and motifs, such as the plum, the cherry, the maple, and the chrysanthemum, which appear again and again in Japanese art. The Japanese love of nature is reflected in the use of such raw materials as lacquer, wood, bamboo, and paper throughout Japanese architecture. The high humidity and frequent earthquakes and typhoons common to Japan discouraged the use of more permanent materials such as stone in architecture and ensured the preference for the more readily mendable and available materials that dominate the Japanese aesthetic.

At the same time, the influence of China, whose culture rests at the heart of East Asian creativity, was particularly felt in Japan; Chinese artistic styles and larger segments of Chinese culture, including the great international tradition of Buddhist art, reached Japan either directly or filtered through the Korean peninsula. Even the famous secular style of the Heian court (794–1185) received notable inspiration from continental shores.

Despite Japan's contact with and absorption of foreign aesthetics from prehistoric times to the present, Japanese art had little, if any, influence on outside cultures, especially Western cultures, until the last half of the 19th century, when European artists discovered its beauties and developed a passion for *japonaiserie*. Exposure to and consciousness of Japanese art through, for example, Japanese ceramics and woodblock prints played a major role in the development of a modern European painting aesthetic, as well as influencing the aesthetic course of the decorative arts. Present-day Japanese artists are making an increasingly active contribution to the development of contemporary international art.

Buddhist art (Bukkyo *bijutsu*) 仏教美術●

Like Japanese Buddhism itself, Japanese Buddhist art was a national variant of an international tradition. In Japan the Buddhist art forms that were periodically introduced from China and Korea were tempered in the crucible of local custom and usage, to yield a rich tradition of religious art and architecture.

Culture

Early Buddhist Art 初期の仏教美術●

Buddhism was formally transmitted to Japan from China and Korea in the 6th century. The forms of Buddhism and Buddhist art that first arrived in Japan were chiefly those of the Mahayana (J: Daijo Bukkyo) tradition, a theistic and catholic system of belief that stressed universal salvation and that was to remain the underlying framework of most sects of Buddhist belief and practice in Japan through the modern era.

From its inception Buddhism in Japan engaged the concern and patronage of ruling interests and became virtually a state creed. Temples and monastic compounds usually consisted of at least seven typical structures, including a *to* (pagoda), a main hall called the *kondo* ("golden hall"), a lecture hall called the *kodo*, and a *kyozo* or sutra repository. They were built as the seats of Buddhist worship and instruction. In the first wave of such construction, numerous temples were erected from the late 6th to the early 7th century in what is now the Kyoto-Osaka region, most notably Asukadera, Shitennoji, and Horyuji. After Heijokyo (Nara) was designated the national capital in 710, a new wave of temple construction in the early 8th century produced the great Nara-period (710–794) metropolitan monasteries, among them Kofukuji, Daianji, and Yakushiji.

A tremendous amount of Buddhist art was commissioned for the halls and chapels of these temple complexes. Paintings and sculptures representing various Buddhas, bodhisattvas, and guardian deities were the icons to which worship and ritual were directed. A corollary art form, that of the illustrated handscroll (*emakimono*), was developed for Buddhist narrative instruction. The oldest in this genre is the 8th-century biography of Shaka called the *Einga kyo* (Illustrated Sutra of Cause and Effect).

The construction of Todaiji from 747 marked the apex of classical Buddhist art and architecture in Japan. The temple's *honzon*, or principal object of worship, is a colossal gilt-bronze image —measuring some 15 meters (49 ft) in height— of the cosmic Buddha called Birushana (Skt:

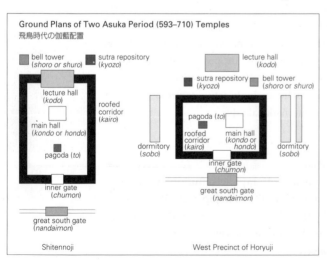

Ground Plans of Two Asuka Period (593–710) Temples
飛鳥時代の伽藍配置

bell tower (*shoro or shuro*)
sutra repository (*kyozo*)
lecture hall (*kodo*)

lecture hall (*kodo*)
roofed corridor (*kairo*)
main hall (*kondo or hondo*)
pagoda (*to*)
inner gate (*chumon*)
great south gate (*nandaimon*)

Shitennoji

sutra repository (*kyozo*)
bell tower (*shoro or shuro*)
pagoda (*to*)
roofed corridor (*kairo*)
main hall (*kondo or hondo*)
dormitory (*sobo*)
dormitory (*sobo*)
inner gate (*chumon*)
great south gate (*nandaimon*)

West Precinct of Horyuji

Vairocana). A technical feat, this giant sculpture—called the Nara Daibutsu ("Great Buddha of Nara")—came to symbolize the power, wealth, and intrusiveness of state-sanctioned Buddhism.

Esoteric Buddhism   密教●

In part as a reaction to the state Buddhism symbolized by Todaiji and the Nara Daibutsu, a new regime moved the capital to Heiankyo (now Kyoto) in 794. Largely coincidental with this move was the emergence into prominence of *mikkyo*, "the secret teachings," a system of esoteric Buddhist belief and practice that was to be articulated in the Shingon sect and the Tendai sect.

The Buddha Dainichi (Skt: Mahavairocana), a cosmic force that was already evident in Buddhist ideology by the time of the Nara Daibutsu, became the organizing principle of esoteric Buddhism and the focus of worship. Esotericism also involved a vastly enhanced pantheon of deities, many culled from non-Buddhist traditions, and an increased emphasis on elaborate ritual as a means of harnessing the power inherent in this pantheon.

Key to Shingon and Tendai practice were the paired mandalas of the Diamond or Thunderbolt Realm and the Matrix or Womb Realm, together referred to as the "Two Mandalas."

The paintings and sculptures that filled Shingon and Tendai temples, in keeping with their function as iconic representations of esoteric deities, displayed an aesthetic and stylistic tenor appropriate to the mystery of ritual and meditation at a remote temple in mountain setting. An important example of this tendency is seen in the 9th-century set of five statues of the Bodhisattvas of the Void (Go Dai Kokuzo Bosatsu), each in painted wood, at Jingoji. Also coincidental with the development of esotericism was a trend in sculpture toward the carving of votive statues out of single blocks of wood, their surfaces left unadorned with paint or lacquer in deference to the inherent sanctity of the sacred tree (*shimboku*). The principal examples of this "plain wood" style are the Yakushi figures at Gangoji (early 9th century) and at Jingoji (ca 783).

Pure Land Buddhism   浄土教●

Even though esotericism remained a major element in Japanese religious life, by the close of the 10th century it had begun to give way as a system of popular belief to Pure Land faith and practice. In the Pure Land tradition worship focused on the Buddha Amida (Skt: Amitabha) and on rebirth in his Western Paradise, or Pure Land, called Gokuraku (Skt: Sukhavati).

A celebrated example of Pure Land art and aesthetics is the *ami-*

The Phoenix Hall of the temple Byodoin got its name because of the symmetrical wings of its ground plan and the bronze birds that ornament its roof.

dado (Amida hall), now called the Phoenix Hall (Hoodo), at Byodoin in Uji, which was constructed in 1053 by Fujiwara no Yorimichi (992–1074), who, with his father, Fujiwara no Michinaga (966–1028), was one of the great patrons of Pure Land Buddhism and art. Like other temples of its day, which were much influenced by descriptions in Pure Land scripture of Amida's palatial residence, Byodoin was at the same time a detached residence in the *shinden-zukuri* mode, where Yorimichi might live as well as pray.

One of the principal treatises of Japanese Pure Land Buddhism—one that had a major impact on art production—was a work by the Tendai monk Genshin (Eshin Sozu; 942–1017) called *Ojoyoshu* (985, The Essentials of Pure Land Rebirth), in which was set forth an exhaustive account of Amida's nine sectors of paradise and the nine degrees of rebirth (*kubon ojo*) therein.

In painting, a key Pure Land genre was the so-called *raigozu* ("welcoming pictures"), in which Amida and his heavenly entourage are shown arriving to welcome and guide the dying to paradise. The raigozu genre was heavily influenced by Genshin's work. An important example is the mid-12th-century triptych *Amida shoju raigozu* (Descent of Amida and the Heavenly Multitude) at Mt. Koya.

In *Ojoyoshu* Genshin did not limit his discussion to paradise; the first part of this treatise provides a horrific vision of the six realms of existence (*rokudo*), and especially various hells, as a means to awakening faith and penitence. This, too, was reflected in contemporary Pure Land painting, particularly in the emakimono format; by the 12th century an imagery of hell and karmic retribution was fully developed. Celebrated examples of this genre are the *Gaki-zoshi* (Scrolls of Hungry Ghosts) and *Jigoku-zoshi* (Scrolls of Hells). Another emakimono genre, that of temple histories (*engi*) and biographies of saints and monks, was also developed. An example of this popular genre is *Shigisan engi emaki* (The Legends of Mt. Shigi).

Zen Buddhism   禅●

In the 13th century the Zen (Ch: Chan) sect, disseminated by Japanese and Chinese monks, took hold among the ruling military elites and introduced new currents in art. Zen monasteries, such as Kenchoji and Engakuji, emerged as both seats of religious discourse and centers for the secular cultural activities for which the Zen monks became increasingly known: literary studies, poetry, painting, and calligraphy.

Zen temples were strongly continental in flavor and differed significantly from the architectural models used in other sects. Layout, nomenclature, furnishings, and even structural details were derived from the Buddhist architecture of south central China. The typical Zen monastic compound, especially the semiautonomous subtemple known as *tatchu*, usually incorporated a carefully composed small garden. In keeping with the austerity of Zen taste, some of these gardens, in a format called "rock and sand garden" (*karesansui*), were landscaped without the standard pond or stream; the flow of water was evoked through the raking of smooth sand and gravel.

Paintings in a variety of genres figured in Zen ritual and monastic life. The private halls and quarters at a Zen compound accomodated an informal imagery, such as painted portraits of patriarchs of the sect.

A category of painting that was particulary favored in Zen circles was the *doshakuga*, a picture of a Taoist or Buddhist subject that was rendered with innovative handling of brush and ink and employed simplified motifs.

The impact of Zen aesthetics and doctrine was by no means limited to the monastic compound. The development of a pure landscape painting genre in Japan, as well as the emergence of a mature *suibokuga* (ink painting) tradition, owes much to the influence of Zen and Zen monk-painters.

Buddhism under the Tokugawa Shogunate   徳川幕府と仏教●

The spread of Neo-Confucian orthodoxy in China and Korea also affected Japan, where the unifying ideology of the Tokugawa shogunate (1603–1867) and its widespread educational system constituted an official state Confucianism. As Buddhism lost its centrality to politics and culture, Buddhist art gave way to secular forms, although Buddhist values remained visible in much of Japanese taste and aesthetics.

The arts, however, were not entirely devoid of Buddhist genres. While not organized into a formal school, the tradition of the Zen monk–amateur painter flourished to the end of the 19th century and has recently been given the name *zenga*, "Zen painting."

Painting (*kaiga*)   絵画●

Japanese painting is characterized by a wide range of styles in a wide array of formats, from horizontal and hanging scrolls to album leaves, fans, walls, and free-standing and sliding screens. Like the history of Japanese art in general, Japanese painting has been dominated by two components, continental and indigenous, in the development of style and technique.

Culture

PREMODERN PAINTING 前近代の絵画●

Until the 19th century, China was the principal source of innovation. Much of the history of painting in premodern Japan can be described as a dialogue between Chinese and native styles.

Painting through the Nara Period (710–794) 奈良時代までの絵画●

The origins of painting in Japan can be traced to the simple stick figures found on Yayoi-period (ca 300 BC–ca AD 300) bells and the murals, both geometric and figural, on the inner walls of Kofun-period (ca 300–710) tombs. With the introduction of Buddhism and Buddhist culture from Korea and China in the 6th century, painting began to flourish as the production of Buddhist art and architecture became a major concern of the ruling class.

A number of paintings from the late 7th and early 8th centuries are preserved at the temple Horyuji. In Horyuji's museum a votive shrine called the Tamamushi Shrine, or "Beetle-Wing Shrine," bears a series of 7th-century paintings on its panels, whose bronze filigree frames were backed originally by the iridescent wings of the *tamamushi* beetle. These paintings illustrate episodes from the life of the Buddha as well as depicting figures of bodhisattvas and other deities. Their style of execution is reminiscent of painting styles in late-Six-Dynasties (222–589) China.

The 7th-century Tamamushi Shrine at the temple Horyuji.

Painting of the Heian (794–1185) and Kamakura (1185–1333) Periods 平安・鎌倉時代の絵画●

With the rise in the early 9th century of esoteric Buddhism as developed by the Shingon sect and the Tendai sect, the painted mandala emerged into prominence. Important examples of this genre are the Diamond Realm (*Kongokai*) and Womb Realm (*Taizokai*) mandalas, dated 824–833, at the temple Jingoji, and the 11th-century *Kojima Mandala* at Kojimadera in Nara. The five-story pagoda at Daigoji, constructed in 952, contains a number of murals depicting various esoteric deities in a mandala format.

After the 10th century, the influence of Pure Land Buddhism—popularized by the Jodo sect and its predecessors—became increasingly apparent in painting. An important new genre was the *raigozu*, a depiction of the Buddha Amida arriving to welcome the dying to paradise.

By the mid-Heian period, Chinese modes of painting (*kara-e*) had begun to give way to a distinctly indigenous style known as *yamato-e*. The earliest paintings in this style were sliding screens and folding screens. Two new painting formats evolved as the native style was developed: the album leaf (*soshi*) and the illuminated handscroll (*emakimono*).

Painting of the Muromachi Period (1333–1568)   室町時代の絵画●

During the 14th century, scroll painting declined as *suibokuga*, or ink painting, took hold in the great Zen monasteries of Kamakura and Kyoto. An austere monochrome style, introduced from Song (960–1279) and Yuan (1279–1368) China, was favored by Zen painters and their patrons. The styles of the Chinese monk-painters Muqi (J: Mokkei; fl ca 1250) and Liang Kai (1140?–1210?) were particularly influential.

By the end of the 14th century, a monochrome landscape painting genre had emerged as the preferred medium among Zen painters and their Ashikaga family patrons in Kyoto. Artists whose works helped form the landscape genre include Mincho (1352–1431) and Josetsu (early 15th century). During the 15th century, Tensho Shubun (d ca 1460) and Sesshu Toyo (1420–1506) developed the Chinese-inspired monochrome landscape style into a fully Japanese format. A key work by Sesshu is *Amanohashidate* (ca 1501, Kyoto National Museum), which depicts the famous scenic spot of that name.

In the last years of Ashikaga rule, a new genre of ink painting was developed largely outside the Zen community by artists of the Ami school and the Kano school. The Kano school was initiated by the layman painter Kano Masanobu (1434–1530) and continued by his son Kano Motonobu (1476–1559). Although Chinese styles and themes remained their model, Kano-school artists introduced a more decorative and plastic sensibility that would come to dominate the landscape painting of the succeeding centuries.

Painting of the Azuchi-Momoyama (1568–1600)
and Edo (1600–1868) Periods   安土桃山・江戸時代の絵画●

The Kano school, promoted by Oda Nobunaga (1534–1582), Toyotomi Hideyoshi (1537–1598), and other powerful patrons, dominated painting in the late 16th century and developed a grandiose polychromed style for screen and wall painting. Kano Eitoku (1543–1590) was commissioned by Nobunaga to decorate Azuchi Castle (1576–1579; destroyed 1582) near Lake Biwa and by Hideyoshi to decorate Jurakudai Palace (1587; destroyed 1595) in Kyoto. Eitoku is believed to be the first painter to have introduced the dramatic use of fields of gold leaf in large mural compositions. Eitoku's pupil and adopted son Kano Sanraku (1559–1635) continued this style into the early Edo period. By the time that Eitoku's grandson Kano Tan'yu (1602–1674) was active, the Kano school was firmly established as the painting academy of the Tokugawa shogunate (1603–1867).

Another genre, one belonging to the yamato-e tradition, was

developed by painters of the Tosa school, whose small-scale works often illustrated the literary classics of earlier generations. The yamato-e tradition also gave rise to the decorative painters of the group called Rimpa. The principal artists of this school were Tawaraya Sotatsu (d 1643?) and Ogata Korin (1658–1716), whose works—taking classical styles and themes and presenting them in a new, boldly decorative format—have come to symbolize the lavish tastes of Edo (now Tokyo) society in the 17th and 18th centuries.

Fuzokuga, or genre paintings, became popular in the late 16th century and gave rise to UKIYO-E, "paintings of the floating world," which captured the transient experiences of the pleasure quarters of Edo and other urban centers. The woodblock print as a significant Edo-period medium emerged out of this tradition.

The late Edo period was one of eclecticism in painting. The influence of European painting, earlier represented by the "southern barbarian" *namban* art of the late 16th century, was increasingly apparent. The port city of Nagasaki acted as the conduit for both Chinese and Western influence in painting. Major artists of this period include Maruyama Okyo (1733–1795) and Matsumura Goshun (1752–1811), founders of the Maruyama-Shijo school, and Ito Jakuchu (1716–1800). The works of these painters show a mixture of Japanese, Chinese, and Western elements and often evidence a heightened concern with naturalistic depiction.

Another major trend in late-Edo-period painting was that of *bunjinga*, "literati painting," whose artists took their inspiration from a tradition of Chinese scholar–amateur painters who, since the Yuan dynasty, had worked in a style called *nanga* ("Southern painting"). This style entered Japan in the 18th century via Nagasaki, where it was introduced by Chinese immigrant painters and described in Chinese painting manuals.

MODERN PAINTING　　　　　　　　　　　近現代の絵画●

During the Meiji period (1868–1912), political and social change was effected in the course of a modernization campaign by the new government. Western-style painting (*yoga*) was promoted officially, and a number of painters such as Harada Naojiro (1863–1899), Yamamoto Hosui (1850–1906), and Asai Chu (1856–1907) traveled abroad for study under government auspices. However, the initial burst of enthusiasm for Western art soon yielded to renewed appreciation of traditional Japanese art, promoted by the art critic Okakura Kakuzo (1862–1913) and the

American educator Ernest Fenollosa (1853–1908). Japanese-style painting (*nihonga*) rose to prominence as its conservative advocates gained control of art institutions. By the 1880s, Western-style painters were barred from exhibitions and widely criticized.

Confronted by the resurgence of traditionalism, Western-style painters formed the Meiji Bijutsukai (Meiji Fine Arts Society) and began to hold their own exhibitions. Prominent among these painters was Kuroda Seiki (also known as Kuroda Kiyoteru; 1866–1924), who introduced pleinairism and established the influential White Horse Society (Hakubakai).

Painting of the Taisho Period (1912–1926)　　　大正時代の絵画●

The Taisho period saw burgeoning Western influence in the arts. After long stays in Europe the painters Yamashita Shintaro (1881–1966), Saito Yori (1885–1959), and Arishima Ikuma (1882–1974) introduced impressionism and early features of the postimpressionist movement to Japan; Yasui Sotaro (1888–1955) and Umehara Ryuzaburo (1888–1986), whose careers would span the modern period, returned to promote the styles of Camille Pissarro, Paul Cézanne, and Pierre Auguste Renoir. The eclecticism that informed Taisho-period painting came as a direct result of the rapid infusion of the full range of contemporary European styles.

Although on a limited scale, Japanese-style painting too was affected by European styles, especially neoclassicism and, later, postimpressionism. Modernizing trends first appeared among second-generation nihonga members of the Japan Fine Arts Academy (Nihon Bijutsuin), which had been reorganized in 1914 to compete with the government sponsored Bunten. Its founding members, Yokoyama Taikan (1868–1958), Shimomura Kanzan (1873–1930), and Hishida Shunso (1874–1911), all to some degree adopted Western-style atmospheric treatment of space and light, for which they were called the Moroha ("Dim and Hazy school"). The second wave of academy painters, while emphasizing yamato-e traditions, embraced certain features of postimpressionism.

Painting of the Showa Period (1926–1989)　　　昭和時代の絵画●

The painters Yasui Sotaro and Umehara Ryuzaburo stood at the forefront of pre-World War II Showa painting. In recognition of their importance, the period 1925–40 is termed the "Yasui-Umehara era." While incorporating notions of pure art and abstraction, both succeeded in surmounting the heretofore largely derivative character of Western-style painting in Japan. Umehara in particular brought aspects of the nihonga tradition to his work and launched Western-style painting on a more interpretative path.

However, neither artist completely dominated Western-style painting of the 1930s. A far more international contemporary of Yasui and Umehara was Fujita Tsuguharu (also known as Fujita Tsuguji, Léonard Foujita; 1886–1968). The Nika Society widened its sphere of influence by absorbing surrealism and abstractionism, and the essentially fauvist Dokuritsu Bijutsu Kyokai (Independent Art Association) was formed in 1931.

Prominent painters' circles formed during the late Taisho and early Showa periods, such as the Nika Society, weathered the war years to emerge as leading interests among painters today. The government-subsidized Japan Art Academy (Nihon Geijutsuin) was formed in 1947 and contains both yoga and nihonga divisions. Government-sponsored art exhibitions like the Bunten have disappeared, replaced by privately sponsored exhibitions on a large scale. The Nitten (Nihon Bijutsu Tenrankai; Japan Art Exhibition) in particular has functioned as the modern counterpart of the Bunten. Initially the exhibition of the Japan Art Academy, the Nitten since 1958 has been run by a corporation, Nitten, Inc. Exhibition of works in the Nitten can lead to membership in the Japan Art Academy and, for a few, decoration with the Order of Culture. Only a handful of non-Nitten artists have received this award, among them Munakata Shiko (1903–1975).

A self-portrait by Fujita Tsuguharu.

Today Japanese artists are active members of a worldwide artistic community. By the 1960s, avant-garde notions of art had been embraced, and an internationalization of Japanese art followed. Postwar trends in the West have been taken up rapidly in Japan, from the abstract expressionism of the 1950s to later developments such as the antiart movement, assemblage, pop and op art, primary structure, minimal art, and kinetic art. After a largely derivative past, modern Japanese painters have emerged as significant contributors to international movements in art. ●

Ukiyo-e   浮世絵 ●

A genre of art, chiefly in the medium of the woodblock print, that arose early in the Edo period (1600–1868) and built up a broad popular market among the middle classes. Subject matter tended to focus on the brothel districts and the KABUKI theaters, and formats ranged from single-sheet prints and greeting cards to albums and book illustrations. Ukiyo-e flourished throughout Japan, attaining their most characteristic form in the prints produced in Edo (now Tokyo) from about 1680 to the 1850s.

Early Ukiyo-e   初期の浮世絵●

The distinctive milieu from which ukiyo-e would emerge was flourishing as early as the Kan'ei era (1624–1644). Genre paintings (*fuzokuga*) of the time depict pleasure seekers of every social class thronging the entertainment district beside the river Kamogawa in Kyoto. It was in such districts, in Kyoto, Osaka, and Edo, that there developed the freewheeling way of life of the *ukiyo*, or "floating world," and the genre of art, ukiyo-e, that glorified it.

Sex manuals (*shunga*; literally, "spring pictures") and courtesan critiques (*yujo hyobanki*) were among the earliest types of printed ukiyo-e. Shunga were either books or albums that depicted highly explicit love scenes, though rarely are couples completely naked. Few of the sex manuals from the 1660s and early 1670s have survived and none are signed; the earliest attributions are to Hishikawa Moronobu and Sugimura Jihei, who were active in the late 17th century, and thereafter shunga remained a genre at which most ukiyo-e artists tried their hand. The critiques of courtesans, essentially picture books with commentary, contained stylized portraits of the leading courtesans of the day, engaged in some casual activity such as reading or adjusting their hair. The interest of such scenes is chiefly in the poses and the draping of *kimono*. A similar type of picture was the *bijin-e* ("beautiful-woman picture"), in which courtesans of the highest rank (*tayu*) were depicted, often with their entourages. Pictures of courtesans remained popular throughout the history of ukiyo-e; the Kaigetsudo school (early 18th century) of ukiyo-e painters rarely turned to any other subject, and many of Kitagawa Utamaro's most memorable prints were of these stylish beauties.

A woman portrayed by Utamaro.

Edo Ukiyo-e   江戸の浮世絵●

By the late 17th century, the center of ukiyo-e had shifted from Kamigata (the Kyoto-Osaka area) to Edo, where the single-sheet print, probably initially intended for mounting on scrolls (*kakemono-e*), seems to have become a specialty in the closing years of the Genroku era (1688–1704).

It was the development of the single-sheet print, that marked a turning point in the history of ukiyo-e, the coming of age of which was closely joined to that of kabuki. A major role in the development of kabuki was played by Ichikawa Danjuro I, who invented a bombastic style of acting known as *aragoto* that became immensely popular in Edo. Portrayals of actors (*yakusha-e*) in popular roles had already become standard subject matter of ukiyo-e, but it was the Torii school that achieved the greatest success in rendering the pyrotechnics of an aragoto performance in graphic terms. Torii Kiyonobu I and Torii Kiyomasu I perfected a style that, with its vigorous use of line and robust forms, was particularly appropriate for theatrical subjects, and their school soon acquired a virtual monopoly over commissions in Edo for painted theatrical posters (*kamban*) and illustrated program notes (*ebanzuke*). The finest of the Torii school prints, recording a pose or entrance popularized by a particular actor, are in the large *kakemono-e* format, and provided a visual catalog of theatrical conventions that reinforced kabuki tradition. A separate theatrical print style arose in Osaka.

Another important ukiyo-e artist of the second quarter of the 18th century was Nishikawa Sukenobu, a native of Kyoto, whose illustrated books presenting scenes from daily life or from classical poetry gained extraordinary popularity throughout the country. His work displayed a delicacy that set it apart from Edo ukiyo-e of the time and influenced the subsequent development of the genre.

Color Prints   色刷り ●

In about 1745, a technique was conceived for registering successive blocks, each printing a different color on a single sheet. The resulting prints, called *benizuri-e* (pictures printed in red) because the most striking color was a red derived from the petals of the safflower (*benibana*), were produced only in two or three colors. It was not until 1764 that the first full-color prints appeared, a development that is closely associated with the sudden popularity of the work of Suzuki Harunobu. By 1766 almost every ukiyo-e artist was working in Harunobu's style. These new prints, called *nishiki-e* (brocade pictures) or *edo-e* (Edo pictures), represented the final stage of technical advancement in color printing achieved in the Edo period.

The stylistic revolution brought about by the development of full-color printing soon affected the traditional genre of yakusha-e. From about 1770, in the work of the major innovators Katsukawa Shunsho and Ippitsusai Buncho, actors were for the first time presented as individuals with distinctive features, whereas previously they could be distinguished only by the crest (*mon*) on their kimono. Shunsho had particular influence as the teacher of Katsukawa Shun'ei and Katsushika Hokusai, and the changes he set in motion laid the foundation for the work of Toshusai Sharaku.

In the 1770s poets of *kyoka*, a type of comic verse, and artists began to collaborate in the production of some extraordinarily handsome books combining kyoka with ukiyo-e illustrations. The success of these works, particularly Utamaro's *Ehon mushi erami* (1788, Insect Book), helped give rise to surimono. Popular in the 1790s, *surimono*, which combined kyoka or *haikai* and ukiyo-e, were prints that were produced on commission and issued in limited editions for use as announcements, invitations, or gifts. The printing was quite elegant, making frequent use of burnished metallic pigments and of embossing, which gave texture and depth to the surface of prints. Some kyoka poets also wrote *kibyoshi* and *sharebon* stories, which were customarily illustrated by ukiyo-e artists.

The Golden Age of Ukiyo-e 　浮世絵の黄金時代●

The late 18th century was largely a period of consolidation rather than innovation; however, development of the more generous *oban* format and the introduction of diptychs and triptychs led to more complex composition. After 1790, ukiyo-e images acquired a new intensity and styles began to succeed one another with greater rapidity. Utamaro and Sharaku achieved a heightened closeness to their subjects by using the format of the *okubi-e* or bust portrait: Utamaro's women are extremely sensuous and the masculinity of Sharaku's female impersonators (*onnagata*) infuses his portrayals. Utamaro was one of the first to isolate his figures against a brilliant mica background, and did so with a flair that other artists of the time, among them Hosoda Eishi and Utagawa Toyokuni, only rarely managed to equal.

Portrait of a *kabuki* actor by Sharaku.

After 1800, there appears to have been a radical change in taste, accompanied by a faltering of inspiration in design and a deterioration in the quality of printing. Short figures with hunched shoulders and sharp features replaced the tall, elegant figures of the 1770s and 1780s, kimono patterns became coarser and more strident, and pictures of actors tended toward the exaggerated and grotesque. One reason for this was change in the print-buying public, which had grown larger and presumably less discriminating, resulting in prints that were produced hastily—many showing faulty registration of colors—and in great numbers.

Landscape 　風景画●

The emergence of the landscape print was a relatively late phenomenon in the history of ukiyo-e. Prior to Hokusai's *Fugaku sanjurokkei* (1823, Thirty-Six Views of Mount Fuji), landscape as independent subject matter for ukiyo-e was largely unknown. Other artists soon followed Hokusai's lead, and landscape achieved a popularity that rivaled the established genres of portraiture. Active as an artist for some 60 years, Hokusai developed a style that was highly individual, combining Chinese and Western influences with elements drawn from the native Kano school, the Tosa school, and the Rimpa tradition. He was also a prolific draftsman who employed a variety of techniques to create the astounding array of images in his famous 13-volume *Hokusai manga*

The Hakone print from Hiroshige's most famous series, *Fifty-Three Stations of the Tokaido Road.*

Culture

(1814–1849, Hokusai's Sketches).

Hokusai's only true rival in landscape was Ando Hiroshige, whose great *Tokaido gojusantsugi* (1833–1834, The Fifty-Three Stations of the Tokaido Road) brought him fame and a host of imitators. Hiroshige displays in this and other works a greater concern than Hokusai with atmosphere, light, and weather. Drawing on the style of certain of the landscape paintings of the Southern Song dynasty (1127–1279), his work was also influenced by the contemporaneous Maruyama-Shijo school and by Western realism.

As an integral element of the Edo-period culture that it mirrored, ukiyo-e was unable to survive that society's demise in the wake of the radical Westernization that transformed Japan during the Meiji period (1868–1912).

Ceramics (*tojiki*)   陶磁器●

Ceramics in Japan has a long history, stretching over 12,000 years. The Japanese archipelago is abundantly supplied with the raw material for ceramics, and an appreciation for clay and its multitude of possible uses has been a steady force in Japanese culture for millennia.

In the development of ceramic materials, China was the great innovator, and all of Japan's advanced technology came directly or indirectly from there; more often than not, China also set the style. Yet also typical of Japan's attitude toward ceramics was the fact that, while newer wares representing advanced technology might be accorded a position of highest status, they by no means obliterated existing wares and techniques, which for the most part continued unaffected. As a result, Japanese ceramics became steadily richer in variety, and the ceramic articles produced in Japan today cover the full range from earthenware directly descended from neolithic precedents to the most demanding Chinese-style glazed wares.

Early Earthenware   初期の土器●

Yayoi-period jar.

It seems to have been almost 12,000 years ago that people in Japan began to use sedimentary clay to form vessels. Jomon pottery, characterized by its "cord-impressed" patterns, dates from as early as 10,000 BC. Its earliest forms resemble deep cylindrical baskets with pointed bottoms.

With the introduction of rice cultivation to Japan in the succeeding Yayoi period (ca 300 BC–ca AD 300), the heavy, elaborate Jomon style gave way to the smooth, thin, symmetrical, minimally ornamented Yayoi style.

The change reflected a shift of habitation centers from highlands to river deltas where rice was grown: whereas Jomon clay is usually stiff, requiring considerable temper, and too coarse to take a fine finish, pots of the Yayoi period are formed from the plastic, fine-grained clay found in such deltas. Whereas ceramics in the Jomon period seems to have been the primary form of artistic expression, Yayoi culture had access to other materials introduced from the continent—most significantly bronze—and this is reflected in the pottery. Certain design elements in Yayoi pots, such as raised horizontal ridges, suggest the aesthetic influence of cast metal.

Sue and *Haji* Wares　　　　　　　　　　須恵器と土師器●

During the Kofun period (ca 300–710) influences from the Korean peninsula wrought radical changes in Japanese culture and technology. By the mid-5th century a method of making high-fired stoneware ceramics known as sue ware had been introduced and was rapidly developed by Korean craftsmen residing in what are now the Nara and Osaka regions, eventually superseding earthenware in production and status. Sue vessels, produced in through-draft or tunnel kilns (*anagama*), were of superior quality for storing liquids.

Earthenware, however, now known as haji ware, remained indispensable for cooking purposes and also for ritual. Pottery grave goods, such as portable clay stoves and tall flanged pots, were placed in the conspicuous aboveground tombs (*kofun*) after which the period is named, and by the 6th century elaborate grave offerings of metal weapons and armor had been replaced with pottery replicas. Clay cylinders, or *haniwa*, were arranged around raised tomb mounds; eventually these cylinders were rendered as figurines and placed atop the tombs.

Glazed Ceramics　　　　　　　　　　釉薬をかけた陶磁器●

By the Nara period (710–794) continental ceramic technology had been introduced: intentional glazing of high-fired wares.

Production of lead-glazed wares began at kilns in or around the modern city of Nara. Plain green-glazed pieces were being made by the late 7th century, and polychrome glazes were added by the early 8th century. These early Nara wares, produced under government control, include three-color wares—usually green, white, and yellowish brown—called *sansai toki*.

Duplication of the celadon technology occurred with the development at the Sanage kilns (in the vicinity of modern Nagoya) of a feldspathic glaze applied to a high-fired gray or white body. Sanage had begun as a sue-ware center, but the fortuitous availability of white clay made it a natural locale for the development of ash-glaze techniques, in which wood ash was sprinkled thinly over the shoulders of vessels prior to firing. Sanage received direct support from the Heian court.

By the end of the 12th century, however, most central Sanage kilns were making only the unglazed, popular tablewares. A movement from eastern Sanage toward better sources of white, kaolin-like clay led to the establishment of a new center for glazed ware in Seto (Aichi Prefecture).

Medieval Ceramics 中世の陶磁器●

Under the patronage of the Kamakura shogunate (1192–1333) and Zen temples, Seto began by copying newly introduced Southern Song (1127–1279) Chinese forms—four-eared jars, flasks, ewers—with amber or green ash glaze applied over carved, stamped, or sprigged designs. By the 14th century Seto had also perfected use of the iron-brown *temmoku* glaze inspired by brown-glazed teabowls brought back from China.

Seto kilns reached their peak in the mid-15th century, but their development was cut short by the outbreak of the Onin War (1467–1477). The center for glazed wares shifted to Mino (now part of Gifu Prefecture), which had also produced first sue, then Sanage-type, and finally Seto-type glazed wares. At the beginning of the 16th century a change occurred in the kiln, as the through-draft or tunnel kiln introduced with sue ware was replaced by the larger, more reliable *ogama* ("great kiln"). Efforts to imitate porcelains from Ming (1368–1644) China led to the development of the opaque, white feldspathic glaze with underglaze iron decoration that became popular as Shino ware late in the century.

Although glazed as well as unglazed wares continued to be produced at Seto, Mino, and other medieval kilns, from the 12th through the 16th century the principal Japanese ceramic product was a sturdy, unglazed stoneware, called *yakishime* or *sekki*, that was made in a limited set of shapes primarily for utilitarian storage. The most important kilns to produce this type of stoneware were those at Tokoname in Owari (now part of Aichi Prefecture). Potters used the clay without alteration, employing simple coiling and scraping construction methods.

With the growing commercial significance of ceramics in the Muromachi period (1333–1568), when unglazed stonewares in particular emerged as valuable sources of cash income, potters became more professional as output increased. Beginning with tea jars, everyday wares began to be glazed, resulting in further improvements in kiln structure. Mino potters were most influential in dispersing glazing technology to stoneware kilns.

Nevertheless, the same kilns that were striving to develop glazes were also influenced by the interest of the tea masters in unglazed pieces (particularly in ceramics imported from Southeast Asia, known as *nam-ban* ware) for use as tea ceremony vessels. This interest reflected an increasing appreciation of simplicity and rusticity, aesthetic values that came to a peak in the tea ceremony school founded by Sen no Rikyu (1522–1591). Bizen produced the outstanding early pieces in this mode. Around 1600 the conscious manipulation at the Iga kilns of the features of unglazed medieval stonewares, including "natural" ash glaze, represented the epitome of the artificial naturalism espoused by many tea ceremony adherents.

Edo-Period Ceramics   江戸時代の陶磁器●

The Edo period (1600–1868) saw a continuation of innovative stylistic and technological developments in stonewares and in glazed and unglazed ceramics—fueled not only by the aesthetic tastes of tea masters but also by the by-now-enormous commercial market for pottery. Innovations involved not only the popular decorated wares, such as Shino ware, Oribe ware, and Karatsu ware, but also the more austere wares, such as Raku ware, Iga ware, and Bizen ware, which underwent more subtle changes in form and design.

Japan's invasions of Korea in 1592 and 1597 gave military leaders the opportunity to bring Korean potters, with their superior skills of throwing and glazing, to Japan to work in their domains. The introduction from Korea of the *noborigama* ("climbing kiln") revolutionized the firing of stonewares and made possible the successful firing of porcelain after suitable clays were discovered in the Arita area of northern Kyushu by Korean potters in the early 17th century.

The desire to make porcelain had been stirred by imported Ming porcelains, and Chinese ware had provided the earliest models, but by the mid-17th century a second crucial influence was added in the form of the European market. The Dutch East India Company not only placed enormous orders but also provided explicit models. Special preference was accorded an Arita-produced decorated ware called Kakiemon ware, which was characterized by application of polychrome enamels and underglaze cobalt to a milk-white porcelain body.

The second half of the 17th century saw the full flowering of such decorated wares. Colorful Imari ware and Kakiemon ware were shipped to Europe from Kyushu in great quantities; the finer Kakiemon and Nabeshima ware porcelains were reserved for local rulers. In Kyoto, a popular form of decorated earthenware or stoneware known as *kyo-yaki* was developed by such potter-decorators as Nonomura Ninsei (fl mid-17th century) and Ogata Kenzan (1666–1743). Only isolated ventures,

An Edo-period Kakiemon bowl.

such as Himetani ware and Kutani ware, attempted the production of porcelain in competition with the dominant kilns in Arita.

Modern Ceramics 現代の陶磁器●

The opening of Japan to the West brought new opportunities for ceramics export and the development of porcelain centers at Kyoto and Yokohama. Through the work of the German technician Gottfried Wagener (1831–1892) in Arita, Kyoto, and Tokyo, and through Japanese participation in international expositions in Europe and the United States, Western ceramic technology and taste were introduced. Major ceramic centers opened training laboratories and began the process of transforming the workshop into the factory.

Contemporary Japanese ceramics may be said to have begun shortly after 1900 with the emergence of the "studio potter" with an individual name and style. The studio potter of the 20th century came to ceramics by choice rather than by birth, and the typical eclectic style was based on a strong knowledge of Japanese ceramic history. Itaya Hazan (1872–1963), for example, was trained as a sculptor, and Kitaoji Rosanjin (1883–1959) began making pottery to supply his own gourmet restaurant.

From 1926, the FOLK CRAFTS movement led by Yanagi Muneyoshi (1889–1961) began to foster interest in the aesthetic value of traditional craftwork and skillfully made simple objects of daily use—among them ceramics. The potters Kawai Kanjiro (1890–1966) and Hamada Shoji (1894–1978) participated in this movement, and it was through the latter, who established his workshop in Mashiko (Tochigi Prefecture), that the town became famous as a center of folk-style pottery. Many foreign potters have studied in the town.

Swords (*nihonto*) 日本刀●

The origins of the Japanese sword go back to the 8th century and the earliest development of steel in Japan. Japanese swords are particularly impressive because of the early technical mastery achieved in Japanese steelmaking and because of the elegant shape, lines, texture, and shades of color of the steel fabric. For more than 12 centuries the sword has had a spiritual significance for the Japanese; along with the mirror and jewels, it is one of the three Imperial Regalia.

Swordsmiths 刀工●

The Japanese swordsmith was traditionally held in high regard. The earliest swordsmiths were often *yamabushi*, members of the Shugendo sect, who with their apprentices lived an austere and religiously dedicated life. The approximately 200 schools of Japanese sword-smith-artists were scattered throughout Japan, each with its own history and its own identifiable and surprisingly consistent blade characteristics that can be traced down through the centuries.

Forging 鍛造●

Iron-working technology was introduced to Japan from about the 3rd to the 5th century AD, and, as early as the 8th to 10th century, sword blades of high-quality steel were being made in Japan. After the steel was forged, the "skin steel" (*kawagane*) was some 10 to 20 times hammered into plates, which were then hardened, broken into coin-sized pieces, stacked, and welded. This hardened steel was later welded onto the surface of the less brittle inner steel (*shingane*). This repeated folding and welding gave the Japanese blade one of its unique qualities—a texture (*jihada*) like that of the grain of wood.

Tempering and Polishing 焼入れと研磨●

The *hamon*, or temper pattern of the blade, is one of the most noticeable and beautiful features of the sword and also an important means of identifying its origin. By the early Kamakura period (1185–1333), this hamon was made to exhibit many shapes and forms. Generally a specific type of temper or group of types was employed by an individual school or smith. The final polishing and sharpening were done by a sword polisher, who set the sword to a series of stones of increasing fineness that were lubricated with water.

Jokoto (Ancient Sword) Period 上古刀時代●

Jokoto, or ancient swords, have come down to us almost exclusively from the ancient burial mounds of the Kofun period (ca 300–710) and are badly rusted. These ancient blades were nearly always straight, with a very small and sharply angled slanted point (*boshi*). Swords of the Nara period (710–794) and the early Heian period (794–1185) were similar to those found in the mounds. Being rather short and lightweight, they were probably used for thrusting rather than slashing. From approximately the 9th and 10th centuries, blades were made longer with a slightly curved shape and with ridge lines on both sides, a far more efficient weapon for mounted warriors.

Koto (Old Sword) Period 古刀時代●

The quality of the sword greatly improved in the middle Heian and early Kamakura periods, or from approximately the 10th to the early 13th century, when its use markedly increased, especially by mounted warriors. The swords of the Kamakura period (*tachi*) are of the highest quality, both artistically and technically, and most of the National Treasure

A 12th-century ceremonial sword mounting with mother-of-pearl inlay and gold fittings on a *nashiji*-lacquer ground.

blades derive from this period. With improvements in armor the sword necessarily became longer and heavier. In the late Kamakura period the sword became very long—in many instances as long as 1 to 1.5 meters (3–5 ft)—and was used exclusively by mounted warriors. Many of these were later shortened for use in hand-to-hand combat.

In the Muromachi period (1333–1568), as a result of prolonged strife and feudal combat, the production of swords increased in number but quality declined. Swords became somewhat heavier and less curved, wider and considerably shorter, so that they could cut through the heavier armor then coming into use. This new blade was called *katana* and was upward of 60 centimeters (2 ft) in length. It was soon accompanied by a somewhat shorter blade, *wakizashi*. The katana and wakizashi were worn thrust through the sash, edge up and parallel to or crossing each other in the sash. These swords were called *daisho*, "long and short."

Shinto (New Sword) Period 新刀時代●

During the Azuchi-Momoyama (1568–1600) and Edo (1600–1868) periods individual swordsmiths founded new schools, and an interest developed in the largely lost skills of the Kamakura period. They attempted to copy the swords of the past but were restricted by the requirements of hand-to-hand combat. Many swords had extraordinarily brilliant tempering patterns, a substantial structure of well-hammered and well-tempered steel, and beautiful chiseled engravings (*horimono*) and grooves. Sword guards (*tsuba*) and other fittings (*koshirae*) for the *samurai*'s long and short swords and for daggers became highly ornate.

The years from 1800 to the close of the Edo period are known in sword history as the Shinshinto (New, New Sword) period. It was a brief renaissance marked by a final effort to revive the beauty and quality of the ancient sword.

Modern Period 現代●

In 1868 the emperor Meiji promulgated regulations forbidding the making or wearing of swords but permitted a small number of smiths to continue their work in order to keep the art alive. A further quickening of interest occurred during the Russo-Japanese War of 1904–1905 and before and during World War II. For the most part these later military swords are not genuine art swords (nihonto) but are made from machine-made steel.

After World War II, the Allied Occupation forces ordered all swords destroyed, but the order was modified to exclude swords of artistic, religious, or spiritual significance belonging to museums, shrines, or private collections.

Even so an enormous number of good swords were destroyed, and many others were taken out of the country as souvenirs.

Since the end of World War II, there has been a gradual renewal of interest in the art of the ancient sword, and a number of smiths are currently attempting to restore the ancient skills.

Folk crafts (*mingei*)   民芸●

The term mingei refers to objects handcrafted for daily use, as well as to the movement begun by Yanagi Muneyoshi (1889–1961), who coined the term in 1926. Yanagi himself preferred to translate mingei as "folk crafts," which emphasizes the utilitarian aspect, rather than "folk arts," although both terms have been used.

The Folk Craft Movement   民芸運動●

Collecting examples of folk crafts from the Korean Yi dynasty (1392–1910) led Yanagi to realize that the most beautiful objects were the products not of individual artists but of the collective genius of the Korean people. He concluded that the approach of modern European art history, which emphasized the creativity of individual artists, was inadequate in understanding mingei.

Instead, Yanagi turned his attention to the work of a Japanese priest, Mokujiki Gogyo (1718–1810), who had carved tens of thousands of rough Buddhist images while traveling throughout Japan. To Yanagi these figures, created in response to the hopes and aspirations of the masses, were more beautiful than the Buddhist images by famous sculptors displayed by great temples. Around this time Yanagi also discovered Tamba ware, with its rich patterns of glaze formed during firing from wood ash randomly falling and fusing with the ceramic surface. Reflecting on this process, he concluded that beauty was not the result of any conscious intent but was born of chance and the cumulative skill of generations of unknown artists. Yanagi saw this process as akin to the Buddhist concept of *tariki*, the attainment of salvation not through one's own merits but through complete reliance on the Buddha's mercy.

Based on these theories Yanagi coined the term mingei to differentiate between *bijutsu*, or fine art, which he saw as created for aesthetic appreciation alone, and *kogei*, or utilitarian craftwork made for practical use. Yanagi saw kogei as a broader term than mingei: kogei included objects made by machine and by individual artists, as well as "aristocratic" works. But he also claimed that the best of kogei belonged to the category of mingei. According to Yanagi, the character of kogei was defined, first, by *yo* (use or function): kogei objects must be simple and sturdy to function effectively. Second, kogei objects must be produced on a large scale at low prices. Third, the beauty of authentic kogei is created by anonymous laborers who have honed their skill by turning out large numbers of articles without thought of self-expression. Fourth, hand-crafted kogei objects are superior to those made by machine.

History of Japanese Folk Crafts　　　　　　日本における民芸の歴史●

Tracing the history of folk crafts following the canons laid down by Yanagi is difficult because so few examples survive. Some scholars consider the earthenware of the Jomon (ca 10,000 BC–ca 300 BC) and Yayoi (ca 300 BC–ca AD 300) periods to be the first folk art in Japan. The "six old kilns" were established in Echizen, Shigaraki, Seto, Tokoname, Tamba, and Bizen during the Heian period (794–1185), each producing pottery with distinct local characteristics. However, pottery then was considered precious and rare. Most of what is today considered mingei survives from the Muromachi period (1333–1568). This is doubtless partly because the traditional Japanese style of living, as presently understood, became widely established at that time: the *shoin-zukuri* type of residential architecture was perfected, and techniques for making lacquer ware and pottery were highly developed. This, along with increased production, led to wider distribution of articles. The popularization of the tea ceremony from the Muromachi period through the Azuchi-Momoyama period (1568–1600) was another important factor. Local pottery and textile producers flourished in the latter half of the Edo period (1600–1868). Many examples from this period can still be found, and they set the standards of beauty in Japanese folk crafts. By the early 20th century, however, with the introduction of synthetics and increasing reliance on machinery, folk crafts began to decline. Folk crafts in Yanagi's sense of the term have nearly become extinct in Japan.

However, folk traditions in a broader sense are thriving. Under the Cultural Properties Law of 1950 the concept of cultural assets was revised and broadened, encouraging governmental participation in the preservation of folk knowledge, folk performing arts, games, and folk utensils used for making clothing, food, and shelter and in trade or communal life.

Classification of Folk Crafts　　　　　　　民芸の分類●

Folk crafts are generally classified in the categories of ceramics; wood and bamboo articles; metal and leather objects; dyeing and weaving; paper; and painting, sculpture, and calligraphy.

With regard to the first category, the kilns of Okinawa produce various types of ceramics called Tsuboya ware. In Kyushu, such ceramics as Karatsu ware, Agano ware, and Takatori ware are produced by techniques learned from Korean potters. Imari ware is also famous for its excellent quality. Other superior ceramics are Koishiwara ware and Onta ware. In the Shikoku region, the only well-known ceramic ware is Tobe ware. In the Chugoku region, some of the most ancient Japanese kilns are found in Fushina, Ushinoto, and Bizen. The Kinki region is noted for Tamba ware, Kyoto ceramics, Shigaraki ware, and Iga ware. The Chubu region, largest of Japan's ceramics centers, is famous for Seto ware and Mino ware. The Kanto region produced unglazed pottery such as Imado ware. The center of the folk crafts movement is Mashiko. Much pottery is also produced in the Tohoku region.

Wood and bamboo craftworks include lacquer work inlaid with gold from Okinawa; dolls from Hakata (Fukuoka Prefecture); lacquer ware and *ikkambari uchiwa* (fans made by painting lacquer over a paper frame) from Shikoku; *yanagi-gori* (wicker trunks made of willow branches) from the San'in region; *funadansu* (ship trunks) from Niigata Prefecture used on ships (*kaisen*) traveling between Osaka and northern Japan during the Edo period; Wakasa and Wajima lacquer ware from Fukui and Ishikawa prefectures; woodcrafts from Hida (Gifu Prefecture) and Matsumoto (Nagano Prefecture); birch, bamboo, and other woodcrafts, including *kago* (woven baskets), *magemono* (round containers), and *kabazaiku* (birch woodcrafts), from the Hokuriku region; lacquer ware such as *aizu-nuri* (Fukushima Prefecture), *shunkei-nuri* (Akita Prefecture), and *tsugaru-nuri* (Aomori Prefecture); and Ainu woodcrafts from Hokkaido.

Craftsmen weaving bamboo ware.

Metalwork includes *kiseru* (smoking pipes), made by town craftsmen in various regions of Japan; tableware made in Tsubame (Niigata Prefecture); hardware and carpentry tools from Miki (Hyogo Prefecture); razors and other cutting instruments from Seki (Gifu Prefecture); metal fittings made in Sendai (Miyagi Prefecture); and iron pots and kettles produced throughout Japan.

Textiles include *bingata* (surface-dyed textile) and *basho* (abaca) cloth from Okinawa; Satsuma *jofu* (linen cloth) from Kagoshima Prefecture; *kurume-gasuri* (Kurume ikat cloth) from Fukuoka Prefecture and *iyo-gasuri* (Iyo ikat cloth) from Ehime Prefecture; indigo (*ai*) from Tokushima Prefecture, which was once valued throughout the country as *awa-ai*, a natural dye; cotton cloth from Tamba (Hyogo and Kyoto prefectures); *saki-ori* (woven from strips made from old clothes) from the Hokuriku and Tohoku regions; *habutae* silk from Fukui Prefecture and *chijimi* (crepe) from Niigata Prefecture; *mikawa momen* (Mikawa cotton) from Aichi Prefecture and *kaiki* (Kai silk) from Yamanashi Prefecture; silk weaving from the Kanto region at Kiryu (Gumma Prefecture), Ashikaga (Tochigi Prefecture), and Hachioji (Tokyo Prefecture); *kogin* from the Tsugaru region; *hishizashi*, distinguished by their embroidered patterns in white cotton thread, from Aomori and Iwate prefectures; and *sashiko* (quiltings) made by the Ainu in Hokkaido.

Washi (Japanese paper), once produced throughout the country, is now rarely used in everyday life. Japanese papers still produced today are *tosa-gami* from Kochi Prefecture and Sekishu *hanshi* and *izumo-gami* from Shimane Prefecture. Washi made in Kyoto and Nara has been famous for centuries. Dyed pattern paper is still produced in Mie Prefecture. Echizen *hosho* and *torinoko-gami* from Fukui Prefecture are well known, as is Yao paper made in Toyama Prefecture. Surviving washi products include kites from Nagasaki Prefecture and *shibuuchiwa* (fans) from Kutami in Kumamoto Prefecture.

Numerous types of paintings and religious sculptures are considered representative of Japanese folk crafts, although in these categories there are different opinions about what is and what is not folk craft. (According to Yanagi's somewhat personal and subjective criteria, *otsu-e* are included among folk arts whereas *ukiyo-e* are not.) Present designations of what can be considered mingei should not be accepted as final, since scholars may develop a more comprehensive method of categorization in the future.

Architecture

Modern architecture (*kingendai no kenchiku*) 近現代の建築●

As Japan launched its modernization drive following the Meiji Restoration of 1868 and began to import Western science and technology as part of its national policy, the government invited foreign engineers and experts to train Japanese and oversee initial construction projects.

At first, Western methods and designs were incorporated into traditional Japanese methods of wood construction.

In 1877 Josiah Conder of Britain arrived in Japan to teach at the Industrial College (forerunner of the Department of Engineering at Tokyo University); he trained many architects, including Tatsuno Kingo and Katayama Tokuma. The Akasaka Detached Palace (1909) by Katayama and the main office of the Bank of Japan (1896) and Tokyo Station (1914) by Tatsuno are typical of the kind of Western-style buildings designed by Japanese at this time.

Meiji-period building of the Bank of Japan.

In the 1880s there was a general reaction against excessive Westernization in many fields, including architecture. Architect and art historian Ito Chuta was among the first to advocate Asian models for Japanese architecture; he was later responsible for the design of the Meiji Shrine (1920). After World War I architects like Frank Lloyd Wright and Antonin Raymond of the United States and Bruno Taut of Germany came to Japan, contributing to the reevaluation of traditional Japanese architecture. Through their work, Japanese architecture influenced Western architecture, in much the same way that *ukiyo-e* had influenced Western painting. The renewed interest in tradition also led to the development by Yoshida Isoya of a new style in residential architecture that assimilated traditional *sukiya-zukuri* techniques.

Since World War II the activities of Japanese architects have increasingly attracted attention overseas. The reconciliation of modern and traditional architectural forms was one of the major issues during the postwar years.

One of the best-known and most influential modern Japanese architects is Tange Kenzo (1913–). He developed a methodology linking Japanese traditional elements with the achievements of science and technology in architectural form and established his reputation with a number of dramatic buildings in the 1950s and 1960s such as the futuristic Yoyogi National Stadium (1963), built for the 1964 Tokyo Olympics, and the Dentsu head office building (1967). These were built at a time when there was a rush, propelled by a new wave of technological innovation and the dynamism of rapid economic growth, to construct very large buildings. The 1960s were a period both of pioneering work by individual architects and of the industrialization and depersonalization of architecture, as fast-working design and construction companies specializing in building groups of standardized, characterless structures came to dominate the field. Cities in Japan as in many other countries were rapidly filled with boxlike buildings.

The reevaluation of architectural priorities was led by Isozaki Arata (1931–), who worked under Tange early in his career. Rejecting the tendency toward the total commercialization of architecture and construction, Isozaki argued that architecture had to regain its independence from commercial and technological imperatives. Examples of his work such as the Museum of Modern Art in Gumma Prefecture (1975) and his many critical writings had an immense impact on the rising younger generation of architects in the 1970s. It was about this time that architects who regarded themselves primarily as artists (as opposed to technicians or builders) began to make their appearance, among the most distinguished being Ando Tadao (1941–), Shinohara Kazuo (1925–), and Kurokawa Kisho (1934–). During this period Japanese architects were preoccupied with reassessing the functional and utilitarian aspects of postwar Japanese architecture and its relationship to Japanese traditions. These more introspective concerns paralleled the relative contraction in the growth and dynamism of the Japanese economy as a whole after the expansion of the 1960s.

In the 1980s, however, the economy once again began to boom, and this was reflected in architectural circles by a union between new commercial imperatives, prompted by government deregulation of the construction industry, and the emphasis on pure design that had resulted from the introspection of the 1970s. The demand of business for imposing buildings with the power to impress customers—which had, for example, led to the construction of the first skyscrapers in the Shinjuku area of downtown Tokyo in the early 1970s—reasserted itself in the 1980s, but now architects responded with buildings that incorporated more artistic design features. Tange Kenzo's Tokyo Metropolitan Government Offices (1991) are a good example of the monumental style that resulted.

The 1980s and early 1990s also saw a rapid increase in the number of works by Japanese architects being built in other countries. Works like Isozaki's Museum of Contemporary Art in Los Angeles (1986) and Tange Kenzo's OUB Center in Singapore (1986) marked the advent of active two-way international exchange in the field of architecture.

Traditional domestic architecture (*dentoteki* Nihon *kenchiku*)

伝統的日本建築●

Traditional residential architecture in Japan is perhaps best viewed as a response to the natural environment. Traditional Japan was a primarily agricultural society, centering on activities associated with rice planting. A feeling of cooperation, rather than an antagonistic relationship, developed between the Japanese and their natural surroundings. Instead of resistance or defense, accommodation and adaptation became the basic stance. Traditional Japanese architecture is characterized by the same attitude toward the natural environment, responding in particular to climatic and geographical conditions.

Japan's climate is distinguished by long, hot, humid summers and relatively short, cold, dry winters, and the Japanese house has evolved accordingly to make the summers more bearable. Since in the past the only relief from the oppressive heat and humidity was found in the cooling movement of air, the choice was toward light and open structures much like those found in Malaysia and other tropical areas. The traditional Japanese house was raised slightly off the ground and the interior opened up to allow for unrestricted movement of air around and below the living spaces. Associated with the heat and humidity of summer were sun and frequent rain. This necessitated a substantial roof structure with long, low overhangs to protect the interior.

With its open structure, the traditional Japanese house is vulnerable to all kinds of intrusion, including dirt, dust, and insects. Noise and lack of privacy are also problems, though screens and *shoji* (translucent paper-covered sliding panels) offer a measure of visual privacy to the inhabitants.

Materials and Construction   建材と構造●

The choice of building materials has been determined by the climate, wood being preferred to stone. Stone is uncomfortable and unhealthy in hot, humid weather, restricting airflow and closing off the structure; it also requires a longer period of time in preparing materials and in building. In contrast, wood responds more sensitively to the climate, being much cooler and absorbing moisture in summer and not as cold to the touch in winter. Wood is also more suited to withstand earthquakes, almost daily occurrences in Japan.

Fusuma sliding panels.

The choice of wood and an open structure allows for flexibility in living arrangements according to seasonal changes and the needs of the family. Inner partitions such as shoji and *fusuma* (opaque paper-covered sliding panels) can be removed to open up the interior, and, except for the roof's supporting columns, a clear space can be exposed.

Apart from the use of wood, the apparently little consideration given to earthquake protection in the structure itself is striking. Diagonal bracing, for example, is hardly ever seen in walls or roof structure. Rigidity, however, is not the only way of protecting a structure against earthquakes. Wood is flexible and can take more shear and torque for its weight than most other materials. The joinery makes use of the strengths of wood. The walls, consisting essentially of bamboo lattices heavily plastered with clay, are not at all substantial by Western standards but are surprisingly resistant to earthquakes. One room of the traditional house is plastered heavily on four walls in this way, with only a minimal entrance in one. This is directly connected to some of the main supports and helps to strengthen the building. The diagonal was not unknown, for wood diagonal compression braces have been found beneath the plaster walls of a few very old structures, but for some reason it was not used generally. In older structures the joint between a foundation stone and the support post or column was not fixed, so that when the earth moved, the column sometimes simply slid off its foundation stone. After the earthquake, the house could be lifted up and the support placed on another stone with no real damage to the structure.

Spatial Concepts in Architecture　　　　建築における空間概念●

A basic spatial concept in Japan is *ma* (written with a Chinese character that is also pronounced *ken* or *aida*). It has no exact English equivalent, variously meaning space, relationship, interval, period, luck, or pause, depending on the context. In architecture the term is applicable to the distance between two posts or the space between two or more walls, rocks in a garden, buildings, people, or other things with a possible relationship.

In constructing a house, the first step is to raise posts and beams until a skeletal structure stable enough to support a roof is completed. The space is organized by the roof and by the modular placement of the posts and columns. From this point on, design concerns itself with filling in the spaces or intervals between the posts and columns. Two things happen as this filling-in process occurs. First, a relationship is developed between the filled-in wall planes, and subdivisions—rooms—are created. Second, the wall itself alters the relationship of the posts by the kinds of materials used in its construction and its value as a barrier. In both cases, one is adjusting ma, or relationships that already exist—a process that lies at the heart of traditional Japanese design. Once the structure is given, design is concerned with the realignment and alteration of already existing relationships. Consequently, in Japanese design the wall has a different conceptual basis than that of Western design. Japanese walls are not defensive. In the West, by contrast, the wall is conceived as defensive, acting as a barrier between two opposing environments, such as winter cold and house warmth.

An important aspect of traditional design is the relationship of the house to its specific environment, particularly the GARDEN; the two are continuous. The Japanese do not see exterior and interior as two separate entities; in other words, there is no definite point at which exterior ends and interior begins. The lack of barriers in Japanese designs has already been discussed. The Japanese veranda (*engawa*) is a concrete expression of this concept, serving as a transition space from inside to outside. Its function is further expressed by the materials used in its construction. Whereas the floors of the interior of the house are covered with *tatami* mats and the exterior is made of earth and rock, the engawa is made of unfinished wood planks, belonging neither to the soft and accommodating interior nor to the harsh and more primitive materials on the outside.

Tatami maker sewing the edge of a mat.

The development of the individual spaces within the house was a gradual process of breaking down the larger open space that was available into smaller, more human-scaled spaces. Individual rooms were later defined by shoji and fusuma, "sliding doors" that could still be removed to form a single large space.

Gardens (*teien*) 庭園●

Japanese gardens possess a unique beauty derived from the combination and synthesis of various elements. There is a compositional beauty derived from a blending of natural plantings, sand, water, and rock, made unique by the natural beauty of Japan's landscape, seasonal change, and a symbolic beauty arising from the expression of Shinto beliefs and Buddhist intellectual conventions.

History 歴史●

It has been said that the use of groupings of rocks is a distinguishing feature of the Japanese garden and provides its basic framework. The ancestors of the modern Japanese referred to places surrounded by natural rock as *amatsu iwasaka* ("heavenly barrier") or *amatsu iwakura* ("heavenly seat"), believing that gods lived there. Dense clusters of trees were also thought to be the dwelling places of gods and were called *himorogi* ("divine hedge"). Moats or streams that enclosed sacred ground were called *mizugaki* ("water fences").

The first gardens amidst the mountains of Yamato (now Nara Prefecture), where the Japanese state was established during the 6th and 7th centuries, imitated ocean scenes with large ponds rimmed by wild "seashores" and dotted with islands. During this period Buddhism was transmitted to Japan, and immigrants from Paekche on the Korean peninsula contributed continental influences to the Japanese garden.

In 794 the capital was moved from Nara to Kyoto. Here several rivers converged, and channels were dug to carry water through the city. In order to provide some relief from the summer heat, waterfalls and ponds were fashioned, and narrow streams (*yarimizu*) were made to pass between buildings and flow through the gardens of the *shinden-zukuri* mansions. The ponds were of simple shape yet were large enough for boating, and at their edges, jutting out over the water, were erected fishing pavilions (*tsuridono*) connected by roofed corridors to the other structures of the mansion. The large area between the main buildings and the pond was covered with white sand and used for formal ceremonies.

With the rise of the cult of the Buddha Amida in the 10th century, the shinden style of garden, modeled on the image of the Pure Land (Jodo) as described in scripture and religious tracts, was developed. A good example of this is the garden of the Byodoin, a temple at Uji near Kyoto that was originally the country residence of Fujiwara no Michinaga.

The Muromachi period (1333–1568) has been called the golden age of Japanese gardens. Skilled groups of craftsmen known as *senzui kawaramono* ("mountain, stream, and riverbed people") were active, and the new *karesansui* ("dry mountain stream") style of garden appeared. Waterless rock and sand gardens (karesansui) arose under the influence of Zen Buddhist doctrine, *shoin*-style architecture (*shoin-zukuri*), and Chinese ink painting, together with potted dwarf trees (*bonsai*), and tray landscapes, the ideal being the symbolic expression of the universe within a limited space.

The TEA CEREMONY (*sado*) as taught by Sen no Rikyu emphasized a quiescent spirituality. The approach to a teahouse was through a tea garden (*roji* or *chaniwa*), the ideal of which Rikyu sought in the desolate tranquility of a mountain trail. Among the contributions of the tea garden to the contemporary Japanese garden are stepping-stones, stone lanterns, and groves of trees, as well as stone washbasins and simply constructed gazebos for guests being served tea.

During the Edo period (1600–1868) a synthesis of preceding forms took place. The garden of the Katsura Detached Palace in Kyoto, which achieved considerable renown through the writings of the German architect Bruno Taut, is made up of a number of tea gardens. This is an example of the *kaiyu* or "many-pleasure" style, which became fully established in the mid-Edo period. A representative garden designer of this period was Kobori Enshu, whose work included the gardens of the Sento Palace in Kyoto.

Castles (*shiro*)   城●

Japanese castles were originally military fortifications designed to provide protection against enemy attack. With the rise of feudalism, however, they became distinctive architectural forms serving as both palatial residence and seat of military and political power of feudal barons. The principal construction material of a castle was wood.

Ancient Fortifications   古代の砦●

Three types of fortification have been identified as existing in ancient Japan. These are the grid-pattern city (*tojo*), the mountain fortress (*yamajiro*), and the palisade (*ki*).

Medieval Castles   中世の城●

Internal wars were frequent in Japan during the medieval period (mid-12th–16th centuries). From the period of the Northern and Southern Courts (1337–92) to the Sengoku period (1467–1568), territorial warlords repeatedly fought each other, and castles were constructed throughout the country. Their forms varied, but many were small, semipermanent fortifications built at the tip of steep mountain ridges. To prevent enemy approach, two or three lines of advance fortifications were built. Along the ridge line a trench was dug, the peak and mountainside were terraced, and palisades were erected around the perimeter. Stone walls were uncommon, and, since these facilities were used only in times of war, they were not built to last.

By the Sengoku period, constant warfare made it necessary to build more permanent structures. Military chieftains built fortifications similar to their own residences, with the addition of raised watchtowers on the roof. This was the beginning of castle architecture in Japan. Most castles of the medieval period were of the mountain castle type and were used only in times of war. Ordinarily the warrior chieftain lived in a fortified residence located on a plain or low plateau. This was the origin of the plain castle (*hirajiro*) and the so-called hill-on-the-plain castle (*hirayama-*

jiro). An example of the hirajiro is Edo Castle in Tokyo. The hirayamajiro was generally sited on a low-lying plateau set in a plain.

Azuchi-Momoyama and Edo Period Castles   安土桃山・江戸時代の城●

There was great development in the building of castles during the Azuchi-Momoyama period (1568–1600), and the castle became a complex of many structures. With the reorganization of the feudal system by the Tokugawa shogunate (1603–1867), the daimyo built castles in the center of their domains, and the hirayamajiro thus became the standard type. The castle included the residences of the castle lord and his chief retainers. Located as it was, near a plain, the feudal castle now required additional fortifications. Stone walls developed, moats (*hori*) were dug, and earthworks were added. Around these castles developed castle towns (*joka machi*). The castle became not just a defensive facility but the administrative and economic center of its region.

Osaka Castle.

The military hegemons Oda Nobunaga and Toyotomi Hideyoshi were responsible for major developments in castle architecture. Between 1576 and 1579 Nobunaga constructed the central part of an enormous castle project at Azuchi in what is now Shiga Prefecture. Azuchi Castle was destroyed after the death of Oda Nobunaga in 1582. It established a tradition of large-scale, sumptuous castles that was continued in Fushimi Castle (1594) and Osaka Castle (1583), both built by Hideyoshi and no longer extant. After the Battle of Sekigahara (1600), the decisive battle in the rise of Tokugawa Ieyasu to the shogunate, through the Keicho era (1596–1615), there was a surge of castle construction by daimyo throughout the country.

By 1615 the Tokugawa shogunate, seeking to secure complete control over the country, ordered that there could be only one castle to each domain. The art of castle architecture went into a gradual decline during the Edo period (1600–1868).

Castle-Building Techniques and Design   築城技術とデザイン●

The most important step in building a castle was the site planning (*nawabari*), in which the building's outline was fixed on the prospective site by stretching ropes. Ideally, a castle was composed of a main compound or ward (*hommaru*) centered around the donjon or main tower (*tenshu* or *tenshukaku*) surrounded by or connected with minor compounds or enclosures. The most important feature of castle architecture from the late Muromachi period (1333–1568) through the Edo period, the donjon originated in the watchtower built atop a warrior's residence. There were several entrances to the castle, but the important ones were called the *ote* and *karamete*. The former was the main entrance and the latter the rear entrance. In case the castle was overrun, the karamete could be used as an avenue of escape. A moat (hori) or system of moats, ponds, waterways, and trenches surrounded the castle, and natural features of the land were also employed in its fortifications. In order to reach the donjon it was necessary to traverse a mazelike route.

Stone foundation walls (*ishigaki*) were built vertically in earlier times on sites with foundation soil, but where the ground was not stable, walls with a concave profile came to be used both for structural and decorative reasons. The early donjon had exposed wood members, but at the height of the castle-building era most surfaces came to be plastered. Arrows could be shot through rectangular openings in the walls, and muskets fired through round, triangular, or square openings. All such loopholes were known as *sama* or *hazama*. Both the inner ward and the outer enclosures were reinforced with small towers (*yagura*), one- to three-storied structures similar in design to the donjon. The entrances to various parts of the castle were sometimes fortified with *masugata* (bastions laid out so as to form a rectangular courtyard), from which flanking fire could be directed upon assailants and in which defenders could group for a sudden sally. So-called mounted exits (*umadashi*) were earthworks constructed in front of the main gateways (*koguchi*) to mask the egress of mounted soldiers from the castle. Two gates peculiar to castle architecture were the *koraimon* and the *yaguramon*. The koraimon was one bay wide, with support posts on either side; it had a main roof over the two supporting pillars and auxiliary roofs projecting from them. The yaguramon was a two-storied gatehouse.

Traditional theater (*koten geino*)   古典芸能●

The five major genres of Japanese traditional theater, all still in performance, are *bugaku*, NO, KYOGEN, BUNRAKU, and KABUKI. Although different in content and style, they are linked by strong aesthetic relationships, derived from a confluence of sources both inside and outside Japan. The assumption of an integral relationship among dance, music, and lyrical narrative governed the evolution of performing arts throughout Asia. The synthesis of the disparate elements of speech, music, and dance led to highly developed styles, of which the five Japanese genres represent supreme examples.

Among the five Japanese genres, bugaku stands apart as a ceremonial dance associated only with court ritual, in which the theatrical element is minimal and music predominates. Ceremonial dance was common in ancient Chinese ritual. Bugaku incorporates aesthetic and structural principles current in the 8th century—admixtures of Central Asian, Indian, and Korean elements assimilated by China and adopted by Japan during a period of cultural borrowing.

No, kyogen, bunraku, and kabuki, by contrast, are indigenous forms representing successive periods of political and social change in Japan. The first two belong to an age when Chinese influences were still potent; the latter two come from a time when Japan was politically isolated. But all adhere to Asian dramatic principles emphasizing symbolism and allusive imagery, as opposed to the Aristotelian concept of mimesis, the imitation of reality, which dominates Western dramatic theory. Japanese theater, whatever the genre, strives to induce a mood, to create an immediate aesthetic experience drawing an instantaneous response from the spectator.

No drama, for example, seeks to reveal the ephemeral nature of reality through stage techniques stressing imagery, metaphor, and symbolism. Medieval Buddhist thought, which profoundly influenced No, rejected factual reality as illusory: in Buddhist theory it is only at the moment of perception that anything exists; thus, all existence is fleeting.

Kyogen, the comic interludes that are an integral part of No performance, poke fun at human frailties as did the traditional Asian storytellers, jesting at social pretensions, marital discord, quackery, and so forth. Through stylized vocal forms, pantomime, and spatial control, kyogen preserves some of the formal elegance of No. In kyogen the comic action is physical and situational, playing off the discrepancies between what people would be and what they really are. The comic actor becomes a catalyzing agent, relieving tension through the arrangement of his appearance between the serious plays.

Bunraku, or puppet theater, is unique in being accepted in Japan as the equal of orthodox drama. Indeed, it is impossible to speak of bunraku without mentioning kabuki, since a sizable part of the latter's repertoire consists of plays originally written for puppet drama, which has also greatly influenced the style of kabuki acting. In turn, bunraku has taken much from the sophisticated technical presentation of kabuki and has incorporated some of its popular dance dramas into its own repertoire.

Kabuki carries even further the deployment of speech, sound, movement, and space as equal contributory forces. Theatrical synthesis reaches a powerful degree of instantaneous communication by using visual and aural techniques cumulatively to assail the playgoer's senses and emotions. Stylization conditions every level of performance. Narrative musical forms are used constantly to convey mood, emphasize emotional tensions, and provide exposition.

N*o*   能●

The oldest extant professional theater; a form of musical dance-drama originating in the 14th century. No preserves what all other important contemporary theater has lost: its origin in ritual, reflecting an essentially Buddhist view of existence. The performance looks and sounds more like solemn observance than life. The actors are hieratic, playing their ancient roles of intermediaries between the worlds of gods and men. To the bare stage come soberly dressed instrumentalists, the six-or-eight-member chorus, then the supporting character (*waki*), handsomely robed, often as a priest. Finally, out of the darkness at the end of the long passageway leading to the stage proper, evoked by drums and flute, the resplendently caparisoned (usually masked) leading character (*shite*) materializes. In strict rhythms, out of music, voice, and movement rather than the artifice of stagecraft, time and space are created and destroyed. Language is largely poetic. Costumes are rich and heavy, movement, even in dance, deliberate. The shite seeks intercession by the waki and, having attained it at the end, returns to the darkness freed of karma.

Origins   起源●

At the middle of the 14th century professional theater was based in Kyoto and Nara, and the actors organized into troupes under the patronage of Shinto shrines and Buddhist temples. They raised money, piously and commercially, with subscription No (*kanjin* No), their performances at religious festivals serving both to propagate doctrine and to entertain.

Some troupes presented *dengaku* No, others *sarugaku* No. At this time little distinguished the two kinds, for both had a common theatrical inheritance. Their masks had origins in the ancient dance-drama called *gigaku*. Their music came from Shinto ritual dance (*kagura*), the Buddhist liturgy (*shomyo*), popular 10th-century songs (*imayo*), and 13th-century "party music" (*enkyoku*). Their dance was influenced by 7th-century dance music (*bugaku*); by *furyu*, an 11th-century dramatic dance accompanied by flute and drum; and by *shirabyoshi*, a type of 12th-century song-and-dance performance. Their plots were drawn from legend, history, literature, and contemporary events, given some literary refinement by the influence of *ennen* No. The players distinguished between comic and serious materials, the comic pieces, kyogen, being played as interludes between serious ones. In spite of their similarities, however, sarugaku eventually emerged as dominant, replacing dengaku in popularity.

The transformation of sarugaku into No, in basically the same form it has today, was accomplished by Kan'ami and his son Zeami, both prodigious actor-dancers and playwrights of the Muromachi period (1333–1568).

In 1374 Kan'ami and Zeami performed before the shogun Ashikaga Yoshimitsu, who, greatly taken by the performance and by Zeami, thereafter sponsored the troupe. Never before had actors attained such social esteem. Kan'ami's troupe, the Kanze school, was preeminent, and three other troupes that now survive, the Komparu school, the Hosho school, and the Kongo school, adopted the Kanze style of performance. It was on the Zen artistic principles of restraint, economy of expression, and suggestion rather than statement that Zeami fashioned his 40 or so plays, his acting, and his productions. His ideas on every aspect of the theater were set down in a series of essays that remain the essential documents of the No.

Evolution   発展●

A civil war, the Onin War, started in 1467 and was fought in and around Kyoto until 1477, when the battles shifted to the provinces. By the end of the century the entire country was engaged in a period of conflict known as the Sengoku, or Warring States, period, which lasted until 1568. The shogunate had little time for No, but for others the war whetted the desire for entertainment and culture. Toward 1500, amateur performances became widely popular. The study of No music and dance spread not only among aristocrats but also among priests, soldiers, and commoners, who wanted professional instruction, which the troupes gladly gave them for a fee. Written copies of the songs and chants (*utaibon*) of the Kanze and Komparu troupes appeared in 1512. By disseminating the performances throughout the country, civil war made No an increasingly integral part of the culture.

No returned to the center of political power when in 1571 the Kanze troupe was summoned to the military headquarters of Tokugawa Ieyasu. But it found its most enthusiastic support when Toyotomi Hideyoshi came to power in 1582. Hideyoshi bolstered his soldiers' morale by having all four troupes perform for them, and he commissioned 10 plays written about himself, in which he played the lead. When Tokugawa Ieyasu became shogun in 1603 he celebrated the occasion with No performances, and in 1609 he employed all of Hideyoshi's performers and established them in Edo (now Tokyo). The Kita school, which still exists today, was added to the original four in 1618. No became the official property and ceremonial art of the Tokugawa line. In 1647 Tokugawa Iemitsu issued regulations for its governance, as stringent as those by which he ran the country: tradition must be maintained, the troupe leader brooking no deviations. Over more than two centuries No became more and more codified, even surpassing Zeami's refined art in solemnity. Performances that took half an hour in Zeami's day take an hour and a half or more today.

During the Edo period (1600–1868) favored commoners were invited to performances at the shogun's castle on auspicious occasions. They were forbidden to learn No music and dance, but they did nonetheless. As the economic life of the military class worsened in the 19th century, that of many commoners improved, and they were able to pay well for No instruction. Large numbers of them also became attracted to the popular kabuki theater. When the shogunate fell in 1867 and government subsidy of No stopped, some of the nobility kept No alive. Their support ended with the end of World War II, however, and the public became No's sole sponsor. Today No has a small but dedicated following, many members of which belong to No study groups.

Stage 舞台●

No performance.

Tokugawa formalization of No also standardized the stage, and today that architecture is requisite for the correct performance of the plays. Although the stage is now usually inside a concrete building, it retains its original appearance as an exterior structure. The elaborate, carved, cypress-bark-covered roof of Shinto shrine architecture extends over the main stage (*butai*), which measures 6 by 6 meters (19.7 by 19.7 ft), as well as the side stage (*wakiza*), the rear stage (*atoza*), and the bridge (*hashigakari*). The bridge joins the main stage at an oblique angle, connecting it with the "mirror room" (*kagami no ma*), the actors' dressing room. Musicians (*hayashikata*) and actors enter and exit on the bridge. The only other entrance to the stage is a 1 meter (39 in) high sliding door (*kirido*), upstage left on the main stage, used by stage assistants (*koken*) and the members of the chorus (*jiutai*).

Along the front of the entire structure, at audience level, is a strip of pebbles. In front of the bridge in this area are three equidistantly placed pine trees. A stylized pine tree, the only scenic background, is painted on the back wall (*kagamiita*) of the main stage. The entire structure is built of polished Japanese cypress (*hinoki*).

Performers
演者●

All performers are male, and their organization is that established in the Edo period. Each of the five schools of No, mentioned earlier, trains its own shite, his "companion" (*tsure*), the child actor (*kokata*), the chorus, and the stage assistants. The waki and his "companion" have their own separate schools, such as Fukuo and Takayasu. Each instrument—the flute, small and large hand drums, and the large drum standing on the floor—is taught in a number of different schools.

The actors' children, trained in the traditional manner beginning at the age of seven, appear in performance in children's roles. Training is strictly by rote, vocally and physically. Each unit of movement, including the No style of walking in which the heel never leaves the floor, is called a *kata* ("form"). Some 200 kata exist, each having a name, but only about 30 are commonly used.

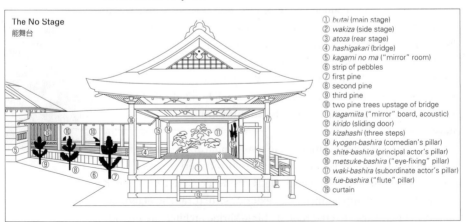

The No Stage
能舞台

① *butai* (main stage)
② *wakiza* (side stage)
③ *atoza* (rear stage)
④ *hashigakari* (bridge)
⑤ *kagami no ma* ("mirror" room)
⑥ strip of pebbles
⑦ first pine
⑧ second pine
⑨ third pine
⑩ two pine trees upstage of bridge
⑪ *kagamiita* ("mirror" board, acoustic)
⑫ *kirido* (sliding door)
⑬ *kizahashi* (three steps)
⑭ *kyogen-bashira* (comedian's pillar)
⑮ *shite-bashira* (principal actor's pillar)
⑯ *metsuke-bashira* ("eye-fixing" pillar)
⑰ *waki-bashira* (subordinate actor's pillar)
⑱ *fue-bashira* ("flute" pillar)
⑲ curtain

Properties, Masks, and Costumes   小道具・面・装束●

The expressiveness of the shite and the waki is enhanced by hand properties, among them letters, umbrellas, rosaries, and the bamboo branch signifying derangement, but most of all by the folding fan (*chukei*). Closed, partly closed, or open, it may represent any object suggested by its shape and handling—dagger, lantern, rising moon. In other kata it represents not objects but actions—listening, moon viewing, sleeping. The abstract or pictorial design painted on the fan is conventionally associated with a type of character such as a ghost, old woman, or demon. Only the shite and waki use them. The other actors and the chorus carry fans (*ogi*) bearing the crest of the school. The chorus place their fans, always closed, on the floor in front of them and pick them up to signal the beginning of a chant.

Han'nya (female demon) mask.

Only the shite and his companions wear masks, carved of wood and painted, though not in plays in which the characters they portray are living men. Each mask is a variation on a general type—holy old men, gods, demons or spirits, men, women—and in many plays the shite changes masks midway through the play, the second mask revealing the character's true being. The shite chooses the mask he prefers for the role, and his choice determines, by association and custom, his costume.

Many of the costumes (*shozoku*) used today were constructed in the 18th and 19th centuries when the patterns, colors, and materials to be worn by a given character were systematized. Costume creates an effect of luxurious elegance but also a bulky, massive figure, that of the shite looming largest. This is effected by at least five layers of clothing, the outermost richly figured damask, brocade, or embroidered silk gauze. No garment completely conceals the one beneath it; surfaces and textures are multiple. Wigs, hats, and headdresses heighten the figure.

Plays   演目●

Okina, the oldest item in the repertory, consists principally of three dances extant in the 10th century that are prayers for peace, fertility (the basis of Shinto), and longevity. Scarcely a play, it is performed only on ceremonial occasions and always first on the program. The usual program today consists of two or three No plays with half-hour comic pieces, kyogen, between them.

The other 240 or so plays now performed, most dating from the 15th century, are grouped into five categories, corresponding to the five parts of the traditional No program called *goban-date. Shobamme-mono* (part-one plays) are sometimes called *wakino-mono* or *kami* (god) plays. *Nibamme-mono* (part-two plays), or *shura-mono*, are often about men or warriors. *Sambamme-mono* (part-three plays) are also called *katsura-mono* ("wig" plays) and are usually about women. *Yobamme-mono* (part-four plays) are also called *zo-mono* ("miscellaneous No") or "madwoman" plays. Some of these are referred to as "present-day" or "realistic" plays. *Gobamme-mono* (part-five plays) are also called "demon" plays, or *kirino-mono* ("final No").

K*abuki*   歌舞伎●

One of the three major classical theaters of Japan, together with the NO and the BUNRAKU puppet theater. Kabuki began in the early 17th century as a kind of variety show performed by troupes of itinerant entertainers. By the Genroku era (1688–1704), it had achieved its first flowering as a mature theater, and it continued, through much of the Edo period (1600–1868), to be the most popular form of stage entertainment. Kabuki reached its artistic pinnacle with the brilliant plays of Tsuruya Namboku IV (1755–1829) and Kawatake Mokuami (1816–1893). Through a magnificent blend of playacting, dance, and music, kabuki today offers an extraordinary spectacle combining form, color, and sound and is recognized as one of the world's great theatrical traditions.

Origin of Kabuki   歌舞伎の起源●

The creation of kabuki is ascribed to Okuni, a female attendant at the Izumo Shrine, who, documents record, led her company of mostly women in a light theatrical performance featuring dancing and comic sketches on the dry bed of the river Kamogawa in Kyoto in 1603. Her troupe gained nationwide recognition and her dramas—and later the genre itself—became identified as "kabuki," a term connoting its "out-of-the-ordinary" and "shocking" character.

The strong attraction of *onna* (women's) kabuki, which Okuni had popularized, was largely due to its sensual dances and erotic scenes. Because fights frequently broke out among the spectators over these entertainers, who also practiced prostitution, in 1629 the Tokugawa shogunate (1603–1867) banned women from appearing in kabuki performances. Thereafter, *wakashu* (young men's) kabuki achieved a striking success, but, as in the case of onna kabuki, the authorities strongly disapproved of the shows, which continued to be the cause of public disturbances because the adolescent actors also sold their favors.

Kabuki after 1652   1652年以降の歌舞伎●

In 1652 wakashu kabuki was forbidden, and the shogunate required that kabuki performances undergo a basic reform to be allowed to continue. In short, kabuki was required to be based on *kyogen*, farces staged between No plays that used the spoken language of the time but whose style of acting was highly formalized. The performers of *yaro* (men's) kabuki, who now began to replace the younger males, were compelled to shave off their forelocks, as was the custom at the time for men, to signify that they had come of age. They also had to make representations to the authorities that their performances did not rely on the provocative display of their bodies and that they were serious artists who would not engage in prostitution.

In the 1660s a broad platform, the forerunner of the *hanamichi* in use today, extending from the main stage to the center of the auditorium, was introduced to provide an auxiliary stage on which performers could make entrances and exits. In 1664 two theaters located in Osaka and Edo (now Tokyo) introduced the draw curtain, which brought unlimited theatrical possibilities to the previously curtainless stage by permitting the lengthening of plays through the presentation of a series of scenes and providing the freedom to effect complicated scene changes unobtrusively. In the meantime the roles played by the *onnagata* (female impersonator) gradually increased in importance; mastery of them came to require many years of training. By the mid-17th century, the major cities, Kyoto, Osaka, and Edo, were permitted to build permanent kabuki playhouses.

Genroku Era Kabuki   元禄時代の歌舞伎●

By the beginning of the Genroku era in 1688 there had developed three distinct types of kabuki performance: *jidai-mono* (historical plays), often with elaborate sets and a large cast; *sewa-mono* (domestic plays), which generally portrayed the lives of the townspeople and which, in comparison to jidai-mono, were presented in a realistic manner; and *shosagoto* (dance pieces), consisting of dance performances and pantomime. In the Kyoto-Osaka (Kamigata) area, Sakata Tojuro I (1647–1709), whose realistic style of acting was called *wagoto*, was enormously popular for his portrayal of romantic young men, and his contemporary Yoshizawa Ayame I (1673–1729) consolidated the role of the onnagata and established its importance in the kabuki tradition. For a period of some 10 years until about 1703, when he returned to the puppet theater, Chikamatsu Monzaemon (1653–1724) wrote a number of kabuki plays, many of them for Tojuro I, which gained public recognition for the craft of the playwright. The commanding stage presence and powerful acting of Ichikawa Danjuro I made him the premier kabuki performer in Edo, and as a playwright, under the name Mimasuya Hyogo, he was once considered the rival of the great Chikamatsu.

Kabuki and the Puppet Theater　　　　　歌舞伎と文楽●

The spectacular success of kabuki in the Kyoto-Osaka area during the late 17th century was followed by a period of diminished popularity due to the flourishing of the bunraku puppet theater. In the years following the departure of Chikamatsu, *maruhon-mono* (kabuki adaptations of puppet plays) were staged in an attempt to draw back the spectators who were now flocking to the puppet theater. The musical and narrative accompaniment of the puppet plays was transported to kabuki performances, and even stage techniques of bunraku, such as the distinctive movement of the manipulated dolls, were imitated by kabuki actors. Chikamatsu's *Kokusen'ya kassen* (1715), an early example of the maruhon-mono, enjoyed tremendous success in both the Kamigata area and in Edo when it was performed soon after its presentation as a puppet play. The works of later writers which are considered masterpieces in both theaters include: *Sugawara denju tenarai kagami* (1746), *Yoshitsune sembon-zakura* (1747), and *Kanadehon chushingura* (1748). In Edo, despite the growing popularity of the bunraku theater, kabuki remained in the ascendancy due to the undiminished power of the Ichikawa Danjuro family of actors and the regional preference for the *aragoto* style of performance, which was not suited for the puppet stage. Nevertheless the tight logical structure of the puppet plays and their realistic character portrayal eventually influenced the Edo kabuki theater. After enjoying immense success during the first half of the 18th century, the puppet theater rapidly declined in the Kamigata area, and kabuki recaptured the support of the townspeople. Today, half of the plays presented on the kabuki stage are adaptations of bunraku plays.

Kanadehon chushingura, Ichiriki at Gion (in Kyoto Prefecture).

After the mid-17th century, the cultural center of Japan gradually shifted from the Kamigata region to Edo. During this transitional period, one of the more notable Kamigata playwrights was Namiki Shozo I (1730–1773), best known as the inventor of the revolving stage (*mawaributai*). It was a pupil of Shozo I, the dramatist Namiki Gohei I (1747–1808), along with Sakurada Jisuke I (1734–1806), who was instrumental in transmitting the social realism traditionally associated with the sewamono (domestic plays) of the Kyoto-Osaka area to Edo. Their plays laid the foundation for the development of the realistic *kizewa-mono* ("bare" domestic plays) written by Tsuruya Namboku IV, Segawa Joko III (1806–1881), and Kawatake Mokuami.

Late-Edo- and Meiji-Period Kabuki　　　江戸後期と明治時代の歌舞伎●

After the death of Namboku IV in 1829, kabuki did not produce any prominent playwrights until the mid-1850s, when Joko III and Mokuami began to write for the theater. Their early successes, embellishments on the genre *kizewa-mono*—the masterpiece of which had been *Tokaido Yotsuya kaidan* (1825) by Namboku IV—intermingled brutality, eroticism, and macabre humor and introduced characters from the underworld. Mokuami created the *shiranami-mono* (thief plays), which had robbers, murderers, confidence men, and cunningly vicious women in the leading roles.

The Meiji Restoration of 1868 marked the collapse of the social order ruled by the *samurai*, whose loss of status was symbolized by a ban on the wearing of swords and by government discouragement of the continued wearing of topknots. During the early years of the Meiji period Mokuami developed the *zangiri-mono* ("cropped-hair" plays), which introduced soldiers dressed in Western-style uniforms and onnagata characters wearing Western dresses. These dramas were little more than caricatures of modern life and failed to draw audiences. Actors such as Ichikawa Danjuro IX (1838–1903) and Onoe Kikugoro V (1844–1903) urged the preservation of classical kabuki, and in the later years of their careers agitated for the continued staging of the great plays of the kabuki tradition and trained a younger generation of actors in the art that they would inherit.

Post-World War II Kabuki　　　　　第二次世界大戦後の歌舞伎●

In the postwar era the popularity of kabuki has been maintained and the great plays of the Edo period, as well as a number of the modern classics, continue to be performed in Tokyo at the Kabukiza and the National Theater. However, offerings have become considerably shortened and, particularly at the Kabukiza, limited for the most part to favorite acts and scenes presented together with a dance piece. The National Theater continues to present full-length plays. The average length of a kabuki performance is about five hours, including intermissions. The roles once played by the great postwar actors Morita Kan'ya XIV (1907–1975), Ichikawa Danjuro XI (1909–1965), Nakamura Kanzaburo XVII (1910–1988), Onoe Shoroku II (1913–1989), Onoe Baiko VII (1915–), and Nakamura Utaemon VI (1917–) are now performed by younger actors, such as Ichikawa Ennosuke II (1939–), Matsumoto Koshiro IX (1942–), Nakamura Kichiemon II (1944–), Bando Tamasaburo V (1950–), Kataoka Takao (1944–), and Nakamura Kankuro (1955–). Dramas in which Tamasaburo V appears in the role of the onnagata and Takao that of the leading man, or tachiyaku, are always well attended.

Kabuki and Tokugawa Thought   歌舞伎と徳川思想●

The kabuki theater often incorporates the prevailing moral notions of Tokugawa society as the mechanism upon which plots turn. For example, *inga oho* (law of retributive justice), a Buddhist notion, may result in the destruction of an evildoer or the bestowal of prosperity and happiness upon a long-suffering woman. The notion of *mujo* (the impermanence of all things), also derived from Buddhism, may be illustrated by the fall of a powerful military leader or the demise of a proud family. Certain ethical notions based on Confucian traditions, such as duty, obligation, and filial piety, may come into direct conflict with personal desires and passions, leading to a series of dramatic situations.

The Kabuki Stage   歌舞伎舞台●

The kabuki theater uses a draw curtain. It has broad black, green, and orange vertical stripes and is normally drawn open from stage right to stage left accompanied by the striking of wooden clappers. The curtain may also serve as a backdrop for brief scenes given before or after the performance on the main part of the stage. *Kamite* (stage left) is regarded as the place of honor and is occupied by characters of high rank, guests, and important messengers or official representatives. *Shimote* (stage right) is occupied by characters of low rank and members of a household; most entrances and exits take place on this side, usually by way of the hanamichi. A unique feature of the kabuki stage is the *mawaributai*, a circular platform that can be rotated to permit a second scene to be performed simultaneously with the scene already in progress or to dramatize a flashback.

Roles in Kabuki Plays   歌舞伎の役柄●

Yakugara, or types of dramatic role, are determined on the basis of the personality, age, or social position of characters. Onnagata are assigned to such roles as housewife, samurai lady, heroic woman, and wicked woman. Within the rich repertory of kabuki plays, the roles of Agemaki in *Sukeroku yukari no Edo-zakura* and Masaoka, the loyal nanny in *Meiboku sendai hagi*, are regarded as among the most challenging. Standard male roles are virtuous hero, handsome lover, evil courtier, wicked samurai, and unscrupulous rake. Versatile performers sometimes play both male and female roles.

Kabuki Dialogue   歌舞伎の台詞●

The dialogue in kabuki plays ranges from the extremely stylized to the intensely realistic. Generally jidai-mono contain more formalized speech and the sewa-mono more colloquial speech. In general, lines tend to be marked by a seven-five syllabic pattern (similar to that of classical

Japanese poetry) and are delivered with a distinctive rhythm and tempo that is closely identified with kabuki. The *tsurane*, a long declamatory speech occurring in jidai-mono, effectively employs this rhythmic pattern. Maruhon-mono, kabuki adaptations from bunraku puppet plays, are in particular noted for their mellifluous lines in the seven-five pattern.

Acting Forms
型●

The powerful influence of a long theatrical tradition is graphically illustrated by *kata* (forms), the stylized gestures and movements of kabuki performers. Since kata are not subject to rejection at the whim of the actor, they have helped to maintain the artistic integrity of kabuki. *Tate* (stylized fighting), *roppo* (dramatic exit accompanied by exaggerated gestures), *mie* (striking an attitude), and *dammari* (silent scene) all belong to this category.

Costumes
衣装●

Costume, wig, and makeup are carefully matched with the nature of a role. In general, the costumes in jidai-mono are more stlyized and elegant, befitting members of the nobility and the samurai class. By contrast, the prevailing fashions of society at large during the Edo period are portrayed quite realistically in sewa-mono plays. The costumes used in shosagoto dance pieces are especially noted for their color, design, and workmanship. Wigs are classified according to age of characters, historical period, social status, occupation, and other considerations. Makeup varies widely depending on the role. The most striking example is *kumadori*, an established set of masklike makeup styles numbering about 100 and used in jidai-mono.

Stage Assistants
後見●

In addition to the regular performers, the *koken* (stage assistant) serves a valuable function on the stage. He is especially important in dance pieces. During the demanding *hayagawari* (quick costume change), the koken must carefully follow the movements of the dancer, all the while remaining close behind him, and at the crucial moment assist in the *hikinuki* ("pulling out"), by which a layer of clothing is quickly removed revealing a costume of different pattern and color. The koken is also known as *kurogo* ("black costume") since he is often dressed all in black.

Shumei
襲名●

The theater Kabukiza in Tokyo.

Each performer belongs to an acting family by whose name he is known. Professionally, he is part of a closely knit hierarchical organization, headed by one of the leading actors, and must spend many years as an apprentice. An actor may eventually receive a new name as a mark of his elevation to a higher position within the professional organization.

It is awarded at a *shumei* (name-assuming) ceremony, and in the company of his colleagues he then delivers from the stage an address (*kojo*) in which he requests the continued patronage of the audience. The name Ichikawa Danjuro, which can be traced back to the formative years of kabuki, is regarded even today as the most illustrious of honors a kabuki actor can receive.

Bunraku 文楽●

The professional puppet theater of Japan. Like the KABUKI theater, bunraku is an enduring form of art developed by city-dwelling commoners of the Edo period (1600–1868).

The term bunraku is of relatively recent origin. Of the many puppet theaters of the Edo period, only that known as Bunraku-za, organized in the early 19th century by Uemura Banrakuken in Osaka, survived commercially in modern Japan, and bunraku came to mean "professional puppet theater." The more precise term, *ayatsuri joruri*, denotes the component elements of the theater: ayatsuri means "puppetry," and joruri refers to the dramatic text and the art of chanting it. Historically, it was the fortuitous joining of two independent art forms, puppetry and joruri, that gave birth to bunraku.

Conventions of the Theater 文楽の仕掛●

The bunraku theater presents dramas both serious and entertaining, as well as beautifully choreographed dances, for an audience primarily of adults with cultivated sensibilities. The performance is a composite of four elements: the puppets, which are approximately one-half to two-thirds life size; the movement given to the puppets by their operators; the vocal delivery by the *tayu* (chanter); and the rhythmical musical accompaniment provided by the player of the three-stringed *shamisen*. To add to the complexity of the performance, each puppet portraying a major character is operated jointly by three men.

Bunraku puppets are not operated by strings. With his left arm and hand the *omozukai* (principal operator) supports the puppet and manipulates the mechanisms that control the movable eyelids, eyeballs, eyebrows, and mouth; with his right hand he operates the puppet's right arm. The *hidarizukai* (first assistant) functions solely to operate the puppet's left arm, and the *ashizukai* (second assistant) operates the puppet's legs. Most female puppets do not have legs, for Japanese women generally wore flowing robes of ankle length or longer, which concealed the lower body. The movements of a female puppet's legs are simulated

Scene from the *bunraku* play *Keisei Awa no Naruto* (1768).

through manipulating and shaping the lower part of the *kimono*.

The puppeteers are usually dressed in black robes of coarse weave; the assistants wear black hoods over their heads to become "invisible" in the audience's eyes. Although the omozukai may be similarly hooded—usually in scenes that require the utmost delicacy in the expression of emotions—he is most often seen full face by the audience, for he is a celebrity in the theatrical world. At times bedecked in a robe of lustrous white silk and ceremonial vest of brilliant hue, he becomes an important part of the total visual spectacle.

A single tayu speaks on behalf of all puppets on the stage—men, women, and children—and so his voice must cover an extremely broad range, from a raspy bass to a silky falsetto. Several tayu may perform simultaneously, as in the spectacular opening scene of the best known of all bunraku plays, *Kanadehon chushingura* (1748; tr *Chushingura: The Treasury of Loyal Retainers*, 1971). Pageantry is, in the main, a borrowing from the kabuki theater.

A distinguishing aural feature of bunraku is the melodious, deep-toned thrumming of the solo shamisen, which contrasts with the lively, high-pitched tone of the tenor shamisen of the kabuki theater. In kabuki, an ensemble of 10 or more shamisen may play in unison or heterophonically in extravaganzas. In bunraku, the exceptional use of a shamisen ensemble may occur when a kabuki spectacle is adapted for performance in the puppet theater.

In bunraku, the puppets' movements must be synchronized with the tayu's chanting and the shamisen accompaniment. Seldom is there visual contact between the puppeteers onstage and the tayu and shamisen player, who face the audience from the *yuka*, an elevated platform projecting from the stage. The shamisen player, by his strumming, normally dictates the pace of the narrative and the timing of the action.

Early History   黎明期●

The earliest extant written reference to puppetry in Japan dates from the 11th century. Doubtless even earlier, itinerant hunters and their women earned money by entertaining in the cities, the men presenting episodic plays with small puppets that they operated with their hands and the women working as prostitutes. Eventually a large number settled in Sanjo on the island of Awaji, which became known as the birthplace of professional puppetry.

During the 15th and 16th centuries, blind bards (*biwa hoshi*) garbed in Buddhist robes were chanting historic episodes described in the *Heike monogatari* (13th century; tr *The Tale of the Heike*, 1975, 1988).

These bards accompanied themselves on the biwa (lute), an instrument that had originated in Persia.

The chanting style of medieval narratives changed remarkably in the 16th century with the evolution of a style of chanting called joruri. Also around that time the shamisen was imported into Japan from Okinawa and came to be preferred over the lute by chanters of joruri. Shamisen players composed new melodies that, in turn, influenced the style of joruri chanting. This collaboration was the beginning of bunraku, which caught the fancy of the townspeople—commoners who were low on the social ladder but who came gradually to dominate the economy, art, and material culture of the new era.

Stages of Development　　　　　　　　　　　　　　発展期●

By the mid-17th century the puppet theater was flourishing in Osaka and Kyoto, where puppeteers and chanters of joruri were reaching new heights of artistry. Bunraku became the rage in 1685, when the tayu Takemoto Gidayu I of Osaka garnered accolades for the virile beauty of his chanting style. It was his collaboration, however, with the greatest playwright of the Edo period, Chikamatsu Monzaemon, that led to the transformation of bunraku from popular entertainment to artistic theater.

Chikamatsu employed the imagery, diction, and literary techniques of classical prose, drama, and poetry in writing plays that focused on both historical and contemporary subjects and that emphasized prevalent codes of morality and ethics as thematic material. The success of his *Love Suicides at Sonezaki* in 1703 started a vogue for dramas treating love affairs between merchants and prostitutes. In most of these the tragedy results from the inability of a pair of lovers to resolve the conflict between accepted social codes and their own emotions.

Many of the techniques, such as movable eyelids and mouths, used in bunraku today were developed after Chikamatsu's death.

Kabuki actors were influenced by the style of the bunraku tayu and even imitated the stylized gestures of the puppets. If a certain innovation in a kabuki production delighted its audience, the bunraku producers would incorporate it into their own productions.

The Final Stage　　　　　　　　　　　　　　　　完成期●

Gradually overshadowed by kabuki, bunraku went into a decline after the mid-18th century even though its performers attained new heights of artistry and skill. With the Japanese welcoming Western forms of theatrical art and developing their own "modern" theater, bunraku fared poorly in the competition to attract audiences. After Japan's defeat in World War II, bunraku languished as many Japanese turned away

from the traditional aspects of their own culture, and in the early 1960s it
tottered on the verge of commercial extinction. It has survived largely
with government support and the establishment of the National Theater
in Tokyo and the National Bunraku Theater in Osaka. Bunraku may
enjoy a mild revival because of a new appreciation of tradition among
younger Japanese, but its future is uncertain.

Traditional music (*hogaku*)   邦楽●

Term applied to the varieties of music performed in Japan in premodern times and to forms of such music that are played today.
Although archaeological materials and Chinese documents provide evidence of music in Japan as far back as the 3rd century BC, the traditional
history of Japanese music normally starts with the Nara period (710–794).
Japanese music had its roots in the music of Buddhism and the vibrant
traditions of Tang dynasty (618–907) China.

History   歴史●

Buddhism was established as an official court religion by the 6th
century, and its sounds and music theories became influential in Japan.
Chinese and Korean courts or monasteries were the sources and models
of most of the music in courts and temples but, because of the international dynamism of continental Asia from the 7th through the 10th
century, influences from South and Southeast Asia can be found as well.
The fact that Japan seemed to be "at the end of the line" in this cultural
diffusion is of particular interest, for many traditions remained in Japan
long after they had disappeared in the lands of their origins. The instrumental and dance repertoires of the court, generically known as GAGAKU,
reflect such origins in their classification into two categories: *togaku*,
pieces derived from Chinese or Indian sources, and *komagaku*, music
from Korea and Manchuria.

During the turbulent change from a court-dominated to a military-dominated culture at the end of the 12th century, more theatrical
genres of music became popular. The *biwa* (lute) of the court became the
accompaniment not only of itinerant priests and evangelists but also of
chanters who recited long historical tales, particularly the *Heike monogatari*. Pantomime theatricals at Buddhist temples and Shinto shrines
gradually combined in the 14th century with the rich heritage of folk theatricals to produce a new form known as NO drama. The 13-stringed *koto*
(zither) tradition is one of the few types of ancient courtly solo and chamber music that continued to develop in the 16th century, primarily in the

mansions of the rich or in temples. At first there were remnants of older traditions, but by the 17th century quite different koto pieces appeared, particularly in the new Ikuta school. The founding of the Yamada school in the 18th century further enriched the repertoire. Both these schools have continued to the present day, and their solo and chamber music form the basis of what most Japanese would consider to be their "classical" music. The end-blown *shakuhachi* (bamboo flute) also developed new schools of performance and repertory during this period, but it is the three-stringed plucked lute (*shamisen*) that best represents the new musical styles and new audiences of the 16th through the 19th century. By the 18th century the narrative tradition of the puppet theater (BUNRAKU) had become a major source of literature, which was performed by skilled chanters (*tayu*) with shamisen accompaniment. The KABUKI theater adopted some of this material for its own plays, but it also developed a combination of other genres of shamisen music plus the percussion and flute ensemble (*hayashi*) of the No, along with an eclectic assortment of folk and religious instruments. A logical outgrowth of an economically and socially supported theater music was the creation in the 19th century of compositions using theatrical genres and instruments but intended for dance recital or purely concert performances. The shamisen genre called *nagauta* was particularly active in this new field.

Musical Characteristics   音楽的特徴●

Most Japanese music shares with its East Asian counterparts a general tendency to be word-oriented. Except for the variation (*dammono*) pieces for the koto, Japanese traditional music has either a vocal part with text or a title that evokes some image. Instrumental genres differ widely in Japanese music, but the general concept of the Western chamber-music sound ideal seems to apply to almost all Japanese traditional ensembles over the past 1,200 years. No matter how large or small an ensemble may be, the tone color of the instruments combined is such that the sounds do not "melt" into a single experience as they do in some Western orchestral music.

Perhaps the most difficult aspect of traditional music for the inexperienced listener is that it is generally through-composed. It does not state a theme and then develop it as in the standard Western classical tradition. Instead it moves on to new musical ideas. What gives it a sense of logical progression is its conventions of form, which are stated most generally by the terms *jo*, *ha*, and *kyu* (introduction, scattering, rushing toward the finale). After becoming used to the music's reduced volume and activity, it is possible to begin to appreciate the artistry of "less action—more meaning". The challenge is to the flexibility of the listener, not the composer or performer.

Gagaku 雅楽●

Traditional music of the Japanese imperial court. The term derived from the Chinese word *yayue*, which denotes ancient ritual music played by a large orchestra of stone chimes, bronze bells, flutes, drums, and numerous other instruments. Gagaku comprises three main bodies of music: *togaku*, music said to be in the style of Tang dynasty (618–907) China; *komagaku*, a music style said to have been introduced from ancient Korea; and, finally, all of the many forms of native Japanese music associated with rituals of the Shinto religion.

The oldest and most carefully preserved of the various forms of Shinto ritual music and dance used in the imperial court is the *kagura*, formally called *mikagura* (court kagura) in order to distinguish it from the various folk forms of Shinto music that are also called kagura. Besides the mikagura, this group of Shinto ritual songs and dances includes the Yamato *uta*, Azuma *asobi*, and Kume *uta*. The mikagura is central to the Shinto ritual style, and the other three forms are in some way modeled on it. Also included in the gagaku repertoire are *saibara* (regional Japanese folk songs reset in an elegant court style), though only a small number of saibara compositions continue to be performed by court musicians.

History 歴史●

During the Nara period (710–794), a great number of styles of music existed, each with its own special musicians, dancers, and types of instruments. In the early Heian period (794–1185), the various styles of foreign music were combined into the togaku and komagaku categories and were performed both by the court nobles and by hereditary guilds of professional musicians. With the fall of the noble classes in the early part of the Kamakura period (1185–1333), the popularity of gagaku waned. It was maintained by guilds and the remaining nobles, each in relative isolation from the other. The guild musicians were divided into three groups and were in service in Kyoto, Nara, and Osaka.

After the Meiji Restoration of 1868 and the relocation of the Imperial Palace to Tokyo, the three groups were brought together as the official musicians of the newly established state. The musicians of the present-day Imperial Palace Music Department are still largely the direct descendants of the members of the first musicians' guilds that performed gagaku in Japan during the 8th century. They perform all the ritual

Gagaku stage at the Imperial Palace.

music and dances required by the court and also give regular public gagaku concerts.

Instruments   楽器●

The instruments used in performances of gagaku are Japanese modifications of those used in the Tang court ensembles. The instrumentation is determined by the type of music being performed. A small double-reed pipe similar to an oboe or shawm, called the *hichiriki*, is used in all the instrumental ensembles. Three different types of flute are used, the *kagurabue* generally for the Shinto rituals, the *komabue* for *komagaku*, and the *ryuteki* or dragon flute for togaku. In addition to these wind instruments, togaku uses a small mouth organ of 17 bamboo pipes called the *sho*, which plays tone clusters of 5 or 6 notes. Togaku and komagaku each use three percussion instruments, two of which are common to both types of music. These are a hanging *taiko*, or large drum, and the *shoko*, a small bronze gong. In komagaku there is also a small hourglass drum called *san no tsuzumi*, played with a single stick; the *kakko*, a small drum played with two sticks, is used in togaku. In Shinto vocal music, the only percussion instrument is a pair of wooden clappers (*shakubyoshi*). Stringed instruments are no longer used in the togaku dance repertoire or in komagaku, but two have been retained in the *kangen*, or chamber music setting of togaku: the *gakuso*, which is usually called by its common name, *koto*, and the biwa. Only one stringed instrument, the *wagon*, is used in Shinto music. The repertoire of gagaku music is played at tempos that, although varied, seem very slow when compared to Western music or even to other forms of Japanese music.

Rakugo   落語●

Popular form of comic monologue in which a storyteller (*rakugoka*) creates an imaginary drama through episodic narration and skillful use of vocal and facial expressions to portray various characters. Typically, the storyteller uses no scenery; the only musical accompaniment is the *debayashi*, a brief flourish of drum, *shamisen*, and bamboo flute that marks his entrance and exit. The storyteller, dressed in a plain *kimono*, crosses to stage center and seats himself on a cushion before his audience, with a hand towel and a fan as his only props. There he remains until he has delivered his final line, usually a punning punch line (*ochi*; literally, "the drop"). This is the characteristic ending from which the term rakugo was coined, the word being written with two Chinese characters meaning "drop" (J: *raku*, also pronounced *ochi*) and "word" (*go*).

In a rakugo performance the interplay between performer and audience is extremely important. Since the repertory of classic rakugo is small, aficionados have heard the basic story many times. They delight in the storyteller's particular version, his arrangement of familiar episodes, and appreciate his timing and the verisimilitude of the details he adds, such as the sound of sake as he pours it into his imaginary cup. The introduction to the story proper must be completely original. The plots of the stories are never as important as the characterizations in them, for rakugo pokes fun at all manner of human foibles.

By the early 1670s professional performers called *hanashika* had emerged. Tsuyu no Gorobei (1643–1703) from Kyoto and Yonezawa Hikohachi (d 1714) from Osaka are regarded as the forefathers of Kamigata (Kyoto-Osaka) rakugo, while Shikano Buzaemon (1649–1699) is credited with founding the Edo rakugo tradition, later perfected by San'yutei Encho.

A regular entertainment feature at roadside shows, private banquets, and makeshift stages set up at restaurants during off-hours, this vagabond art found a home in 1791 when the first permanent Japanese-style vaudeville theater, or *yose*, was opened in Edo (now Tokyo). Soon afterward the popularity of yose spread to Kyoto and Osaka.

After surviving the challenge of cinema in the 1920s and 1930s, which significantly reduced yose attendance, rakugo performers met with increasing official disapproval during World War II, because they did not adapt their material to complement national ideology.

With the resumption of civilian broadcasting at the end of World War II, rakugo recovered its popularity. Although the proliferation of new entertainment media has greatly reduced the number of yose, the adaptability of rakugo to both radio and television has ensured its survival. There are still four traditional yose in Tokyö, along with rakugo halls, larger and more expensive, where all-rakugo programs are presented for devotees, often on a monthly basis. Many universities also sponsor rakugo clubs whose members study and perform rakugo for their own entertainment.

Manzai 漫才●

Performing art in which a comic dialogue is carried on by two comedians. Said to have had its beginnings in the Nara period (710–794), manzai spread throughout Japan in the Edo period (1600–1868).

Toward the close of the Edo period, manzai was performed in makeshift theaters, and by the first decade of the 20th century its popularity, especially in Osaka, increased rapidly. After World War II, passing from the age of radio to that of television, manzai has continued to flourish. Today the repartee of manzai performers—the wit is now called *tsukkomi* and the straight man *boke*—is distinguished by its fast pace, its use of current events, and its swift shifts, often by bizarre association, from topic to topic.

Japanese Film (Nihon *eiga*) 日本映画●

The Japanese first imported motion pictures in 1896. By 1899 they were filming their own. Until the coming of talkies, movies in Japan were accompanied by a *benshi*, a live performer who sat by the side of the screen and orally interpreted the images of the film. Because benshi supplied expository connections and full dialogue, the first filmmakers replicated Japanese stage plays and generally ignored film techniques being developed in the West by such film directors as D. W. Griffith (1875–1948).

Early History 草創期●

Makino Shozo (1878–1929), the father of the Japanese period film, gradually dropped KABUKI elements from his costume dramas to concentrate on stories from juvenile literature and the traditional genre of oral storytelling known as *kodan*. Films with contemporary stories drew on the *shimpa* theatrical repertoire throughout the early 1900s. After World War I, would-be filmmakers, influenced by the ideals of *shingeki* ("new theater") and by the flood of movies from abroad, cried for "modernization and realism." They sought naturalistic acting and the casting of actresses instead of traditional *onnagata* (female impersonators), subject matter that stretched beyond the narrow range of shimpa and kabuki plays, and the adoption of expressive techniques seen in foreign films.

The First *Jidaigeki* and *Gendaigeki* 最初の時代劇と現代劇●

The early 1920s marked the emergence of jidaigeki (period films), the genre that encompasses all films set before the Meiji period (1868–1912). In 1924 Makino Shozo collaborated with the Shinkokugeki drama troupe in a movie version of its swashbuckling hit *Kunisada Chuji*. The head of Shinkokugeki, Sawada Shojiro (1892–1929), had earlier developed *chambara* (spectacular sword-fighting scenes) as the basis for his popular theater. The plays staged by Sawada were derived, in part, from the *taishu bungaku* (popular literature) movement that had originated a decade earlier in the sword-fighter novels of Nakazato Kaizan (1885–1944). Jidaigeki subsequently evolved over 60 years through a symbiotic relationship among literary, theater, and film works focused on swords and solitary heroes.

Gendaigeki, the other genre of the post-1920 Japanese cinema, encompasses all stories with modern settings. Until 1926 the only gendaigeki that outdrew jidaigeki at the box office were either adventure stories patterned after foreign serials or sentimental love stories based on popular songs. Meanwhile, former Hollywood actor Abe Yutaka (1895–1977) led an "Americanism" school with his "smart, modern, speedy" comedies. Mizoguchi Kenji (1898–1956), the most eclectic of early gendaigeki directors, drew on sources ranging from the German film *The Cabinet of Dr. Caligari* to traditional shimpa drama.

The Late 1920s and Early 1930s　　1920年代後半から1930年代前半まで●

The economic depression that hit Japan before 1929 engendered left-wing tendencies in literature, shingeki, and films. Nihilistic, egocentric swordsmen became fighting protectors of the downtrodden in jidaigeki. After the invasion of Manchuria in 1931, more stringent government censorship ended these mildly radical efforts. The cutting edge of jidaigeki moved to satire and comedy after Itami Mansaku's (1900–1946) *Kokushi muso* (1932, Peerless Patriot). The most important new direction for jidaigeki was initiated by Yamanaka Sadao (1909–1938) and Inagaki Hiroshi (1905–1980), who brought the slice-of-life, lower-class urban milieu of many gendaigeki to the period film. In gendaigeki, Shimazu Yasujiro (1897–1945), with his *Tonari no Yae-chan* (1934, Our Neighbor Miss Yae), turned toward stories focused on the small joys and passive endurance of the world. The works of Ozu Yasujiro (1903–1963) best reflected the continuing development of the *shoshimin geki*, "dramas about the petite bourgeoisie." For three years in a row, critics chose his stories of imperfect fathers—*Umarete wa mita keredo* (1932, I Was Born, But ...), *Dekigokoro* (1933, Passing Fancy), and *Ukigusa monogatari* (1934, A Story of Floating Weeds)—as the best pictures of their respective years.

The Talkies　　トーキー●

Gosho Heinosuke's (1902–1981) family comedy *Madamu to nyobo* (The Neighbor's Wife and Mine) was Japan's first technically successful talkie as well as the critical and popular success of 1931. Although talkies strained the capital resources of the industry (and drove the live benshi out of movie theaters), the innovation did not displace established film talent as it did abroad. Not until 1934–35 did talkies constitute more than half of all Japanese feature production.

The bulk of jidaigeki continued to be nihilistic chambara adventures. Several small studios survived throughout the 1930s by turning out cheap, silent jidaigeki for the surviving benshi market. Although feature production had risen to a steady average of 650 per year by the mid-1920s, the average annual output stabilized at 550 throughout the 1930s. Under wartime restraints this number suddenly decreased to 232 in 1941 and fell to 26 in 1945.

Censorship, the War, and the Postwar Era　検閲および第二次世界大戦から終戦直後まで●

Film censorship was consolidated under the control of the national Police Bureau (Keihokyoku) of the Home Ministry in 1925 and gradually tightened during the 1930s. In 1939 the Home Ministry ordered filmmakers to follow its list of essential "national policy" subjects, which accented patriotic home life and sacrifice for the nation. Despite strong official encouragement, fewer than one-fifth of all wartime features complied with government guidelines. Fewer than 2 percent of all films produced between the 1937 start of war in China and the 1945 surrender of Japan were stories about the military.

The American Occupation abolished Home Ministry censorship and set up its own office to supervise film content. In 1949 Occupation authorities eased their controls in return for the industry's establishment of a self-regulatory body, the Motion Picture Code Committee (Eirin), which administered a production code patterned after Hollywood's. Japanese cinema was without official, formal censorship and within a year sword fighting was back.

After disrupting production for two years, striking union militants occupied the Toho studios in 1948. Japanese police, aided by American tanks, quickly quashed the strike. Activists quit Toho and began to make a scattering of low-budget, independent features that had a defiant leftist sensibility long missing from the Japanese cinema. In 1947, during the union turmoil, a large anticommunist faction left the parent Toho company to establish Shin Toho as the fourth major studio of the postwar period. (The two major studios in the late 1930s were Shochiku and the parent Toho company. In 1942, the government had engineered the amalgamation of the faltering Nikkatsu company with two lesser studios to create the third major studio, Daiei). Two small postwar studios combined in 1951 to produce the fifth major studio, Toei. A new Nikkatsu production company, with no connection to Daiei, became the sixth major studio in 1953. The six major studios controlled the industry through a cartel-like hold on film distribution and exhibition. The number of movie theaters reached an all-time high of 7,457 in 1960. This was 8.8 times as many as when the war ended. Two men whose directing careers had begun during

Film director Kurosawa Akira.

the war came to the forefront during the early Occupation era: Kurosawa Akira (1910–) and Kinoshita Keisuke (1912–). Along with two other directors of their generation, Imai Tadashi (1912–1991) and Yoshimura Kozaburo (1911–), they dominated the 1947–1950 period with films about postwar life.

The 1950s 1950年代●

The decade of the 1950s, apart from being the most prosperous in the history of the Japanese cinema, is considered by many to be its creative Golden Age. Five times during this decade critics voted a film by Imai the best of the year, a streak that began with *Mata au hi made* (1950, Until the Day We Meet Again). When Kurosawa's innovative *jidaigeki Rashomon* (1950) won the top prize at the Venice Film Festival in 1951, it opened the Japanese cinema to international audiences. Kurosawa's cosmopolitan style alternated between such social issue–oriented gendaigeki as *Ikiru* (1952, To Live) and such seminal jidaigeki epics as *Shichinin no samurai* (1954, *Seven Samurai*).

Kurosawa's rival for international attention, Mizoguchi, abandoned his early postwar love stories to refashion the period film with such exquisite works as *Saikaku ichidai onna* (1952, The Life of a Woman by Saikaku; shown abroad as *The Life of Oharu*) and *Ugetsu monogatari* (1953, *Ugetsu*). Starting with *Banshun* (1949, Late Spring), Ozu Yasujiro and his scenarist Noda Kogo (1893–1968) concentrated on the emotional complexities of middle-class family life, while Naruse Mikio (1905–1969) and Gosho Heinosuke continued the prewar *shoshimin geki* tradition. Naruse later turned to a new major interest: portraits of women fighting the domination of men in such films as *Ukigumo* (1955, Floating Clouds). Gosho's major work was *Entotsu no mieru basho* (1953, Where Chimneys Are Seen).

Comedy grew in sophistication. Shibuya Minoru (1907–1980) perfected the well-wrought farce in *Honjitsu kyushin* (1952, Clinic Closed Today), Kawashima Yuzo (1918–1963) created the definitive postwar jidaigeki comedy in *Bakumatsu taiyo den* (1957, A Tale of the Sun during the Last Days of the Shogunate), and Ichikawa Kon (1915–) pioneered black humor in *Kagi* (1959, The Key; shown abroad as *Odd Obsession*). The new Toei company captured a large new audience for jidaigeki by creating young chambara stars, and it also backed jidaigeki old masters: Ito Daisuke (1898–1981), Uchida Tomu (1898–1970), and Makino Masahiro (1908–1993). Toho and Daiei countered Toei with their own brands of jidaigeki program pictures, while they supported new directions for period films by Kurosawa, Mizoguchi, and Inagaki. To strengthen its principal market among urban, middle-class audiences, Toho made pop

Film director Ozu Yasujiro.

musicals and dozens of comedies about middle-aged white-collar workers. In 1954 Toho created Japan's first film monster in *Godzilla (Gojira)*. A horde of Toho and Daiei monsters followed for two decades. Kinoshita's *Karumen kokyo ni kaeru* (Carmen Comes Home) inaugurated a decade of technical innovation in 1951 with the first Japanese color feature. Three years later Kinugasa Teinosuke's (1896–1982) *Jigokumon* (1953, Gate of Hell) won the highest international acclaim for innovative use of color. Anamorphic wide-screen features appeared in 1957, but it took more than seven years for the new frame dimensions to become standard in Japan. In the late 1950s, a new short-lived genre, *taiyozoku* (sun tribe) films, so called after a group of young people portrayed in the best-selling novel *Taiyo no kisetsu* (1955, Season of the Sun; tr *Season of Violence*, 1966) by Ishihara Shintaro (1932–), exploited the hedonism of affluent postwar youth. This accelerated interest in movie sex and violence.

Television and a New Wave   テレビとニューウェーブ

In 1958, five years after television broadcasting had begun, there were 1.6 million television sets throughout the country. By 1969 there were 21.9 million sets, a figure almost equal to the number of households. Attendance at the movies fell from the all-time high of 1.1 billion in 1958 to 300 million in 1968. The Shin Toho studios went bankrupt in 1961. Half of the movie theaters in the country closed during the 1960s.

In 1958 Masumura Yasuzo (1924–1986) called for the destruction of the established Japanese cinema and soon was joined by other young directors. Oshima Nagisa (1932–) demanded an end to lyricism, heaviness, naturalism, *mono no aware*, and the omnipotent conventions of the international cinema of realism. Oshima and two tradition-breaking fellow directors at Shochiku, Shinoda Masahiro (1931–) and Yoshida Yoshishige (1933–), were dubbed the "Shochiku Nuberu Bagu" (*nouvelle vague*, or new wave). Oshima's Brechtian *Koshikei* (1968, Death by Hanging) and *Shinjuku dorobo nikki* (1969, Diary of a Shinjuku Thief) established him as the principal new talent of the cosmopolitan 1960s. Imamura Shohei (1926–) rivaled Oshima with a call to destroy the illusionistic pretensions of fiction and documentary films. Imamura searched for clues to Japanese national identity in the pseudobiography *Nippon konchuki* (1963, Story of a Japanese Insect; shown abroad as *The Insect Woman*) and the modern primitive myth *Kamigami no fukaki yokubo* (1968, The Profound Desire of the Gods; shown abroad as *Kuragejima: Tales from a Southern Island*).

Film director Oshima Nagisa.

In jidaigeki, major directors looked occasionally to the classical theater. Kurosawa adapted elements from the No theater to his syncretic

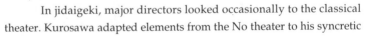

version of Macbeth, *Kumonosujo* (1957, Throne of Blood). Uchida Tomu in *Naniwa no koi no monogatari* (1959, Naniwa Love Story) and Shinoda Masahiro in *Shinju Ten no Amijima* (1969, Love Suicide at Amijima; Double Suicide) used plays by Chikamatsu Monzaemon (1653–1724) and borrowed respectively from kabuki and *bunraku* drama. In 1963 Toei originated a new direction for ultraviolent chambara: the *yakuza* (gangster) genre. The plots of these films were invariably formalistic variations of intricate *giri-ninjo* sword-fighting dramas, portraying a righteous gangster amid low-life corruption in prewar Japan. The immediate popularity of Toei yakuza pictures soon wiped out jidaigeki as the main arena for chambara.

Since the Late 1970s　　　　　　　　1970年代後半以降●

The dominant director of the 1970s was a major-studio man, Yamada Yoji (1931–) of Shochiku. Although his principal works were prize-winning portraits of lower-class family life, his overwhelmingly popular success was the *Tora san* series. Beginning in 1969 and continuing for more than two decades, Yamada has written and directed more than 40 films in this series, which fuses the two bedrock motifs of Japanese film: the everyday collective life of a family and the adventures of a lonely wanderer.

Film director Yamada Yoji.

From the late 1960s most major directors as well as promising newcomers could not depend on the studios for employment. As independents, they had to raise money bit by bit themselves. After 1985, cash-heavy Japanese companies (including media conglomerates but not the poor movie studios) were backing Broadway shows and Hollywood movies. By the time Sony bought Columbia Pictures in 1989 as an investment in American, not Japanese, filmmaking, Oshima, Kurosawa, Shinoda, and Itami Juzo (1933–) were looking abroad for production funds.

Comedies dominated Japanese film production in the 1980s, especially Itami's satires *Tampopo* (1985, Dandelion) and *Marusa no onna* (1988, A Taxing Woman). Exceptions are the serious films of Oguri Kohei (1945–), who won the jury prize at the 1990 Cannes Film Festival for *Shi no toge* (1990, The Sting of Death). By 1990 total annual movie admissions had declined to 143 million in a market now dominated by American blockbusters; the number of theaters decreased to about 1,900, and overall annual feature production dwindled to 239.

Culture

Language

Japanese language (*nihongo*) 日本語●

The native language of the overwhelming majority of the more than 100 million inhabitants of the Japanese archipelago, including the Ryukyu Islands, and significant numbers of Japanese immigrants in other countries, especially in North and South America.

Although the Japanese and Chinese languages are entirely unrelated genetically, the Japanese writing system derives from that of Chinese. Chinese characters were introduced sometime in the 6th century, if not before, and the modern writing system is a complex one in which Chinese characters are used in conjunction with two separate phonetic scripts developed from them in Japan. Japanese has also absorbed loanwords freely from other languages, especially Chinese and English, the former chiefly from the 8th to the 19th century and the latter in the 20th century.

Genetic Relationships 起源●

Some scholars have maintained that no genetic relationship of Japanese to any known language can be demonstrated. However, the syntactic similarity of Japanese to Korean is widely acknowledged, as is its resemblance in certain respects to the Altaic languages in general. The situation is complicated by similarities in vocabulary between Japanese and the Malayo-Polynesian languages. There seems to be a growing consensus among Japanese scholars that syntactically Japanese shows an Altaic affinity, but that at some time in its prehistory it received an influence in vocabulary and morphology from the Malayo-Polynesian languages to the south.

The Japanese Dialects and the Speech of Tokyo 方言と東京弁●

Modern Japanese language has a large number of local dialects, existing alongside, but gradually being overwhelmed by, the officially recognized standard language (*hyojungo*), which is based on the speech of the capital, Tokyo. The Japanese dialects, however, show less variety in syntax and morphology than do the strong regional languages of Italy, for example, or Austria.

Two important urban dialects that flourish alongside the standard language of Tokyo are those of the cities of Kyoto and Osaka. Kyoto was the imperial capital for more than 1,000 years, and, though it was not always the seat of real political or economic power, both it and its language continued to have the highest prestige. The language of its court nobility during the Heian period (794–1185) as preserved in the literary works of that period became the basis of Classical Japanese, which remained the standard for the written language until the beginning of the 20th century. During the Edo period (1600–1868), Edo (now Tokyo), which was the seat of the Tokugawa Shogunate, grew into an important commercial and administrative city. Both it and the older commercial city of Osaka became thriving centers of the culture and language of the merchant classes (*chonin*), and the language of Edo in particular—the locus of political power and the home of the *samurai* bureaucracy—gradually developed a prestige of its own. When Edo was renamed Tokyo and made the new imperial capital, the language of its educated elite was gradually systematized and transformed. Incorporated into this language were a number of expressions from the language of the nobility from Kyoto. The resulting mixture became what is now the standard language, sometimes loosely referred to as "the Tokyo dialect."

The Phonology of the Standard Language   標準語の音韻●

The short or unit vowels of standard Japanese, *a, i, u, e,* and *o,* are pronounced more or less as in Spanish or Italian. (In this description the phonemes of Japanese will be written in the standard Hepburn romanization, phonetic symbols being added only when necessary for clarity.) The long vowels, *â, ii, û, ei,* and *ô,* are pronounced double the length of the short vowels (*a:, i:, u:, e:,* and *o:*), except that *ei* is often pronounced as a sequence of two separate vowels. The distinction between long and short vowels is essential for meaning. Aside from *ei,* sequences of vowels such as *ai, au, ae, oi, ue,* and so forth are so pronounced that the individual vowels retain their identity, although a glide often occurs; they are treated as separate syllables.

The consonants are *k, s, sh, t, ch, ts, n, h, f, m, y, r, w, g, j, z, d, b,* and *p.* The fricative *sh* (as in English "shoe") and the affricates *ch, ts,* and *j* (as in English "church," "patsy," and "judge," respectively) are treated as single consonants. *G* is always pronounced as in English "good" (never as in "genetics"). The rest are pronounced more or less as in English except that *f* is a bilabial rather than labiodental fricative, *r* is flapped, and *t, d,* and *n* are dental. When *n* is used at the end of a syllable as opposed to the beginning, it expresses a uvular syllabic nasal "N"; this changes to

The Japanese Syllabaries (*gojuon zu*)
五十音図

あ ア a	か カ ka	さ サ sa	た タ ta	な ナ na	は ハ ha	ま マ ma	や ヤ ya	ら ラ ra	わ ワ wa	ん ン n
い イ i	き キ ki	し シ shi	ち チ chi	に ニ ni	ひ ヒ hi	み ミ mi	い イ i	り リ ri	ゐ ヰ i	
う ウ u	く ク ku	す ス su	つ ツ tsu	ぬ ヌ nu	ふ フ fu	む ム mu	ゆ ユ yu	る ル ru	う ウ u	
え エ e	け ケ ke	せ セ se	て テ te	ね ネ ne	へ ヘ he	め メ me	え エ e	れ レ re	ゑ ヱ e	
お オ o	こ コ ko	そ ソ so	と ト to	の ノ no	ほ ホ ho	も モ mo	よ ヨ yo	ろ ロ ro	を ヲ o	

Note: In each box the *hiragana* character is on top with the corresponding *katakana* character below.

Culture

one of three different types of nasals when followed by certain consonants: *n* (dental) before *t*, *d*, or *n*; (velar, as in English "thank") before *k* or *g*; and *m* (bilabial) before *p*, *b*, or *m*. The older Hepburn spelling used in this book reflects the last named of these pronunciations by changing *n* to *m* before *p*, *b*, or *m* as in *san* (three) versus *sammai* (three sheets); however, the modified Hepburn romanization used in many recent publications retains the *n* in all cases (*sanmai*). When followed by a vowel or *y*, this syllable-final *n* must be distinguished from syllable-initial *n*. In this book an apostrophe is used after the former for this purpose (e.g., *jin'in* "personnel" as opposed to *jinin* "resignation"). In the double consonants, *-kk-*, *-pp-*, *-tt-*, and *-ss-*, and in the combinations *-ssh-* and *-tch-* (all of which are always medial) the consonants are pronounced—without release but with, in effect, a short interval of silence—much as in the English "bookcase," "shirttail," and "hatcheck."

Japanese has no stress accent like that of English. Each syllable is given equal stress, successions of syllables being pronounced with metronomic regularity. Standard Japanese and a number of the dialects do have, however, a high-low pitch accent system, accent in a word or sequence of words being marked by the syllable after which the pitch drops. The way in which the same word (or the same set of contrasting homophones) is accented can differ significantly among those dialects that have pitch accents.

Another characteristic of standard Japanese is the strong tendency to devoice the vowels *i* and *u* when they fall between two voiceless consonants, so that *shitakusa* (undergrowth) becomes *sh'tak'sa*. The vowels are not always dropped entirely, however: often they are sounded faintly, or at least their metronomic beat preserved. The vowel *u* at the end of a word after a voiceless consonant is also often devoiced or dropped, most notably in *desu*, the polite form of the copula, and in the polite verb ending *-masu*, which are often pronounced *des'* and *mas'*, respectively.

The Grammar of Modern Japanese　　　　　　　現代日本語の文法●

Nouns（名詞）Japanese nouns are uninflected words that have neither number nor gender and do not influence the inflection of the adjectives modifying them.

In Japanese the grammatical function of nouns within a sentence is not indicated by word order as in English; neither are nouns inflected for grammatical case as in some languages. Instead grammatical function is indicated by grammatical particles (sometimes called postpositions), which follow the noun. Among the more important of these are *ga*, *o*, *ni*, and *no*, which function as case markers, *ga* indicating subject of verb, *o* direct object of verb, *ni* dative or indirect object, and *no* genitive. For example, in *kaze ga fuku* (the wind blows/will blow), *ga* marks *kaze* as the subject of the verb *fuku*; in *kodomo ga tomodachi no inu ni mizu o yaru* (the child gives/will give water to his/her friend's dog), *ga* marks *kodomo* (child) as the subject of the verb *yaru*, *no* marks *tomodachi* (friend) as possessor of *inu* (dog), *ni* marks *inu* as indirect object, and *o* marks *mizu* (water) as direct object of the verb. A particularly important particle is *wa*. This is not a case marker but rather marks the topic or theme of the sentence. In *zo wa hana ga nagai* (elephants have long noses; literally, "as for elephants, the nose is long"), *wa* marks *zo* (elephant/elephants) as the topic of the sentence and *ga* marks *hana* (nose/noses) as the subject of the adjective *nagai* (is long). All of these particles also have various other functions and meanings depending on grammatical structure and context. There are a number of other postpositions that function much as prepositions do in English.

Verbs (動詞) Japanese verbal inflections do not indicate person or number. The dictionary forms of all verbs in the modern language end in the vowel -*u*. When citing the dictionary form of Japanese verbs in English, it is conventional to refer to them by the English infinitive; thus *kaku* is often cited as "to write," although this form is actually the present (more precisely the nonpast) tense, which means "write/writes" or "will write." Other inflectional forms include *kakanai* (negative: "does not/will not write"), *kako* (tentative or hortatory: "someone may write"; "let's write"), *kakitai* (often called "desiderative": "wants to write"), *kaita* (past: "wrote"), *kakeba* (provisional or conditional: "if someone writes"), and *kake* (nonpolite imperative: "write!"). Verbs can be used not only to form the predicate of a sentence or clause but also attributively to modify nouns (e.g., *kaku hito*, "the person who writes").

Verb conjugations are classified in two main types. One of these consists of the consonant-stem verbs (verbs whose stems end in consonants), including verbs such as *kaku* (write), *hanasu* (talk), and *utsu* (hit), whose stems are *kak-*, *hanas-*, and *uts-*, respectively (as mentioned above, ts is treated as a single consonant). The other type comprises the vowel-stem verbs, which are themselves of two types, with stems ending in either the vowel *i* or the vowel *e*; e.g., *miru* (see) and *taberu* (eat), whose stems are *mi-* and *tabe-*, respectively. (The dictionary forms of vowel-stem verbs all end in -*iru* or -*eru*; however, not all verbs so ending are vowel-stem verbs. Some are consonant-stem verbs with stems ending in r; e.g., *kiru* "cut"). In modern Japanese there are two fully conjugated irregular verbs, *kuru* (come) and *suru* (do), bringing the total number of standard verb conjugations to five.

The copula (連辞)   The Japanese copula or linking verb (plain form *da*; polite form *desu*) is used to link two nouns (or nominal phrases) in the pattern A *wa* B *da* or A *wa* B *desu* (A is B). The literal meaning of this pattern is "as for A, it is B" or "as for A, it is in the category of B," e.g., *neko wa dobutsu da* (cats are animals; literally, "as for cats, they are animals"). For this reason the Japanese copula cannot always be translated by the English "to be." For example, *watakushi wa biru desu* does not mean "I am beer" but "I am having beer" (literally, "as for me, it is beer").

Adjectives (形容詞)   Japanese adjectives are inflected in some ways like verbs, and like verbs they can function either attributively, coming before the nouns they modify, or as the predicates of sentences or clauses, in the latter case appearing at the end of the sentence or clause. The dictionary forms of all adjectives end in one of four vowels (*a*, *i*, *u*, or *o*) followed by a final *i*. The stem of the adjective is obtained by dropping the final *i*; e.g., *takai* (high; stem *taka*), *utsukushii* (beautiful; stem *utsukushi*), *samui* (cold; stem *samu*), and *shiroi* (white; stem *shiro*).

Levels of speech (話法)   Japanese expresses a consciousness of social relationships by various grammatical means. Plain versus polite verb forms distinguish between easy informality and abruptness on the one hand and a correct, neutral politeness on the other. In the system of levels known as HONORIFIC LANGUAGE (*keigo*), the speaker chooses among a number of alternative ways of saying the same thing, the choice being determined by such factors as relative age, sex, and social status. One uses respectful or exalting forms with reference to an addressee or third person of higher status and humble terms with reference to oneself or a third person who falls into the same category as oneself.

Some actions often referred to in social situations, such as "go," "come," "be," "say," "look," "eat," "give," and "receive," are represented by sets of three completely different verbs, one neutral, one humble, and one exalting. There are also sets of humble and exalting nouns for common kinship terms, and so forth. The passive forms of verbs are also often used as honorific verbs (with active meaning) when referring to actions of the exalted.

The sentence (文)   The typical Japanese sentence is built on the pattern of subject-object-verb (SOV), as in *neko ga nezumi o tsukamaeta* (the cat caught the mouse). However, since the particle *ga* marks *neko* (cat) as the subject, and the particle *o* marks *nezumi* (mouse) as the object of the verb *tsukamaeta*, a certain amount of inversion, as for stylistic purposes, is possible; *nezumi o neko ga tsukamaeta* (OSV) would have virtually the same meaning as the SOV sentence, whereas in English such inversion of subject and object would change the meaning entirely. To return to the basic SOV sentence, if an adverbial modifier, for instance *subayaku* (swiftly), is inserted, it may come before the subject, the object, or the verb, with slight differences of emphasis.

There are no relative pronouns in Japanese as in the English "the cat that caught the mouse died." In Japanese the entire subordinate clause is placed directly in front of the noun as a modifier: *nezumi o tsuka-maeta neko ga shinda* (literally, "the caught-the-mouse cat died"). A sentence can also be made into a subordinate clause in another sentence by inserting either the nominalizing particle *no* (not to be confused with the genitive particle *no* mentioned earlier) or the function word *koto* (thing; matter) after the final verb of the sentence, which then modifies the particle, forming a noun clause.

Vocabulary (語彙) Japanese has an extremely rich and varied vocabulary, not only its large stock of native words, which are felt to be particularly expressive and sonorous, but also a great quantity of words of Chinese origin. To these are added the many LOANWORDS from English and other European languages that have come into Japanese, especially during the 20th century. Many of the loanwords from Chinese have been so thoroughly absorbed into the daily vocabulary that their foreign origin is no longer felt. Much of the intellectual and philosophical vocabulary is of Chinese origin, but not all of this is due entirely to Chinese cultural influence; an important part of the modern intellectual vocabulary consists of words coined in Japan in the late 19th and early 20th centuries by devising new combinations of Chinese characters as translations of concepts then being introduced from the West. This process of coinage still continues, but there is a growing tendency, particularly in the sciences, to use Western words intact. Aside from the sciences, words are often used with meanings quite different from those of their original languages, and new Japanese words are sometimes coined by combining parts of Western language words in startling ways. One particularly interesting feature of the native Japanese vocabulary is the large number of established onomatopoeic words it contains. These include not only words imitating sounds but also words expressing abstract qualities or subjective feelings.

Writing System   文字●

The Japanese writing system uses Chinese characters (KANJI) in combination with two separate forms of the phonetic syllabic script known as KANA: *hiragana* and *katakana*. Some words are written entirely in kana, others entirely in Chinese characters, and others in a combination of the two. In the latter case the stem of the word is written with a Chinese character, or characters, and inflectional endings or other suffixes with kana. Grammatical particles and function words (such as demonstratives and auxiliary verbs) are written in kana. The resulting text is sometimes sprinkled with Roman letters (e.g., acronyms such as PTA, model numbers, and occasionally entire foreign words), so that the number of scripts needed to write modern Japanese actually comes to four.

There are 1,945 Chinese characters in the *joyo kanji*, the list approved by the government for use in publications for the general public and for writing personal names. There are an additional 284 characters approved for writing names alone. The joyo kanji are learned (or at least taught) by the end of the ninth grade. Kanji in scholarly publications may exceed the government guidelines. Tens of thousands of kanji are contained in large dictionaries; however, the number of characters in actual use probably did not exceed 5,000 or 6,000 even before the post–World War II language reforms that led to adoption of the government-approved list.

Most Chinese characters have more than one pronunciation or "reading." There are two types: *on* readings and *kun* readings. The former are the pronunciations that result when characters are used to write Chinese loanwords. They reflect an original Chinese pronunciation of the character, but as pronounced in Japan. Some characters have two or three possible on readings, reflecting loanwords brought in from different parts of China or in different historical periods. *Kun* readings are native Japanese words that have the same meaning as the character (or more precisely, the Chinese morpheme the character represents); they are, in effect, the Japanese words that the character stands for.

Japanese is normally written or printed in vertical lines reading from top to bottom, with the lines starting at the right-hand side of the page and proceeding across from right to left.

Kana 仮名●

General term for a number of syllabic writing systems developed in Japan, all based on Chinese characters (KANJI), used to express the sounds of Japanese rather than the meanings of individual words.

Since kana can express all the sounds of Japanese, the language can be written entirely in kana. However, the normal practice is to use a mixture of Chinese characters and kana; the Chinese characters are used to express the meanings of most words (from which the pronunciation can be inferred) and the kana to write inflectional endings, grammatical particles, and certain words officially designated not to be written in characters (see JAPANESE LANGUAGE). Two sets of kana are used in the present-day Japanese writing system: *hiragana*, a cursive form (and the one commonly used for native words and any words of Chinese origin not to be written in characters), and *katakana*, a noncursive form. The latter can be used in place of hiragana, but it is most typically used to write loanwords from other languages, for emphasis, or for representation of onomatapoeic words, thus performing functions similar to the use of italics in Western orthography. Both katakana and hiragana derive from an earlier set of kana known as *man'yogana*, and hiragana in particular derives from the cursive form of man'yogana known as *sogana*.

cursive

Man'yogana   万葉仮名●

Man'yogana are a set of unmodified Chinese characters that were once used as phonetic symbols to represent Japanese syllables. As the name suggests, man'yogana was the writing system used in the *Man'yoshu*, an 8th-century poetry anthology. Most attempts to write Japanese prior to the Heian period (794–1185) fall into the category of man'yogana.

The man'yogana differs from the two currently used kana systems in at least three important aspects. First, there is no one-to-one relationship between syllables and characters. There were 87 syllable types in 8th-century Japanese, but more than 970 Chinese characters were used to write them. Second, the Chinese characters were used as written in Chinese, without modification or simplification. For this reason a text written in man'yogana superficially resembles a text in Chinese; however, because many of the characters are used only for their pronunciation and not for their meaning and because the language represented is Japanese, the text is likely to be unintelligible to a Chinese reader. Third, the types of character pronunciation represented in man'yogana are more varied than in hiragana and katakana, including the *on* reading and *kun* reading of the character.

Katakana   片仮名●

In its modern, standard form, katakana is a system of 48 syllabic writing units for writing non-Chinese loanwords, onomatopoeia, emphasized words, and the names of flora and fauna. The *kata* in katakana means "partial," "not whole," "fragmentary." It is so named because many of the katakana are a part and not the whole of a Chinese character.

In its earlier stages, katakana was used as a mnemonic device for pronouncing Buddhist tests written in Chinese. Next appeared Japanese texts written in a mixture of Chinese characters and katakana. This writing system is called *kanamajiri bun* (sentences mixing kana and characters). By the middle of the 10th century, anthologies of Japanese verse (WAKA) came to be written in katakana and by the 12th century collections of folktales came to be written in a mixture of Chinese characters and katakana.

Hiragana 平仮名●

In its modern, standard form, hiragana is a system of 48 syllabic writing units for writing indigenous Japanese words and often for Chinese loanwords that cannot be written with the 1,945 characters officially approved for general use. *Hira* means "commonly used," "easy," "rounded." Hiragana is so named because the letters are considered rounded and easy to write compared with the full forms of the original Chinese characters. In its early forms hiragana was used by women, while the unsimplified Chinese characters were used by men; for this reason, the earliest hiragana was also called *onnade* (women's hand). By the end of the 9th century onnade ceased to be a system limited to women and became an accepted device for recording poems. Hiragana gained full acceptance when the imperial poetic anthology *Kokin wakashu* (905) was written in onnade.

Kanji (Chinese characters) 漢字●

Ideographs of ancient Chinese origin that are still used in China, Korea, and Japan and were formerly used in other areas influenced by Chinese culture such as Vietnam. Chinese characters are ideographs in that essentially each character or graph symbolizes a single idea and, by extension, the sound (i.e., spoken word or morpheme) associated with that idea. For example, the Chinese character is "dog" in English, *quan* in modern standard Chinese, and *ken* or *inu* in Japanese.

On and Kun Readings 音読みと訓読み●

Since in the Japanese writing system Chinese characters can be used to write either words of Chinese origin or native Japanese words, the pronunciations that can be assigned to them in reading fall naturally into two categories: (1) the Japanese imitations or approximations of the sound of the original Chinese syllable and (2) the native Japanese word that translates the meaning of the character. The former are called on readings (*on yomi*), on being written with a character that means "sound" (i.e., the original Chinese sound); these are often referred to as "Sino-Japanese" readings in English. The latter are called kun readings (*kun yomi*), kun being written with a character that originally meant "to interpret the meaning" (i.e., the meaning of the character as expressed by the Japanese word).

Number of Characters in Use　　　　一般に使われている漢字の数●

The number of Chinese characters currently used in Japan is limited to a small percentage of the 40,000 to 50,000 contained in the larger dictionaries. A list of characters called *toyo kanji* (Chinese characters for daily use) was selected by the Ministry of Education in 1946, limiting the number of characters for official and general public use to 1,850. In 1981 this list was superseded by a similar but larger one (the *joyo kanji*) containing 1,945 characters.

Honorific language (*keigo*)　　　　敬語●

Often referred to in English as "polite speech" or "honorifics." The Japanese language has an extensive system of honorific language to show respect by the speaker to the addressee. Keigo in the broad sense refers to the entire system of speech levels. In its narrow sense keigo means "terms of respect" and refers to honorific words and expressions. In speaking, a choice is made as to the degree of politeness to be expressed. Depending on the status of the speaker relative to the addressee and on the context of the conversation, a simple question can be phrased in as many as two dozen different ways.

Choice of Speech Style　　　　話法の選択●

The speech style adopted in any two-person interaction is basically determined by the status of the speaker and the addressee and the degree of intimacy between them. The general rule is that when the addressee is of higher status than the speaker, or when the two are not very intimate, the polite style (with *desu-masu* verb forms) is to be used. Relative status is determined by a combination of factors, such as age, sex, rank, or social status and favors done or owed. Observance of the status hierarchy is particularly strict within an in-group situation. Being members of the same club or working in the same section of the company results in greater intimacy than otherwise. In general, however, status superiority supersedes intimacy in the above cases, and the junior-ranking person normally is expected to use the polite style of speech in addressing friends or colleagues of a slightly higher status. In the reverse case, where the speaker is of higher status in an in-group situation, the speaker has a choice of plain (with da verb forms) or polite style. The choice depends partly on how great the status difference is and partly on the personal preference of the person of higher status. When two individuals who do not belong to the same group meet for the first time, both individuals will use the polite style unless there are some obvious differences in age or social status as reflected in dress, manner, or occupation.

The speech style chosen by women is often a step politer than that selected by men. Women are not as likely to speak in the plain style to a junior-ranking adult as men are. They tend to use the polite style much more widely and indiscriminately, restricting the use of the plain style to immediate family members, close friends, and children.

Types of Honorifics 敬語の種類●

The final verb phrase of the sentence that differentiates the speech styles is only one aspect of keigo. There are innumerable other honorifics to be found in various parts of speech, including nouns, pronouns, verbs, adjectives, adverbs, and conjunctions. These honorifics, also referred to as keigo, are normally classified into three groups: *sonkeigo* (exalted terms), *kenjogo* (humble terms), and *teineigo* (polite terms). Exalted terms are used to refer to the addressee and anything directly associated with the addressee, such as kin, house, or possessions, while humble terms are used to refer to the speaker and anything associated with the speaker. By elevating the addressee through exalted terms and lowering the speaker through humble terms, a greater distance is created between the two, thereby expressing deeper respect for the addressee. Exalted terms are also used to refer to a third person of higher status if he is not a member of the speaker's in-group. Teineigo or polite terms are used without reference to the addressee or speaker and are found in increasing numbers as the speech level goes up.

The give-receive verbs play an important role in the keigo system. These verbs are used as main verbs in describing the giving and receiving of gifts and as auxiliary verbs in compound verb phrases to express the giving and receiving of actions done as a favor. The rules in using the give-receive verbs are complex, and group membership becomes an important factor.

In comparison with verbs, honorific nouns are relatively simple. There are underived exalted and humble nouns, but the majority of these are used in writing. Most exalted nouns are created through grammatical rules. In general, the prefix *o-* is attached to neutral nouns of Japanese origin, such as *oniwa* (garden), *otegami* (letter); and the prefix *go-* to Chinese compounds, such as *gobyoki* (illness), *goiken* (opinion). In the case of nouns referring to people, *-san* is suffixed in addition to the prefix o-, such as *otetsudaisan* (maid), *oishasan* (doctor).

Rules exist for the use of keigo in referring to a third person, as well as for first- and second-person pronouns. The result is an all-pervasive system that allows for fine gradations in the level of politeness within each speech style.

Loanwords (*gairaigo*)   外来語●

Foreign loanwords and phrases that are extensively used in Japanese and normally written in the *katakana* syllabary are called gairaigo. Loanwords from China are not normally treated as gairaigo, since they are not only numerous but written in Chinese characters and hence are not easily distinguishable from native words. The most important *gairaigo* are American and European loanwords.

Foreign words were introduced along with new things and new ideas from foreign cultures; many of these, such as the large number of technical terms, had no adequate Japanese equivalent. Even when Japanese had equivalent expressions, foreign words were in many cases employed for their novelty or the sense of prestige they gave the speaker. A foreign word is often substituted as a euphemism for a Japanese word, as in the case of "WC" and *toire* (from "toilet").

The earliest foreign loanwords, many from Sanskrit, Ainu, or Korean, are hardly recognized as such by present-day Japanese speakers. Most of them are written in Chinese characters rather than katakana. Many were introduced quite early in Japanese history and often refer to things closely associated with everyday Japanese life. After the arrival of the Portuguese in 1543, Christian and commercial terms were borrowed from Portuguese.

The Spanish also entered Japan about the same time as the Portuguese, but the number of Spanish words that remained in Japanese is limited. The Dutch arrived in 1600 and continued to have limited access to Japan even during National Seclusion, bringing a number of Dutch words into the language.

In the late Edo period (1600–1868), English, French, and Russian words began to arrive. At present English loanwords outnumber all others; among the countless examples are *sutoraiki* (labor strike), *depato* (department store), and *kare raisu* (curried rice). French words are especially numerous in fashion, cooking, foreign affairs, and politics. Russian has supplied words for foods and things Russian. After Japan reopened to foreign countries in the second half of the 19th century, a great number of German words also entered. They are most numerous in medicine and the humanities and among mountaineering and skiing terms. Italian words were also introduced beginning in the Meiji period (1868–1912), especially for music and food.

Feminine language (*joseigo*)   女性語●

A variety of Japanese, called joseigo or *onnakotoba*, that is typically used by females as a reflection of their femininity. The existence of clearly marked, gender-differentiated language styles is a frequently mentioned characteristic of Japanese.

Feminine language can be described in terms of features that occur almost exclusively in the language of females and features that are, in a given context, more typical of the language of females. Aside from the high pitch, distinctive voice quality, and particular sentence-final intonations that are associated with the speech of Japanese females, and aside from the vocabulary associated with topics predominantly of interest to females, feminine features include lexical items, such as: (1) the self-reference terms *atashi* and *atakushi*, as less formal equivalents of *watakushi* (I); (2) the sentence particle *wa* in sentence-final position with rising intonation—or prefinal before *yo* or *ne*—indicating gentle assurance; (3) sentence-final *koto* occurring in exclamations, for example: *Kirei da koto* (How pretty it is!); (4) particular interjections, for example: *Ara, ma, uwa* (indicating surprise).

Most commonly, feminine language is characterized by certain features that occur in a particular context or with a marked frequency. The most striking example is the feature of politeness. Given the socialization process, which trains Japanese women to be polite and subservient to men, it follows that the honorific and formal varieties of Japanese language are used more frequently by women. This does not mean that the forms themselves are feminine, but rather that their frequent use and their occurrence in certain social situations are typical of female usage. Thus, a polite form that would be used by a man only when talking to a person of extremely high position might be used by a woman in talking to a casual acquaintance.

Names (*namae*)   名前●

Proper names in Japan present a problem since virtually all

Chinese characters used in names have a multiplicity of readings—both *on* readings, based on Chinese pronunciation, and *kun* readings, based on native Japanese words. Moreover, since most names are written with two or more characters, it is often impossible to be sure of the combination of readings needed in any particular case without having personal knowledge. Conversely, the same name element usually can be found written with a number of different characters. In the case of personal names, for example, more than 130 characters have 10 or more possible name readings, and the common name elements *taka* and *nori* are found written with 168 and 225 different characters, respectively. Since some characters and readings are much more common in names than others, it usually is possible to arrive at the likely reading of a name, and the number of characters available for use when registering the personal names of children is now limited by law. However, since there is no restriction on the readings that can be given to these characters, many uncertainties remain in all types of names.

People's Names 呼称●

In Japanese usage the family name comes before the personal name, but otherwise the treatment of names is much the same as in the West. A Japanese has a family name and an official personal name; artistic or professional names also are often used. Suffixes equivalent to titles such as Mr. or Mrs. (san) or Dr (sensei) are used after the family name in formal reference, and within the family or among intimates the familiar ending chan is used after personal names, often in abbreviated form, very much as -y is used in diminutives such as Willy or Lizzy.

Group (Clan and Family) Names 集団（閥・家）名●

Up to the end of the 8th century, the two main types of group names within society were *uji*, to indicate lineage groups or clans, and *kabane*, hereditary titles of nobility granted to *uji* and individuals. In the case of an individual, the *kabane* was used between the name of the uji and the personal name; for example, Nakatomi no Muraji Kamako indicates one Kamako of the Nakatomi clan who had the rank of *muraji*.

During the Heian period (794–1185), clans such as the Ariwara, Minamoto, and Taira, which were related to the imperial line and had been granted their names by the court, increased in size so much that subdivisions became necessary. These smaller groups usually were distinguished by their locations.

From the 13th century on, military families in rural areas distinguished themselves from others of the same clan by using as their standard family name the name of their locality, and all types of group names

Culture

had become wholly fixed by the early 17th century. With a few exceptions, the use of family names remained limited to the upper classes of society, with the lower orders generally being referred to only by their personal names or, where necessary, by prefixes indicative of their trade or location.

Two years after the Meiji Restoration of 1868, however, everyone was allowed to take a family name, and in 1875 family names were made compulsory. Certain names came to be adopted more generally in some areas than others, but the whole process led to the appearance of family names of every conceivable kind, and the frequent mistakes made in writing the characters for newly acquired names have in some cases survived to add to the present confusion of Japanese name readings.

At the present time, the names Sato and Suzuki each account for more than 1.5 percent of the population, and other common family names are Tanaka, Yamamoto, Watanabe, Kobayashi, Saito, Tamura, Ito, and Takahashi. In the case of family names, native Japanese readings are more frequent than *on* readings.

Personal Names 個人名●

Various considerations may apply in the naming of children in modern Japan—seniority in the case of brothers, for example, or the advice of fortune-tellers in choosing characters deemed appropriate to the family name. In nearly all cases, though, names and characters are chosen primarily for their auspicious meanings and happy associations, that is, as talismans of good fortune.

The choice of characters permitted for use in personal names was first limited in 1948 and was restricted as of 1990 to the 1,945 *joyo kanji* and the 284 characters selected for use only in personal names.

Men's Names 男性の名前●

In premodern Japan men of the upper ranks of society could have a variety of personal names. The main categories were as follows: (1) *Yomyo* or *domyo* (child name). Often ending in -*waka*, -*maru*, -*maro*, or -*o* (e.g., Ushiwaka), a name of this type was customarily given to a boy on or by the seventh day after birth (*shichiya*) and generally was used until superseded by other names at *gempuku* when he was about 15. Men of the lower classes normally used these child names throughout their lives. (2) *Tsusho* or *yobina*, *zokumyo*, *kemyo* (current name). This name was given to a male at gempuku together with his *jitsumyo* and was the one by which he generally was known (e.g., Taro). Some of these names could take prefixes to indicate a particular generation (Kotaro for Taro II) or lineage (Heitaro for a member of the Heike i.e., Taira clan). (3) Jitsumyo or *nanori* (true name). This was a formal adult name used in association with the clan name (Minamoto no Shitagau for Shitagau of the Minamoto clan) and so closely associated with the individual that other people would use it of him very rarely or never at all if he was their superior. Upon the death of a dignitary, his jitsumyo would be used as his *imina* (posthumous name).

Many other types of name were, and still are, used in special circumstances. Nicknames (*adana*) were not uncommon, used either alone or in conjunction with a *tsusho*—for example, Nossori Jubei ("Plodder" Jubei). More current are the *yago* (house names) traditionally associated with *kabuki* actors and families, which are shouted out by members of the audience during performances.

Women's Names   女性の名前●

Before the 9th century most women's names seem to have ended in -*me*, -*iratsume*, or -*toji*, as in Shima-me. From then on, high-ranking court ladies had formal personal names consisting of one character followed by the suffix -*ko*—for example, Sadako—but the taboos against the general use of such jitsumyo led also to the wide use of yomyo, tsusho (e.g., Murasaki Shikibu), and, later, to the use of various elegant names, many of them derived from *The Tale of Genji*. Among humbler women the -*ko* suffix was never used, but the 16th century saw the introduction of the prefix *o*-, as in Oichi. This practice spread during the Edo period (1600–1868), when most women had two-syllable names, often written in *kana* (phonetic syllabic characters) and a woman's status was immediately evident from her name.

The changes brought about by the Meiji Restoration (1868), however, led to a vast increase in the use of Chinese characters. The employment of the formerly aristocratic suffix -*ko* grew steadily from about 3 percent in the mid-1880s to 80 percent in 1935. Today women follow the ancient court practice of having two-syllable names plus -*ko* or having elegant three-syllable names such as Harue with no suffix.

Place Names   地名●

Accounts of the origins of place names are a common feature of the earliest written works in Japan, especially those known as *fudoki* (regional chronicles), but many of their etymologies are still uncertain. In general, though, they can be said to derive from natural features or historical causes.

The names of geographical origin generally refer to such obvious features of the land as a river, mountain, valley, plain, moor, ford, or beach. These designations often are combined with prefixes describing such aspects as size, length, depth, or direction, such as Nagasaki (long cape), Yokohama (side beach), or Hiroshima (broad island).

History-based names include some derived from the Ainu, most typically those ending in -*betsu* or -*nai* in northern parts of Japan. Names such as Shinden (new rice fields) indicate the development of an area, while others show religious associations by the use of such components as *kami* (god), *miya* (shrine), and *tera* (temple). Also, Edo was renamed Tokyo (eastern capital) in 1868 in contrast to its predecessor Kyoto (capital metropolis).

Makuuchi (top division) *sumo* wrestlers waiting for the *dohyo-iri* (ring-entrance ceremonies) prior to the start of the day's bouts.

Clothing (*ifuku*)   衣服●

Clothing in Japan is broadly categorized as either *wafuku* (Japanese style) or *yofuku* (Western style). KIMONO is the modern designation for the traditional Japanese robelike garment that is worn belted at the waist, but this garment was historically called a *kosode* ("kimono" can also mean traditional dress in general). The history of Japanese clothing is in large part the history of the evolution of the kosode and the Japanization of imported styles and textiles.

Ancient Clothing (to AD 794)   古代の衣服●

The type of clothing worn during the Jomon period (ca 10,000 BC–ca 300 BC) is unknown, although jewelry from that period has been found. People probably used fur and bark to cover themselves. With the Yayoi period (ca 300 BC–ca AD 300) came the rise of sericulture (silkworm breeding) and weaving techniques.

Influenced by the importation of Buddhism and the Chinese government system, Prince Shotoku (574–622) followed the practice of the Sui court (589–618), establishing rules of dress for aristocrats and court officials. Figures depicted in paintings and embroideries wear long, loose clothing that shows the influence of Han-dynasty (25–220) fashion. The Taiho Code (701) and Yoro Code (718; effective 757) reformed clothing styles, following the system used in Tang China (618–907). Garments were divided into three categories: ceremonial dress, court dress, and working clothes.

Heian Period (794–1185)   平安時代●

As Japan drew away from continental influence, clothing became simpler in cut but more elaborate in layers. For formal occasions the male aristocrat's layered outfit (*sokutai*) included loose trousers stiffened by divided skirts (*oguchi*), worn underneath, and many layers of long, loose upper garments (*ho*).

The formal costume of the Heian lady-in-waiting was the *karaginumo*, often referred to after the 16th century as the 12-layered garment (*junihitoe*). Its most important element was the *uchiki*, the layers of lined robes (5, 10, or more) also called *kasane-uchiki* or *kasane* (layers). Great consideration was given to the combination of colors in the layers of uchiki. Each layer was longer than the one over it, so that the edge of each color showed, creating a striking effect.

Kamakura (1185–1333) and Muromachi (1333–1568) Periods

鎌倉・室町時代●

With the establishment of the Kamakura shogunate and the decline of the prestige of the imperial court, stiffened military garments replaced luxurious silk. The highest officials wore the formal sokutai of the Heian period, but the informal hunting jacket (*kariginu*) became the standard uniform of the *samurai*, along with a stiffened cloak (*suikan*).

At the beginning of the Kamakura period, women wore a combination of uchiki robes and *hakama* skirt-trousers as the formal outfit. Later these were replaced by the small-sleeved undergarment, the kosode, worn with hakama. In the Muromachi period an extra jacket (*uchikake* or *kaidori*) was worn over the kosode to complete the formal dress; today it is part of the bridal outfit.

Azuchi-Momoyama Period (1568–1600)

安土桃山時代●

In the late 16th century the powerful generals Oda Nobunaga and Toyotomi Hideyoshi, great patrons of the arts, encouraged a wave of bold, decorative brilliance. The samurai continued to wear matched upper and lower garments (*kamishimo*). The upper garment was sleeveless. Gradually the material was made stiffer and the shoulders more flared; together with trailing pleated trousers (*nagabakama*), this continued as formal wear for samurai throughout the Edo period.

Edo Period (1600–1868)

江戸時代●

During the 250 peaceful years of Tokugawa government, the wealthy merchant community (*chonin*) supported new forms of artistic expression. The KABUKI theater and the entertainment quarters led fashion. The kosode, the basic garment for both men and women, was more brilliantly decorated after the development of *yuzen* dyeing and tie-dyeing patterns.

Over the kosode the Edo man often wore a *haori* jacket, a loose garment with a straight collar. The Tokugawa shogunate reformed clothing regulations for the military class toward the close of the period. The standard uniform became a kosode, ankle-length hakama, and haori. A number of early-Edo-period fashions reflected Portuguese influence. From the Portuguese large cape came the *kappa* raincoat. The *juban* kimono, worn under the kosode, derived its name from the Portuguese word for underwear: *gibao*.

Yuzen dyeing allowed detailed, painterly patterns on textiles for the first time.

Modern Developments

現代●

After the Meiji Restoration of 1868 the Japanese slowly changed over to Western clothing. The process began with a government decree that civil servants, such as soldiers, police, and postmen, should wear

Western dress. Soon students were also wearing Western uniforms. By World War I, almost all men dressed in trousers, shirts, and jackets.

Women were generally slower in adopting Western styles. The aristocracy, however, sported imported Western gowns and accessories at the European-style balls held at the Rokumeikan from 1883 to 1889, and after World War I professional and educated women began to adopt Western clothing as their daily wear. It was not until after World War II that the habit of wearing Western clothing became the norm for all classes. Today most Japanese women wear their traditional kimono only on special occasions, such as festivals and weddings. Men wear traditional clothing even more rarely. The cotton summer kimono or *yukata* is worn by both men and women at resorts and summer festivals.

Kimono 着物●

The word kimono (literally, "clothing") is usually used in the narrow sense for the traditional Japanese wrap-around garment, worn by both men and women, with rectangular sleeves, and bound with a sash (OBI). The word is occasionally used in the broad sense as a term for clothing or for the native dress in general as opposed to Western-style clothing (*yofuku*). The predecessor of the kimono is the *kosode* ("small sleeves"), which was worn as an undergarment from about the Nara period (710–794) and as the everyday outer garment from about the mid-16th century. The term kimono gained favor over kosode only in the 18th century (see also CLOTHING).

In the Meiji period (1868–1912) many men began wearing Western-style clothes, reserving kimono for formal occasions or when relaxing at home, but only from the beginning of the Showa period (1926–89) did the new style of dress become popular among women. Today most women wear kimono mainly for social and ceremonial events or when performing certain traditional arts. Children and young men and women may wear kimono for such occasions as New Year, the Shichigosan festival, Adulthood Day, graduations, and weddings.

Kimono, obi, nagajuban, and accessories.

Kimono may be unlined (*hitoe*), lined (*awase*), or cotton-quilted (*wataire*). Unlined kimono are worn from June through September; for everyday wear, stencil-dyed cotton *yukata* are most common. For street or formal wear, materials such as silk gauze (*ro* and *sha*) or fine linen (*jofu*) are used. Lined kimono are worn from October through May and are mainly made of silk or wool. Cotton quilted kimono, or cotton-quilted robes called *tanzen* worn over kimono, are for midwinter at home.

The ceremonial kimono for men is made of black *habutae* silk and decorated in several places with the family crest in white. Women wear different types of formal kimono. The dazzling wedding costume consists of a white or red silk kimono with embroidery or brocade. Married women wear dark-colored silk, with a lighter design, for festive occasions and black silk, without a design, for funerals.

Generally when dressing one first dons *tabi* (socks); top undergarment and wrap-around underskirt; and then the underkimono (*nagajuban*), which is tied tightly with a wide belt (*datemaki*). The nagajuban has a collar (*han'eri*), usually white, which should show about 2 centimeters (1 in) above the collar of the kimono that is worn over it. The left side of the kimono is lapped over the right in front.

O*bi* 帯●

The long sash worn with traditional Japanese KIMONO. Until the early 8th century people wore loose, one-piece robes or upper garments with wide trousers for men and pleated skirts for women, secured by a narrow obi. With the introduction of new weaving techniques from Korea and China during the Nara period (710–794), obi became more elegant. In the Heian period (794–1185) gems and other stones were used to adorn men's leather obi, but the court ladies did not wear obi. Clothing styles did not call for obi again until the end of the 15th century through the Edo period (1600–1868).

Men's obi have changed little over the centuries. The obi worn by men today are either stiff, about 9 centimeters (3.5 in) wide, and tied in a half-bow (*kakuobi*), or of soft gray or black silk that is often tie-dyed (*hekoobi*). The latter is at least 50 centimeters (20 in) wide; when folded over it forms a narrow band that is worn tied or tucked in just under the waist.

A festive knot used for *obi* worn by young women.

Early in the Edo period women's obi measured approximately 30 centimeters (1 ft) in width and 2 meters (6.6 ft) in length, eventually reaching their present length of about 3–4 meters (10–13 ft). Women's obi were usually made of silk. Girls and unmarried women tied their obi at the back, while married women tied them in front.

Today most women, married or single, wear their obi tied in back in a square-shaped bow (*otaiko*). The season of the year and the nature of the occasion usually determine what kind of obi a woman wears. Formal obi are made of brocade (*nishiki*) or figured brocade (*tsuzure-ori*); daily-wear obi are made of figured satin or *habutae* silk. The obi is often considered a more important element of dress than the kimono, and a good one may cost several times as much as a kimono.

Modern housing (*gendai no sumai*) 現代の住まい●

Housing in Japan has changed dramatically in the past century as a result of rapid urbanization, population pressures, changes in family and social relationships, and the influence of Western architecture. Especially in large cities, multiunit dwellings have become the norm, although the majority of people still aspire to own their homes.

The Modern Japanese House 現代の日本の家●

Developer-built houses in Asaka, Saitama Prefecture.

There has been a progressive shrinking of the living space available to the middle-class household, from an average total floor space of 165 square meters (1,776 sq ft) at the turn of the century to 100 square meters (1,076 sq ft) by the beginning of the Showa period (1926-89), and by 1988 average total floor space had shrunk to 89 square meters (958 sq ft). In the 1980s this trend was exacerbated by the rapid rise in the cost of land, which forced would-be homeowners into the suburbs and into the market for small *tateuri jutaku* (developer-built houses). Large tracts of tateuri jutaku housing have become a common sight within a two-hour commuting distance of major urban centers such as Tokyo, Osaka, and Nagoya.

Whether built by the owner on his or her own property or by a developer, the two-story detached house with a tiled roof, a small (sometimes tiny) ornamental garden enclosed by a high stone wall or hedge, and garage space for the family automobile remains the ideal for the majority of Japanese. Such houses are basically wooden structures with overlaid plaster walls. The average total floor area in a house built by a salaried worker about 40 years of age is about 115.48 square meters (1,242 sq ft). There is a dining room-kitchen, two or three Japanese-style rooms with TATAMI mats, and one or two Western-style rooms with carpeted, tiled, or wooden floors.

Typical Japanese-style room with a *tokonoma* (alcove).

Passage through traditional houses was from room to room rather than along a corridor. Rooms were separated by sliding screens and sliding doors (SHOJI and *fusuma*), which allowed for a more flexible multipurpose use of the rooms than is possible in Western houses, in which rooms tend to have fixed functions. The introduction of Western features such as corridors, hinged rather than sliding doors, Western-style furniture, and beds has tended to make many modern Japanese houses more compartmentalized and somewhat more private than traditional houses. Eighty percent of all newly constructed single-family dwellings have Western-style toilets and living or dining rooms; the entry (*genkan*) of 60 percent has Western-style doors rather than sliding doors. However, since almost 90 percent of these new houses also have a traditional Japanese *tokonoma* (alcove), it is clear that many Japanese prefer a blend of Japanese and Western styles. Modern elements are common in urban areas, while rural homes often retain the multifunctional rooms of the old style. Rural homes tend to be larger, reflecting the lower price of land in rural areas, and ceremonial functions still take place at home there rather than in restaurants or community buildings.

Multiunit Dwellings   複合住宅●

Overall, multiunit dwellings increased to 52.8 percent of total housing constructed from 1986 to 1988. Wood-construction rental apartments continue to be a widespread form of multiunit housing. The earlier small units had shared kitchens and toilets, but in recent years the majority of apartments of this type have private kitchen, bath, and toilet facilities.

A building of condominium type units called *manshon* ("mansion").

In 1955 the Japan Housing Corporation (JHC) was established, and apartment buildings and housing projects (*danchi*) became a familiar sight in Japan. The JHC standardized apartment layouts, introducing the concept of the dining room-kitchen ("dining-kitchen"; DK), a space of about 8 square meters (86 sq ft) used for both cooking and dining. This soon became a popular feature.

The most common unit in early JHC housing was the 2DK, or two rooms and the dining-kitchen area; in such apartments one of the rooms would serve as a living room during the day. An enlarged DK is called an LDK, or living room-dining-kitchen area. The emphasis in recent JHC housing has been on 3DK and 3LDK units.

In addition to the publicly subsidized danchi apartments, there are a great number of mid- to high-rise buildings constructed by private developers since the 1960s; these have individual units for sale or rent and are known as *manshon* (the English word "mansion" was borrowed to distinguish them from the more spartan 1960s public danchi apartment buildings). Townhouses—basically, connected rows of single-unit, rather more expensive dwellings—are an increasingly popular alternative to apartment dwelling. See also ARCHITECTURE, MODERN; ARCHITECTURE, TRADITIONAL DOMESTIC; HOUSING PROBLEMS.

Tatami   畳●

Mat used as a flooring material in traditional Japanese-style rooms. Even today, most Japanese houses have at least one room done in the traditional style, with tatami and sliding doors.

Since the Muromachi period tatami have been made of a thick base of straw covered with a soft surface of woven rush (*igusa*). The size of tatami was gradually standardized within each region of Japan, and today tatami continue to be used as a unit of measure (pronounced *jo*) for Japanese and sometimes even for Western-style rooms. For example, a room with floor space for six mats is called a *rokujoma* ("six-mat room"). A tatami generally measures 1.91 by 0.95 meters (6.3 by 3.1 ft) in the Kyoto area, 1.82 by 0.91 meters (6.0 by 3.0 ft) in the Nagoya area, and 1.76 by 0.88 meters (5.8 by 2.9 ft) in the Tokyo area. The thickness is on the average 6 centimeters (2.4 in).

Shoji 障子●

Sliding screen, used since the Heian period (794–1185) to set off a room from a hallway or another room. The present *fusuma*, a wooden sliding door frame with cloth or paper applied on both sides, was initially called fusuma shoji, but now the term shoji refers only to screens comprising a wooden frame on one side of which translucent paper (*shojigami*) is applied. Since shoji admit light, they are also used for window fixtures and ornamentation. With the contemporary trend toward Western-style interiors, shoji are becoming less common as fittings in modern buildings.

Bath (*furo*) 風呂●

Public bath.

The typical Japanese bath consists of a tub deep enough for the bather to immerse the body up to the neck when sitting. Water is piped to the tub from a water heater or heated in the tub by a gas burner at one end. There is a drain in the floor of the bathroom, and the bather washes and rinses the body completely before entering the tub to soak, thus keeping the bathwater as clean as possible for other bathers, who usually use the same water throughout the day.

Modern public baths (*sento*) now have separate entrances, dressing rooms, and bathing rooms for men and women. Plastic stools and basins are provided for the use of customers, who sit in rows before sets of hot- and cold-water faucets where they wash before entering one of the large tubs to soak. However, because people increasingly have baths in their own homes, many sento are going out of business. In 1964 there were 23,016 public baths in Japan, but in 1991 there were only 9,704.

Modern-day baths in the home are in small rooms, usually separate from the toilet. The room is usually tiled. Although traditionally made of wood, tile, or, more rarely, metal, tubs are now often made of polypropylene reinforced with fiberglass. On Children's Day (5 May) many people still put the fragrant leaves of the *shobu* plant in the bathwater. Several customs of the furo have entered other aspects of Japanese life. For example, the square cloth known as *furoshiki* ("bath spread"), used since the Edo period (1600–1868) to carry toilet articles into the sento and to stand on while dressing, is now a common article used to wrap gifts or to carry many other items.

Japanese cooking (Nihon *ryori*)　　　　　日本料理●

There are three fundamental types of traditional full-course Japanese cuisine: *honzen ryori*, an assembly of dishes served on legged trays at formal banquets; *chakaiseki ryori*, a series of dishes sometimes served before the TEA CEREMONY; and KAISEKI RYORI, a series of dishes for parties, often served at restaurants specializing in Japanese cuisine (*ryotei*). Other types are *osechi ryori*, dishes traditionally served on important holidays such as NEW YEAR's, and *shojin ryori*, Buddhist vegetarian dishes.

The main ingredients in Japanese cooking are seafood, vegetables, and rice. The consumption of raw seafood has long been a distinguishing feature of native cuisine, and its preparation requires that fish be very fresh and that it be skillfully cut with a very sharp knife (*hocho*). Because of the abundance of foods supplied by the seas surrounding Japan and the influence of Buddhism, which militated against the killing of animals, Japanese cooking formerly made little use of the flesh of animals and fowl, dairy products, and oils and fat. Principal seasonings are fermented products of soybeans, such as SOY SAUCE (*shoyu*) and MISO (soybean paste), or of RICE, such as SAKE, vinegar, and *mirin* (sweet *sake*). Mirin has a smoother sweetness than sugar and is used in small amounts to enhance the taste of soy sauce and miso, as well as to mitigate the acidity of vinegar. To preserve the natural flavors of ingredients, strong spices are avoided in favor of milder herbs and spices, such as *kinome* (aromatic sprigs of the tree known as *sansho*), *yuzu* (citron), *wasabi* (Japanese horseradish), ginger, *myoga* (a plant of the same genus as ginger), and dried and ground sansho seeds.

The *kaiseki ryori* style of Japanese cuisine.

In preparing foods for serving one arranges them in a manner that harmonizes colors and textures, on plates or in bowls that accord with the season of the year; for example, glass and bamboo are considered appropriate for summer. Dishes of contrasting shapes, sizes, and patterns are used during the course of a meal to achieve an aesthetic balance between food and receptacle that pleases the eye and stimulates the appetite.

The basis of all Japanese cooking is stock (*dashi*), the standard form of which is made with the type of seaweed known as sea tangle (*kombu*) and dried bonito-fillet (*katsuobushi*) shavings.

The categories into which all Japanese cooking falls are described below. Each Japanese term that appears in subheadings not only expresses the method of cooking but also denotes the dish itself.

Shirumono   汁物●

Shirumono (soups) can be roughly divided into two types, *sumashijiru* and *misoshiru*. Ingredients may include white-fleshed fish, prawns, shellfish, *tofu*, fowl, seaweed, and seasonal vegetables; one or two ingredients that accord with the remainder of the menu are selected from among these. To add more zest and aroma, yuzu, kinome, sansho, ginger, or *mitsuba* (a trifoliolate herb of the same genus as honewort) may be added.

A Japanese breakfast with a bowl of *misoshiru* on the lower right.

For sumashijiru, or clear soup, dashi, to which salt and soy sauce have been added, is customarily used.

Yakimono   焼き物●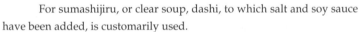

The principal ingredients of yakimono (grilled foods) are fish, shellfish, meat, and vegetables. Foods are pierced with a skewer or placed on a wire net and grilled over an open fire. One may also make yakimono using an iron skillet or oven broiler. The basic type of yakimono is *shioyaki*, in which salt is sprinkled over the food before grilling. The distinctive flavor of fish is best enjoyed in this way. For *tsukeyaki* the food is first marinated for about an hour in *awase-joyu*, a mixture of soy sauce and sake or mirin. *Teriyaki* is a yakimono prepared with a stronger-flavored awase-joyu. For *misozukeyaki*, the food is marinated in miso flavored with sake or mirin. In arranging a grilled whole fish on a plate, the head of the fish is positioned to the left with the belly facing the diner.

Nimono   煮物●

Nimono are stewed dishes seasoned with salt, soy sauce, sake, mirin, sugar, vinegar, or other condiments. The most common nimono is *nitsuke*—fish or shellfish cooked briefly in a relatively thick mixture of sake, soy sauce, mirin, and sugar. In the case of the white-fleshed fish *tai* and *buri* (yellowtail), the fillets are removed and used for *sashimi* or yakimono and the head and backbone chopped in pieces, washed in hot water, and cooked with a relatively light mixture of water, sake, mirin, and soy sauce until the juice is almost entirely absorbed. Bluefish, such as mackerel, sardines, and saurel, are first cooked in a mixture of water, sake, and mirin. Miso that has been diluted with a ladleful of the broth (*nijiru*) is then added to mask the strong flavor of the fish. This is called *misoni*.

Agemono 揚げ物●

Agemono, or deep-fried foods, are of three basic types. *Suage*, in which foods are fried without a coating of flour or batter, is appropriate for freshwater fish, eggplant, green peppers, and other vegetables whose color and shape can be utilized to good effect. *Karaage* frying, in which food is first dredged in flour or arrowroot starch, preserves the natural water content of the food and crispens the outer surface. In *tatsutaage*, a variant of karaage, pieces of chicken are marinated in a mixture of sake, soy sauce, and sugar, lightly covered with arrowroot starch, and deep-fried. *Tempura* belongs to a third type of agemono, in which foods are coated with batter.

Mushimono 蒸し物●

Mushimono are steamed foods. With this method, natural flavors do not escape and the taste is very light. Foods may be sprinkled with salt and steamed (*shiomushi*) or sprinkled with salt and sake (*sakamushi*). The latter method is particularly appropriate for clams or abalone. Mushimono are served with seasoned dashi thickened with arrowroot starch and sprinkled with grated ginger, yuzu rind, or chopped scallion. The foundation of *chawan mushi* is a mixture of beaten eggs and lukewarm dashi (about three times the volume of the eggs). Ingredients such as shrimp, mushrooms, and chicken are placed in individual bowls. The egg mixture is poured in and the bowls covered and steamed over medium heat.

Sunomono and Aemono 酢の物・和え物●

Sunomono are vinegared fish or vegetables; aemono are fish or vegetables with a dressing, the basic ingredient of which is ground sesame seed, miso, or mashed tofu. Fish and shellfish are sometimes broiled or steamed, or they may be sliced, sprinkled with salt, and marinated in vinegar or sea-tangle stock. Vegetables are either blanched, rubbed with salt, boiled, or steamed. Excess water should be eliminated.

Yosemono and Nerimono 寄せ物・練り物●

Yosemono are molded dishes made with agar-agar or gelatin. Foods such as rock trout, flounder, and chicken that have a relatively high gelatin content are used. Nerimono are foods that have been mashed into a paste. For one such dish, fish or shellfish is chopped into small pieces and mashed in a mortar with a pinch of salt. The paste is mixed with beaten eggs, grated *yamanoimo* (a type of yam), and dashi and divided into portions for boiling, deep-frying, or steaming. It is eaten with soy sauce and grated ginger.

Gohammono   御飯物●

Gohammono are dishes consisting of rice combined with other ingredients. *Takikomigohan* is made by cooking rice and another ingredient—in spring, green peas or pieces of bamboo shoot; in autumn, *matsutake* mushrooms or chestnuts—in seasoned water or dashi. *Gomokumeshi* (also known as *kayakugohan*) is prepared by adding finely diced chicken, carrot, fried tofu, *shiitake* mushroom, and burdock to rice and cooking it in dashi seasoned with soy sauce, sake, and sugar. *Domburimono* are dishes in which cooked rice is placed in a bowl (*domburi*) that is larger than the usual rice bowl and then topped with various prepared ingredients.

Menrui   麺類●

Menrui is a category of dishes, served hot or cold, whose chief ingredient is noodles. The most common types of noodles are *udon*, *somen*, and *soba*. The first two are made with wheat flour, and soba with buckwheat flour. Somen is always dried; soba and udon may be either fresh or dried.

Nabemono   鍋物●

Nabemono are dishes cooked in a pot of simmering broth at the table. Ingredients are arranged on platters so that each person may cook what he or she likes. The chief types of nabemono are *mizutaki*, *yudofu*, *udonsuki*, *kanisuki*, *dotenabe*, *shabushabu*, and *sukiyaki*. Mizutaki is prepared by cooking fillets of white-fleshed fish with vegetables, tofu, and *harusame* (thin potato-starch noodles) in a pot of *kombu* stock, or chicken and vegetables in chicken broth. Grated white radish, red pepper, and chopped onion are used as condiments, and the food is dipped in *ponzu*, a sauce made from citron and soy sauce.

In *tenzaru* dishes such as this one, *tempura* is served with cold *soba* noodles.

Kaiseki ryori   会席料理●

One of the three basic styles of traditional JAPANESE COOKING. Kaiseki ryori is a type of cuisine served at *sake* parties and developed in its present form as restaurants became popular in Japan in the early 19th century. Although the basic features of kaiseki ryori can be traced to the more formal styles of Japanese cooking—*honzen ryori* and *chakaiseki ryori*—in kaiseki ryori diners are able to enjoy their meal in a relaxed mood, unrestricted by elaborate rules of etiquette. Today this type of cooking can be found in its most complex form at first-class Japanese-style restaurants (*ryotei*). Sake is drunk during the meal, and, because the

Japanese customarily do not eat rice while drinking sake, rice is served at the end. Appetizers (*sakizuke* or *otoshi*), *sashimi* (sliced raw fish; also called *tsukuri*), *suimono* (clear soup), *yakimono* (grilled foods), *mushimono* (steamed foods), *nimono* (simmered foods), and *aemono* (dressed saladlike foods) are served first, followed by *miso* soup, *tsukemono* (pickles), rice, Japanese sweets, and fruit. Tea concludes the meal. The types and order of foods served in kaiseki ryori are the basis for the contemporary full-course Japanese meal.

Sushi   鮨●

Vinegared rice topped or combined with such items as raw fish, shellfish, or cooked egg. Served in restaurants and sold at supermarkets and take-out shops, sushi can also be prepared at home. It is enjoyed in many regional varieties all over Japan and is one of a handful of Japanese foods, along with TEMPURA, that have become popular internationally.

Sushi cuisine originated in ancient China as a method of preserving fish. After packing the fish in rice and salt, the mixture was left to ferment for anywhere from two months to one year. After fermentation the rice was discarded and the pickled fish was eaten. This method probably came to Japan with the introduction of wet rice culture sometime in the Yayoi period (ca 300 BC–ca AD 300); a variant of the ancient process is used today in making certain regional varieties of sushi. Variations on the fermentation process reduced the waiting time and introduced vinegar as a flavoring agent, and after a time the rice came to be eaten along with the pickled fish. It was not until the early 19th century, however, in Edo (now Tokyo), that the pickling process was dropped and fresh raw fish was served on freshly cooked vinegared rice. The sushi of this period was sold from stalls as a snack food; the stalls were the precursors of today's sushi restaurants.

Examples of *nigirizushi* (hand-pressed *sushi*).

Today sushi can be divided into four broad categories:

Nigirizushi (hand-pressed sushi) is the sushi developed in Edo in the 1800s. It is also known as *edomaezushi*. It consists of a bite-sized portion of vinegared rice topped with a small slice of raw fish or shellfish (cooked shellfish is also used) and seasoned with a dab of *wasabi* (Japanese horseradish) between the rice and the topping. Some of the most popular fish used in nigirizushi are tuna (*maguro*), and sea bream (*tai*). Also used are shrimp (*ebi*), salmon roe (*ikura*), octopus (*tako*), and squid (*ika*). Nigirizushi is dipped lightly in soy sauce before eating.

For *makizushi* (rolled sushi), vinegared rice is spread over a sheet of lightly toasted seaweed (*nori*) and various types of seafood and/or vegetables are arranged along the center; a thin bamboo mat placed beneath the seaweed beforehand is used to roll the makizushi into a cylinder, which is sliced crosswise into bite-sized pieces. Some of the most popular types of makizushi are *tekkamaki* (tuna roll), *kappamaki* (cucumber roll), *kampyomaki* (gourd roll), and *futomaki* (a thick roll of omelet, gourd, bits of vegetables, and other ingredients). For *temakizushi* the seaweed and other ingredients are loosely rolled by hand (without the bamboo mat) into a conelike shape that is not cut into pieces. The various types of makizushi may also be dipped in soy sauce for eating.

The category of *chirashizushi* ("scattered" sushi) is divided into two regional varieties. In the Tokyo variety cooked and uncooked seafood, vegetables, and sliced omelet are arranged over a bowl of vinegared rice. Soy sauce is served on the side for dipping. In the Osaka version cooked seafood and vegetables are chopped and mixed into the vinegared rice, and the whole is topped with thin strips of omelet.

Oshizushi (pressed sushi) is a specialty of the KANSAI REGION (Kyoto-Osaka-Kobe) made by pressing marinated seafood and vinegared rice in a small, boxlike wooden mold. It is sliced into bite-sized pieces and eaten dipped in soy sauce. *Battera* is oshizushi topped with marinated mackerel. *Inarizushi* consists of a pocket of deep-fried bean curd (*aburaage*) filled with vinegared rice mixed with roasted poppy or sesame seeds.

Tempura   天ぷら●

Fresh fish, shellfish, or vegetables dipped in a batter (*koromo*) of flour mixed with egg and water and then deep-fried. Tempura tastes best eaten right after frying, accompanied by a side dish of special tempura dipping sauce and grated radish. The sauce is a mixture of SOY SAUCE, *mirin* (sweet sake), and *dashi* (stock).

The origins of tempura date to the mid-16th century, a time when many items of Portuguese and Spanish culture, including methods of frying game, were brought to Japan (the word tempura is generally thought to be a corruption of the Portuguese *tempero* or cooking). Open-air tempura stalls became popular in early-19th-century Edo (now Tokyo), and many of these stalls developed into full-scale tempura restaurants.

A wide variety of foods can be used as ingredients for tempura. Low-fat fish such as smelt (*kisu*), a kind of whitebait (*shirauo*), conger eel (*anago*), cuttlefish (*ika*), shrimp, and such shellfish as scallops are commonly used. Vegetables used include lotus root, mushrooms, ginkgo nuts, beefsteak plant (*shiso*), and green peppers. Shrimp tempura is commonly served in a bowl atop a bed of rice in a dish known as *tendon*, or atop noodles as tempura *soba* or tempura *udon*.

Sukiyaki すき焼き●

Thinly sliced beef, vegetables, *tofu*, and other ingredients cooked at the table in a large skillet or iron pot in a broth of SOY SAUCE, *mirin* (sweet SAKE), and sugar.

Although meat dishes such as sukiyaki are now popular among the Japanese, traditional Buddhist injunctions against the consumption of the flesh of four-legged animals effectively prevented the widespread eating of meat in Japan for much of its history. The word sukiyaki first appears in documents from the early 19th century as the name of a dish in which goose, duck, or venison was broiled on top of a spade (*suki*) and basted with *tamari* (a thick soy sauce). However, sukiyaki as it is known today was created during the Meiji period (1868–1912), after Western influence helped make the consumption of beef and other types of meat common among large segments of the Japanese population. "Western-style" restaurants began by serving a dish of thinly sliced beef with chopped scallions. Flavoring the meat with soy sauce, mirin, and sugar soon became popular.

Ingredients for *sukiyaki*.

Today, the most typical recipe for sukiyaki, among many regional and personal variations, calls for beef (usually a high-quality, well-marbled variety), spring onions (*negi*), a type of thin, gelatinous noodle known as *shirataki*, tofu, chrysanthemum leaves (*shungiku*), and a type of mushroom (*shiitake*). After first browning the sliced beef, the soy-sauce-based broth and other ingredients are added, and the resulting stewlike mixture is brought to a boil. The cooked meat is dipped in beaten raw egg before eating. In the KANTO (Tokyo area) version of sukiyaki, the meat and vegetables are cooked together, while in the Kansai (Kyoto-Osaka-Kobe area) variety they are cooked separately.

Traditional confections (*wagashi*) 和菓子●

The development of what are now considered "traditional" Japanese confections was affected by a series of stimuli from abroad, beginning in the Nara period (710–794) with the introduction of Chinese confections by Japanese scholars studying in China, then the spread of

ZEN Buddhism (also from the continent, where wagashi were an integral part of the priests' vegetarian diet) during the Kamakura period (1185–1333), and later by such *namban-gashi* ("southern barbarian" confections) as *kasutera*, brought to Japan by Portuguese missionaries during the Muromachi period (1333–1568).

The popularization of the tea ceremony during the Edo period (1600–1868), especially in the Genroku era (1688–1704), saw a dramatic increase in wagashi varieties, many of which have remained unchanged into the present. Around this time the first stores specializing in confections (*kashiya*) began to appear in Edo (now Tokyo), in Osaka, and particularly in Kyoto, where confections called *kyogashi* were developed as religious offerings and to be presented to the imperial household.

Among the defining characteristics of wagashi are their distinctive ingredients. The principal ingredient is *an*, a sweet paste made of red *azuki* beans or white bush beans, sugar, and water, which was first developed in the Kamakura period. Wheat and rice flours are also used, but dairy products and vegetable oils are not. Instead, sparing use is made of such ingredients as walnuts, peanuts, or sesame seeds, which have their own natural oils. Artificial flavoring is not added, and even natural flavorings with strong aromas are avoided. Another characteristic is the way seasonal change is incorporated in the shapes and colors of wagashi, as well as in the names chosen for each variety. For instance, *sakuramochi* ("cherry" confections) are the color of cherry blossoms (white or light pink) and are wrapped in pickled cherry leaves. Until recently, many varieties were available only during specific seasons.

Rice *(kome)*   米●

Principal Japanese staple crop; an annual marshland plant of tropical origin; introduced into Japan in the Yayoi period (ca 300 BC–ca AD 300), either from China or the Korean peninsula. Rice cultivation was traditionally regarded as a religious act—an invoking of the *inadama* or spirit of the rice plant. Supplications to the deity survive today in various forms of folk performing arts. Many festivals in honor of tutelary deities are also harvest festivals. It is generally agreed that the Japanese extended family (*ie*) system evolved within the context of the rice culture, which required intensive farming, a sophisticated system of water control, and communal cooperation. In this sense rice may be said to have determined the very contours of Japanese society.

More than 100,000 varieties of rice are grown in more than 100 countries, with several thousand in Japan alone. In Japan, improvement of rice plants on an institutionalized and modern scientific basis was started in 1904 with hybridization experiments; pure line selection and, later, radiation breeding have also been utilized. These experiments have resulted in improved productivity, early maturity, and resistance to disease, cold weather, and lodging (stalk collapse). Koshihikari and Sasanishiki, both grown in the northeast, are among the most popular types of Japanese rice and command a high price. Since World War II, with land improvement, breeding of varieties responsive to fertilizers, improvement of fertilizing techniques, and the development of chemical fertilizers, herbicides, and insecticides, average yields have increased to more than 4.0 metric tons per hectare (1.8 short tons per acre). Since the beginning of the 1960s agricultural machinery has largely replaced human and animal labor, and threshing and hulling as well as transplanting of seedlings are now done by machines. At the same time, because of herbicides, there has been a reduction in the work load.

Rice consumption has decreased dramatically in Japan since the early 1960s. This phenomenon may be explained by the increased consumption of bread and animal food products. Rice contains somewhat less protein than wheat, but the quality of the protein is superior. Although customarily boiled and eaten plain, rice can be processed in many ways. Cooked glutinous rice is pounded into a kind of dough called *mochi*, which is then prepared in various ways. It may also be thinly sliced and then dried, roasted, and flavored with soy sauce to be made into a variety of rice crackers called *arare*. Rice confections, such as *dango*, are made from rice flour, as are the type of rice crackers known as *sembei*. Rice is also brewed as rice wine (SAKE), rice vinegar, and cooking wine (*mirin*), and by adding *koji*, a fermenting agent, is made into a sweet, fermented rice drink (*amazake*) or used as a pickling base.

Despite the decrease in rice consumption, rice is still considered a staple, and rice production and supply is a key element in agricultural policy. The present policy regarding rice production is based on the 1942 Foodstuff Control Law, which put the pricing and distribution of rice under government control. The import of rice, which has also been strictly controlled by the government, was permitted early in the postwar era when Japanese domestic production was unable to meet demand. As domestic production increased, imports were curtailed, and since 1983 the import of rice for table use has been prohibited. Japan has been under strong pressure from the United States and other countries to open its rice market to imports.

California rice on its way to Japan after a partial opening of the rice market in 1994.

In December 1993 Japan officially announced a partial opening of its rice market. Japan will open 4 percent of its domestic rice market to imports in the first year (1995) with the rate increasing each year until it reaches 8 percent in 2000.

Sake 酒●

A brewed alcoholic beverage made from fermented RICE. Sake is also used as a generic term for all alcoholic drinks. The formal name for refined sake, the kind most commonly drunk in Japan, is *seishu*; it is often referred to as *nihonshu* to distinguish it from Western liquors (*yoshu*). The other traditional Japanese alcoholic beverage is a distilled spirit called *shochu*. Malted rice (*koji*) is the fermenting agent in both refined sake and shochu.

Sake.

Today there are about 3,000 manufacturers of refined sake in Japan. The chief producing districts are Kyoto and Hyogo prefectures. A few national brands are also produced in places such as Akita and Hiroshima prefectures. *Jizake* (local brands) are numerous and are produced all over Japan.

Sake is made with a yeast of rice, malted rice, and water. This is placed in a vat, additional amounts of the three yeast ingredients are added, and the mixture is left to ferment for 20 days (the drained solids of the mixture, called *sakekasu* or dregs, are used in cooking and in the preparation of *tsukemono* or pickles). After fermentation the mixture is ready for pressing, filtration, and blending. The sake is then pasteurized, bottled, and stored. The alcohol content of crude sake is about 40 proof; sake on the market is about 32 proof. A good-quality sake has a subtle blend of the so-called five flavors (sweetness, sourness, pungency, bitterness, and astringency) and a mellow fragrance. Older sake has a soft, mellow taste, but sake is rarely stored for more than a year. There are also carbonated, sweet, dry, hard, and aged types. Unrefined sake is called *nigorizake*. A sweet sake called *mirin* is made especially for cooking.

Soy sauce (*shoyu*) 醤油●

Basic flavoring agent used in Japanese cuisine; made by fermenting water, salt, and a yeast of soybean and wheat—a process that may take over a year. Its prototype, a pasty substance called *hishio*, made by adding fish to salt, is known to have been made in the Yayoi period (ca 300 BC–ca AD 300). Shoyu as it is known today was first made in Japan in the Muromachi period (1333–1568).

Shoyu is distinguished according to the ingredients used in its preparation and the length of fermentation. *Koikuchi* shoyu, widely used, is fermented for a longer time and is thick; *usukuchi* shoyu is fermented for a shorter period. The addition of *mirin* (sweet *sake*) gives the latter a delicate color, flavor, and aroma, making it suitable for seasoning vegetables, white-fleshed fish, and clear soups. Both types are now produced mainly in Chiba and Hyogo prefectures. There are also local variations: the sweeter *tamari*, made in central Honshu; the pale yellow *shottsuru* of Akita Prefecture, made with fish; and the white *shiroshoyu* of the Nagoya area.

Miso (bean paste)   味噌●

Miso is made by mixing steamed soybeans with salt and a fermenting agent (*koji*) made of rice, wheat, or soybeans; together with SOY SAUCE (*shoyu*), it is the basic flavoring of Japanese cuisine. Miso is a good source of protein, especially the amino acids lysine and threonine, but it also contains a large amount of salt, as much as 8 to 15 percent. Introduced from China in the 7th century, it became popular during the Muromachi period (1333–1568). The color, aroma, and taste of miso differ according to the combination of ingredients, which vary from place to place.

Miso is most commonly used for making miso soup, which along with rice is an indispensable part of a Japanese-style meal. Because of its strong flavor miso is often used for marinating or cooking fish. It is also used as a preservative.

Tableware (shokki)   食器●

Almost contemporaneous with the perfection of what is now considered "traditional" Japanese cuisine, the development of Japanese tableware culminated during the Edo period (1600–1868) in nearly the same form that it has today. The use of *hashi* (CHOPSTICKS) as eating utensils was a shaping force in that development. Unlike metal knives and forks, hashi are usually made of softer materials such as wood or lacquered wood, so dishes could be made of similar materials as well as ceramics. Also, because hashi can be maneuvered in smaller areas, dishes could be made in a variety of shapes and sizes. The *wan* (bowl) was developed so that, in the case of soup for example, one could alternately drink the broth and use hashi to pick up the solid ingredients. Since hashi cannot readily be used for slicing, food is usually cut into small

Examples of the different types of traditional Japanese tableware.

pieces beforehand and served in individual dishes. The amount of tableware needed for a Japanese meal, therefore, is much greater than that for a Western meal.

Characteristic of Japanese cuisine is the emphasis placed on seasonal awareness, and tableware plays an important role in conveying this sense. There are fixed designs and patterns that distinguish seasonal tableware, and the way in which chefs select and combine tableware from various regions, made of diverse materials, is a measure of their skill.

Traditional forms of Japanese cuisine include KAISEKI RYORI, *honzen ryori*, and *chakaiseki ryori* (see TEA CEREMONY). The fundamental rule governing the menu for all of these is formulated as "one soup and three side dishes." For example, a meal of kaiseki ryori (the typical cuisine for banquets and gatherings) corresponding to a Western dinner would consist of the following: *shirumono* (soups), *sashimi* (raw fish), *yakimono* (grilled foods), and *nimono* (simmered foods). At the conclusion of the meal, rice and pickles are served. The kind of tableware necessary for such a meal includes individual place settings of hashi, lacquer soup bowls (*shiruwan*), plates for sashimi as well as tiny dipping bowls for soy sauce, plates for yakimono, bowls for nimono, rice bowls (*chawan*), and small dishes for pickles. Also, if SAKE is served, *sakazuki* (sake cups) and *tokuri* (sake decanters) might be added. Depending on the menu, the number of side dishes for kaiseki ryori can be increased to 5, 7, or as many as 11. As a rule, tableware for chakaiseki ryori is made of lacquered wood, but in actual practice ceramic dishes are often mixed in with the lacquer ones. Noodles (such as *udon* and *soba*), SUSHI, and foods for formal ceremonies all have their own specialized tableware.

With increasing availability of Western food, Western tableware has come to play a prominent role in Japan. Recently tableware that can be used for both Japanese and Western foods has become prevalent. However, almost every home is supplied with chawan, soup bowls, and hashi, since these are the basic eating utensils for Japanese food. Most tableware come in sets of five, but generally all members of a family have their own individual chawan and hashi for daily use.

Chopsticks.

Chopsticks (*hashi*)   箸●

All Japanese dishes are eaten with hashi; in the case of soups, the solid ingredients are eaten with hashi and the stock sipped directly from the soup bowl. Hashi are commonly made of light but strong wood, such as cypress or willow, and then lacquered; they are also made of bamboo or, increasingly, of plastic. It is customary in the Japanese household for each person to have a pair of hashi reserved for his or her exclusive use. Disposable plain-wood chopsticks (*waribashi*), which the diner splits apart before using, are common in restaurants. Long chopsticks made of bamboo and used for cooking are called *saibashi*. Long metal chopsticks with wooden handles are used for deep-frying. When not in use during a meal, hashi are rested upon small ceramic, wooden, or glass stands called *hashioki*.

Bento (box lunch)

弁当●

In premodern Japan box lunches, usually consisting of dried rice, rice balls (*nigirimeshi*), or sweet potatoes, wrapped in a leaf or in the sheath of a bamboo shoot, were eaten chiefly by travelers and people who worked outdoors. In the Edo period (1600–1868) elaborate meals were prepared and carried in tiered lacquer boxes (*jubako*) on outings. Bento sold at theaters to be eaten during intermission were called *maku-nouchi bento* ("entr'acte box lunches"), the prototype of today's *shidashi bento*, which are usually ordered in quantity and delivered by the restaurant that prepares them. Since the middle of the Meiji period (1868–1912) bento known as *ekiben* ("station box lunches") have been sold at railway stations. In recent years there has been a proliferation of shops that specialize in take-out bento.

A Kyoto-style *bento*.

Restaurants (*inshokuten*)

飲食店●

Today among the more than 1 million restaurants in Japan there are many that offer foreign cuisines. Chief among these are restaurants that specialize in Chinese, Korean, French, or Italian cooking, and recently Southeast Asian cuisines, such as Thailand's, have enjoyed particular popularity.

Restaurants serving Japanese cooking range from elegant *ryotei*, which provide elaborate multicourse meals, to simple eating houses. Many restaurants specialize in one type of Japanese food, such as SUSHI, TEMPURA, SUKIYAKI, broiled eel (*unagi*), deep-fried pork cutlets (*tonkatsu*), grilled chicken (*yakitori*), simmered foods (*oden*), pancakes containing vegetables (*okonomiyaki*), or *tofu*. There are also restaurants that serve regional cuisine, such as that of OKINAWA PREFECTURE or Akita Prefecture, as well as locally brewed brands of SAKE.

Entrance to a *sobaya* type restaurant.

One of the more popular noon meals consists of Japanese noodles (*soba*; *udon*), which are served at restaurants known as *sobaya*. Many such restaurants also serve *domburimono*, a bowl of rice topped with any of a variety of ingredients. *Ramen*, a Japanese version of Chinese-style noodles, is also a common lunchtime repast. *Ramen'ya*, the Chinese restaurants that specialize in it, serve other simple Chinese dishes as well, such as fried rice (*chahan*) and fried or steamed pork dumplings (*gyoza*). *Yoshokuya*, which specialize in Japanese variations of Western dishes, offer such foods as sauteed pork cutlets, spaghetti, and beef stew.

On their way home office workers often stop at drinking houses (*nomiya* or *izakaya*) that serve a variety of foods such as yakitori, grilled fish (*yakizakana*), raw fish (*sashimi*), chilled *tofu*, and pickles (*tsukemono*) to go along with beer, *sake*, or the distilled liquor known as *shochu*. Young people in particular have acquired a taste for Western-style fast foods, and a number of franchise chains have established restaurants throughout the country. There is also a type of large restaurant known as a family restaurant that serves a wide range of Western foods from club sandwiches to steak and to which parents often take their children.

Bottles of *sake* line the wall in this *izakaya*.

Coffeehouses (*kissaten*)   喫茶店●

Establishments that serve coffee, tea, and other beverages and snacks. Japan's first modern coffeehouse, the Kahii Sakan, opened its doors in 1888 in the Ueno district of Tokyo. In addition to serving coffee, it provided magazines and board games for customer use. Soon after, similar establishments began springing up around the Ginza area. After World War II "specialty" coffeehouses, establishments that play a particular type of music (such as jazz or classical) or are designed with some special theme in mind, became popular. Today coffeehouses can be found all over Japan, especially in urban areas. Certain coffeehouses have breakfast and lunch menus and are more like American-style coffee shops. Although a cup of coffee can be expensive, ranging from ¥300 to ¥500 (US $2.35-$3.90), customers are permitted to stay as long as they like and are not required to order anything else. Coffeehouses are popular places for meeting with business associates or, informally, with friends.

Tea ceremony (*chanoyu*; also called *chado* or *sado*) 茶の湯●

A highly structured method of preparing powdered green tea in the company of guests. The tea ceremony incorporates the preparation and service of food as well as the study and utilization of architecture, gardening, ceramics, calligraphy, history, and religion. It is the culmination of a union of artistic creativity, sensitivity to nature, religious thought, and social interchange.

History of Tea in Japan 日本における茶の歴史●

According to tradition, Bodhidharma, who left India and introduced ZEN (Ch: Chan) Buddhism to China in 520, encouraged the custom of tea drinking for alertness during meditation. In Buddhist temples during the Tang dynasty (618–907), a ritual was performed using tea in brick form. This was ground to a powder, mixed in a kettle with hot water, and ladled into ceramic bowls.

Buddhism was brought to Japan sometime in the first half of the 6th century. During the Nara period (710–794), the influence of Chinese culture included the introduction of tea in conjunction with Buddhist meditation. Early in the Kamakura period (1185–1333), the Japanese priest Eisai (1141–1215) returned from Buddhist studies in China, bringing the tea ritual practiced in Chinese Buddhist temples during the Song dynasty (960–1279). In this ritual, called *yotsugashira* ("four heads"), powdered green tea (*matcha*) is whisked in individual conical bowls called *temmoku* ("heaven eye"), after the Chinese mountain where they were used in Buddhist temples. The bowl is supported on a lacquered stand (*dai*). Eisai also brought tea seeds from the plant that was to become the source of much of the tea grown in Japan today. Although wild tea grew in Japan, it was considered inferior, and the tea grown from Eisai's seeds became known as "true tea" (*honcha*).

In Sakai, south of Osaka, there was a group of wealthy merchants called the *nayashu* ("warehouse school"), which espoused a modest manner of tea drinking. Out of this tradition came Takeno Joo (1502–1555), who taught the use of the *daisu* (the stand for the tea utensils), as it had been handed down from Murata Shuko (1422–1502, tea master to shogun Ashikaga Yoshimasa), as well as a sensitive connoisseurship and the aesthetic sensibility known as WABI, the contrast of refinement and rusticity. His influence was widely felt but was most important in his instruction of his student Sen no Rikyu (1522–91).

Tea master Sen no Rikyu.

Rikyu transformed the tea ceremony, perfected the use of the daisu, and substituted common Japanese objects for the rare and expensive Chinese tea utensils used previously. Tea was no longer made in one room and served to guests in another, but rather was made in their midst. Many people began to practice the tea ceremony following the precepts and example of Rikyu.

Rikyu's successor, Furuta Oribe (1544–1615), introduced a decorative style that some considered superficial. Oribe's pupil Kobori Enshu (1579–1647) continued the grand style and was teacher to the Tokugawa shoguns, moving freely among the nobility, while also designing gardens and teahouses.

There were many masters of tea, with heirs and followers who eventually gathered into schools. Ura Senke and Omote Senke are the leading schools in Japan today.

Gathering for the Tea Ceremony   茶会●

The manner of preparing powdered green tea may be influenced by many styles and techniques, depending on the practices of the various schools. The following procedure is adapted from the Ura Senke way of preparation. A full tea presentation with a meal is called a *chaji*, while the actual making of the tea is called *temae*. A simple gathering for the service of tea may be called a *chakai*. The selection of utensils (*dogu*) is determined by time of year, season, and time of day or night, as well as special occasions such as welcoming someone, bidding farewell, a memorial, a wedding, flower viewing, and so on.

The tea is prepared in a specially designated and designed room, the *chashitsu*. It is devoid of decoration with the exceptions of a hanging scroll (*kakemono*) and flowers in a vase (*hanaire*). The scroll, inspired by Buddhist thought, provides the appropriate spiritual atmosphere for serving tea. The Buddhist writing, usually by a recognized master, is called *bokuseki* ("ink traces"). Flowers for tea (*chabana*) are simple, seasonal, and seemingly "unarranged," unlike those in *ikebana* (flower arrangement).

Nodate (outdoor tea ceremony).

The following are some of the highlights of a chaji: The guests, ideally four, assemble in a *machiai* (waiting room) and are served *sayu* ("white" hot water) by the host's assistant, the *hanto*, in order to sample the water used in making tea. The guests enter the *roji* ("dew ground"), a water-sprinkled garden path devoid of flowers, in which the guests rid themselves of the "dust" of the world. They take seats at the *koshikake machiai* (waiting bench), anticipating the approach of the host, who is called *teishu* (house master).

The host replenishes the water in the stone basin set in a low arrangement of stones called *tsukubai* (literally, "to crouch"). The host purifies his hands and mouth and proceeds through the *chumon* (middle gate) to welcome the guests with a silent bow. This gate separates the mundane world from the spiritual world of tea. The guests purify their hands and mouths and enter the tearoom by crawling through the small door, or *nijiriguchi*, which the last guest latches. Individually they look at the scroll in the *tokonoma* (alcove), the kettle, and the hearth and take their seats.

Prior to the guests' entry, the kettle of water (*kama*) is placed in the room on a portable hearth (*furo*) with a charcoal fire. In winter a *ro*, a hearth set into the floor, replaces the furo to provide warmth. The host greets the guests. A charcoal fire to heat the water is built in the presence of the guests; this presentation (*sumi-demae*) is performed after the meal in the furo season and before the meal in the ro season. Incense, held in a *kogo* (incense container), is put into the fire; sandalwood (*byakudan*) is used in the furo, kneaded incense (*neriko*) in the ro.

The Tea Meal 茶懐石●

The host serves the tea meal, which is called *kaiseki* or *chakaiseki*. The foods are fresh, seasonal, and carefully prepared without decoration. The meal concludes with a sweet. In order to make preparations for serving the tea, the host then asks the guests to leave the room.

Preparing and Serving Tea 支度と点前●

Alone, the host removes the scroll and replaces it with flowers, sweeps the room, and sets out utensils for preparing *koicha* (thick tea), which is the focal point of the gathering. The *mizusashi*, a jar filled with fresh water, is displayed; the water represents the *yin* to complement the fire in the hearth, which is *yang*. The *chaire*, a small ceramic jar containing the powdered tea, covered by a fine silk bag (*shifuku*), is set in front of the water jar. An appropriate *tana*, or stand, on which to display the tea utensils is chosen for the occasion. A gong (*dora*) is struck to summon the guests during the day; at night a small bell (*kansho*) is rung. The guests once again purify their hands and mouth at the *tsukubai* and reenter, look at the flowers and displayed utensils, and latch the door.

Tea ceremony utensils.

The host enters with the *chawan* (teabowl), which holds the *chakin* (tea cloth), a bleached white linen cloth used to dry the bowl; *chasen* (tea whisk); and *chashaku* (tea scoop), a slender bamboo scoop used to dispense the tea powder. The chashaku often bears a poetic name. These are set next to the tea jar, which represents the sun (symbolic of yang); the bowl represents the moon (symbolic of yin). The host brings in the *kensui*, a waste-water bowl; the *hishaku*, a bamboo water ladle; and the *futaoki*, a rest for the kettle lid made of green bamboo, and closes the *sadoguchi* (tea way entrance). The host uses a *fukusa*, a silk cloth representing the host's spirit, to purify the tea container and scoop; examining, folding, and handling the fukusa deepen the host's concentration and meditation. Hot water is ladled into the bowl to warm it; the whisk is examined and rinsed. The emptied bowl is dried with the linen cloth. Three scoops of tea in increasing amounts are put into the bowl; then the tea jar is emptied into the bowl. Hot water is ladled into the bowl, sufficient to form a thin paste when kneaded with the whisk. A little more water is added to bring it to a drinkable consistency. The bowl is offered to the guests.

The first guest takes the bowl, drinks, and passes it to the others. The bowl is returned and rinsed. The whisk is rinsed, the chashaku wiped, and the kettle replenished. The tea jar is cleaned and, with the tea scoop, is offered to the guests to examine more closely. The utensils are taken from the room. During the presentation, the utensils and related subjects are discussed.

The fire may be rebuilt in anticipation of serving *usucha* (thin tea), which helps to rinse the palate and to prepare the guests psychologically for their return to the mundane world. Smoking articles—a *hiire* (fire receptacle), a ceramic cup with a lighted piece of charcoal set in a bed of ash; a *haifuki* (ash blow), a length of green bamboo containing water to extinguish the ash; and a *kiseru* (pipe)—are offered on a *tabakobon* (tobacco tray). Since one rarely smokes in the tearoom, the tray is presented as a sign for relaxation. *Zabuton* (cushions) and *teaburi* (hand warmers) may be offered. *Higashi* (dry sweets) are served on a wooden tray to complement the bitterness of the thin tea. Thin tea is prepared in a way similar to that of thick tea, except that less tea powder, of a lesser quality, is used, and it is dispensed from a *natsume*, a date-shaped lacquered wooden container; the bowl has a more casual or decorative character; and the guests are served individually prepared bowls of frothy, light tea. At the conclusion, the guests thank the host and leave; the host watches their departure from the open door of the tearoom.

The Japanese tea ceremony, a social act founded on reverence for all life and all things, is enacted in an idealized environment to create a perfect life. Its quiet atmosphere of harmony and respect for people and objects, with attention to cleanliness and order, strives to bring peace to body and spirit.

Flower arrangement (*ikebana*)   生け花●

Also called *kado*, or the Way of flowers. Japanese flower arrangement had its origin in early Buddhist flower offerings and developed
into a distinctive art form from the 15th century, with many styles and
schools. The attention given to the choice of plant material and container,
the placement of the branches, and the relationship of the branches to the
container and surrounding space distinguished this art from purely decorative uses of flowers.

Traditional Ikebana   伝統的生け花●

Buddhist ritual flower offerings (*kuge*) were introduced to Japan
from China early in the 7th century by Ono no Imoko, from whom the
Ikenobo school of arranging claims descent. The important "three-ele-
ment" (*mitsugusoku*) offering placed in front of a Buddhist image
consisted of an incense burner flanked by a candlestick and a vase of
flowers. These flower offerings were arranged with the main stem
approximately one and a half times the height of the container and set
vertically at its center; two additional stems were placed symmetrically
to the left and right.

Aside from religious offerings, there is no record of any systematized form of flower arrangement in Japan prior to the late 15th century.
From the *mitsugusoku* tradition developed the style known as *rikka*
("standing flowers"), a more sophisticated arrangement that sought to
reflect the majesty of nature and from which all later schools of Japanese
flower arrangement derive.

During the 16th and 17th centuries, although the Ikenobo school
predominated, various schools of rikka rose and flourished under the
patronage of the aristocracy.

In the late 16th century, a new form of flower arrangement called
nageire ("to throw or fling into") emerged for use in the tea ceremony. An
austere and simple form was required for *chabana*, a general term for
flower arrangements used in the TEA CEREMONY, rather than the increasingly elaborate rikka styles. Sen no Rikyu (1522–1591) is regarded as the
founder of both the ritualistic tea ceremony and the accompanying
nageire style of flower arrangement, in which a single vase might hold
only one flower disposed with deceptively simple elegance.

An example of *ikebana*
(flower arrangement).

The late 17th century saw the emergence of a thriving merchant
class and a shift away from aristocratic and priestly forms of flower
arrangement. A growing demand for simplification of the increasingly
contrived rikka styles gave rise to a new form of arrangement called

shoka or *seika* (living flowers), basically consisting of three main branches arranged in an asymmetrical triangle. Whereas rikka expressed the majesty of nature by symbolic representation of a landscape, the ideal in shoka was to convey the plant's essence. Shoka combined the dignity of rikka with the simplicity of nageire, and by the end of the 18th century it had become the most popular style. Diverse angles of placement and varying lengths of branches define the styles of the various schools of shoka. Early in the 19th century, the three main branches used in shoka became commonly known as *ten* (heaven), *chi* (earth), and *jin* (man). The height of the jin varies, but the ten is two-thirds as high as the jin, while the chi is one-third as high.

Modern Ikebana　　　　　　　　　　　　現代の生け花●

After the Meiji Restoration of 1868, traditional Japanese arts, including ikebana, were temporarily overwhelmed by enthusiasm for Western culture. In the late 19th century, however, there was a revival of ikebana when Ohara Unshin (1861–1914), founder of the Ohara school, introduced his *moribana* (piled-up flowers) style. Based on the classic principles of the three-branch design, moribana stressed color and natural plant growth, utilizing low arrangements that sometimes nearly touched the sides of shallow, wide-mouthed containers. It was probably designed to employ newly introduced Western flowering plants.

In the late Taisho (1912–1926) and early Showa (1926–1989) periods, the foundations of modern ikebana were laid in the work of Ohara Koun (1880–1938) and Adachi Choka (1887–1969), among others. Up until about 1930, ikebana was taught exclusively by private instructors in upper-class homes, but now masters began to concentrate on developing ikebana schools that could attract large numbers of students from all social classes. They emphasized three-dimensional arrangements that were loosely derived from the traditional triangle pattern of the ten-chi-jin (heaven-earth-man) form of shoka.

Teshigahara Sofu, founder of the Sogetsu school of *ikebana*.

In the postwar era, avant-garde ikebana (*zen'eibana*), spearheaded by Sogetsu school founder Teshigahara Sofu (1900–1979), Ohara Houn (1908–), and Nakayama Bumpo (1899–1986), revolutionized the materials considered acceptable. These artists used not only live flowers and grasses but also plastic, plaster, and steel to express surrealistic and abstract concepts in their arrangements.

Today, there are approximately 3,000 ikebana schools in Japan, with 15 million to 20 million students, mostly women between the ages of 18 and 26. The most popular styles are the Ikenobo, Ohara, and Sogetsu, each of which attracts some 3 million students. Still practiced are rikka and shoka, as well as more modern styles.

Before World War II, foreign interest in, and knowledge of, ikebana was scant. After the war, however, ikebana became popular with the wives of Allied military officers stationed in Japan, and many returned home as certified teachers, bringing the influence of ikebana to untold numbers of students abroad. Ikebana International, founded in Tokyo in 1956 by Ellen Gordon Allen (1898–1972), encourages the teaching of ikebana as an art form throughout the world. Overseas expansion of ikebana schools, which began seriously in the 1960s, continues today.

Calligraphy (*shodo*) 書道●

In Japan, as in other countries in the Chinese cultural sphere, calligraphy is considered one of the fine arts. In China, the birthplace of the East Asian tradition of calligraphy, the three disciplines—poetry, calligraphy, and painting—were considered the proper attainments of every cultured person, and excellence in writing thought to be a manifestation of the practitioner's character. The respect accorded to calligraphy in Japan is essentially an extension of its status in China.

The history of Japanese calligraphy begins with the introduction into Japan of the Chinese writing system in about the 5th century AD. Initially the Japanese wrote in Chinese, but they soon began using Chinese characters, or KANJI, in new ways to suit the requirements of their native language. The poetry anthology *Man'yoshu* (mid-8th century), for example, was written using Chinese characters to convey either Japanese words or syllables. The latter phonetic method of writing is now known as *man'yogana*. This practice ultimately led to the creation in the early 9th century of Japanese syllabaries, or KANA, that were used either alone or in combination with Chinese characters. The Japanese kana script was in wide use in the 10th century and emerged as a major calligraphic form after the 11th century. Nevertheless, for a long time the Chinese language retained its status as the literary language of the elite, and to varying degrees it was favored in later periods as well.

Scripts 書体●

Various types of Chinese-character scripts, or *shotai*, representing the historical development of writing in China, are practiced. *Tensho*, or archaic script, is traditionally used for carving official seals. *Reisho*, or clerical script, was once used for official documents. These are very ancient Chinese scripts and did not come into extensive use in Japan until the Edo period (1600–1868), when Chinese historical studies received much attention. More common is *kaisho*, or block-style script, perhaps the most popular style since the characters are easily recognizable. *Gyosho*, or "running-style" script, is created by a faster movement of the brush and some consequent abbreviation of the character. This script is frequently used for informal writing. *Sosho*, or "grass-writing," is a true cursive style that abbreviates and links parts of a character, resulting in fluid and curvilinear writing. In sosho writing, variations in the size of different characters may occur in the flow of a column, and some characters may be joined to the next, creating rhythmic and artistic forms.

Implements 道具●

Compared to writing styles, calligraphy implements have changed very little since the early days of the art. There are two basic kinds of brush: *futofude* (thick brush) and *hosofude* (slender brush); the former is generally used for the main body of a text, and the latter for inscriptions and signature at the end of a work, or for small-character calligraphy or fine cursive writing. *Sumi*, or Chinese ink, is usually made of soot from burned wood or oil mixed with fishbone or hide glue and dried into a stick. To make liquid ink the stick is rubbed on an inkstone, or *suzuri*, that has an indentation at one end to hold water that gradually darkens as the stick is rubbed. The *suiteki*, or small water dropper, which is either ceramic or metal, completes the basic paraphernalia. When not in use, writing equipment is kept in a box called a *suzuribako*, which is usually lacquer ware and often elaborately decorated.

Brushes, ink stone, and other calligraphy implements.

Early History 初期の歴史●

With the introduction of BUDDHISM and Confucianism to Japan around the 6th century, numerous examples of Chinese writing entered Japan, mostly sutras and Buddhist commentaries written in brush and ink on paper in varied script styles. The earliest extant handwritten text by a Japanese is thought to be the *Commentary on the Lotus Sutra*, which is purported to have been written by Prince Shotoku (574–622). It is written in a typical clerical-cursive style that was current in China from the late 4th century to the late 6th century.

From the late 7th century through the 8th century, early Tang (618–907) dynasty calligraphic styles were rapidly mastered in Japan, notably through increased sutra-copying activities that began in earnest with the establishment of the Shakyojo, or Sutra-Copying Bureau, in the capital city of Nara.

An early influence upon the development of Japanese calligraphy was the monk Kukai (774–835), who introduced the calligraphic style of Yan Zhenqing (709–785), then popular in metropolitan Tang China, and promoted an awareness of calligraphy as an aesthetic form. Kukai and his contemporaries, Emperor Saga (786–842) and the courtier Tachibana no Hayanari (d 842), were known to later generations as the Sampitsu (the "Three Brushes").

A major transformation in calligraphy from a rigid emulation of Chinese styles to creative assimilation occurred in the 10th and 11th centuries. This was the time of the Sanseki (Three Brush Traces): Ono no Tofu (894–966), Fujiwara no Sukemasa (944–998), and Fujiwara no Yukinari (or Fujiwara no Kozei; 972–1028).

Kamakura and Muromachi (1333–1568) Periods　　　鎌倉・室町時代●

Chinese Song (960–1279) calligraphy had a great impact on Japanese practitioners, especially through ZEN monks. Eisai (1141–1215) and Dogen (1200–1253) returned from pilgrimages to China in the late 12th and early 13th centuries, respectively, and their surviving calligraphic works reflect the influence of the Southern Song revival of Northern Song calligraphy, a trend embodied in the works of Su Shi (1036–1101) and Huang Tingjian (1045–1105). Huang Tingjian, in particular, was eagerly emulated by the monks of the Gozan Zen temples, such as Kokan Shiren (1278–1346), who mastered both the semicursive gyosho and cursive sosho modes. No calligrapher, however, was so artistically aware of the expressive potential of Song calligraphy as Soho Myocho (1282–1337). His powerful style follows in the Song tradition, particularly that of Huang Tingjian, without being overly imitative. Lanqi Daolong (J: Rankei Doryu; 1213–1278), one of a number of Chinese monks who came to Japan, wrote in the style of the Song calligrapher Zhang Jizhi (1186–1266), best known for his regular script.

Works of calligraphy by Zen monks came to be known as *bokuseki* ("ink traces") and were prized by monastic communities, which treated them as icons symbolizing spiritual transmission from master to master.

Edo (1600–1868) Period　　　江戸時代●

The establishment in 1661, largely by Chinese monks, of the Obaku sect of Zen in Uji, south of Kyoto, contributed to an influx of Ming-dynasty (1368–1644) styles of calligraphy. They were enthusiastically received by Japanese men of letters, who created a new orthodoxy called *karayo* (Chinese mode), which eventually overshadowed the *wayo* tradition. Hosoi Kotaku (1658–1735), Rai San'yo (1781–1832), and Sakuma Shozan (1811–1864) are among the more famous calligraphers who wrote in this mode, which was greatly favored by literati scholars and artists throughout the Edo period.

Contemporary Calligraphy 現代の書道●

In the modern era, calligraphy has continued to thrive, and it is represented, along with painting and sculpture, at the government-sponsored annual Nitten exhibitions. In post-World War II Japan, avant-garde calligraphy (*zen'ei shodo*) was born—a genre in itself. This recent trend in calligraphy asserts new artistic forms of pure abstraction, coming close to some aspects of 20th-century Western pictorial art and deviating sharply from the traditional script styles and emulative aspects of the age-old art of calligraphy.

B*onsai* 盆栽●

The art of dwarfing trees or plants by growing and training them in containers according to prescribed techniques. The word bonsai also refers to the miniature potted trees themselves. Bonsai, which first appeared in China more than 1,000 years ago, was introduced to Japan in the Kamakura period (1185–1333) on the wave of cultural borrowings that included ZEN Buddhism. In Japan the art was refined to an extent unapproached in China.

Bonsai can be developed from seeds or cuttings, from young trees, or from naturally occurring stunted trees transplanted into containers. Most bonsai range in height from 5 centimeters (2 in) to 1 meter (approximately 3 ft). Bonsai are kept small and trained by pruning branches and roots, by periodic repotting, by pinching off new growth, and by wiring the branches and trunk so that they grow into the desired shape.

Grown in special containers, bonsai are usually kept outdoors, although they are often displayed on special occasions in the *tokonoma*, the alcove in traditional Japanese rooms designed for the display of artistic objects. An unglazed, dark-colored container is usually chosen for a classic bonsai or to impart a look of age, but glazed containers are often used for flowering trees. As a rule, oval containers complement deciduous trees; rectangular ones, evergreens.

Growing Bonsai 仕立て方●

Given proper care, bonsai can live for hundreds of years, with prized specimens being passed from generation to generation, admired for their age, and revered as a reminder of those who have cared for them over the centuries. Venerable bonsai are generally more respected than young ones, but age is not essential. It is more important that the tree produce the artistic effect desired, that it be in proper proportion to the appropriate container, and that it be in good health. The two basic styles of bonsai are the classic (*koten*) and the informal or comic (*bunjin*). In the former, the trunk of the tree is wider at the base and tapers off toward the top; it is just the opposite in the bunjin, a style more difficult to master.

Bonsai are ordinary trees or plants, not special hybrid dwarfs. Small-leaved varieties are most suitable. In Japan varieties of pine, bamboo, and plum are most often used. The artist never merely duplicates nature but rather expresses a personal aesthetic or sensibility by manipulating it. The miniaturized tree may suggest a scene from nature, a family grouping, a scene from a play, or a foolish or even grotesque character. But in all cases the bonsai must look natural and never show the intervention of human hands.

Aesthetics and Philosophy 美学と哲学●

The bonsai with its container and soil, physically independent of the earth since its roots are not planted in it, is a separate entity, complete in itself, yet part of nature. This is what is meant by the expression "heaven and earth in one container." A bonsai tree should always be positioned off-center in its container, for not only is asymmetry vital to the visual effect, but the center point is symbolically where heaven and earth meet, and nothing should occupy this place. Another aesthetic principle is the triangular pattern necessary for visual balance and for expression of the relationship shared by a universal principle (life-giving energy or deity), the artist, and the tree itself. Tradition holds that three basic virtues are necessary to create a bonsai: *shin-zen-bi* (truth, goodness, and beauty).

Origami 折紙●

Folded paper; also the art of folding paper to form shaped figures and ornamental objects. Origami ranges from a simple form of child's play to a complex art form. It is used in certain Japanese ceremonies and rituals, as well as for practical, educational, and entertainment purposes.

Background 背景●

Origami as a form of entertainment probably began during the Heian period (794–1185). Origami with only folding and no cutting developed first in the Muromachi period (1333–1568). In the Edo period (1600–1868) other techniques of folding, cutting, and dyeing paper were developed. By the Taisho period (1912–26) patterns for some 150 different kinds of origami figures had been established. The new art of creative origami does not, generally speaking, use cutting or coloring techniques, and the main pattern of expression is cubic.

Uses for Origami   折紙の利用●

The oldest known use of origami in Japan is found in the *katashiro*, used from ancient times in Shinto ceremonies at the Ise Shrine. The katashiro is a symbolic representation of a deity. Vestiges of katashiro can still be found in the paper cutouts of human figures currently used in various purification ceremonies and in the paper dolls displayed on the occasion of the DOLL FESTIVAL in March.

Origami also plays an important part in formal etiquette. There are many different ways to fold wrapping paper for gifts presented on ceremonial occasions or on special days in the cycle of annual events. Weddings and funerals, in particular, require elaborate folded paper ornaments such as the male and female butterflies that adorn SAKE bottles. Paper folding has been an important part of Japanese folk ritual as well; for example, it is used in making *noshi*, a kind of traditional ornament attached to gifts.

During the late Meiji period (1868–1912) and the Taisho period, origami was used as a teaching device in kindergartens and primary schools. In the beginning of the Showa period (1926–89), creativity came to be emphasized in Japanese education, and origami was criticized because children were required to handle the paper in standardized ways. Recently, however, origami has come to be appreciated once again as an educational technique. In particular, it is used to teach such concepts as the relationship between a plane and a solid.

Origami in the World   世界の折紙●

There are a few examples of early paper folding to be found in other parts of the world. Some folded paper considered Asian in origin was brought to Europe by the Moors in the 8th century. There is evidence that the Japanese origami for dog was imitated in Spain, England, and France in the form of a bird, horse, or hen.

The number of devotees of origami and origami associations in Japan and abroad has rapidly increased in recent years.

G*o*   碁●

Also called *igo*. A game for two players in which black and white stones are alternately placed at the intersections of lines on a board with the object of capturing the opponent's stones and securing control over open spaces on the board.

Some historical accounts place the origin of go in ancient China, while others trace the game to India, where early forms of chess were also played more than 4,000 years ago. Whereas chess spread widely throughout the West and the East (it is called SHOGI and played by somewhat different rules in Japan), go was until recently played only in China (where it is known as *weiqi*), Korea (*paduk*), and Japan. It is somewhat hard to understand why the game did not spread further in early times, for some have called it the world's most intellectual game, and many aficionados in Japan consider it a true art. Its rules are simple and few, yet the number of possible play sequences is staggering; it is calculated to be 10^{750} or 1 followed by 750 zeros.

Basic Rules

ルール●

Modern go is played on a wooden board, the surface of which is engraved with 19 vertical and 19 horizontal lines, thus producing 361 intersections. Nine of the intersections are specially marked with a small dot and called *hoshi* (star); these serve to orient the players and are also used as positions for handicap stones in official matches.

Only four basic rules are necessary to describe go, the second of which contains the central premise of the game: (1) Two players (Black and White) alternate in placing their stones on unoccupied intersections of the board, Black being the first to play. A stone cannot be moved once it is played, except when it is captured. (2) If a stone or a group of stones is completely surrounded by the opponent's stones with no empty points within the surrounding area, it is captured, removed from the board, and retained by the opponent. (3) Each captured stone or surrounded intersection counts as one point. (In China the stones on the board are also counted.) (4) If a move would result in the reversal of the previous move by the opponent, the player is required to abstain from that move until other plays have been made; this is called *ko* and is meant to prevent stalemates through perpetual repetition.

Match between two *kudan* (ninth grade) *go* masters, Takagawa Kaku (right) and Kitani Minoru.

The game ends when all stones have been placed or the possibilities for gaining territory or capturing the opponent's stones have been exhausted. At this point all captured stones are placed in the opponent's vacant spaces, and the player with the most remaining vacant spaces under his control wins.

History

歴史●

Legend attributes the invention of go to a vassal named Wu in ancient China, perhaps 4,000 years ago, although some accounts state that the game developed in India. From China go was brought to Korea and later to Japan by Chinese missionaries in the 5th or 6th century. The oldest go board in Japan is displayed at the Shosoin in Nara, and the game is mentioned in the 11th-century *Tale of Genji*.

Modern go history begins in 1612, when the Tokugawa shogunate set up four go schools, called Hon'imbo, Hayashi, Inoue, and Yasui. Intense competitions were held to determine the best player of the game, who was installed in the position of *godokoro*. Annual official games were held in the presence of the shogun at his castle in Edo (now Tokyo); these were called *oshirogo*. Dosaku, Hon'imbo IV (1645–1702), was the most outstanding player of the early modern period and is referred to as the "saint of go."

Professional go players met hard times after the Meiji Restoration (1868) when their stipends were discontinued by the government. Top professionals formed a study group called Hoensha in the Meiji period (1868–1912), and the Japan Go Association was formed in 1924. At this time Shusai, Hon'imbo XXI (1874–1940), gave the title Hon'imbo to the association to be awarded in regular competition thereafter.

Professional and International Go　　　　　　プロと碁の国際化●

There are millions of go fans in Japan but only about 400 professionals. Amateurs are ranked from the ninth *kyu* or degree, the lowest, to the first kyu; from there the rankings advance to *shodan* (first grade), with *rokudan* (sixth grade) usually the highest amateur ranking. A small number of *nanadan* (seventh grade) amateurs are as strong as professionals of the professional first grade; the top of the professional rankings is *kudan* (ninth grade). The ranks are used to decide handicaps for official matches; each rank represents a one-stone handicap for amateurs and a one-third-stone handicap for professionals. Promotions are granted on the basis of official games (*oteai*). Newspapers sponsor regular competitions; professionals make their living through prize money offered in these matches.

Go is slowly but steadily spreading in the Western world. The International Go Federation, based in Tokyo, was organized in 1982. As of 1989 there were go associations in 35 countries, with an estimated combined membership of 13 million.

S*hogi*　　　　　　　　　　　　　　　　将棋●

A board game involving two players and 40 pieces; commonly referred to in the West as "Japanese chess." The object of the game is to checkmate the opponent's king. There are many similarities to chess in the way the pieces move, but what is different is that a captured piece can be used again as one's own piece. There are an estimated 20 million shogi players in Japan. The present-day Japan Shogi Federation (Nihon

Shogi Remmei) was founded in 1947.

The prototype of shogi is believed to have originated in India. From there it made its way to Europe via Persia, becoming what is known today as Western chess. It also moved east, to China, where it became known as xiangqi (Japanese pronunciation shogi). Shogi may have been introduced to Japan in the Nara period (710–794) by Japanese envoys who were sent to Tang dynasty (618–907) China. In the Heian period (794–1185) several forms of shogi were popular among the nobility, but by the Muromachi period (1333–1568) the rules of the game had been modified, and the game had become very much like present-day shogi.

In 1607 the Tokugawa shogunate established an office for shogi and GO, under the jurisdiction of the commissioner of shrines and temples; a monk named Hon'imbo Sansa (1558–1623) was made its head. Later the office was turned over to Ohashi Sokei (1555–1634), who was installed as its first lifetime *meijin* ("master"). The meijin rank was inherited within a shogi "family"; a meijin remained one for life, with no alteration of status despite any change in his actual ability. The lifetime meijin system was abolished in 1935, and annual contests for the title of meijin were begun. Kimura Yoshio (1905–86) was the first to win the title. Championship matches, usually sponsored by newspaper companies, are held regularly, and game moves in such matches are featured daily in newspaper columns.

The *osho* (king) *shogi* piece.

The Game   ルール●

The shogi board is a square wooden block with a grid of 81 squares. Each player uses 20 flat wooden pieces of an elongated, irregular pentagon shape. Each piece is placed on the grid with its apex pointing toward the opponent. The pieces are distinguished by characters written on each side. Captured pieces are placed to the player's right and returned ("dropped") to the board at the discretion of the player who captured the piece, for his or her own use.

The *osho* (king; *o* for short) and *gyokusho* (jewel; *gyoku* for short) are in essence the same piece, i.e., a king. Making one king a "jewel" (by adding one stroke to the character for "king") avoided having two kings on the same board, a custom that supposedly originated on the request of an emperor in ancient times. The better player has the king and the other player has the jewel. The osho or gyokusho can move one square in any direction, like a king in chess.

Shogi match between Oyama Yasuharu (right), holder of the special *judan* (tenth grade) rank, and Masuda Kozo, holder of the *kudan* (ninth grade) rank.

The other pieces are the *hisha* (abbreviated, only in writing, as *hi*), which moves like a rook in chess; the *kakugyo* (*kaku* for short), which corresponds to the chess bishop; the *kinsho* (*kin* for short), or "gold," which can move one square in any direction except diagonally backward; the *ginsho* (*gin* for short), or "silver," which moves one square in any direction except sideways or straight backward; the *keima* (*kei* for short), which is similar to the knight in chess except that it may jump only to one of two squares two ranks ahead and one file to the left or right; the *kyosha* (*kyo* for short), or "lance," which moves any number of squares straight forward only; and the *fuhyo* (*fu* for short), which corresponds to the chess pawn except that it captures forward, not diagonally. The forward, sideways, backward, or diagonal movement of each piece is therefore restricted in shogi, in ways similar to (but not exactly corresponding to) the various moves permitted to the pieces in chess.

The pieces can take enemy pieces that are in range of their movements. The two aspects of shogi that distinguish it from chess are *utsu*, the use of captured pieces, and *naru*, the promotion of one's own pieces. All the pieces except the o or gyoku and kin can be promoted after penetrating enemy territory. The piece is turned over to show its new name. The hisha becomes a *ryuo* (*ryu* for short), which has the combined powers of a rook and a king. The kaku becomes a *ryuma* (*uma* for short), which has the combined powers of a bishop and a king. The ginsho becomes the *narigin*, which has the same powers as the kin. The kei, kyo, and fu can all be promoted to the powers of a kin. Their names after promotion are, respectively, *narikei*, *narikyo*, and *tokin*. To promote or not is a matter of choice. A promoted piece returns to its original status when captured.

To begin play, the board is placed between two players and the pieces are lined up. Players alternate, moving one piece at a time. There are three important restrictions: one cannot drop a fu on a file in which there is already a friendly fu, one cannot drop a piece where there is no room for its next move, and one cannot checkmate the enemy gyoku by dropping a fu. It is permissible to checkmate using a fu on the board. One forfeits immediately upon violation of any of the above three rules. In the case of a stalemate, the game must be played over. When both players' kings enter enemy territory and neither player can check the other, victory is determined by the number of pieces left.

Japanese businessmen playing Mah-Jongg.

Mah-Jongg (J: *majan*)   麻雀●

Game of Chinese origin usually played by four persons with 136 pieces called tiles. The two Chinese characters for Mah-Jongg literally mean "house sparrow," and the name is said to derive from the way the shuffling of the tiles sounds like the twittering of sparrows. It is thought that the game itself derives from tarot cards introduced to China from Europe. Mah-Jongg is similar to the Western card game of rummy in that the object is to collect combinations of sequences and sets of identical tiles.

Mah-Jongg was introduced to Japan early in the 20th century. By the 1920s it had become especially popular in urban areas, and it achieved an unprecedented level of popularity after World War II. Today there are more than 25,000 Mah-Jongg parlors in the country and more than 14 million players. In Japan Mah-Jongg has traditionally been a man's game, frequently played for money.

Pachinko　　　　　　　　　　　　　パチンコ ●

Japan's most popular arcade game; a variety of pinball. First played commercially in Nagoya in 1948, it rapidly became popular throughout the country. It has been estimated that more than 30 million Japanese play the game on a regular basis. Pachinko is played in brightly lit, gaudy parlors. A player buys a number of steel balls, loads them into a pachinko machine, and (in one of the original mechanical models) flips a lever in order to propel a ball to the top of the machine. The ball then bounces down through a maze of pegs, either falling into a winning hole on the way down or becoming lost in a hole at the bottom of the machine. When the ball enters a winning hole, the machine discharges additional balls, which can be fed back into the machine or redeemed for prizes (which are sometimes illegally exchanged for cash). Today, mechanical pachinko machines have been completely replaced by computer-controlled machines in which a knob is turned and the balls are propelled automatically. Some newer types of pachinko machines have number displays similar to those of slot machines. A winning combination earns the player bonus points. The illegal use of certain types of these machines for gambling has led to their regulation.

Karaoke　　　　　　　　　　　　　カラオケ ●

Prerecorded musical accompaniment, usually on compact or laser disc. An essential part of one of the most popular leisure-time activities in Japan: the singing of songs backed by karaoke musical accompaniment at bars and pubs, at parties, or at home. Recording studios and radio stations started using music-only karaoke tapes in the mid-1960s, and in the 1970s bar owners hit upon the idea of outfitting their establishments with karaoke sound systems so that patrons could sing along (today's systems display the song lyrics on a separate video monitor, and smaller systems are available for home use). Most karaoke establishments have a large and eclectic catalog of songs; the sentimental songs known as *enka* and contemporary music are among the most popular selections.

Comic magazines (*komikku zasshi*)　　　コミック雑誌●

The flourishing of a "comic culture" is one of the significant features of mass culture in present-day Japan. Comic magazines fall into four categories: boys' comics, girls' comics, youth comics, and adult comics. Comic magazines are published weekly, biweekly, and monthly.

Boys' and girls' comics average around 400 pages, and a given issue usually contains some 15 serialized stories. Especially popular serials may continue for 10 years. Total combined circulation of the major weekly boys' comic magazines is about 10 million, and it is estimated that two-thirds of all boys aged 5 to 18 read these magazines on a regular basis. More than one-sixth of Japanese girls in the same age group are regular readers of girls' comics. Youth and adult comics average about 250 pages and contain about 10 serialized "story cartoons" and 5 "nonsense cartoons" in each issue. Including the so-called vulgar comics, 40 to 50 different youth and adult comic magazines are published.

Hot springs (*onsen*)　　　温泉●

Hot springs are numerous in Japan, and for centuries the Japanese people have enjoyed hot spring bathing. Visits to hot spring resorts were hailed not only as a means of relaxation but also for the beneficial medicinal properties attributed to thermal spring water. Hot springs are still major attractions for vacationing Japanese, and many have been modernized and developed into large-scale resort complexes. Under the 1948 Hot Spring Law (Onsen Ho), the Japanese government recognizes as onsen only those hot springs that reach certain standards regarding temperature and mineral composition; the number of these as of 1990 was about 2,300. Since 1954 the Ministry of Health and Welfare has accorded special recognition to 64 hot spring resorts capable of providing medical treatment.

Dogo Hot Spring.

History of Utilization　　　利用の歴史●

Dogo Hot Spring in Iyo Province (now Ehime Prefecture) is reputedly the oldest hot spring in Japan. It was the site, according to tradition, of therapeutic bathing by several legendary or early historical emperors. Buddhist monks developed hot springs for medicinal purposes and used hot springs for the bathing that is part of the Buddhist purification ritual. Farmers and fishermen engaged in ritualistic baths at various times of the year.

Goto Konzan, a doctor in Edo (now Tokyo), noticed the effectiveness of hot spring bathing as a cure for certain disorders and in 1709 initiated the first medical study of hot springs, advocating the use of baths as therapy for various ailments. In 1874 the Japanese government undertook the chemical analysis of mineral springs. After the founding of the Balneotherapy Institute (now called the Medical Institute of Bioregulation) at Beppu Hot Spring in Oita Prefecture by Kyushu University in 1931, the medical study of hot springs began to be systematized, with many universities establishing research facilities at various hot springs. After World War II, national hot spring hospitals were created, making hot springs for medical treatment available around the country. Hot springs are utilized in the treatment of chronic rheumatism; neuralgia; chronic diseases of the stomach, intestines, liver, and gallbladder; hypertension; hemiplegia; glucosuria; and gout. They are also used for treating external injuries and for postoperative treatment and rehabilitation.

Martial arts (*bujutsu*) 武術●

Also called *bugei*; now usually called *budo* or "the martial Way." The Japanese terms encompass such martial arts as KENDO (fencing), JUDO, and KYUDO (archery). The old expression *bugei juhappan* (the 18 martial arts) refers to the arts of archery, horsemanship, spearmanship (*sojutsu*), fencing, swimming, *iai* (sword drawing), the short sword, the truncheon (*jitte*), dagger throwing (*shuriken*), needle spitting, the halberd (*naginata*), gunnery, roping, *yawara* (present-day judo), *ninjutsu* (spying), the staff, *mojiri* (a staff with numerous barbs on one end), and the chained sickle (*kusarigama*). KARATE is not considered one of the traditional Japanese martial arts, although it is sometimes referred to as such outside of Japan. In the Edo period (1600–1868), in addition to academic subjects, warriors were required to learn six martial arts: fencing, spearmanship, archery, horseback riding, *jujutsu* (now known as judo), and firearms. These six, together with military strategy, were called the seven martial arts. These were taught under the name *bushido* (the Way of the warrior).

After the Meiji Restoration (1868) the content of martial arts changed greatly, reflecting the fact that they were no longer meant to be used in combat and were no longer exclusive attainments of the warrior class. Reflecting this new circumstance, bujutsu was replaced by the term budo, implying that one would be trained in spiritual principles rather than for combat.

Modern budo seeks the development of skills through physical exercise and, by establishing objective standards of skills, provides opportunities for competition. In this sense it can be considered a form of sport. Yet behind the martial arts lie the philosophies of Confucianism, Buddhism, and Taoism. Japanese martial arts started with *waza* (skills) for killing and fighting and, through searches for *kokoro* (or *shin*, heart), the heart that transcends victory and defeat, were led to the Buddhist view of life and death and the Confucian way of natural harmony, yawara (pliancy).

The martial arts entail danger. As soon as one has dodged the enemy's attack through proper posture and body movement, one counters by attacking when the enemy is off guard. The means and methods for this are the basis for classification of the various martial arts. They can be roughly divided into those that use weapons and those that use the hands. Skills employing weapons aim to "strike and kill." Even when attacking the enemy empty-handed, the purpose of blows, thrusts, and kicks is to "strike and kill." On the other hand, unarmed skills such as throwing, restraining, squeezing, and immobilizing do not necessarily aim to kill and injure, but to "control violence yet not hurt life." However, these too, depending upon how they are employed, can be dangerous.

After World War II, there was a need to modify certain views of the martial arts, and the emphasis shifted from practical arts to sports that stress harmony and universality.

Judo 柔道●

One of the martial arts; a form of unarmed combat that stresses agile motions, astute mental judgment, and rigorous form rather than sheer physical strength. The Chinese character for *ju* derives from a passage in the ancient Chinese military treatise Sanlue, which states, "softness (*ju*; Ch: rou) controls hardness well." Judo techniques (*waza*) include throwing (*nagewaza*), grappling (*katamewaza*), and attacking vital points (*atemiwaza*). The first two techniques are used in competition, but the *atemiwaza* is used only in practice. Developed as a sport by Kano Jigoro (1860–1938) from *jujutsu*, judo has been valued as a method of exercise, moral training, and self-defense.

Throw executed by Nakamura Yukimasa, gold medal winner at the 1993 World Judo Championships.

Jujutsu began with *sechie-zumo* (court banquet wrestling), a court event popular in the Nara (710–794) and Heian (794–1185) periods. During the sustained peace of the Edo period (1600–1868) jujutsu developed as a self-defense martial art and was used in making arrests. Jujutsu schools proliferated during this period but declined with the collapse of the *samurai* class after the Meiji Restoration of 1868. In 1882 Kano Jigoro organized the Kodokan *judo* school at Eishoji, a temple in Tokyo.

Kano Jigoro set up a system of ranks (*dan*) and classes (*kyu*) as an encouragement for his disciples. These designations have been recognized internationally. There are ranks from 1 to 10, with 10 the highest. Those in ranks 1 to 5 wear a black belt, ranks 6 to 8 have a scarlet and white striped belt, and those in ranks 9 to 10 have a scarlet belt. The classes are below the ranks and range from the fifth class to the first and highest class. Adults in the first to third class wear a brown belt; children in the first to third class wear a purple belt. Those in the fourth and fifth class wear a white belt.

Kendo 剣道●

Japanese fencing based on the techniques of the two-handed

sword of the *samurai*. Before the Showa period (1926–1989) it was customarily referred to as *kenjutsu* or *gekken*. Kendo is a relatively recent term that implies spiritual discipline as well as fencing technique.

Fencing with the single-edged, straight-blade sword was probably introduced from Sui (589–618) or early Tang (618–907) China. The cultivation of sword skills flourished during the Kamakura shogunate (1192–1333). With the establishment of nationwide peace by the Tokugawa shogunate in the early 17th century, kenjutsu went into a decline. The moral and spiritual element became prominent, drawing on Confucianism, SHINTO, and BUDDHISM, especially ZEN. Kenjutsu became an element for training the mind and body. In the late 18th century protective equipment and bamboo training swords (*shinai*) were introduced.

The weapon is a hollow cylinder made of four shafts of split bamboo. It is bound with a leather grip and cap connected by a silk or nylon cord and a leather thong wound three times around the bamboo cylinder and knotted. The length varies for different age groups. Fencers are protected by the *men* (face mask); the trunk of the body is protected by the *do* (chest protector). The thighs are protected with five overlapping quilted panels (*tare*), and the hands with padded mittens (*kote*). Training is based on a variety of movements of attack and defense known as *waza*. Most fundamental are stance, footwork, cuts, thrusts, feints, and parries.

Match during the national championship *kendo* tournament for female university students.

Kyudo (Japanese archery)   弓道●

Kyujutsu, the technique of the bow, was the term more commonly used until well into the 19th century. Under the influence of Chinese culture from the 6th century, Japanese archery was divided into military and civil archery. Military archery was primarily mounted archery, while civil archery was shooting in the standing position, with emphasis on form and etiquette. Over the centuries the rules of archery became systematized, and schools began to proliferate. Those of the Ogasawara school, the Heki school, and the Honda school dominate modern kyudo.

The bow is usually 2 meters 21 centimeters (7 ft 3 in) in length. It is an eccentric bow; that is, two-thirds of its length is above the grip and one-third below. Two target distances are used in modern kyudo competition. Usually the archer stands 28 meters (92 ft) from a circular target 36 centimeters (14 in) in diameter. In contrast to Western archery, in *kyudo* the emphasis is on form rather than accuracy. Certain schools are strongly influenced by ZEN.

K*arate* 空手●

Art of self-defense that uses no weapons and relies instead on three main techniques: arm strikes (*uchi*), thrusts (*tsuki*), and kicks (*keri*). A distinction is made between offensive and defensive techniques, which are modified according to the position of one's opponent. For defense, there are various parrying methods (*uke*) corresponding to each of the methods of offense. There are two sections in karate competitions: form (*kata*) competition and sparring (*kumite*) matches.

Karate was historically most widely practiced in China and OKI-NAWA and thus is not considered one of the traditional Japanese martial arts. Current forms of karate developed from a style of Chinese boxing called *quanfa* (literally, "rules of the fist"; known as kung fu in the West; J: *kempo*), which is thought to have been transmitted by the Indian Buddhist monk Bodhidharma (d ca 532) along with ZEN Buddhist teachings to Chinese disciples at Shaolin temple (J: Shorinji) in the southern province of Henan. The method of self-defense traced to these beginnings is called Shorinji kempo in Japan; it had spread widely through China by the time of the medieval Ming dynasty (1368–1644), but it was suppressed in the Qing period (1644–1912) because it was used by a secret society aspiring to reestablish Ming rule. The subsequent develop-

A *karate* practitioner throws a reverse punch.

ment of karate took place primarily in Okinawa. Chinese fighting techniques (referred to in Japanese as *tode*; literally, "Tang hand") merged with indigenous techniques (called *te*; literally, "hand") to produce the karate style. A karate club was established at a middle school in Okinawa in 1905 after the islands had become a prefecture of modern Japan, and the sport thereafter began to emerge from obscurity. It became known throughout mainland Japan in 1922, when Funakoshi Gichin, an Okinawan master, performed a demonstration in Tokyo.

After World War II, karate and the other martial arts experienced a decline that lasted until around 1955. After that the sport increased in popularity, and it is more widespread now than ever.

S*umo* 相撲●

A 2,000-year-old form of wrestling that is considered by many to be the national sport of Japan. Sumo became a professional sport in the early Edo period (1600–1868), and although it is practiced today by clubs in high schools, colleges, and amateur associations, it has its greatest appeal as a professional spectator sport.

The object of this compelling sport is for a wrestler to force his opponent out of the center circle of the elevated cement-hard clay ring (*dohyo*) or cause him to touch the surface of the dohyo with any part of his body other than the soles of his feet. The wrestlers may spend as much as the first four minutes in the ring in a ritual of stamping, squatting, puffing, glowering, and tossing salt in the air, but the actual conflict is only a matter of seconds. To decide who has stepped out or touched down first is often extremely difficult and requires the closest attention of a referee (*gyoji*), dressed in the court costume of a 14th-century nobleman, on the dohyo and judges (*shimpan*) sitting around the dohyo at floor level.

The Japan Sumo Association (Nihon Sumo Kyokai), the governing body of professional sumo, officially lists 70 winning techniques consisting of assorted throws, trips, lifts, thrusts, shoves, and pulls. Of these, 48 are considered the "classic" techniques but the number in actual daily use is probably half that. Of primary concern in sumo are ring decorum and sportsmanship.

Unique to sumo is the use of a belly band or belt called a *mawashi*, which is folded, looped over the groin, wrapped tightly around the waist, and knotted in the rear. Most sumo matches center on the wrestlers' attempts to get a firm, two-handed grip on their opponent's mawashi while blocking him from getting a similar grip on theirs. With the right grip they then have the leverage to execute a throw, trip, or lift. During tournaments, but not in practice, a string apron (*sagari*) is also worn tucked into the front folds of the mawashi, whence it falls frequently in the heat of the match.

Dohyo-iri (ring-entrance ceremonies) by *makuuchi* wrestlers.

The Wrestlers 力士●

Traditionally sumo has drawn the majority of its recruits from rural communities. Most wrestlers start in their mid-teens and retire from this rigorous sport in their early thirties. Top-ranking wrestlers have an average height of 185 centimeters (6 ft) and an average weight of 148 kilograms (326 lb), with successful exceptions running from as light as 102 kilograms (225 lb) to as heavy as 239 kilograms (527 lb).

The wrestlers in professional sumo are organized into a pyramid. Progress from the ranks of beginners at the bottom to the grand champion's pinnacle at the top depends entirely on ability. The speed with which a wrestler rises or falls depends entirely on his win-loss record at the end of each tournament. Based on this, his ranking is calculated for the next tournament and then written with his name and those of other wrestlers in Chinese characters on a graded list called the *banzuke*. The only permanent rank is that of *yokozuna*, "grand champion," but a

yokozuna who cannot maintain a certain level of championship performance is expected to retire.

Only wrestlers in the top two divisions, *juryo* and *makuuchi*,
receive regular salaries. They also enjoy the title *sekitori*, "top-ranking
wrestler," and the right to have their long, oiled hair combed into the elegant *oichomage* (ginkgo-leaf knot) during tournaments.

Annual Tournaments 本場所●

Traditionally only two tournaments were held each year, but by
1958 this number had grown to six, where it stood in the early 1990s. The
big six are held every other month in four different cities.

In 1949 the length of a tournament increased from the traditional
10 days to 15 days. A tournament day starts with the apprentices of
maezumo (pre-*sumo*) fighting in the qualifying rounds, then the long
march of the four lower divisions across the dohyo begins. The boy-men
in these divisions—*jonokuchi, jonidan, sandamme*, and *makushita*—wrestle
on 7 of the 15 days of the tournament. For them a winning record
(*kachikoshi*) begins with 4 wins against 3 losses, which ensures promotion.
Anything less is a losing record (*makekoshi*) and demotion. A *zensho*
record (all wins, no losses) of course boosts a wrestler way up the ladder,
usually into a higher division.

A *sumo* match of *makuuchi* wrestlers.

Sekitori in the juryo and makuuchi divisions wrestle once a day
for 15 days. Sekitori must win 8 of their 15 bouts for a kachikoshi record.
Makekoshi starts with 8 losses. The entire tournament is won by the
makuuchi wrestler with the most wins.

The Stable System 部屋制度●

The sumo stable system has as its purpose the training of young
wrestlers into senior champions while inculcating them with the strict
etiquette, discipline, and special values of sumo.

Physically, a stable (*heya*; literally, "room") is a self-contained unit
complete with all living-training facilities. Every professional sumo
wrestler belongs to one, making it his home throughout his ring career and
often even into retirement. The only exceptions to the live-in rule are the
married sekitori, who may live outside with their wives and commute to
daily practice at the *heya*. As of June 1992 there were 44 active heya.

A stable is managed under the absolute control of a single boss
(*oyakata*). All oyakata are former senior wrestlers and members of the
Japan Sumo Association. The stable they run is usually the stable where
they wrestled. Oyakata are generally married and live in special quarters
with their wives, known by the title of *okamisan*, the only women to live
in heya. Okamisan play an important behind-the-scenes role in the

smooth operation of a stable, but their duties never include cooking or cleaning for the wrestlers. These and all other housekeeping chores outside the oyakata's quarters are performed by apprentices and low-ranked wrestlers. Heya expenses are paid for by regular allowances from the Japan Sumo Association and gifts from the heya fan club.

Sumo Practice   稽古●

Keiko, "practice," is a sacred word in sumo, and a brief description of the morning practice that takes place every day in every heya will give an idea of the sumo way of life.

The day begins at 4:00 or 5:00 AM for the youngest, lowest-ranked wrestlers, who ready the ring and begin their exercises. The higher a wrestler's rank, the longer he may sleep. Makushita are up at 6:30 and in the ring at 7:00. Juryo wrestlers enter the ring around 8:00 and makuuchi shortly after.

At 11:00 AM the wrestlers head for the baths, seniors first, followed by the lower ranks. Next is brunch, the first and largest sumo meal of the day. This consists of *chankonabe*, a high-calorie stew made with a seaweed-base stock and containing chicken, pork, fish, *tofu*, bean sprouts, cabbage, carrots, onions, and other vegetables. The senior wrestlers eat bowl upon bowl of this stew together with bowl upon bowl of rice washed down with quarts of beer; the younger wrestlers get what is left.

The Japan Sumo Association   日本相撲協会●

Every aspect of professional sumo is controlled by the Japan Sumo Association, composed of 105 retired wrestlers known as elders (*toshiyori*) and including representation from sumo's "working ranks," i.e., active wrestlers, referees, and ring stewards (*yobidashi*). The Japan Sumo Association is organized in several divisions such as Business, Judging, Off-Season Tours (Jungyo), Out-of-Tokyo Tournaments (Chiho Basho), Training, and Guidance, supervised by an elected 10-man board of directors under the leadership of a president or managing director (*rijicho*).

Yakult Swallows manager Nomura Katsuya held aloft by his team after they won the Central League championship in 1993.

Professional baseball (*puro yakyu*)   プロ野球●

The first professional baseball team was organized in Japan in 1934, when the mass media entrepreneur and politician Shoriki Matsutaro formed the core of the team that is known today as the Yomiuri Giants. Six additional teams had been established by 1936, when the first professional baseball league was organized. Since 1950 there have been two professional leagues: the Central League and the Pacific League. In 1995 the following teams constituted the Central League: the

Yomiuri Giants, the Chunichi Dragons, the Hanshin Tigers, the Hiroshima Toyo Carp, the Yakult Swallows, and the Yokohama BayStars. In the same year, the Pacific League comprised the following teams: the Kintetsu Buffaloes, the Seibu Lions, the Fukuoka Daiei Hawks, the Nippon-Ham Fighters, the Orix BlueWave, and the Chiba Lotte Marines. Each team plays the five other teams in its league 26 times each season for a total of 130 games. The teams with the highest winning percentage in each league face each other in the Japan Series to decide that year's championship team. Approximately 20 million fans attend baseball games annually in Japan, and millions more watch it on television, making baseball one of the nation's most popular professional sports.

Japan Professional Football League
(Nihon Puro Sakka Rigu)   日本プロサッカーリーグ●

The first professional soccer league in Japan. Commonly referred to as the "J. League," the Japan Professional Football League was founded in February 1991. It held its first professional tournament, the Cup Matches, in the fall of 1992. Games for the regular season, known as the League Matches, began in May 1993. The ten original member teams are: the Kashima Antlers, JEF United Ichihara, Urawa Red Diamonds, Verdy Kawasaki, Yokohama Flügels, Yokohama Marinos, Shimizu S-Pulse, Nagoya Grampus Eight, Gamba Osaka, and Sanfrecce Hiroshima. Two new teams, Júbilo Iwata and Bellmare Hiratsuka joined the league in 1995, bringing the total current membership to twelve teams. To gain membership in the league, teams are required to meet four conditions. Each team must: 1) be a legally incorporated body; 2) have the official local support of a designated "hometown"; 3) have access to a home stadium with a seating capacity of over 15,000; and 4) foster the development of future soccer players by maintaining its own youth division.

The Japanese team playing in a World Cup preliminary round match in Qatar in 1993.

Golf (gorufu)   ゴルフ●
Golf was introduced to Japan by Arthur H. Groom, an English merchant, in the early 20th century. Since World War II, the popularity of golf has increased tremendously, even though golf is one of Japan's most costly sports. Many corporations buy company memberships in golf clubs for entertaining and other business purposes; however, the number of college-student and women golfers is on the increase. As of 1994 the number of professional golfers was well over 3,000, including 400

women. The same year there were approximately 2,000 golf courses, which were being used by some 12 million golfers.

Ekiden kyoso 駅伝競争●

Long-distance relay race in which the distance to be run is divided into sections and a cloth sash is passed among the runners on a team and worn by each member as they run their section. The word ekiden derives from the names of two ancient Japanese relay systems of transportation using horses. The average number of team members ranges from 5 to 10. The distance run per section by men ranges from 5 to 20 kilometers (3–12 mi); women runners run from 2 to 10 kilometers (1–6 mi) per section. The first ekiden kyoso was run in 1917 between Kyoto and Tokyo. Today a wide variety of ekiden kyoso are held in Japan, one of the oldest of which is the Tokyo-Hakone Ofuku Daigaku Ekiden, a competition for male college students. There are also international competitions to which foreign teams are invited.

The Waseda University team won its second straight All Japan Inter-University Ekiden Championship in 1994.

CONSTITUTION OF JAPAN 日本国憲法 (1946)

**Promulgated on November 3, 1946;
Put into effect on May 3, 1947**

We, the Japanese people, acting through our duly elected representatives in the National Diet, determined that we shall secure for ourselves and our posterity the fruits of peaceful cooperation with all nations and the blessings of liberty throughout this land, and resolved that never again shall we be visited with the horrors of war through the action of government, do proclaim that sovereign power resides with the people and do firmly establish this Constitution. Government is a sacred trust of the people, the authority for which is derived from the people, the powers of which are exercised by the representatives of the people, and the benefits of which are enjoyed by the people. This is a universal principle of mankind upon which this Constitution is founded. We reject and revoke all constitutions, laws, ordinances, and rescripts in conflict herewith.

We, the Japanese people, desire peace for all time and are deeply conscious of the high ideals controlling human relationship, and we have determined to preserve our security and existence, trusting in the justice and faith of the peace-loving peoples of the world. We desire to occupy an honored place in an international society striving for the preservation of peace, and the banishment of tyranny and slavery, oppression and intolerance for all time from the earth. We recognize that all peoples of the world have the right to live in peace, free from fear and want.

We believe that no nation is responsible to itself alone, but that laws of political morality are universal; and that obedience to such laws is incumbent upon all nations who would sustain their own sovereignty and justify their sovereign relationship with other nations.

We, the Japanese people, pledge our national honor to accomplish these high ideals and purposes with all our resources.

Chapter I.

The Emperor 天皇

Article 1. The Emperor shall be the symbol of the State and of the unity of the people, deriving his position from the will of the people with whom resides sovereign power.

Article 2. The Imperial Throne shall be dynastic and succeeded to in accordance with the Imperial House Law passed by the Diet.

Article 3.	The advice and approval of the Cabinet shall be required for all acts of the Emperor in matters of state, and the Cabinet shall be responsible therefor.
Article 4.	The Emperor shall perform only such acts in matters of state as are provided for in this Constitution and he shall not have powers related to government.
	(2) The Emperor may delegate the performance of his acts in matters of state as may be provided by law.
Article 5.	When, in accordance with the Imperial House Law, a Regency is established, the Regent shall perform his acts in matters of state in the Emperor's name. In this case, paragraph one of the preceding article will be applicable.
Article 6.	The Emperor shall appoint the Prime Minister as designated by the Diet.
	(2) The Emperor shall appoint the Chief Judge of the Supreme Court as designated by the Cabinet.
Article 7.	The Emperor, with the advice and approval of the Cabinet, shall perform the following acts in matters of state on behalf of the people:

    (i) Promulgation of amendments of the constitution, laws, cabinet orders and treaties;

    (ii) Convocation of the Diet;

    (iii) Dissolution of the House of Representatives;

    (iv) Proclamation of general election of members of the Diet;

    (v) Attestation of the appointment and dismissal of Ministers of State and other officials as provided for by law, and of full powers and credentials of Ambassadors and Ministers;

    (vi) Attestation of general and special amnesty, commutation of punishment, reprieve, and restoration of rights;

    (vii) Awarding of honors;

    (viii) Attestation of instruments of ratification and other diplomatic documents as provided for by law;

    (ix) Receiving foreign ambassadors and ministers;

    (x) Performance of ceremonial functions.

Article 8.	No property can be given to, or received by, the Imperial House, nor can any gifts be made therefrom, without the authorization of the Diet.

Chapter II.

Renunciation of War   戦争の放棄

Article 9.	Aspiring sincerely to an international peace based on justice and order, the Japanese people forever renounce war as a sovereign right of the nation and the threat or use of force as a means of settling international

disputes.

(2)　In order to accomplish the aim of the preceding paragraph, land, sea, and air forces, as well as other war potential, will never be maintained. The right of belligerency of the state will not be recognized.

Chapter III.

| | Rights and Duties of the People | 国民の権利及び義務 |

Article 10.　The conditions necessary for being a Japanese national shall be determined by law.

Article 11.　The people shall not be prevented from enjoying any of the fundamental human rights. These fundamental human rights guaranteed to the people by this Constitution shall be conferred upon the people of this and future generations as eternal and inviolate rights.

Article 12.　The freedoms and rights guaranteed to the people by this Constitution shall be maintained by the constant endeavor of the people, who shall refrain from any abuse of these freedoms and rights and shall always be responsible for utilizing them for the public welfare.

Article 13.　All of the people shall be respected as individuals. Their right to life, liberty, and the pursuit of happiness shall, to the extent that it does not interfere with the public welfare, be the supreme consideration in legislation and in other governmental affairs.

Article 14.　All of the people are equal under the law and there shall be no discrimination in political, economic or social relations because of race, creed, sex, social status or family origin.

(2)　Peers and peerage shall not be recognized.

(3)　No privilege shall accompany any award of honor, decoration or any distinction, nor shall any such award be valid beyond the lifetime of the individual who now holds or hereafter may receive it.

Article 15.　The people have the inalienable right to choose their public officials and to dismiss them.

(2)　All public officials are servants of the whole community and not of any group thereof.

(3)　Universal adult suffrage is guaranteed with regard to the election of public officials.

(4)　In all elections, secrecy of the ballot shall not be violated. A voter shall not be answerable, publicly or privately, for the choice he has made.

Article 16.　Every person shall have the right of peaceful petition for the redress of damage, for the removal of public officials, for the enactment, repeal or amendment of laws, ordinances or regulations and for other matters, nor shall any person be in any way discriminated against for sponsoring such a petition.

Article 17. Every person may sue for redress as provided by law from the State or a public entity, in case he has suffered damage through illegal act of any public official.

Article 18. No person shall be held in bondage of any kind. Involuntary servitude, except as punishment for crime, is prohibited.

Article 19. Freedom of thought and conscience shall not be violated.

Article 20. Freedom of religion is guaranteed to all. No religious organization shall receive any privileges from the State nor exercise any political authority.

(2) No person shall be compelled to take part in any religious acts, celebration, rite or practice.

(3) The State and its organs shall refrain from religious education or any other religious activity.

Article 21. Freedom of assembly and association as well as speech, press and all other forms of expression are guaranteed.

(2) No censorship shall be maintained, nor shall the secrecy of any means of communication be violated.

Article 22. Every person shall have freedom to choose and change his residence and to choose his occupation to the extent that it does not interfere with the public welfare.

(2) Freedom of all persons to move to a foreign country and to divest themselves of their nationality shall be inviolate.

Article 23. Academic freedom is guaranteed.

Article 24. Marriage shall be based only on the mutual consent of both sexes and it shall be maintained through mutual cooperation with the equal rights of husband and wife as a basis.

(2) With regard to choice of spouse, property rights, inheritance, choice of domicile, divorce and other matters pertaining to marriage and the family, laws shall be enacted from the standpoint of individual dignity and the essential equality of the sexes.

Article 25. All people shall have the right to maintain the minimum standards of wholesome and cultured living.

(2) In all spheres of life, the State shall use its endeavors for the promotion and extension of social welfare and security, and of public health.

Article 26. All people shall have the right to receive an equal education correspondent to their ability, as provided by law.

(2) All people shall be obligated to have all boys and girls under their protection receive ordinary educations as provided for by law. Such compulsory education shall be free.

Article 27. All people shall have the right and the obligation to work.

(2) Standards for wages, hours, rest and other working conditions shall be fixed by law.

(3) Children shall not be exploited.

Article 28. The right of workers to organize and to bargain and act collectively is guaranteed.

Article 29. The right to own or to hold property is inviolable.

(2) Property rights shall be defined by law, in conformity with the public welfare.

(3) Private property may be taken for public use upon just compensation therefor.

Article 30. The people shall be liable to taxations as provided by law.

Article 31. No person shall be deprived of life or liberty, nor shall any other criminal penalty be imposed, except according to procedure established by law.

Article 32. No person shall be denied the right of access to the courts.

Article 33. No person shall be apprehended except upon warrant issued by a competent judicial officer which specifies the offense with which the person is charged, unless he is apprehended, the offense being committed.

Article 34. No person shall be arrested or detained without being at once informed of the charges against him or without the immediate privilege of counsel; nor shall he be detained without adequate cause; and upon demand of any person such cause must be immediately shown in open court in his presence and the presence of his counsel.

Article 35. The right of all persons to be secure in their homes, papers and effects against entries, searches and seizures shall not be impaired except upon warrant issued for adequate cause and particularly describing the place to be searched and things to be seized, or except as provided by Article 33.

(2) Each search or seizure shall be made upon separate warrant issued by a competent judicial officer.

Article 36. The infliction of torture by any public officer and cruel punishments are absolutely forbidden.

Article 37. In all criminal cases the accused shall enjoy the right to a speedy and public trial by an impartial tribunal.

(2) He shall be permitted full opportunity to examine all witnesses, and he shall have the right of compulsory process for obtaining witnesses on his behalf at public expense.

(3) At all times the accused shall have the assistance of competent counsel who shall, if the accused is unable to secure the same by his own efforts, be assigned to his use by the State.

Article 38. No person shall be compelled to testify against himself.

(2) Confession made under compulsion, torture or threat, or after prolonged arrest or detention shall not be admitted in evidence.

(3) No person shall be convicted or punished in cases where the only proof against him is his own confession.

Article 39. No person shall be held criminally liable for an act which was lawful at the time it was committed, or of which he has been acquitted, nor shall he be placed in double jeopardy.

Article 40. Any person, in case he is acquitted after he has been arrested or detained, may sue the State for redress as provided by law.

Chapter IV.

The Diet　　　　　　　　　　　　　　　　　　　　　　　国会

Article 41. The Diet shall be the highest organ of state power, and shall be the sole law-making organ of the State.

Article 42. The Diet shall consist of two Houses, namely the House of Representatives and the House of Councillors.

Article 43. Both Houses shall consist of elected members, representative of all the people.

(2) The number of members of each House shall be fixed by law.

Article 44. The qualifications of members of both Houses and their electors shall be fixed by law. However, there shall be no discrimination because of race, creed, sex, social status, family origin, education, property or income.

Article 45. The term of office of members of the House of Representatives shall be four years. However, the term shall be terminated before the full term is up in case the House of Representatives is dissolved.

Article 46. The term of office of members of the House of Councillors shall be six years, and election for half the members shall take place every three years.

Article 47. Electoral districts, method of voting and other matters pertaining to the method of election of members of both Houses shall be fixed by law.

Article 48. No person shall be permitted to be a member of both Houses simultaneously.

Article 49. Members of both Houses shall receive appropriate annual payment from the national treasury in accordance with law.

Article 50. Except in cases provided by law, members of both Houses shall be exempt from apprehension while the Diet is in session, and any members apprehended before the opening of the session shall be freed during the term of the session upon demand of the House.

Article 51. Members of both Houses shall not be held liable outside the House for speeches, debates or votes cast inside the House.

Article 52.   An ordinary session of the Diet shall be convoked once per year.

Article 53.   The Cabinet may determine to convoke extraordinary sessions of the Diet. When a quarter or more of the total members of either House makes the demand, the Cabinet must determine on such convocation.

Article 54.   When the House of Representatives is dissolved, there must be a general election of members of the House of Representatives within forty (40) days from the date of dissolution, and the Diet must be convoked within thirty (30) days from the date of election.

(2) When the House of Representatives is dissolved, the House of Councillors is closed at the same time. However, the Cabinet may in time of national emergency convoke the House of Councillors in emergency session.

(3) Measures taken at such session as mentioned in the proviso of the preceding paragraph shall be provisional and shall become null and void unless agreed to by the House of Representatives within a period of ten (10) days after the opening of the next session of the Diet.

Article 55.   Each House shall judge disputes related to qualifications of its members. However, in order to deny a seat to any member, it is necessary to pass a resolution by a majority of two-thirds or more of the members present.

Article 56.   Business cannot be transacted in either House unless one-third or more of total membership is present.

(2) All matters shall be decided, in each House, by a majority of those present, except as elsewhere provided in the Constitution, and in case of a tie, the presiding officer shall decide the issue.

Article 57.   Deliberation in each House shall be public. However, a secret meeting may be held where a majority of two-thirds or more of those members present passes a resolution therefor.

(2) Each House shall keep a record of proceedings. This record shall be published and given general circulation, excepting such parts of proceedings of secret session as may be deemed to require secrecy.

(3) Upon demand of one-fifth or more of the members present, votes of the members on any matter shall be recorded in the minutes.

Article 58.   Each House shall select its own president and other officials.

(2) Each House shall establish its rules pertaining to meetings, proceedings and internal discipline, and may punish members for disorderly conduct. However, in order to expel a member, a majority of two-thirds or more of those members present must pass a resolution thereon.

Article 59.   A bill becomes a law on passage by both Houses, except as otherwise provided by the Constitution.

(2) A bill which is passed by the House of Representatives, and upon

which the House of Councillors makes a decision different from that of the House of Representatives, becomes a law when passed a second time by the House of Representatives by a majority of two-thirds or more of the members present.

(3) The provision of the preceding paragraph does not preclude the House of Representatives from calling for the meeting of a joint committee of both Houses, provided for by law.

(4) Failure by the House of Councillors to take final action within sixty (60) days after receipt of a bill passed by the House of Representatives, time in recess excepted, may be determined by the House of Representatives to constitute a rejection of the said bill by the House of Councillors.

Article 60. The Budget must first be submitted to the House of Representatives.

(2) Upon consideration of the budget, when the House of Councillors makes a decision different from that of the House of Representatives, and when no agreement can be reached even through a joint committee of both Houses, provided for by law, or in the case of failure by the House of Councillors to take final action within thirty (30) days, the period of recess excluded, after the receipt of the budget passed by the House of Representatives, the decision of the House of Representatives shall be the decision of the Diet.

Article 61. The second paragraph of the preceding article applies also to the Diet approval required for the conclusion of treaties.

Article 62. Each House may conduct investigations in relation to government, and may demand the presence and testimony of witnesses, and the production of records.

Article 63. The Prime Minister and other Ministers of State may, at any time, appear in either House for the purpose of speaking on bills, regardless of whether they are members of the House or not. They must appear when their presence is required in order to give answers or explanations.

Article 64. The Diet shall set up an impeachment court from among the members of both Houses for the purpose of trying those judges against whom removal proceedings have been instituted.

(2) Matters relating to impeachment shall be provided by law.

Chapter V.

The Cabinet 内閣

Article 65. Executive power shall be vested in the Cabinet.

Article 66. The Cabinet shall consist of the Prime Minister, who shall be its head, and other Ministers of State, as provided for by law.

(2) The Prime Minister and other Ministers of State must be civilians.

(3) The Cabinet, in the exercise of executive power, shall be collectively responsible to the Diet.

Article 67.   The Prime Minister shall be designated from among the members of the Diet by a resolution of the Diet. This designation shall precede all other business.

(2) If the House of Representatives and the House of Councillors disagrees and if no agreement can be reached even through a joint committee of both Houses, provided for by law, or the House of Councillors fails to make designation within ten (10) days, exclusive of the period of recess, after the House of Representatives has made designation, the decision of the House of Representatives shall be the decision of the Diet.

Article 68.   The Prime Minister shall appoint the Ministers of State. However, a majority of their number must be chosen from among the members of the Diet.

(2) The Prime Minister may remove the Ministers of State as he chooses.

Article 69.   If the House of Representatives passes a non-confidence resolution, or rejects a confidence resolution, the Cabinet shall resign en masse, unless the House of Representatives is dissolved within ten (10) days.

Article 70.   When there is a vacancy in the post of Prime Minister, or upon the first convocation of the Diet after a general election of members of the House of Representatives, the Cabinet shall resign en masse.

Article 71.   In the cases mentioned in the two preceding articles, the Cabinet shall continue its functions until the time when a new Prime Minister is appointed.

Article 72.   The Prime Minister, representing the Cabinet, submits bills, reports on general national affairs and foreign relations to the Diet and exercises control and supervision over various administrative branches.

Article 73.   The Cabinet, in addition to other general administrative functions, shall perform the following functions:

> (i)   Administer the law faithfully; conduct affairs of state;
>
> (ii) Manage foreign affairs;
>
> (iii) Conclude treaties. However, it shall obtain prior or, depending on circumstances, subsequent approval of the Diet;
>
> (iv) Administer the civil service, in accordance with standards established by law;
>
> (v)   Prepare the budget, and present it to the Diet;
>
> (vi) Enact cabinet orders in order to execute the provisions of this Constitution and of the law. However, it cannot include penal

provisions in such cabinet orders unless authorized by such law.

(vii) Decide on general amnesty, special amnesty, commutation of punishment, reprieve, and restoration of rights.

Article 74. All laws and cabinet orders shall be signed by the competent Minister of State and countersigned by the Prime Minister.

Article 75. The Ministers of State, during their tenure of office, shall not be subject to legal action without the consent of the Prime Minister. However, the right to take that action is not impaired hereby.

Chapter VI.

Judiciary 司法

Article 76. The whole judicial power is vested in a Supreme Court and in such inferior courts as are established by law.

(2) No extraordinary tribunal shall be established, nor shall any organ or agency of the Executive be given final judicial power.

(3) All judges shall be independent in the exercise of their conscience and shall be bound only by this Constitution and the laws.

Article 77. The Supreme Court is vested with the rule-making power under which it determines the rules of procedure and of practice, and of matters relating to attorneys, the internal discipline of the courts and the administration of judicial affairs.

(2) Public procurators shall be subject to the rule-making power of the Supreme Court.

(3) The Supreme Court may delegate the power to make rules for inferior courts to such courts.

Article 78. Judges shall not be removed except by public impeachment unless judicially declared mentally or physically incompetent to perform official duties. No disciplinary action against judges shall be administered by any executive organ or agency.

Article 79. The Supreme Court shall consist of a Chief Judge and such number of judges as may be determined by law; all such judges excepting the Chief Judge shall be appointed by the Cabinet.

(2) The appointment of the judges of the Supreme Court shall be reviewed by the people at the first general election of members of the House of Representatives following their appointment, and shall be reviewed again at the first general election of members of the House of Representatives after a lapse of ten (10) years, and in the same manner thereafter.

(3) In cases mentioned in the foregoing paragraph, when the majority of the voters favors the dismissal of a judge, he shall be dismissed.

(4) Matters pertaining to review shall be prescribed by law.

(5) The judges of the Supreme Court shall be retired upon the attainment of the age as fixed by law.

(6) All such judges shall receive, at regular stated intervals, adequate compensation which shall not be decreased during their terms of office.

Article 80. The judges of the inferior courts shall be appointed by the cabinet from a list of persons nominated by the Supreme Court. All such judges shall hold office for a term of ten (10) years with privilege of reappointment, provided that they shall be retired upon the attainment of the age as fixed by law.

(2) The judges of the inferior courts shall receive, at regular stated intervals, adequate compensation which shall not be decreased during their terms of office.

Article 81. The Supreme Court is the court of last resort with power to determine the constitutionality of any law, order, regulation or official act.

Article 82. Trials shall be conducted and judgment declared publicly.

(2) Where a court unanimously determines publicity to be dangerous to public order or morals, a trial may be conducted privately, but trials of political offenses, offenses involving the press or cases wherein the rights of people as guaranteed in Chapter III of this Constitution are in question shall always be conducted publicly.

Chapter VII.

Finance	財政

Article 83. The power to administer national finances shall be exercised as the Diet shall determine.

Article 84. No new taxes shall be imposed or existing ones modified except by law or under such conditions as law may prescribe.

Article 85. No money shall be expended, nor shall the State obligate itself, except as authorized by the Diet.

Article 86. The Cabinet shall prepare and submit to the Diet for its consideration and decision a budget for each fiscal year.

Article 87. In order to provide for unforeseen deficiencies in the budget, a reserve fund may be authorized by the Diet to be expended upon the responsibility of the Cabinet.

(2) The Cabinet must get subsequent approval of the Diet for all payments from the reserve fund.

Article 88. All property of the Imperial Household shall belong to the State. All expenses of the Imperial Household shall be appropriated by the Diet in the budget.

Article 89. No public money or other property shall be expended or appropriated for the use, benefit or maintenance of any religious institution or association, or for any charitable, educational or benevolent enterprises not under the control of public authority.

Article 90. Final accounts of the expenditures and revenues of the State shall be audited annually by a Board of Audit and submitted by the Cabinet to the Diet, together with the statement of audit, during the fiscal year immediately following the period covered.

(2) The organization and competency of the Board of Audit shall be determined by law.

Article 91. At regular intervals and at least annually the Cabinet shall report to the Diet and the people on the state of national finances.

Chapter VIII.

Local Self-Government 地方自治

Article 92. Regulations concerning organization and operations of local public entities shall be fixed by law in accordance with the principle of local autonomy.

Article 93. The local public entities shall establish assemblies as their deliberative organs, in accordance with law.

(2) The chief executive officers of all local public entities, the members of their assemblies, and such other local officials as may be determined by law shall be elected by direct popular vote within their several communities.

Article 94. Local public entities shall have the right to manage their property, affairs and administration and to enact their own regulations within law.

Article 95. A special law, applicable only to one local public entity, cannot be enacted by the Diet without the consent of the majority of the voters of the local public entity concerned, obtained in accordance with law.

Chapter IX.

Amendments 改正

Article 96. Amendments to this Constitution shall be initiated by the Diet, through a concurring vote of two-thirds or more of all the members of each House and shall thereupon be submitted to the people for ratification, which shall require the affirmative vote of a majority of all votes cast thereon, at a special referendum or at such election as the Diet shall specify.

(2) Amendments when so ratified shall immediately be promulgated by the Emperor in the name of the people, as an integral part of this Constitution.

Chapter X.

| Supreme Law | 最高法規 |

Article 97.   The fundamental human rights by this Constitution guaranteed to the people of Japan are fruits of the age-old struggle of man to be free; they have survived the many exacting tests for durability and are conferred upon this and future generations in trust, to be held for all time inviolate.

Article 98.   This Constitution shall be the supreme law of the nation and no law, ordinance, imperial rescript or other act of government, or part thereof, contrary to the provisions hereof, shall have legal force or validity.

(2) The treaties concluded by Japan and established laws of nations shall be faithfully observed.

Article 99.   The Emperor or the Regent as well as Ministers of State, members of the Diet, judges, and all other public officials have the obligation to respect and uphold this Constitution.

Chapter XI.

| Supplementary Provisions | 補足 |

Article 100.   This Constitution shall be enforced as from the day when the period of six months will have elapsed counting from the day of its promulgation.

(2) The enactment of laws necessary for the enforcement of this Constitution, the election of members of the House of Councillors and the procedure for the convocation of the Diet and other preparatory procedures for the enforcement of this Constitution may be executed before the day prescribed in the preceding paragraph.

Article 101.   If the House of Councillors is not constituted before the effective date of this Constitution, the House of Representatives shall function as the Diet until such time as the House of Councillors shall be constituted.

Article 102.   The term of office for half the members of the House of Councillors serving in the first term under this Constitution shall be three years. Members falling under this category shall be determined in accordance with law.

Article 103.   The Ministers of State, members of the House of Representatives, and judges in office on the effective date of this Constitution, and all other public officials, who occupy positions corresponding to such positions as are recognized by this Constitution shall not forfeit their positions automatically on account of the enforcement of this Constitution unless otherwise specified by law. When, however, successors are elected or appointed under the provisions of this Constitution, they shall forfeit their positions as a matter of course.

日本国憲法

1946年（昭和21）11月3日公布
1947年（昭和22）5月3日施行

　日本国民は，正当に選挙された国会における代表者を通じて行動し，われらとわれらの子孫のために，諸国民との協和による成果と，わが国全土にわたつて自由のもたらす恵沢を確保し，政府の行為によつて再び戦争の惨禍が起ることのないやうにすることを決意し，ここに主権が国民に存することを宣言し，この憲法を確定する。そもそも国政は，国民の厳粛な信託によるものであつて，その権威は国民に由来し，その権力は国民の代表者がこれを行使し，その福利は国民がこれを享受する。これは人類普遍の原理であり，この憲法は，かかる原理に基くものである。われらは，これに反する一切の憲法，法令及び詔勅を排除する。

　日本国民は恒久の平和を念願し，人間相互の関係を支配する崇高な理想を深く自覚するのであつて，平和を愛する諸国民の公正と信義に信頼して，われらの安全と生存を保持しようと決意した。われらは，平和を維持し，専制と隷従，圧迫と偏狭を地上から永遠に除去しようと努めてゐる国際社会において，名誉ある地位を占めたいと思ふ。われらは，全世界の国民が，ひとしく恐怖と欠乏から免かれ，平和のうちに生存する権利を有することを確認する。

　われらは，いづれの国家も，自国のことのみに専念して他国を無視してはならないのであつて，政治道徳の法則は，普遍的なものであり，この法則に従ふことは，自国の主権を維持し，他国と対等関係に立たうとする各国の責務であると信ずる。

　日本国民は，国家の名誉にかけ，全力をあげてこの崇高な理想と目的を達成することを誓ふ。

第1章

天皇

第1条　天皇は，日本国の象徴であり日本国民統合の象徴であつて，この地位は，主権の存する日本国民の総意に基く。

第2条　皇位は，世襲のものであつて，国会の議決した皇室典範の定めるところにより，これを継承する。

第3条　天皇の国事に関するすべての行為には，内閣の助言と承認を必要とし，内閣が，その責任を負ふ。

第4条　天皇は，この憲法の定める国事に関する行為のみを行ひ，国政に関する権能を有しない。
　②天皇は，法律の定めるところにより，その国事に関する行為を委任することができる。

第5条	皇室典範の定めるところにより摂政を置くときは，摂政は，天皇の名でその国事に関する行為を行ふ。この場合には，前条第1項の規定を準用する。
第6条	天皇は，国会の指名に基いて，内閣総理大臣を任命する。
	②天皇は，内閣の指名に基いて，最高裁判所の長たる裁判官を任命する。
第7条	天皇は，内閣の助言と承認により，国民のために，左の国事に関する行為を行ふ。

1 憲法改正，法律，政令及び条約を公布すること。
2 国会を召集すること。
3 衆議院を解散すること。
4 国会議員の総選挙の施行を公示すること。
5 国務大臣及び法律の定めるその他の官吏の任免並びに全権委任状及び大使及び公使の信任状を認証すること。
6 大赦，特赦，減刑，刑の執行の免除及び復権を認証すること。
7 栄典を授与すること。
8 批准書及び法律の定めるその他の外交文書を認証すること。
9 外国の大使及び公使を接受すること。
10 儀式を行ふこと。

第8条	皇室に財産を譲り渡し，又は皇室が，財産を譲り受け，若しくは賜与することは，国会の議決に基かなければならない。

第2章

戦争の放棄

第9条	日本国民は，正義と秩序を基調とする国際平和を誠実に希求し，国権の発動たる戦争と，武力による威嚇又は武力の行使は，国際紛争を解決する手段としては，永久にこれを放棄する。
	②前項の目的を達するため，陸海空軍その他の戦力は，これを保持しない。国の交戦権は，これを認めない。

第3章

国民の権利及び義務

第10条	日本国民たる要件は，法律でこれを定める。
第11条	国民は，すべての基本的人権の享有を妨げられない。この憲法が国民に保障する基本的人権は，侵すことのできない永久の権利として，現在及び将来の国民に与へられる。
第12条	この憲法が国民に保障する自由及び権利は，国民の不断の努力によつて，これを保持しなければならない。又，国民は，これを濫用してはならないのであつて，常に公共の福祉のためにこれを利用する責任を負ふ。
第13条	すべて国民は，個人として尊重される。生命，自由及び幸福追及に対する国民の権利については，公共の福祉に反しない限り，立法その他の国

政の上で，最大の尊重を必要とする。

第14条　すべて国民は，法の下に平等であつて，人種，信条，性別，社会的身分又は門地により，政治的，経済的又は社会的関係において，差別されない。
②華族その他の貴族の制度は，これを認めない。
③栄誉，勲章その他の栄典の授与は，いかなる特権も伴はない。栄典の授与は，現にこれを有し，又は将来これを受ける者の一代に限り，その効力を有する。

第15条　公務員を選定し，及びこれを罷免することは，国民固有の権利である。
②すべて公務員は，全体の奉仕者であつて，一部の奉仕者ではない。
③公務員の選挙については，成年者による普通選挙を保障する。
④すべて選挙における投票の秘密は，これを侵してはならない。選挙人は，その選択に関し公的にも私的にも責任を問はれない。

第16条　何人も，損害の救済，公務員の罷免，法律，命令又は規則の制定，廃止又は改正その他の事項に関し，平穏に請願する権利を有し，何人も，かかる請願をしたためにいかなる差別待遇も受けない。

第17条　何人も，公務員の不法行為により，損害を受けたときは，法律の定めるところにより，国又は公共団体に，その賠償を求めることができる。

第18条　何人も，いかなる奴隷的拘束も受けない。又，犯罪に因る処罰の場合を除いては，その意に反する苦役に服させられない。

第19条　思想及び良心の自由は，これを侵してはならない。

第20条　信教の自由は，何人に対してもこれを保障する。いかなる宗教団体も，国から特権を受け，又は政治上の権力を行使してはならない。
②何人も，宗教上の行為，祝典，儀式又は行事に参加することを強制されない。
③国及びその機関は，宗教教育その他いかなる宗教的活動もしてはならない。

第21条　集会，結社及び言論，出版その他一切の表現の自由は，これを保障する。
②検閲は，これをしてはならない。通信の秘密は，これを侵してはならない。

第22条　何人も，公共の福祉に反しない限り，居住，移転及び職業選択の自由を有する。
②何人も，外国に移住し，又は国籍を離脱する自由を侵されない。

第23条　学問の自由は，これを保障する。

第24条　婚姻は，両性の合意のみに基いて成立し，夫婦が同等の権利を有することを基本として，相互の協力により，維持されなけれぱならない。
②配偶者の選択，財産権，相続，住居の選定，離婚並びに婚姻及び家族に関するその他の事項に関しては，法律は，個人の尊厳と両性の本質的平等に立脚して，制定されなければならない。

第25条　すべて国民は，健康で文化的な最低限度の生活を営む権利を有する。
②国は，すべての生活部面について，社会福祉，社会保障及び公衆衛生

の向上及び増進に努めなければならない。

第26条　すべて国民は，法律の定めるところにより，その能力に応じて，ひとしく教育を受ける権利を有する。

②すべて国民は，法律の定めるところにより，その保護する子女に普通教育を受けさせる義務を負ふ。義務教育は，これを無償とする。

第27条　すべて国民は，勤労の権利を有し，義務を負ふ。

②賃金，就業時間，休息その他の勤労条件に関する基準は，法律でこれを定める。

③児童は，これを酷使してはならない。

第28条　勤労者の団結する権利及び団体交渉その他の団体行動をする権利は，これを保障する。

第29条　財産権は，これを侵してはならない。

②財産権の内容は，公共の福祉に適合するやうに，法律でこれを定める。

③私有財産は，正当な補償の下に，これを公共のために用ひることができる。

第30条　国民は，法律の定めるところにより，納税の義務を負ふ。

第31条　何人も，法律の定める手続によらなければ，その生命若しくは自由を奪はれ，又はその他の刑罰を科せられない。

第32条　何人も，裁判所において裁判を受ける権利を奪はれない。

第33条　何人も，現行犯として逮捕される場合を除いては，権限を有する司法官憲が発し，且つ理由となつてゐる犯罪を明示する令状によらなければ，逮捕されない。

第34条　何人も，理由を直ちに告げられ，且つ，直ちに弁護人に依頼する権利を与へられなければ，抑留又は拘禁されない。又，何人も，正当な理由がなければ，拘禁されず，要求があれば，その理由は直ちに本人及びその弁護人の出席する公開の法廷で示されなければならない。

第35条　何人も，その住居，書類及び所持品について，侵入，捜索及び押収を受けることのない権利は，第33条の場合を除いては，正当な理由に基いて発せられ，且つ捜索する場所及び押収する物を明示する令状がなければ，侵されない。

②捜索又は押収は，権限を有する司法官憲が発する各別の令状により，これを行ふ。

第36条　公務員による拷問及び残虐な刑罰は，絶対にこれを禁ずる。

第37条　すべて刑事事件においては，被告人は，公平な裁判所の迅速な公開裁判を受ける権利を有する。

②刑事被告人は，すべての証人に対して審問する機会を充分に与へられ，又，公費で自己のために強制的手続により証人を求める権利を有する。

③刑事被告人は，いかなる場合にも，資格を有する弁護人を依頼することができる。被告人が自らこれを依頼することができないときは，国でこれを附する。

第38条	何人も，自己に不利益な供述を強要されない。
	② 強制，拷問若しくは脅迫による自白又は不当に長く抑留若しくは拘禁された後の自白は，これを証拠とすることができない。
	③ 何人も，自己に不利益な唯一の証拠が本人の自白である場合には，有罪とされ，又は刑罰を科せられない。
第39条	何人も，実行の時に適法であつた行為又は既に無罪とされた行為については，刑事上の責任を問はれない。又，同一の犯罪について，重ねて刑事上の責任を問はれない。
第40条	何人も，抑留又は拘禁された後，無罪の裁判を受けたときは，法律の定めるところにより，国にその補償を求めることができる。

第4章

国会

第41条	国会は，国権の最高機関であつて，国の唯一の立法機関である。
第42条	国会は，衆議院及び参議院の両議院でこれを構成する。
第43条	両議院は，全国民を代表する選挙された議員でこれを組織する。
	② 両議院の議員の定数は法律でこれを定める。
第44条	両議院の議員及びその選挙人の資格は，法律でこれを定める。但し，人種，信条，性別，社会的身分，門地，教育，財産又は収入によつて差別してはならない。
第45条	衆議院議員の任期は，4年とする。但し，衆議院解散の場合には，その期間満了前に終了する。
第46条	参議院議員の任期は，6年とし，3年ごとに議員の半数を改選する。
第47条	選挙区，投票の方法その他両議院の議員の選挙に関する事項は，法律でこれを定める。
第48条	何人も，同時に両議院の議員たることはできない。
第49条	両議院の議員は，法律の定めるところにより，国庫から相当額の歳費を受ける。
第50条	両議院の議員は，法律の定める場合を除いては，国会の会期中逮捕されず，会期前に逮捕された議員は，その議院の要求があれば，会期中これを釈放しなければならない。
第51条	両議院の議員は，議院で行つた演説，討論又は表決について，院外で責任を問はれない。
第52条	国会の常会は，毎年1回これを召集する。
第53条	内閣は，国会の臨時会の召集を決定することができる。いづれかの議院の総議員の4分の1以上の要求があれば，内閣は，その召集を決定しなければならない。
第54条	衆議院が解散されたときは，解散の日から40日以内に，衆議院議員の総選挙を行ひ，その選挙の日から30日以内に，国会を召集しなければならない。

②衆議院が解散されたときは，参議院は，同時に閉会となる。但し，内閣は，国に緊急の必要があるときは，参議院の緊急集会を求めることができる。

③前項但書の緊急集会において採られた措置は，臨時のものであつて，次の国会開会の後10日以内に，衆議院の同意がない場合には，その効力を失ふ。

第55条　両議院は，各々その議員の資格に関する争訟を裁判する。但し，議員の議席を失はせるには，出席議員の3分の2以上の多数による議決を必要とする。

第56条　両議院は，各々その総議員の3分の1以上の出席がなければ，議事を開き議決することができない。

②両議院の議事は，この憲法に特別の定のある場合を除いては，出席議員の過半数でこれを決し，可否同数のときは，議長の決するところによる。

第57条　両議院の会議は，公開とする。但し，出席議員の3分の2以上の多数で議決したときは，秘密会を開くことができる。

②両議院は，各々その会議の記録を保存し，秘密会の記録の中で特に秘密を要すると認められるもの以外は，これを公表し，且つ一般に頒布しなければならない。

③出席議員の5分の1以上の要求があれば，各議員の表決は，これを会議録に記載しなければならない。

第58条　両議院は，各々その議長その他の役員を選任する。

②両議院は，各々その会議その他の手続及び内部の規律に関する規則を定め，又，院内の秩序をみだした議員を懲罰することができる。但し，議員を除名するには，出席議員の3分の2以上の多数による議決を必要とする。

第59条　法律案は，この憲法に特別の定のある場合を除いては，両議院で可決したとき法律となる。

②衆議院で可決し，参議院でこれと異なった議決をした法律案は，衆議院で出席議員の3分の2以上の多数で再び可決したときは，法律となる。

③前項の規定は，法律の定めるところにより，衆議院が，両議院の協議会を開くことを求めることを妨げない。

④参議院が，衆議院の可決した法律案を受け取つた後，国会休会中の期間を除いて60日以内に，議決しないときは，衆議院は，参議院がその法律案を否決したものとみなすことができる。

第60条　予算は，さきに衆議院に提出しなければならない。

②予算について，参議院で衆議院と異なつた議決をした場合に，法律の定めるところにより，両議院の協議会を開いても意見が一致しないとき，又は参議院が，衆議院の可決した予算を受け取つた後，国会休会中の期間を除いて30日以内に，議決しないときは，衆議院の議決を国会の議決とする。

第61条	条約の締結に必要な国会の承認については，前条第2項の規定を準用する。
第62条	両議院は，各々国政に関する調査を行ひ，これに関して，証人の出頭及び証言並びに記録の提出を要求することができる。
第63条	内閣総理大臣その他の国務大臣は，両議院の一に議席を有すると有しないとにかかはらず，何時でも議案について発言するため議院に出席することができる。又，答弁又は説明のため出席を求められたときは，出席しなければならない。
第64条	国会は，罷免の訴追を受けた裁判官を裁判するため，両議院の議員で組織する弾劾裁判所を設ける。
	②弾劾に関する事項は，法律でこれを定める。

第5章

内閣

第65条	行政権は，内閣に属する。
第66条	内閣は，法律の定めるところにより，その首長たる内閣総理大臣及びその他の国務大臣でこれを組織する。
	② 内閣総理大臣その他の国務大臣は，文民でなければならない。
	③ 内閣は，行政権の行使について，国会に対し連帯して責任を負ふ。
第67条	内閣総理大臣は，国会議員の中から国会の議決で，これを指名する。この指名は，他のすべての案件に先だつて，これを行ふ。
	② 衆議院と参議院とが異なつた指名の議決をした場合に，法律の定めるところにより，両議院の協議会を開いても意見が一致しないとき，又は衆議院が指名の議決をした後，国会休会中の期間を除いて10日以内に，参議院が，指名の議決をしないときは，衆議院の議決を国会の議決とする。
第68条	内閣総理大臣は，国務大臣を任命する。但し，その過半数は，国会議員の中から選ばれなければならない。
	② 内閣総理大臣は，任意に国務大臣を罷免することができる。
第69条	内閣は，衆議院で不信任の決議案を可決し，又は信任の決議案を否決したときは，10日以内に衆議院が解散されない限り，総辞職をしなければならない。
第70条	内閣総理大臣が欠けたとき，又は衆議院議員総選挙の後に初めて国会の召集があつたときは，内閣は，総辞職をしなければならない。
第71条	前2条の場合には，内閣は，あらたに内閣総理大臣が任命されるまで引き続きその職務を行ふ。
第72条	内閣総理大臣は，内閣を代表して議案を国会に提出し，一般国務及び外交関係について国会に報告し，並びに行政各部を指揮監督する。
第73条	内閣は，他の一般行政事務の外，左の事務を行ふ。
	1 法律を誠実に執行し，国務を総理すること。
	2 外交関係を処理すること。

3 条約を締結すること。但し，事前に，時宜によつては事後に，国会の承認を経ることを必要とする。

4 法律の定める基準に従ひ，官吏に関する事務を掌理すること。

5 予算を作成して国会に提出すること。

6 この憲法及び法律の規定を実施するために，政令を制定すること。但し，政令には，特にその法律の委任がある場合を除いては，罰則を設けることができない。

7 大赦，特赦，減刑，刑の執行の免除及び復権を決定すること。

第74条　法律及び政令には，すべて主任の国務大臣が署名し，内閣総理大臣が連署することを必要とする。

第75条　国務大臣は，その在任中，内閣総理大臣の同意がなければ，訴追されない。但し，これがため，訴追の権利は，害されない。

第6章

司法

第76条　すべて司法権は，最高裁判所及び法律の定めるところにより設置する下級裁判所に属する。

②特別裁判所は，これを設置することができない。行政機関は，終審として裁判を行ふことができない。

③すべて裁判官は，その良心に従ひ独立してその職権を行ひ，この憲法及び法律にのみ拘束される。

第77条　最高裁判所は，訴訟に関する手続，弁護士，裁判所の内部規律及び司法事務処理に関する事項について，規則を定める権限を有する。

②検察官は，最高裁判所の定める規則に従はなければならない。

③最高裁判所は，下級裁判所に関する規則を定める権限を，下級裁判所に委任することができる。

第78条　裁判官は，裁判により，心身の故障のために職務を執ることができないと決定された場合を除いては，公の弾劾によらなければ罷免されない。裁判官の懲戒処分は，行政機関がこれを行ふことはできないい。

第79条　最高裁判所は，その長たる裁判官及び法律の定める員数のその他の裁判官でこれを構成し，その長たる裁判官以外の裁判官は，内閣でこれを任命する。

②最高裁判所の裁判官の任命は，その任命後初めて行はれる衆議院議員総選挙の際国民の審査に付し，その後10年を経過した後初めて行はれる衆議院議員総選挙の際更に審査に付し，その後も同様とする。

③前項の場合において．投票者の多数が裁判官の罷免を可とするときは，その裁判官は，罷免される。

④審査に関する事項は，法律でこれを定める。

⑤最高裁判所の裁判官は，法律の定める年齢に達した時に退官する。

⑥最高裁判所の裁判官は，すべて定期に相当額の報酬を受ける。この報

酬は，在任中，これを減額することができない。

第80条　下級裁判所の裁判官は，最高裁判所の指名した者の名簿によつて，内閣でこれを任命する。その裁判官は，任期を10年とし，再任されることができる。但し，法律の定める年齢に達した時には退官する。

②下級裁判所の裁判官は，すべて定期に相当額の報酬を受ける。この報酬は，在任中，これを減額することができない。

第81条　最高裁判所は，一切の法律，命令，規則又は処分が憲法に適合するかしないかを決定する権限を有する終審裁判所である。

第82条　裁判の対審及び判決は，公開法廷でこれを行ふ。

②裁判所が，裁判官の全員一致で，公の秩序又は善良の風俗を害する虞があると決した場合には，対審は，公開しないでこれを行ふことができる。但し，政治犯罪，出版に関する犯罪又はこの憲法第3章で保障する国民の権利が問題となつてゐる事件の対審は，常にこれを公開しなければならない。

第7章

財政

第83条　国の財政を処理する権限は，国会の議決に基いて，これを行使しなければならない。

第84条　あらたに租税を課し，又は現行の租税を変更するには，法律又は法律の定める条件によることを必要とする。

第85条　国費を支出し，又は国が債務を負担するには，国会の議決に基くことを必要とする。

第86条　内閣は，毎会計年度の予算を作成し，国会に提出して，その審議を受け議決を経なければならない。

第87条　予見し難い予算の不足に充てるため，国会の議決に基いて予備費を設け，内閣の責任でこれを支出することができる。

②すべて予備費の支出については，内閣は，事後に国会の承諾を得なければならない。

第88条　すべて皇室財産は，国に属する。すべて皇室の費用は，予算に計上して国会の議決を経なければならない。

第89条　公金その他の公の財産は，宗教上の組織若しくは団体の使用，便益若しくは維持のため，又は公の支配に属しない慈善，教育若しくは博愛の事業に対し，これを支出し，又はその利用に供してはならない。

第90条　国の収入支出の決算は，すべて毎年会計検査院がこれを検査し，内閣は，次の年度に，その検査報告とともに，これを国会に提出しなければならない。

②会計検査院の組織及び権限は，法律でこれを定める。

第91条　内閣は，国会及び国民に対し，定期に，少くとも毎年1回，国の財政状況について報告しなければならない。

第8章

地方自治

第92条　地方公共団体の組織及び運営に関する事項は，地方自治の本旨に基いて，法律でこれを定める。

第93条　地方公共団体には，法律の定めるところにより，その議事機関として議会を設置する。

②地方公共団体の長，その議会の議員及び法律の定めるその他の吏員は，その地方公共団体の住民が，直接これを選挙する。

第94条　地方公共団体は，その財産を管理し，事務を処理し，及び行政を執行する権能を有し，法律の範囲内で条例を制定することができる。

第95条　一の地方公共団体のみに適用される特別法は，法律の定めるところにより，その地方公共団体の住民の投票においてその過半数の同意を得なければ，国会は，これを制定することができない。

第9章

改正

第96条　この憲法の改正は，各議院の総議員の3分の2以上の賛成で，国会が，これを発議し，国民に提案してその承認を経なければならない。この承認には，特別の国民投票又は国会の定める選挙の際行はれる投票において，その過半数の賛成を必要とする。

②憲法改正について前項の承認を経たときは，天皇は，国民の名で，この憲法と一体を成すものとして，直ちにこれを公布する。

第10章

最高法規

第97条　この憲法が日本国民に保障する基本的人権は，人類の多年にわたる自由獲得の努力の成果であつて，これらの権利は，過去幾多の試練に堪へ，現在及び将来の国民に対し，侵すことのできない永久の権利として信託されたものである。

第98条　この憲法は，国の最高法規であつて，その条項に反する法律，命令，詔勅及び国務に関するその他の行為の全部又は一部は，その効力を有しない。

②日本国が締結した条約及び確立された国際法規は，これを誠実に遵守することを必要とする。

第99条　天皇又は摂政及び国務大臣，国会議員，裁判官その他の公務員は，この憲法を尊重し擁護する義務を負ふ。

第11章

補則

第100条　この憲法は，公布の日から起算して6箇月を経過した日から，これを施行する。

② この憲法を施行するために必要な法律の制定，参議院議員の選挙及び国会召集の手続並びにこの憲法を施行するために必要な準備手続は，前項の期日よりも前に，これを行ふことができる。

第101条   この憲法施行の際，参議院がまだ成立してゐないときは，その成立するまでの間，衆議院は，国会としての権限を行ふ。

第102条   この憲法による第1期の参議院議員のうち，その半数の者の任期は，これを3年とする。その議員は，法律の定めるところにより，これを定める。

第103条   この憲法施行の際現に在職する国務大臣，衆議院議員及び裁判官並びにその他の公務員で，その地位に相応する地位がこの憲法で認められてゐる者は，法律で特別の定をした場合を除いては，この憲法施行のため，当然にはその地位を失ふことはない。但し，この憲法によつて，後任者が選挙又は任命されたときは，当然その地位を失ふ。

Japanese History	World History

Prehistory
(Before ca 300–710)

Before 30,000 BC ● Paleolithic culture (*kyusekki bunka*); crude stone tools produced by a preceramic hunting and gathering society.

Ca 10,000 BC ● Manufacture of Jomon pottery and polished stone tools marks the beginning of the Jomon period.

Ca 300 BC ● Yayoi culture emerges in northern Kyushu with the introduction of wet-rice cultivation from the Korean peninsula.

Ca 1300 BC● Chinese characters engraved on tortoise shells and animal bones.

334 BC● Alexander the Great begins his conquest of the East.

Ca 1 AD ● Japan mentioned in Chinese historical records (J: *Gishi*) as the land of Wa, composed of a number of states.

57 ● King of the state of Na (Nakoku) in Wa offers tribute to Emperor Guangwu of the Chinese Later Han dynasty (25–220) and is awarded a seal in return (Kan no Wa no Na no Kokuo no In).

239 ● Himiko, queen of Yamatai, sends an envoy to the kingdom of Wei in China, receiving from Emperor Ming a gold seal and the title *qin wei wowang* (J: *shingi wao*; Wa ruler friendly to Wei).

Kofun period
(ca 300–710)

The Kofun period was characterized by the construction of large tomb mounds (*kofun*), indicating the stratification of the agricultural society inherited from the Yayoi period. The Kofun period witnessed the introduction of Buddhism and the Chinese writing system from the Asian continent and the rise of the Yamato court, a powerful dynasty which established Japan's earliest unified state. The last period of the Kofun period is called the Asuka period, which is generally considered Japan's first historical age.

350 ● By this time the Yamato court has been established in what is now Nara Prefecture.

552 ● Traditional date of introduction of Buddhism to Japan, when Buddhist images and sutras are sent from Korea by King Song of Paekche. An earlier date, 538, is assigned to this event by many scholars.

589● Beginning of the Sui dynasty (589–618) in China.

600 ● First embassy to Sui-dynasty (589–618) China (*kenzuishi*) dispatched.

604 ● *Kan'i junikai* system of court ranks instituted. Prince Shotoku promulgates Seventeen-Article Constitution.

607 ● Ono no Imoko appointed leader of the second embassy to Sui China.

● Construction of the Buddhist temple Horyuji completed.

622● Prophet Muhammad arrives in Medina; the Islamic Era begins.

Japanese History	World History

630 ● First embassy to Tang-dynasty (618–907) China (*kentoshi*) dispatched.

645 ● Prince Naka no Oe (later Emperor Tenji) and Nakatomi no Kamatari (later Fujiwara no Kamatari) destroy the Soga family and initiate the Taika Reform.

667 ● Imperial palace Otsu no Miya established by Prince Naka no Oe (later Emperor Tenji) on the southwestern shore of Lake Biwa. Capital until 672.

672 ● Prince Oama (later Emperor Temmu) usurps the throne from his nephew and designated heir Prince Otomo (Jinshin Disturbance).

684 ● System of eight cognomens (*yakusa no kabane*) instituted, under which members of lineage groups (*uji*) are assigned titles of rank, forming a social pyramid with the emperor at its apex.

694 ● Capital city Fujiwarakyo established. Capital until 710.

World History column:

624 ● China unified under the Tang dynasty (618–907).

668 ● Silla unifies Korea.

....

701 ● Compilation of the Taiho Code of penal and administrative laws completed (*ritsuryo* system); becomes effective the following year.

708 ● Minting of the Wado *kaiho* initiated; it is the first coinage minted in Japan.

Nara period
(710–794)

The establishment of the capital city Heijokyo (Nara) marked the beginning of the Nara period, which was characterized by the maturation of the Chinese-inspired *ritsuryo* system of government and the active adoption of other aspects of Chinese culture and technology. Buddhism gained official recognition as the state religion, and temples were constructed throughout Japan in an effort to buttress the authority of the central state.

710 ● Capital city Heijokyo (Nara) established. Capital until 784.

712 ● Compilation of the historical narrative *Kojiki*, Japan's oldest extant chronicle, is completed by O no Yasumaro.

720 ● Historical narrative *Nihon shoki* completed.

733 ● Regional gazetteer *Izumo fudoki* completed.

743 ● Konden Eisei Shizai Ho promulgated; recognizing the permanent privatization of reclaimed lands, this law lays the legal basis for the emergence of the landed estates called *shoen*.
● Construction of a huge Buddha image (*daibutsu*) at the temple Todaiji initiated by imperial decree; it is completed in 752.

751 ● *Kaifuso* compiled; it is the oldest extant collection of Chinese poetry by Japanese poets.

759 ● Ganjin founds the temple Toshodaiji.
● The *Man'yoshu*, the oldest extant anthology of Japanese poetry, is completed around this time.

784 ● Capital moved to Nagaokakyo. Capital until 794.

788 ● Saicho, founder of the Japanese Tendai sect of Buddhism, establishes the temple Enryakuji.

Japanese History	World History

Heian period
(794–1185)

The Heian period, which began with the establishment of the imperial capital at Heiankyo (Kyoto), saw the full assimilation of Chinese influences and the flowering of an indigenous aristocratic culture. The development of the Japanese *kana* syllabary gave birth to a truly native literary tradition, including some of the finest works of Japanese poetry and prose. Politically, the Heian period was characterized by the domination of the imperial court by regents of the Fujiwara family.

794 ● Capital moved to Heiankyo (Kyoto). Capital until 1868.

905 ● The *Kokinshu*, the first imperial anthology of *waka* verse, is completed.

960 ● Beginning of the Northern Song dynasty (960–1126) in China,

985 ● The Buddhist monk Genshin completes the religious tract *Ojoyoshu*; the work contributes to the spread of Pure Land Buddhism among the aristocracy.

995 ● Fujiwara no Michinaga becomes head of the Fujiwara family; golden age of its domination of the imperial court begins.

996 ● A portion of Sei Shonagon's *Makura no soshi* is now in circulation; this elegant and whimsical diary brings alive the social and aesthetic values of the court aristocracy.

1008 ● Entry in Murasaki Shikibu's diary indicates that a substantial part of the *Tale of Genji*, her long novel depicting the lives of the aristocracy, has now been written.

1087 ● Emperor Shirakawa abdicates, establishes the system of "cloister government" (*insei*).

1156 ● Hogen Disturbance: rivalry between the Taira family and the Minamoto family for political power at court begins.

1127 ● Beginning of the Southern Song dynasty (1127–1279) in China.

1160 ● Heiji Disturbance: influence of the Taira family over the imperial court established.

1175 ● Honen begins to preach in Kyoto and founds the Jodo sect of Buddhism.

Kamakura period
(1185–1333)

Minamoto Yoritomo's victory in the Taira-Minamoto War (Gempei no Soran) heralded the beginning of the Kamakura period and the rise to political power of the provincial warrior class. His appointment of provincial governors (*shugo*) and estate stewards (*jito*) established the foundations of the Kamakura shogunate, the first in a series of military governments that would rule Japan until the mid-19th century.

1192 ● Minamoto no Yoritomo appointed shogun by Emperor Go-Toba.

1203 ● Hojo Tokimasa assumes the office of shogunal regent (*shikken*).

1205 ● The *Shin kokinshu*, the most important of the imperial anthologies of *waka* poetry after the *Kokinshu*, is submitted to the throne.

Japanese History	World History
1219 ● Minamoto no Sanetomo assassinated, ending the line of Minamoto shoguns. Members of the Hojo family continue to rule as regents for a series of figurehead shoguns.	**1215** ● Magna Carta issued, duress, by King under John of England.
1221 ● Jokyu Disturbance: abdicated emperors Go-Toba and Juntoku sent into exile by the shogunate.	
1224 ● Shinran establishes the Jodo Shin sect of Buddhism.	
1227 ● Dogen establishes the Soto sect of Zen Buddhism.	
1232 ● Goseibai Shikimoku promulgated; it is the first codification of warrior house law.	
1253 ● Nichiren establishes the Nichiren sect of Buddhism.	
1274 ● First of the Mongol Invasions of Japan.	**1271** ● Marco Polo sets out on his journey to the
1281 ● Second of the Mongol Invasions of Japan.	court of the Mongol emperor Kublai Khan.
1330 ● Yoshida Kenko completes his masterwork, the collection of essays *Tsurezuregusa*, around this time.	

Muromachi period
(1333–1568)

The destruction of the Kamakura shogunate by the forces of Ashikaga Takauji signified the beginning of the Muromachi period, an era of great cultural achievement and persistent social instability. The first decades of the Muromachi shogunate were disrupted by conflict between two rival imperial lines (Northern and Southern Courts). The shogunate was unable to restrain the ambitions of powerful provincial governors (*shugo daimyo*) and collapsed entirely after the Onin War, which ushered in a century of civil strife known as the Sengoku period (1467-1568).

Japanese History	World History
1333 ● Kamakura shogunate collapses; power restored to Emperor Go-Daigo (Kemmu Restoration).	
1336 ● The Kemmu Shikimoku, a code of governmental principles, is promulgated by Ashikaga Takauji.	
1337 ● Emperor Go-Daigo escapes to Yoshino; declaring that the regalia he had surrendered to Prince Toyohito were imitations and denying his abdication, he establishes the Southern Court.	**1337** ● Hundred Years' War, waged by England against France, begins.
1338 ● Ashikaga Takauji receives the title of shogun from the Northern Court, founds the Muromachi shogunate.	**1368** ● Zhu Yuanzhang founds the Ming dynasty (1308–1644) in China.
1392 ● Northern and Southern Courts reconciled with the acceptance of Emperor Go-Komatsu as sole sovereign.	**1392** ● Yi Song-gye declares himself king of Korea. founds the Yi dynasty (1392–1910).
1397 ● Shogun Ashikaga Yoshimitsu begins construction of the temple Kinkakuji in Kyoto.	
1400 ● Zeami completes the first three chapters of his *Fushi kaden*, a treatise on No drama.	
1404 ● Tally trade initiated with Ming-dynasty (1368–1644) China.	**1455** ● Johannes Gutenberg completes the Forty-Two Line Bible, the earliest book printed in Europe from movable type.
1467 ● Onin War begins (1467–77); Kyoto laid waste.	
1483 ● Retired shogun Ashikaga Yoshimasa settles at the villa that later becomes the temple Ginkakuji; located in the Higashiyama section of Kyoto, this becomes known as the center of Higashiyama culture.	**1492** ● Christopher Columbus lands in the Bahamas.

Japanese History	World History
1488 ● Adherents of the Jodo Shin sect of Buddhism vanquish the army of the governor (*shugo*) of Kaga Province and establish autonomous rule there (Ikko Ikki).	**1498** ● Vasco da Gama, after a voyage around the Cape of Good Hope, reaches Calicut in India.
1543 ● Matchlock muskets (*hinawaju*) are introduced to Japan by the Portuguese on the island of Tanegashima off the coast of Kyushu. **1549** ● Francis Xavier establishes Japan's first Christian mission at Kagoshima.	**1517** ● Martin Luther nails the Ninety-Five Theses to the church door at Wittenberg. **1534** ● Founding of the Society of Jesus (Jesuits) by Ignatius of Loyola.

Azuchi-Momoyama period
(1568–1600)

The Azuchi-Momoyama period was defined by the rise of three successive hegemons, Oda Nobunaga, Toyotomi Hideyoshi, and Tokugawa Ieyasu, who brought about the political unification of Japan following a century of civil war. During this brief period, Japan was exposed to Western (*namban*) culture through contact with European traders and missionaries.

Japanese History	World History
1568 ● Oda Nobunaga enters Kyoto, installs Ashikaga Yoshiaki as shogun; Yoshiaki driven into exile in 1573.	**1571** ● Spain founds Manila.
1575 ● Battle of Nagashino: the 3,000 musketeers deployed by Oda Nobunaga in his victory over Takeda Katsuyori mark Japan's shift to modern warfare.	
1576 ● Oda Nobunaga begins construction of Azuchi Castle.	
1582 ● Honnoji Incident: hegemon Oda Nobunaga commits suicide after a surprise attack by his vassal Akechi Mitsuhide. ● Toyotomi Hideyoshi initiates the Taiko *kenchi*, a national survey of lands and their productive capacity.	
1587 ● Toyotomi Hideyoshi issues an edict expelling all Christian missionaries from Japan (anti-Christian edicts).	
1588 ● Toyotomi Hideyoshi issues an edict prohibiting possession of weapons by peasants (*katanagari*).	
1590 ● Toyotomi Hideyoshi destroys the Later Hojo family (Odawara Campaign), pacifies all of Japan.	
1592 ● First of the invasions of Korea in 1592 and 1597.	

Edo period
(1600–1868)

Victory in the Battle of Sekigahara established Tokugawa Ieyasu's hegemony over Japan, commencing the Edo period. Over two centuries of peace followed under the rule of the Tokugawa shogunate, which instituted a political structure known as the *bakuhan* system and isolated Japan from potentially disruptive foreign influences through its policy of National Seclusion (Sakoku). The vibrant bourgeois spirit of the period's thriving merchant class (*chonin*) found expression in dramatic forms such as *kabuki* and *bunraku*, in the popular literature known as *gesaku*, and in artistic genres such as *ukiyo-e*. In the turbulent period following Commodore Matthew Perry's arrival in 1853, the shogunate lost its ability to assert national authority, and the Tokugawa regime collapsed.

Japanese History	World History
1600 ● Battle of Sekigahara: Tokugawa Ieyasu establishes hegemony over Japan.	**1600** ● British East India Company incorporated by royal charter.
1603 ● Tokugawa Ieyasu is granted the title of shogun, founds the Tokugawa shogunate.	**1602** ● Dutch government grants the Dutch East India Company a monopoly on trade in the East Indies.
1609 ● Dutch Factory (Oranda Shokan) established at Hirado;	

Japanese History	World History
Dutch trade begins.	1607● English settlement established in North America at Jamestown, Virginia.
1612 ● Shogunate issues directives aimed at restricting Christianity (anti-Christian edicts; *kinkyorei*).	
1635 ● Revision of the Buke Shohatto (Laws for the Military Houses); system of mandatory alternate residence in Edo by *daimyo* formalized (*sankin kotai*).	
1636 ● Buildings on the artificial island of Dejima at Nagasaki completed; Portuguese merchants, who since 1571 had lived freely in the city, are removed there.	
1639 ● Edicts establishing National Seclusion (Sakoku) are completed: Portuguese merchants are evicted from Dejima; all Westerners except the Dutch are prohibited from entering Japan.	1644● Manchus establish the Qing dynasty (1644–1912) in China.
1641 ● Dutch Factory shifted from Hirado to Dejima in Nagasaki.	
1657 ● Meireki Fire ravages Edo, killing more than 100,000 people; much of Edo Castle and more than 350 shrines and temples burn.	
1682 ● Ihara Saikaku publishes the amorous adventure tale *Koshoku ichidai otoko*.	
1688 ● Beginning of the Genroku era (1688–1704), a time of cultural flowering known in particular as the golden age of *kabuki* and *bunraku*.	
1689 ● Matsuo Basho departs on the journey through northern Honshu that he later chronicles in the *haiku* travel diary *Oku no hosomichi*.	
1703 ● Band of former retainers of the Ako domain, under the leadership of Oishi Yoshio, carry out a vendetta against Kira Yoshinaka (Forty-Seven Ronin Incident).	
1707 ● Last eruption of Fujisan (as of 1994).	
1716 ● Tokugawa Yoshimune becomes shogun; Kyoho Reforms (1716–1745) commence.	
1732 ● Locust plague and unseasonable weather cause Kyoho Famine in southwestern Japan.	
1774 ● Anatomical text *Kaitai shinsho* published by Sugita Gempaku and Maeno Ryotaku; it is the first complete Japanese translation of a Western medical work.	1776● Continental Congress issues the US Declaration of Independence.
1782 ● Temmei Famine begins; estimates of the nationwide death toll during the five years of its duration range from 200,000 to 900,000.	1789● George Washington becomes the first president of the United States.
1792 ● Adam Erikovich Laxman arrives at Nemuro in eastern Ezo (now Hokkaido) with Daikokuya Kodayu; the following year Laxman negotiates unsuccessfully with shogunal officials in Matsumae for the establishment of trade relations between Japan and Russia.	● French Revolution begins. 1796● Edward Jenner performs first smallpox inoculation.
1798 ● Motoori Norinaga completes the *Kojiki den*, a comprehensive annotation of the early historical narrative *Kojiki* and a major work in the Kokugaku (National Learning) movement.	

	Japanese History	World History
1800	● Ino Tadataka begins his cartographic survey of all Japan; it is completed in 1816.	
1802	● Jippensha Ikku publishes the first volume of his serial comic novel *Tokaidochu hizakurige.*	
1804	● Russian envoy Nikolai Petrovich Rezanov reaches Nagasaki, unsuccessfully seeks the establishment of trade relations with Japan.	**1804** ● Napoleon crowns himself emperor of France.
1809	● Mamiya Rinzo discovers the Tatar Strait, proving that Sakhalin is an island.	
1820	● Kobayashi Issa completes the poetical diary *Oraga haru.*	
1823	● Philipp Franz von Siebold arrives in Japan to serve as physician to the Dutch Factory; the following year he opens the boarding school Narutakijuku and teaches Western medicine and science to Takano Choei, Ito Gemboku, and Ito Keisuke.	
1833	● Tempo Famine (1833–36) begins; by 1836 rice harvests are estimated to have been only one-third of the normal crop; some 200,000 to 300,000 people are thought to have died of starvation and disease.	**1837** ● Victoria becomes queen of England (1837–1901). **1839** ● Opium War begins in China (1839–1842).
1853	● Four warships of the US East India Squadron, commanded by Commodore Matthew Perry, call at Uraga at the mouth of Edo Bay.	
1854	● Fleet of nine US naval vessels, led by Commodore Matthew Perry, anchors in Edo Bay. ● Treaty of Peace and Amity between the United States and the Empire of Japan signed.	
1856	● US consul general Townsend Harris arrives at Shimoda to initiate negotiations with the shogunate on what will become the Harris Treaty (Nichibei Shuko Tsusho Joyaku).	
1858	● Ansei commercial treaties (Ansei gokakoku joyaku) are concluded between the shogunate and the United States, the Netherlands, Russia, Great Britain, and France.	
1860	● Shogunal mission to the United States leaves aboard the American ship *Powhatan* to ratify the Harris Treaty. It is accompanied by the *Kanrin maru*, with a Japanese crew under the command of Katsu Kaishu. ● Assassination of Ii Naosuke (Sakuradamongai Incident).	**1861** ● Civil War begins in the United States (1861–1865).
1862	● Richardson Affair (Namamugi Jiken): murder of a British merchant by retainers of the Satsuma domain.	
1864	● Shimonoseki Bombardment (Bakan Senso): naval expedition by the Western powers against the Choshu domain in retaliation for attacks on its ships passing through the Shimonoseki Strait.	**1864** ● The International Workingmen's Association (commonly known as the First International) is founded in London.
1866	● Satsuma-Choshu Alliance (Satcho Domei) formed against the Tokugawa shogunate.	
1867	● Formal return of political authority to the emperor by the last shogun, Tokugawa Yoshinobu (Taisei Hokan).	

Chronology of Japanese History

Japanese History	World History

Meiji period
(1868–1912)

The Meiji Restoration of direct imperial rule commenced the Meiji period and began Japan's transformation into a modern industrial society. Restoration leaders welded former feudal domains into a modern nation-state, established centralized bureaucracy, enacted a new land tax system, and created a modern conscript army. Abolition of feudal classes and the establishment of universal education helped create a unified national polity.

1868 ● Restoration of imperial rule (Meiji Restoration; Osei Fukko).
● Charter Oath (Gokajo no Goseimon) promulgated; Gobo no Keiji (Five Public Notices) issued by Emperor Meiji.
● The city of Edo is renamed Tokyo ("eastern capital"); it becomes the official seat of government the following year.

1869 ● Formal return of domainal registers to Emperor Meiji (Hanseki Hokan).

1871 ● Postal Service established.
● Domains dissolved and prefectures established (*haihan chiken*).

1872 ● Railroad begins operation between Shimbashi and Yokohama.
● The Education Order of 1872 (Gakusei) establishes Japan's first modern school system.

1875 ● Treaty of St. Petersburg (Karafuto-Chishima Kokan Joyaku) gives Sakhalin to Russia and the Kuril Islands (Chishima Retto) to Japan.

1876 ● Treaty of Kanghwa (Nitcho Shuko Joki), signed with Korea, gains unequal privileges for Japan.

1876 ● The first successful telephone transmission is achieved by Alexander Graham Bell.

1877 ● Satsuma Rebellion (Seinan Senso); Saigo Takamori commits suicide.

1883 ● Completion of the Rokumeikan, a two-story brick building designed by Josiah Conder; it is the site for Western-style social events attended by prominent Japanese and foreigners.

1883 ● Sino-French War (1883–1885) begins; in 1885 China recognizes Vietnam as a protectorate of France.

1889 ● Constitution of the Empire of Japan promulgated.

1890 ● Imperial Rescript on Education (Kyoiku Chokugo) distributed to all schools.

1894 ● Sino-Japanese War of 1894–1895 (Nisshin Senso) begins.

1895 ● Tripartite Intervention (Sangoku Kansho): Japan forced by Russia, France, and Germany to relinquish territory ceded to it by China.

1899 ● US secretary of state John Hay sends his Open Door notes concerning China to Great Britain, Germany, France, Russia, Italy, and Japan.

1902 ● Anglo-Japanese Alliance (Nichiei Domei) signed.

1903 ● Wilbur and Orville Wright achieve the first sustained flight in a power-driven airplane.

1904 ● Russo-Japanese War (1904–1905; Nichiro Senso) begins.

1910 ● Korea is made a colony of Japan (Annexation of Korea; Nikkan Heigo); Government-General of Korea (Chosen Sotoku Fu) established.

1911 ● Treaties signed with the Western powers that restore tariff autonomy to Japan.

Japanese History	World History

Taisho period
(1912–1926)

The Taisho period was marked by the advent of true party government, increased popular involvement in politics, the growth of organized labor and left-wing movements, and a domestic economic boom fueled by World War I. The democratic tendencies of the period, often referred to as Taisho Democracy, were supported by the emergence of an educated urban middle class and the rise of new forms of mass media.

1914 ● Japan enters World War I on the side of Great Britain and its allies.

1915 ● Japan presents China with its Twenty-One Demands for territorial and other concessions.

1918 ● Commencement of the Siberian Intervention (1918–1922).

1920 ● League of Nations established; Japan is granted permanent membership in the League Council.

1921 ● Washington Conference (1921–1922) begins; it will result in the signing of the Four-Power Treaty, the Nine-Power Treaty, and the Washington Naval Treaty of 1922.

1923 ● Tokyo Earthquake (Kanto Daishinsai); assigned a magnitude of 7.9, this earthquake resulted in more than 100,000 deaths.

1925 ● Enactment of the Peace Preservation Law of 1925 (Chian Iji Ho); freedoms of speech and assembly severely restricted.
● Universal Manhood Suffrage Law (Futsu Senkyo Ho) passed.

1912 ● Republic of China established with Sun Yat-sen (Son Issen) as president; Emperor Puyi abdicates.

1914 ● Archduke Francis Ferdinand assassinated at Sarajevo; World War I begins.

1917 ● October Revolution in Russia.

1922 ● Benito Mussolini forms a cabinet of Fascists and Nationalists in Italy.

Showa period
(1926–1989)

The Showa period was one of the most turbulent in Japanese history. In its first decades an ultranationalist coalition of right-wing politicians and army officers seized control of the country, engaging in domestic political repression and setting Japan on a course of militarist expansionism in continental Asia that culminated in the Sino-Japanese War of 1937–1945 and entry into World War II. Japan's defeat ushered in a period of Occupation by Allied military forces and sweeping democratic reforms that included a new Constitution of Japan. The postwar decades saw recovery from the war, reentry into the international community, and phenomenal economic growth that transformed Japan into the world's second largest economy by the end of the period.

1927 ● Financial Crisis of 1927 (Kin'yu Kyoko).

1932 ● Guandong Army (Kantogun) establishes the state of Manchukuo; the last Qing-dynasty (1644–1912) emperor, Puyi (J: Fugi), appointed as head of state.
● May 15th Incident: Prime Minister Inukai Tsuyoshi assassinated during an attempted coup by young naval officers.

1933 ● Japan withdraws from the League of Nations to express its opposition to a report criticizing it as an aggressor in Manchuria.

1936 ● February 26th Incident: 1,400 troops participate in an unsuccessful coup d'état.

1937 ● Marco Polo Bridge Incident (Rokokyo Jiken): Sino-Japanese War of 1937–1945 (Nitchu Senso) commences.

1927 ● Chiang Kai-shek (Sho Kaiseki) sets up a Nationalist government in Nanjing.

1929 ● US stock market crashes, prolonged depression begins.

1933 ● Adolf Hitler becomes chancellor of Germany.

Japanese History	World History

1938 ● Passage of the National Mobilization Law (Kokka Sodoin Ho).

1939 ● Nomonhan Incident: heavy fighting between Japanese and Soviet troops along the Manchurian-Mongolian border ends in a rout of Japanese forces.

1939 ● Germany invades Poland; World War II (1939–1945) begins in Europe.

1940 ● Tripartite Pact (Nichidokui Sangoku Domei) signed by Japan, Germany, and Italy.

1941 ● Soviet-Japanese Neutrality Pact signed.
● Japanese attack Pearl Harbor, the Malay Peninsula, and the Philippines; war declared against the United States, Great Britain, and the Netherlands.

1945 ● Atomic bomb dropped on Hiroshima and Nagasaki.
● Japan accepts the terms of the Potsdam Declaration.
● Douglas MacArthur, supreme commander for the Allied powers (SCAP), arrives at Atsugi Airfield near Tokyo to oversee the Occupation of Japan (1945–1952).

1945 ● US president Harry Truman, Soviet premier Joseph Stalin, and British prime minister Winston Churchill call for the unconditional surrender of Japan in the Potsdam Declaration.

1946 ● Emperor Showa renounces his divinity in New Year's address to the Japanese people.
● Implementation of the Land Reforms of 1946 begins.
● Constitution of Japan promulgated; it goes into effect in 1947.

1948 ● Republic of Korea established in the southern part of the Korean peninsula and the Democratic People's Republic of Korea in the north.

1949 ● Yukawa Hideki awarded the Nobel Prize for physics; he is the first Japanese to receive a Nobel Prize.

1950 ● National Police Reserve created.

1950 ● Korean War begins (1950–1953).

1951 ● San Francisco Peace Treaty and the United States-Japan Security Treaty signed.

1953 ● Television broadcasting begins in Japan.

1954 ● Defense Agency and the Self Defense Forces established.

1955 ● Japan joins GATT (General Agreement on Tariffs and Trade).
● Liberal Democratic Party formed.

1956 ● Soviet-Japanese Joint Declaration reestablishes diplomatic relations between the two countries.
● Japan granted membership in the United Nations.

1957 ● Soviet Union launches the first space satellite, Sputnik 1.

1964 ● High-speed Shinkansen trains begin operations between Tokyo and Osaka.
● Eighteenth Summer Olympic Games, the first sponsored by an Asian city, held in Tokyo.

1961 ● Organization for Economic Cooperation and Development (OECD) organized; Japan joins in 1964.

1962 ● Algeria gains independence from France.

1965 ● Korea-Japan Treaty of 1965 signed; diplomatic relations between Japan and the Republic of Korea restored.

1965 ● US airplanes begin bombing North Vietnam.

1968 ● University upheavals of 1968–1969 (*daigaku funso*) begin.

1966 ● Cultural Revolution sweeps across China.

1969 ● US Apollo 11 spacecraft puts the first man on the moon.

1970 ● Expo '70 opens in Osaka.

1972 ● Okinawa returned to Japanese sovereignty by the United States.
● China-Japan Joint Communiqué of 1972 issued; it announces the establishment of diplomatic relations between Japan and the People's Republic of China.

1973 ● Floating exchange rate introduced.

		Japanese History	World History
		● Oil crisis of 1973: oil prices spiral.	*1973* ● Fourth Arab-Israeli War triggers the oil crisis.
1976		● Lockheed Scandal: Japanese government officials charged with taking bribes from Lockheed Aircraft Corporation.	*1975* ● North Vietnam achieves the unification of Vietnam.
1978		● New Tokyo International Airport (Narita Airport) opens.	*1979* ● Peace treaty signed by Egypt and Israel.
1985		● Enactment of the Equal Employment Opportunity Law For Men and Women.	*1986* ● Nuclear accident at Chernobyl in the Soviet Union.
1988		● Recruit Scandal: it comes to light that the staffs of a number of leading politicians received gifts of stock shares from Recruit Co. in 1986.	

Heisei period
(1989–)

The Heisei period commenced at the peak of an economic boom, but the recession that began in 1991 has continued to the present (1995). With the end of the one-party rule of the Liberal Democratic Party, politics in the period has been marked by short-term governments, changing coalitions, and the creation of new parties. In an increasingly interdependent world, Japan has continued slow but steady efforts to internationalize its society and to shoulder international responsibility consistent with its economic power.

	Japanese History	World History
1989	● Death of Emperor Showa; accession of Emperor Akihito.	*1989* ● Tiananmen Square Incident; thousands of demonstrators for democratization in China are killed by government troops.
	● Sohyo disbands and is largely absorbed into Rengo.	● Berlin Wall demolished.
1993	● Non-LDP coalition government is formed, marking the end of the LDP's 28 years in power.	*1990* ● Reunification of Germany.
1994	● Political reform bills pass in the Diet.	*1991* ● Soviet Union dissolved.
	● Kansai International Airport opens.	
1995	● Kobe Earthquake; this magnitude 7.2 earthquake resulted in more than 5,000 deaths.	

INDEX

HOW TO USE THE INDEX

Typography

Boldface type indicates entries
for which there are articles in this book
while lightface type is used for words
appeared within articles. Number in italics
direct the reader to photographs.

Alphabetization

The entries in the index are alphabetized
letter by letter, not word by word,
so that not all of the entries
beginning with the same word
will fall together.

A

■H

I

■L

■N

■O

■T

Y

Z

英文日本小事典

Japan: Profile of a Nation

定価はカバーに表示してあります

1995年6月16日

第1刷発行

発行者	野間佐和子
発行所	講談社インターナショナル株式会社
	東京都文京区音羽1-17-14 (〒112)
	電話：東京 03-3944-6493 編集局
	東京 03-3944-6492 営業局

組版	guild
印刷	大日本印刷株式会社
製本所	株式会社堅省堂